PENGUIN BOOKS

THE PILLARS OF HERCULES

Paul Theroux was born and educated in the United States. After graduating from university in 1963, he travelled first to Italy and then to Africa, where he worked as a Peace Corps teacher at a bush school in Malawi, and as a lecturer at Makerere University in Uganda. In 1968 he joined the University of Singapore and taught in the Department of English for three years. Throughout this time, he was publishing short stories and journalism, and he wrote a number of novels. Among these were *Fong and the Indians*, *Girls at Play* and *Jungle Lovers*, all of which appear in one volume, *The Edge of the Great Rift* (Penguin, 1996). In the early 1970s Paul Theroux moved with his wife and two children to Dorset, where he wrote *Saint Jack*, and then on to London. He was a resident in Britain for a total of seventeen years. In this time he wrote a dozen volumes of highly praised fiction and a number of successful travel books, from which a selection of writings were taken to compile his book *Travelling the World* (Penguin, 1992). Paul Theroux has now returned to the United States, but he continues to travel widely.

Paul Theroux's many books include *Picture Palace*, which won the 1978 Whitbread Literary Award; *The Mosquito Coast*, which was the 1981 *Yorkshire Post* Novel of the Year and joint winner of the James Tait Black Memorial Prize, and was also made into a feature film; *Riding the Iron Rooster*, which won the 1988 Thomas Cook Travel Book Award; and, most recently, *Millroy the Magician* and *The Pillars of Hercules*. Most of his books are published by Penguin.

PAUL THEROUX

THE PILLARS OF HERCULES

A GRAND TOUR
OF THE MEDITERRANEAN

PENGUIN BOOKS

PENGUIN BOOKS

Published by the Penguin Group
Penguin Books Ltd, 27 Wrights Lane, London W8 5TZ, England
Penguin Books USA Inc., 375 Hudson Street, New York, New York 10014, USA
Penguin Books Australia Ltd, Ringwood, Victoria, Australia
Penguin Books Canada Ltd, 10 Alcorn Avenue, Toronto, Ontario, Canada M4V 3B2
Penguin Books (NZ) Ltd, 182–190 Wairau Road, Auckland 10, New Zealand

Penguin Books Ltd, Registered Offices: Harmondsworth, Middlesex, England

First published by Hamish Hamilton 1995
Published in Penguin Books 1996
3 5 7 9 10 8 6 4

Acknowledgement is gratefully made to the following for permission to use extracts from: *The Odyssey* by Homer, translated by Robert Fitzgerald, reprinted by permission of William Heinemann Ltd; "The Next Time" by Robert Graves, reprinted by permission of Carcanet Press Ltd; "At Algeciras – a Meditation upon Death" by W. B. Yeats, reprinted by permission of Linda Shaughnessy of A. P. Watt Ltd on behalf of Michael Yeats

Printed in England by Clays Ltd, St Ives plc

To the Memory of My Father
Albert Eugene Theroux
13 January 1908
30 May 1995

Contents

FRANC

Nîmes

Montpellier

Narbonne

Perpignan

Cerbère

Port Bou

Gerona

Costa Brava

Sitges

Barcelona

Tarragona

R. Ebro

Saragossa

PORTUGAL

S P A I N

Sagunto

Valencia

Sóller

Valdemosa

Palma

MAJORCA

Denia

Benidorm

Alicante

A N D A L U S I A

Murcia

Granada

Cartagena

Malaga

Almeria

Algeciras

La Linea

Tangier

Ceuta

M E D I T E R R A N

Melilla

Rabat

M O R O C C O

A L G E R

West Mediterranean

Ljubljana

Trieste

Venice

Opatija • Rijeka

Chioggia

Ferrara

YUGOSLAVIA
(Former)

R. Po

Genoa

Rapallo

Carrara

Rimini

Zadar

Menton • Ventimiglia

Nice

Monte Carlo

seilles

Cannes

St Tropez

Cote d'Azur

Pisa

Livorno

oulon

Sibenik

Split

Mostar

R. Neretva

Cap Corse

Elba

ITALY

Ancona

ADRIATIC

Calvi

Bastia

CORSICA

Ajaccio

Corte

Dubrovnik

SEA

Sartène

Pescara

Bonifacio

Rome

Olbia

Sassari

Bonorva

Oristano

SARDINIA

Mt Vesuvius

Naples △

Bari

Potenza

Taranto

Sorrento

Salerno

Aliano

Metaponto

Cagliari

Crotone

Lipari

A   N   S   E   A

Palermo

Messina

Reggio

Trapani

Taormina

Catania

Siracusa

Annaba

Tunis

Carthage

SICILY

Sousse

Gozo

Valletta

MALTA

N

TUNISIA

A

Sfax

Kerkennah
Islands

0   200 Miles

0   200 km

East Mediterranean

Have you ever reflected on what an important sea the Mediterranean is?

— James Joyce in a letter to his brother Stanislaus

The Mediterranean is an absurdly small sea; the length and greatness of its history makes us dream it larger than it is.

— Lawrence Durrell, *Balthazar*

I

The Cable Car to the Rock of Gibraltar

People here in Western civilization say that tourists are no different from apes, but on the Rock of Gibraltar, one of the Pillars of Hercules, I saw both tourists and apes together, and I learned to tell them apart. I had traveled past clumps of runty stunted trees and ugly houses (the person who just muttered, "Oh, there he goes again!" must read no further) to the heights of the Rock in a metal box suspended by a cable. Gibraltar is just a conspicuous pile of limestone, to which distance lends enchantment; a very small number of people cling to its lower slopes. Most of them are swarthy and bilingual, speaking intelligible English, and Spanish with an Andalusian accent. Mention Spain to them and they become very agitated, though they know that as sure as eggs are *huevos* the British will eventually hand them over to the King of Spain, just as they chucked Hong Kong into the horny hands of the dictator of China.

The Rock apes of Gibraltar are Barbary macaques (*macaca sylvanus*), the only native apes in Europe. The apes are still resident, and have lived there longer than most Gibraltarian families. There is a social order among the ape tribes, as well as ape rituals that are bizarre enough to be human. Ape corpses and skeletons are never found on the rock. Somewhere in the recesses of this rock that looks like a mountain range there is said to be a secret mortuary established by the apes; ape funerals, ape mourning, ape burials. The apes are well established, but disadvantaged – unemployed, unwaged, destitute welfare recipients. The municipal government allocates money to feed them.

But there might be a darker motive in this food aid. A powerful superstition, held by locals, suggests that if the apes vanish from Gibraltar, the Rock will cease to be British. For hundreds of years – since 1740, in fact – the apes have been mentioned by travelers – Grand Tourists, in whose footsteps I was following. But Gibraltar has been visited almost since Hercules, patron of human toil, flung it there on his journey to capture the Red Oxen of Geryones, the monster with three bodies (Labor Ten). He tossed another rock across the straits, to become Ceuta in Morocco. These two rocks, Calpe and Abyla to the Greeks – the Mediterranean bottleneck – are the twin Pillars of Hercules.

My idea was to travel from one pillar to the other, the long way, with the usual improvisations *en route* that are required of the impulsive traveler; all around the Mediterranean coast, the shores of light.

"The grand object of traveling is to see the shores of the Mediterranean," Dr Johnson said. "On those shores were the four great Empires of the world; the Assyrian, the Persian, the Grecian, and the Roman. All our religion, almost all our law, almost all our arts, almost all that sets us above savages, has come to us from the shores of the Mediterranean."

"Our" of course is as questionable as "savages," but you get the idea. A great deal happened on this coastline. It was not until the second century B.C. that the Romans sailed through the Pillars of Hercules. The reason for this late, if not timid, penetration of the straits was not the current, nor was it the inconvenient westerlies that blow through this narrow opening of the inland sea; it was the Mediterranean notion that nothing lay beyond the pillars except the Isles of the Hesperides and the lost continent of Atlantis, and hellish seas.

The pillars marked the limits of civilization, "the end of voyaging," Euripides wrote; "the Ruler of Ocean no longer permits mariners to travel on the purple sea." And later in the second century B.C., Polybius wrote, "The channel at the Pillars of Herakles is seldom used, and by very few persons, owing to the lack of intercourse between the tribes inhabiting those remote parts . . . and to the scantiness of our knowledge of the outer ocean."

Beyond the pillars were the chaos and darkness they associated with the underworld. Because these two rocks resembled the pillars at the temple to Melkarth in Tyre, the Phoenicians called them the Pillars of Melkarth. Melkarth was the Lord of the Underworld

– god of darkness – and it was easy to believe that this chthonic figure prevailed over a sea with huge waves and powerful currents and ten-foot tides.

The point is not that the Mediterranean peoples had never ventured westward through the straits, but that they had dared it – the Phoenicians had reached Britain by a sea-route – and verified that it had a wicked and destructive turbulence. From this they conceived the idea that nothing useful lay beyond the straits, only the spooky Mare Tenebrosum, the dark and dangerous ocean which lay beyond the Middle Sea, a purple river of furious water. The Greeks named this the Stream of Ocean. It circled the earth of which they were privileged to live at the center, its precise location at Delphi, where a stone like a toad stool marked the Navel of the World. Mediterranean, after all, means "middle of the earth."

The surface current moves through the straits at a walking pace to the east, streaming through the 15-mile-wide channel into the Mediterranean; but 250 feet below this another sub-current rushes in the opposite direction, westward, into the Atlantic, pouring over the shallow sill of the straits, "that awful deepdown torrent," Molly Bloom murmurs in her bedtime reverie. The unusual circular exchange of water at the straits is the only way this just about landlocked sea is kept refreshed and alive. Very few large rivers flow into it. For thousands of years, until the Suez Canal was opened in 1875 to the strains of Verdi's *Aida*, the Straits of Gibraltar "the Gut," to the English sailors, "The Gate of the Narrow Entrance" (*Bab el Zaka*) to the Moors – was the only waterway to the world.

Even so, the Mediterranean has an odd character. It has almost no tides at all, and except for a whirlpool here and there (notably at Messina) an absence of distinct marine currents. It is dominated by winds rather than currents, and each wind has a name and is associated with a series of specific traits: there is the Vendaval, the steady westerly that blows through the Straits of Gibraltar; the Tramontana, the strong wind of the Spanish coast; the Bora, the cold wind of Trieste; the Mistral, the cold, dry north-westerly of the Riviera, and so on, through the Khamsin, the Sirocco, the Levanter, and about six others (often the same wind, with a different name) to the Gregale, the north-east wind of Malta that blows in winter and was more than likely the wind that caused St Paul to be shipwrecked on the Maltese coast as described in the Bible (Acts 27–28).

It is not a sea that is affected by the phases of the moon; it has moods rather than monthlies. Its nervous character has been mentioned by sailors, and its color – purple, wine-dark, and its blueness in particular. The Mediterranean was the White Sea to the Greeks – the Turks still use that name for it: *Akdeniz*, and the Arabs use a variant, the White Central Sea. If the oceans can be compared to vast symphonies, the German traveler Emil Ludwig wrote, then the Mediterranean "is subdued in a way that suggests chamber music." It is tentative, and its waves with their short fetch, and its strange swells, are unlike any to be found in the great oceans.

All over the Rock of Gibraltar there were signs in six languages (English, Spanish, Italian, Japanese, Arabic, French) that said "Do Not Feed the Apes!" and "Apes Might Bite!". These signs were more frequent at the top, where one of the ape tribes – the friendlier of the two – lived.

Here at the top of the Rock, an ectoplasmic middle-aged woman, a French tourist, plump and pushy and grinning, picked up a pebble and approached an ape. It was a mother ape that was nuzzling her child, urging it against her pink nipple, with that serene and happy expression that mothers have when they breast-feed their young. The tourist's name, I felt sure, was Grisette. She poked the pebble at the mother ape, giggling, while her three friends watched. One of the friends jerked the arm of her small boy, forcing him to watch Grisette tease the ape.

The mother ape took the pebble and considered it carefully for a few moments before dropping it to the ground. Grisette laughed very hard and then went even closer, making a hideous face. Grisette wore glasses with lenses so thick and distorting that her eyes swam and changed shape as she nodded and grinned at this cornered ape. The mother ape expressed concern, and when Grisette reached over and touched her young suckling baby the mother ape raised a cautioning hand – a shapely hand, wonderfully pink, human in miniature, with fine nails. There were enough lines on the ape's palm to occupy a fortune-teller for a whole session of palmistry.

Provoked and a bit irritated by the cautioning mother ape, Grisette poked the baby ape as though testing a door jamb with a "Wet Paint" sign. Grisette's friends laughed again. The ape mother raised her cautioning hand again, and when Grisette pinched the baby, the mother ape rapped Grisette's knuckles. This went on, back and forth, for a minute or so. I thought that the ape was going to leap into Grisette's face and bite and claw her – Apes Might Bite!

But the mother ape showed enormous patience, as though she knew she was dealing with someone simple-minded and unpredictable, someone who was a nuisance rather than a threat. She merely raised one of her hands and restrained the stupid woman, and when Grisette put her big googly-eyed face nearer – simpering and calling her friends as she tormented the mother and child – all the mother ape did was show her teeth and she crept away, off the little rail, out of the sunshine where she had been suckling her infant. And as she padded away, still graceful in the face of all that provocation, the mother ape growled, just audibly, to me, "This is unconscionable."

Grisette moved heavily over to her fellow tourists, one of whom was hitting her child and saying, "I'm not a millionaire!" and an English one – a British Army spouse, I supposed – "Get off me before you get a smacked bottom!" Grisette was chattering and scratching herself and looking to her friends to praise her for having pinched the ape baby and maddened the mother ape and driven them away.

And I thought: Yes, the apes are better-mannered than the tourists, and while the tourists brutalized and screamed at their kids, the apes were tender towards their young. The apes did not say, "I told you to stop it – I'll give you a clout!" The tourists yakked and giggled, the apes were quiet and thoughtful. The tourists teased the apes, the apes never teased the tourists. When the apes played they rolled over and over on the steep slopes or on the walkways of the Rock; when the tourists' children played they hurt each other and made a noise and it always seemed to end in tears. And the apes never made faces unless the tourists made faces at them first. Ape funerals were held in pious secrecy, a tourist death or funeral was accompanied by howling grief and hysterics. The tourists were obstreperous, the apes were dignified and·correct. Yet every year apes are shot and killed on the Rock of Gibraltar for biting tourists.

The woman of course was a French tourist. She might have been a tourist from any country in the Mediterranean. She fitted the description of "the Mediterranean sub-racial group" I found in a textbook entitled *Advanced Level Geography* (1964): "brown-skinned, long-headed, wavy-haired, dark-eyed, slightly-built." These people traveled back and forth across this interesting stretch of water all the time, keeping to their particular basin. But Mediterranean tourists were generally so offensive and ill-natured that I made a vow early in my trip to ignore them, the way I ignored the flies in Australia; to avoid writing about tourists at all. Far better to write about the apes.

"This ape is cruel," the tourist says, and it is like an epitaph for the world's animals. "When I pinch him he bites me."

For years I was happy flopping along elsewhere, avoiding the Mediterranean. Such a trip had always been regarded as the Grand Tour, a search for wisdom and experience. Yet at the age of fifty I still had never been to Spain. All I had seen of Yugoslavia was the main line from Ljubljana to the Bulgarian border. Yugoslavia was now five separate nations. I had never been to Israel or Egypt or Morocco or Malta. Most people I met had been to many of these countries. Everyone knew much more of the Mediterranean than I did. Everybody had been there. I suspected that from one end to the other it was nothing but urbanization and clip-joints. James Joyce once wrote, "Rome reminds me of a man who lives by exhibiting to travelers his grandmother's corpse." I assumed the whole Mediterranean was like that, tourism as ancestor-worship and the veneration of incoherent ruins.

Then I began to think that this was perhaps the best reason for going to see this part of the world, that it was so over-visited it was haunted and decrepit, totally changed. Change and decay had made it worth seeing and an urgent subject to record. I was the man for it. Half a lifetime of traveling had given me a taste for the macabre.

Some countries swallow the traveler; certainly in Africa and Polynesia and South America I found this to be true. But Europe and the Mediterranean in particular is like a stage set. It gives drama to a trip – it is a background.

You know this already. You have been to Italy – very likely to Sicily, perhaps to Siracusa, and you stayed at the same little hotel I found. Near the harbor? Run by a grumpy man who wrote poetry? About twenty-five dollars, with breakfast? And you might read this and say: It was not that way at all! Siracusa was delightful, the hotel was clean, the poet was a cheery soul. Or it might be somewhere else we both visited, in Spain or Greece or Egypt. Never mind.

That was your trip, that was your Italy. This book is about my trip, my Italy. This is my Mediterranean.

My idea was to begin in Gibraltar, and go to Spain, and keep going, hugging the coast, staying on the ground, no planes; to travel by train, bus, ferry, ship; to make a circuit of the sea from the Rock of Gibraltar all the way around to Ceuta, from one Pillar of Hercules to the other. To travel the whole shore, from the fish-and-chip shops of Torremolinos to the gun emplacements of Tel Aviv, by way of the war in Croatia and the nudist beaches of Crete.

The Mediterranean, this simple, almost tideless sea the size of thirty Lake Superiors, had everything: prosperity, poverty, tourism, terrorism, several wars in progress, ethnic strife, fascists, pollution, drift-nets, private islands owned by billionaires, gypsies, seventeen countries, fifty languages, oil-drilling platforms, sponge fishermen, religious fanatics, drug smuggling, fine art, and warfare. It had Christians, Muslims, Jews; it had the Druzes who are a strange farrago of all three religions; it had heathens, Zoroastrians and Copts and Bahais. It is over 2,000 miles from end to end. It is noted for being salty. It ranges from the shoals and shallows of the northern Adriatic to the almost 16,000-foot depths in the Ionian Basin, west of Crete. Although it is deficient in plankton, it is still the home of dolphins, and in the deeps around Majorca sperm whales (some of them entangled in drift-nets) are often sighted.

Giant loggerhead turtles – an endangered species in the Mediterranean – return in diminishing numbers every year to the Greek
island of Zakinthos, where they struggle among tourists and beachside restaurants for nesting sites.

One of the many strange facts about the Mediterranean people
is that compared with the British and the Northern Europeans
they are not great fish-eaters. This is Emil Ludwig's observation
and it is generally true. One of the more anticlimactic experiences
in a Mediterranean market is surveying the fish goggling on
marble slabs. There are not many, they are rather small, and the
larger proportion have been caught outside the Mediterranean.
Tuna is the exception, because it makes an annual journey through
the Pillars and across the Mediterranean to spawn in the Black
Sea. Dolphins are protected. With the exception of illegal drift-net
vessels that use nets of up to ten miles long (for example, Greenpeace France detected and documented 137 illegal Italian drift-
netters between April and June 1994), fishing is small-scale and
unrewarding. Deep-sea fishing in the Mediterranean is almost
unknown, apart from the illegal drift-netters and the competition
for the migrating tuna.

It is not a fishy sea, but it is blessed with a beautiful climate, and
though Mediterranean storms and high winds can be devastating,
it was always noted for its calm waters. The very word Mediterranean signified sunny skies and balmy weather, and for thousands
of years these shores had been a kind of Eden, fruitful with grapes
and olives and lemons.

But soon after I set off, I mentioned my itinerary to a young
French student on a train. Pointing to my map, I remarked on
how easy it was to travel around the Mediterranean.

"Croatia! Albania!" the student said. "And what about Algeria
– are you going there?"

"Of course. I've always wanted to see the souk in Algiers, Albert
Camus' Oran, taking the night train from Tunis to Annaba."

"In the past two years, twenty thousand people have been
killed in fighting in Algeria, most of them on the coast," he said.
"You didn't know that the most recent election was annulled and
the Muslim fundamentalists have a policy of killing all foreigners?"

No, I did not know that.

"Maybe I'll skip Algeria." And I thought: *Maybe they'll stop killing each other before I get there.*

Gibraltar is tiny, just two square miles of it, mostly uninhabited cliffs, and there are almost as many apes as there are humans. The name is from Tarik el Said, the Moorish conqueror who named it "Geb-el-Tarik" (Hill of Tarik). I arrived on a cheap flight from London sitting with Mr Wong, from the People's Republic. We looked at the Rock.

"Like a small mountain," Mr Wong said.

Like a beheaded sphinx, I thought, all buttocks and trunk, crouching with its paws on the water, and the more impressive for there being no other monstrosities or mountains near it.

Mr Wong told me he was planning to start a Chinese restaurant in the town. "And why did you come here?"

"Because I've never been here before," I said.

I had never been to Spain either. Once I had been to the South of France, to see Graham Greene in Antibes. That tiny fishing-port was all I knew of the Riviera. I had seen a little bit of Italy and had spent one day in Athens, but apart from that had not traveled in the Mediterranean, not even to the most obvious places. Israel, no. Lebanon, no. Egypt no – I had never seen the pyramids. Most English people I met had been to Majorca; I had never been there. Because I had not been to any of these Mediterranean places I had vigorous and unshakeable prejudices, and those prejudices amused me and kept me from wanting to visit the places.

And in the way that you don't really understand great novels until you are older and experienced, you needed to be a certain age to appreciate the subtleties of the Mediterranean. I had re-read *Anna Karenina* and felt that it was a different novel from the one I had read when I was twenty-one. I had also re-read *Tender is the Night*, and *The Plague*, and *The Secret Agent*. I wondered whether they would have the same impact. They did, but for different reasons; they were different books, because thirty-odd years later I was a different man.

By a happy coincidence these books all had Mediterranean connections. Dick and Nicole Diver singlehandedly invent the Riviera by turning the sleepy fishing village of Juan-les-Pins into a fashionable resort. Anna Karenina and her lover Vronsky escape Russia, and the scandal of their liaison, and experience bliss in a romantic interlude in Venice, Rome, and Naples; but after an extended stay in a palazzo in a small Italian town, they are disillusioned with Mediterranean life, "and the German tourists became so wearisome, that a change became absolutely necessary. They decided to return to Russia."

Joseph Conrad wrote the whole of his London novel in the South of France, in Montpellier; and Camus — who was born on the Algerian coast — set his novel in Oran. I had also recently read Hemingway (on bullfighting in Spain), Naguib Mahfouz and Cavafy (both on Alexandria), Flaubert (*Salammbô*, set in Carthage), Cyril Connolly (the Riviera again in *The Rock Pool*), and Evelyn Waugh's *Labels*, which takes in almost the whole of the Mediterranean. One of the most neglected post-war American novels of the Mediterranean coast — in this case southern Italy — is William Styron's complex and brilliant *This House on Fire*. I reread it with renewed admiration for its portraits of expatriate artists and drunks and poseurs, their brains baking in the Amalfi sunlight. And I had finally got around to reading *Christ Stopped at Eboli*, by Carlo Levi. The miserable little village he writes about, which he called Gagliano, isn't on the Mediterranean, but it is near enough; the real place, Aliano, is only about twenty miles from the sea, at the arch on the sole of Italy's boot. All these books fueled my desire to travel in the Mediterranean. Perhaps unconsciously I had been doing homework.

There was a time when I wanted to see only wild places, and was reluctant to go to a place that had been written about extensively. But then — it is so funny about travel — I would go to a place that everyone had written about and it was as though I was seeing something entirely new. I felt that when I was writing about Britain: my Britain was different from anything I had read. It made the going good because I was unprepared for what I saw. That was always the best part of travel, the sense of discovery. When there was none and it was all predictable, I wanted to go home.

The Mediterranean was not one place, but many; and I was at last calm enough to venture into its complexity without the risk of getting lost. I was happier with love in my life. I was not looking for a new home, traveling hopefully down the road rejecting places as I passed through. I was traveling in the purest way, without envy or a spirit of acquisition. I was setting out on an extensive trip around the shores of the Mediterranean, Christian, Muslim, Jewish and heathen; to meet the people, eat the food, get rained on and shot at.

My idea was to see it out of season, when the tourists were back home, to spend the fall and winter in the northern half, the spring and summer in the Levant and North Africa, going from one Pillar to the other; and to make a modern Grand Tour, seeking out wise people.

An inland sea is perfect for a journey, because the coastline determines the itinerary.

The day I arrived in Gibraltar, the Chief Minister of Gibraltar, Joe Bossano, was at the United Nations, explaining to the assembly why Gibraltar wanted to remain itself, autonomous. But Gibraltar has nothing but the Rock and its strategic location. It makes nothing, it sells nothing, it imports everything it needs to sustain life; it is tiny both in land area and population (a mere 28,000 people, of whom 16,000 are voters). It is just a few streets at the base of the Rock, and on the lower slopes there are some luxury homes and gun emplacements. There is not enough room for an airport, and so when a plane is due the main road into Spain is closed – barriers swing shut – and traffic is halted until the plane has landed. The aircraft taxis across the road and the portion of Gibraltar known as The Neck, and continues to the terminal. At the All Clear, the road reopens.

The Spanish dictator Franco, El Caudillo – his title was deliberately chosen to imitate Hitler's "Führer" and Mussolini's "Duce" – with his iron hand in a choke-hold on the throat of every Spaniard until just the other day, closed his border with Gibraltar in 1969.

"He died in 1975," a Gibraltarian told me, "but it was another ten years before the border was opened again."

That was ordered by Prime Minister Felipe Gonzalez in 1985. But Spain has never wavered in its insistence that Gibraltar be given back to Spain.

So for sixteen years Gibraltar was hemmed in like a little penal colony. And it did no good for the people in Gibraltar to harangue the Spaniards with the terms of the Treaty of Utrecht, which gave Britain sovereignty over the Rock in 1713. In this same treaty the island of Manhattan was swapped for Surinam. In the most casual conversations in Gibraltar, people quoted the relevant clause of the Treaty of Utrecht. I took a closer look at the Treaty and saw that the terms of Article 10 prevented "residence or entry into the town of Gibraltar by Jews and Moors."

The anonymous author of *How to Capture and Govern Gibraltar* (1865) stated that Protestants ought to be encouraged and given low rents and hospitality. But "Papists, Moors and Jews" should be discouraged.

And in some ways this sentinel rock became a bigoted British island at the entrance to the Mediterranean. As a large British garrison it could hardly fail to be reactionary, backward, philistine and drunken, as it upheld the long Royal Navy tradition of rum, sodomy and the lash. For many years it had been noted for its vast number of taverns. But there is something so wonderful and stark about the Rock − and it is the only grand work of nature for miles around − that its enchantment is transferred to the people who live on its lower slopes and at its base. It stands enormous and immutable, dwarfing everything and everyone nearby; and so Gibraltarians seem like a tribe of tiny idolaters, clinging to their mammoth limestone shrine.

It is pretty clear that shrunken, bankrupt Britain finds Gibraltar too expensive to run, no more than an inconvenient relic of a former age. It even looks it. Apart from the Rock it looks like an English coastal town, much smaller but with the same seediness and damp glamour of, say, Weston-super-Mare; a little promenade, and teashops, and fish-and-chip shops, and ironmongers, and respectable-looking public houses, and bus shelters and twitching curtains. Its Englishness makes it safe, tidy, smug, community-minded.

Gibraltar's historical notes satisfied my curiosity for meaningless facts and colorful atrocities. First there was the list of sieges, fourteen of them, going back to the year 410 when the Vandals overran the Roman Empire, and the later incursions of the Visigoths and the Ostrogoths. Franco's closure of Spain's frontier with Gibraltar is known as the fifteenth siege. In the seventh century King Sisebut persecuted Gibraltar's Jews, tortured thousands, and forcibly baptized 90,000 of them. Then there were 700 years of Moors in Gibraltar. And this: "In 1369, when Pedro the Cruel, who had succeeded Alfonso XI, was assassinated, the Count of Translamara seized the throne of Castile and became Henry II. The following year, 1370, Algeciras was destroyed by Mohammed V." And on 13 December 1872, "the mystery derelict *Marie Celeste* arrived in Gibraltar."

Lastly, Gibraltar is known as the scene of a sudden shocking multiple murder. The woman who told me where it had taken place described it in a whisper: "Walk down Winston Churchill Road, and just before the overpass, across from the Shell station, that's where it happened."

One day in 1988, much to the horror of Gibraltarians, three civilians were shot dead by men wearing masks. Witnesses described the suddenness of it, all three cut down, and one masked man lingering over a supine wounded man and finishing him off. And then the masked men vanished. It was not hard for them to get away, since they were members of the British SAS sent on this deadly mission by Margaret Thatcher.

No one mourned the murder victims – two men and a woman. They were Irish. It was claimed that they were going to plant a bomb at The Convent, the Governor's House, during a parade. That was not firmly established – the whole affair was obscured by official secrecy. Two years after the killings, a British minister in Mrs Thatcher's government blandly explained that the government briefings to journalists at the time of the incident had been inaccurate. The dead had not been armed, as had been suggested. And the car parked in Gibraltar had not contained explosives. So why were they killed?

The minister, Sir Geoffrey Howe, said: "They made movements which led the military personnel operating in support of Gibraltar police to conclude that their own lives and the lives of others were under threat."

The official version stressed that a bomb would have been devastating. The blast would have damaged two schools and a Jewish home for old folks and the marchers and the spectators. It would have been on a par with the bomb hidden under the bandstand in Hyde Park, that killed eleven members of a military band, one of the nastiest IRA crimes; it is very easy to plant a bomb in a peaceful, trusting place. But no one ever knew whether there had been any good reason for the murders of three Irish people that day.

Gibraltar is still a garrison, though greatly reduced in numbers of men, and the steep town looks severe but is actually rather friendly. In common with an English village, the Gibraltarians are friendly to the point of nosiness. It is small enough for everyone to know everyone else, except the Moroccans, who come and go. The Gibraltarian family names are all known – the English, the Spanish, the Jewish ones, especially. The great thing in Gibraltar is to be able to date your ancestry to the Genoese who emigrated early in the eighteenth century.

Because Gibraltarians asked me questions, I returned the compliment and pestered people about their origins.

"I'm a Gibraltarian," a man named Joe told me. His real name was José, and his surname sounded Spanish too. I asked him about that.

He said, "I'm not Spanish, I'm not English."

"What does your passport say?"

"Colony of Gibraltar," he said. "But we would rather be an English colony than part of Spain. The majority of people here want autonomy."

In other words, for Gibraltar to govern herself and for Britain to pay the bills.

"We want independence and to be part of the EEC. The frontier was opened in 1985 only to satisfy the EEC – the Spanish were trying to make friends."

"What did you do all those years when it was impossible to go across the road to Spain?"

"I went to Morocco." He shook his head. "It was not like anything I ever saw before."

"Interesting?"

"Awful."

We talked about the absence of any manufacturing in Gibraltar.

"But we have shipyards," he said. "We can repair ships."

"You speak Spanish?" I asked.

"And English."

In Gibraltar, the Spaniards were considered to be vastly inferior to the Gibraltarians; they were held in contempt for their passionate gesticulation, their forty years of Franco's fascism, their twanging guitars, their provincialism and irrationality and bean-eating and bull-torturing. Prejudices in Gibraltar were quite similar to those I had encountered in English seaside resorts, an enjoyable mixture of bluster and wrong-headedness, the Little Englander in full spate. But these poor rock-hoppers were, it seemed to me, about to be abandoned. In the fullness of time, I could imagine this place being handed over to the Spaniards just as ruthlessly as Hong Kong had been served up like a *dim sum* to whining Chinese plutocrats and executioners. Gibraltarians would very soon discover how bankruptcy could make a nation unsentimental and self-serving.

I wanted to talk to someone in power about this – someone other than people I casually encountered in public houses and at bus stops; so I sent a note to the distinguished former Chief Minister Sir Joshua Hassan, and waited for a reply.

It was rainy and cool these October days. I became fond of this weather for various reasons. It was good for writing, and it kept the tourists away. In such grim weather there was always a place to stay and it was seldom necessary to make onward arrangements. I liked feeling that I could leave a town at a moment's notice and be assured that I would find a hotel farther up the line. In the whole of the Mediterranean, all seventeen countries, traveling off-season, I never had a problem of that sort, showing up in a place that was full of "No Vacancy" signs. In fact, most hotel-owners complained to me that there weren't half enough tourists these days.

In the several days that I waited to hear from Sir Joshua, I climbed the Rock. There was a lovely view from a vantage point at 1,350 feet, at the summit. To the west was Algeciras on a sweep of bay; to the north, the low brown hills of San Roque beyond The

Neck; to the south, beyond the lighthouses at Europa Point, across the Straits, was Morocco – Ceuta, the other Pillar, and farther west, Tangiers.

At that altitude, wandering among the tourists and apes, learning to distinguish between them, I concluded that because the apes were both intelligent and deprived they are quite like the homeless people in big cities, soft-voiced, panhandling, desperate and yet chastened creatures. They are, horribly, like the poor in Europe – ragged and dispossessed, tenacious and yet fatalistic, as they hang on, knowing they are despised; they have that resentful but fatalistic look of natives who have been displaced by swindling late-comers. The apes on the Rock are one of the underclasses of Gibraltar. Another underclass are the Moroccans. Coincidentally, the apes also originated in Morocco – in 1740 a whole tribe of apes was imported.

There was a strong sense of community in Gibraltar, which made it much odder for me to reflect that I was in a place that was both a racial hotchpotch and also deeply paranoid about admitting aliens. It was partly a result of Gibraltar's insularity – the Rock is significantly an island. But tribalism and xenophobia were also Mediterranean character traits. Never mind that the history of the Mediterranean is a history of mongrelization; these days the most common sound was the native mongrel yapping about his pedigree and driving off foreign mutts.

After I saw the French tourist taunting the mother ape I asked a Gibraltarian who worked on the Rock whether many people were attacked.

"Lots of people are bitten," he said, "but the strange thing is that nine out of ten are women – the women get the bites. We had one yesterday – a woman – big bite on her arm."

His name was Jerry. One of his jobs was operating the cable car. I asked him whether the apes had rabies.

"No. These apes are medically looked after. But we send the people to the hospital anyway."

I told him what a policeman in New York had once told me, that a human bite is much more dangerous than an animal bite, and that a tourist who bit you would do more harm than an ape.

From the top of the Rock it was possible to see that Gibraltar was little more than a harbor and a cluster of tenements, and like many towns with hills nearby the higher you live on the slopes the posher your house. The cable car passed over swimming-pools and hot tubs and foaming whirlpool baths attached to luxury homes. Later, I looked at an 1810 map of Gibraltar and it reminded me of a colonial map of Boston: fifteen batteries – Queen's Battery, King's, Norman's, Cockaigne's, Prince of Hesse's, Mungo's, and so forth. Then The Neck and the Spanish lines and all the papists on the Spanish side. It was as though Dorchester Heights remained British while the rest of America went its own way – just as odd and inconvenient and anachronistic.

Major Brian Cooper Tweedy of the Royal Dublin Fusiliers was posted in Gibraltar late in the last century. His daughter Marion, known to all as Molly, lost her virginity to one Harry Mulvey in Gibraltar. Later, particularly at bedtime, she ruminated on her sexual encounters in Gibraltar. This woman, literature's earth mother, is of course Molly Bloom, and her girlhood in Gibraltar, being kissed under the Moorish Wall, is vividly recounted in her drowsy soliloquy at the end of *Ulysses*.

Molly remembers "those awful thunderbolts in Gibraltar as if the world was coming to an end," and the obscene Gibraltarian graffiti that "used to be written up with a picture of a woman on that wall in Gibraltar with that word I couldn't find anywhere." The Rock in her memory is emblematic and powerful, "looking across the bay from Algeciras all the lights of the rock like fireflies."

She ruminates on the weather: "the rain was lovely just after my beauty sleep I thought it was going to get like Gibraltar my goodness the heat there before the levanter came on black as night and the glare of the rock standing up in it like a big giant." And even the apes: "I told him it was struck by lightning and all about the old Barbary apes they sent to Clapham without a tail."

Most of all, Molly's remembrance is of her first sexual encounter, one of the most passionate in literature. She hardly remembers Mulvey's name but the incident is vivid: "we lay over the firtree cove a wild place I suppose it must be the highest rock in existence the galleries and casemates and those frightful rocks and Saint

Michaels cave with the icicles or whatever they call them hanging down . . ." And the moment itself: "he was the first man kissed me under the Moorish wall my sweetheart when a boy it never entered my head what kissing meant till he put his tongue in my mouth." And the glorious Gibraltarian conclusion: ". . . I put my arms around him yes and drew him down to me so he could feel my breasts all perfume and his heart was going like mad and yes I said yes I will Yes."

There could be a Molly Bloom Defloration Tour of the Rock, but there isn't. James Joyce never visited Gibraltar; he was scribbling and studying maps in another corner of the Mediterranean – Trieste. But it is a testimony to his imaginative powers that it is impossible to be in Gibraltar and not hear Molly's sensuous voice. The presence of Jews in Gibraltar interested Joyce greatly – after all, his Ulysses figure, Leopold Bloom, was a Dublin Jew. In spite of Gibraltar being associated with Jewish expulsions, its Jewish community has deep roots. There are five synagogues in the little town.

Still waiting for a reply from Sir Joshua Hassan, I met Stephen Leanse, a Jewish entrepreneur.

"I was born in the Bahamas," he said, "but my wife's family, the Serruyas, came here in 1728."

The majority of Gibraltarians trace their origins to Genoa and are Catholic. Some others are Maltese. A few are British expatriates – shopkeepers, ex-servicemen. No one admits to being Spanish. Stephen was one of a thousand or so Jews in Gibraltar, members of about a hundred Jewish families. It was not a large number, but it was an influential – and cosmopolitan – segment of the population. They were all Sephardic Jews, some of them speaking Spanish – the word Sephardic means "of Spain." Others were speaking Ladino – the Sephardic language that combined Renaissance Spanish with elements of Hebrew.

Like most other people I met in Gibraltar, Mr Leanse told me that the place was small, perhaps too small; and business was poor; and the future was uncertain.

"I would love to live in Israel, but my family is here."

"Are the Jews in Gibraltar associated with any particular business?"

"No. All sorts of businesses. We don't manufacture anything.

Some of us are in banking, or we have shops, or restaurants. Some are politicians."

One of the Jewish restaurants was the Bomb House Lane Glatt Kosher Restaurant, where I heard Yiddish, Ladino, Spanish, English and Hebrew spoken, all at once, sometimes in the same sentence, under a picture of David Ben-Gurion and another of a girlish Queen Elizabeth II. Everyone in the place wore a yarmulka, even the funny little man depicted on the menu. Because this glatt kosher restaurant was in Gibraltar, some of the dishes on the menu were Moroccan. The cook – along with most cooks, cleaners, bus-drivers and waitresses in Gibraltar – was Moroccan. A good proportion of the Jewish diners had come from Morocco.

Glatt indicates a specific sort of kosherness in meat. The word is Yiddish for "smooth" and signifies that after the animal was ritually slaughtered by a *shochet* its lungs were examined and found to have no punctures. It also suggests that in life it had no imperfections on its skin: a cow with no spots, a calf an even shade of brown, a monochrome chicken, a fluffy little prancing lamb, a goat that was above reproach. The opposite of *glatt* is *trayfe* (or *terefah*), meaning "torn" – and that could be a creature with a punctured lung, or a fatal laceration, or a suppurating wound. All this is discussed in the Talmud (which advocates the eating of several species of locusts, provided they are not *trayfe*). It is also somehow related to the idea of sacrifice – that if a lamb is worthy to be slain, it had to be the sort of lamb that would win a blue ribbon at a country fair. God loved you for sacrificing your best, most impressive animal.

Dietary laws fascinate me for the way they mingle good sense with utter foolishness. But for me the *glatt* concept was purely academic. I told the waiter I was not a meat-eater and ordered fish.

My sea bass was grilled. It was a kosher fish, no imperfections, with both fins and scales. (Every fish that has scales also has fins, but not vice versa.) But when I stuck my fork into it the middle was still frozen and tasted *trayfe*. When I sent it back to be thawed and re-cooked, they obliged me. The bill was nineteen dollars – twelve handsomely engraved Gibraltar pounds, and so I com-plained, but it was no use.

Soon they would have competition from Mr Wong and his joint-venture Chinese restaurant.

In the Jewish Social and Cultural Club a leaflet on a notice-board announced Hillel Tours' "Annual Trip to Spain." It sounded as though this destination was remote – a journey to a far-off land, when in fact if you walked down Bomb House Lane and looked west you could see Algeciras, and after a ten-minute stroll north you could spit in La Linea, where once there had been bullfights (Molly Bloom: "the bullfight at La Linea when that matador Gomez was given the bulls ear").

But because Gibraltar has turned its back on Spain, Spain seems remote; and the Gibraltarian's face is averted from Morocco. It seems irrelevant that Gibraltar occupies one side of the Bay of Algeciras. It is an inward-looking place, and in spite of its majestic position on the Mediterranean, hardly anyone seems interested in the water.

The exception to this apparent hydrophobia are the members of the Mediterranean Rowing Club, who scull a thirty-foot four-man boat called a *yola*, a very beamy craft made in Florence.

I went to the club, hoping that I would be able to go for a row, but the Gibraltarians who showed me around said that the day was too windy.

The prevailing wind is a westerly – "a fresh, cool one, like today," said Alfie Brittenden, one of the club's rowers. "The Levanter is an easterly that brings humidity. Sometimes the Levanter makes a cloud form on the Rock."

"Do you ever row across the Straits?" I asked.

"Occasionally we row to Morocco, for an annual charity event. But it's very hard. There's a four-knot current and rough water."

"I was wondering whether I might bring my kayak here."

"It would be suicide to try it alone," Alfie said.

But another man at the club told me that I should not be intimidated.

"Ees there, Morocco," he said. "Ees eesie."

"That's what I thought."

"You can't loose eet."

That night I went along to the NAAFI at one of the military barracks near the harbor and watched a World Cup qualifying match. It was England versus Holland and the room was packed with hundreds of screaming, chanting England fans. At first England seemed to be holding its own. The whole room was united in its howling, but when Holland scored two goals in quick succession and England failed to make any reply there was disappointment and then real anger among the soldiers who earlier had been screaming for blood. That loss cast a heavy pall over Gibraltar, and the next day the Rock was in mourning for England's interment by the Dutch.

Hearing nothing from Sir Joshua Hassan, I called his office and told him I was planning to leave soon. He apologized and said I could visit him that same afternoon.

He is the grand old man of the Rock, the father of modern Gibraltar. "Sir J. Hassan & Partners" was on the top floor of a bank. On the wall of Sir Joshua's office there was a large photograph of the man himself at the time he was Chief Minister, addressing a vast crowd in Gibraltar's main square. A framed charter signed by the Queen. A gilded document: "We have inscribed your name in the Golden Book of Jewish Unity." And a telegram from Prince Philip: "Congratulations on your well-deserved honour" – Sir Joshua's knighthood.

He was dark and small and stout and lined, a kindly sloping presence, and he had the softest hands, and the limp handshake of an old woman. His Ladino accent and his solemn face made him seem at times not Jewish but Spanish, but his confidence and fits of sudden jollity transformed him into a Dickensian barrister. He was seventy-eight.

Realizing I did not have much time, I bluntly asked him about the status of Gibraltar.

"The person who says 'I want Gibraltar to be Spanish' does not exist in Gibraltar," he said. "If Gibraltar is not my country, where is my country? Ha! We consider ourselves Gibraltarians irrespective of where we came from. We get along very well together."

"So you are totally committed to Gibraltar," I said.

Sir Joshua said, "Jews have a second loyalty – to Israel. But that is an emotional loyalty. My daughter lives there."

His own people, he said, the Hassan family, had emigrated to the Rock in 1788, from Morocco — from a town just across the water, Tetuan. On his mother's side, the Cansino family came from Minorca. "We're all settlers here," he said, "dating from roughly 1704."

I said, "It amazes me how everyone quotes the terms of the Treaty of Utrecht when they talk about Gibraltar."

"Because of the clause about Jews and Moors being forbidden to stay in Gibraltar more than a month. But they needed us. They had to look to Morocco for victuals. Because of realities they drove a coach and horses through the treaty."

He shuffled some documents.

"I wrote a paper about it. My thesis was that Gibraltar developed despite the treaty."

"Do you think the Chief Minister made any headway the other day at the UN?"

"Joe Bossano doesn't know what he wants," he said, and leaned towards me. "When people go berserk they ask for something they don't understand. The idea of a colony smells bad."

"So what's the best solution?"

"It is very difficult! There are three choices for Gibraltar. Independence is one. Or, to be part of a state – but Spain is out of the question. Or free association, like the Cook Islands and New Zealand."

"The Cook Islanders go fishing and New Zealand pays the bills. Something like that?"

This made Sir Joshua wince. He said, "The best solution would be the utmost autonomy in internal matters, and a treaty with Britain that would remove the wide powers of the Governor."

"What would Spain say to that?"

"Spain would never agree that Gibraltar should have its own government," he said. "But I don't want to be colonized by Spain. I was colonized already by Britain!"

"Weren't you worried when Franco was in power?"

"Yes, because he had a tyrannical government. But just the other day the Spanish foreign minister made a speech demanding sovereignty over us and calling us 'the last colony in Europe.' The Spanish say, 'It is a matter of honor!' But we have honor too."

"Isn't Gibraltar a colony?"

"We call ourselves a dependent territory."

"I have the impression that business is rather poor, with most of the British troops pulled out."

"Business isn't good. We get tourists, and some day-trippers from Spain" – the tormentors of the Rock apes, the souvenir-hunters that arrived in buses from Torremolinos and Marbella. "We used to have day-trippers from Morocco, but because of French paranoia against North Africans the Moroccans now need visas to enter EEC countries. It's ridiculous and very bad for business."

"Gibraltar's in the EEC?" This was news to me.

"Yes. We are a full member politically. But we are excluded from VAT and other taxes."

I asked him, "Are you aware of being a sort of folk hero and father figure of Gibraltar?"

He smiled at this, as though agreeing with what I said but forbidden by modesty to say so.

"I am speaking to you candidly now," he said. "I go to Spain every now and then. My wife shops for vegetables there. On one trip I said to a guard, 'Why are the Spanish police and guards here so courteous to me, when they know that I want to keep Gibraltar independent from Spain?'"

The order in Sir Joshua's office and the way he was dressed, with that excessive neatness that is common to morticians and lawyers, told me that he was fastidious. Perhaps this was why he pursed his lips and narrowed his eyes as though an unpleasant thought was passing through his mind.

"The guard said to me, 'Because you put *sus cojones sur la mesa* –'"

"Your balls on the table," I said.

"Yes. He continued, 'And you haven't offended anyone.'"

"That's a pretty neat trick."

"Oh, yes. I was flattered."

It was time for me to go. I thanked him for seeing me and speaking frankly, and I told him sincerely that I had enjoyed myself in Gibraltar. Though I did not tell him this, fearing he would misunderstand, I liked it best because it was unexpected; the rain, the gusting wind, the dignified apes. It was not at all the Mediterranean port I had expected but more like an English seaside resort in autumn, full of plucky retirees and gasconading soldiers.

"The only thing wrong with us," Sir Joshua said, ruefully rather than in anger, "is our bloody size!"

2

The *Mare Nostrum* Express to Alicante

To prove a point to myself about Gibraltar's smallness I picked up my bag and walked from my hotel in the middle of Gibraltar to the Spanish frontier; got my passport stamped, and then sauntered into Spain; another stamp. The whole international journey from my thirty-dollar room in Gibraltar to the cheese-colored suburbs in the foothills of Andalusia was less than half an hour.

My first day in Spain. I thought of a line from the Spanish writer, Pio Baroja, that V.S. Pritchett quotes: "It may look as if I am seeking something; but I am seeking nothing." (*Parece que busco algo; pero no busco nada.*)

There were no coastal trains from Algeciras, no useful trains at all, until Malaga. The Algeciras bus was waiting at the station at La Linea, over the border, a town cauchemaresque in its littleness and its sense of being unpeopled and nowhere. Its nondescript beach was noted for its smugglers – drugs, cigarettes, appliances. This bus was just a rattly thing, full of locals who were heading home from work to the ferry port that lay beneath the brown hills. I looked back and saw that Gibraltar was no more than its dramatic Rock. The town was not visible until darkness fell, and then all you saw were lights on its lower slopes like candle flames flickering around an altar. As we passed around the bay the Rock receded, changing shape as the prospect altered.

The best view of Gibraltar is from Algeciras, across the bay, where the Rock appears as a long ridge, like a fortress, something man-made and defensive rather than the recumbent and misshapen monster at the edge of the sea. The Neck, Gibraltar's land connection to Spain, is so low, almost at sea-level, that the enormous citadel of rock seems to be detached from the mainland.

That low-lying neck gave Oliver Cromwell a bizarre idea. He decided to make Gibraltar an island; to detach it – dig a wide trench that would quickly fill with water, and sever the Rock from the Spanish mainland. Presto! the English island of Gibraltar. According to Samuel Pepys, Cromwell authorized a ship loaded with picks and shovels to set sail in 1656 to accomplish this God-like task of fiddling with the landscape. The ship was captured by the Spaniards. Then Oliver Cromwell died. The scheme was abandoned.

Algeciras was merely my starting-point. "An ugly town of very slight interest," the guidebook said. But this was the sort of guidebook that recommended a town when it had a building that it could praise in these terms: "The central dome is supported on a hexadecagonal beading over squinches."

A scruffy little Spanish man took me aside.

"You German?"

"American."

"Good, I like Americans," he said. "You want to buy one kilo of hash?"

"No, thank you. It may look as if I am seeking something, but I am seeking nothing."

"You no like me?" he said, and turned abusive.

I ignored him and walked to the harbor where the ferry, *Ciudad de Zaragoza*, was setting out for Tangiers. Another ferry left from Tarifa, where in the past Barbary pirates demanded payment from all ships passing through the Straits (and so this tiny haven of extortionists, Tarifa, gave us our taxation word "tariff"). Morocco, across the water, was as near as Falmouth is from Vineyard Haven. It was my intention to end my trip there, and to get there by the most roundabout route, via France and Italy, Croatia, Albania, Malta, Israel, and every other Mediterranean shore, even Algeria, if I had the stomach for it. It gave me pleasure to turn away from the ferry landing and walk to the bus station, and buy a ticket to Marbella. I assumed it would take a year or so to reach Morocco.

The bus had plenty of empty seats, and yet when a couple got on wearing matching warm-up suits, the woman sat at the front alone and the man sat right next to me.

He was in his mid to late sixties, with a big intrusive face and mocking frown and hairy ears. He looked careless and lazy, and he stared at me in a meddling way. He said, "Hi there."

My dim smile was meant to convey that I was perhaps Spanish. I said nothing. I wanted to concentrate on this, my first experience of Spain.

We rolled out of town, past the bullring. The man next to me muttered "Plaza de Toros" in a self-congratulatory way, though he merely squinted at the graffiti on the walls next to the Autovia di Mediterraneo, most of it very angry: *Yanqui = Terroristas* and *Republica Si! – Monarchia No!* and *No Vote – Lucha!* ("Don't Vote – Fight!") The grandly named highway was just a winding two-lane road along the coast, running past scrubby fields and truck stops and low rocky hills under a gray sky on a Saturday afternoon, the market closed, the beaches empty – the water much too cold for swimming – and even the little old men fishing from the jetties wearing foul-weather gear.

The piles of cork-oak bark stacked by the side of the road suggested that a traditional harvest ritual was taking place – not right here, but inland, away from the shore. And that was my first Mediterranean epiphany, the realization that life on these shores bore little relation to what was happening five miles inland, no matter what the country. Somewhere over this Andalusian hill a peasant was hacking bark off trees to sell. That hinterland was not my subject, though; I did not care about the perplexities of Europe. My concentration was on the edge of this body of water, the ribbon of beach and cliff, and all the people who shared it, used and misused it, even the snorting old man who for some reason had chosen to sit next to me on the bus.

The Spanish newspaper I had bought in Algeciras told of a murder scandal involving wealthy English expatriates – the wife dead in mysterious circumstances, the husband a prime suspect – in Sotogrande, the next town.

"Cops," the man next to me said.

It was a road block; he had seen it before me, about six policemen at a bend in the road, directing cars to an area where they were to park and be searched. This was a throwback to Franco, surely. The police, the Guardia Civil, masters of intimidation

and search-and-destroy missions, were plundering the trucks of cars
and interrogating drivers and passengers.

This had nothing to do with the Sotogrande murder. It was a
search for illegal drugs, items such as the kilo of hashish that the
Algeciras punk had tried to sell me. The police, who were heavily
armed, had sniffer dogs and mirrors, and two of them moved
through the bus, poking luggage, looking under seats, and harass-
ing the dirtier male passengers. The most woeful-looking passenger
was ordered to stand up in the aisle while a policeman examined
each cigarette in the pack he had in his pocket. The police dog
slavered at me and padded on.

"This is unreal," the man next to me said, perhaps to me,
perhaps to himself.

When they were satisfied that the bus did not contain any drugs,
we were allowed to continue on our way.

"Spain is a land to flee across. Every town, and every capital, is
a destination; and the names, which ring with refuge to the
fugitive, mount with finality to him traveling relentlessly
unpursued."

That accurate description of my mood that day (even if it
sounded a bit too orotund for the landscape I was looking at) is by
William Gaddis in *The Recognitions*, the great American novel of
counterfeiting and forgery. Gaddis's vision of Spain was one of the
many that filled my head. The experience of Spain had been an
inspiration to some of my favorite writers. If I read enough about
one country I sometimes found that the intensity of the reading
removed my desire to travel there. I did not want to risk disappointment – the reality displacing the fabulous land in my imagination.
Arthur Waley, the great Chinese scholar and translator, refused to
go to China; he did not want to risk having his illusions shattered.
He was wise. His illusions of the harmony and grace inspired by the
Chinese classics would not have survived for two stops on the Iron
Rooster.

It was impossible to be in Spain and not think of Hemingway,
lover of fiestas, whose literary reputation was partly based on his
passion for bullfighting, and whose notions of honor and heroism,
not to say the human condition, were derived in greater measure
from the *toreros* he mooned over than from the foot-soldiers in the

Spanish Civil War he also wrote about. I personally had an aversion to Hemingway's work, but that was a matter of taste; I did not dismiss him. Hemingway appears in Gaddis's book, not by name but as a sententious old bore and boozer known as the Big Unshaven Man (BUM for short). I disliked *A Farewell to Arms* because it seemed to me to be written in Pilgrim Father English. I preferred Orwell's account of the Spanish Civil War in *Homage to Catalonia*, and his version of how the war had challenged his political ideas. Gerald Brenan was for me the best guide through Spanish history in *South from Granada*, Jan Morris's *Spain* provided all I needed to know about the Spanish landscape, and V.S. Pritchett's *The Spanish Temper* seemed the shrewdest possible examination of Spanish literature and of the passions and pastimes of the Spaniards.

I had read as much as I could – everything mattered – but it struck me on this Spanish bus that I had never seen a landscape like this described anywhere, in any book I had read about Spain. That cheered me up. This was as remote from the Spain of Cervantes and Hemingway and Pritchett and everyone else as it was possible to be. This was the Spain of the absurd travel brochures, the cheap flights, the package tours and the more mendacious travel magazines.

It was a sort of cut-price colonization, this stretch of coast, bungaloid in the extreme, bungalows and twee little chalets and monstrosities in all stages of construction, from earthworks and geometrically excavated foundations filled with mud puddles to brick and stucco condos and huts and houses. There were cheap hotels, and golf courses, and marinas, and rain-sodden tennis courts and stagnant swimming-pools at Estepona, where "Prices Slashed" was a frequent sign on housing developments in partly-built clusters with names such as "Port Paradise" and "The Castles" and "Royal Palms" – no people on the beach, no people on the road, no golfers, no sign of life at all, only suggestions here and there that the place was known to English-speaking people. "English Video Club" was one, and another that was hardly out of view from Gibraltar to the French frontier at Port Bou: "Fish-and-Chips."

And it was only the other day that this whole coast had sprung up and become vulgarized as the object of intense real-estate speculation. My guidebook said of awful overgrown Estepona, "As recently as 1912, the road ended here."

Then, this end of Spain was just mules and goats; and peasants hoeing the rocky hillsides, cutting cork oak, gathering barnacles and praying on their knees. And now they are mopping the floors of the bungalows at "Port Paradise."

"It's all English people here," the man next to me said. "You speak English?"

"Yes."

"Your pants don't have a fly," he said.

I did not have an answer for this. He was smiling. I said, "Does that bother you?"

"Seems to me that makes them kind of inconvenient."

I am on my Grand Tour, on this Spanish bus on a gray day out of season, minding my own business, and this foolish old man who insists on sitting next to me points out that my Patagonia pants don't have a fly. I did not ask for this at all.

He was still smiling. He said, "See my wife? That's her up there."

Commenting on the cut of my pants was merely a way of breaking the ice. He wanted to talk about his wife.

"She was an X-rated showgirl," he said, and out of the corner of my eye I saw that he was watching my reaction.

She had the face of an elderly baby. Her hair was stiff and blonde. She was looking out the bus window, giving me her profile. She was big, hefty even, and her baggy warm-up suit conveyed an impression of physical plenitude. Yet there was a soft and faded beauty about her, a carefulness in her make-up that told she was still trying, that she still cared, and perhaps it was the absurdity of her husband that made me think she was very unhappy.

"No, I'm kidding you. Not X-rated. She was a Las Vegas showgirl."

He was not looking at me any more. His forearms rested on the seat-bar in front of him, and he was staring.

"Imagine what she looked like forty years ago."

We were passing gray sand, weedy yards, hillsides of condominiums – some with turrets, some with battlements, all of them empty; and houses and villas helter-skelter.

To this man who had offended me by commenting on the way I was dressed I said, "I imagine she looked twenty-five."

"She was beautiful," he insisted. Hadn't he heard me? "She's still beautiful."

You pimp, I thought, why aren't you sitting with her?

"She knows I'm talking about her."

The woman had glanced back and her face darkened.

"She'd kill me if she knew what I was saying. She hates having been a showgirl. That's where I met her. Vegas. If she knew what I was saying to you she'd murder me."

We had come to Guadalmina, which looked old-fashioned and pleasant. I wanted to make a note, but the man beside me was talking again.

"She's tough. You wouldn't think it, but she is. She makes all the decisions. She wears the pants in the house."

"You seem to be an expert on pants," I said. In my mind I imagined his wife, this bulky woman, in big brown tweedy pants and clomping shoes, walking through a house in which this man cowered.

"I once said to her, 'I'm going to marry a rich woman next time. I don't care if she's fat or ugly, as long as she has money.'"

The man laughed, remembering this conversation.

"My wife says to me, 'And what are you going to offer her?'"

"What did you say to that?"

"What could I say? She shot me down."

We came to San Pedro de Alcantara, which was older and more settled, something like a town. *Few trees to speak of*, I wrote in my innocence, little knowing that on the thousands of miles of Mediterranean coastline there are few trees to speak of, no forests except for one in Corsica, hardly any woods abutting the shore. It made for a rather stark coastline, but it revealed everything – here at San Pedro the ruins of a Roman villa, a Visigoth's basilica and a Moorish castle, and all those bungalows.

I had not planned to get off the bus at Marbella, but this man irritated me. I had the feeling that it gave him a perverse pleasure to sit with me at a distance and leer at his wife, in the way that some men enjoy watching their spouse have sex with strangers; at the very least, he wanted to go on talking. I am out of here.

Passing the woman just before I got off, I turned to her. She looked at once alarmed and suspicious.

Laughing a little, I said, "Your husband tells me you were a Las Vegas showgirl. I would never have known."

The last sound I heard was this woman's howl ringing through the bus and the pusillanimous whine of her husband's hollow denial.

In Marbella I met a Spaniard, Vicente, who had just spent a year in Mexico. He worked for a company that exported Spanish olive oil. He had liked his time in Mexico, but – buttoned-up, self-conscious, innately gloomy, cursed with an instinctive fatalism, and envious in a class-obsessed way – patronized the Mexicans much as the British patronize Americans, and for the same reasons.

"They talk like this," Vicente said, and did an imitation of a Mexican talking in slushy mutterings with his teeth clamped shut.

It seemed accurate and clever to me, and I told him so, though he seemed to be embarrassed by his effort and he was too shy to continue. And, naturally, having mocked them, he then said what wonderful people the Mexicans were.

"Did you go to any bullfights there?"

"Yes. Very small bulls in Mexico. Our bulls are much bigger and stronger – more brave. We breed them especially to fight."

"Any other differences?"

"We use the horses more. And much else. I cannot explain all the differences."

Everything I knew about bullfighting, including "There is no Spanish word for bullfight," I had learned from *The Sun Also Rises*. Rose Macaulay's appreciative book about Spain, *Fabled Shore* (1949) – an account of a trip down this coast – mentions bullfights only once and briefly: "I do not care for them."

I said, "I was thinking of going to a *corrida*."

"Have you never seen one?"

"No – never."

This made Vicente laugh, and he insisted I should go to one.

"We love football, but the *corrida* is here," he said and tapped his heart. "It is our passion. And, listen, one of the most popular *toreros* in Spain is from America – Colombia."

I was grateful for Vicente's encouragement, but I did not really need it. I had intended to go to the first bullfight I saw advertised.

In the meantime I had found a place to stay in Marbella. As an experiment in budget travel I had found a ten-dollar-a-night room in a *pensione* behind the oldest church in the town, the Iglesia de la Encarnacion. This was in the Old Town. An effort had obviously been made in Marbella to renovate this older neighborhood and reclaim some of its narrow alleys and small lanes. I regarded this as a challenge. Anyone can go to a strange town and buy comfort and goodwill. With the single exception of limping, vandalized Albania, which is in a state of disrepair and anarchy, luxury is available in most places on the shores of the Mediterranean.

I knew from experience that the de luxe route was the easy way out, and that it was unreal, the fast lane, where I would meet stuffy travelers and groveling locals. I did not require luxury, I needed only modest comfort and privacy, and it was often possible to find what I wanted for ten or fifteen dollars. This was particularly so in the off-season, as the wind blew through these coastal resort towns, where business was terrible.

Even Marbella, which had the reputation of being one of the more salubrious resorts, was hurting. The summer had been bad and nothing was happening now; it would be a long winter. The rise in inflation and the cost of living generally had surprised the British who had retired here. Many were in the process of selling their houses – at a loss in some cases – and moving elsewhere.

"And to think that there were British people who went to Estepona to retire and find the good life," I said to an Englishman in Marbella.

"I've met a number of expats on the Costa del Sol who are trying to sell up and go home. Prices are high, taxes are high – to pay for the redevelopment and the improvement. That's why Marbella looks nice. The people came because life was so cheap here in the 1970s and 80s, and now it's more expensive than Britain. They want to go home."

"You see all these houses being built?" a Spanish real-estate agent told me. "It's all Kuwaiti money. Middle East people."

This was impossible to verify, though other locals mentioned it — that this building boom had been a result of Arab investment in the late eighties and early nineties, punters hoping to make a killing in the Spanish property market. It had the look of a bubble, though: too many houses, too much development. The "For Immediate Sale!" and "Prices Slashed!" signs had a desperate note of hysteria in them.

I hung around Marbella for a day and a half, noted the youngsters prowling the empty discothèques and clubs, and ate paella.

When I inquired about the bullfight I hoped to see, I was told to go to Malaga . . . to Granada . . . to Barcelona . . . to Madrid — anywhere but Marbella; and so I left on a bus, heading north along the shore to Torremolinos. There were no coastal trains here — none until Valencia or thereabouts — but the buses went everywhere.

The utterly blighted landscape of the Spanish coast ("Oh, there he goes again," someone just muttered, reading that — but please wait for the end of the paragraph) — Europe's vacationland, a vile straggling sandbox — begins about here, north of Marbella, and continues, with occasional breaks, all the way up the zigzag shore to France. The meretriciousness, the cheapo appeal, the rankness of this chain of grease-spots is so well known it is superfluous for me to describe it; and it is beyond satire. So why bother?

But several aspects of this reeking vulgarity interested me. The first was that the debased urbanization on this coast seemed entirely foreign, as though the whole holiday business had been foisted on Spain by outside investors hoping to cash in. The phenomenon of seaside gimcrackery was familiar to anyone who had traveled on the British coast and examined the Kingdom by the Sea. Spain even had the same obscene comic postcards, and funny hats, and junk food. It was also ridiculously cheap, in spite of the retirees' complaints about the high cost of living. The Spaniards did not mock it, and they were grateful for the paying guests; for many years this was the chief source of Spanish prosperity. It was also remarkably ugly, and this was especially true in these out-of-season months. In full sunshine it might have had a cheap and cheerful carnival atmosphere, but under gray skies it hovered, a grotesque malignancy, sad and horrible, that was somewhere between tragedy and farce. And Spain seemed distant.

I felt intensely that the Spanish coast, especially here on the Costa del Sol, had undergone a powerful colonization – of a modern kind, but just as pernicious and permanent a violation as the classic wog-bashing sort. It had robbed the shore of its natural features, displaced headlands and gullies and harbors with futile badly-made structures. It did not repel me. It showed what unruly people were allowed to do to a magnificent shoreline when they had a little money and no taste. It had a definite horror-interest.

The landscape was obliterated, and from the edge of the Mediterranean to the arid gravely inland slopes there were off-white stucco villas. There were no hills to speak of, only sequences of stucco rising in a hill shape, like a collapsing wedding cake. There were no people, there were few cars, and after dark only a handful of these houses were lit. In the poorer, nastier coves there were campsite communities and the footprint foundations in cement for caravans and tents.

A poisonous landfill, a dump with a prospect of the sea dominated Fuengirola, which was otherwise just high-rises and huts. Ugly little towns such as Arroyo de la Miel sometimes had the prettiest names – in that case "Honey Gulch" – but the worst indication of blight on this coast was the gradual appearance of signs in English: "Cold Beer" and "Afternoon Tea" and "Authentic English Breakfast" and "Fish and Chips" – and little flapping Union Jacks. They were also the hint that we were nearing Torremolinos, which was grim and empty and dismal and sunless; loud music mingled with the stink of frying, souvenir letter-openers and ashtrays and stuffed animals and funny hats stacked on a narrow strip of gray sand by the slop of the sea.

There were some tourists here – British, French, German – making the best of things, praying for the sun to shine. Instead of staying I found a train and took it back to Fuengirola, which was just as awful as Torremolinos. That night strolling along the promenade – the sea was lovelier at night – I saw a bullfight poster, announcing a *feria* the next day at Mijas, not far away.

There was a bullfight on television in a café near my hotel that night. The café was filled with silent men, smoking cigarettes and sipping coffee. A few disgusted tourists left. I watched for a while with these attentive Spaniards. It seemed just a bloody charade of ritual slaughter, a great black beast with magnificent horns trotting around the ring, snorting and pawing and full of life, reduced in minutes to a kneeling wreck, vomiting blood, as a narrow-hipped matador gloated – this was something that made me deeply curious, even as it filled me with dread.

I went to Mijas and took a seat in the bullring. It was a *novillada*, a bullfight with young bulls. The matadors here were also young – trainees (*novilleros*) – nervous, tentative teenagers. One walked out, stiffly in tight pants. People cheered. The bull appeared from a gate. It was a small bull, because the matador was still learning; but even so, this beautiful bewildered animal made him look like a punk. Attempting to be fearless, the matador knelt and was almost immediately gored. He tumbled, the bull was on top of him. The cape-men distracted the bull and after a while stuck banderillas into the bull's neck. This tore the neck muscles, the bull lowered its head – an easy target. The matador made an attempt with his sword, but so badly the bull was crazed – surprised, fearful, fighting for its life – and chased the matador into a "blind." Confused, dying, the bull bled against its own flanks for a while and then, weak and kneeling, was dispatched with a sword thrust, and the dead thing was dragged away by a mule team.

This was all worse, more farcical, more horrible than I had imagined, because it was so inefficient. People cheered, but pointlessly – the bull was doomed from the start. The bullring is round: there is nowhere for the bull to hide; but the blinds allow the matador to hide with ease.

The second bull was less lucky – though all bulls are unlucky – and ended up howling, bellowing as the matador fumbled with the sword and cape. He was butted. The bull was bleeding and roaring. At last the bull was stabbed. At this point about fifteen English tourists left the bullring, muttering with indignation. A third bull entered. A new matador faced this creature and was downed inside a minute. He tried three times to stab this bull, but succeeded only in enraging him. The matador was gored and limping. He lost his cape. He then stabbed the bull, but ineptly,

skewering the bull so grotesquely that the animal was given courage, and it cantered around, bleeding and complaining, with the
sword bobbing from its neck. The Mijas church bells tolled, and
the pigeons flew out of the belfry, the matador was chased, there
was great confusion, until at last the bull was slowly, amateurishly,
painfully put to death.

There is nothing in bullfighting except blood – the anticipation
of blood, the letting of blood, and the brutally choreographed
death of a ramping animal which just a moment ago was bucking
and snorting with life. It is the sight of terrible beauty victimized
and killed, in style. The word "matador" is unsubtle. *Matar* is the
verb to kill. Matador means killer. In the larger bullrings, the
great *corridas*, the bulls are enormous, monstrous even, but in
minutes, the bull is reduced to a slobbering, drooling wreck,
shitting in alarm and desperation, and finally knifed to death. *Olé*.

The small bullring at Mijas, about the size of a circus ring at a
state fair, was almost a century old. Mijas, a lovely town in the
hills above Fuengirola, is the scene of *In Hiding*, by Ronald Fraser,
which describes how a Republican was forced to remain hidden in
his house for thirty years; a good example of the absurd cruelties
brought about by the Franco government, which by the way
encouraged bullfighting.

Bullfights are as frequent on Spanish television as football games.
It is not unusual to find them on three channels simultaneously,
three different bullfights. Spaniards, not a people noted for finding
common agreement on anything, are almost unanimous in their
enthusiasm for bullfighting. It is not a sport, Hemingway said; it is
a tragedy, because the bull dies. But the bull dies in the worst
possible way, first tortured by knives in its neck and then stabbed –
usually clumsily by a prancing man with a sword – and then it
bleeds to death.

A tragedy? Isn't it pretty to think so. It is certainly not a sport.
It is a gruesome entertainment, on a par with bear-baiting or the
exquisitely nasty Chinese "Death by a Thousand Cuts." It is a
cruel farce, and since cheating is involved (shaving the bull's
horns, drugging the animal), it is often no more than a charade,
just a gory spectacle. It woke in me an unholy pleasure at the
prospect of seeing a matador gored.

This debased form of the *corrida* is not ancient; it dates from the late eighteenth century, with many gory modernisms. Yet elaborate cultural explanations are made on behalf of bullfighting. I found them all laughable, and the only satisfying part of a bullfight to me was seeing a gored matador lying in the sand being trampled flat by the bull's hooves, the bull's horns in the supine *torero*'s gut. It is what ought to happen to anyone who dares to torment an animal. It was a reminder of the ape and the tourist: *This bull is cruel – when I stab him he tries to gore me.*

Give it a chance, Spaniards told me. You will become an aficionado. "Somehow it was taken for granted that an American could not have *aficion*," Hemingway writes. But his hero and *alter ego* Jake Barnes has *"aficion"* (enthusiasm), he proves it, he is loved for it. Spaniards buy him drinks! "We're talking bulls," Jake says, when he is invariably talking balls. The novel is a pretentious sermon on the nobility of the *corrida*, one bloody bull after another, and all the pedantry of bull fever. It is an example of how badly *The Sun Also Rises* fails that the blood and the physical cruelty of the bullfight is never touched upon. "We had that disturbed emotional feeling that always comes after a bullfight, and the feeling of elation that comes after a good bullfight."

I went to bullfights in Malaga, in Lorca, in Barcelona. What perversity in the Spanish character demanded this sickening spectacle? You couldn't blame Franco for this, although it must have been a tremendous safety-valve for all the frustration of fascism. The *corridas* depressed me, and I was glad to abandon the effort. But the events were inescapable, always on television, constantly in the newspaper. Even the small provincial papers in Spain have a page or two devoted entirely to news of bullfights. The section is headed "Bulls" and it deals with local *ferias* and ones that are much farther afield. Cartagena was a modest-sized town up the coast. The Cartagena paper had reports of bullfights in Lorca nearby, in Murcia, farther away in Saragossa, and in Lima, Peru.

Nearly all the matadors had nicknames: El Tato (The Kid), El Niño, El Balsiqueño, Niño de la Taurina, El Quilas. There was a popular matador called Jesulín de Ubrique. The reports were detailed, using the numerous terms that are applied in a bullfight for the movements of the matador, or the bull's defensive manoeuvers, or the disposition of the severed ears. All this for a staged hemorrhaging.

The Spaniards were well-mannered with one another, restrained, seldom aggressive, seldom drunk in public, and they were generally kind to their animals. The idea that as members of the European Community the Spaniards might have to curb their appetite for bull-torturing just made them laugh. They also jeered at the thought that they might have to abandon the practice of what could only be termed "chicken-yanking" − riding on horseback and snatching a live chicken from a row that hung on a line.

"Spain must not give this image!" an animal rights poster announced, showing various cruelties to animals, and it included bullfighting. But for this Spanish organization, ADDA (the Association for the Defense and the Rights of Animals), it was all uphill. It was hard for me to imagine that Spain would ever get rid of this institutionalized sadism.

I took the train to Malaga. A Malagueño said to me, "Everything in Spain is expensive. Also we have no money. Also there is twenty per cent unemployment."

The man was direct and pleasant and unsentimental, and I realized that I had wandered so widely in poor, envious, demoralized places that I had become accustomed to surliness and delay. The promptness of Spanish life was unexpected. Buses and trains traveled on time. Spanish politeness made me take the people and their pastimes more seriously.

Malaga was proud, tidy, a city of substance, with a pleasant harbor and a busy port. Ferries left here for the Spanish toehold of Melilla in Morocco, trains for Granada. The university was not far from my hotel and so I had the impression of Malaga as a place with a youthful population.

It was all so familiar, though, not just the overlay of Europe − banks, post offices, telephones − but the fact that many aspects of Euro-culture had been inspired by America. On the cosmopolitan shores of the Mediterranean, our electronic modernity had been absorbed along with our crass popular culture. Communications were so efficient that they left few opportunities for people to meet each other. There is nothing like a bad ride or a long wait to inspire friendship and get strangers talking. But the simplicity of these features of Spain meant that people traveled quickly, efficiently, in silence. Not long ago in Europe if you wanted to make anything but a local telephone call you went to the telephone exchange and filled out a form and waited to be directed to your booth. In the smallest village in Spain, France, Italy, Croatia, Greece, Turkey – everywhere in Mediterranean Europe except Albania – you can now make a phone call from a public phone, using an access code. In the park in Malaga I stepped into a phone booth and called my brother Peter who happened to be in Casablanca. The next day in Guadix, in the barren mountains beyond Granada, I called Honolulu from the phone on the wall in the local bar.

Who's that singing in Spanish?

I was on my way in a bouncing bus via Almeria and Cartagena to Alicante.

Just inland in the villages above Almeria, there were cave-dwellers: caves had been cut or enlarged in the rubbly biscuit-colored hills and house fronts fixed to the cave entrances. The slopes were devoid of trees. It was a land of little rain, and of so few people, of such dust and emptiness, that it could have been the far west of the United States – Arizona or New Mexico. When I remarked on this to a Spaniard in Almeria he told me that it had been the location for many of the Sergio Leone so-called spaghetti westerns.

Almost in sight of the overbuilt coast, this countryside was lovely in its grandeur and in its sunlight and emptiness, its white huts and grazing goats and olive groves, its houses of stacked stone, some with grape arbors and others hung with garlands of drying red peppers, shielded by stands of pines or clusters of broom; olive-pickers riding in the backs of trucks, their faces masked against the dust, and elderly shepherds in blue suits in postures so intense they seemed to be preaching to their flocks. Beyond a sun-baked ravine there were thirty black goats in a field, and a mass of swallows diving into a small bush. It was no wonder that Spaniards felt at home in Mexico and Peru.

There were no foreigners in Lorca, in a Mexican landscape which was only twenty miles from the coast where the majority of people were tourists. Lorca was a town of granite and gravel quarries, a center for ceramics and every sort of porcelain object from toilet-bowls to vases. There were luxuriant palms along the main street, Avenida Juan Carlos. But even in the center of town so much dust had collected on the roofs of houses – dust raised by a stiff wind blowing over the dry riverbed, the brown fields, the stony hills – that a wild straggling variety of cactus had taken root in the tiles. There was no sightseeing here, the bullfights were a local matter, and so it was just the quarries and the bathroom fixtures, the drugstores, the supermarkets, and the candy stores which were also retailers of pornographic picture-books.

Mazarron lay at the far end of a series of wide grassy valleys, but the grass was dry as dust. A bit farther on was Puerto Mazarron, by the sea, a tiny place which had somehow escaped the ravages of tourism. I arrived in darkness, found a place to stay, and left early on another bus for Cartagena.

"There is another Cartagena in Colombia," I said to a man in Cartagena.

"Yes, I have heard of it," he said. "Maybe people from Cartagena went there and named it."

"Maybe."

"Cartagena of the Indies – that's what we call it," he said.

And this one founded by Hasdrubal over two thousand years ago had been named for the original Carthage, farther along my route, in Tunisia. An important and much-coveted town for that whole time, it was noted for having the safest and best natural harbor on the Spanish Mediterranean coast. Most Mediterranean ports like this, perhaps every port on the entire sea, had a history of being raided and recolonized. After Hasdrubal, Cartagena had been plundered by everyone from Scipio Africanus in 210 B.C., through the Moors and Francis Drake, to the Nationalists in 1938.

The harbor was filled with ships even on this cold day, and there were yachts in the marina. There was no beach. One of Cartagena's relics was a big old submarine in a garden near the harbor. It looked like a vast iron cigar, and it had been placed there because the supposed inventor of the submarine was born in the town.

I spent my day walking in the hills behind the town, and that night, having a drink in a bar, ran into a drunken crowd of British soldiers. From their conversation I gathered they had just recently been on manoeuvers in Belfast, Northern Ireland; they were full of angry stories, and they were telling them, interrupting each other.

"I knew it was the same fucking bloke we were looking for because the car was fucking traced —"

"He comes up to me and I says to him, 'Don't you fucking move!'"

"The RUC didn't give us any fucking help —"

"But Simpson was like a father to me. I wouldn't have stayed in the fucking army if it wasn't for Simpson —"

"The RUC ran a check on him —"

"Remember that little fucker?"

"What little fucker?"

"From Hull."

"Oh, that little fucker."

I wondered whether to ask them what they were doing in Cartagena, but they became restive and even louder as they went on drinking, and so I thought, *Never mind*, and went out to look for a restaurant.

I knew only two things about Spanish politics — that General Franco ruled Spain as a dictator from 1937 until 1975, when he died. On his deathbed, so the story goes, he heard the grieving crowds crying out, "Adiós, great general!" and he said, "Where are they going?"

The second thing I knew was that Felipe Gonzalez was the current Prime Minister and that he was being given a hard time because of the current economic situation.

Later, I was watching TV in a small restaurant with the waiter, when a fat smug man appeared on the screen and began declaiming, about his struggle (*mi lucha*).

"Politician?"

"Yes," the waiter said. "That's Fraga. He is very right-wing."

"He must hate the socialist government."

"Yes, but we have plenty of right-wing politicians here in Murcia."

"Friends of Franco?"

"Fraga was a member of Franco's government," he said, seeming to make a distinction between friend and colleague.

Fraga was crowing, having just won another election, the presidency of "La Xunta de Galicia." This in itself was not so surprising. What was remarkable was that Manuel Fraga had been a great friend of Franco. Indeed, he had been Minister of Tourism, with responsibility (so this waiter told me) for carrying out Franco's ambitious pro-tourist effort – so much so that Fraga was today identified with all the hastily thrown up hotels and apartment blocks on the tourist-ravaged coasts – the Costa del Sol, the Costa Blanca and the Costa Brava. Franco wanted this tourist boom for the foreign exchange it provided, though he could not have foreseen what a corrupting influence, in all senses, it would prove to be.

Introducing the topic of Franco was regarded as rather impolite. Spaniards were reluctant to talk about this pious monster and their own part in his holding power. It was bad taste in Spain to talk about the fascist past at all, those years of collaboration and repression. That was the theory. But for a note-taker like myself, only the unpopular subjects are worth raising in any country.

My questions brought forth from the waiter a story about Fraga's strange career, which included Fraga's friendship with Fidel Castro – he was friendly both with Fidel and Fidel's parents who, along with many other Cubans, traced their origins to the northern province of Galicia. Fraga had cultivated Fidel and created an understanding that made Spain an ally and a refuge for many Cubans.

"When Fidel visited the grave of his grandparents in Galicia," the waiter said, "Fraga stood beside him and burst into tears, while Fidel simply stared at the tombstone."

Meanwhile, on the TV screen, Fraga was still howling in victory. He was a survivor from a time of shame, a relic and a reminder of the dictatorship, but none the less he was still popular.

"So what is his secret?" I asked.

"He is a little rich."

"So that makes him powerful?"

"Well, he just won – they can't stop him."

I looked at the florid, triumphant face of this Galician. He was said to have all the Galician traits – above all, Galicians were inexplicable and enigmatic. A Spaniard named Alberto gave me a vivid illustration of this. "If you meet a Galician on a stairway," he said, "it is impossible to tell whether he is going up or down."

"Trains do not depart: they set out, and move at a pace to enhance the landscape, and aggrandize the land they traverse."

That is William Gaddis, and although my train was small and slow, this seemed to me a fair description. I was leaving Cartagena on a misty morning at 9:05 and heading north to Murcia via Torre Pacheco and Balsicas. Murcia, noted for its abundant fruit trees, is just inland from the town of Los Alcazares – The Fortresses – on its own enclosed Mediterranean lagoon, called Mar Menor. The train passed through a plain of orange groves, bushy trees with dark green leaves, many of the trees still with fruit on them – the last fruit of the season. And at Murcia itself there were orange trees in most gardens and by the front doors of the houses.

I was not stopping in Murcia, just changing trains for Alicante up the coast on the Costa Blanca, catching the express *Mare Nostrum*.

Onward past Orihuela to Elche, home of the only palm forest in Europe, and at the very end of the trip we traveled by the beach, where there was a bit of wind-blown surf and the train was so close to the sea some spray flew against the windows.

It had become a stormy day, and the rain and wind made the city interesting. My idea was to spend a day or so here and then try to find a ship going to the Balearic Islands, Majorca or Ibiza. It did not matter to me where the ship was going. I thought that if I got to one of those islands I would look around and then take another ship back to the mainland, farther up the coast, perhaps to Valencia or Barcelona.

"It is low season," a Spanish travel agent told me. "The ferries to Majorca might not be running."

He shrugged – he didn't know. He told me to fly. I said there had to be a ferry.

"Yes. Perhaps. You might have to go to Valencia. It is low season."

I liked that expression. Low season was a good expression, indicating the strange and the unpopular and the unpredictable.

There was a ferry. I found out, from the insignificant seaside village of Denia, about fifteen miles away on a headland. It was leaving the next day, at the inconvenient hour of eleven at night. When I asked the agent whether he had any tickets for the ferry he said, "Many!" and laughed.

A statue on the esplanade in Alicante greatly resembled Franco. I asked a man whether this was who it was. He said, "No" – angrily, and did not pause to enlighten me. This was an example of the risk of raising the forbidden topic of Francisco Franco. I seriously wondered whether there were statues of the man still standing in Spain; and what of the question of Franco's robust and reactionary Catholicism and his sinister and cabalistic movement Opus Dei?

"But this is a Catholic country?" I said to a man in Alicante later that day.

"No, no," he said. "Just the people are Catholic. It was a Catholic country when Franco was in power, but not any more. Now it is a democratic country."

We were talking about birth control. Spain has the lowest birth-rate in Europe. This seemed unbelievable to me – that it was lower even than that of Germany or Denmark. But it was apparently true. Abortion was legal and there were measures afoot to make it even easier to secure one. It was also a fact that little kiddies were not much in evidence. This could have been a result of the dire economic situation: Europeans kept their families small in times of recession.

The waves were breaking on the beach below the Castello de Santa Barbara, and the rock above it, which was more impressive than the castle where I was headed – restless for something to do; though it was a clear sign of desperation when I contemplated sightseeing. My lowest points were visiting churches and ruins, and famous graves were rock bottom. It was a cold day. The beach stretched for miles. One person splashed in this gray sea, a small blue girl.

I wandered over to the harbor and found a cruising sailboat, the *Legrandbois* out of Guernsey, and had a chat with the captain, John Harrison, who had sold up, got rid of all he owned, and left Blyth, near Newcastle, to cruise the Mediterranean with his wife.

"I bought this sailboat four years ago and sailed it here slowly, coming down along Portugal, taking my time," he said. "We were at Gibraltar for a long time. Did you see those semi-inflatables, the black ones, piled with cargo? They're used for smuggling cigarettes across to Morocco and Algeciras and La Linea."

"I heard there was smuggling at La Linea."

"The smugglers buy the cigarettes legally. They're dealers and there's no tax. They have cellular phones and everything else. Now and then the police stop them, but usually they come and go as they please."

"I thought the Spanish police were supposed to be tough," I said, and told him about the road block I had seen.

"They had a reputation for being bureaucratic and unfriendly, but they've eased up. They've been friendly to us. I think they're smashing."

"How long are you going to be here in Alicante?"

"I don't know. We stay weeks or months in a place, depending on how much we like it. It's true there are very few people out there sailing in this weather, but this isn't bad. I used to sail at Christmas and New Year's out of Newcastle, and I can tell you that the North Sea at that time of year is pretty rough."

"Is that fishing tackle?" I asked, indicating some odds and ends on the deck.

"Yes. We occasionally fish. I catch small mackerel and we grill them."

"I thought there were hardly any fish at all in the Mediterranean."

"There's no question it's overfished. The hake and mackerel you see in the market is all local, and there are still squid and octopus. But it's going to be dire if they keep catching these undersized fish."

"I haven't seen many commercial fishermen."

"I saw one at Torrevieja with six small boxes, all filled with tiny fish. A man said to him, 'Why are you keeping these little fish? This is the fish stock. If you don't leave them to be fattened up there won't be any for the rest of us.' The fisherman said, 'Sorry, but I've got a family. I've got mouths to feed.' They went at it a bit more and were finally fighting with fists."

We talked about the Mediterranean.

"If I wanted I could sail right across from here to the Turkish coast and it wouldn't take me much more than three weeks. It's only 1,500 miles or so – not such a large area, either. But I want to poke into the corners of it and take my time."

"Do you see much pollution?"

"The most polluted part of the Med is said to be that corner between France and Italy, around Genoa. But I've seen some very rough beaches here in Spain – raw sewage on the beach, for example. Estepona had some."

He was about sixty. He told me he had simply chucked everything, his job, his house, the lot, and sailed away from Britain. He was planning to spend the coming year sailing from port to port in the Mediterranean, in all seasons, in all weather. North Africa did not interest him, but "They say Turkey is very pleasant and very cheap." He had no long-term plan. "We just take it a month at a time."

I liked him for being dauntless and self-sufficient, as well as appreciative, easygoing, reliable, all the qualities of a single-handed sailor. He could even fix his own engine – his father had taught him how.

"Where are you headed?"

"Barcelona, by way of Majorca."

"We'll be looking out for you," he said.

Alicante was a town in which it helped to be self-sufficient, because of the downturn in tourism and the low season. People seemed to go their own way, many stores had closed, no one was touting for business. It was a small city, but with an air of friendliness. The pedestrians seemed fairly elderly, the old Spaniard and his wife hobbling along, she with a string bag, he with a cane, the thick-and-thin marriage that seems so enviable from the outside, that you only seem to see in provincial towns like this.

And the other people in Alicante: mending phone lines, painting shutters, diddling with adding machines, counting money, leading children down the street, selling lottery tickets, sweeping – such people made me feel idle and superfluous. as a traveler. The worst part of travel, the most emotional for me in many respects, is the sight of people leading ordinary lives, especially people at work or with their families; or ones in uniform, or laden with equipment, or shopping for food, or paying bills.

V.S. Pritchett speaks of "the guilt of being a tourist who is passing through and is a mere voyeur." I did not share that guilt. I felt sorrow, horror, compassion, joy. Observing how people worked and lived their lives is one of the objectives of travel. It sometimes made me feel bad and fairly useless. But I was not a "mere" voyeur. I was a very hard-working voyeur.

In Alicante I saw for the first time on my trip the dark, shiny, plum-colored West Africans with their trinkets and leather bags and beads laid out on mats in the middle of the wide and pretty Esplanada de España. They were from remote villages in Senegal, so they said; they had come here via France. There were also Moroccans selling sunglasses, Spanish peasants selling nuts in paper cones, gypsies selling wilted flowers. One man held a hand-lettered sign in Spanish: "I have no job and I have three mouths to feed." But no one took any notice.

Killing time on the day I was to leave Alicante, I fell into conversation with a man in a café who was casually watching a bullfight on TV along with a number of other men. I realized once again how much I hated bullfights – the preening matador, the tortured bull – and yet I was still trying to account for this Spanish *aficion* for them.

I said, "The bull always loses. So what's the sport?"

"The matador has to work in order to win," the man said.

"Is it really so dangerous for the matador?"

"Oh, yes. Think of the horns of the bull – how sharp they are, how big they are."

"Yet the bull dies."

"It is very complicated," he said. He mentioned all the moves a matador needed to have in his repertoire. "And the matador needs so much practice."

Elias Canetti has an epigram about wishing to see a mouse eat a cat alive, but to toy with it first. Thinking about bullfighting I wanted to see a bull torment a matador to death, not trample him but gore him repeatedly and make him dance and bleed to death. This vindictive thought might have been shared by some people who went to bullfights: to see the matador trampled.

As an ignorant foreigner I had a right to ask him the obvious: "So people really enjoy it?"

"It is a Spanish thing," he said.

"What about you – do you enjoy it?"

"No. It is not for me," he said. "For me it is all suffering."

3

The MV *Punta Europa* to Majorca

A small coach left every few hours from Marina Station on the beach at Alicante and chugged north-east on a narrow-gauge railway, through Villajoyosa and Benidorm and Altea, to the old port village of Denia, where I had been told I could catch the late-night ferry to Palma in Majorca.

Benidorm was a mass of beachside high-rises, the worst place I had seen on the coast so far, worse than Torremolinos, which was slap-happy seaside tackiness of a familiar and forgivable kind. But Benidorm was ugliness on a grand scale – tall blocks of apartments, hideous hotels, winking signs, the whole place as badly built and visually unappealing as a suddenly thrown-up town on the shores of the People's Republic of China. Everything that Spain was said to stand for – charm, dignity, elegance, honor, restraint – was denied in the look of Benidorm. And because this was wet chilly winter, the wide streets were empty, most of the hotels were shut, no one sat on the beach or swam in the sea: the useless horror, naked and raw in the low season, was demoralizing and awful.

In 1949, Benidorm was a tiny impoverished fishing village, "said to be an open door for smugglers," an English visitor wrote. I walked around. I had a pizza. I sat on a bench surveying the Mediterranean, and then the wind picked up and the rain began.

The rain delighted me. It whipped against the sea. It darkened the stone of the hotels and tore at the signs. It coursed down the empty streets and flooded the gutters and cut gullies through the beach sand. A bit more wind and the lights would fail, a bit more rain and it would be a real flood. And that would be the answer, the cure for Benidorm – nature's revenge, an elemental purifying storm that would wipe the place out.

It lifted my spirits to imagine the destruction of such a place, and I boarded the onward train feeling joy in my heart at the prospect of the wholesale destruction. The rain swept loudly against the side of the railway car like a shower of gravel. I was the only passenger. Darkness fell as we shuttled towards Denia in the storm. "Of all the lovely places down the Iberian seaboard, I believe Denia (the Roman Dianium) to be the most attractive and the place I would most like to spend my days," Rose Macaulay wrote in *Fabled Shore*. Her confidence is understandable; when she drove down the coast in 1948 she saw only one other British car. But the day I was at Denia the rain was torrential. I could not see Denia's famous lighthouse. There were flooded streets in the little town, the station was drenched, the rain glittered in the lights of the port, where the ferry was moored by an empty puddled quay.

It was possible that this look of desertion meant that I had the departure time wrong.

"You are sure this ferry goes to Palma tonight?"

"Yes. No problem."

"Where are the other passengers?"

"Perhaps there are no other passengers tonight."

It was ten o'clock. I bought my ticket and boarded ten minutes later. The ferry *Punta Europa* had space for 1,300 passengers. A sign in Spanish on the upper deck spelled it out:

> Maximum authorized passengers – 1,300
> Crew Members (*Tripulantes*) – 31
> Total of passengers and crew – 1,331

Then a man and his son came aboard. That made three of us on the *Punta Europa*. There were five inside saloons for passengers, filled with seats; every seat was the same, narrow, hard-edged molded plastic, and so we sat bolt upright as the ferry sailed out of Denia, roaring like an express train in the storm. The saloon lights still burned, the crew stayed below, the wind made the doors bang, the whole ferry stank of oil and the reek of decaying cork on its interior decks. A television set had been left on in each saloon – a man loudly reading the news. Outside was the black, furious Mediterranean. It was my first storm on this sea and it thrilled me, because I had been seeing it as a sink of gray slopping water, and the wind and waves tonight gave it the look of a great ocean.

Four hours of this, the ferry pitching and rolling, and then the wind eased and the sea grew calmer as we approached Ibiza. It was three in the morning. An English couple boarded, murmuring, but they were not talking to each other, they were reassuring their pets, a nervous dog on a leash, a whining cat in a hand-held cage. Now the passengers numbered five, and two animals. The lights still glared, the television screen flickered, still on but no program.

All those seats and yet not a single one was comfortable – straight backs, hard armrests, no leg room in front. None of them reclined. I propped myself up and when I could not stand the discomfort and the burning light bulbs any more I went on deck. The black swell of sea sighed against the hull, while I yawned and fiddled with my short-wave radio. After three hours the eastern sky grew lighter.

In the misty light of daybreak there was nothing, not even a sunrise – only the whitish water of dawn, no land. We did not raise Majorca until seven-thirty or so – the west coast, Dragonera Island – and then rounded Cabo Cala Figuera where there was a light-house. I could see tawny hills and a mountainous interior, a lovely rugged place, looking nothing at all like what I had expected. At the edge of some beaches there were white hotels stacked up, and dense settlement, but there were stretches of coast on which there was very little evidence of any building.

Majorca, sometimes called the heart of the Mediterranean for embodying all its virtues, is known in Britain as a package holiday destination, and so is a synonym for cheapness. It is one of those place-names which, like Frinton or Bognor, carries with it so many dubious associations that it has been given the status of a household word; just pronouncing it, deliberately twanging it, calling it "Majorca" and sounding the "j," has the same effect as cracking a joke.

"Yes, it is lovely," the Spanish passenger said, when I remarked on the beauty of the island. His son was still asleep as we pulled into the harbor. "When I was growing up this island was all natural."

I asked him his age. He was fifty. He remembered the coming of the package tours, the rise of the hotels. He said there were parts of

Majorca that were still very beautiful. "But in the summer it is terrible all over."

He said that business was awful here at the moment – worse than on the mainland. "But things are improving. There is a fiesta at the weekend."

Arriving by ferry gave me a good look at the place. I had resolved not to fly anywhere in the Mediterranean anyway, and the decision was useful in forcing me to make elaborate detours (like the one to Denia) which gave me a perspective on places I would not otherwise have had.

Majorca looked elegant from the sea as we crossed the wide Bahia de Palma. Nearer the port I could see the old town of Palma, the ornate cathedral dominating the city walls, and the stucco buildings, some of them ancient, and the newer suburbs to the west, the fertile fields and valleys at a greater distance to the north.

I walked down the gangway and through the port building to the main street, by one of the marinas. Over breakfast, studying a map, I debated whether to take the narrow-gauge train through the mountains to Sóller on the rocky north coast. "As beautiful a run as any in Switzerland," one brochure said. But I also wanted to see the more remote seaside villages on the west coast which were nowhere near the railway. A rental car seemed a good idea.

The phone book listed a number of rental agencies. And because of the large British population there were many British businesses, a whole sub-directory listing importers of sausages and beer and books and jam, as well as advertising clothes, haircuts and houses.

There was even an English radio station, beaming sentimental songs from Palma to British residents on the island. I discovered this after I had rented the car. I tuned to that station, which was all the more affecting because it was so amateurish.

"Valerie is on her way to London," the woman announcer said. "She'll be in Mayfair tomorrow. Safe trip, Val. Here's a song for Valerie."

It was "A Nightingale Sang in Berkeley Square."

"I was thinking how I first heard that song at the Hammersmith Palais," the announcer said, after it had ended.

I had driven out of Palma and I was passing small fertile farms and stone houses, heading for the mountains.

"Change Partners and Dance" began to play – Fred Astaire, and soon my favorite, a wobbly melody,

> Wuddle Ah do
> When you
> Are far away?
> Just dream of you,
> Wuddle Ah do?

The music made me homesick, but homesickness seemed a natural condition of travel. I can only travel when I am happy, but when I am happy I miss the productive routines of my life, and the woman at the center of it. Each morning these days I woke to the questions, *Where am I and what am I doing here?* and then got up and attempted to make something of the day.

"I've got to say cheerio now. But remember, if you do it, do it good. And if you don't do it good, don't do it at all."

The mountainside rose abruptly from the flat Palma plain, and it was steep, a vertical ascent of hairpin bends. At the ridge I looked across the rocky cliffs and saw green slopes and a bay and blue ocean. But as I descended a storm crowded the coast, and it was raining like hell as I entered Sóller.

I was so wet and bedraggled that at least four Spaniards took me for a native and asked me difficult questions. One question was, "Where is the office that processes insurance claims for injured workers?"

Walking around the town to get my bearings I saw three coin-operated machines in the plaza. One dispensed gum. One dispensed plastic toys and beads. The third dispensed (for 200 pesetas) pairs of condoms encased in small plastic globes. I could see them in the fishbowl top of the dispenser. I was trying to decide where I should spend the night when I saw a sign to Deyá.

"An English poet lived in Deyá, isn't that so?" I asked a man near Sóller harbor.

"Robert Graves," the man said, without hesitating. "His house is still there. Now his son and daughter live there."

"I think he was a wonderful poet. Do the people here know his poems?"

"Yes. We have a high regard for his work. We compare him with the great poets, not just of Spain but of the world."

It seemed a pleasant idea to make a trip to Deyá – maybe walk there along the cliffs, and look at the landscape that Graves had praised for so many years.

I found a hotel within sound of the harbor. Sóller had such a placid harbor, such magnificent cliffs, that I decided to stay a few days and catch up with my note-taking. I hadn't written much since Alicante. I had lost a night's sleep on the *Punta Europa*. I was delighted to find this peaceful place. On most trips I kept rolling until I found a place I liked, and when I got a certain feeling I came to a stop. This was another reason I traveled alone, because it was rare for two people to see the same qualities in a place ("Why do you want to stop here? I thought we were supposed to keep going"). Sóller was pleasant. But even in this low season there were some tourists here – hikers mostly.

That seemed a good idea to me. I bought food in the supermarket, yogurt, sardines, fruit juice, picnic food for home-made *bocadillos* – fat sandwiches. I bought Sóller's prized oranges and a topographical map; and when the rain stopped and the sea glittered with sun, I spent two days hiking, looking at birds, making notes, glad that I had found such a lovely corner of this supposedly hackneyed island.

All places, no matter where, no matter what, are worth visiting. But seldom-visited places where people were still living settled traditional lives seemed to me the most worthwhile, because they were the most coherent – they were readable and nearly always I felt uplifted by them. What I had missed intensely in my trip so far was a chance to look at a landscape that was not wall-to-wall hotels and condos and clip-joints and "English Spoken Here." Perhaps I was too ignorant for ruins; whatever the reason, they did not interest me greatly, nor did tombs, nor churches. It was not my philistinism, it was my desire to see the life of the coast, no matter what form it took. I made some exceptions. Big crumbling Roman or Greek amphitheaters were another story. They looked absurd and ancient, and there they lay with all their ambitious symmetry in the oddest settlements. "Here is where the gladiators entered," "Notice the ruts of the rich people's chariots." (I was to see such structures in Albania in a slum in Durazzo and in Tunisia in the otherwise ramshackle town of El Djem.)

Not long before, I had been thinking that it was seldom possible to be alone at any point on the Mediterranean coast; and then, by chance, I found this part of Majorca. True, it was dotted with villages and parts of it were jammed with houses, but it was the prettiest coast I had seen so far. I hiked to the village of Fornalutx on the slopes of Sóller's mountain, Puig Major, in the shape of a witch's hat, and went bird-watching on the vertiginous path along the sea-cliffs.

At the end of my two days' hiking I caught up with my chores, my notes and laundry. If it seemed strange to be alone on the cliffs, no sounds except sea birds and the occasional Teutonic squawk, it seemed even stranger to be in a launderette in Sóller, with young mothers and children, folding clothes.

"Hello. How are you?"

"Very well. You are a visitor?"

"Yes. I like Sóller. Very pretty."

"Not spoiled," the woman said.

"I wonder why."

"Because there are no flat places. It is all cliffs and crags and steep slopes. The few hotels we have are all at the harbor and on the road leading out of the village."

That seemed a good explanation. It was not possible to put up a big hotel here, and there was no money in a small hotel – no room for the package tours.

"It's a quiet time of year."

"Mostly the Germans now."

Only Germans, really, big chunky waterproof hikers, pairs of them, in parkas and knickerbockers, carrying walking-sticks and binoculars. And when I saw Germans like that I did not think of hiking but invasion. They were Germans of a robust pink-cheeked sort, wearing thick-soled hiking boots, taking advantage of the cheap rates and marching up and down the mountain paths as though unintentionally auditioning for a production of "The Private Life of the Master Race."

"Once the British came, but when the prices went up, the French and Belgians took their place. Now it is Germans in the winter. Some British people still come in the summer months."

She knew who frequented Sóller. She was a cleaner in one of the hotels. Her husband was a fisherman. He caught shrimp in these months and in the spring he would look for sardines. Fishing was a hard living, she said.

Her little girl goggled at us and used a small square of cloth to imitate her mother's clothes-folding.

I bought gas for the car – 4,000 pesetas to fill the tank, about $35 for this tinky-winky Renault 5, another revelation of the high cost of living in Spain. But generally speaking in the Mediterranean a liter of gas cost twice as much as a liter of table wine.

The next morning, my last in Sóller, I woke once again to the sound of the waves sloshing against the beach, regretting that I had to leave.

In my two days of hiking I had walked almost to Deyá. Today I drove there on the narrow, winding coast-road, and early on came upon the sight of a head-on collision (no one hurt, but a car and a truck badly damaged). I was cautioned by the consternation of the young man standing by his smashed jeep, his face dark with anxiety; the busy movements of the truck-driver who had rammed him on the sharp bend in the road. A tunnel was being dug through the mountains. The shout "No Tunnel!" was scrawled all over this part of the island. I agreed. There was a train. There was a road. There were already too many cars in Majorca.

The village of Deyá was for so many years the home of the poet Robert Graves that the villagers passed a resolution and in 1969 made Graves "an adopted son," the only one in the long history of the village. He had come there in 1929 on a hunch and lived there for more than half his life.

It is hard for me to work up any interest in a writers' birthplace, and I hate pilgrimages to writers' tombstones, but I do enjoy seeing where they lived and worked; writers' houses fascinate me. And writers often choose magnificent landscapes to live in, whether they have money or not. Henry Miller settled in Big Sur and lived in a cabin long before Big Sur became a coveted piece of real estate; D.H. Lawrence was in pre-chic Taos; Hemingway was in Key West for the fishing, and moved on to Cuba for much the same reason. Robert Louis Stevenson was an early visitor to California and Hawaii, and at last a pioneer in Samoa.

In the literary history of the Mediterranean, many places became famous and fashionable long after foreign writers discovered them and wrote about them. Very often the writers were residents. Usually it was a case of putting a fishing village on the map, and that ended when the tiny port was turned into an expensive resort. This is pretty much the story of F. Scott Fitzgerald glorifying the Riviera, of Norman Douglas in Capri (*South Wind*), Lawrence Durrell in Corfu (*Prospero's Cell*) and Cyprus (*Bitter Lemons*), and of Somerset Maugham in Cap Ferrat. There are scores of other examples – people in Greece looking for Zorba or the Magus, literary pilgrims in Alexandria looking for Justine. The *reductio ad absurdum* of this, and probably the worst thing that can happen, is for the writer's paradise to turn into hell while he or she is still living there – the hell of traffic and hotels, visitors and literary pilgrims. The writer may have unintentionally caused this to happen, by raving about the place.

In her typical gnomic way, saying that it was "Paradise – if you can stand it!", Gertrude Stein suggested that Robert Graves try Majorca. And so, having left his wife and children, he went there with his lover, the impossible Laura Riding. In the course of his lifetime, this idyllic island almost sank under the weight of package tourists. Yet Deyá was still a somewhat remote and pretty village, high on sea-cliffs, surrounded by the lovely Teix mountains. He went there because it was cheap and off the beaten track. It also seemed a happy blend of two landscapes he loved – those of North Wales and Corfu. He was determined not to leave. He wrote in "The Next Time,"

And when we passengers are given two hours,
  The wheels failing once more at Somewhere-
    Nowhere,
To climb out, stretch our legs and pick wild flowers –
  Suppose that this time I elect to stay there?

I easily found Graves's house. It was named Canneluñ and, made of local stone, it occupied a lofty position on a ledge outside the village. It was a dignified house on a steep slope, crags behind it, and the rocky shore far below it. There was an unexpectedly luxurious hotel in the center of Deyá, La Residencia, the sort of hotel I had been avoiding, since this was supposed to be a breezy trip. My idea was to press on; it was an enormously long coastline, and I was trying to avoid being corrupted and detained by luxury and lotus-eating.

Graves had bought Canelluñ in 1932 with his profits from *I, Claudius* and had lived there for many years with Laura Riding, who like so many other mistresses in literature began as his muse and ended as a nag. It has been said that one of the reasons this powerful novel of the decline of Caesardom is so convincing is because Graves "used it as a vehicle for expressing the dark side of his feelings for Laura Riding." He saw her character in the wicked and manipulative poisoner Livia. Laura was known in the village as "a bossy eccentric who wore strange clothes." After some years and some suffering, Graves tossed her out and took up with another White Goddess.

An interviewer once asked Graves a boring question about his living in Deyá: "Has living in Deyá, isolated from what you call the mechanarchic civilization, led you to what you call handicraft in your poetry?"

This produced an interesting answer from Graves. "I once lived here for six years without moving out – in 1930 to '36," he replied. "Didn't even go to Barcelona. Apart from that I've always made a point of traveling. One's got to go out, because one can't live wholly in oneself or wholly in the traditional past. One's got to be aware of how nasty urban life is."

By keeping his head down, he had tried to get through the Spanish Civil War. He had fought in the First World War (and written a book about his disillusionment in his precocious – he was thirty-three – autobiography, *Goodbye to All That*). Franco kept threatening to invade Majorca, and when the time came, and the island grew dangerous, Graves fled.

The village of Deyá is lovely. How to account for the fact that it remained so long after other parts of the island had fallen to the crassest of developers? Perhaps it was as the woman in Sóller had said to me, "no level places" – that and the narrow roads. If a place was inaccessible it had a chance of keeping its identity and – remaining untainted.

"Deyá had little to recommend it except the Graves magic," Anthony Burgess wrote dissentingly in his autobiography, speaking of a period when he had lived in the village. He went on: "A literal magic, apparently, since the hills were said to be full of iron of a highly magnetic type, which drew at the metal deposits of the brain and made people mad. Graves himself was said to go around sputtering exorcisms while waving an olive branch."

The Majorcans I spoke to in the north of the island all knew of Graves, they knew the village and the house. They knew everything except Graves's poetry. That was the way of the world. The man's reputation was good enough for them, and it inspired their respect. A celebrated writer who lives in a small town or a village has an odd time of it. It is amusing when the local philistines disparage the writer in the neighborhood, but it is downright hilarious when the writer is strenuously championed by the local illiterates. Graves lived among olive-squashing peasants and fruiterers and shepherds, as well as prosperous retirees and aristocrats. He shocked some, but his love for the island and for the village in particular impressed them to the point where most of the locals were his well-wishers.

As Graves's son and daughter still lived at the house, I decided not to ring the bell – for fear of intruding but also for fear of being turned away, rebuffed for invading their privacy. Apart from curiosity I had no profound reason for poking my nose in. I was simply interested in what his desk looked like, the room, the books, the pictures; it gave some idea of the writer's mind.

I looked too disreputable for La Residencia; I had a cup of coffee in the village and spent the day walking around the steep lanes, admiring the fruit trees and the tidy houses. The village had great dignity and enormous physical beauty. It was a place, I decided, I would gladly return to.

In Deyá, in casual conversation, I did not find anyone who knew Graves's poetry. But no matter. The question that was in my mind was about Franco, and in particular his hold on Majorca. Because the Spaniards are so polite generally and reserved it was a long time before I could steel myself to ask. Also, asking about a dictator who had been in power so long was also a way of asking people about themselves, a question like "What did you do in the war, Daddy?"

Anyway, in Deyá I popped the question. The man I asked was of that generation, in his early seventies, a thoughtful person out walking his dog. I had caught him unawares, while we were discussing the route to Valdemosa. He considered my Franco question.

"In that time" – he seemed to be avoiding saying Franco's name – "we could not do certain things. We could not say certain things. Some things we could not think."

"So there was political repression?"

"Yes. We were not as free as we are now," he said. "But there was work for everyone and there were tourists. When you have work you are satisfied and you don't ask questions. You get on with your life. If you have work and food you don't think about political matters."

"And if there's no work?"

"Ah, then you ask questions."

"So under Franco there was full employment?"

"The country was growing. But that was a different time. Now everything has changed."

"Was the Catholic church stronger then?"

"Much stronger."

He was talking about Spain's entering the modern world. Long after the rest of Europe had joined it, little had changed in Spain. I took "that was a different time" to mean that it was ancient history. And in a short time, only since the late seventies, Spain had worked to catch up – to lighten its mood and learn how to vote; most of all to cope with the humiliation of having lived so long under a dictator who presumed to think for them. It must have been like living in an abusive household.

Rather than spend the night here in Deyá I decided to stay at Valdemosa, another lovely place above a fishing port; more olive trees, more fruit trees and fincas, but an altogether more level town. Part of Valdemosa's fame rests on the fact that George Sand had brought her lover Chopin here in the winter of 1838–9; while he recovered from an illness and wrote his Preludes, she quarreled with the locals. Afterwards she had written a famously cruel book about their sojourn.

This seemed the perfect place to read the copy of *A Winter in Majorca* that I had bought in Palma. It was a locally published edition, translated and extensively annotated by Robert Graves — most of his notes were rebuttals or else cleared up her misapprehensions or her willful judgments.

At the time of their visit, Chopin, younger than George Sand, was twenty-eight; she was thirty-four. Her real name was Baroness Aurore de Dudevant, neé Dupin, "the child of a *mésalliance* between an aristocrat and an ex-milliner, the uncrowned queen of the Romantic," Graves wrote.

Chopin passed as her husband, but it was known that they weren't married and perhaps that was why the locals did not warm to the foreigners, suspecting that she was pursuing a secret love-affair. It was the worst, most rainy winter in years, the olive crop was a failure, and George Sand's writing was not going well. As if that were not enough, Chopin suffered an attack of virtuousness and began to think Godly thoughts. This provoked his anti-clerical mistress, who liked to think of herself as a liberated soul. It was not a happy household. The village disapproved. The island was cold.

The book was George Sand's way of settling scores. She wrote it, raging, after she got back to France. She railed about the vulgarity and spitefulness of the people; she complained about everything, from the way the Majorcans built their houses and looked after their animals, to the poor quality of their olive oil, which she called "rancid and nauseating." She called them monkeys, barbarous, thieves and "Polynesian savages," as if the civilized navigators of the Pacific had not already been ill-used enough by the French.

At one point, she quotes a French writer who begins a sentence, "These islanders are very well-disposed, gentle and hospitable," and suddenly interrupts with, "We know that in every island, the human race falls into two categories: the cannibals and the 'very well disposed.'"

In another aside, she used the Majorcans in order to generalize about Spain, how easily offended and thin-skinned the Spanish were. "Woe betide the traveler in Spain who is not pleased with everything he encounters! Make the slightest grimace on finding vermin in a bed, or scorpions in the soup, and you draw upon yourself universal scorn and indignation."

"We nicknamed Majorca, 'Monkey Island,'" she writes, "because when surrounded by their crafty, thieving yet innocent creatures, we grew accustomed to defending ourselves against them," and then, showing a certain ignorance about the natural world's distribution of primates, she goes on, "but felt no more scorn than Indians feel toward chimpanzees or mischievous, timid orang-outangs."

Soon after the book appeared it received solemn rebuttals. It is one of the livelier and funnier Mediterranean travel books, and for gratuitous rudeness it is on a par with Evelyn Waugh's *Labels* as an example of a traveler's bad temper in the Mediterranean.

I mentioned *A Winter in Majorca* to a man in Valdemosa.

"It's a silly book. And it's old. I'm surprised that people still read it."

"I'm reading it because it's funny."

"It's full of lies about Valdemosa."

"It's not about Valdemosa," I said. "It's about George Sand."

"Yes." He was relieved and saw me as an ally. "That is right."

I drove the next day down the long hill back to Palma, across the island. It seemed to me that tourist Majorca was at the beach, the masses of hotels in the south and the east. But even the town of Palma seemed traditional Spanish, not touristy, and it even had a venerable look to it – the lovely thirteenth-century cathedral, one of the few in Europe that had never been sacked or bombed.

"This place is nice now," a man from Cordoba told me. "But it is madness in July and August."

I stayed in a small hotel in a suburb to the north-east, where there were just working people and inexpensive boarding-houses. People getting by. I shopped in the supermarket, drank in the bar and watched football and bullfights like everyone else. And living in this way I tried to sum up the Spanish contradictions. They still puzzled me: the way the independent spirit of Spain had endured a dictatorship for forty years; the way Spanish passion seemed at odds with Spanish courtesy. They were church-going Catholics who were loudly anticlerical. And how could one reconcile the

strenuous libido (the papers crammed with personal ads for everything from boyfriends to sado-masochism) with the low birth-rate?

The elderly people in Spain were often the most broadminded.
Pornography was the most vivid example of their tolerance. There
were porno shops and movies in all the Spanish towns and cities,
and even the smaller places like Cartagena had at least one or two
porno outlets.

It seemed incontestable to me that a country's pornography was
a glimpse into its subconscious mind, revealing its inner life, its
fantasy, its guilts, its passions, even its child-rearing, not to say its
marriages and courtship rituals. It was not the whole truth, but it
contained many clues and even more warnings. Japanese porno is
unlike anything in Germany, French is unlike Swedish, American
unlike Mexican, and so forth.

Spanish pornography baffled me. It seemed beyond sex, most of
it. It involved children and dogs and torture; men torturing
women, women being beastly to men; much of it was worse than
the German varieties, possibly the most repellent porno in the
world. Some of it was homegrown – hermaphrodites and toilet
training. One film I saw concerned a woman, a man and a
donkey. Another, one of the strangest I have ever seen, concerned
a Moroccan boy of about thirteen or fourteen, and a very bewildered goat.

In the primmest little districts in Alicante or Murcia or Majorca,
such films were on view next to the candy store or the hairdresser's.
And the candy stores themselves sometimes sold porno – not just
tit-and-bum magazines, but hard-core porn. Here is Granny
behind the counter selling Juan a lottery ticket, and on the
magazine rack with the kiddies' books and the evening papers and
How to Knit is *S & M Monthly*, with page after page of women
being tortured, burned, tied up, sexually mutilated, spiky objects
being forced into vaginas, their arms being twisted, their screams
recorded: 'Help! *Socorro*!'

Porno comic books seemed to me the worst of all, because the
sexual torture was idealized and easily accessible, in a realm of
unreality and fantasy that seemed dangerous. I had presumed that
photographs would be off-putting and disgusting, yet such photographs, showing torture and death, hardly existed. But anything

was possible in the comics, anything could be pictured and usually was, including bestiality and necrophilia.

"If you are not going to buy that magazine, please put it down, señor."

One sunny morning I boarded the ferry at Palma and sailed past the lump of Ibiza under blue skies back to the mainland port of Valencia. It was eight hours, mostly sunshine. There were about thirty of us on a ship that could accommodate 1,500. I sat on deck, scribbling. Inside, a roomful of men watched the day's bullfight on television, and each time the *coup de grâce* was delivered, the whole length of the matador's sword driven into the stumbling bull, a thrill of satisfaction went through the room, an intense sigh of passion.

4

The *Virgen de Guadalupe* Express to Barcelona and Beyond

If a quest for the Holy Grail began in Valencia it would be a very short quest, because the Holy Grail is propped on an altar in a small chapel of the cathedral, in the Plaza de la Reina in the middle of Valencia. It is the real thing, that was drunk out of by Jesus at the Last Supper, and then passed around to the Apostles. This chalice, teacup size, was carved from greenish agate (chalcedony), as is the base, an inverted cup set with pearls and emeralds, with gold handles, and it is held together by a gold post and jeweled bands. The whole thing is seven inches high, small but complex. The simple cup might have acquired the gold and jewels since Jesus used it. The cathedral's authorized pamphlet offers all this conjecture as fact.

The Last Supper was held in the house of St Mark. After this, Joseph of Arimathea collected drops of blood in it from Jesus's crucified body. The cup – usually called the Grail – was taken to Rome by St Peter, where it was used as the papal chalice until the time of Sixtus II. It was then sent to Huesca by St Lawrence, first Deacon of the Roman Church, where it stayed until 713. It was carried as part of the portable paraphernalia of the court of Aragon. In the eleventh century it was in Jaca, in the twelfth century at the Juan de la Peña monastery; in the fourteenth it was taken to Saragossa by King Martin the Human, and in 1437 it was presented to Valencia cathedral by Don Juan, the King of Navarre. Most of the churches in Valencia were vandalized or bombed during the Spanish Civil War (euphemistically called "the National Uprising"), but the Grail remained intact. It had been taken out and hidden in the village of Carlet, in the mountains south-west of Valencia, so that it would not be smashed.

It is venerated. It "receives a continuous growing cult . . . The cup is very ancient work and nothing can be said against the idea that it was utilized by the Lord during the first eucharistic consecration," J. A. Oñate writes in his definitive book on the subject.

Oh well, all of this might be true. But even if it isn't, the Holy Grail, the agate cup, is much prettier than the chunks of the True Cross that are displayed all over Italy – enough pieces of the Cross, it is said, to rebuild the Italian navy.

A priest was saying mass in the Holy Grail chapel each time I took my skeptical self to examine it. This continuous mass struck me as being exactly analogous to the plot device in Paul Bowles's short story, "Pastor Dow at Tacate," where an American preacher can only attract Indians to his church by playing "Fascinatin' Rhythm" on a wind-up Victrola. As long as the song plays the Indians sit quietly, and when the music stops (and the Indians get up to leave the church) the preacher rushes over and gets the music going again.

In the same way, godless visitors looking for the cup enter the chapel where a priest is saying mass and as the Holy Grail is fairly small and far-off these idly curious people are forced to sit down or kneel. Then, gawking at the Holy Grail, they are trapped by the mass. And there they remain, squinting, listening to the mass and the preaching and the denunciations.

There was once a mosque where this cathedral stands. The mosque had itself displaced a Christian church. That early church had been built on the ruins of a Roman temple to Diana. These layers of history, like sedimentary rock, are less typical of Spanish history than of the historical multiplicity of the Mediterranean coast. Very similar layers existed on the coasts of Italy and Albania and Egypt, and elsewhere. Nine cultures on the same spot.

The city center of Valencia was mobbed with beggars jostling for the best begging spots. Beggars tended to congregate around the churches (as they do around mosques in Muslim countries). They were not all old women selling prayer cards, or the lame, or the blind. There were some pale youths, and harridans, and bearded junkies in black leather, all haranguing passers-by or churchgoers. Some others held elaborate signs. "I am the father of three young children and I have no job."

Valencia, an old provincial capital on the sea, had a pleasant aura. It was low and gray; it was not busy; it seemed to me happily unfashionable, and though it is Spain's third-largest city it had an air of friendliness. The central part of Valencia was labyrinthine, dusty, full of shabby shops selling hardware and groceries and cheap clothes. This was Valencia in the winter, a city returned to itself, with no tourists and little traffic; but even in the summer I imagined that the tourists would be at the beach.

Fishermen headed out of the nearby port of El Grao and netted sardines, farmers grew oranges near the city in the irrigated plain the Spaniards call a *huerta*. I had a sardine sandwich for lunch, and two oranges. Then I walked in the sunshine to the Torres de Serrano, not to marvel at the antiquity of these towers, but to see the flea market in the same neighborhood. This flea market told sad stories. It was a mass of old and semi-destitute people selling things no one could possibly want – broken eyeglasses, bent coathangers, old plastic toys, rusted alarm clocks, faded cassette tapes, faucets, battered board games, old magazines, beads, books, and more. It was very grubby stuff. Only the old clothes were moving. Most of the people were browsing and chatting. This was one example of hard-up Spain, but it could not have been typical since nearly all the stuff was worthless.

A man selling postcards caught my eye and said, "These are valuable."

"How much is this one?" It was General Franco.

"Four hundred pesetas." Three dollars.

"Why so much?"

"That's El Caudillo in his military uniform. That's from 1940."

Because I wanted to get him on the subject of Franco, I haggled a little, offered him less than he had demanded, and he said okay.

"Why is it I never see statues of Franco?" I asked, pocketing the picture.

"Here in Valencia there are none. But you'll see them in Madrid, and in Barcelona. Plenty in Galicia."

"Why aren't there any here?"

"Politics!" he exploded, and threw up his hands.

The portrait made Franco look like a Roman emperor, just the sort of image that a man noted for being personally timid would choose. He praised and attempted to flatter the Nazis, who returned the favor by nicknaming Franco "The Dwarf of the Pardo." Paul Preston in his exhaustive thousand-page biography, *Franco*, writes: "the hunger for adulation, the icy cruelty and the tongue-tied shyness were all manifestations of a deep sense of inadequacy.

"Despite fifty years of public prominence and a life lived well into the television age, Francisco Franco remains the least known of the great dictators of the twentieth century." This is how Preston begins his book. "That is partly because of the smoke-screen created by hagiographers and propagandists. In his lifetime he was compared with the Archangel Gabriel, Alexander the Great, Julius Caesar, Charlemagne, El Cid, Charles V, Philip II, Napoleon, and a host of other real and imaginary heroes."

Valencia railway station, picked out with ceramics of figures and fruit, and prettily painted, with flags stirring and a gold ball and eagle: it had the whimsy and hospitality of the front gate of a fairground. Entering it gave a pleasant feeling of frivolity, if not recklessness, to any onward train journey.

The bullring next to the station was huge and handsome and well made, elaborate brickwork, arches and colonnades, not old, but handsome and a bit sinister, like the temple of a violent religion, a place of sacrifice, which was what it was. There were no bullfights that week in the Valencia bullring, but there were plenty on television. Televised bullfights I found to be one of the irritations of eating in cheap restaurants – the way the diners stopped eating when the bull was about to be stabbed, the close attention they gave to the stabbing – a silence in the whole place – and then the action replay, the whole length of the sword running into the bull's neck, the bull dropping and vomiting blood in slow motion.

It's not really a Catholic country, the Spaniards told me, but this express train to Barcelona was dedicated to the Virgin Mary. I asked the conductor why this was so. "It's just a name," he said.

The Virgin sped out of Valencia and along the Mediterranean shoreline of gray sand and blue sea, a plain of gardens and trees and square houses of brown stone, the hills rising to mountains in the background, a classic Spanish landscape of dry over-grazed hills, some of it hardly built upon. But most of it, especially around the coastal town of Tarragona and beyond, over-developed, full of houses. Yet even the most unsightly place was relieved by vineyards or lemon trees, orchards, palm trees. It did not have the nasty urban desolation of industrialized Europe.

There were mainly Spaniards on the train. A few foreigners were heading to Barcelona, others to Cerbère, the first stop after the train entered France. They were clusters of Japanese, and French businessmen, and Moroccans. And Kurt, who was heading back to Germany. He was very fat and bearded, in a leather vest, with a tattoo on his wrist, and very drunk at two in the afternoon in the buffet car.

"This tattoo – I made it myself! I got drunk and took a needle and just went *plunk-plunk-plunk* for three hours."

The tattoo seemed to show a hot-dog in a man's hand, but Kurt helped me to see that it depicted a bulky submarine being crushed by an enormous hairy fist. Above it were the words *Germany – Navy* and below it, *Killer Submarine Crew*.

"Why are those words in English?"

We were speaking German. Kurt did not speak English.

"They just are."

"Were you in the navy?"

"For twenty years, based in Wilhelmshafen, but I also traveled."

It seemed an unlikely question because he was not much older than I was, but I asked, "Did you destroy any submarines?"

"No, but I would have if I had to. I knew how."

"Why did you leave the navy?"

"Family problems. My son is a diabetic. He needs my help. And my wife is in the hospital."

"Serious?"

"Yes. She jabs herself – with a needle, you know. She is not a fixer, not really. She is sick."

"What brought you to Valencia?"

"Football. Karlsruhe was playing Valencia."

"Who won?"

He growled and made a face. "Valencia," he said, and uttering the word seemed to make him thoughtful. He was probably thinking of the defeat, the details of the game. He drank for a while longer, and while he was lost in his thoughts I started to slip away.

"Wait," he said. "See this tattoo?" He rolled up his sleeve. "This one was much easier to do. I did this one myself, too."

Eventually I went back to my seat. As this was an express, the Virgin had a TV in each car. The video that trip was a soft-porn film of the 'Blue Lagoon' variety – castaways, jungle, friendly parrot, and plenty of excuses for the man and woman to get their clothes off.

Headphones were sold, though hardly anyone bought them. Most of the passengers looked out of the train windows at the pretty coves and the rocky shoreline, the steep cliffs and the pines and the small port villages. We had passed Sagunto and Castellón, and the Desierto de las Palmas, a high ridge with an eighteenth-century monastery to the west. Past miles of fruit trees and tenements by the sea, and after Tortosa on the river Ebro we were traveling ten feet from the sea, known in this corner of the Mediterranean as the Balearic Sea.

In spite of its fragrant herbaceous name, Tarragona was a grim place. That seemed to be the rule on this part of the Mediterranean shore. The town had been the subject of poems by Martial. The wines had been praised by Pliny: "The emperor himself wintered here in 26 B.C. after his Cantabrian campaign." Now it was mainly an oil-cracking plant and a strip of littered shore. The sour stink of sulfuric acid is an unmistakable indication that you have entered an industrial suburb. Sitges, farther along, once a fashionable resort, was now known mainly for its strip of homosexual beach.

Big cities seem to me like destinations, walled-in stopping places, with nothing beyond their monumental look of finality, breathing *You've arrived* to the traveler. But I did not want to have a destination on the Mediterranean coast. I had planned to push on and to avoid places like Barcelona; or at least see them glancingly and not linger. Such a rich place seemed perfect for the person who wants to write a book about a city. There were many with the title *Barcelona*. Yet I hung on.

It was a sunny afternoon when I arrived on the Virgin from Valencia. I was in no hurry. And Barcelona seemed a bright and lovely place, pleasant for walking around, with parks and wide boulevards and a brightness and prosperity. The prosperity might have been an illusion. One of the city's car factories, a division of Fiat, shut down the day I arrived, putting 9,000 people out of work. The graffiti were almost instantaneous: *Fiat...Mafia*.

But I had other reasons for liking Barcelona. In its bookstores, along with pornographic comics and pornographic photo magazines, the many bullfighting magazines, treatises on the occult, and dreams, and witches; knitting magazines, marriage manuals, motor-cycle monthlies, sadistic and romantic novels, dictionaries, gardening books, gun digests, and hagiographies, were *La Costa de los Mosquitos* and *Mi Historia Secreta*, *San Jack*, *La Calle de la Media Luna*, *Zona Exterior*, and many more books in Spanish translation, written by me.

People in Barcelona were apparently buying and reading my books. Knowing that gave the city an air of sympathy and erudition and it made me want to stay a while.

I had not had a good meal since starting. Spanish food was – what? Undistinguished, unmemorable, regional. In several Spanish towns I had been encouraged by locals to eat at Italian restaurants; in Cartagena I was told the best place was Chinese. Spaniards often disparaged their own food and said the restaurants were terrible, and when I asked them what they liked to eat they would mention something their mother made.

Barcelona, full of great restaurants, was the exception to all this. The city had been spruced up for the Olympics but even so it had always had a reputation for good living and great art, the Picasso Museum, the Gaudí cathedral. And that was odd for me because in my mind it was the bombed and besieged city at the heart of Orwell's *Homage to Catalonia*, fiercely contended for by fascists, communists and anarchists.

What was the Spanish view of all that? Presumably there were many Spanish books about "the National Uprising."

"There are almost no books of that kind," Antonio was saying.

We were eating sea-urchins' eggs with julienne of seared tuna at his restaurant, La Balsa. There are seldom any lapses in service when you are seated with the owner.

"We have no memory. For example, no one in Spain writes biographies. There are no memoirs at all."

"It is as though we do not want to remember the past," his companion Beatriz said. "It's strange, but that's Spain."

"We live for today and tomorrow. We don't think about yesterday. It's not good. Maybe it's better to have no memories at all than have bad memories," Antonio said. "My family was okay. They were not for Franco, but they were monarchists."

Beatriz said she had been an anarchist, an unexpected announcement from a prosperous and well-turned-out woman, who had just praised the wine, or perhaps it was my ignorant presumption that an anarchist was an outlaw. And I should have known better because Orwell, who had been a member of a Trotskyite militia, had described the anarchist brigades.

She smiled and said that anarchists greeted each other with the word, "*Salud!*"

"Let's say your great-great-grandfather went to Cuba and made a fortune buying and selling slaves," Antonio said. "If someone writes a book about that, a biography, and claims this relative of yours was a slaver, the family will be hurt, eh? Better not to hurt the family. I think this."

"Tony uses that example because his great-great-grandfather sold slaves in Cuba," Beatriz said.

"Maybe he sold slaves and maybe not, but anyway he made his fortune in Cuba."

"Doing what?"

"Many things." Antonio was smiling sheepishly. "That is why I say, better not to ask."

I said, "But when I asked about the past I wasn't thinking of the eighteenth century. I was thinking about thirty years ago, or less."

I had yet to accustom myself to such remote allusions. This example of colonial Cuba was typical of a certain Mediterranean way of thinking. Antonio might easily have mentioned the ancient Iberians. The Gibraltarians casually quoted the Treaty of Utrecht, the coastal French could talk about the Roman occupation until the cows came home, and the Italians reminisced about the Etruscans. Even this was nothing compared with a Greek in full cry, describing his glorious Hellenic heritage ("Euripides once said . . ."), or a Turk animadverting about the Ottoman Empire.

And references to Masada, Moses, and the wisdom of the prophet Abraham were part of most Israelis' small-talk. Much of this was romance, or at least sentimental. The Frenchmen who talked about the Romans would be evasive when the subject of the German occupation was raised. Israelis might not be happy talking about something that occurred in South Lebanon last year. There was a book to be written about Mediterranean notions of time.

Nor, in the Mediterranean, were there clear divisions between the dead and the living, between the mythical and the real. That was another book.

Meanwhile, Antonio was answering my question.

"For some people there is a clear memory of Franco," he said. "It is not good. Everything changed after he died – in fifteen years we changed totally. But maybe we had changed before, and kept it to ourselves."

Beatriz said, "The taxi-drivers are sentimental, they say things were better before – less crime, no drugs, more order."

"Taxi-drivers all over the world say that," I said.

"And the young people say, 'Franco? Wasn't he a general?' "

"It was the tourists who kept us up-to-date," Antonio said.

Was he talking about individual travelers, or the vast numbers of predictable and frugal package tourists, the English out of Monty Python's Flying Circus, wearing socks under their sandals and demanding Watney's Red Barrel and the *Daily Express* and complaining of garlic in the food and joking about tummy upsets and diarrhea, and overdoing it on the first day and – too late – putting Timothy White's sun-cream on their big sunburned beaks. *The Spannies don't have our clean ways, innit?*

Them, he said, the lower-middle-class hearties and trippers.

"We learned a lot from them," he said. "Ideas, style, what they thought of us and our government. We learned about the rest of the world. And Franco thought he had closed the door."

But the reason might also have been that in the twilight period of the seventies, Franco was on his deathbed, and book and movie censorship had been relaxed. Of these years, Colm Toibin writes in *Homage to Barcelona*, "People [in Barcelona] lived in a free country of their own invention, despite the police, despite the dying Dictator."

My dinner companions asked me about my trip so far, about the provinces of Andalusia and Murcia and Valencia.

This raised a common Mediterranean theme. There was another book to be written, based on the text: "This is not one country – this is many countries." Italy was several countries; so were Turkey and Israel and France and Cyprus. Yugoslavia was quite a few countries. And Spain?

"Spain is not a country," Antonio said. "It is many different countries, with many different languages. Andalusia is so different from Castile and Galicia. Yet, somehow, Andalusian culture got exported – the guitar, the dances, the songs, all that. Foreigners think that Spanish culture is Andalusian only. But this is many nations."

"That's why the Spanish can't write about it," Beatriz said. "Only outsiders can."

We talked about the Spain of Gerald Brenan, and Pritchett, and Jan Morris, and H.V. Morton, and Hemingway, and George Borrow, and Rose Macaulay, and Robert Graves. It was true, Spain had been thoroughly anatomized by foreigners, the British especially.

"Mario Vargas Llosa comes here quite a lot," Antonio said, referring to the novelist, essayist and unsuccessful presidential candidate in the last Peruvian election. He says, 'People in Spain talk in a lively and intelligent way. They are very perceptive and sometimes very rude. Then they go home and do nothing.'"

One night in Barcelona I had been invited to one of those parties where everyone was witty. There was a poet, a moviemaker, a philosophy professor, a publisher, a painter, a musician, about fifteen people around a table, all intellectuals and artists, and all of them friends, all drunk on champagne – the empty bottles littered the table – celebrating the director's forty-fourth birthday. They laughed and poked fun and quoted each other, while I sat and marveled. It was a bright, cliquey, old-fashioned, unselfconscious gathering of people, neither fashionable nor wealthy, but all of them talented – and, incidentally, every person at the table was smoking a cigarette.

Antonio went on quoting Vargas Llosa, "'The English meet at

London parties. They are very polite, they hardly talk. Then they go home and write amazing things – rude, wicked, funny, lively.'"

"Paul is so polite," Beatriz said. "Maybe that means he is going to write something wicked!"

On the contrary, in Barcelona I was thinking kindly of the Spanish; what I saw (and it made me hopeful for the rest of my trip) was simple affection. In other travels I had not seen much affection between men and women, that is open displays of physical intimacy – kissing, hand-holding, snogging, canoodling, a sudden hug; not lust but affection, friendship, reassurance, paddling palms and pinching fingers. I had hardly seen it in China. It was rare on the islands of Oceania. It did not exist in India.

I saw it in Spain: old married couples holding hands, young people kissing, married ones embracing. It was not submissive and sexist. It was deeply affecting, spontaneous and candid. I thought: *I like this*.

Even at the Barcelona bullfight, my last bullfight, couples held hands there too.

"He is a show-off," a woman behind me said, calling him a *presumido*. The matador was kissing the tips of the bull's horns, kneeling just in front of the bleeding, drooling animal, and teasingly flicking the bull's head with his finger.

Then the bull came alive and rewarded the matador for taunting him. It bore down on the matador and tore him with its hoofs and gored him, as the cape-waggers tried to distract the murderously provoked creature. The matador got up. There was blood on his arm and his hip. The crowd cheered him, but in a robust and almost satirical way. Then I saw why. The bull in goring him had torn the matador's tight trousers just at the crotch, and as he limped his dick was exposed, a small pink sausage.

I fell into conversation with the man next to me and said I wondered what happened to the bull after it was dragged away dead.

They were butchered and eaten, he said. He described the broth that was made from the bull's tail, the steaks that were cut from its haunches; and hamburgers that were made from chopped bull.

"And tomorrow morning you can find the bull's *criadilla* on the menu of certain restaurants in Barcelona," he said.

Criadilla?

"*Cojones*," he said. "But *cojones* is not polite. Better to say *criadilla*.

"The bull's testicles are served like brain. And it is like eating kiwi fruits. You think they are going to be tough, then you bite, and it is soft and tender and mushy."

After the Picasso Museum and the climb to the top of the hill Montjuic and through the Parc Guell, I made a tour of Gaudí's masterpiece, the Sagrada Familia. Colm Toibin, in his book on Barcelona, tells the story of Gaudí's being interrogated by a visiting bishop. Why had Gaudí decorated the tops of towers which no one would ever see?

Gaudí said, "Your Grace, the angels will see them."

And then I set out again, up the flat tame coast they call the Costa de Maresme, which would lead me to the rugged cliffy Costa Brava, the "Wild Coast," and the French border.

Badalona, just outside the city, was both Roman ruins and a grotesque power plant. One stop out of Arc de Triunfo station, going north along the Mediterranean, and Barcelona out of the back window seemed like a small town at the foot of a wooded hill – an illusion perhaps, but that was how it seemed.

There was enough surf for surfers and boogie-boarders on the first stretch of shore, at Banys Mortgat; I could see them in black wet-suits in the cold water. The train loped along next to the shore, and on this overcast day there were nudists sheltering from the wind at Afrenys de Mar, and more just before St Pol, a nude man and a clothed man lying together; and a nude woman reading a book that she had clasped between her knees; a nude man on his back, a nude woman on her stomach, smooth ones, hairy ones. In the winter!

For the rest it was the Mediterranean shuffle, people walking dogs, families, pipe-smokers, men in berets walking arm in arm, and old crippled nuns not only dressed up like penguins but walking like penguins, side to side, in that flat-footed way. And a man swaying and pissing in the Mediterranean in full view of the train passengers – couples, families, children, nuns, priests, monks, dogs, lovers.

St Pol de Mar was a dense but well-maintained seaside resort, and I could see that the towns improved as the train moved north and the coast became rockier. There were palms on the promenade at Calella, where "Fisioculturismo" was announced on a poster, the "25th Championship of Body-building – the Calella Finals." At Pineda del Mar, apart from the pines, there were cabbages planted by the sea and vineyards inland. The bigger and busier places had signs in German and English.

There were shouting girls on the train, and there was sexual defiance in the way they seemed to challenge the boys across the aisle with their loud laughter. Others were pushing each other and calling out. A poor old woman ate potato chips out of her handbag. A snotty infant clutched a paper bag. Two mustached nuns nodded as the train jogged on the tracks. The painter Constable said, "Nothing is ugly in this world."

Blanes was a cut above the others in this strung-out shore of small resorts, and not on the main line. Although I was going farther, it is the limit of a day-trip, as far as it is possible to go on an outing from Barcelona. It lies in a bay, the beginning of the Costa Brava, with a rocky bluff and a rocky promontory and a harbor with fishing-boats and sailboats, and only its terrible post-war architecture identifies it as Spanish – a wall of stucco flat-fronted tenements and apartment blocks, with rusty balconies facing the sea. Today the sea looked like iron, and the beach was brown sand and chilly palms, with a cold sun glowing behind the thick clouds.

And at Blanes the same signs I had been seeing everywhere since I had left Gibraltar: "Snak Bar,", "Snaks," "Pizza," "Helados," "Loteria," "Motel," "Pizzeria," "Hamburguesa," "Hotel del Mar," "Bar Paraiso," "Camping," "Teléfono," "Heladeria," "Bistro," "Bodega," "Viajes," "Peluqueria," "Cambio-Exchange-Change-Wechsel," "Bebe Coca-Cola," "Discoteca," "Piscina," "For Rent," "For Sale," "Cerveceria," "Club Nautic," "Hostel," but also – because this was militant Catalonia – the angry graffiti, *Puta Espanya* and *Puta Madre* and *En Catalan* and *Free Catalunya!*.

Blanes, with its trampled sand, its masses of footprints, its blowing paper, its empty promenade, could stand for them all.

In the morning I got back on the main line, traveling north to Figueras and the frontier. At each station on the line, stocky men puffing cigarettes were cutting the smaller branches from the plane trees, turning them into ugly stumps, some of the trees looking castrated and others like amputees, and the slighter ones seeming as though they had had brutal haircuts. The neat bundles of branches, the procession of ladders, all the saws and axes, and the many men carrying out the operation, gave it the appearance of a solemn ritual – so methodical, unhurried, tidy and self-important, the cutters almost priestly as they went about their business. The ritual element might also have meant that they were members of a labor union. I had the feeling that they would never allow a woman to do a simple job. This was going on at Sils and Flassa and Camallera and Vilamatta.

The heart of Gerona is medieval, yet from the train Gerona was like a view in China – the plain brick buildings, the leafless trees, the bright dry hills outside, the harshness, the streets being swept by men with twig brooms, the stick-like trees and tiled roofs; it looked to me like any Chinese town of the same size, even to the turgid river Onar with its water a dubious color. Outside it, the way the gardens were planted in narrow allotments, the look of the tile roofs of the stucco cottages, the neatness, the fruit farms, an absence of decoration, all made it seem intensely Chinese.

There were so many trains on this line that I got off, walked around Gerona; caught another train north, went to Figueras, got off, walked around Figueras.

In a café in the middle of Gerona an Arab – who was perhaps a Moroccan – was sprawled on the floor. He was tangled in the chair legs, as a policeman nagged him and people stared. The Spanish are both very polite and very curious, an awkward combination of traits, and so they have developed an economical and yet piercing way of eavesdropping, an unintrusive way of being nosy. The policeman and another man helped the Arab to his feet and then sat him down. And then the policeman began hitting the Arab on the arm as he questioned him. The Arab looked too drugged and dazed to care. He looked as though he was being picked on; but in such a provincial town in Spain every outsider looked like a Martian.

On the way to Figueras a little sorority of Japanese girls twittered among themselves. They lacked the characteristic Nipponese submissiveness, but as their giggles grew louder and a bit frenzied an old Spaniard stood up and turned his evil eye upon them and silenced them, and they became enigmatic. They were the first of many young Japanese women I saw who were boldly traveling along the shores of the Mediterranean, some of them taking advantage of the low season, others refugees from language schools in France and Italy.

One of the first buildings I saw in Figueras was the Asilo-Vilallonga – the town asylum for mental cases. In 1904, Salvador Dali was born in Figueras. This was nine months after his brother (also named Salvador) died, and the second Salvador might have ended up in this asylum if his madness had not also brought forth paintings and sculptures of great ingenuity. As a sixteen-year-old he wrote in his diary, "Perhaps I'll be misunderstood, but I'll be a genius, a great genius. I am sure of it."

Dali's parents always kept a huge ("majestic") painting of the first Salvador, who died at the age of seven, in their bedroom. Dali said he lived two lives, his brother's and his own. In Madrid as a young art student he met Federico García Lorca, and later in life Dali reminisced about his friendship with the distinguished poet and playwright:

"[Lorca] was homosexual, as everyone knows, and madly in love with me. He tried to screw me twice ... I was extremely annoyed, because I wasn't homosexual, and I wasn't interested in giving in. Besides, it hurts. So nothing came of it. But I felt awfully flattered vis-à-vis the prestige. Deep down I felt that he was a great poet and that I did owe him a tiny bit of the Divine Dali's asshole."

Sentiments of this sort in Dali's autobiography shocked George Orwell, who regarded him as abnormal, without any morality, and James Thurber, who jeered at him. Dali simply laughed: his book had succeeded in upsetting readers. He spent his life attempt-

ing to outrage people's sense of decency; he played at perversion
and then came to believe in it, even in the nonsense he uttered. In
his eyes there was no portrait or landscape that could not be
improved by adding another breast, or a corpse, or a handful of
ants.

Yet Dali was also the consummate Spaniard – a Catalan to boot
– and throughout his work are the Spanish preoccupations and
iconography: bulls, Christs, Quixotes, Virgins, nakedness, fetishism,
eroticism, humor, anti-clericalism, dry hills, matadors. A Dali
crucifixion is erotic and pious at the same time. In Dali's work, as
in Spanish life, there is no dividing line between the sacred and the
profane, between a shrine and a boudoir, a sport and a sacrifice,
between sexual passion or spiritual ecstasy. Dali made the fetishes
and relics of the Church his own obsessions; and his wife Gala
(who had been the wife of the French poet, Paul Éluard) was at
once virgin, whore, Venus; his mother, his madonna and his
coquette.

"I am the king of cuckolds!" Dali shrieked as he saw Gala being
rowed out to sea by a young fisherman who fancied her. Dali
indulged Gala in her preference for young handsome men. Gala
was active with these studs well into her seventies, though the
sexual athletics may also have shortened her life. When Gala died
Dali stopped eating and went off his head – or rather went madder
in such a melancholy way that he ceased to paint.

He had delighted in being a spectator to Gala's numerous
romances and, intensely voyeuristic, he took his pleasure in watching the sexual act being performed live by hired hands in his
castle. He inspires a similarly voyeuristic impulse in anyone
who looks at his pictures. He invites voyeurism: you don't enter
his pictures, or even feel them much. You stand a few feet
away, fascinated. It is hard to know what to think of the
cannibals and giraffes and amputees in the pictures; it is also
hard to look away, because Dali has a diabolical mastery of
space. And so you gape, a bit ashamed, a bit amused, mostly
bewildered.

Although he cheerfully mutilated his pictorial subjects he was
capable of painting the human body in its most idealized form;
and perhaps since the act of sodomy fascinated Dali – he paid

couples to perform it privately for him – he was at his most expressive and naturalistic when painting human buttocks. The shapely curves of thigh and back are found all over his work – not shocking at all, but lovingly presented, not an ant in sight, no disfigurement at all. A good example of this, one of his most brilliant bums, is the painting "Dali Raising the Skin of the Mediterranean Sea to Show Gala the Birth of Venus."

That painting hangs in the quirky Dali Museum, one of Figueras's former theaters, Dali's legacy and living joke. Dali is also buried there, which ranks it as one of the more bizarre mausoleums in the world. Entering the museum is like walking inside Dali's teeming brain. He designed the museum and so it is as much his house as his head – his life's work, perhaps his masterpiece of surrealism. It is an eccentric but well-arranged building, with a gift shop where you can buy Dali tarot cards and Dali scarves and even a melted wristwatch that gives the exact time.

Rooms and corridors, painted ceilings, monsters, masks, junk, a 1936 Cadillac with a fat seven-foot goddess straddling the hood and opera music blasting from the radiator grille. Elsewhere there are skeletons – dog skulls, croc skulls, an entire gorilla skeleton with the head of the Virgin Mary encased in the rib-cage. The gorilla bones are gilded. There are ants everywhere. The unlikeliest objects such as chamber pots are covered in feathers; machine parts are coated in fur, human bodies in soup spoons.

A fetching photo of Dali shows him wearing a loaf of bread on his head. His Venus de Milo has desk drawers for breasts. There is a shrine with big buckets and even bigger nudes, and the "Sala de Mae West" is a pair of enormous lips and nostrils, with a specially erected viewing stand.

Much of it is mockery – of classicism, the Church, authority, women, convention, Christ, Spain. He did riffs on Velasquez, copies of 'Las Meninas,' a satire of Millais in the style of Seurat, a satire of Picasso in the style of Picasso.

You need to be a talented Spaniard maddened by all that history and culture to explode like this. Obviously brilliant, often childish, at his best he seems as great as an old master, and then you see that it is pastiche – his originality is a kind of comedy, the comedy of outrage, and perhaps the personification of the Spanish temper.

One of the highest compliments in Spain is the dedicatory bullfight. On 12 August 1961 this honor was accorded to Dali, in the Plaza de Toros in Figueras: "An Extraordinary *Corrida* to Pay Homage to the Eminent Artist Salvador Dali."

In his later years he supported Franco, and this alienated those friends of his who had endured his nonsensical and dotty utterances. They drew the line at fascism. Once, after a lunch with Franco, Dali said, "I have reached the conclusion that he is a saint." Before then he had not been particularly political – he was not yet scatterbrained enough for that. He had chosen to be oblique, and had said, apropos of "Autumn Cannibalism" (two semi-humans, feeding on each other, propped up with crutches and garnished with ants), that it showed "the pathos of the Civil War considered (by me) as a phenomenon of natural history, as opposed to Picasso who considered it a political phenomenon."

Luis Buñuel made *The Andalusian Dog* (*Un Chien Andalou*) with Dali, in which a celebrated image in the notorious fifteen-minute film is an eyeball being sliced with a razor. But Buñuel eventually came to regret and finally loathe Dali for his self-promotion and irresponsible encouragement of Franco. Buñuel had said in his memoirs that he considered surrealism "a poetic, a revolutionary, and a moral movement."

Dali did not reply to this, though he might have said that all war was inevitable because we are so unpredictable and impulsive, and because all human life involves savagery and fetishism. Religion and politics, in the Dali scheme of things, are the primitive expression of our fears and desires. There is no question that he succeeds at depicting this.

The Dali Museum is a repository of flea-market cast-offs and visual paradoxes; it is junkyard art, found objects, ceramic ambiguities, and perverse natural history. It is a monument to Dali's exhibitionism. He occupies the middle ground, somewhere between a buffoon and a genius, wearing his deviation on his sleeve a bit too obviously for many people's comfort, hiding very little. He is somewhat like the youths of Figueras who spray the old walls of the town with graffiti as they chew Bubbaloo ("The gum stuffed with liquid!") and are watched by old men who wear vast floppy berets. Dali has been belittled as a buffoon. The proof of Dali's gift is that he knows how to arouse us, and outrage us, and make us laugh.

Apart from this artistic funfair, Figueras is an ordinary town, of whiny cars and narrow streets, and working people. It is conventional to see Dali as an aberration. But I had the feeling, seeing the Spaniards of Figueras, that Dali was speaking for them, perhaps for all of us, from the depths of our unconscious.

There was no train to Cadaqués. I took a bus to this vertical village. Here, nearby at Port Lligat, Dali lived, on the Costa Brava, the real, wild thing, with rocks and cliffs and a dangerous shore. It is steep and stony, with precipitous cliffs and headlands with some vineyards. There are few beaches to speak of, only small tight harbors and coves, littered beaches with masses of flotsam. Another bus took me across a steep cape of land, back to the railway line.

This was Llansa. It was sunset. I hated traveling after dark, because it meant I could not see anything out of the window. So I stayed in Llansa, a pretty bay with horrid condos by the sea, looking (perhaps this was surrealism suggested by my recent experience of Dali) like kitchen appliances. They were all shut for the winter. After writing my notes and having a drink I walked to the beach, where some fishermen stood under a cold purple sunset sky. They were casting and standing by their rods rubbing their hands, waiting for a nibble as night fell, and to the north there was a shadow, a black sky, winter in France.

5

Le Grand Sud to Nice

What threw me was the sameness of the sea. The penetrating blue this winter day and the pale sky and the lapping of water on the shore, continuous and unchanging, the simultaneous calm in eighteen countries, and those aqueous and indistinct borders, made it seem like a small world of nations, cheek by jowl, with their chins in the water. And it was so calm I could imagine myself trespassing, from one to the other, in a small boat, or even swimming. So much for the immutable sea.

On land, the station at Port Bou, the edge of Spain, was like a monument to Franco. Fascism shows more clearly in the façades of buildings than in the faces of people. This one was self-consciously monumental, austere to the point of ugliness, very orderly and uncomfortable, under the Chaîne des Arbères, a gray range of mountains. The train rattled, and it moved slowly on squeaky wheels through the gorge to the station at Cerbère, the beginning of France.

There were no passport formalities, the bright winter light did not change, and yet there was a distinct sense of being in another country. And that was odd because all we had done was jog a short way along the shore. Gibraltar is a marvel of nature — it looks like a different place. But the border between Spain and France (and France and Italy, and so on) looks arbitrary, vague in reality and only distinct on a map. But some aspects of it spoke of a frontier: the different angle of the mountains, and especially the way the lower slopes were covered in cactuses, plump little plants, sprouting from every crevice and ledge on the rock face and cliffs that overlooked the harbor at Cerbère; an odor, too — disinfectant and the sea and the cigarette smoke; but most of all the Arabs. There had been none in the small port towns over the border, but there was a sudden arabesque of lounging cab-drivers, porters, travelers, lurkers.

"There are a lot of them in Marseilles," a young man said in English. He was sitting just ahead of me, with his friend, and holding a guitar-case on his lap. He was addressing two Japanese travelers, still saying "them."

He was referring to the Arabs without using the word.

"We're going there," one of the Japanese said.

"That's a real rough place."

"What? You mean we'll get ripped off?"

"Worse."

That stopped them. What was worse than being robbed?

"Like I got robbed on the subway train," the first American said. "And then they tried to steal my guitar. There are gangs."

"Gangs," the Japanese man said.

"Lots of them," the American said.

"Where do you think we should stay?"

"Not in Marseilles. Arles, maybe. Van Gogh? The painter? That Arles. Like you could always take a day trip to Marseilles."

"Is it that bad?"

The second American said, "I'd go to Marseilles again if I could leave my stuff behind. That's why I didn't go to Morocco. What would I do with my guitar?"

"You speak French?" the Japanese traveler asked.

"I can read it. Do you know any other languages?"

"Japanese."

"Your English is great."

"I grew up in New Jersey," the Japanese man said.

At this point I took out my notebook, and on the pretext of reading my newspaper wrote down the conversation. The Japanese man was talking about Fort Lee, NJ, his childhood, the schools. The man with the guitar was also from New Jersey.

"Fort Lee's not that nice," the man with the guitar said. It seemed a harsh judgment of the Japanese fellow's home town.

"It used to be," the Japanese man said. "But I'd be freaking out when I went to New York."

"My brother loves sports, but he's too scared to go to New York and watch the games."

"Like, I never took the subway in ten years."

"I don't have a problem with the subway."

"Except, like, you might get dead there."

The Japanese man was silent. Then he said, "How did these guys attempt to rob you?"

"Did I say 'attempt?'"

"Okay, how did they do it?"

"The way they always do. They crowd you. They get into your pockets. One guy went for me. I kicked him in the legs. He tried to kick me when he got off the train."

"That's it. I'm not going to Marseilles," the Japanese man said.

I got tired of transcribing this conversation, which was repetitious, the way fearful people speak, when they require reassurance. It all sounded convincing to me, and it made me want to go to Marseilles.

The landscape had begun to distract me. Almost immediately a greater prosperity had become apparent – in the houses, the way they were built, the trees, the towns, the texture of the land, the well-built retaining walls, the sturdy fences, even the crops, the blossoms, the way the fields are squared off, from Banyuls-sur-Mer to bourgeoisified Perpignan.

With this for contrast, I saw Spain as a place that was struggling to keep afloat. It had something to do with tourism. The Spanish towns from the Costa Brava south are dead in the low season; the French towns just a few miles along looked as though they were booming even without tourists. They did not have that soulless appearance of apprehension and abandonment that tourist towns take on in the winter: the empty streets, the windswept beach, the promises on signs and posters, the hollow-eyed hotels.

The train was traveling next to the sea – or, more precisely, next to the great lagoon-like ponds: Étang de Leucate, Étang de Lapalme. Nearer Narbonne and the Étang de Bages et de Sigean, the railway line bisected the Étang de l'Ayrolle, making it resemble a low-lying Asiatic landscape feature, a traverse between fish farms or paddyfields.

Towards Narbonne there were fruit trees in bloom – apples, cherries, peach blossoms. And shore birds in the marshes, and at the edges of the flat attenuated beach. There were Daliesque details in all this — I put this down to my recent visit to the crackpot museum. The first was a château in the middle of nowhere, with vineyards around it, turrets and towers and pretty windows, a smug little absurdity in the seaside landscape, a little castle, like a grace note in a painting. There was no reason for it to be there. And much stranger than that, what looked like an enormous flock of pink flamingos circling over the *étang* a few miles before the tiny station of Guissan-Tourbelle. I made a note of the name because I felt I was hallucinating. *Flamingos? Here?*

That night, in Narbonne, in Languedoc, I was wondering about those flamingos I thought I had seen flying out of the salty lagoons by the sea on the way into the city. Having a cup of coffee in the cool blossom-scented air of Mediterranean midwinter I struck up a conversation with Rachel, at the next table. A student at the university in Montpellier, she was spending a few days at home with her family. She was twenty, a native of Narbonne.

"They are flamingos, yes — especially at Étang de Leucate," Rachel said.

The tall pink birds had not been a hallucination of mine; yet it was February, fifty degrees Fahrenheit. What was the story?

"All the *étangs* have flamingos" — the word is the same in French — "but in the summer when there are a lot of people around they sometimes fly off and hide in the trees."

Rachel did not know more than that.

She said, "The *étangs* are very salty, very smelly at low tide, but there are fish in them and lots of mussels."

"I associate flamingos with Africa," I said.

Rachel shrugged. "I have not traveled. You are traveling now?"

"To Arles, and then Marseilles."

"I have never been to Arles," she said.

It was thirty miles beyond her college dorm at Montpellier.

"Or Marseilles, or Nice," she went on. "I went to Spain once. And to Brittany once. I prefer the sea in Brittany — it is rough and beautiful."

"What about the Mediterranean?"

"It is not exciting," she said.

I could have told her that the Mediterranean extended to the shores of Syria, was tucked into Trieste, formed a torrent at Messina, hugged the delta of the Nile, and even wetted a strip of Bosnia.

"And will you stay in Nice?" she said.

"For a few days. Then I'll take the ferry to Corsica."

"I have a friend from Corsica. He told me that the people are very traditional there. The women are suppressed – not free as they are here."

"Is his family traditional?"

"Yes. In fact, when they heard that he was talking about life there they got really angry. Corsicans think it's bad to repeat these things. I feel bad that I am telling you."

So to change the subject, I asked her about her studies.

"I am studying psychology. It's a six-year course. I chose it because I want to work with autistic children after I graduate."

"Have you ever worked with autistic children?"

"In the summer, yes, several times," she said. "Ever since I was twelve I knew I wanted to work with handicapped people. I knew it would be my life."

"That's hard work, isn't it?"

"Yes, it's hard. You give a lot. You don't get back very much. But I don't mind. Not many people want to do it."

Such idealism seemed to me rare. These were not sentiments I had heard expressed very often and they lifted my spirits.

The next day was sunny, and Arles was not far. I left my bag at Narbonne railway station and went for a walk along the *étangs*, and watched the flamingos feeding and flying.

This Mediterranean sunshine was like a world of warmth and light, and it was inspirational, too. It was easy to understand the feelings of T.E. Lawrence who took a dip here in 1908 and wrote to his mother, "I felt I had at last reached the way to the South, and all the glorious East; Greece, Carthage, Egypt, Tyre, Syria, Italy, Spain, Sicily, Crete . . . they were all there, and all within reach of me."

I had thought that I had left Narbonne in plenty of time, but the early darkness of winter fell upon Arles just as the train pulled into the station. I had wanted to arrive in daylight. It was the seven-teenth of February; Vincent Van Gogh had first arrived in Arles on the twentieth (in 1888), and because of that timing his life was changed.

"You know, I feel I am in Japan," he wrote to his brother Theo.

It was the light, the limpid colors. It was, most of all, the trees in bloom. And strangely that February was very cold and snowy. To see branches covered in snowflakes and white blossoms thrilled Van Gogh – and this in a low Hollandaise landscape of flat fields and windbreaks by the Rhône. They were almond blossoms mostly, but also cherry, peach, plum and apricot. Van Gogh painted the almond flowers on the branches, a Japanese-style picture that resembled a floral design that he had seen before on a screen panel.

Even in the dark I could see some blossoms, and in the glarey light of street lamps the almond petals were like moths clustered on the black branches and twisted twigs.

Arles had three or four large luxury hotels, but I was put off by their ridiculous prices. I had found the name of a twenty-dollar hotel in a guidebook. This was called La Gallia. It was apparently a café and pizza joint.

The man at the coffee machine said, "Go outside, turn right, go around to the back and up the stairs. Use this key. The light switch is on the wall. Your room is on the second floor. You can't miss it."

"Do you want me to sign anything?"

"No name needed. No signature. Just the money in advance. No passport. Sleep well!"

"Is there a toilet?"

"It's in the hall. But you have a sink."

It was a medieval tenement on a back street, with a cobblestone courtyard and a winding staircase. I was halfway up the stairs when everything went black; the timer on the light ran out. I struggled in the dark to the landing, where I fumbled my flashlight out of my bag. I used this to find the light switch on the next landing. It seemed so difficult contriving to enter and leave this odd, empty building that I stayed in my room and went out at the first sign of dawn.

That morning there was an old man with a wooden leg trying to climb the stairs.

"Softly," I said.

There was only room for one person at a time on these precipitous stairs.

"This wooden leg of mine is heavy," he panted. "It was the war."

"My uncle was here in the war."

Corporal Arthur Theroux of Stoneham, Massachusetts.

"Fighting?"

"Running a blood bank. He was a medic. 33rd Station Hospital."

We had to throw most of the French blood away, Paulie. They all had syphilis. The American whole blood was the stuff we used.

In the watery morning light I saw a profusion of almond blossoms. But I would have noticed them without the suggestion of Van Gogh; there was no subtlety. It was an explosion of flowers, the trees frothing with blossoms. The cherry blossoms of early spring in London and on Cape Cod always indicated to me that winter was over; there is something magical about their appearing before the trees are in leaf.

Walking towards the river a man – American – asked me directions to the railway station. He was Jim, from Connecticut, relieved to be in Arles after a harrowing trip – so he said – through Portugal and Spain.

"I hated Spain. I almost got robbed in Madrid."

He was a recent graduate of Bucknell. Philosophy major.

"Ever heard of Philip Roth? He went to Bucknell," Jim said. "We had to study him. Everyone at Bucknell reads him. I hated that stuff."

I asked him whether he was on vacation.

"No. I quit my job. I hate the job market. I worked a little while for Cadbury-Schweppes. They were developing a home soft-drink dispenser. The whole bit. Syrup, gas, water – your own soft drinks on tap. It was like a coffee machine."

"What were you doing?"

"Test-marketing it."

"Did it fly?"

"It was a failure. It was too expensive — and who needs it?" He kicked along beside me. "They weren't open to new ideas, so I quit."

"I'm sure you did the right thing — and here you are, a free man, seeing the world."

"What are you doing?"

His lack of interest in writing or reading encouraged me, and so I said, "I'm a publisher."

"What do you look for in a novel?" he asked suddenly. It was a good question.

"Originality, humor, subtlety. The writing itself. A sense of place. A new way of seeing. Lots of things. I like to believe the things I read."

I pulled a novel, *The Rock Pool* by Cyril Connolly, out of my back pocket and waved it at him.

"This has some of those qualities, but not enough."

"What's it about?"

"People going to pieces on the Riviera."

"Another one of those!"

True enough, I thought. "Do you do any writing?"

"No. I'm planning to go to art school, but at the moment I'm heading for Bratislava."

"Any particular reason?"

"Supposed to be a pretty nice place."

With that, he jogged off to the railway station, and I continued strolling through the back streets of Arles to the river. In many respects this was much the same place that Van Gogh saw; many of the same buildings still stand, the same streets and squares and boulevards. There is a vast Roman arena in the town, a splendid hippodrome the size of a small football stadium, used at certain seasons for bullfights. One series had just been held, another, the Easter Feria (*Feria de Pâques*) was coming soon.

Not far from here, the town of Nîmes was the center of French bullfighting and had been for a decade or so, since the revival of the nauseating — what? recreation? pastime? you could hardly call it a sport. It had been dying out, but Nîmes's right-wing backward-looking mayor, Jean Bousquet, provided guidance and enthusiasm. There are three bullfighting festivals a year in Nîmes, one attracting almost a million people. Of course French bullfighting had been denounced by animal rights activists and foreigners, but nothing encourages the French so much as disapproval, especially from aliens.

"Do you go to the bullfights?" I asked a man walking his dog along the river.

"Sometimes. But you know these special events are to bring in the tourists," he said. "I prefer football."

Arles was a small town and it had the two disfigurements of pretty French towns in the provinces: dog merds and graffiti. The sidewalks were so fouled they were almost impassable because of the merds. As for the graffiti, there was something particularly depressing about spray-painted scrawls on the stone of ancient façades. *Paris, t'encule* ("Up your ass, Paris") and *Gilly = pute et salope* ("Gilly = a whore and a slut") were two of the more picturesque obscenities.

The town had prepared itself for tourists, but on this winter day it looked especially empty: too many brasseries, hotels, gift shops and stores; in July it would be packed, the people said. But Arles had an off-season friendliness and lack of urgency. The waiters were not surly. One explained the drinks available and laughed with me over the odd names – Foetus Whisky, Delirium Tremens Beer ("It's from Belgium") and the blue cordial liqueur called "Fun Blue."

I eavesdropped in Arles, though it annoyed me when people were talking and I could not understand them because of the intrusive background music or other voices. It was like looking at something interesting while someone intruded on my line of vision. I felt stifled and frustrated.

Some of the snippets tantalized me:

A man said, "Let's do in Italy what we did in France, back at the hotel –"

A woman said, "I am not going to go to another place like that again, because, one, it's too complicated, and two, what if we got sick? And three, the other people look really strange –"

There were almond blossoms everywhere, which gave a great freshness to Arles and all its fields and made it seem still rural, still

provincial, picturesque and even inspirational. I liked the provinci-
ality of the place, and its clear light.

But Arles was not all floral, and tweeting with sparrows. The
mailman was doing his rounds, a hard-working housewife with big
red hands down at the grocer's was complaining about the high
price of morel mushrooms. This so-called cup fungus was selling at
168 francs for 100 grams, which worked out at $126 a pound. And
even in the early morning there were drinkers leaning on bars. It
was never too early for a drink in provincial France. Two ladies
were tippling Pernod. And down the street a florid blowzy woman
was nursing a beer. This was at seven in the morning in an Arles
back street.

To verify that Arles is a seaport, I walked along the east bank of
the Rhône in a southerly direction for a day of sunshine and sweet
air. There were windbreaks of twigs and boughs, and the wide flat
fields. There had been floods a few months before, which showed
on the banks of the river. Some sections of it had been strengthened,
parts of the retaining wall and the embankment filled in.

In the late afternoon I walked back to town to take the train the
short distance to Marseilles. At the small railway station at Arles
there were almond trees on each platform and they were in
blossom. Such a pretty station! Such lovely trees! And then the
TGV was announced. The TGV is the French high-speed train,
much too fast and too grand to stop at a little station like Arles. It
screamed past the platforms with such speed and back draft that a
special yellow TGV line was painted on the platform, so that
people would stand at a safe distance, giving the train six feet of
leeway. It howled like an earthbound jet, doing about 160 miles
an hour, and with such a rush of air that petals were blown from
the almond trees. The sight, the sound, the rush of air, made it a
deafening event, the train slicing the day in half and leaving such a
vacuum that I had the sense that my brain was being sucked out
of my ears.

Anyone who hankers for the romance of railways, of the branch
lines jogging through Provence, ought to consider the fact that the
newest trains are nearly as obnoxious – as noisy and intrusive – as
jets.

*

But even by the little blue, normal, stopping train of French National Railways it was an hour or less to Marseilles – about sixty miles away. We crossed the low delta of the Rhône, the fields of horses and flowers and vegetables, thriving in the winter sunshine; through the towns of Entressen and Miramas and along the shore of the Étang de Berre. I stayed as close as possible to the shore of the Mediterranean, which meant bypassing Aix-en-Provence and all the rest of the romanticized and much-written-about villages of Provence. They were not on my coastal route, which was neither a gastronomic tour nor a sentimental wallow in the life of rural Europe. That seemed a good thing too – from what I saw of those clumps of cottages, the tarted-up villages seemed more pretentious and expensive than the jammed ports and cities of the Mediterranean, where settlements were too active to be stuffy. And I had a sense that these coastal places had stronger links with each other than they had with the inland capitals and gentrified villages.

That was true of Marseilles, a wonderful city to arrive in by train, certainly one of the best in the world, because the ornate St Charles railway station is on a bluff. You walk outside and all of Marseilles is spread out below – the Old Town, the Old Port, the boulevards, the rooftops, the chimneys and church steeples, and on the far hill the cathedral of Notre Dame de la Garde, a gold statue on its dome. I could see the islands, the bluffs, the earthworks and fortresses and lighthouses. All this from the high stairs of the railway station.

"I read so much about the crime in Marseilles in my guidebook that I'm going to skip it altogether," Jim, the American, had told me in Arles.

I was suitably warned, not to say terrified. Until I found a hotel I left my bag in a station locker; I carried nothing in my hands; I had no camera and very little cash. I walked briskly, as though I had somewhere to go.

Marseilles was a frightener; it was famous for its boasters and liars, for the way its people exaggerated, and it had a wicked reputation – for its gangs, its badly-housed immigrants, its racism, and most of all for its crime. No wonder people compared it to New York City. It was certainly a center for drugs. The cocaine was produced in the former French colonies in West Africa, the raw paste was smuggled into Marseilles to be processed, made into crack or base or crystal, or else powdered and cut with dry milk from Italy and sold all over Europe. Petty crime was commonly spoken of in Marseilles; I kept my head down and was safe. Such wickedness as drugs and racketeering, which kept both the police and the gangsters busy, did not affect the idle wanderer that I was.

It seemed to me to be the ultimate Mediterranean city, for its size and its diversity. As soon as I left the station and started down the marble stairs to the city, I saw a gypsy woman smoking a pipe in the sunshine, and another counting coins she had made from playing tunes on her accordion. These gypsies were as sorry-looking here as in Spain, where they are relentlessly romanticized by travel journalists and persecuted by locals. Gypsies are generally despised in the Mediterranean, as they are in the rest of Europe. The same could be said for the Moroccans and Algerians, who were said to account for Marseilles being notorious for crime. But every Mediterranean race was represented here; the Arabs were as common as the French, and there were Greeks, Spaniards and Italians; there were tall loping Tuaregs in blue robes, and Berbers from Tunisia, and Senegalese selling handbags and watches. Arab women begged, each one squatting and holding a snotty-nosed child instead of a pleading sign, in a futile attempt – the Marseillaise seemed impervious to the pleas – to elicit sympathy.

In Marseilles the foreign men linger on street corners in small groups, because they come from cultures without telephones, where men linger on street corners in small groups. There they stood, dusky men, yakking and smoking. The so-called Foreign Quarter is in the Old Town, just below the station. The Baedeker Guide *Mediterranean* for. 1911 mentions this area: "On the N. side of the Quai du Port, the scene of motley popular traffic (pickpockets not uncommon), lies the Old Town, with its narrow and dirty streets, inhabited by the lower classes, including numerous Italians of whom the city contains about 100,000." Now it is Arabs and Vietnamese in the Old Town; and the same perceptions – motley, pickpockets, lower classes, cut-purses, parasites.

I walked down the Canebière ("Can o' Beer") along the Prom-enade Louis Brauquier ("poet and painter") to the mouth of the

Old Port. Out of the wind, sitting in the sunshine against a wall, was a line of people in various postures – old Moroccan women in shawls, men in berets, dog-walkers, men with their shirts off, other men stripped to their underwear grinning into the sunshine.

Farther on, standing at the limit of the fort, I looked out, and the Mediterranean seemed like a limitless ocean. I walked on to the Gare Maritime, where ferries left for Algeria and Tunisia, and Corsica. I was headed for Corsica but the station timetables told me that I could continue down the Côte d'Azur and catch the once-a-week (in the winter) ferry from Nice to Bastia, a port in the north of Corsica. At the ferry station passengers were boarding the French ship to Algiers, all of them Algerian Arabs. Not a single Frenchman, nor any foreigners. There was a good reason for this: at that point seventy-one foreigners, and tens of thousands of Algerians, had been killed by Islamic terrorists in Algeria in a fifteen-month period.

I kept walking. Because of Marseilles' pleasant thoroughfares, its absence of heavy traffic, its venerable architecture and its hills, it is pleasant for walking in and full of views. It was not particularly expensive either. My hotel, near the railway station, was about forty dollars a night.

It was fairly easy to get lost in Marseilles, particularly in the Old Town. As the Arab quarter, it had the fiercest reputation, though all I saw were cats and stragglers and the mindless defacing of the ancient walls with spray-painted graffiti. From behind bolted shutters I heard Algerian hilarity and screechy music.

My greatest fear walking down these back streets was of being killed by a garbage truck. These vehicles came quickly around the corners and did not slow down, and as they filled the entire street I found myself diving for a doorway and flattening myself against it.

Because Marseilles was so frightening to visitors it lacked the touristic triteness that was so common on the rest of the Riviera: expensive hotels, and sluttish recreations, and piggy food, and curio shops. The day after I arrived I walked in a different part of the city and found a market crowding the narrow lanes of the town around the Place du Marché des Capucines that was more like an Arab souk. Sacks of nuts and piles of dates, ten kinds of olives, fish and fruit and couscous, and French, Arabs and Africans mingling and haggling. The Arabesque of Marseilles, loathed and feared by the French, was one of its most interesting and liveliest aspects.

The maddening thing was my inability to speak to any Arabs. Their French I found peculiar and I don't speak Arabic. I felt there was the same vast cultural gulf between the French (Catholic, bourgeois, monoglot) and the Arabs (Muslim, peasants, Arabic-speaking). They really did not know each other at all.

Walking past a police station, I decided to go in and bluntly inquire about crime in Marseilles, since that was all that travelers talked about. I had seen no sign of it, not even on the previous night, as I loitered and lurked.

There was an ante-room where five policemen sat smoking cigarettes and twirling their truncheons.

One policeman said, "Yes, we have one big problem here in Marseilles. My colleague will tell you what it is."

The others laughed, as – on cue – a policeman said, "Arabs, Arabs, Arabs, Arabs, Arabs."

"They are the cause of all the trouble," the first policeman said. "Be very careful."

In such circumstances, talking to someone who was generalizing in such a racist way, I had a choice of challenging his logic, scolding him for uttering such offensive things, and so ending the conversation; or to keep listening, without interrupting, nodding and smiling in mild encouragement.

"What will the Arabs do to me?"

"They will steal your bag, your money, anything."

"Are they armed?"

"This is not New York! No, no guns. The knife is the favorite weapon of the Arab."

"Who are these Arabs? From what country?"

"They are Algerian. Also Moroccans, but mainly Algerians. They are awful. And they are everywhere."

The French are entirely frank in expressing their racism. I wondered whether this lack of delicacy, indeed stupidity, was an absence of inhibition or simply arrogance. Their public offensiveness ranged from smoking in restaurants to testing nuclear bombs in the Pacific. Perhaps they did not know that the world had moved on, or perhaps they just did not care; or, more likely, they delighted in being obnoxious.

I thanked the policemen for this information and pushed on, pondering the relationship between racism and xenophobia. By a coincidence I saw an article that day in a Marseilles newspaper describing a bill put forward by Jacques Toubon, the French Minister of Culture. This bill was intended to cleanse the French language; it would ban all foreign words – anglicisms mainly – and enforce linguistic purity. Everyone knew the words, everyone used them. In the course of traveling along the French part of the Mediterranean I picked up a number of them which were specifically denounced by the minister and which would have been banned by the bill.

Most English-speakers are aware that the French – indefatigable trend-spotters – have picked up words such as *le weekend, un snack* and *le club*; and as a result of this quest for novelty French is rife with anglicisms. The French feel the same *frisson* from saying *le smoking* (meaning a tux) that English-speakers feel from saying *frisson*. There are roughly 3,000 entries in the *Dictionnaire des Anglicismes*. For example, *le paddock* (also used for bed), *l'autostop* (hitchhike), *le ketchup*, and *le leader. Le jamesbonderie* is French for a daring feat; *surbooker* means to over-book, *le best-of, le challenge* and *le hit parade* are obvious, and *se faire lifter* means to have a face-lift.

But a large element in French officialdom (representing an element in public life) hated this. It seemed to me that hating foreign words was perhaps related to hating foreigners, and was another example of French insecurity. Three months later the bill was ratified – fines of up to 20,000 francs ($3,500) for the public use of an English word when a French one would do; the next problem lay in its enforcement, particularly in a polyglot city such as Marseilles.

On my last day in Marseilles I treated myself to a bouillabaisse, the dish that Marseilles gave to the world. The fish broth was pungent and flavorful, saffron-colored as in the classic recipe, presented with croutons and cheese and rémoulade and potatoes. And the vital ingredients were the fruit of the Mediterranean – rouget (mullet), rascasse (red, spiny hog-fish found only in the

Mediterranean), Saint-Pierre (John Dory), moules, whiting, monk-fish, bass, gurnet, weever, conger eel, crab, crawfish, clams.

The crab was very small. The waiter lifted the shell with a fork.

"And this, as they say in English, you suck."

This one meal cost nearly as much as my hotel room, but it was worth it to sit with a view of the port, stuffing myself and reading a book and glancing at the boats. Marseilles was obviously a tough place, but it was neither irritatingly sophisticated nor conspicuously poor. That was what I liked most about it, its air of being a cultural bouillabaisse, made up of distinctly Mediterranean ingredients. I also had a confidence that I could go anywhere in the city – not a confidence I had ever had in New York or London. There were no mansions in Marseilles. The rich stayed in outlying villages, behind high hedges and barbed wire and *Chien Méchant* ("Wicked Dog") signs, pretending they were in the bosom of Provence, and not in the city of stray cats and prostitutes and wanderers from the Barbary Coast. The reality of Marseilles was Arabs, skateboarders, hookers, the drug trade, and people working, all of them together, usually in the same narrow lanes.

I took a boat – a small launch – to the islands in the Bay of Marseilles, to the tiny Château d'If of *The Count of Monte Cristo* (Dumas lived in Marseilles) and to the Frioul Islands. Château d'If was a combination of Alcatraz and the Magic Kingdom, a Disney prison, and like the nearby islands of crumbly sun-faded rock that looked like stale cake. No trees here, but ashore there were dry treeless headlands dusted with green, which were the last of the bushes.

I liked being out on the blue Mediterranean, among the sail-boats, again that feeling of being at the edge of the sea that obliterated any clear idea of nationhood – the ports having mixed populations and a common destiny, living by the sea.

"The Mediterranean is beautiful in a different way from the ocean, but it is as beautiful," Victor Hugo wrote on a visit to Marseilles. He made some pleasing distinctions. "The ocean has its clouds, its fogs, its glaucous glassy billows, its sand dunes in Flanders, its immense vaults, its magnificent tides. The Mediterranean lies wholly under the sun; you feel it by the inexpressible unity that lies at the foundation of its beauty. It has a tawny stern coast, the hills and rocks of which seem rounded or sculptured by Phidias, so harmoniously is the shore wedded to gracefulness."

When I returned from the little cruise I decided to take another launch, and let it be my departure from Marseilles. We sailed along the coast, past the offshore islands of Tiboulen, Maire, Jane, Calseraigne, stopping briefly at Sormion and Morgiouy, and ending up at Cassis, where I caught another train. It was *Le Grand Sud*, stopping at Toulon, St-Raphael and Cannes, passing St Tropez, Fréjus and Antibes. Most of the time the line was within sight of the sea, and the Aleppo pines and the palms at the shore, but as the train approached Nice the large apartment blocks and tall buildings obstructed the sea view.

The dream of the Mediterranean is not the Albanian coast or the docks of Haifa or the drilling-rigs at the edge of Libya. It is the dream of this part of France, the sweep of the Riviera as a brilliant sunlit lotophagous land − the corner of the Mediterranean from the outskirts of Toulon eastward to Monte Carlo, a hundred-odd miles of Frenchness − food, wine, style, heat, rich old farts, gamblers and bare-breasted bimbos. All that and art too. It is the Cagnes of Renoir, the Nice of Matisse, the Antibes of Graham Greene; the Cannes Film Festival, the casinos. In describing the machismo of the *corrida*, Hemingway had put Spain on the map, Fitzgerald in his short stories and in *Tender is the Night* was the first chronicler of the Riviera, the bon vivants and drunks and flappers and phoneys of Antibes or Juan-les-Pins. It could be said that Fitzgerald invented the Riviera as a fashionable place, but he had many collaborators in keeping it in business.

Ten years after Fitzgerald the names had changed. "All along the coast from Huxley Point to Castle Wharton to Cape Maugham, little colonies of angry giants had settled themselves," the dissolute Naylor ponders in Cyril Connolly's novel *The Rock Pool*, summing up the literary Riviera in the thirties. "There were Campbell in Martigues, Aldington at Le Lavandou, anyone who could hold a pen at St Tropez, Arlen in Cannes, and beyond, Monte Carlo and the Oppenheim country. He would carry on at Nice and fill the vacant stall of Frank Harris."

Yet it rains on the Riviera too, the traffic is awful, and there is no elbow room. It has been called the *zone nerveuse* and a special sort of madness attributed to residence in this part of the Mediterranean, "the arid foreshore of that iodine-charged littoral." Here there are mainly older people, retirees, crooks, tax exiles – who else can afford it? – and meretricious businesses and dog-walkers and stony beaches on the sluggish sea. Nothing is sadder than a resort out of season, no matter how good the food. And there are times when even this dreamland is crammed with all the stale and wilted lotuses that no one wants to eat.

It was a rainy February night in Nice and I was walking down the wet gleaming street from the station. I was pleased with myself for having arrived here at the lowest point of the season. The hotels and restaurants were empty. No need for reservations: I felt liberated from having to plan ahead. And so I kept walking, to evaluate the likely hotels, avoiding the ones directly on main streets (car noise, motorcycle blast), or near churches (organ music, yakking), or schools (screams, bells), or restaurants (drunks, music, banging doors). A hotel on the seashore would have been perfect – silence, a light breeze, the slop and wash of little waves; but not even the great hotels of Nice are on the sea. As in Brighton, with which Nice is often compared, a busy main road separates the sea front from the hotels.

On a quiet square, the Place Mozart, a little old woman rented me a room for forty dollars, and just to see what I was missing I walked down to the Promenade des Anglais to the Hotel Negresco for a drink at the bar. It is said to be the most expensive hotel in Nice, if not the best. Ha! Built in 1913, but imitating the *belle époque* style, it is a hotchpotch of fatuous Frenchness, the bellmen and concierges and flunkies in footmen's breeches and frock coats bowing and scraping, and groveling for tips under gilt and chandeliers and red flock wallpaper, candlesticks with light-bulb flames and copies of bad paintings.

There was a placard in front of the Negresco's Chantecler restaurant with a quotation from my friend Eric Newby, cobbled together from the six pages he devotes to the Negresco in his book on his trip around the Mediterranean: "One of the greatest restaurant (sic) in France ... newest Mecca for gourmets ... most beautifully presented meal ... my entire life ... best I ever ate or am ever likely to eat," blah-blah-blah.

Newby! Singing for his supper! Hang it up, Eric!

Never catch me doing a thing like that, I was thinking, as I had my fish soup (quite pleasant) in a restaurant (fairly empty), all the while chatting to the proprietor (a big bore).

"The Americans didn't come this past season," he said. "The exchange rate was bad."

And perhaps they reached the conclusion that they could be overcharged and could tramp around in dogshit in Atlantic City, NJ – no? But the inclement weather set Nice apart from New Jersey. What I liked the best about Nice that night was the heavy rain. Nice was smack against the sea, and so the many lights from the apartment houses and the old-world street lamps created a Whistlerish effect of glowing bulbs and reflections, like one of his wet nocturnes. Yes, that was possible in New Jersey, too.

The next morning I walked down to the port of Nice, the Genoese-looking harbor, which is not a fanciful comparison – Nice belonged to Italy until 1860, Garibaldi was born there – and I saw the *Rainbow Warrior* at one of the docks.

This Greenpeace ship – one of three or four in the world – had sailed there to educate the French about environmental threats to the Mediterranean. The crew members were selling T-shirts and bumper stickers and handing out leaflets detailing terrible pollution statistics.

"Pollution is only one of the problems," Catherine Morice said. She was from the Paris office of Greenpeace. "Drift-nets are legal in the Mediterranean. And Italian drift-nets are extremely long. Many kilometers. Spain and France also use drift-nets. That's something that has to be stopped."

She showed me some reports detailing the drift-netters' abuses – and the length of the nets, ten and fifteen miles long. I told her I was traveling along the Mediterranean coast, and had just come from Marseilles and Arles.

"That is one of the worst regions for pollution."

"But Arles is pretty – you mean the Rhône?"

"The Rhône at Arles stinks and it's dangerous. It's a terrible

river. We call it the *couloir chimique* – chemical corridor. It makes
the Camargue a mess."

And where travel-writers rhapsodize about gypsies and horses
and Van Gogh – well, I had done a little bit of that, hadn't I? –
she said the oil and chemical factories of the Camargue are the
source of a lot of Mediterranean pollution.

"Are there nuclear plants along the Mediterranean as there are
along the coast of Britain?" I asked.

At this point Catherine called over to Jean-Luc Thierry, the
Greenpeace nuclear expert.

Jean-Luc said, "No. They are not built on the Mediterranean,
they are inland. But they are not far. There is a nuclear reprocess-
ing plant at Marcoule, a hundred kilometers up the Rhône. We've
found traces of plutonium in the river and in the estuary."

Where there were gypsies and horses and almond blossoms,
there was plutonium.

"What sort of a reception are you getting with your campaign
in the Mediterranean?"

"The French are very suspicious of efforts like this. The first
question we always get is, 'Where does your money come from?' "

"That's true of a lot of countries."

"France is worse. They suspect us of having foreign influence –
the French paranoia – money from America or Russia."

As though, if this were true, it would cast doubt on the statistics
or invalidate the effort to clean up the Mediterranean.

"Does the pollution vary from country to country, according to
the part of the Mediterranean?"

"Yes, but the most serious division is the north against the
south," Jean-Luc said. "A lot of the waste and pollution on the
European side affects North Africa."

The next morning *Rainbow Warrior* sailed for Calvi in Corsica, to
carry the environmental message.

Later that afternoon, reading *Nice-Matin* on a bench on the
promenade, I saw there was a symphony concert that night at the
Acropolis, Nice's cultural center. It was a twenty-minute walk
from my hotel, and when I got there a man was waving his arms
and saying, "No tickets – all sold" to some disappointed people. I
suppose I had a look of consternation on my face, because a

woman came up to me and asked me whether I wanted a ticket. Her mink coat, her look of evasion and aloofness, and even her air of innocence made her seem like a tout; and yet she did not scalp me, but asked for the exact price that was printed on the ticket.

She vanished a moment later, and only then – as I was congratulating myself on my luck – did it occur to me that she had sold me a fake ticket.

Soon afterwards, I found my seat, and in the seat beside it was the woman in the mink coat. She smiled at me.

"My husband is sick," she said. "So you are lucky. This is a popular concert."

She was not a tout, or anything near it. She was a good, kind, compassionate and honest person, whom I had wrongly suspected of being a hustler.

"My husband is so sorry to miss it," she said. "But now you can enjoy it. May I look at your program?"

She was Madame Godefroy, and, for the duration of the concert, I became her husband. We shared the program. We agreed that the playing was wonderful. It was Berlioz (the overture to "Beatrice and Benedict") and the Beethoven Piano Concerto No. 3, and a Dvořák symphony (No. 5). The soloist was French and warmly applauded. The conductor was Chinese, Long Yü, and young (born in 1964). We chatted about the weather, what a terrible winter it was! What a wet day! What a lovely concert!

Flushed and breathless with all these exclamations, Madame Godefroy and I went into the foyer and had a glass of wine.

"We were living in Clermont-Ferrand, where my husband was working," she said. "After he retired, about eight years ago, we came here."

"Is it more expensive here in Nice?"

"The apartments cost twice as much, or more, as in Clermont-Ferrand. Property is very expensive in Nice. But everything else is the same – food, clothes, whatever."

"I liked Marseilles," I said.

Madame Godefroy winced but said, "Yes, there are the Le Corbusier buildings. But Marseilles is dangerous. It has all the problems, too – drugs, immigrants, AIDS."

She was too polite perhaps to mention blacks and Arabs, but I was reminded of how the young blacks in Marseilles imitated American dress code: baseball hats on backward, tracksuits, baggy pants, expensive running-shoes, and the same unusual haircuts. There were no other role models in France, or in Europe, but the Americanized look marked these youths out and must have seemed like a threat.

"So you're happy here, Madame?"

"Nice is safe," she said. "The weather is good, except for this year. It is youthful, because of the universities and language schools. There are many retired people – perhaps thirty per cent. But Cannes is worse – it doesn't have universities, so it's mostly retired people."

"I always imagined that the French were settled people. I didn't realize that they retired and moved to the coast the way people do in Britain and the United States."

"My parents never retired and moved," she said. "It happened after the war, when children moved away from their parents to find work. Before, in France, everyone lived together, the children looked after their parents, and they lived in the father's house. But – no more."

So the break-up of the family home was an economic necessity dating from the recent past, when the young were uprooted and had to search for jobs. And the nature of jobs changed – the decline of agriculture, and manufacturing, the rise of the service industries; all of this since the war.

"Do you have any relatives living in Nice?"

"No, and I miss them. I miss my children and my grandchildren. All my children are married. Well, my younger son has been living with his girlfriend for so long they are good as married."

She sipped her wine.

"My father is dead. He was ninety-three when he died. My mother is alive. She is ninety-one – but in good health and very alert."

"Where are your roots in France?"

"Strasbourg. I was born there and my family lived there for many generations."

"Hasn't Strasbourg also been German at times?"

"Yes, it has gone back and forth, from French to German and

back again. During the war" — she sighed —"we had to leave Strasbourg. It was a bad time. The Germans occupied it. We fled to Aix-en-Provence."

She told me about the fighting, the house-searches, the crowded train, the hunger. This woman in furs in the foyer of the concert hall in Nice, the very picture of bourgeois serenity, had once been a refugee, fleeing from town to town, ahead of the Huns, in a desperate struggle for survival.

The mention of the war and this talk clearly depressed Madame Godefroy, who perhaps realized that she was talking with a stranger who had been sitting in her husband's seat, an inquisitive American. I liked her, though — her rectitude, her stoicism, her clearsightedness: law-abiding, polite, married for life.

"Are you staying in Nice?"

"For a while. I want to travel in this immediate area. And then I'm going to Corsica."

"I have been there. Once. It is very different. The people, especially the ones in the mountains, are very severe."

At her request, because it was late, and there were lurkers here and there, I walked Madame Godefroy to the taxi-stand. I said goodnight, and then headed back to the Place Mozart, through the empty city, and detoured down the promenade that was bright with wet reflections, and the water of the Bay of Angels a sea of gleaming liquefaction.

The concert had been a local event, part of this wintry low season, not a tourist attraction. There were other events – dances, plays – and this week, because the Lenten season had just begun, a two-week festival of parades and exhibitions. I went to one of the parades because I had nothing better to do, and it seemed to me to have been put on expressly for people who lived in Nice and the surrounding towns.

The parade was called "La Bataille des Fleurs," and it involved floats and flower-tossing. It interested me as local events often did for the way they roused people from their homes, children and spouses, and revealed their fantasies and enthusiasms. Families lined the streets, and so did soldiers and policemen and priests and punks. These French punks were grubby youths, swigging wine, looking dirty and dangerous. They jeered and shouted at the floats which were piled with flowers, and on each float a pretty girl in a ballgown or a tight dress or sequins stood flinging mimosa (which had just come into bloom) to the bystanders. The sprigs of mimosa, with tufty yellow fluff, had the look of baby chicks.

One of the flower girls was black and attractive, wearing a white wedding-dress and a veil.

"She's a good one," said a man beside me to his friend.

"Oh, yeah," the friend said, and leered at the girl. "Amazing."

And they clamored for her to throw them some mimosa.

There were military bands with blaring trumpets. A Tyrolean oompah band. Another: St Georg's Bläser from Haidenbach. A brass band called *Les Loups* ("The Wolves") playing loud and wearing baggy wolf costumes. More floats, more skinny fox-faced girls in pretty dresses flinging mimosa, and when they ran out of mimosa they tore flowers from their floats and threw those. There were Germans dressed as Mexicans. French cowgirls and drum majorettes, medieval knights and wenches, many playing trumpets and twirling elaborate flags. Twenty little girls in traditional Provençal costumes tossing flowers and inviting the stares of elderly gentlemen. Zouaves, clowns, and a band of pink teddy bears. Musical policemen and "Miss Galaxie" and the forty-piece band of Stadtkapelle Schongau (Bavaria) in *lederhosen*: more oompah. "Los Infectos Acelerados" and a down-home band from East Texas State University – baton-twirling cuties in black leotards and short skirts.

Seeing Americans, the French children became hysterical and began spraying strings of goo at them out of aerosol cans, screaming, "*Mousse!*"

The day after the parade, I tiptoed to Nice station. It is impossible to stride confidently through Nice, city of dog merds.

When the English painter Francis Bacon was seventeen he saw dogshit on a sidewalk and had an epiphany: "There it is – this is what life is like." What enchantment he would have found in Nice, where pavements are so turdous that a special one-man turdmobile trundles along sucking them up its long snout. Even that ceaseless activity hardly makes a dent.

The turdmobile is defeated by an unlikely enemy: an older overdressed French woman, a widow, a retiree, a prosperous landlady, someone precisely like Madame Godefroy. She is the last person you would associate with dogshit, and yet this delicate and dignified woman spends a good part of the day calculating the urgencies of her dog's bowels. There are thousands of these women and their dogs all over the Riviera. They are forever hurrying their tiny mutts down the sidewalk and looking the other way as the beasts pause to drop a stiff sausage of excrement just where you are about to plant your foot.

At the station, I said to myself: If the next train goes east, I'll head for Ventimiglia and eat spaghetti in Italy. If it goes west, I'll eat in Antibes or Juan-les-Pins.

It was an eastbound train to Menton, and once again I was struck by the courtesy of the older French rail passengers, strangers to each other, who chatted about trivial things and seldom departed in silence; nearly always when they left a train compartment they said, "Bye, now" or "Bon voyage" or "Take care."

There was something else about the train, that Fitzgerald mentions in *Tender is the Night*. "Unlike American trains that were absorbed in an intense destiny of their own, and scornful of people on another world less swift and breathless, this train was part of the country through which it passed. Its breath stirred the dust from the palm leaves, the cinders mingled with the dry dung in the gardens. Rosemary was sure she could lean from the window and pull flowers with her hand."

Beyond the pretty bay at Villefranche-sur-Mer, a little jewel among rocky cliffs, I could see St Jean Cap Ferrat, where King Leopold of the Belgians, sole proprietor of the Congo, had built a regal estate that was so complete that even his mistresses and his private priest, his confessor, lived in a mansion in the grounds. The idea was that the king could sin all he wanted, for the priest was on call to give him absolution on his deathbed. Somerset Maugham had bought the priest's house, the Villa Mauresque – named for its Moroccan decor. I had planned to stop here, but the whole kingly place was now a set of condominiums.

Past Beaulieu-sur-Mer, palmy, sedate, piled against the hillside, with mansions on ledges; past Èze, less grand, with great clusters of banana trees at the station. The bays beyond Èze were beautiful but the beaches were stony, the cliffs perpendicular, a wall-like coast similar to the one I had seen on the Costa Brava. After Cap d'Ail came Monte Carlo – bigger, sleepier, nastier than I had expected, and it was impossible to tell the condos from the mausoleums. I decided to stop there for lunch.

I walked from the station, trying to figure out where I was. There are three regions in the Principality of Monaco – Monaco Ville, the hill where Prince Rainier's palace dominates; the valley of the Condamine; and another hill, Mount Charles – Monte Carlo. The whole place owes its existence to Grace Kelly who provided Rainier with a son, thus maintaining the Grimaldi line. She met Rainier when the prince became involved as a human prop in a photo shoot in Monaco to promote one of Grace Kelly's films; and then he pursued her, with a priest acting as a go-between. He was well aware of the clause in Monaco's treaty with France asserting that Monaco would be absorbed into France if Rainier did not somehow produce an heir. Now it is for the young balding playboy, Albert Grimaldi, to secure the Grimaldi line with an heir of his own.

The Grimaldi family, said to be the oldest monarchical line in Europe, is – like most of those families – royally dysfunctional; filled with stressful and unsatisfying relationships, though Grimaldi self-esteem is not in short supply. They are well aware that their home was a dump until the mid-nineteenth century when Prince Charles III built a casino. He did it in much the same spirit that the Pequot Mashantucket Indians introduced gambling to Connecticut, because it was forbidden everywhere else (France and Italy had banned it). So Monaco got rich, as the Pequots got rich, on suckers being encouraged to throw their money away.

But the wealthy people who live in Monaco are the opposite of gamblers. They are mainly anal-retentive tax exiles with a death grip on their cash and a horror of spending, never mind gambling. There are 30,000 residents. Fewer than ten per cent of them are natives, which says a great deal. Tax havens are by their very nature boring or else actively offensive; if they were pleasant, everyone would want to live in them. But only by promising tax incentives do the places attract their resident populations. This is not Happy Valley. For one thing, the chief characteristic of wealthy people is that they are constantly whining about how poor they are; the rest of us can take a malicious satisfaction in the fact that these tycoons have only each other at which to cry poormouth.

I had a pizza, and walked around, but all my attempts to start conversations with the Monégasques ended in failure. That was another unhelpful personality trait of tax exiles – paranoia.

Farther down the railway line, nasturtiums grew like weeds at Roquebrune, and at Cabrolles there was space and light and a great valley slotted into a range of high snow-dusted mountains, with stony features that matched those of the local bourgeoisie.

Menton was a Victorian-looking seaside resort of indescribable dullness. The fat, philandering Edward VII used to like it here, for the apparently limitless opportunities it afforded him to eat and chase women. Menton was having its own celebration today, the Lemon Festival (*Fête du Citron*). This one was obvious and programmatic, and it was watched without much enthusiasm. The floats were constructed of lemons and oranges in the shape of whales, dinosaurs, the Eiffel Tower, airplanes, full-figured women, windmills and so forth. It was neither as rich nor as revealing as Nice's parade, with its flowers and odd-balls.

I had decided that if I grew cranky I would simply move on to a better place, but it was not convenient for me to leave Menton. I did see the reality of United Europe at Menton station. Here we were on the border between France and Italy. A group of elderly Italians, none of them younger than seventy or so, were trying to buy cups of coffee and some cookies. The French woman at the counter was snarling at them.

"If you don't have the money, stop wasting my time," she said.

They did not have French money; they did not speak French. The woman at the counter, a mile or so from Italy, did not speak Italian.

"What is she saying?" a man asked plaintively in Italian.

"She is asking for money."

"If you want to buy, change your money!" the woman said in French.

"For francs, I think."

An Italian said to her in Italian, "All we want to buy is coffee. It's not worth changing money for that."

Another Italian said to her in Italian, "We will give you a thousand lire apiece. You can keep the change."

"Don't you understand me?" the French woman said.

So there was no sale, nor were the Italians able to eat or drink anything; the border between France and Italy was simple to pass through, but the language barrier was insurmountable.

The European Union, seen from the Mediterranean was full of misunderstandings which made that argument a trifle. People were so confused about EU regulations in the Mediterranean that Euro-rules had become Euro-myths. They were ludicrous, but still they were believed, and they made EU nationals angry. Fishermen will have to wear hairnets, it was said. All fishing trawlers will have to carry a supply of condoms. There would be a ban on curved cucumbers. British oak would no longer be used in furniture because it was too knotty. Donkeys on beaches would have to wear diapers because of droppings. Henceforth, all European Union coffins will have to be waterproof.

There were advantages to being in the European Community, but the Mediterranean was a community, too. At the fruiterer's in Menton in February there were grapes from Tunisia, strawberries from Huelva in Spain, tomatoes from Morocco and Sicily, mandarin oranges from Sicily, and North African dates, figs, prunes, nuts. Clementines from Corsica. And locally-grown artichokes and lemons, and apples (Bertrannes and Granny Smiths) – all from Provence. In addition, there was cheese, sausages, honey and preserves, and ten varieties of olives. Almost the whole of the world's production of olive oil came from these neighboring Mediterranean countries. The suburban density in Menton and on the Riviera generally was misleading; the shoreline catered to the hordes of tourists and the complacent rich, but just across the coastal highway and railway tracks the land was still profoundly agricultural – both in mood and culture.

Back in Nice, I did my laundry, sitting in "Albertinette," the launderette, and writing notes. On my right was a housewife folding clothes, on my left an Arab watching his clothes revolve in the washer. With maintenance in mind, I got a haircut afterwards. The woman cutting it was interrupted by a man who came up and began gesticulating and complaining.

He said in French, "Your hair is too long!"

"That's why I am here," I said.

"But it's still too long, the way you have it."

"You don't approve of my hair?"

"No. You need to emphasize your body," he said, becoming passionate, plucking at my hair. "Cut the hair shorter, show the energy of the face. Make it so you can run fingers through it – like this! Get some harmony!"

I was not sure whether he actually believed this or was simply teasing me by pretending to be a stereotypical Frenchman and demonstrating how passionately he could talk about trivialities. On the other hand, maybe he was serious. In any case, I ended up with very short hair.

I had traveled east to Menton; my ferry to Corsica was not leaving for another day and a half; and so I went westward to Antibes on the stopping train – Nice, St-Laurent-du-Var, Cros-de-Cagnes, Cagnes-sur-Mer, Villeneuve-Loubet, Biot, Antibes.

A lovely blonde Frenchwoman got off the train at Antibes, and as she was struggling with a suitcase I offered to help. She gladly accepted, and we were soon walking from the station in Antibes together, her suitcase banging against my leg.

"I am sorry my suitcase is so heavy," she said.

"I don't mind," I said. "I'm fairly strong. Ha-ha!"

"You are so kind."

The thing weighed about fifty pounds. If I had not offered, how would she have carried it?

"I suppose you have tools in it, or guns of some kind?"

"Cosmetics," she said.

"That's all?"

"It is full of cosmetics," she said. "I have just come from Nice where I was demonstrating them in a store."

She was that attractive, rather formally dressed and businesslike coquette with mascara and red lips you sometimes see in the aisle of a department store waving a tube of lipstick or else offering to squirt perfume on your wrist.

I put the bag down. I said, "Just resting. Ha-ha!"

"Ha-ha."

"What about having lunch?" I said.

"Thank you. But I have an appointment."

"A drink, then? Or a coffee?" I said. "I am a stranger here."

The word "stranger" had an effect on her. It is not the way a French traveler would describe himself. He would say, "*Je ne suis pas d'ici*," I am not from here. My way of saying it was odd and existential, something like "I'm a weirdo," and it did the trick. Moments later we were clinking glasses.

"Menton is for the old," she said. Her name was Catherine. "So is Nice. St Tropez is superficial. Money, drugs, rich people, lots of Italians. No culture, no mind at all."

As a demonstrator of cosmetics who did nothing but travel from town to town with her leaden suitcase, she knew France very well and the Riviera like the back of her dainty hand.

"And Monaco is just a joke," she said.

"That's what I decided, but I thought it was because I am an American."

"Believe me, it is a joke. I spent five days there and it was like a year. I spend five days everywhere, showing the products. I was recently in St Malo. Brittany is good, but it's cold."

She was about thirty, not married, slightly enigmatic. She said that in spite of its superficiality she liked the South of France.

"Where this wine comes from," I said.

"Cassis, yes," she said. "What are you doing here?"

"Just looking around," I said. "I was in Antibes about fifteen years ago, visiting a man. I want to see if his apartment is still here. Want to see it?"

Catherine smiled, and it seemed to mean yes, and so we finished our glasses of wine and walked down the street, to where Graham Greene's old apartment, "La Résidence des Fleurs," stood.

On the way she said, "Some men disapprove of cosmetics."

"Not me," I said. "A woman wearing make-up likes to appear in a certain way." I tried to explain this, but did not have the words.

"*Attrayante*," she said.

It sounded right. I said yes, definitely, vowing to look the word up.

"As you do."

She seemed pleased and embarrassed, and touched my hand. She said, "I know this address."

"An English writer lived here. Graham Greene."

"I don't know the name. What did he write?"

"Novels, stories. Some travel books."

"A good writer?"

"Very good."

"I think you are a writer," she said. "From your questions."

"Yes. I want to write something about the Mediterranean."

"You should go to a different part – not here. Nothing to write about here! Ha-ha."

"Plenty to write about here," I said.

I was thinking about my previous visit to Antibes. Then, I had not wondered why a millionaire novelist would choose to live in a small apartment three blocks from the harbor, with no sea view at all. But I wondered today. How could Greene have lived so long by the Mediterranean in a flat where all he saw from his windows were other houses? He had lived there more than twenty years, and I found it hard to spend a single afternoon in the place – the foreshore packed with apartment houses, the harbor jammed with yachts and sailboats, no beach to speak of, the little town blocked with traffic. Greene had wanted to avoid paying his British taxes – but what a way to go about it.

"It's almost time for lunch," I said.

"But I must go. My friend will be wondering where I am. He can get very excited."

"He lives in Antibes?"

"No. He is visiting from Paris. He has a dangerous job." She smiled at me. "A stuntman for films."

So I ate lunch alone, more fish soup and *fruits de mer* and wine. I had not been trying to pick her up – I had love in my life. Yet I thought how there was no mistaking this word "stuntman," which she had said in English. It seemed to me, as she spoke it, to suggest one of the most intimidating professions imaginable. If she had said he was a boxer or a marksman I would not have been more seriously cautioned. You could see this lover of hers defying explosions and car crashes and hurtling through flames, enough for anyone's manhood to shrink to the size of a peanut.

Attrayante means alluring.

After lunch, I hurried out of town, walking to Juan-les-Pins. In 1925, Gerald and Sara Murphy took up residence in their "Villa America," at this end of Antibes. They were the bright couple who inspired F. Scott Fitzgerald to create the civilized and generous hosts Dick and Nicole Diver in *Tender is the Night*. He and Zelda supplied the dark side, the most interesting part, hysteria, madness and desperation, in those characters, "in the grip of fashion . . . while up north the true world thundered by."

In great contrast to Nice, where the beach is shingly and stony, the beach at Juan-les-Pins is sandy, though it is small and narrow. "The hotel and its bright tan prayer rug of a beach were one," Fitzgerald writes in his brilliantly observed novel. "In the early morning the distant image of Cannes, the pink and cream of old fortifications, the purple Alp that bounded Italy, were cast across the water and lay quavering in the ripples and rings sent up by the sea-plants through the clear shallows." To the west, under a reddened sky, a complex and lovely view, where Cannes lay under a headland.

"A shameless chocolate-box sunset disfigured the west," runs a line in *The Rock Pool*. That, in a single observation, is the English writer's embarrassment in the face of natural beauty.

Since almost every other writer who has described the Riviera has praised it, it is worth looking at a paragraph of Riviera abuse, that is, a generally unfavourable review of the whole Mediterranean Sea. It is rare to find a body of water accused of being so hideous and worthless.

"The intolerable melancholy, the dinginess, the corruption of that tainted inland sea overcame him [Connolly writes]. He felt the breath of centuries of wickedness and disillusion; how many civilizations had staled on that bright promontory! Sterile Phoenicians, commercial-minded Greeks, destructive Arabs, Catalans, Genoese, hysterical Russians, decayed English, drunken Americans, had mingled with the autochthonous gangsters – everything that was vulgar, acquisitive, piratical, and decadent in capitalism had united there, crooks, gigolos, gold-diggers and captains of industry through twenty-five centuries had sprayed their cupidity and bad taste over it. As the enormous red sun sank in the purple sea (the great jakes, the tideless cloaca of the ancient world), the pathos of accumulated materialism, the Latin hopelessness, seemed almost to rise up and hit him. Like Arab music, utterly plaintive, utterly cynical, the waves broke imperceptibly over the guano-colored rocks."

The insults are almost comic – Connolly was actually a sucker for the voluptuousness of the Riviera, and returned to that landscape in one of his other books, *The Unquiet Grave*, where he wrote of "swifts wheeling round the oleanders . . . armfuls of carnations on the flower stall . . . the sea becomes a green gin-fizz of stillness in whose depths a quiver of sprats charges and counter-charges in the pleasure of fishes."

Under the pines in the Jardin de la Pinède and at the Square F.D. Roosevelt in Juan-les-Pins, there were friendly folks playing boules. Why was this interesting? Because they were all men, they were all polite – they all shook hands before and after a match; and most of all because they seemed the antithesis of what people wrote about Juan-les-Pins. They were obviously hard-up, blue-collar, manual workers, fishermen and cabbies and farmers. They completely possessed the center of the square. A number of them were Vietnamese. I watched three Vietnamese trounce three Provençal players – their winning technique lay in lobbing the steel ball in a perfect arc, so that it bombed the opponent's ball and sent it skidding.

One of the players walked towards me to sit down and smoke, and so I talked to him. But he waved his hands at me, to get me to stop talking.

"It is not necessary regulation to speak to my face in the French," he said in English. "I can catch all the majority of what you are saying."

"I was watching you playing boules."

"The game of bowlings is a genius, and you can perform so many skilltricks to gain the winnership and shock the opponent, your enemy."

"Of course."

"So you see the French games nothing like American – hit people with ball and fight with hands or take – ha! ha! – your gun and gain. What you see is typical French bowlings."

"It is a sort of club?"

"Also" – he wasn't listening to me – "wonderful alimentation in Provence."

"Where did you learn English?"

"From the war. From people," he said. "But explain me one thing, why Americans speak English in France the manner they speak in Los Angeles, Chicago, New York, everywhere, and so we cannot catch at all. But if I speak French to them the way I speak with my wife, ah, whoof! They will never catch!"

This went on a bit more. Then I walked back to Antibes by way of the lighthouse, the Phare de L'Îlette on the Cap d'Antibes.

The Mediterranean here was an enigma. It was corrupt, it was pure. There were horrible apartments, there were beautiful headlands. There were nasty tycoons, there were friendly folks. The sea was polluted and blue, the sea was a green gin-fizz of stillness. Everything that had been written about the Riviera was true.

6

The Ferry *Île de Beauté* to Corsica

It took all night, a twelve-hour trip in the *Île de Beauté*, a ferry as large as an ocean liner, to get to this other part of France; but it is a French province in name only. Corsica is Corsica.

I liked being on the water again, and I liked the empty ship, hardly anyone on the quay at Nice, just a few people in the cafeteria buffet which was open all night – spaghetti and rice and salad, and calamari that looked and tasted like shredded gym shoes. Some men were playing video games, Germans among them, bikers in tight leathers with shaven heads that gave them odd blue skulls. There was a lounge where people were drinking wine, some unruly children ran among the chairs, and there were the usual bronchitic French people coughing their guts out and chain-smoking.

The deck was empty, except for a man muttering solemnly to his dog in French, and a Tibetan woman clinging to the rail. The night was black, almost starless, like a pierced blanket, and not cold but cool in late February. I stood watching the foaming wake in this emptiness that was like a great ocean, and thinking how it must have been so easy for the Mediterranean people to believe that this was the whole world.

After a while I looked up and saw the Frenchman and the Tibetan were gone. I went to my cabin, and crept into my bunk and read a bit more of the biography of the painter Francis Bacon. "The truth comes in a strange door," Bacon said. And as for his gory paintings and his frequently bloody subjects: "It's nothing to do with mortality but it's to do with the great beauty of the color of meat."

The purr of the ship's screws put me to sleep, and when I woke the sun was rising on a calm sea, a rubious dawn lighting Cap

Corse and the distant mountains in the island's interior, the great granite peaks and the ridge above the port of Bastia. There are twenty tall peaks on the island, which is the most mountainous in the Mediterranean.

The *Île de Beauté* (which is also a name for Corsica) docked, and I hoisted my bag and walked down the gangway into the middle of Bastia, empty at this early hour of the morning – only pigeons cooing and shitting on big bronze statues in the Place Nationale. I had breakfast in a café and immediately became aware that the men around me were not talking French, but amiably and incoherently, showing their teeth and joshing, gabbling in a sort of Italian. Corsican is a variety of old Tuscan, tumbling and Italian-sounding, like a secret tongue. I imagined that it seemed to an Italian the way a Scottish accent sounds to an English speaker, a regional dialect that was familiar even when it was incomprehensible. When I addressed the men – asking some directions – they became serious and polite and slipped into French or Italian.

The language business – no outsider I met spoke Corsican – heightened my sense of Corsica's being a colonized place, with the secret life that all colonies have: the parallel culture lived in another language. The fact that Corsican life is known to be explosive makes it all the more enigmatic.

Bastia is a seaport in the shadow of a granite mountain. Most of the travelers who have passed through it express a measure of disappointment when speaking of the city, perhaps because it seems Italian rather than Corsican. Prized for its harbor rather than its fortifications (being hard to defend it was frequently captured), Bastia's architecture is Genoese. In its older quarters it is still an Italian-looking town, with a picturesque old port. In Bastia I walked all over, in a way that I had not done on the Riviera, and I realized that it was probably true, as I had read, that a great deal of the pleasure to be had in Corsica was from walking – not only along cliff paths and mountain tracks, but on country roads and in the back streets of the handsome city.

That night at dinner, the Corsican waiter approached me shyly and asked in French, "How do you say *bon appétit* in English?"

Bastia is also well served by ferries and is a simple place to leave. I could have gone to Nice or Sardinia or Tunis. I could have gone to Italy, leaving Bastia on the *Corsica Regina* in an hour or two for Livorno, and be in Florence in time for lunch.

There are small districts within the city, including a Moroccan – or perhaps Arab – quarter, near the old port. This exotic corner was also where the city's only synagogue was located. Very small, in a narrow passage, Rua du Castagno, which is a long flight of stone stairs, it is called Beth Meir synagogue.

There was a recently erected sign on the wall, putting all the blame for the wartime anti-semitism on the French government that had existed during the war: "*La République française/En hommage aux victimes/Des persécutions racistes et antisémites/Et des crimes contre l'humanité/Commis sous l'autorité de l'état/Dite 'Gouvernement de l'état français' (1940–1944)/N'oublions jamais.*"

It seemed to me ironic that Arabs had taken up residence in what in former days had been the Jewish ghetto, and that they were being harassed at the moment.

Arabs in France are like the Tribe That Hides From Man, and so I deliberately sought one out in this district in Bastia, just to talk to. His name was Sharif – eyes close together, skeletal, skinny, his narrow shoulders showing through his burlap gown.

"I am from Gardimaou, in Tunisia, near Djanouba, on the border of Algeria. But the Algerians are – oh, well!"

"Are there many Tunisians here?"

"Lots of them in Corsica. Moroccans, too. But no Algerians."

"Why is that?" And I was aware when I asked the question that Corsicans believed that the island was full of Algerians because no one differentiated among North Africans.

"There is something wrong with Algerians," Sharif said. "In their heads. They are very nervous types. And you see, that makes them dangerous. They cause all sorts of trouble on the mainland. They are not like other people. And some of them hate foreigners."

"Like me."

"Unfortunately."

Sharif had worked in Corsica for twelve years, but still the Corsican language was a mystery to him. He did not know a word of it. "It is too difficult."

But no language is difficult. Language is an activity, a kind of play, learned through practice. It requires little intelligence. It is social. So you had to conclude that in his dozen years no one had ever spoken to Sharif in Corsican. That activity was closed to him.

There was no mosque in Bastia, indeed none in Corsica. He made a tentative face, as though he wanted to say more, then thought better of it. "Lots of Muslims, though.

"In my village in Tunisia, life is good, but there is no money. In other places where there are tourists, life is fine but it is expensive. I came here for work."

I pressed him about the non-existent mosque. He said, "Yes, it is odd that there is none, but who can say why?"

It was later that I found out that two houses where Muslims met to pray, near Bonifacio, had been blown up. And later, after the French government took over an oriental-style building in Ajaccio (crescent, archway, arabesque doorways, domes – it had been the headquarters of a company selling Turkish tobacco), that too had been torched by arsonists, who believed – because of its unusual décor – that it was going to be used by Arabs.

Some people in Bastia seemed impartial in their abuse. Not far away on an ancient pillar of Bastia's cathedral, the fifteenth-century Église Sainte-Marie: *Jésus est mort* ("Jesus is dead").

I gathered that there were many ways to see Corsica. The most strenuous is on foot on the many paths, or from north to south on the famous high-level trail, the Grande Randonnée 20; more than two weeks of trudging at such an altitude and you see the whole island, but hardly meet Corsicans. There are the local ferries, from Bastia to Bonifacio, Ajaccio to Propriano. There is renting a car and driving through Corsica, the simplest and most popular way of traversing the island – on good roads and nightmarish ones, some of them vertiginous, all of them spectacular.

And there is the little train from Bastia to Ajaccio, with a spur line to Calvi. There were two trains a day to Calvi, four to Ajaccio. It was hardly a train, just a rail car, a *navette*, literally a "shuttle." It moved in jerks like a tram or a trolley. When I started the next day from Bastia there were only two of us on board; a few miles down the track, at Furiani, two boys got on.

It is not a popular train, though the Corsicans do everything they can to persuade people to use it. On an island of notoriously bad roads a trip on the Chemin de fer de la Corse is one of the most restful ways to spend a day. The motto is: *Prenez le train, c'est plus malin!* ("Take the train, it's smarter!").

The mountains were still snowcapped, and I was told that there would be snow at their summits until July. I had seen them in Bastia, and even from the train I could see them. In the towns and villages men stood in clusters on street-corners – talking, smoking, shaking hands, gesturing – as I had seen them in Bastia. There were few women on the streets, and those who were there walked briskly, not looking either left or right, giving an impression of great modesty and rectitude. This was the old world of the Mediterranean, the man's world.

Winter had given the island a dramatic starkness that revealed the rugged landscape, the cliffs and peaks, the moorland that lay exposed through bare branches. This, and the behavior of Corsicans on the street, I was able to study at Biguglia, where the rail car stopped and the driver took out a newspaper and spread it on the console of his controls, and read it with close attention.

"I am going to look around," I said.

"Don't go far," he said, without glancing up.

Twenty minutes passed. I smiled at a man on the platform, and we began talking harmlessly about the weather: how bright and cold it was, no rain, very nice, and then I said: "Have you ever been to Sardinia?"

He did not say no. He shook his head as though my question was insane, and he walked away. I wanted to tell him that I was going there. Sardinia is only four miles from Corsica's south coast.

Another train pulled in, what in India would be called the "up train," and because this was a single-line track we had to wait for it at this station in order to pass it. Then we were off again and deep in the low, dense Corsican bush, universally known as the *maquis*. Corsica is famous for having its own fragrant odor – the herbaceous whiff of the *maquis* – lavender, honeysuckle, cyclamen, myrtle, wild mint and rosemary. After he left Corsica as a young man, Napoleon never returned to the island, but was exiled on Elba, which is just off the coast of Italy; he said he often savored the aroma of Corsica in the west wind. It smells like a barrel of potpourri, it is like holding a bar of expensive soap to your nose, it is

Corsica's own Vap-o-Rub. The Corsican *maquis* is strong enough to clear your lungs and cure your cold.

This was not the Riviera, not France, it was definitely another country, and yet there were resemblances, Mediterranean similarities. The hint of herbs on a hot day in Provence was a fragrance in the breeze; here it was an aromatic feast, gusting through the window of the rail car. Here there were oleanders and palms and olive trees; and also dumps, and junkyards, and automobile graveyards. Yellow villages on the summits of high hills. There were miles of vineyards surrounding venerable half-ruined villas. And there were fruit trees, some of the groves heavy with ripe lemons and pendulous bunches of clementines.

Two boys got off at Casamazza, one got on.

The villages were strange and lovely. They had the look of monasteries or fortresses, twenty stucco structures and a sentry-like church steeple, gathered at precipitous angles, and the deeper into the island we went the higher up the villages were sited until they almost crowned the summits. I could not imagine how the villagers lived their lives at such a steep angle, though it was obvious that these high and easily fortified villages were the reason the Corsicans had survived and had beaten off invaders. In these steep retreats Corsicans had kept their culture intact.

At the head of the valley looking west from the station of Ponte-Nuovo I saw the snow-capped peak of Monte Asto, and there was nowhere else I wanted to be. Here, now, on this rail car rattling across Corsica under the massive benevolence of this godlike mountain top – this for the moment was all that mattered to me, and I was reminded of the intense privacy, the intimate whispers, the random glimpses that grant us the epiphanies of travel.

We came to Ponte-Leccia where the line branched to Île Rousse and Calvi, and moved along through the mountain passes and the *maquis* in sunshine, and it all seemed so lovely that I felt frivolous, almost embarrassed by my luck at this thirteen-dollar train ride past the nameless villages plastered against the mountainsides, visited only by the soaring hawks.

I was writing this, or something like it, at a little place called La Regino, with its chickens on the line, and thinking: In German there is a word, *Künstlerschuld*, which means "artist's guilt," the emotion a painter feels over his frivolity in a world in which people work in a rut that makes them gloomy. Perhaps there is also a sort of traveler's guilt, from being self-contained, self-indulgent, and passing from one scene to another, brilliant or miserable makes no difference. Did the traveler, doing no observable work, freely moving among settled, serious people, get a pang of conscience? I told myself that my writing – this effort of observation – absolved me from any guilt; but of course that was just a feeble excuse. This was pleasure. No guilt, just gratitude.

At Île Rousse the deep blue sea, the bluest I had so far seen, was beaten and blown by the west wind, and the sea foam of the white caps lay piled like buckets of egg-white whipped into fluff against the beach of the pretty town. It had a snug harbor and a headland and a lighthouse and yet another – there was one in every Corsican town, perhaps obeying a local ordinance – Hotel Napoleon.

The surf beat against the rocks near the train tracks that ran along the shore, and then in minutes we were at the next town, Calvi.

Some of Corsica's highest, snowiest mountains lay in sight of the harbor at Calvi, from a table at a harborside restaurant where I was drinking the local wine, a crisp white Figarella made from the Calvi grapes, and reading my Francis Bacon book ("Later, when we were alone . . . Francis showed me the weals across his back . . . The masochist is stronger than the sadist . . .") and the owner of the restaurant was telling me that Christopher Columbus had been born here in Calvi, which was not true at all, so I had read (some Calvi families of that name gave rise to the myth). I thanked him for the information, and had fish soup that was heartier and more flavorful than in Nice, and *rouget* – four small red snappers *en papillote* – whole pink fish on a pink plate, like a surrealist's lunch.

Apart from this restaurant and the post office and a pair of inexpensive hotels (the Grand Hotel was closed until April), everything was shut in Calvi, closed and locked and shuttered. Still, I stayed for the novelty of the sight of snow, and the exposed crags in the sunshine. After dark the town twinkled a bit, but it was empty, and the chill in the air and the black sea at its shore gave it a ghostly quality.

Retracing my steps, I returned to the same restaurant that night, had the fish soup again, finished the Bacon book, and then walked around the harbor, looking at the lights over Calvi's fortress. I passed by the little railway station and saw there was an early train out of here. Life had vanished, disappeared indoors. Walking back towards the harbor, I saw a woman whom I had seen just before sundown. She was perhaps selling something – she had that ready smile, and a ring-binder thick with brochures – samples of furniture, maybe, or hotel accessories.

"Good evening," I said.

"Good evening," she replied, and she passed into the darkness.

The next sound made me jump, because it erupted behind me, a shrill cautioning voice, saying, "You spoke to that woman."

It was English but accented.

"How do you know I speak English?"

"I know, I know. You spoke to that woman. You make a mistake. In Corse you never, ever speak to a woman. Never ever, never ever."

"Why not?" I said, trying to discern this man's features in the dim light of the harbor's edge.

"They put a bomb in your car."

"I don't have a car," I said.

"They fight you – they kill you."

He had been sitting in the shadows, speaking confidently. He got up and came nearer, still nagging. He was young, balding, with a large pale face and an explosive and scolding way of talking. His French accent had something else in it that I could not place.

"You're English?"

"American," I said.

"I hate the English."

"Why?"

"I don't know," he said. "I never went there. I just hate them. I meet them sometimes. They swear all the time."

To give me an impression of this, he mimicked an Englishman

swearing and it sounded as though he had swallowed something foul and was retching.

"Where do you live?" I asked.

"Nizza," he said.

Calling Nice "Nizza" – it rhymed with pizza – seemed to indicate that he was Italian; I was sure he was not, yet there was something Mediterranean in his manner, in his irritating certainty.

"And you're traveling in Corsica."

"Not just Corse, but all over. And I don't talk to women, like you just done. I don't talk to anyone. I keep my mouth like so. These Corse people are giving problems if they don't like you."

"How do you know?" It was not that I doubted him, everyone said this; but I wanted some colorful evidence, preferably first-hand.

"I live in Nizza, I know. I read newspapers. If you are a tourist one week, two weeks, is okay. But you maybe want to stay long, buy a house, talk to people – talk to women. Then they put a bomb in your car, burn your house, fight you."

"You're sure of this?"

"Nazionalists, you know? And fanatics."

"The Corsicans seem friendly," I said, though I had hardly done more than exchange pleasantries. Actually they seemed, not friendly, but bluff, offhand, taciturn, rough and ready, with weather-beaten faces and horny hands, men and women alike.

"Maybe they are more friendly than the French. I hate the French."

There is a point in every conversation with a stranger when you decide whether to end it or else press on. As soon as he said, "I hate the French," I realized he was reckless and probably good for a laugh.

"Why do you hate the French?"

"Because they hate everybody. You have seen Nizza? You see all the peoples has dogs? Ha! Is the reason!"

"Reason for what?"

"They has no friends, so they has dogs."

"The French prefer dogs to people?"

"Is the truth. Even me, when I stop traveling I buy a dog, a *caniche*, how you say it?"

"Poodle."

"Everyone in the Côte d'Azur has a poodle."

"But you can't sleep with a dog," I said.

"The dog is your best friend always."

"Better than people?"

"Yes, I think."

He said he had just arrived from Ajaccio and before that had traveled through Sardinia, Sicily and Croatia. This was helpful, since I was headed in the direction he had just come from. I asked him what Croatia was like. "No fighting in Zagreb," he said. He did not know about the Croatian coast, which was my destination. But he had had no visa problems, and he had traveled most of the way by train.

"What sort of work do you do?" I asked.

"No work. Just trains and going, going, going."

In life, it is inevitable that you meet someone just like yourself. What a shock that your double is not very nice, and seems selfish and judgmental and frivolous and illogical.

I questioned him closely, of course, but I was merely verifying his answers; I was not surprised. His life was the same as mine. Wake up in the morning, walk somewhere. Drink a coffee, take a train, look out of the window. Talk to strangers, read the paper, read a book, then scribble-scribble. Now and then, passing a phone booth, punch in numbers – anywhere – and get a clear line to Honolulu and some love and reassurance. Then leave the solitude of the confessional phone booth and enter France again, back in Juan-les-Pins, the click of boules, the salt-sting of wind and waves at Calvi. Is this a life?

"You write things down?" I said.

I suspected from his eccentricity alone that he was a writer.

"No. Just looking. Just going."

"It's expensive."

"Trains are cheap."

"Eating is expensive." The meal I had just eaten in Calvi had cost fifty dollars.

"I eat sandwiches."

"What about Corsican food?"

"What is Corsican food? It is French food! They have no spécialité, but I buy things to eat in the boulangerie."

"What about Nizza?" I said. I was thinking: What does this guy do for money? He wasn't more than thirty-five or so – and he was dressed fairly well, from what I could see. "Nizza is expensive."

"I spend one thousand US dollars a month. Six hundred for room, the rest for food."

"Isn't it boring, not working?"

"Sometimes I buy something, sell something, get money."

That was as specific as he got, regarding his employment.

"Then I take a train. But here I am careful. You are not careful. Ha-ha! Is still a nice place. Corse has the bombs. Amsterdam has the drugs. San Francisco has the homosexuals."

"I don't see the connection. Do you hate homosexuals too?"

I had just finished the Francis Bacon biography and was indignant on Bacon's behalf.

"I never went to America," he said, being evasive. "Is too many people. And I like Nizza. But here in Corse" – now he was becoming agitated – "these people cannot get food if the French don't give them money. They want freedom but they has no food."

"You're not French, are you?"

"No. Israel."

"Oh, God."

"You don't like Israel?"

I laughed. "I was thinking of the four billion dollars a year America gives to Israel, so the Israelis can eat."

"We don't need the money," he shrieked. "They give it, so we spend it. They are stupid to give it."

"I agree. But where would Israel be if they didn't get the money?"

"No problem. Israel don't need it."

"Maybe we should give the money to Corsica."

"Planes! Guns! Israel buys planes for millions. Some politicians steal it. Spend it. Throw it away. Israel is not stupid like America!"

"And yet you live in France."

"I hate the Arabs in Israel, the way they make trouble," he said. "There are thirty thousand Jewish in Nizza. Synagogues.

Everything. I feel it is like home, all these Jewish. So I am happy there."

"But you travel all the time."

"All the time," he said.

"In the Mediterranean."

"Only in the Mediterranean," he said.

"Jew-lysses," I said. "That's what an American writer called himself, because he traveled all the time, like Ulysses, and he was Jewish. Henry Roth – Jew-lysses."

"I don't understand."

He was instantly suspicious, thinking I was mocking him. He had that harsh, cynical, everyone-else-is-a-sucker attitude that is common among certain citified Levantine Arabs and Jews in the Mediterranean. The country folk were capable of idealism. His sort were selfish and scolding.

Oddly, for a traveler in the Mediterranean, he confessed that his great fear was of the sea itself – any water. He got sick on all boats, on ferries, any vessel, whatever the size. Instead of taking the overnight ferry from Sicily to Sardinia, he had caught a plane and flown from Palermo to Cagliari. He had flown from Sardinia to Ajaccio, even though (as he said) it was a one-hour trip by ferry across the straits that separated Sardinia from Corsica.

"I get headaches. I get frights. I get sick," he said.

But he loved trains. He was leaving for Bastia in the morning, and the same train connected to Ajaccio.

"So we go together?" he said.

"Maybe," I said, but I knew better. He had seemed at first like a version of myself, shuttling around in a solitary way on trains, from one part of the Mediterranean coast to another, from island to island. But talking to him I had verified that he was not my double – perhaps that was why I had provoked him and interrogated him: to prove that we were not alike. I had proven to myself that we were utterly different.

Two days later the news from Israel was that twenty-nine Arabs praying in a mosque had been machine-gunned to death by a Jewish settler, Baruch Goldstein. Born in Brooklyn, a Kach member and a militant supporter of Meir Kahane, Goldstein was beaten to death by some of the surviving Arabs in the mosque. More Arabs were shot soon afterwards by Israeli soldiers.

This incident was the first in a wave of violence that continued throughout my trip. In a reprisal, some Arabs blew up a bus in Tel Aviv. After that an Arab leader was shot in his house. Then an Arab suicide-bomber killed himself, and took three Israeli soldiers with him, at a checkpoint; and this was answered with more killings. Each side answered the other, as in a blood feud; each side was unforgiving.

That was happening in the Mediterranean too, and reading these reports I was always reminded of this irritating little man, nagging me that night at Calvi harbor.

He was not on the noon train the next day. Rather than go all the way south to Ajaccio I bought a ticket to the old capital in the interior, the high-altitude and almost hidden town of Corte. In the early part of the trip, as we circled the shoreline, the strong winds picked up foamy veils of spoondrift and flung this delicate froth at the windows of the clattering *navette*.

The line to Corte, by way of the junction at Ponte-Leccia, wound through the valleys of the snowy mountains and ascended through fields of lavender and herbs, past trees of madly twittering birds, towards the center of the island, a spine of mountains, the highest of which, Monte Cinto (2,710 m), was bleak and beautiful, gray and cracked rock, ledges and crevasses surmounted by a massive shawl of snow. Above it all, over the whole granite island, was a zone of blue, a winter sky – nothing but blue skies, smiling at me.

I was happy in this descent through the island, knowing that I would be island-hopping for a few weeks: Corsica, then Sardinia, then Sicily, and finally the Italian mainland.

Corte was only a few hours away. The little place is almost perpendicular. It is the heart of Corsica, and the apotheosis of the steep Corsican village. This small town was chosen as the capital for its remoteness, its altitude, its seemingly impregnable topography. "Seemingly" – you wonder how it could ever be captured, yet it had been captured a number of times, by the Saracens, the Genoese, the Corsicans, the Italians. It was at last snatched by the French (in 1768) after Pascal Paoli, the father of Corsican independence, established it as his capital, the site of the national assembly. Paoli is still regarded in Corsica (his portrait is everywhere) as *U Babbu di a Patria*. Paoli's name is a sort of rallying cry even today for Corsican patriots, whose efforts at expression range from eloquent appeals for sovereignty and assertions of cultural identity to command-detonated bombs and the systematic torching of foreigners' houses.

I had been here before and found it so moribund and spooky I wrote a short story about it ("Words are Deeds"). That was on a brief visit to the island in 1977. In 1982 it became a university town and it was now a bustling place, filled with youthful students and cafés. Many Corsicans told me that after this university started there was a greater feeling of Corsican identity and more resistance. This was also a way of saying that the graffiti on the ancient walls of Corte were of a political character: *Liberta pa i Patriotti!* ("Freedom for the patriots!"); *Speculatori Fora!* ("Out with speculators!"); *Colon Fora!* ("Out with colonists!"), and so forth.

Corsican courtesy is deferential, a sort of shy dignity, and it is in great contrast to that sort of defiant graffiti scrawled in the Corsican language on most public walls. I had lunch at a café, sitting in the sunshine. The town I had thought of as forbidding had been rejuvenated by the presence of students. I talked to some of them at the café, and when I asked them about Corsican politics they suggested that I attend a lecture later that afternoon.

"Which sandwich did you choose?" one girl asked.

"It's a Freud," I said.

The sandwiches were named after great thinkers or writers, Pascal, Newton, Verlaine, Rimbaud. Rimbaud was ham and cheese, Freud was mozzarella, tomato, basil, olive oil.

I had no luck understanding the lecture, "The Clan is the Cancer of Corsica," which was given by a Corsican, Professor Sinoncelli. It was highly technical, it concerned the social structure, the family, and the relationship of politics to the Corsican activists, who had organized themselves into marauding gangs.

My problem was linguistic. I had no trouble chatting with people on trains or in casual encounters, but the intensity of an academic lecture, full of jargon and unfamiliar terms, was beyond me. It was clear, though, that a problem of identity was being debated, and that there were contradictions. Here was a large island, with a remote and mountainous interior, and a people whose culture meant everything to them. How to reconcile this with being a province of France? The professor seemed to be suggesting that the nationalist movement had been subverted by a selfish and violent minority, who did not represent the Corsican people.

"This word 'clan'," I asked a student afterwards, "does it have some special meaning in Corsica?"

"In Corsica as in France it is a word to describe any political group, not only of the Corsican nationalists," he said. "But the underlying meaning is that the group is close-knit and militant."

The girl with him said, "That is what we have made of democracy!"

Corsican pride ranges from ferocious nationalism to quiet dignity, and it has been remarked upon by every visitor since James Boswell, who got interested in the cause of Corsican independence and introduced Dr Johnson to Paoli.

The most common generalization I had heard before I returned to Corsica after those seventeen years was that it had changed a great deal. The island had always been well known for being dangerous – an unjustified reputation, partly based on some highly-publicized bombings by the nationalist group Resistenza as well as the Corsican separatists' proclivity for defacing signs. I had seen such signs in Spain, where they had been scribbled over in the Catalan language. Few acts of vandalism are more threatening to the visiting stranger than road signs that have been messed with, and they are usually the very ones you need to avoid getting lost. Most signs in Corsica had either been rewritten or, worse, obliterated.

There are many such signs on the road from Corte to the high village of Evisa, through the Niolo region and the towering Forest of Valdoniello. I had been told that this area is best experienced on a bicycle. I was lucky enough to be able to rent one in Corte for an excursion here.

Valdoniello is perhaps the only genuine forest in the Mediterranean. In the whole of my trip I did not see anything like it. It is a world of pines, but not just pines – it is valleys and rushing streams, snowy peaks and granite crags. The pines are gigantic and elegant, very tall and straight. While it was still a wilderness of primeval trees, this forest was first described and depicted in etchings by Edward Lear. Some of the earliest images of the Corsican landscape, especially its interior, are those of Lear.

Lear, who was famous for writing light verse with his left hand and painting Mediterranean landscapes with his right, came to Corsica just a few months after writing "The Owl and the Pussycat." He traveled all over the island in a mule-cart. In his time Lear was better known as a brilliant watercolorist, as well as a painter in oils, than a writer of nonsense poetry. He had the idea of illustrating large-format bird books, much as Audubon had done, and Lear's book of parrots is a masterpiece. But the book made no money. He abandoned ornithology. Looking for new subjects, and restless by nature, Lear became a great traveler in the Mediterranean — France, Italy, Greece, Egypt — and also in India; he wrote and illustrated books on Albania and Corsica. His book about Corsica, *Journal of a Landscape Painter in Corsica* (1869), introduced Corsica as a wild paradise to British readers, and created Corsica's first tourist boom. Lear was the twentieth of twenty-one children. He was a kindly, whimsical man, but given to periods of great sadness and loneliness. So ashamed was he of being an epileptic that he hid his affliction — never spoke the word — and so he remained a lonesome traveler.

He was one of the first foreigners to penetrate the Corsican interior, though in the 1860s the French had already begun to exploit Corsica for its fine trees. By the time Edward Lear ventured into the forest he saw "the ravages of M. Chauton's hatchets; here and there on the hillside are pale patches of cleared ground, with piles of cut and barked pines . . . giant trees lie prostrate . . ."

I was told that the French had recently made this forest a national park, but being colonists in Corsica — the activists' slogans were justifiably indignant — French lumber companies were still intensively cutting trees. The signs of logging were everywhere — marked trees, cut timber, clear-cut slopes, every sort of abuse that goes under the weasel term "forest management."

The narrow road traversed the valleys, westward, through the trees. The best way of seeing this forest was on a bike, in the open air, for the fragrant scent of the tall pines. The valleys were dappled with shadow and spread thickly with a litter of pine cones and needles, warmed and made fragrant by the sunlight.

Lear had rhapsodized about it. He wrote in a letter (to Emily Tennyson): "I have seen the southern part of the Island pretty thoroughly. Its inner scenery is magnificent – a sort of Alpine character with more southern vegetation impresses you, & the vast pine forests unlike those gloomy dark monotonous firs of the north, are green and varied Pinus Maritima. Every corner of the place not filled up by great Ilex trees and pines and granite rocks is stuffed with cistus and arbutus, Laurustinus, lent & heath: and the remaining space if any is all cyclamen & violets, anemones & asphodels – let alone nightingales and blackbirds."

It is much the same today. The trip through this region is a combination of forest, meadow and mountain, all this leading from one side of Corsica to the other; and after Evisa, with its tall narrow houses and graceful church steeple, the road descends through the sheer rocky gorges of Spelunca to Porto, haunt of tourists.

At Evisa I met the Dunnits, from England. I was admiring the steep striated gorges and the sloping ledges of pinkish stone, the pinnacles and scalloped ridges, when a car drew up. The driver asked me how far to Corte.

"An hour or so, through the forest," I said.

"You just come by push-bike?"

"Right."

"Stopping in Corte?"

"I have to go back there to return my bike. I'm on my way to Ajaccio."

"We were there – we done that."

"Calacuccia's very pretty."

"We done it, as well."

I decided to tease them.

"Bonifacio – have you done it?"

"Done it."

And then the Dunnits began to reminisce about the Hebrides, how they had done it, and how the people were just like the Corsicans, insisting on speaking Celtic ("Or Gaelic," said Mrs Dunnit). Eventually the Dunnits drove off.

This was just a day off for me – a picnic. Instead of bicycling all the way downhill to the seaside village of Porto, I pedaled back to Corte and caught the train to Ajaccio.

It was the last train to Ajaccio. I arrived in darkness, passing through the back of the city, and hardly entering it on the train, because the station is some distance from the center. It was only eight in the evening, but the streets were empty. I was later to discover that Ajaccio is a city of convulsions – busy from seven until noon, the market, the banks, the fruit stalls, the fish shops, the bus station, the stores, all bustling; then dead from noon until three or so; and then convulsed until six-thirty, when it expired until the following morning. And the streets, like the streets in many Mediterranean towns, were a men's club.

The other train passengers quickly vanished. I walked out of the tiny station down the main street, the Cours Napoléon, past the Napoleon Restaurant, and the Boutique Bonaparte, to the Hotel Napoleon. The Napoleon was never the luxury hotel in a Corsican town but it was always one of the better ones.

As soon as I got into my room and shut the door, which had a strange device for locking it, the lights went out. I struggled to find my flashlight in the darkness and then got the door open.

"My room has no electricity," I said to the manager.

He smiled at me. He said. "You are the writer, eh? You wrote *Le Royaume des Moustiques*, *Voyage Excentrique*, and *Les Îles Heureuses d'Océanie*."

"That's me."

"Are you making a trip here to write a book?"

"I don't know."

It was the truth. It was too early in my Mediterranean journey for me to tell whether it might be a book, and what had I seen so far? Only Gibraltar, Spain and France. I did not want to jinx it by being confident, so I said that I was still groping around.

His name was Gilles Stimamiglio, a Corsican from the Castagno region in the north-east, the province of chestnut trees and Roman forts.

"Where are you going from here?" Gilles asked.

"South, to Sartène and Bonifacio."

"Bonifacio is a very pretty place. You know Homer's *Odyssey*? Bonifacio is where the Laestrygonians live."

That was beautiful, that he referred to the distant little port, not for a good restaurant or a luxury hotel or its fortress or a trivial event, but as the place where a group of savage giants had interfered with Ulysses. When it comes to literary allusions you can't do better than use the authority of the *Odyssey* to prove that your home town was once important. In Gibraltar Sir Joshua Hassan had jerked his thumb sideways towards the Rock and said to me, "That's one of the Pillars of Hercules."

I went for a walk through the empty town, got a drink at an empty bar, then went back to my room to read Anthony Burgess's autobiography, *You've Had Your Time*. I liked this book because it was about his writing life as well as the various places in the Mediterranean where he had become a tax refugee: Monte Carlo, Malta, Italy, all of them more or less disastrous for him.

The next day I tried to get information about the ferries to Sardinia. The travel agents could give me precise details of the flights to Dallas or Miami, they could make reservations for me at Disneyland; but they had no idea if, or from where, or when, a ferry traveled the few miles from Corsica to Sardinia. I inquired at eight agencies before I found one with the right information.

"So a ferry leaves at four every afternoon from Bonifacio," I said. "What time does it arrive?"

The clerk did not know.

"Where do I get a ticket?"

The clerk did not know, but guessed that someone in Bonifacio would be selling them.

"Is there a bus or a train that meets the ferry in Sardinia?"

This made her laugh. "That is in Italy!" she cried, highly amused, as though I had asked her the question about New Zealand.

I spent the day walking up the coast road, which went past a cemetery and some condominiums and a hotel to a point where I could have caught a little boat to Les Îles Sanguinaires. I took a bus back to Ajaccio and as the sun had still not set – not yet the hour for a drink and diary-writing – I walked along the Ajaccio beach and saw a Tibetan woman mourning in the sand, being watched by three beefy Corsican soldiers.

This Tibetan looked familiar. It happens traveling in the Mediterranean that you often keep seeing the same people on your route. I had seen this small roly-poly woman on the quay at Nice boarding the *Île de Beauté*. I had even seen her at Bastia, where she had hurried down the gangway and vanished. Here she was again, round-faced, brownish, orientalish, in a thick jacket and heavy trousers, hardly five feet tall, pigeon-toed, with a floppy wool hat.

The men were leaning over her. You never saw men talking to a Corsican woman this way. I suspected they were pestering her. Having seen her at Nice and Bastia, I felt somewhat responsible for her welfare, even if she did not know that I was observing her.

So I walked over to her and said hello in English.

The men – young mustached Corsican soldiers – were startled into silence.

"Are these men bothering you?"

"I'm not sure," she said.

But as I was speaking, the men stepped aside. Just like soldiers to pick on a solitary woman sitting on the cold beach in the winter. She had been scribbling – probably a letter; it lay on her lap.

The hairy Corsicans looked like potential rapists to me, with the confident, hearty manner of soldiers who would not dare to defy a superior officer but would be very happy bullying a subordinate.

I said, "Look, you should be careful. Are you alone?"

"Yes," she said. She peered at me. "Do you know me?"

"I saw you on the ferry from Nice."

Hearing English conversation, a novelty to them, the soldiers goggled like dogs, their mouths hanging open.

"She is my friend," I said in French.

"Okay, okay." And they went away, muttering and laughing, and kicking sand.

"Thank you," the young woman said.

"You are traveling alone?"

She replied in French. She said, "My English is no good. Do you understand French? Good. Yes, I travel alone. Usually I have no problems."

"Where are you from?"

"Japan."

She said that she was studying French in Lyons and that she wanted to learn it well enough to read French literature when she got back to Japan. She was twenty-two. Her English was poor, her French was shaky.

I said, "I was under the impression that Japanese people traveled in groups."

"Yes. But not me."

"Aren't Japanese women taught to be dependent and submissive?"

"Now they are the equal to men."

Her name was Tomiko. She was four foot ten. She hardly spoke any language but her own. Here she was sitting on the beach at Ajaccio, alone.

I said, "Would you do this in Japan? I mean, go to a place alone, where people were all strangers?"

"No, I would go with a friend. But my friends did not want to come with me here to Corsica."

"Maybe you're brave. Maybe you're foolish."

"Foolish, I think," she said.

"I admire you, but please be careful."

All this convinced me that she was a good person, and she followed me back into town, talking ungrammatically. I realized that by being disinterested I had won her confidence, and she clung for a while, until I sent her on her way.

That night, Gilles Stimamiglio gave me the telephone number of Dorothy Carrington, author of the best modern book in English on Corsica, *Granite Island*. I called her from a phone booth and asked whether we might meet for a meal.

She said, "I am very old. It has to be lunch – I am no good in the evenings. And I'm slow. I have 'intellectual's back' – the discs are all bad from sitting. Or it might be called 'hiker's back.' I've done so much hiking here."

She gave me elaborate instructions for finding her apartment ("I am in what the French call 'first basement'") and I said I would take her to lunch the next day.

*

James Boswell visited Corsica in 1765; Flaubert visited as a young man and filled nineteen notebooks in ten days; Lear traipsed around in 1868 and produced pictures and his *Journal*. Mérimée roamed Corsica, looking for settings for his novels. But although these people raved about Corsica's beauty, they left after their visits.

One person visited and stayed: Dorothy Carrington. Frederica, Lady Rose (her proper name) was in her eighties, with a radiance that certain serene people achieve in old age, with pale eyes and the gasping expression of the elderly that is also a look of perpetual surprise. She warned me over the phone that she was frail, and yet in person she gave an impression of being unusually hardy, game, alert, not deaf at all; one of those down-to-earth aristocrats that the English have always exported to thrive in hardship posts.

She had once been truly gorgeous – the proof was a Cecil Beaton photograph propped on the mantelpiece in her small damp apartment. In the photograph she was a willowy blonde, languid, reclining on a sofa, a cigarette holder in her dainty fingers. A frowning man stood over her, and they were surrounded by hideous paintings. Beaton had been a friend. She had had many friends in her long and interesting life.

"I'd like to take you to a good restaurant," I said.

"That would be Le Maquis. It's a bit out of town, but it's good food."

It was a fifteen-minute drive to a spot on the coast south of Ajaccio, a five-star hotel with a restaurant which had been awarded three forks by the Michelin Guide. Only one other table was taken.

"No one can afford to come to Corsica any more," Dorothy said. "Now what would you like to know?"

"How did you happen to come here?"

She began, at my insistence, with her birth in England. Her mother had been diagnosed as having cancer. "Have another child and you'll be cured," the local quack had assured the woman. And so Dorothy was born, and when she was three her mother died, of cancer. Her father, General Sir Frederick Carrington, had (with Cecil Rhodes) helped conquer Rhodesia and claim it for Britain.

Dorothy was raised by uncles and aunts in rural Gloucestershire, in Colesbourne, "in a very grand house, much of it built by my Elwes grandfather when he was having an attack of megalomania."

They were landed gentry, with the usual mix of soldiers and misfits. It was not a farming family. "We thought the soil was too bad and we were too high – three hundred meters."

"What did the family do?"

It is an American question, *What do you do?* but there it is.

Perhaps reflecting on the intrusiveness of the question, Dorothy Carrington's pale eyes grew even paler.

"We rode to hounds," she said.

She attended Oxford, and scandalized her family by having an affair with an Austrian in Spain. "Nowadays I would have spent some time with him and moved on. My uncles and aunts showed up – in Paris, where I was living with the man. They dragged us off to be married." And so she was forced to leave Oxford University. This was in the 1920s.

"I went to Vienna and lived with my mother-in-law while my husband was in Rhodesia. I thought as my father had conquered Rhodesia I'd have all sorts of welcomes. We went. My first husband was good with horses. He could tame a wild horse, fix a roof. Clever farmer. But he had no mind at all."

"What did you do in Rhodesia?"

She didn't smile.

"We rode to hounds," she said.

"Of course."

"We chased every animal in Rhodesia. They were in great supply then. We lived about thirty miles from Marandellas – that was where we went for supplies, fording streams on the way. It was a rough life. We hardly knew the Africans. I spoke what they called 'kitchen kaffir.' It would have been different in Kenya. There were all sorts of diversions there. Rhodesia was second-rate."

Everything was fine until Germany invaded Austria. "My husband could not claim to be Austrian any more. He automatically became German. And I had no choice. I had to take his nationality, as his wife. We eventually divorced. Have I mentioned that he was

excellent with horses but he had no mind? I went to London. I was
a German national!"

"That must have been inconvenient."

"We were at war with Germany, you see," she said. "I put that
right by marrying an agreeable little Englishman, to get a passport.
It was a marriage of convenience."

After a spell in Paris, she returned to London, and by chance
entered an art gallery where paintings by Sir Francis Rose were
being exhibited.

"Very strange ones. People either loved or hated his paintings. I
thought to myself, I'm going to marry that man. I just had that
feeling."

And so it happened. She married Sir Francis Rose, and lived, as
she put it, "absolutely at the center of things." She was photo-
graphed by Beaton, knew Gertrude Stein and Picasso. "Picasso
was a bit of a Sun King, such a personality. And such a libido."
Picasso had made a fruitless attempt on her virtue. Gertrude Stein,
surprisingly, had not; but she had bought sixty-eight of Sir Francis's
paintings, and immortalized him by mentioning him in *The Autobiography of Alice B. Toklas*.

We had ordered our meal – "Notice the stew on the menu?
Corsicans stew everything." Dorothy had the charcuterie for which
Corsica is famous, and then oxtail. I had the soup and the fish.
Meanwhile we were drinking wine, Patrimonio, from the north of
the island; tippling and talking in the bright still restaurant by the
sea.

"I am not betraying a secret when I say that Francis was
homosexual," Dorothy said. "Everyone knew. What's the secret?
And, well, men are unfaithful to their wives. That is how men are,
that is what they do. But when a man is unfaithful in a homosexual
way, there is a sort of guilt that comes over him. That was the bad
part."

"You knew that he was homosexual when you married him?"

"Um, yes. I thought I could cure him."

"What was his libido like? Not on the Picasso scale, was it?"

"He had a libido, yes. And very low friends. Francis Bacon –
you know who I mean?"

"I've just read a book about him."

"He had a very grisly talent. *Nostalgie de la boue*, perhaps. And my husband's friends were very rough."

Ready for yer thrashing, now, Frawncis? the young men muttered to Bacon, flexing a leather belt, and then the whipping began. So the book (written by Bacon's friend Daniel Farson) had said. I told this to Dorothy Carrington.

"Oh, yes, I suppose so. All of that," she said. "But these low friends kept him going. Our marriage didn't last. After he died I felt a duty to go back. I met some of them. They had given him money, they had kept him."

"They were loyal to him?"

"Yes. In a strange way. I think they were atoning for something in their own past."

It cannot have been a blissful marriage, yet she was as compassionate and uncritical as it was possible to be.

"Francis always had his own set. Cyril Connolly was one. He was frightfully rude to me in 1972 – he snubbed me. I said hello to him. He turned away. 'I was always Francis's friend, not yours,' he said."

"I just read Connolly's novel, *The Rock Pool* – about the Riviera."

"He was horrid."

"What about Corsica?" I asked. It seemed the right question – we were now on dessert

"Francis and I started coming to Corsica when we were absolutely penniless," she said. She began to describe episodes in a marriage that greatly resembled the plot of a D.H. Lawrence novel: aristocratic couple, escaping England, find an earthy people and life-affirming landscape, living in peasant huts, hiking the hills, sailing the coast in fishing smacks. It does not cost much. He paints, she writes. Even the sexual ambiguity was Lawrentian. Eating bad food, catching cold, moving slowly up and down the island; most of all, making friends and growing to understand Corsica.

"Francis was an artist, and I was a writer, so we didn't expect any more. After the war, it was amazing here – mule tracks, nowhere to live, very primitive, still the code of the vendetta."

Sir Francis and Lady Frederica! Artist and writer! People with class living on the margins! I remarked on that, but she dismissed it. "A title is nothing. I think it is no use at all – it is probably a disadvantage these days."

And then she let drop the fact that she had been a communist: Comrade Frederica, Lady Rose, waiting for the socialist millennium in a muleteer's hut on a Corsican mountainside.

"But I left the party when I realized they were trying to influence my mind. I didn't want anyone to tell me how to think."

There were other parties for Sir Francis and his lady. Because of their bohemian habit of just scraping by, living at the edge, they got to know Corsica well; and after Sir Francis decamped to overdo it with his cronies in London, Dorothy stayed on and made Corsica her passion, seeing Corsican culture as something distinct from anything in Europe.

"People talk about the Arab influence, but they overrate it. Here, sentiment as we know it does not exist. Very violent feelings exist. This mind-set still exists among the older people – revenge and superstition."

"For example?"

"Marrying for love, our idea of love, is quite remote here. I know a woman who had an affair with a young man. She became pregnant. The man went to the mainland to make some money, he said, but when he returned he was still dithering about marrying her. By then she'd had the child. She met him secretly and they talked, and when he made it plain that he was not going to marry her she took out a pistol and shot him."

"That happens in other countries."

"Perhaps. But she got a very light sentence," Dorothy said. "Women occupy a special position in Corsica. In spite of what you see, the absence of women in the streets and in the cafés, they have their little trysts and assignations. I know it. There is a great risk." And she smiled. "That is part of the attraction."

She seemed to be speaking from intimate knowledge.

She said that if I saw nothing else in Corsica I should visit Filitosa – it was on the way to Bonifacio, where I would be catching the ferry to Sardinia. I had seen Bastia and Calvi and Corte and the Niolo region. Yes, get out and about, she said. It was how she herself had become acquainted with Corsica. *Granite*

Island, still in print almost twenty-five years after it was first published, is full of excursions, long walking tours and risky and difficult journeys to the interior. It is a book without sarcasm or belittling or any complaints; only gratitude that she had been accepted as an honorary islander. It is no wonder she had lived there happily for almost fifty years.

We went together to Chiavari, one of those little villages high on a mountainside. I was interested in the Italian name, a place-name from coastal Liguria. On the way we passed wildflowers – many of the same kind, a meager flower on an attenuated stalk.

"Asphodels," Dorothy said. "They call it 'the poor people's bread,' because the poor ate the bulb. Until Paoli introduced potatoes to Corsica, everyone ate them. The Greeks called it 'the flower of death,' but it is edible. It is the flower of life. Lear mentions them."

"I've got his book with me, *Journal of a Landscape Painter*."

"Lovely book."

The village was empty, though the church had been recently renovated, and the war memorial, commemorating the Corsicans who had died resisting the Italians in the Second World War, had fresh flowers on it.

Michael Bozzi, Héros de la Résistance. Fusillé le 30.8.1943.

"*Fusillé* – shot?"

"Executed," she said. "They like the word 'resistance' – better to resist than be for something. Corsicans can be so negative. A greater feeling of Corsican identity has caused more and more bombing incidents – against quite nice people, in some cases. The Williamses are a lovely couple. Lived here for years. They had a watermill. They were bombed."

I said, "Corsicans have had a history of invasion. Maybe that accounts for their resistance."

"The Corsican way of life is a resistance to foreigners," Dorothy said. "And Catholicism gives a life to the villages, like the Good Friday observance in Sartène, which is a jolly good picnic, and the men take their hats off as the statue of the Virgin goes by. Many of those men are gangsters, who rehabilitate themselves through the Church."

In the churchyard of Chiavari's lovely church, looking down at the bay of Propriano and beyond to Ajaccio, Dorothy became thoughtful.

She said, "Corsicans helped the French run their empire, they worked in the colonies in Indo-China and Africa." We were walking among gravestones with foreign place-names chiseled into them, where each deceased Corsican had breathed his last – Algiers, Oran, Tonkin.

"The Corsicans had always gone abroad, from the turn of the century until the 1960s. The nationalist movement started when there were no more colonies to exploit and no more jobs. It's a Marxist argument, yes, but there it is."

We went back to Ajaccio and had tea in her apartment. There were some of Francis's paintings on the wall. I understood what she meant when she said people either loved them or hated them. I did not love them. It was an austere apartment; and yet Dorothy made no apologies. It was a writer's apartment, a sitting-room, a narrow kitchen, a bedroom – books and papers, an old typewriter, notes, drafts, notebooks, and some flowering plants in pots. But it was chilly there. The winters could be cold, she said.

She was frail, and yet she gave classes in poetry appreciation to get some income. She had just finished a book about belief in the supernatural in Corsica, *The Dream Hunters of Corsica*. "My rationalist friends will hate it." Her life was full. She was settled here. "This is all I want," she said, and it was not clear whether she meant the apartment in the first basement or the island of Corsica; but it came to the same thing.

Over tea we were talking about England.

"Margaret Thatcher!" Dorothy said. "Isn't she awful? Look at her, a very humble upbringing in a grocer's shop. But listen to her. That's why she's so careful in the way she talks, so 'refained.' And so careful in the way she dresses. And she is so intolerant."

She had ceased to be a Marxist, but Lady Rose was still a bohemian.

In heavy rain, I left Ajaccio the day after my lunch with Dorothy, detouring around the village of Petreto-Bicchisano and down a winding road to Filitosa. Seeing the strange, almost monstrous beauty of Filitosa helped me to understand passages in *Granite*

Island where Dorothy had been transformed in something akin to a spiritual experience – in her brisk practical way Lady Rose probably would not use that word, though Dorothy Carrington might. But she was changed: "On that day I entered Corsican life and became part of it," she wrote.

In slippery mud and pouring rain I made my way through the cold forest to the simple settlement of stones. I saw no other people until I reached the place, and then as if in a bizarre re-enactment I saw a wet family sheltering from the rain in the remains of a Filitosa stone hut – beefy father, red-cheeked mother, two pale children. Two thousand years fell away, as the cliché goes. They were German tourists, but it was a vivid glimpse of early man in the Mediterranean, in his hide-out in the hills. At first the little tableau startled me, and then I walked on, laughing.

The little glade below Filitosa, where there were upright sculptures, was full of wildflowers. Now I knew what an asphodel was, and there were two varieties growing here, with buttercups and broom and pink lavender. A big middle-aged man and woman, wearing yellow raincoats, were embracing and kissing in a stone shelter farther down the hill, and still the rain fell. There was thunder, so loud a horse was spooked from where it stood under a tree, and it bolted into the downpour.

In the late forties and early fifties, this tiny village in the south of the island was just a place of mythical prehistory, a litter of strange stones, a nameless Stonehenge. Dorothy mentions in her book how a Corsican farmer realized that a convenient flat stone he had been using as a bench for years turned out to be a priceless historical object, an ancient carving of a man with a sword.

Only in the 1960s did the knowledgeable archeologists arrive in Filitosa; then the megalithic ruins of Corsica became codified and the apparently barbarous carvings were more elaborately described and seen for what they are, wonders of Mediterranean prehistory. Dolmens, menhirs, and statue-menhirs – the most ancient of them probably four thousand years old. The terminology is not especially helpful, but it is almost irrelevant when you see the settlement at Filitosa, the shelters, the high walls, the battlements, the altar and the standing stones, the weird mask-like portraiture of the heads on slender stalks of stone – perhaps gods or warriors – of this enigmatic culture.

Such stones have been found elsewhere in Europe, but Corsica seems to represent the whole culture, not just the strange carved faces but weapons, implements and shelters, a whole community. And it is interesting that this community is inland, with access to the ocean but on a hill that offers protection, just as the Corsicans were to plan their towns so much later. No one knows who these people were.

It was only an hour or so by bus from here to the town of Sartène, where I stayed that night. Sartène was a classic Corsican town, like Corte, perpendicular, fortress-like, unwelcoming, piled against a hill. But once inside it, in the small main square, it seemed hospitable. I found a place to stay and that night had a hearty dinner in a Sartène restaurant. *They stew everything*, Dorothy had said. It was the tradition of cooking on the hearth that kept them faithful to the stewpot. Lamb, boar, mutton – even their fish soup was as thick and brown as stew. And this sauce? *Oursin*, the waiter told me. I had to look it up: sea-urchin.

There was a man eating alone, not a tourist, probably a traveling salesman. He ate slowly, the way unhappy people do, with a downturned mouth, like someone taking medicine.

The rain continued all night and I lay under a damp, lumpy quilt planning my onward trip. Out of Sartène tomorrow; to Bonifacio, the ferry to Sardinia, and then . . .

The bus from Ajaccio passed through Sartène at nine or so. I got up early and walked on the winding road to the edge of town with a book in my hand.

One day in April 1868, Edward Lear paused on this road, then a mule track just above Sartène. On that track he spent the day composing a little picture of the town. It is a severe but atmospheric portrait, of tall gloomy houses and a slender church steeple, a bluff of brooding masonry, its dark rain-dampened stone giving the town a look of mystery.

One hundred and twenty-six years later, I stood on the same curve of the road where Lear had sat sketching. I had with me Lear's *Journal of a Landscape Painter in Corsica*, and held up his picture of Sartène. The rugged houses still stood, as unaltered as though they were rocks and boulders and cliffs, which is how Corsican dwellings seem – somewhat severe, defiant, and everlasting, vernacular aspects of the landscape. Corsica can seem a melancholy place ("Everything's somber in Corsica," Prosper Mérimée said). The misty afternoon gave the town the look of an etching in an old book. And I had the book in my hand. Hardly anything in Sartène had changed.

Nor had the landscape from here to Bonifacio. I could see this on the ride there, in the small country bus, four old women on board, and me, and the chain-smoking driver. The coastal towns were fuller of houses and people, but the hinterland was still the land of Lear's etchings – its steep cliffs, its small ports, its mountain roads and mule tracks, its remote settlements, small villages clinging as though magnetized to steep slopes.

What modernity existed was superficial; Corsica's soul of indestructible granite remained intact. But it was more than just the look of the land. Corsica is physically nearer to Italy. Its nearest neighbor is Sardinia, but there is hardly any traffic between the islands. Because Corsica is so far from the French mainland, with its own language and culture and dignity and suspicions, and visited mainly in the summer, its differences endure. Corsica is small enough and coherent enough for people to feel free to generalize about. Corsicans themselves, when they are encouraged to speak to strangers, are tremendous generalizers. The statements are usually debatable, but there is a grain of truth in some of these Corsican comments: the haunted quality of the island, its vigorous language, its folk traditions, the sweet aroma of its *maquis*, the fatuity of its cult of Napoleon.

It was two hours to Bonifacio, because the bus took a long detour to the town of Porto-Vecchio to drop off one of the old women. There were no cars on the road, no one on the move. I liked Corsica for that, the low-season flatness, the rain, and finally just me on the bus that moved down the coast, past steep white sea-sculpted cliffs, the wind moaning in the brushy vegetation.

Bonifacio at noon was empty, a narrow harbor flanked by hotels shut for the season. Some fishing-boats, honey-colored cliffs, an enormous fortress.

In travel, as in most exertions, timing is everything. There is the question of weather; of seasons. In the winter Corsica was stark and dramatic, the mountains were snowier, the valleys rainier; at the coast the tourist tide was out. Traveling to places at unfashionable times, I always think of the Graham Greene short story "Cheap in August," or Mann's "Death in Venice." All I had to do was show up. I never had to make a reservation. I liked Corsica's cold days of dazzling sunshine, its cliffs of glittering granite, the blue sky after a day of drizzle, its lonely roads. It was an island absent of any sense of urgency. I could somehow claim it and make it my own.

Four hours until the ferry left for Sardinia, and no restaurants open. I bought a croissant and a cup of coffee, and then climbed to the fort and walked along the cliff path and found a warm rock and read my Burgess book, and snoozed and thought of the Laestrygonians.

I could see Sardinia clearly on the far side of the channel, beyond a scattering of rocks that they called islands. At three I walked down the slope to the quay, as the Corsican men were coming out to congregate and smoke and banter.

A few Bonifacians left their ancient tenements to see the ferry appear. Apart from them, this port town was motionless. Out of season a place is at its emptiest, and most exposed, but also it is most itself. Bonifacio had been a garrison and a fishing-port. It was now suspended in time; the summer strangers would seem to alter it for a few months, but its soul was its own. If, like Corsica, an island is remote enough and self-possessed, it can seem – far beyond merely insular – like another planet.

7

The Ferry *Ichnusa* to Sardinia

My reward after all the fuss and delay of getting to Bonifacio harbor was a classical glimpse of the harbor itself, the pale fissured limestone, the caverns at the shoreline, as the *Ichnusa* plowed past the last ramparts of the citadel; and then, as though splashing from between the rhythmic chop of two Homeric couplets, a pair of dolphins appeared, diving and blowing, with that little grunt and gasp that all good-sized dolphins give out as they surface, as though to prove they are worried little overworked mammals just like you.

That triumphant sight of Mediterranean dolphins made the whole inland sea seem ancient and unspoiled, peopled by heroes, terrorized by Laestrygonian giants, and all the goddesses and warriors that Ulysses encountered. It was the sea of triremes and sea-monsters and big fat-faced gods like the ones from the corners of old maps, with pursed lips and blown-out cheeks that created strong winds.

Bonifacio was the first place I had come to that could be identified in the *Odyssey*. The bay and harbor of Bonifacio is described in Book 10, and Robert Fitzgerald's translation depicts it clearly, with the directness that characterizes the whole epic:

> . . . a curious bay with mountain walls of stone
> to left and right, and reaching far inland, –
> a narrow entrance opening from the sea
> where cliffs converged as though to touch and close.

Curious about this island ("Lamos"), Ulysses moors his black ship against a rock and climbs the cliff to get his bearings. He and his men meet a young girl carrying water, and she directs them to the haunt of the queen ("a woman like a mountain crag") and the

blood-drinking Laestrygonian king, Antiphates. The rest is cannibalism and rout, as the crew face a whole howling tribe of Laestrygonians: "more than men they seemed,/gigantic when they gathered
on the skyline/to shoot great boulders down from slings."

And the water where those angry boulders splashed was now
stirred with dolphins gasping onward towards the little rocky islets,
Lavezzi and Cavallo, that trickle south from Corsica's south-eastern
shore. In an old quarry on Cavallo an ancient bust of Hercules has
been carved into the side of a large rock, perhaps by Romans,
more likely by ancient troglodytic islanders needing a god to
bother.

Back in Ajaccio, at our last meeting, Dorothy Carrington had
told me a story about an experience she and her husband had had
almost fifty years ago in Sardinia.

"We took a boat from Bonifacio to Sardinia just to have a
picnic," she said. "We gave all the money we had to a fisherman
and when we got there we sat on the beach eating our sandwiches.
Then we saw a great line of women wailing and a boy sitting in
the sand. The women were throwing sand on to his head and
shrieking. It was because his father had decided to go to Corsica.
This was their way of showing grief."

At the time there was no work in Sardinia and the Sards – as
she called them – were resented for going to Corsica and taking
jobs and working for very low wages.

"The man came with us on our boat and when he saw the lights
of Bonifacio he went mad, and so he wouldn't overturn the boat
we held him down by sitting on him."

This brought to mind another of Dorothy's amazing tableaux:
Sir Francis and Lady Rose, imprisoning a demented Sardinian by
jamming him against the deck of a fishing-boat with the combined
weight of their aristocratic bottoms.

"A few days later I saw the Sard in a café in Ajaccio," she said.
"He was having a drink with two nuns!"

The *Ichnusa* was no larger than the Martha's Vineyard ferry
Great Point, perhaps smaller. The distance it traveled was hardly
more than from the Cape to the Vineyard – the Strait of Bonifacio
is only seven miles wide between Cape Pertusato and Punta del
Falcone. There were about ten passengers on board, all returning

Sardinians, and two medium-sized trucks carrying stacks of cork bark from trees that had been stripped somewhere on Corsica's east coast. Corsica was an island of no heavy industry. It grew and exported fruit and wine, and some lumber, and this cork. But in fact Corsica depended for revenue on the tourist trade. The island was the Corsicans' own solemn stronghold for eight months or so; for the other sunny months they shared it with bargain-hunting vacationers from all over Europe, but mainly the despised French and the ubiquitous Germans who shocked the prudish locals with their petty stinginess and their assertive nudity.

"The people are very unlike Italians in some respects: wanting their vivacity – but with all their intelligence and shrewdness," Edward Lear had written about the Corsicans. The same seemed true of the Sardinians. (Or was it the Sardines? Or was it the Sards?)

The ferry passengers were all returning Sardinians, not very jolly, but friendly enough. The crossing only took an hour, but the few people on board and the infrequency of the ferry – once a day, in the afternoon – made it seem something of an event. There was also the fact that it was traveling from France to Italy. This was only technically the case. Corsica was no more France than Sardinia was Italy. Both were strange little islands in the Tyrrhenian Sea, whose islanders were more interested in differences than similarities. Neither of them was fond of the mainland, and they rather disliked each other.

"I'm not comfortable with those people," a Sardinian woman told me in Santa Teresa Gallura, the little port at the top of Sardinia, where the ferry landed. She was wagging her finger at Corsica, just across the strait. "I find that I have – what? – no rapport with them. So?"

It had been a fairly long walk from the port to the town – so long that darkness had fallen just as I reached the piazza of Santa Teresa. With darkness, the town began to roll down its shutters and put an end to the day's business. But even in daylight business could not have been very brisk. Santa Teresa, in the narrow bay of Longo Sardo, was a small place, hardly bigger than a village, that sprawled along the cliffs, but with a cheerier feel than its equivalent in Corsica. People were perambulating in the square, and doing the last of their shopping; there were raised voices and even some loud laughter.

I wanted to go to Olbia, where there was a train south. There was a bus to Olbia, but no bus station. It stopped on a back street, no one was quite sure where. And the bus tickets – ah, yes, I should have known. They were sold at a small coffee-shop three streets away. Having established all this I was told that the bus had left. I would not have been able to buy a ticket anyway. The café owner only took Italian money, and all I had were francs, and the banks were closed. So I had a pizza and found a hotel. The hotel owner said, "The Corsicans in Bonifacio speak a very similar dialect to us, but they are neither French nor Italian. And – you know? – we don't really understand them."

Never mind the delay, I went to bed contented, and I woke in a good mood. The weather seemed milder than in Corsica, and I was happy to be in a place where I spoke the language reasonably well – the lingua franca, actually, since there were four distinct Sardinian dialects, several of them closer to Latin and Spanish than Italian (*yanno* – from *janua* – for door; *mannu* – from *magnus* – for huge; *mesa* for table). A Sardinian told me that there is an organization which is committed to bringing Corsica and Sardinia closer by twinning towns, sending schoolchildren back and forth, and arranging cultural exchanges. Having disclosed this idealistic plan he then burst out laughing, as though he had just described something absurdly far-fetched, something like a scheme for teaching dogs to walk on their hind legs.

Santa Teresa was only on the map for its port and the ferry landing; it was otherwise ignored, and yet it was the sort of provincial place that I liked. It had a hill and a pretty church and a dramatic view of the sea; and everyone knew everyone else. The local dish, a man told me, was wild boar (*cinghiale*, he said, with big *zanne* – tusks), and it was prepared in a variety of ways.

"But I'm a vegetarian," I said.

"You want vegetables? You came to the right place." And then he remembered that he had an uncle in Vermont.

In daylight everything was simple: I changed money, I bought a bus ticket, I found out the times of the buses, and then I was headed east across the top of the island on my way to Olbia.

At Palau, the bus stopped for passengers and a coffee break.

"There's a place in the Pacific called Palau," I said to the driver.

"Another one! Amazing."

After talking casually for a little while, I nerved myself to ask, "There used to be a lot of kidnappings in Sardinia?"

"You mean, a long time ago?"

"No, fifteen years ago, maybe a little more," I said.

"Yes, I've heard there were a few kidnappings."

A few! In the 1970s kidnapping of foreigners had amounted almost to a cottage industry, and Sardinia was known to have developed a culture of kidnapping. The style of crime had deep roots in mountainous regions of the island. Almost anyone with a little money visiting Sardinia was snatched and held in a peasant hut in the mountains by semi-literates demanding millions from their desperate family.

"Kidnapping is labor-intensive," a Sardinian, Questore Pazzi, told Robert Fox, who described the encounter in his chronicle of the modern Mediterranean, *The Inner Sea*. "A band needs at least twelve men to act as look-outs, messengers and negotiators, as well as to seize and guard the victim. Unlike the Mafia families of Sicily and Calabria, the gang works together for one crime only and then disperses."

"So this was long ago?" I asked the driver. "Who was responsible?"

"Bandits."

"I read that it was sheep-stealers" − I did not know the Italian term for sheep-rustling − "but they ran out of sheep to steal, and so they decided to kidnap people."

"Who knows these mountain people?"

His pride dented, he had become a trifle cool towards me, because I had impugned something in his culture.

"More people get killed in America," he said.

"So true," I said.

"Let's go."

It was only an hour or so from here to Olbia. After we arrived I walked the streets like a rat in a maze, looking for a likely place to stay: quiet, not expensive. As in most of the towns I had visited since Spain, business was terrible and in this wintry low season there were plenty of available rooms.

The weather was pleasant, brilliant sunshine, mild temperatures, lemons on the trees; and March was only a few days off. Olbia was on a gulf, but the port that served it was about five miles away at Golfo Aranci, the end of the train line. Just to see where these Italian ferries left from I took the train and walked around Aranci, marveling at how easy it was – generally speaking – to travel in this part of the Mediterranean. There were several ferries a day to different parts of Italy. But my idea was to take a train the length of Sardinia and then get a ferry to Sicily.

The woman who ran my boarding-house in Olbia urged me to go to a particular restaurant that night where they were serving Sardinian specialities.

"No wild boar, thanks."

"Many good things," she said.

The first dish I was served was, appropriately, sardines. The root is the same, related to Sardinia, just as the word for a Sardinian plant ("which when eaten produced convulsive laughter, ending in death") had given us the word sardonic – derisive, sneering – because *sardonios* in Greek meant "of Sardinia."

"People in the country around here eat these all the time," the waiter said.

Squid with celery and tomatoes; chickpea and bean soup; goat cheese covered with dried oregano; seaweed fried in batter; then fish, grilled triglia, and finally pastries.

Normally I hated eating alone, but this was Italy, the waiter was talkative, and after the emptiness and general solemnity of Corsican restaurants, this one was noisy and friendly. It was not a fancy place, and yet several grinning middle-aged men were talking on cellular phones as they ate. It was not business, it was just yakking in Italian. *Uh, and then what did she say? Oh, yeah? Did you tell her you had the money? You imbecile!*

After dinner I took a walk through the town and Olbia seemed, as many places seem while they are twinkling in the dark, a magical place – and I was glad I had come. The reality of daylight was that it was a rough place, and the more I walked the more miserable it seemed, with clusters of mean houses, or else apartment houses, and beyond them stony fields and sheep and goats. The poverty and all the talk of emigration in search of work made Sardinia seem like Ireland, an offshore island that had plenty of culture but no money. Apart from the touristy parts, the Costa Smeralda of the speculating Aga Khan, there was little development. This was a remote Italian province of narrow villages and a hinterland of sheep and emptiness.

One of the Sardinian habits that was inescapable was the advertising all over town of a death or an anniversary of a death by sticking up posters of the deceased on any vertical surface. Many of the posters were as large as a bath towel, and except for the black border could have been mistaken for election posters. With the photo, many in color, was a name in bold letters – PADRE or FRANCESCO or MARIOLINA or PIERO or SALVATORE. It is a variety of lugubrious advertising of grief, common in Irish newspapers, but fairly bizarre when it appears on fences and walls, though the funereal faces had a strange appropriateness on the sides of derelict or condemned buildings.

I was copying down some names and sentiments from these grieving flyers when I looked over and saw that an African was staring at me. I had seen such Africans, very dark and silent, in Palau and also at Santa Teresa. They were in Marseilles and in some of the other large cities in the Riviera, and I guessed they were from the former French colonies in West Africa. Tall, unsmiling, with swollen eyes and matted linty hair, with clawed and scarified cheeks, they hovered near squares of plastic on which were arranged various items for sale, sunglasses, watches, belts, purses, wallets, toys – junk, on the whole, and one unsmiling African's junk was identical to another's. It had not seemed odd to me to see them in the South of France – it was the modern version of the empire striking back; after all, innumerable French people had insinuated themselves into Africa for hundreds of years, hawking all sorts of dubious merchandise. But what were these Africans doing in a small town in Sardinia?

"Hello – good-morning," I said to that staring man in Italian. "Are you looking at me?"

"No," he said, his reddened eyes, with dark-flecked whites, fastened to me.

Almost purple, with dusty hair, his wool coat wrapped around him, long legs, discolored and broken teeth, and those spotty staring eyes; he could not have been a stranger apparition in this small town with its unaccommodating provincial air.

"What are you selling?"

"Whatever you want."

"It looks like a lot of Chinese merchandise to me."

"No. These are good things."

His Italian was shaky, supplemented by French, which was better than mine. His name was Omar.

"Chinese watches. Chinese glasses. Chinese picture-frames. Cigarette lighters from China."

"What do you want to buy?"

"One kilo of hasheesh."

Omar did not smile.

"Just a joke," I said.

Two of his friends, thinking that he was in trouble with a plain-clothes policeman, stepped over to listen. Their names, they told me, were Yusuf and Ahmed.

"Three Muslims in a little Catholic town."

They stared at me.

"From what country?"

"Senegal," Omar said. He was older and taller than the others. "I come from a place ten kilometers from Dakar. My town is called Tuba."

"How long have you lived here?"

"More than ten years," Omar said.

By "here" he meant the Mediterranean generally – out of Africa. He explained that he had lived for six years in Cannes, and also in Livorno and Florence. He had lived in Olbia for two years.

"And them?" I nodded at Yusuf and Ahmed.

"A few months."

"Why here?"

"Olbia is a good place – not expensive," Omar said. "We have two rooms. We all live together."

"Do you have any Italian friends?"

"No – well, maybe a few."

"What about North Africa? There are lots of Muslims in Algeria and Morocco, and business might be better than here."

Business might have been better anywhere but here in Olbia where they stood, ignored and idle, while the townsfolk hurried past them looking slightly nervous. There were no tourists in Olbia.

"We can't go to those places. No documents. But here I have a paper. So I come and go. The police don't bother us at all."

"When you say, 'come and go,' do you mean you return to Africa occasionally?"

"Yes. I plan to go there in a few months. My family is there. Wives. Children. All that."

He had a clumsy clacking way with Italian, and I thought I might have misheard. "Did you say 'wives'?"

"Yes."

"More than one?"

"Only two."

"Children?"

"Only a few," he said. "Six."

The young ragged man and his apprentices fascinated me, and seemed to represent an entirely new kind of penetration in the Mediterranean, a region which had known so many immigrants over thousands of years. It was a poor town on an island that was so poor the local people left it to find work. But it was also a town which had never before seen Africans.

There were some more Africans at the railway station. I asked them the question I had meant to ask Omar. Why not get a job?

"There is no work. We would work in a factory if we could find one. But there are no factories."

"So what's your plan?"

"No plan. Stay here."

Heading south, I took the train to a town in the north-central part of the island, Chilivani, a railway junction. Out of Olbia, the rocky sheep-nibbled hinterland of scrubby trees and low hills were all tumbled together and blown by the wind, like the Scottish lowlands. There were rocky peaks in the distance where, in the manner of Corsicans, the Nuraghic people of Sardinia had tradition-ally made their homes, away from the coasts, and fought off the numerous invaders. Beyond Chilivani, the people in the mountainous region of Barbagia ("extreme examples of the Sardinian national character") had never acknowledged any rule over them and had never paid taxes. The Romans had failed to make them citizens (which was why they called these people Barbagians – barbarians). Sardinia had been annexed but so little did it figure in Rome's plans that it was used as a place to which Jews were deported under the rule of Tiberius (A.D. 14–37). More recently, the Italians had no more luck than the Romans in bringing Sardinians under control, even with enormous numbers of policemen sent from the mainland to pacify the remote districts. Still, rural crime – murder, sheep-stealing, extortion – were unusually high in Sardinia. The Barbagians had been Barbagians for 2,000 years.

There were stone walls everywhere along the line, and as far as I could see, every mile of landscape was demarcated. I was in a two-coach train filled with yelling youngsters on their way home from school. They were going fifteen or twenty miles, and though they were very loud, even rowdy, cackling in their incomprehensible dialect, when a woman straightened up and said, "Excuse me, but would you please close that window?" two of them instantly obeyed.

It was a bleak, untidy beauty in a sparsely populated island. We were among vineyards, running past a range of granite peaks. There were sheep grazing inside the walls in the foreground and in some places cork trees, like those in Corsica, stripped of their bark.

The noisiest youngsters got off at a country station called Berchidda, where there was a small settlement, and others at Fraigas, which had the look of a penal colony. Many Sardinian towns looked like that; others looked ancient, and some had the prefabricated look of having been thrown up last week.

Chilivani was no more than an intersection of two railway lines, in a strong wind. I sat for a while and eventually connected with a train that was coming from Sassari, a bigger, faster train that sped past a continuous landscape of walled-off pastures, all over the hillsides, under a large sky of tumbling woolly clouds that somewhat resembled the unshorn sheep here.

We were less than twenty miles from the western coast, but so little connection was there between these sheep farms and the coast that we might have been a thousand miles from the sea. That was a Mediterranean feature. Life was different away from the shore. Five or ten miles inland from anywhere in the Mediterranean and you were in a separate world.

Much of what I saw was solid rock, long slopes of veined and wrinkled stone, and meadows of stone too, the whole place like an ancient lava flow, except that this was not fertile and volcanic but iron-like crusts of granite. Some of the smooth stone slopes were also partitioned with bouldery walls. I had never seen such a landscape before, nor had I ever imagined it except on a distant planet.

At the town of Bonorva all the newer houses were made of gray cinder blocks. Out of town, a vast stony landscape of tussocky grass and dark twisted trees, the big sky full of smoky clouds. I made a note: *The landscape looks abused*, and only later discovered that many mining companies, foreign as well as Italian, had come and ransacked it for minerals, for antimony, coal, lead, silver and zinc.

Farther south, the sight of a mustached man in the middle of nowhere, leading sheep down a path from one field to another. A shepherd — the first of many I saw. Shepherding was as old an occupation in the Mediterranean as fishing, and this man with his flat cap and his crook and his dog represented to me a timelessness that was both melancholy and indestructible.

Around four, I looked at my map, saw that we were near the town of Oristano, and decided to get off here and spend a night and a day, what the hell.

Oristano seemed to be a port on the map, but my map was not very accurate. Oristano, five miles inland, might have been a hundred, for it had no real connection to the sea. It was just another small simmering town in the middle of a hot plain, the most provincial of places, at a great remove from the world. The far-off whistle of my departing train gave me a pang of regret, but then I thought: *No — this is the Mediterranean, too! Everything matters!* and generally consoled myself with the thought of all the money I was saving by staying here for the night, rather than in the bright lights of big city Cagliari.

Oristano had a moribund atmosphere that was almost palpable, enervating heat, and an audible monotony that was like the drowsy buzz of a single futile bumblebee. I felt a sort of ghastly frivolity in the idea that by parachuting off the train with no plan in my head I was pointlessly insinuating myself in a small Sardinian town which was off the tourist trail – not because it was obscure and hard to reach but because it was utterly boring.

It was a market-place for the nearby farms, and the townies measured themselves against the peasants who turned up to sell vegetables or meat at the market. These peasants, Barbagians to their gnarled fingertips, were toothless and skinny and undersized people. The women wore shawls and four skirts and argyle knee socks and were more whiskery than their menfolk, who chewed broken pipestems and looked oppressed. After the Oristano market closed I imagined them scuttling back to the hills and sheltering under toadstools. But they were also noted for their toughness – *ferrigno*, they were called, made of iron.

The only aspects of the outside world that had penetrated here were extremely violent American videos and Disney comics – we are cultural leaders, after all, specializing in the criminal and the infantile. Italian culture in Oristano was represented by the Church, porno comics, chain-smoking, a plethora of shoe stores. The rest was harmless obsession – Italian here, but generally true of the Mediterranean region – the mild ostentation of the middle-class women in cutting a good figure, and the male passion about sports that bordered on the homo-erotic.

Italy had allowed Sardinia to be self-governing and had given it a degree of autonomy that prevented the island from nursing the sort of political grievances that were so common in Corsica. There were no bomb-throwers in Sardinia. It was a rugged place – none of the poodles and lapdogs of France, only functional mutts that had to work to earn their keep – sheepdogs and guard dogs.

My landlady in Oristano, Regina, was a voluble Italian whose husband worked in Cagliari. "I want you to be happy. I want this to be like your own house." Her flunkeys and room-cleaners were Sardinian women from the interior, who were not forthcoming when I asked them about their own language and culture. It seemed a vaguely colonial arrangement of the memsahib and her native servants, but they all got on well and worshipped in the same church.

The more I saw of Oristano the more strongly I felt that my chief objection was that it was the sort of inbred town, with its own rules and snobberies, that I grew up in. It was full of low-brows but it was neighborly. Strangers in the boarding-house always greeted each other, and when someone entered a restaurant everyone said hello, calling out "How are you?" from where they sat. It was perhaps not very different from Medford, Mass., and friendly and frightening in about equal parts. Excessive friendliness is perhaps a philistine trait; in a place where no one reads, no one values or understands contemplative solitude, and so they need each other to be friendly and talkative.

I was on my way to the station in Oristano when I was accosted by an oriental man. He said, in Italian, "A hundred lire," and clicked a cigarette lighter in my face.

"Where do you come from?"

"China."

Another Chinese man appeared.

"You want a lighter?" he asked in English.

"How did you get here?"

"Cargo ship."

"Do you live here?"

Yet another Chinese man joined us, and he muttered to his friends. They were all in their thirties, and were decently dressed. They spoke little Italian and even less English. They had chosen an unpromising place to hawk cigarette lighters. Perhaps this was a town that was not dominated by African hawkers. My questions and my lack of interest in their twenty-cent cigarette lighters seemed to drive them away, but where to?

Africans living by their wits in Olbia, Chinese seamen boosting lighters in Oristano. What was this all about? The natives of the Mediterranean were always harking back to the past, which was glorious; but the present was much stranger, and baffling.

The railway to Cagliari rattled down the long flat valley of Campidano. I dozed and made notes, and I was surprised by how warm the weather was – sunny and lovely this day in early March.

Along with the Catholic chapel in the midst of Cagliari station, with the Holy Eucharist present in the tabernacle (a mass every Monday at ten-thirty, and every feast day at ten), there was also a pornographic bookstore, a photocopy machine, a barber shop, a coffee shop, and three public telephones. This was the new Italy, after all.

The city itself, built on a slope, old brown houses and offices, resembled Marseilles but without the Marseillaise air of criminality. Cagliari seemed huge after my experience of Sardinia's provincial towns, but after a day it seemed very small. I had the impression that no one ever went there, but when I mentioned this the local people said, "This place is crowded in the summer. You should see Spiaggia de Poetto!"

I went there, to this beach, and walked and saw the flamingos in the nearby lagoons. On this weekday in winter the beach was almost deserted, but that hardly mattered. I sat in the sunshine, read for a while, and walked back to town.

In a Cagliari restaurant that night I was writing my diary, having finished my meal, when I noticed that the place was empty – all the customers had gone. The waiters, the cashier and the cook were just about to sit down to eat, having put a sign saying *Closed* on the front window.

I caught a waiter's eye. "I'd like to pay."

"But you're not finished," he said.

"Yes, the meal was good."

"Your work," he said, and gestured to my notebook, my papers and paraphernalia. "Look, I can see you're busy. Finish your work. It's no problem for us. We're just eating here."

After I was done they invited me to join them. I asked them about Sardinia, but they said it was a horribly dull place, nothing ever happened here, and so they engaged me on their favorite subject, American basketball. *Now about this Michael Jordan . . .*

There were Africans in the streets of Cagliari. The next day, on my way to buy a ferry ticket, I asked a man about them.

"They're Africans," he said, and he shrugged, the Italian gesture: Who cares? "They're here in the summer, lots of them. They sell little things."

"They're from?"

"Who knows? Africa. Ghana – down there." He shrugged again.

"What do Sardinians think of them?"

He jerked his shoulders again and grunted, the fatalistic "Eh!" His tolerance was a variety of indifference. Italians are not threatened by abstractions, and unless they are directly provoked they are great live-and-let-livers. In spite of their manic stereotypes, their refusal to fuss is one of their most endearing characteristics. Coping with disorder is part of Italian life; and conscious of this they often make a virtue of not getting excited.

The scariest-looking people in Sardinia were not the Barbagians, the Senegalese, the toothless shepherds, sheep-rustlers, kidnappers and gypsies, but rather the punks of Cagliari. Young, filthy, ragged, with greasy hair and dreadlocks, rings through their noses, their lips, they were sniffing glue, gagging on wine and shouting vicious abuse at passers-by.

There were plenty of these strange young people hanging about in gangs near the castle, where I had gone for its good view of the harbor.

"So what have we got here?" I asked a man, while six punks quarreled over a bottle. They wore studded dog-collars and chains, and one had a tin cup that clinked at his belt.

"It's a shame," the man said.

"Anarchists?"

"No. They believe in nothing."

"Nihilists, then?"

"No. They are abandoned."

"There are young people like that in England and America."

"I've seen them in Latin America," the man said.

Now we were walking along, up a steep cobblestone street.

"In Brazil," he said. "I lived in Brazil for three years. I never thought I would see them here. It was very strange there. It was ridiculous, really. Brazil is a huge country – rich too."

He laughed out loud.

"So there were these paupers sitting on a mountain of gold!"

The expression made me laugh, and my laughter encouraged him.

"Here it's the opposite. We're rich, but we're sitting on a mountain of ruins."

I asked him whether he ever went to Sicily.

"Why would I want to go there?" he said, and tapped my shoulder. "Just a joke. It's surely a nice place. But when I leave here I go to the continent" – by which he meant the Italian mainland.

The travel agent who sold me the ferry ticket to Palermo said, "You'd be better off taking the plane. It costs the same."

It was $67 for the ferry from Cagliari to Palermo, but this way I had a first-class cabin and because it was an overnighter it was both my fare to Sicily and a bed. And there was the added pleasure of setting out from Cagliari in the evening, watching the lights of the city recede; and after a good night's sleep, seeing the coast of Sicily appear with the sunrise.

8

The Ferry *Torres* to Sicily

It would have been quicker for me to sail to Africa. It was a much shorter trip from Sardinia to Tunisia. Cagliari was only about 120 miles from Bizerta, city of Berbers; it was more like 180 to Palermo, Sicily. But it was generally bad manners, if not heresy, to mention Italy's proximity to Africa and its *melanzane* – "eggplants," as black Africans are described in Italian slang.

Under a full moon in a cloudless night sky the ferry glided out of the Gulf of Cagliari, past the lighthouses and beacons, and soon the city and its twinkling hill were far astern. We were at sea and, as another Ulysses – James Joyce's – saw it, "the heaventree of stars hung with humid nightblue fruit."

The Sicilian crew were offhand and seemed to make a virtue of being unhelpful, so busy were they being themselves, smiling at each other with yellow faces and fangy teeth, muttering backtalk in slushy accents, and shrugging, and avoiding eye-contact with any of the passengers, and all the while preserving their shabby dignity. At first there had been few passengers, but just before we left a great number hurried on board, though few of them were cabin people. They slept in chairs, smoked on the deck, lurked in the passageways, played cards in the lounge.

The galley steward fussed when he saw me showing up for dinner.

"You're late – I can't help you."

"The ship's just leaving," I said. "What time do you close?"

It was a buffet, there was food all over the place and not many eaters. But this was just a little spirited obstinacy on the part of the steward.

"We were going to close right now," he said, and sighed and looked overworked, and shook his head. "Oh, I don't know."

"I am just an ignorant American, but I'm hungry."

"Where did you learn Italian?"

"From my mother."

"Okay, go ahead. But all we have is menu food. No natural."

"What's 'natural'?"

That set off in him a virtuoso flurry of gestures, hurried shrugging, the what-do-you-expect-me-to-do? pursing of hands, and he looked around in his impatience, as Italians do, as though pleading for a witness.

I paid my money, I got my receipt, I chose my food, as the ship's engine made a meat-grinder noise of departure. "Natural" was a sign of the times, the theory of sensible eating had arrived in the island of spaghetti-benders: it meant health-food, low-fat mozzarella and low-sodium pasta. The rest was fried and fatty.

A young man, monotonously complaining and stuffing his face with pasta, had put one foot on the arm of his girlfriend's chair in a sort of misplaced tenderness, as though chunking his big clumsy foot against her elbow was a romantic gesture.

> I hate the noisy way you eat,
> I hate your nose, I hate your feet.

Because in Italy there was such an ingrained contempt for the law, *la legge*, it continued to amaze me that anything as orderly as meals and departures and arrivals were timely; yet my experience of boats and trains was favorable – there were very few hitches. Mealtime, for example, was sacred. It would have been unusual if the steward had turned me away from the buffet. Traveling in Italy, I could nearly always depend on a meal at the end of the day and a cheery person to serve it. I was seldom disappointed.

The life of the mind was something else. Any honest, thoughtful effort, any attempt at seriousness or intellectual ambition, was usually ridiculed. I knew that I would have been made a fool of for my diligent note-taking and – though I tried to hide it – my air of scholarly industry. Only suckers tried to get ahead, bookish people were laughable, and already I could sense that once again I was among philistines, with all the responsive jollity and hearty appetite that was usual with philistinism.

As far as I could tell there were very few Sardinians on the *Torres*, but there were all sorts of Sicilians: city slickers (Armani suits, pointy shoes), smug Palermitanis (overcoats draped on their shoulders like capes), sinister toughs (sunglasses at midnight); and all the rest, the students, the punks, the poor, from "men of respect" (as the mafiosi called themselves) who looked stylish and unreliable, to gypsies with gold teeth and long skirts and scarves, squatting on the floor and breast-feeding babies.

I saw a sign – *Il Vostro Punto di Riunione é* – ("Your Muster Station is –") and it filled me with alarm.

Supine in my cabin, listening to the engine's drone and the thumping of the screws, I could just imagine the panic and clawing and yelling and colorful language and class-warfare if the ship ran into trouble. I thought: *Do I want to be in a sinking boat with these people. Do I dare to share a lifeboat with them?*

In a sunny Sicilian dawn, the sun blazing behind a golden haze, we entered the Bay of Palermo, mountains on either side and a great harmonizing background of stucco-colored peaks behind the ancient buildings. The tallest man-made structures were the church steeples and cathedral domes.

Rather than stay in Palermo, where I had been before, I wanted to spend a day in Cefalù, just down the railway line; and then go to Messina and Taormina and Siracusa, places I had never seen. Still, I needed to walk in order to stretch and get the stiffness out of my legs, and I wanted just to browse in the city. So I left my bag at the station and then looked around, and decided on a hike.

Whenever I asked directions I was usually told the place I wanted was "very far" (*lontanissimo*), even when it was a fifteen-minute walk. I was urged to catch a bus.

"But you'll need a ticket."

"Of course."

"You buy one there."

Silly me for not knowing that bus tickets were sold in a seedy little tobacco and porno shop, *Bar "T"* – *Café Stagnitta* – *Articoli da Fumo, Articoli da Regalo, Articoli da Gioca* – smoking paraphernalia, presents and games. And bus tickets, of course. It was preposterous to think that a bus ticket would be sold in a bus or in a vending machine. A man who sold bus tickets had to have a large stock of cigarettes, and candy, and tit-and-bum magazines.

The swagger of the Sicilian men in Palermo, swarthy as Arabs, shouting to each other, was remarkable for its confidence. Anthony Burgess once heard a young man in Palermo telling his friends how he had devised a foolproof method for discovering whether his new bride was sexually innocent on his wedding night. "He was going to paint his penis purple, he said, and if his bride evinced surprise he was going to cut her throat."

I was fumbling with my wallet, when a woman took me aside. She said, "You're a stranger?"

"Oh, yes. American."

"Watch your pockets," she said.

"Thanks. I'll do that."

"You see, Palermo is very beautiful – eh –"

She lifted the fingers of her right hand and flicked forward, beneath her chin.

"We're good people – eh –"

Again she grazed her chin with her fingers.

"And you'll be all right here – eh –"

Her gesturing continued, as she looked slightly away, and then with a final caution, she walked off.

I had seen this chin-flick gesture before. I had understood it to mean a deep defiance – Up yours, so to speak. But that is another, more severe use of it, as understood from Naples northward. Here, the flicking fingers were meant as a contradiction. *Yes, I am saying this is a nice place but notice that I am indicating with my hand that it is not true in every instance; be warned.*

That was nicely candid. The gestures were more subtle as a priest joined the little crowd standing at a bus stop. There were some mutters, but no one spoke to the priest. Italians – men especially – squint at priests' skirts. They believe that priests who pass butcher shops turn the meat bad. Priests are neither men nor women. They have the evil eye.

I was alert to everyone around me when I saw a priest in Italy. A silence fell when this one appeared, but often there would be a series of simultaneous gestures, because of this belief that priests have the evil eye. For an Italian man, the commonest and most effective way of dealing with the clerical evil eye was to touch his own testicles and subtly prong his fingers at the priest. I never found out what Italian women did. Perhaps they prayed, but in any case they were less anxious than the men in matters that related to the supernatural.

I took a bus to Monte Pellegrino, on the recommendation of Goethe, who had written about it. The high hill was outside the north-west corner of the city, and as this was a weekday in March, there was hardly anyone else on the footpath. I had been told that I could see as far as the Lipari islands from the summit of Pellegrino; the day was too hazy to see any distance, yet the view of Palermo and its bay was splendid, enough of a reward for a two-hour walk.

But the view had stirred something in me. Walking down the slope towards the bus I became agitated about my trip. Perhaps it was the sight of all that coast, and the thought that almost two months into it, where was I? Kicking along a dusty path in Sicily made me feel tiny, overwhelmed by everything that lay ahead of me – Italy, Greece, Turkey, Israel, Egypt, all the rest of North Africa, the islands of Cyprus and Malta, not to mention the war in Croatia and Bosnia.

Then I remembered that I had plenty of time. I had no job, no deadlines, nothing else; and I reminded myself why I had come here. To eat spaghetti and talk to people and, first of all, to see Cefalù.

Cefalù was where the English satanist Aleister Crowley had lived in the 1920s and 1930s, studying yoga and black magic and writing dismal poetry. He was also a mountaineer, and had climbed a number of high peaks – had even worked out a method for climbing Mount Everest, "rushing the summit." His *Confessions*, published only in 1970, showed him to be one of the loonier figures in recent history. He was a dabbler and a dilettante, and as a wealthy man – he had inherited a fortune from the family brewing business – he could afford to be. There was no end to his high spirits. He filed his teeth to points. He showed these fangs to women and said, "Would you like a serpent's kiss?" A number of women doted on him. Today he would be called a New Age guru and they would be called groupies or cultists. He had named his favorite sex partner the Ape of Thoth.

So, after a late lunch, I traveled about twenty miles down the coast on the line to Messina and stopped at Cefalù to see whether anything remained of the Crowley ménage. But no one in town recognized the name of Aleister Crowley and, though I walked the streets, I could not find the house where he had worked black magic and tried to bamboozle visitors and wore a sorcerer's funny hat.

But mine was not a wasted trip. There was something pagan and animistic in the monstrous lions carved in the façade of Cefalù's cathedral – how appropriate that Crowley had chosen to live in a place where the supernatural still mattered. There were oranges and lemons on the trees, and behind the little town, snow-capped mountains. And from the cliff at Cefalù, I could at last see to the east the Lipari cluster of islands, also known as the Aeolian Islands. The volcano Stromboli was regarded in ancient times as the home of Æolus, god of the winds.

Late in the day, I caught an express train to Messina. It was called the *Archimedes* (the mathematician was born in Siracusa, on the other side of Sicily) and it was due in Messina in a couple of hours.

More interesting than the fruit trees and the sight of the sea and the snowy peaks was the man next to me in the compartment, scribbling notations on sheets of paper lined for musical scores. He was murmuring, but he was not humming. He was thoroughly absorbed in his scribbling. Occasionally he tapped his foot. He was writing music?

I would not have believed such a thing was possible except that various people had claimed they had done it, the most famous example being Beethoven in his deafness.

The man was small and bald, about fifty, with a pleasant face. He quickly filled three sheets of paper with music. Then I interrupted him with a grunt.

He stopped tapping his feet. He smiled. "Yes?"

"Are you writing music?"

"Yes," and he showed me the sheet with beads and squiggles on it. "I usually write music on this train. It's not hard."

"But you have no instrument. There's no music."

"This is music. And I don't need an instrument. I write from memory."

"Amazing."

"The music is already in my mind before I write it. When I get home I will continue."

"In silence?"

"I use a piano at home for composing, but my favorite instrument is an accordion."

This odd word *fisarmonica* I had learned in high school as a joke, and this was the first time in my life I had ever heard it spoken. And this man was a *fisarmonicista*.

"It's a typical Sicilian instrument. But I am the only composer of accordion music that I know. I think I might be the only one in Sicily. I love modern music, and mine has folkloric melodies in it."

His name was Basilio. He had just been in Palermo playing in a piano bar, both piano and electronic keyboard. Not only his own music but Frank Sinatra hits.

"'*Staranger Een Danah*,' '*Conflowah Me*,' '*Myweh*' — they are the most beautiful," he said, mingling English and Italian.

"You spend a lot of time traveling back and forth to Palermo."

"I don't have a problem. I'm not married," he said, and laughed. "I have a girlfriend, though. My family is always asking me when I'm getting married, but I say to them, 'Eh, what about my music?'"

We were passing more orchards and a stretch of coast where there were empty beaches.

"Look, all empty," he said, seeing that I had glanced out of the window. "It's so lovely. Sicily is warm from March until October, but no one comes here — why?"

"Maybe something to do with the Mafia?"

"The newspapers! The newspapers! It's all lies," Basilio said. "All the news is about Mafia and danger. Eh, where's the Mafia? Do you see them?"

"I haven't looked," I said, startled by his sudden energy.

"Forget it — it's lies. As for beauty, listen to me — three-fourths of Sicily is untouched. Absolutely untouched! No one comes here — they're afraid. Of what?"

"Yes, it is very pretty," I said, wishing I had not roused his fury.

He was now talking to the other person in the compartment, a man in a heavy sweater and purple socks, holding on his lap a damp and stained parcel that stank of cheese.

"We have – what – a million people or so?" Basilio said.

"About a million," the man agreed.

Surely more? I thought. In fact, there are more than five million people in Sicily.

"A little island. Not many people. And so that makes it all the more friendly," Basilio said. "What do you do for a living?"

"I'm a writer, Basilio."

"That's great. Please, when you write" – he put his hands together in a little prayer gesture, then he held them apart, cupping them in Do-me-a-favor mode – "tell people it's nice here."

It's nice here. Lemons, oranges. Composers on trains. *Staranger Een Danah!*

"I travel a little myself," he said. "We find Sicilians everywhere. You don't have to speak French or English. There's always a Sicilian taxi-driver!"

"You've been in Sardinia?"

"To my shame, no, not to Sardinia. The purest dialect is Sardinian – the worst is Bergamo. As for Corsica – what's wrong with them? Why don't the Corsicans admit they're Italians?" He was laughing. "I love to travel, of course. Although I haven't been to other places in Italy, I have been everywhere in Sicily."

He sounded a bit like Henry David Thoreau who wrote, "I have traveled widely in Concord."

"Sicily fascinates me, the way the dialects here reflect Spanish, French, and Arabic."

"I am headed for Siracusa."

"One of the best places," Basilio said. "Ancient. And natural too. Up north, the beaches are filthy. But here they are clean."

We happened to be passing one that was brown with muddy water from run-off.

"Some of the beaches are a little muddy from the recent rains."

"Very muddy, I'd say." And they were strewn with such rubbish and rocks, and bounded by trash-filled streams and open sewers. Italians were such litterers.

"It will pass! Listen, Germans come here in November and go swimming. For them the water is warm!"

Protesting that I was a wonderful person, and urging me to tell people how delightful Sicily was at all times of the year, he called out, "See you again!" and got off at Sant' Agata di Militello. Then it was just small hot stations and embankments and so many tunnels it was as though we had traveled to Messina in the dark.

The most God-fearing places in Italy were those that had experienced a natural disaster. Such an event was inevitably a goad to Italian piety, and nothing provoked prayer like a flood or an earthquake or a tidal wave. Messina had all three just after Christmas in 1908, when almost the entire city, in fact this whole corner of the island, was destroyed. Part of Calabria was also leveled. Almost 100,000 people died in the one-day disaster (earthquake at 5 a.m., tidal wave just after that, then flooding; cholera came later) – it was equivalent to the entire population of the city.

That is why there are no ancient buildings in Messina, though quite a lot of talk about how the Virgin Mary engaged in vigorous correspondence with Messina's city fathers and reassured them, "We bless you and your city." There is a large pillar in the harbor of Messina, too, with a statue of Mary, making a gesture of blessing that also looks as though she is dropping a yo-yo, and under it, for every ship to see, the same message in Latin, *Vos et ipsam civium civitatem benedicimus.*

A melancholy plaque at Messina railway station records the fact that 348 railway workers died in the earthquake:

A pietoso ricordo dei 348 funzionari ed agenti periti nel terremoto del 28 Dec MCMVIII.

It was easy enough to find a place to stay in Messina, and no problem eating, but apart from strolling along the harbor and admiring the Calabrian coast across the straits – lumpy gray mountains streaked with snow – there was not much to do in this rebuilt city. It had obviously been brought back to life, but it was not quite the same afterwards. Or perhaps it was something else.

I fell into conversation with a man in Messina who told me,

without any hesitation, that Catania was an absolute haunt of crime.

Catania is a port about halfway between Messina and Siracusa on the south-east-facing side of the Sicilian triangle.

"The Mafia control the whole city," he said.

Now and then you got one of these Sicilians who admitted flat-out that the Mafia was pervasive and dangerous; and they could be specific, too, about certain towns or cities.

"How do you explain it?"

"Business is good there. They get a share of it. And the drugs."

"Because it's a port?"

"That's probably the main reason."

"Palermo and Messina are also ports. So perhaps the Mafia is strong in these places as well."

His reply was the Italian lip-droop and finger signal, a combination of affirmative gestures, that meant "Indubitably."

I could well believe that Messina was one of the Mafia strong-holds. Such a place seemed shut and unwelcoming and buzzing with suspicion. There was plenty of money to be made by getting a stranglehold on the port; it was so easy to be disruptive if you controlled the wharves. Organized crime was seldom entrepren-eurial; it was mainly a lazy business of bullying and intimidation. The idea was to find someone with a cash-flow and strong-arm that person or business.

All areas of Italian life, even the Church, had been penetrated by the Mafia. In 1962, the Franciscan monks of the monastery of Mazzarino in central Sicily were put on trial, charged with extortion, embezzlement, theft, and murder. The prior, Padre Carmelo, was the *capo* of this band of Mafia monks. He was a sinister, sprightly man – greedy and libidinous, with Mazzarino in his foxy jaws. The monks were eventually found guilty of most of the charges at their trial in Messina. What emerged as perhaps the most surprising aspect of their criminality was that it had not interfered with their religious routines. The fact that they entertained prostitutes, and ordered killings, and amassed large sums of money in their extortionate activities never prevented their hearing confessions, saying masses, or preaching at funerals – in at least one case, the monk in question saying a funeral high mass and preaching piously over the body of a man he had ordered to be killed.

Italians use obscure gestures and elaborate euphemisms whenever they talk about criminal organizations – the Mafia in Sicily, the 'Ndrangheta of Calabria, the Camorra of Naples. Even the most specific word in Italian for the fees the gangsters charge to businessmen they threaten is somewhat vague – *tangenti*. It is a simple word, meaning "extras." But anyone in the know defines it as "extortion."

Bored with Messina – and anyway I would be back here next week to take the ferry to Calabria – I caught a train to Taormina, twenty-five miles down the coast.

"Lovely beaches!" Basilio had said to me, but the beaches outside Messina were littered with old fridges and rusty stoves, junked cars, hovels, plastic trash and rusty tomato cans. Then it was just driftwood, and finally stony beaches. At Nizza di Sicilia station I saw my first tourists in Italy. They were of course Germans, two young women wearing army boots and heaving forty-pound rucksacks and studying their handbook *Sizilien*; they were sturdy, shorthaired, sapphic.

They got off with me at Taormina, the elegant shoreline station. The town itself is high on a cliff, glittering and vertical.

At the station a man approached the conductor of a train going in the opposite direction and said, "Where are we?"

"Taormina Giardini," the conductor said.

"And where are you going?"

"Venice." And the conductor turned his back and reboarded the Venice Express, Siracusa to Venice, a long haul of more than 700 miles.

I began walking up the hill, thinking that it was not far, but a shrewd taxi-driver followed me, guessing that I would get sick of the climb. He laughed when I got in.

"Gardens, lovely view," he narrated, then glanced at the people by the road. "Germans."

Farther along, he said, "English church. Beautiful, eh?" and paused. "Germans."

They were the inevitable low-season people wherever I went.

The main attraction at Taormina was said to be its ancient

theater, built by the Greeks and completely remodeled by the
Romans. But that was simply a backdrop, the classical excuse.
Taormina had been taken up by the Edwardians as a place to
droop and be decadent. It was a lovely town, but it was now
entirely given over to tourists. There was nothing else generating
income for the local people. It was one of the more anglicized
seaside resorts of Italy, and though it was now simply a tourist
trap, retailing ceramics, and postcards, and letter-openers, and
clothes of various kinds, it had once known true scandals, mainly
imported ones, perpetrated by the northern Europeans escaping
the cold winter. It was strictly seasonal. In the early part of this
century all the hotels in Taormina were closed in the summer.

Taormina had been mainly for wealthy foreigners, though a title
helped. Any number of sponging aristocrats idled away their time
among Taormina's flower gardens, and a German baron who was
an unrepentant pederast became something of a local celebrity for
taking photographs of young Italian boys holding what certainly
looked like lengths of salami. These pictures were sold with views
of Mount Etna in Taormina's shops.

D.H. Lawrence had spent time in Taormina, writing poetry. His
well-known poem "Snake" he had written in Taormina, describing
how he had been standing in his pajamas and had seen a thirsty
snake and bashed it over the head; and how he had to expiate his
pettiness. But snakes were not Lawrence's problem in Taormina.
His daily chore was finding ways to control his wife Frieda in her
adulteries.

Night in Taormina was silence and skulking cats. These tourist
towns shrank in the off-season, and yet at this time of year eighty
years ago the place would have been thronged with visitors.
Taormina's season was the winter. Now it was busy mainly in the
summer.

The next day, I found Lawrence's house on the Via Fontana
Vecchia, and walked up and down the main street, looking at the
shops. I looked at the old amphitheater. The only other people
there were the two German women from yesterday's train.

But the spectacle here was not the amphitheater – it was the
volcano, Mount Etna. I had not expected to get such a dramatic
view. With lantana and palms and bougainvillea and marigolds,

sunny and serene, it was hard to imagine a prettier place or a more dramatic setting. The ancient Greeks praised Taormina in similar terms. But these days it exists only to be patronized and gawked at. It was not a place to live in, only to be visited, one of the many sites in the Mediterranean that are almost indistinguishable from theme parks.

Looking down the coast, I was startled by the sight of the volcano, an old bulgy mountain covered in snow, with a plume of smoke rising from its cone. The morning light took away its shadows and its grandeur and made it clumsy and pretty, with a splendor all of its own, because its pot-bellied shape was unique for a mountain on this coast – and the sea so near emphasized its height.

In a fit of self-aggrandizement, Empedocles jumped into the crater of Mount Etna. In doing so, the Greek philosopher, who believed in reincarnation, hoped to inspire the sense in others that he was godlike.

In a different fit of self-aggrandizement, the writer Evelyn Waugh, passing through here on a cruise ship and refusing to go ashore to visit Taormina, peers from the deck and gets a glimpse of the volcano beyond.

"I do not think I shall ever forget the sight of Etna at sunset," he writes in his first travel book, *Labels* (1930), "the mountain almost invisible in a blur of pastel gray, glowing on the top and then repeating its shape, as though reflected, in a wisp of gray smoke, with the whole horizon behind radiant with pink light, fading gently into a gray pastel sky. Nothing I have ever seen in Art or Nature was quite so revolting."

Sudden and strange, the description is marvelous for its utter perversity. You have to read it twice to make sure you haven't missed a word. *Labels* is full of such snap judgments and hilarious generalizations. It recalls Cyril Connolly, who wrote "a chocolate box sunset disfigured the West" – Waugh and Connolly were friends and in mocking a sunset they believed they were against nature. Theirs was the ultimate rebellion – so they thought; defying every notion of harmony by refusing to be impressed or admit that such loveliness could be moving. It was a self-conscious and envious way of needling other writers, but most of all it was diabolical blasphemy, for isn't criticizing a brilliant sunset an English way of blaming God?

Waugh's work is always a salutary reminder that satire is usually more purposeful than veneration, and that one of the virtues of a good travel book is the chance to see a traveler's mind, however childish, ticking away.

Nothing held me in Taormina. I took a taxi down the hill and caught the train to Siracusa. Traveling towards Catania we crossed the lava flow from the volcano. At Carruba there were blackish cedars by the shore, and lemon groves sagging with fruit. Then, Cannizaro, Lentini, Paterno: almost every town in Sicily reminded me of the names of my high school friends, and a Sicilian railway timetable looked like a list of the Medford High class of '59.

Catania was big and grim, the sort of place only a *mafioso* would tolerate, and that for its opportunities to whack it for money. The coast here was miles of great ugliness, oil storage depots, refineries, cracking plants, and cement factories. Offshore, a man was rowing backwards in the sea, pushing the oars instead of pulling them. By the side of the track, the scrawl *Cazzo* − Italian slang for the male member, when spoken sounding like *gatz*.

The end of the line was Siracusa.

"But what could I do at Syracuse? Why did I come there? Why did I buy a ticket just to Syracuse and not to any other place? Choice of destination had certainly been a matter of indifference. And certainly being at Syracuse or elsewhere was a matter of indifference. It was all the same to me. I was in Sicily. I was visiting Sicily. And I could just as well get on the train and return home."

This paragraph from Elio Vittorini's novel *Conversation in Sicily* had a definite resonance for me. Vittorini was born in Siracusa the year of the earthquake, 1908, and was a young man in the fascist era, the period described in this novel and some of his stories. All this I discovered in Siracusa.

I had stopped inside a bookstore on the long walk from the station to the old city, which was across a bridge, on a small island, Ortygia. The bookstore owner told me about Vittorini and recommended his writing.

"This was a great city once – capital of Sicily," he said.

He named for me the famous Siracusans – Theocritus, the Greek playwright Epicharmus, Santa Lucia, Vittorini.

"So many people have come and gone. We've been Phoenician, Greek of course, from long ago. But also more recently Arab, Spanish, French. You can hear it in the names. Vasqueza is a Siracusa name – Spanish. We have French ones too. Take my name, Giarratana – what do you think it is?"

"Can't imagine." But the truth was that I did not want to guess wrong and risk offending him.

"Pure Arab," said Mr Giarratana. "Giarrat is an Arab word."

"What does it mean?"

"I don't know. I'm not an Arab!"

Later I checked with my Arabic-speaking brother Peter and discovered that Giarrat was probably a cognate of Djarad, meaning locust.

"Our dialect is amazing," Mr Giarratana said. "It would be hard for someone like you to understand. Even other Sicilians have trouble with it."

He had a growly Sicilian voice, deepened with dust and smoke. I asked him for some examples of the incomprehensible dialect.

"Wango," he said. "Asegia. Stradon. What do those words mean?"

"No idea."

"Bank. Chair. Street," he said, smiling because he had stumped me. "We don't say orange [*arancia*], we call them *portugalli*."

That was also from an Arab word for orange, which was *burtugal*, probably from one of the countries which grew them, Portugal.

The most Sicilian of Sicilian words, known and used throughout the world, is *mafia*. It is identical to the obsolete Arabic word *mafya'*, meaning "place of shade," shade in this sense indicating refuge, and is almost certainly derived from it. Norman Lewis, in his book about the Mafia, *The Honored Society* (1964), describes how, after the orderliness of Saracen rule in Sicily was obliterated by the Normans in the eleventh century, Sicily became feudalistic. "Most of the Arab small-holders became serfs on the reconstituted estates. Some escaped to 'the Mafia.'" It became an alternative – and secret – system of justice, society and protection; a refuge.

I bought the Vittorini novel Mr Giarratana had spoken about and also a copy of *Frankenstein*, which I had been meaning to reread. Then I continued down the street and across the bridge to find a hotel. It was not much of a decision. Nearly all the hotels in Siracusa were closed, or being renovated, but not the nameless one run by Dr Calogero Pulvino, poet and philosopher. One star, $23 with breakfast and the occasional impromptu seminar by Dr Pulvino.

He sat surrounded by books, looking harassed, as if inspiration had just deserted him or he had momentarily mislaid his lyric gift. He kept his hat on, as though it was his badge of authorship, if not part of his uniform, and he amazed me with his pedantry.

I said, "So many books, doctor."

"This is not many," he said, dismissing my question. "I own lots more than these."

"What sort of books are they?"

"They are not books." He smiled at my ignorance.

"What are they?"

"They are my friends."

To him this sort of excruciating exchange was sheer poetry.

"Are you writing one yourself?"

"Yes." He showed me some closely typed pages. He wanted me to admire them, but when he had an inkling that I was reading them he snatched them away, saying, "These are unfinished chapters."

"A novel?"

He laughed a big hollow theatrical laugh. He then said, "I am not interested in fantasy, my friend!"

"Are novels fantasy?"

"Completely."

"A waste of time?"

"You have no idea."

"What are these chapters then?"

"Philosophy," he said, in a reverential way, savoring the word.

"What books have you published?"

His arm snaked to the shelf and he withdrew a hard cover book, which he handed to me.

I read the title, *Il Riparo delle Rosse Colline d'Argilla* ("The Shelter of the Red Hills of Clay").

"A volume of my poems," said Dr Pulvino.

"About Sicily?"

He sniggered slightly at my ignorance of geography. He said, "Tunisia. I went there for inspiration. You want to buy a copy?"

I had just bought two books that morning. Books are heavy, especially hardcovers. My method was to buy paperbacks, and read and discard them. I only bought new ones when I had nothing more to read. It was pointless to explain this to Dr Pulvino.

"Not now."

"The price is twenty thousand." That was thirteen dollars. No way.

"I'll pick it up in a bookstore."

"Impossible."

"I'll bet Mr Giarratana has it in his store."

"Mr Giarratana does not have it. You see, my friend, this book is out of print. This is one of very few copies left."

"I'm sure I'll be able to find it."

"Only I can supply you with one."

After that, whenever I saw him, he said, "Have you decided about the book?"

Dr Pulvino was one of a number of people in Siracusa who warned me to be careful of thieves. Mr Giarratana had mentioned "clippers" – bag-snatchers, known as *scippatore*. They were notorious in Sicily for their merciless efficiency, and I heard many stories of people who had lost passports, wallets, handbags, watches, jewelry. But perhaps because this was not the tourist season the thieves were on holiday.

There was "A Very Important Notice" displayed in each of Dr Pulvino's tiny rooms. "The hotel's esteemed guests, especially our lady guests, because of unpleasant incidents which have already happened, are advised, when going out of the hotel, to avoid taking any bags, or handbags, for the possible risk of becoming victims of bag-snatchers and even of being hurt. The manager Dr

Calogero Pulvino, together with the entire City of Syracuse, apologizes for this situation."

The next time I saw him I said, "You speak English."

"Without any doubt," said Dr Pulvino.

Another amphitheater, more broken columns, assorted marble slabs. Just by three pizzerias was the Fountain of Arethusa, with ducks bobbing in it. It is not really a Greek ruin. It is a place Siracusans take their kids and say, "Look at the duckies!" and throw pizza crusts at them. Probably the Greeks did the same thing. The Temple of Apollo was just down the street from Emporio Armani. The Catholic cathedral had been built into and around a Doric temple, probably of Athena, and so you could see Grecian columns inside and out, and crucifixes, and bleeding hearts, and gilded haloes, and more old columns than even Cicero had praised ("in his oration against Verres").

The exaggerated attention given in Siracusa, as in much of Italy, to all this guff about Greeks and Romans, all glory and harmony, was followed by silence, as though nothing else had happened in the last two thousand years. Nothing about the years of lecherous and satanic popes settling into big feather beds with their mistresses and fondling them under gilt crucifixes, or plotting murder, stranglings and poisonings in the Vatican cellars. Never a word about Pope Innocent VIII (1484–92), who commercialized the papacy and sold pardons, and who had a hooligan son by one of his mistresses whom he set up in style; nothing about Pope Alexander VI and his seven children, one of whom was Lucrezia Borgia, another Cesare Borgia, who was made a cardinal along with his uncle. Apart from the poisonings and murders, one of the highlights of Alexander VI's papacy was a bullfight that was held in the piazza of St Peter's to celebrate a victory over the Moors. Nor anything about Leo X, who handed out cardinal's hats to his cousins, or Sixtus IV, another murderer. Not relevant? But surely these were the ancestors and inspiration for Padre Carmelo and his Mafia monks at the Franciscan monastery in Mazzarino.

The Middle Ages had not occurred. There was never anything about the centuries of rape and pillage, cities destroyed by hairy Vandals or Ostrogoths in furry pelts; nothing about bubonic

plague or cholera; nothing about the thirteenth-century Hohen-
staufens, who goose-stepped all over Sicily; nothing about those
religious fanatics and show-offs, the Crusaders, who went clanking
around the island in their rusty suits of armor building castles and
sniffing out Muslims to murder for Christ; nothing about Muslims
and their weird depredations (though the occasional mutter about
"Saracens"); nothing about the Jewish expulsions, the cruelty and
intrigues, little villagers ratting on the local rabbi and then seeing
the old bearded Jew carted off or tortured; and never anything
about the war that ended just the other day, how they had
changed sides; and nothing about their cowardly little dictator –
just the mention of his name in polite company was immeasurably
worse than farting.

"Never mind Mussolini, look at the exquisite statue of
Archimedes," was the exhortation of people who couldn't put two
and two together. Or it was classical trivia: "Archimedes said
'Eureka!' in Siracusa," or "The philosopher Plato was made a
slave in Siracusa!" the Siracusans said, which was just about all
they knew of Plato.

Looking at glorious ruins always puts me in a bad mood. I
walked around instead. I saw a cake sale in a piazza. Cakes and
pies were stacked on a number of tables, and there were about
thirty people hawking them.

"Buy a cake," a woman said, as I slowed down to look at them.
"They are really delicious."

"I'm traveling. I don't have room."

"Where have you just come from?"

"Sardinia."

"Lovely place. Rocky. Natural. Unspoiled. Not like here at all,"
the woman said. And then, "Buy a small cake," she said. She
showed me two or three.

Some other women gathered around, boosting their baked goods,
all seeming very earnest.

"Are you trying to raise money for a particular purpose?" I
asked.

"Not for us. It is for the families in Bosnia."

That touched me. So the larger world and its disorder intruded
on this small, settled place. But in fact Bosnia was not very far

away. And when I gave them five dollars in Italian lire and wished them well, a woman chased me through the piazza with a bag of cookies.

The town was dedicated to one of its native daughters, Santa Lucia. But it was the Madonna of Tears who had produced the most miracles – people cured of blindness, deafness, gammy legs, blights, poxes and diseases, and an enormous sanctuary was being built in her honor outside Siracusa in the shape of a vast cement wigwam.

The low season might have meant poor business and hotel and restaurant closures and grumbling entrepreneurs, but it also meant that people had their towns to themselves. In Siracusa this took the form of the *passegiata* – the streets dense and chattering with promenading citizens. The streets and squares of the Ortygia were thronged on weekend nights with Siracusans of all ages walking, families with small children, lovers, groups of girls flirting with groups of boys; punks, lovers, scolding crones in widows' black bombazine, old shysters wearing sunglasses. Some walked dogs, or carried cats, or pushed infants in carriages. They swarmed among the ruins and shops and the pizza joints, buying ice creams or candy but not much else. It was all friendly – no suggestion of pickpockets, no aggression, just good humor.

It was a night-time turnout, and I had never seen such a thing anywhere. Frenchmen played boules under the trees, while their womenfolk walked the family dog. Spanish men met outside cafés, and yakked. Men in Corsica and Sardinia gathered on street corners and whispered. Some Arabs did the same in Marseilles. But never the whole family, never little children and old people and lovers and animals; and never at night. This was extraordinary and carnival-like, beginning just after dark and going on until eleven or so, the tramping up and down the cobbled streets, swarming around the fountains and the squares, everyone well-dressed and cheery.

They talked among themselves. They greeted and kissed and shook hands. They whispered and laughed. It was an old ritual of sharing – sharing the street, the air, the gossip; it was a respectable way for women to be allowed out, after the meal was cooked and the dishes were done. It was something the telephone or urban crime or traffic had done away with elsewhere. It probably had medieval origins. It was the way old friends and neighbors caught up with news, the way people met and wooed each other; the way they courted; the way people showed off a new hat or coat. The air was full of greetings and compliments. "Nice to see you! Beautiful hat! Sweet little child! God bless him!"

The next day they were all back at work. I was tempted to take a ferry from here to Malta, but there was only one a week and I had just missed it. I went to the fish market and noted the prices of the clams and oysters and octopus. There was not much fishing here, the fishmongers told me. These had come from Venice and Marseilles. The only local product was mussels, sold bearded in black clumps, the sort that are left to the seagulls on Cape Cod.

"You're traveling, eh?" the fishmonger said. "Sardinians – cordial people!"

This was typical. Italians seldom spoke ill of each other. Compliments warded off aggression, and while Italians could be seriously quarrelsome when they were cross they got no satisfaction in carping, and were not interested in nit-picking, which was why chatting to them was nearly always a pleasure. Of the Calabrese they said, "They're like us!" Of Neapolitans, they said, "Musical people!" Of Romans, "Clever! Cultured!" They knew that, putting it mildly, Sicily had its problems of under-development and poverty and organized crime, and so they were not quick to judge other parts of Italy. The worst they would venture was something like, "Up north? It is very hard sometimes to understand the way they speak."

That day I hiked out of town to the hill called Belvedere. Along the way there were tumbled villages thick with orange groves, laundry hanging from every balcony, prickly pear cactus growing wild, schoolchildren shrieking or else holding hands; an old mustached woman in black howling her hello to another passing crone, and in her garden a crucified Michelin man – fatso as a scarecrow; and the village street-sweeper going about his job using a seven-foot palm frond – more effective than a push-broom. I thought with a retrospective shudder of the chilly streets of Nice, and the South of France generally, all the skinny widows and their lapdogs, and their way of studiously refusing to see that this otherwise impeccable Riviera was awash in dogshit. Sicily had its sanitation problems, but dogshit was not one of them.

On my walk back I took a different route, by way of the Anapo river, and reaching the shore saw ahead of me twelve nuns in black habits waving their arms and strolling by the blue sea. It was a Sicilian combination of the bizarre, the religious, the humorous, the tender, and the surreal.

9

The Ferry *Villa* to Calabria

Instead of entering Messina on the way back, I stayed on the train, and the train and I were rolled on to the clanging deck of the ferry *Villa* – railway tracks were bolted to the deck. This shunting was done in jolting instalments, sections of three or four coaches at a time, uncoupled, lined up side by side until the whole train was on board, sixteen coaches. The whole railway train, minus its engine, physically transferred to the vessel, was then floated across the Straits of Messina.

Standing in the darkness of the steel-hulled *Villa* among the greasy train wheels, I heard a man's hoarse, pleading voice.

"I lost my arm."

It was too dark to see anyone, though I could hear the laborious pegging of a crutch or a cane knocking against the metal deck.

"Help me," the voice said.

I stepped back, and the noise I made gave me away and directed him to me.

"Give me something," he said. "I lost my arm."

He then dimly emerged from the soupy darkness and I smelled him more clearly than I saw him. The smell was stale bread and decaying wool, spiked with a hum of vinegary wine.

"Please," he said. And then, "No, I can't take it!"

My coins were clinking because he bumped them with the stump in his ragged sleeve.

"No arm! Put them in my pocket!"

All this was in the stinking darkness of the ship's hull, among the detached coaches of the train.

"Have a good trip," he said, and pegged past me, rapping his crutch, and I heard other passengers giving him money – not out of mercy, but in exchange for his blessing, out of superstition.

On deck with the departing Sicilians and the returning Calabrese, all of them munching sandwiches, I saw that we were
pulling out of Messina's harbor. Sicily had clouds the shape and
color of old laundry billowing over it, and the straits were windy
too, but except for white caps and blown froth it did not seem to
be a bad sea. This could have been just an illusion. A whirlpool
might make a low howling sound, but it is not usually visible until
you are on top of it.

The *Odyssey*'s whirlpool Charybdis ("Three times/from dawn to
dusk she spews . . . a whirling maelstrom . . .") is not fanciful; it
actually exists near Messina, on the Sicilian side, opposite the
small village of Ganzirri. Scylla, the six-headed monster with
twelve great tentacles, has not been sighted recently, but she is
always heard. At just the spot where Scylla "yaps abominably"
the sea-swells roll into the stone caverns on the Calabrian side,
where they make a gulping sound, audible to anyone on the water
– a familiar yapping to anyone who lives within earshot of the
cavernous seashore. This could easily be mistaken for the voice of
Scylla Ulysses heard, "a newborn whelp's cry, though she is huge
and monstrous."

Much of the *Odyssey*'s Mediterranean geography is either misleading or imaginary (I had passed the Islands of the Cyclops near
Catania, but didn't recognize them), yet occasionally, as in Bonifacio and here, the topographical description is so specific that I got
a thrill in matching it to the text. The art in Homer's lines still
precisely reflected nature. There was also a private satisfaction in
savoring the ways in which Ulysses managed to have a pretty bad
time. Homer's epic seldom celebrates the joys of seamanship or
marvelous landfalls. It is about delays and obstructions and messy
deaths. Ulysses' crew is nearly always complaining or fearful, and
the captain himself rather dislikes the gray sea and the fickle
winds, the toil of shipboard life, the distances, the inconveniences,
the dangers. Among many other things the Odyssey is a poem
about the frustrations and miseries of travel, and the long voyage
home; in a word, an epic of homesickness, greatly consoling to a
traveler reading it.

The Calabrians had cracked a ghoulish joke by naming a village
on the shore after the monster that had to eat six sailors at a time

("she takes,/from every ship, one man for every gullet"); in fact, Scilla was a little place nearby on the railway line to Naples and Rome, where this train was going. Above the shore here were great eroded slopes of steep hills, all settled and scraped bare, and like Sicily the landscape was mostly urbanized or settled. No hill existed in Italy without an antenna planted on it, or a fort, or a dome, or a crucifix. Italians fulfill themselves by building and re-organizing the landscape. It is as though nature has no interest for them until it has been improved by digging and urbanizing it. That is one thing Italians have in common with the Chinese. Another is a love of noodles. Yet another, an ancient belief in dragons.

It was a one-hour crossing of the Straits of Messina, and then the train was slung out of the ferry in sections and reconnected at Villa San Giovanni, which was just a ferry port and a mass of chanting signs. "Al Treno," "To the Train," "Au Train," "Zum Zug."

At a certain hour of the day in Italy, one of the more demoraliz-ing aspects of being in a forlorn little station like Villa San Giovanni was seeing a big comfortable express train that would be departing in ten minutes for Rome, arriving tomorrow, just as the shutters were being flung up in the bookstores and restaurants. The passengers on the Rome Express looked out at me, probably thinking *Poor sucker*, because they knew that I was just another peasant waiting for the branch-line train to Reggio, fifteen minutes down the line, on the toe of Italy's boot.

Twenty-three Italian soldiers, wearing maroon nightcaps with dangling blue pompoms, stood with me, and soon after the Rome Express moved importantly north, our little choo-choo went clinkety-clank south, to Reggio, which was dark and cold and windy. It was Sunday night in this poor town – it had once been the capital of Calabria but it had fallen on hard times, like most of the south. It too had been flattened by the 1908 earthquake that had destroyed Messina. Strangely, even after pacing up and down, the only hotel that I could find open in Reggio turned out to be the most expensive one of my trip, so far ($81), though hardly better than the rest of them.

Almost a hundred years ago the English writer George Gissing (born poor, wrote *New Grub Street*, married a prostitute) made a

record of a solitary and often melancholy trip around southern
Italy, which he called *By the Ionian Sea*. He stopped in Reggio and
saw "few signs of activity; the one long street, Corso Garibaldi, has
little traffic; most of the shops close shortly after nightfall, and then
there is no sound of wheels . . . the town is strangely quiet,
considering its size and aspect."

That was precisely what I reported to my diary, until around
seven in the evening I heard a loud commotion, and a howl of
human voices, and I asked a man in the doorway of the hotel,
"What's happening?"

"Nothing," he said in the local dialect, not *niente* but *ninte*.

So accustomed was he to the sound that it meant nothing to
him. But I should have known.

"You from around here?"

"Squillace," he said, and it seemed a very grim name.

"And you?"

"United States."

"Good. I got relatives there." From his agitated hand gesture
and his pursed lips, I was to understand that there were very many
of them.

It was Sunday night in Reggio and that meant the parade of
locals, great and small, old and young, male and female, the ritual
of the *passegiata* — that was the sound I heard. It fascinated me,
more there than in Siracusa, because the weather was colder. On
this foul, windy night in the small town of Reggio, in the depths of
winter dampness, the whole populace turned out to march, bundled up against the weather. It was a gentle mob scene, the loud
scuffing of their shoes, their chattering voices, up and down the
Corso Garibaldi, or milling around the piazza, on street corners,
talking, laughing, walking three or four abreast, about a quarter of
a mile and then back again, commandeering the main street.

The most remarkable thing to me was the controlled fury of it,
all the voices creating one loud, almost deafening drone, everyone
talking at once; that and the motion of the people in the street on
which there were no cars — not that they were specifically excluded,
but who in a little Fiat would risk facing all those tramping arm-
swinging Calabrians? This was a cheery event. It started round
about seven, and by ten everyone had gone home.

Obviously, George Gissing had not seen Reggio at a weekend (though he had seen it just before the earthquake brought it down). It was still true almost a century later that Reggio was just a little lighted place with darkness all around it – not wilderness or woods, but dry tiny villages set amid the strange and infertile landscape of rocks and ravines and dusty hills of Calabria. They were remote and forgotten places even now. People in the nearby village of Bova spoke a dialect that was nearer Greek than it was Italian, and it has been suggested that the people in this region had been yakking happily in Greek during the whole Roman era, speaking Latin to officials only when they had to. When Roman rule was supplanted by the Byzantines, Greek came back into vogue and was once again the language of commerce and the greater empire. None the less, for all this classicism and all the civilizations that had come and gone, there were villages in Calabria that still had no electricity or running water.

No wonder so many Italians said goodbye here. Near the port of Messina, in the poorest region of Italy, Reggio was the last landscape tens of thousands of emigrants saw before they boarded ships for America; Reggio was less a town than a jumping-off place.

The ones in the *passegiata* were the ones who had stayed behind. Eating pasta, drinking wine, I watched them from the window of a restaurant while I scribbled. The idea that most of them had relatives in the United States made them seem resolute, if not defiant, to me, and it was as though they were celebrating the fact that they were still there, carrying on after all these years, proudly rooted in the peculiarly stony soil of their native land.

Again, I seemed to be the only guest of the hotel. That suited me. The empty foyer, the shadowy corridors, my gloomy cubicle – this was an appropriate setting. I was reading the copy of *Frankenstein* I had bought in Siracusa, to put myself in the mood for the gothic darkness of Calabria. And that night I read how Dr Frankenstein had been born in Naples, when his parents were passing through.

I was not heading for Naples. The next day I bought a ticket to Metaponto, half a day's train ride in the other direction, in the arch of the Italian boot. Usually I just rattled to a new place and

hoped for the best; but today I had a specific objective at
Metaponto.

After Reggio there was a succession of straggling settlements by
the sea, and some dilapidated vineyards crowded by factories and
junk heaps. It was a view of the Mediterranean that was new to
me, mile upon mile of empty stony beaches, here and there some
fishermen venturing out in small wooden dinghies. Inland on the
sea-facing slopes there were hamlets of houses, some of them
ancient-looking, many of them with great cracks in their walls
which could have been produced by the 1908 earthquake. There
were newer houses, but they seemed as ruinous as the old ones.
The soil looked infertile, much of it white chalky clay plowed into
clods at Brancaleone, and sluiced into stony gullies at Bova, where
a dialect of Greek was still spoken.

The beaches were littered but there was no one on them, even at
Locri, one of the bigger towns. Albichiara was one of those old
yellow villages built high on a ridge, almost at the skyline ("against
the barbarians"), and in the plains below it were fruit trees and
olive groves. The station at Soverato was crowded with people
clamoring to board this train – which was going to the distant
provincial capital, Taranto, and terminating at the city of Bari on
the Adriatic. But not all the people were boarding, many were
there to say goodbye.

"Have a good trip!"

"Bye, Grandma!"

A priest joined me in my empty compartment. He had the evil
eye, of course. So no one else came in, and those who passed in the
corridor averted their eyes and hurried past.

Squillace was not as ugly as its name suggested. It was Virgil's
"ship-wrecking Scylaceum" and in Gissing's time was squalid:
"Under no conditions could inhabited Squillace be other than an
offense to eye or nostril." But this was only the settlement around
the station. The village itself was five miles inland and was perhaps
still offensive.

Spivs, little old women in black, nuns whose noses were longer
than their bonnets, salesmen with crates, and fussing couples got
on at Catanzaro, which was a good-sized town among ferocious-
looking cliffs of dusty clay. After the desolate grandeur of the great

sweeping fields and valleys littered with stones, the hills near Cutro were so scored with erosion they seemed covered with heavy folded drapes of clay. The redeeming feature was the glittering sea; no waves, no swell, just placid water nudging and sloshing at this arid edge of Italy.

Crotone was a port with fields and factories around it, and a statue of the Virgin at the station. Cape Colonna just at the south side of town was also known as Capo di Nau, a corruption of the Greek word *naos*, meaning temple. The Greek temple of Hera, made up of forty-eight marble columns, had stood on the headland for hundreds of years, but was torn down in a fit of militant piety in the sixteenth century by the Bishop of Crotone. The columns were then broken up and used to build the bishop's palace. The earthquake of 1783, which had devastated this whole area and much of Sicily, knocked down the palace, and the remainder of the temple was used to strengthen Crotone's harbor. Many of those marble slabs were still in place.

"This squalid little town of today has nothing left from antiquity." What George Gissing said of Crotone could have been said of hundreds of places in Sicily and Calabria.

The priest got off at Crotone; a quarreling couple and an old woman took his place in my compartment. As soon as we drew out of Crotone a nun ambushed us, passing out holy cards: the Virgin on one side, a calendar of holy days on the reverse. I accidentally dropped my card and before I could retrieve it the old woman pounced and snatched it up, then brought it to her mouth and kissed it, in a kind of greedy veneration. She looked up at me and handed it over – reproachfully, I thought. I kept the card as a bookmark in *Frankenstein* and for weeks afterward, whenever I came across it, I thought of that old woman rescuing it from the indignity of a train floor and planting a kiss on it as a way of propitiating the Madonna. I saw stranger manifestations of religion in this trip but I remembered that gesture for its passion.

The starkness, the emptiness, the yellow-gray slopes and stones, the stucco houses, the bare hills matching them, the exhausted-looking soil: except for the vineyards, places like Strongoli and Torre Melissa looked like places I had seen in rural China, in the poverty-stricken regions of Gansu and Ningxia, just as poor and as hard to till.

The sea was almost irrelevant here, and it was as though Mediterranean culture did not penetrate beyond the narrow beach. The towns were a little inland or else on hills, with fortifications. There were no fishing-boats for miles here, no boats at all. No marina, no docks, nothing that hinted at recreation. It was too cold for swimming, but even so, no one walked along the beach. So the blue coast was more like a barrier, a use I saw it put to in other places on my trip: the Mediterranean as a moat.

Great snow-covered peaks rose behind Sibari − wholly unexpected, like the first glimpse I had gotten of the snowy crater of Mauna Kea on the Big Island of Hawaii. Mountains seemed so unlikely, and the snow was an added bonus. I looked at my map and guessed it to be Monte Pollino, 7,400 feet high.

And Sibari itself, this insignificant railway station in a wide dusty valley in Calabria, deserted by peasants (who had fled to Naples or Brooklyn), where no one got on or off the train, where all I remember was the glimpse of a snowy peak − this place that passed in the blink of an eye was once the rich Greek town of Sybaris, whose inhabitants were so hoggishly self-indulgent, living in such luxury, that their lifestyle had given a new word to the language, sybaritic.

I alighted at Metaponto and accustomed as I was to small and squalid places I was surprised by the smallness of Metaponto.

My intention was to leave here as soon as possible. I had another book in mind, that I had read years ago, that filled me with a sense of mission. Metaponto was the nearest coastal town to Aliano, which was the scene of Carlo Levi's brilliant memoir, *Christ Stopped at Eboli*. The title of the book is slightly confusing. Levi was quoting a local maxim in Aliano: the point was that Christ stopped at Eboli, fifty miles away (near Salerno), and never got as far as Aliano, in the benighted province of Basilicata, where the people regarded themselves as heathens and savages, living on a crumbling hill.

Carlo Levi, a Florentine Jew and a medical doctor, was banished to Aliano in 1935 because of his anti-fascist views (the Abyssinian war had just begun: Italian machine-guns against African spears), and in this obscure and distant village (Aliano is called Gagliano in the book) he stayed for an entire year. He languished under a casual form of house-arrest, *confino*. There was no chance of escape: Aliano was the Italian equivalent of Siberia. Levi kept a diary, he painted pictures, he attended to the medical problems of the people in the village, and after he left he wrote his book, which is a masterful evocation of life in a remote place. He got to know everyone in the village. The book is unclassifiable in the best sense: it is travel, anthropology, philosophy; most of all, it is close and compassionate observation.

I had been avoiding inland places, but Aliano was near enough to the Mediterranean shoreline to be on my route. I wanted to go there, just to see it. In *The Inner Sea*, Robert Fox wrote of a trip he took to Aliano in 1983, and of the mayor, Signora Santomassimo, who said that Donna Caterina "is still alive, over ninety – you can hear her shrieking at the moon on some nights, mad as a hatter."

Now, twelve years later, the old woman was almost certainly dead, but that compelling description roused me. What about the rest of them? What of the village itself, which is such a strong presence in Carlo Levi's book? There were other details that I wondered about, too. For example, there was a fascinating description in the book of a church at the nearby village of Sant'Arcangelo which contained the actual horns of a dragon. People went to look at the horns. The dragon had terrorized the whole region: "it devoured the peasants, it carried off their daughters, filled the land with its pestiferous breath, and destroyed the crops." The strongest lord of the region, Prince Colonna of Stigliano, had the encouragement of the Virgin Mary ("Take heart, Prince Colonna!" the Virgin said). He slayed the dragon, cut off its head, and built the church to enshrine the dragon's horns.

From Metaponto I could easily reach to Sant'Arcangelo and see the dragon's horns. It was only about fifteen miles to Aliano. And I was lucky to have chosen to get off at Metaponto, because in the summer it welcomed tourists, and although the summer was far off, there were facilities here that did not exist in the places I had come through.

By the time I had found a car to rent, the day was almost gone.

"You can see the ruins," Mr Gravino said.

"I want to drive to Aliano."

"It's a very small place," he said. "You might be disappointed."

"If it is very small I will be very happy," I said.

I spent the night in Metaponto and early the next morning drove up the flat valley to Pisticci and Stigliano (where the dragon-slayer had lived) and beyond. It was a sunny day, and there were green fields beside the shrunken river, and yet the sense of remoteness here was powerful, not merely because the region was so rural and empty, but more because of the condition of the houses, which looked very poor and neglected. A branch-line train had once run through here but it was gone and the stations were ruined. Many houses were in a state of disrepair; many had been abandoned. It was that look of old Ireland you see in book plates that show the effects of the potato famine – collapsed roofs, dead animals, weedy fields. This was also a region from which many people had migrated and no one else had moved in to reoccupy it. It was both the prettiest and certainly the poorest area I had seen so far in the Mediterranean.

It was also a land almost without signposts, and the signs that existed were unhelpful, directing me to the road for the distant cities of Potenza and Salerno.

I saw three men on an embankment and when I slowed down I saw that they carried long worn poles. They were goat-herds, two old men and a young man in his twenties. Their goats were grazing in the meadow just below the road.

"I am looking for Aliano."

"Up there."

They indicated a cluster of old buildings on the crest of a steep dry hill.

Then I asked them about their goats – was there enough grazing here? – just small-talk, because I wanted to hear their voices, I wanted to study their faces. They were as Levi described the peasants hereabouts – short, dark, with round heads, large eyes, thin lips. "Their archaic faces do not stem from the Romans, Greeks, Etruscans, Normans, or any of the other invaders who have passed through their land, but recall the most Italic types." He goes on: "They have led exactly the same life since the beginning of time, and History has swept over them without effect."

Aliano exactly crowned the hill. I had not expected it to be so high up, but of course the height of a village here did not indicate its importance. The poorer and weaker peasants put their villages in these almost inaccessible places. All around it was dry light-brown soil, and some olive trees with grayish leaves and gnarled trunks, and tussocky grass.

A narrow, winding road led to the summit and, climbing it, I could see that the village was not at the top of the hill, but rather spread on the ridge between two steep ravines.

Ahead, an old woman laden with two pails, a shovel, and a bag of freshly picked spinach was laboring up the road. She wore a kerchief on her head, and a black skirt, and an apron – the uniform of the peasant in the deep south of rural Italy. I slowed down and saw that she was perspiring, gasping from the effort of carrying all that paraphernalia.

"Please, I am looking for the house of Dr Levi."

"It is on the other side of the village."

"Far?"

"Yes. Very far."

"Do you want a ride?"

"No," she said, not out of pride or obstinacy, I guessed, but because of the impropriety of it. She was a poor old woman carrying more than she could manage, but still it was wrong for her to ride with a strange man. Levi had something to say about that too. As a young unmarried man he had to be careful not to cause a scandal by appearing to compromise the virtue of an Aliano woman. That meant he could never be alone with any woman.

The houses were built so close to the edge of the hill that the walls of some of them were flush with the sides of the cliffs. Between the upper part of the town and the lower part there was a small square and at its edge a precipice, still known as "the Fossa del Bersagliere, because in earlier days a captured *bersagliere* [infantryman] from Piedmont had been thrown into the ditch by brigands."

The old woman had said "Very far," but I knew it was nothing

like that. I left my car at the edge of the upper village and walked
down the narrow street. Passing cave entrances that had doors on
them, I thought of China again, how I had seen people near
Datong, in a landscape just like this, living in the hollowed-out
sides of mountains. But these were wine cellars.

An old man in a cloth cap sitting on a wooden folding chair
near the main square smiled at me and said hello. We talked a
while, and then I told him what I was looking for.

"Yes. Levi's house is down there," he said. "There is a sign on
it. There is a museum near it."

As we were talking, another man approached. He was small,
wrinkled, smiling, welcoming. He was Giuseppe DeLorenzo. His
friend was Francesco Grimaldi.

"Grimaldi is a good name," I said. "Your family rules
Monaco."

"My family is all dead," he said. But he liked the joke. "That is
another family."

They offered to show me where Carlo Levi's house was, and so
we walked to the lower village, on the other part of the saddle, on
the ridge. I was aware of being very high, of being able to see the
plain stretching south to Metaponto and the sea. We were on a
steep pedestal of dry mud and brush and from the street that
connected the two crumbling parts of Aliano you could look
straight down the Fossa del Bersagliere, 150 feet to a ledge of olive
trees, and then another drop.

"You call this a gorge?" I said, using the word *gola*.

"No. A *burrone*." And he grinned at me. When I checked I saw
that this word might have come from the Arabic *burr*, for land of
wild slopes.

We walked down the hot cobbled street, the sun beating on our
heads. Flowers all over the valley gave it color and perspective,
especially the poppies, which glowed a brilliant crimson against
the dust.

We were passing some squarish crumbling houses.

"You have to see this," Francesco said. "This is the historic part
of Aliano. It is very old."

"The palazzo," Giuseppe said.

Another crumbling house.

"The signorina's palazzo."

"Where is the signorina?" I took this to be the Donna Caterina, "mad as a hatter," who was said to bay at the moon.

"Dead. The whole family is dead."

"What was the family's name?"

"The family Scardacione."

We walked down the cobbled street to Piazza Garibaldi, though "piazza" gives the wrong impression – this square was hardly bigger than the floor of a two-car garage, to DeLorenzo's house. The house was ancient, a section of cracked stucco attached to a row of stucco boxes. His cat yowled at me and crawled into a strangely-made clay contraption that looked like a large bird-house fixed to the wall of the house.

"What's that?"

"A chimney."

He reached over and removed a large brick from under the shelf where the cat had taken cover.

"See? It's an oven. For making bread."

Now I saw that it was a small, scorched fireplace. The cat was curled up on the shelf where the loaf was placed; the chimney flue was connected to the firepit, where Giuseppe was replacing the brick. It was an artifact from another age, and brought to mind the hard, simple labor of bread-making that also involved someone toting faggots of wood to use as fuel. I had seen small blackened bread-ovens similar to this in Inca villages in the Andes.

"It's very old," I said.

Giuseppe made the Italian gesture of finger-flipping that meant "An incredible number of years – you have no idea."

"When was the last time it was used for bread?"

"This morning," Giuseppe said, and then barked an unintelligible word.

A wooden shutter flew open and banged against the wall of the house. A woman, obviously Signora DeLorenzo, stuck her head out of the window and groaned at her husband, who made another demand, unintelligible to me.

The woman was gone for a moment and then appeared and handed down from the window an iron key ten inches long.

I greeted the old woman. She jerked her head and clicked her teeth. Meaning: I acknowledge your presence but I am much too distracted to return your greeting.

"Follow me," Giuseppe said.

We went down the sloping cobbled street to a narrow road that lay against the steep hillside. A little fence and a steel gate surrounded a weedy garden and a grape arbor. Francesco dragged the gate open.

"A doctor came here," Giuseppe said, slotting the key into a wooden door in the hillside. "He was like you. Just traveling. He told me a good thing. 'Worlds can't meet worlds, but people can meet people.'"

"That's very nice."

"Very wise," Francesco said. "See, worlds are big. Worlds can't meet worlds."

"But people can meet people," Giuseppe said, entering the cavernous room.

"So who was this wise doctor?"

"Just a traveler!" Giuseppe beckoned me into the dark room.

It was cool inside, with a musty earthen smell of stale wine and damp dust and decayed wood. As I asked what it was, my eyes grew accustomed to the darkness and I saw some large wooden casks set on racks.

"It is a *cantina*," he said, gesturing in the vinegary coolness. He was using the word in its precise sense, for "cellar." "In the Aliano dialect we call this *una grota*" – a cave.

Apart from the six wine casks, there was also a wine press that had been taken apart, and a great deal of dusty paraphernalia – rubber tubes, glasses, bottles, pitchers, buckets.

"What do you call this?" I said, tapping a cask.

"In Italian it's a *botte*, but we call it a *carachia*," Giuseppe said, using a word that was not in any Italian dictionary. "Please be seated."

Francesco drew off a pitcher of wine and with this he filled three glasses. We toasted. Francesco downed his in two gulps. Giuseppe and I took our time.

Sitting at a rough wooden table in the semi-darkness of the little cave, the bright white day glaring in the doorway, I asked the men their ages. Francesco was seventy-two, DeLorenzo was seventy. They were little boys at the time Carlo Levi had lived as an exile in the village.

"You must have seen Carlo Levi," I said.

"Oh, yes," Francesco said. "I remember him well. I was a small boy at school."

"Have you read his book?"

"Yes, yes," both of them said.

I had a strong feeling this was not true, yet as it was the book that had put Aliano on the map they had a civic duty to say that they had read it, even if they had not.

"He was a doctor," I said. "Did he ever take care of you or your parents?"

"Doctor? He was no doctor," Francesco said, and poured more wine for us.

We toasted again, and I recalled how on his first day in the village, and almost the first page of the book, Levi was asked to cure a man stricken with malaria. Levi asked why the man was in such a bad way (he died soon after) and he was told that there was no doctor in the village. So, in addition to being an exile, he was Aliano's doctor.

The men smiled at me.

"Carlo Levi was a writer," Francesco said. "A very intelligent man. He was writing most of the time."

"We saw him writing!" Giuseppe said.

According to the book, which Levi began (so he said) in 1943, some seven years after leaving Aliano, Levi sketched pictures, and went for walks, and tended the sick. Because of his status, an anti-fascist political prisoner in a village whose mayor boasted that he had been described as "the youngest and most fascist mayor in the province of Matera," Levi was hardly likely to be seen writing in public.

"We would see him walking up and down." Francesco got up and walked a few steps, swinging his arms. "He would be writing the whole time."

"What did the village people think of him?"

"We put up a statue of him!" Francesco said. "That's what we thought of him!"

"Thanks very much," Giuseppe said, as Francesco filled his glass again. "He's buried in our cemetery! You can visit his grave!"

Francesco was urging me to finish my wine so that he could fill my glass again. It was red wine, strongly flavored with a dusty aftertaste, and drinking it in the cool shadows of the *cantina* with the full glare from the doorway in my eyes I quickly became dizzy. None the less, I obliged, because I liked talking to these two hospitable men.

They were recognizable from the book. It was the first feeling I had had when I encountered the woman with the buckets toiling up the hill. She had looked at me as though at another species and had turned away. The men were small and compact, the old Italic round face and large eyes and thin lips. Their language was different and they were proud of that. But there was something more, a greater difference, the very thing that Levi wrote about. The sense in which the villagers felt they were regarded as not Christians, not even human. "We're not thought of as men but simply as beasts, beasts of burden, or even less than beasts, mere creatures of the wild. They at least live for better or worse, like angels or demons, in a world of their own, while we have to submit to the world of Christians, beyond the horizon, to carry its weight and to stand comparison with it."

Levi had written a great deal about the language. Their word *crai*, for tomorrow, was a version of the Latin *cras*, but it also meant for ever and never. Yes, Giuseppe laughed, that is our word, and he was delighted that I used it.

"This is a lovely village, not a prison," I said, my happiness fueled with wine.

"Who said it was a prison?" Francesco said.

"For Carlo Levi it was a prison," I said. "He was sent here by the police."

"Because we are so isolated," Francesco said. "There was no road, nothing at all, just a path. We had no water, no electricity."

"I remember when the electricity came," Giuseppe said. "And the water for drinking."

"Oh, sure," Francesco said. "Before that it was just candles, and getting water from a well. That meant a long walk down the hill."

"I didn't mean to say that Aliano was a prison."

"Not a prison at all. Just far!"

"And full of fascists," I said.

"Yes, it was all fascists," Francesco said. "But I'll tell you one thing. The police liked Levi a lot."

This was not true, according to the book, but if it allowed the men to take pride in the village and not be ashamed, that was all right with me. In fact, the police had from time to time made life difficult for Levi, who was prohibited from leaving the village. This was enforced. The limit of his world was the boundary of Aliano. "The surrounding lands were forbidden territory, beyond the Pillars of Hercules."

Meanwhile we were still at the table, in the little wine cave, drinking and talking. Levi himself had spoken of the hospitality of the people, how they would share whatever they had, how attentive they could be in the presence of strangers.

"Was he tall or short?" I asked. "What was his face like? Very kind, I imagine."

Giuseppe considered this. He said, "A strange face, of course."

"Why strange?"

"Well, he wasn't Italian."

"Yes. He came from Florence."

"No. He came from another country – far away."

People in Aliano looked upon strangers from the north as though they came from another world, Levi had written, "almost as if they were foreign gods."

"I'm sure it was Florence," I said.

"He was a Brega," Francesco said. "He had a foreign face."

What was this "Brega"? I tried to think of a country that it might apply to, but I drew a blank. I asked each man to repeat the word. Still it sounded incomprehensible to me.

"If he was a Brega," I said, using the word, "then where did he come from?"

"From far away."

"Not Italy?"

"No. Maybe Russia," Giuseppe said.

This seemed pretty odd. His Italian-ness was the whole point of *Christ Stopped at Eboli*: an Italian from Florence was exiled to a village in the south of Italy, and living with such a strange breed of

Italians he felt as though he was "a stone that had dropped from the sky."

"This word 'Brega,' is that his nationality?"

"Yes," Francesco said, and he could not imagine why I did not understand him.

Then the light dawned. I said, "Are you saying *Ebraica*?"

"Yes."

Two syllables, four syllables, what was the difference, the word meant Jew, like our word Hebraic. He was no Italian – he was a Hebrew!

And so sixty years and twenty-three printings of the book in English, and twice that in Italian, and fame, and literary prizes, and a world war and the fall of fascism – none of these had made much difference. The man who had suffered exile and made Aliano famous in this wonderful book was not an Italian after all, but just a Jew.

These two men were not anti-semites. They were villagers. Everyone who visited was measured by the standards of the village, and when it came to nationality the standards had strict limits.

By this time all of us were full of wine. I stood up and staggered and said, "I have to go. I want to see Levi's house. And then I want to go to Sant'Arcangelo."

"A lovely place."

"There are said to be the horns of a dragon in the church."

"That's true. A lovely church."

Francesco stacked the tumblers that we had used for the wine, and outside he used his enormous key to lock the door to the cavern.

"I imagine this historic part of town is old," I said.

"Very old," Giuseppe said.

"Probably fourteenth or fifteenth century," I said.

Francesco laughed so hard I could see his molars and his tooth stumps and his tongue empurpled with his own wine.

"No! Before Christ!" he said. "Some of this was built in the ancient times."

And walking back up the narrow road to the piazza and the edge of the ravine they went on encouraging me to share their belief that the village of Aliano – many of these same buildings, in fact – had existed for the past two thousand years.

Because of our drinking – almost two hours of it – the lunch hour had passed. I was dazed from the alcohol and dazzled by the sun. They pointed me in the direction of Levi's house, and there I went and found it locked. It was high, at the top of a steep street off the crooked Via Cisterna, and faced south. It was signposted *Casa di Confina*, and it had not been renovated, only preserved, with a crumbling wall around it, the shutters broken and ajar. There were two small hilltop villages in the distance, Sant'Arcangelo and Roccanova, each one "a streak of white at the summit of a bare hill, sort of miniature imaginary Jerusalem in the solitude of the desert."

I sat on Levi's porch in the shade, among the broken chunky walls of stucco and brick, the tiled roofs sprouting weeds, broken paving stones and ceramic shards and dusty cobbles. It was all poor, and lovely, and primitive, with no charm but a definite warmth of a savage kind. Its height was part of its beauty, so close to the blue sky, the clouds, the enormous view across the ravine to the sea.

There I stayed until I regained my balance, and then in the coolness of the afternoon I walked back through the village, noting the little quotations from the book, written on tiles, many of them not complimentary at all: " . . . *coni, piagge di aspetto maligno, come un paesaggio lunare*" ("cones, slopes of an evil aspect, like a lunar landscape").

Some students were sketching pictures of an old house in the town.

"Do you live here?" I asked.

"No. We're art students," one of them, a young woman, said. "We're from Eboli. Where the book is set."

"Have you read the book?"

"No," she said.

I said, "The meaning of the title is that Christ stopped at Eboli. The Savior didn't get as far as Aliano."

They smiled at me, looking incredulous, and perhaps thinking that I was wrong – that Carlo Levi was a man from Aliano who had written a book about their home town of Eboli.

The cemetery was beyond the top of the town in a grove of junipers. Some old women were tending a grave there, weeding a flower-bed, digging, their fatigue giving them a look of grief. The graves were of marble and granite, sarcophagi the shape of small cottages, with flowers and portraits of the dead in niches in their façades.

Levi's grave was the smallest, the most modest in the place, a gray slate stone: *Carlo Levi 29.11.1902–4.1.1975.*

Some birds were chirping in the junipers and on the gate of the cemetery was another quotation from the book, referring to this spot as "*il luogo meno triste,*" a less sad place than the village itself.

How strange, the unusual power of a book to put a village this small on the map. It was also strange that this region was full of villages as obscure and poor as this one. It did not seem to me that Aliano had changed much. Already Levi was partly mythical, but one of the characteristics of Aliano he had described was the way the people did not distinguish between history and legend, myth and reality.

I was both uplifted and depressed by the visit. The village was unchanged, the people were as enigmatic as those he had described: good people, but isolated, bewildered, amazed at the world. I was uplifted because it was a solitary discovery; depressed because the National Alliance was part of the coalition government. That was the new name for the neo-fascist party. There were fascists in power once again in Italy. The Ministries of Agriculture, Posts, Environment, Cultural Affairs, and Transport all had neo-fascist ministers; and at least one of them was still publicly praising Mussolini.

It was growing dark. I hurried back to Metaponto. I dropped off my rental car, because it was too dark, too late to go to Sant'Arcangelo to see the dragon's horns.

From Metaponto to Taranto on the coastal railway line there were miles of pine woods and pine barrens on a flat plain stretching inland from the wide sandy coast, and there were dunes nearer the shore covered with scrub and heather, some of the pines twisted sideways by the strong onshore wind. This counts as wilderness in

Italy, which has little or none of it – about twenty miles of empty beach, no road, no people.

A suddenness of scrappy settlements was a warning of Taranto and its smokestacks, its fearful-looking outskirts, depots and docks and freighters. Almost everyone in the train piled out at Taranto – youths, old people, nuns, and a Japanese girl who seemed terribly confused.

The Japanese girl, another solitary wanderer who had yet to master the language, asked me in basic Italian whether I was also getting out here.

"No. I am going to Bari," I said. "Do you speak English?"

"*Poco.*"

"What about Italian?"

"*Poco.*"

"How long have you been in Italy?"

"One week, but I have studied Italian for four years."

She was going to Alberobello, but where was the Taranto bus station? And did the bus go to Alberobello?

My map showed Alberobello to be a tiny hamlet some distance to the north. What was there?

"A certain building," the Japanese girl said. "Very old."

"A church?"

"I do not know."

"A pretty building?"

"I do not know."

"Why are you going there?"

My question bewildered her, but after I made myself understood she showed me a guidebook, in Japanese, filled with ugly pictures the size of postage stamps.

"This is the most popular guide in Japan," she said. "It says to go to Alberobello."

"Good luck," I said. "But you should also be careful."

"The Italian men," she said, and compressed her face in consternation. "They say, 'Let's eat,' or 'Come to my house.' I always say no, but they still ask. I think they are dangerous."

Off she went to an uncertain fate. I boarded the train again and it swung inland, crossing the top of Italy's heel through gullies and rocky ravines and a shattered-looking landscape. Seeing ruined and cracked houses at Palagiano and Castellaneta, I turned to an old man near me.

"The war?"

"The earthquake."

Dust and yellow clay and rock gave way to flatness and agriculture, vineyards and vegetable fields, then the poor suburbs of Bari.

I finished reading *Frankenstein*, sad that it was over. "I am ... the fallen angel ... Everywhere I see bliss, from which I alone am irrevocably excluded. I was benevolent and good; misery made me a fiend. Make me happy and I shall again be virtuous." Also, I noted, the monster was a vegetarian: "My food is not that of man; I do not destroy the lamb and the kid to glut my appetite; acorns and berries afford me sufficient nourishment."

It had been cold and windy at Taranto, and the people were dressed unfashionably in sturdy clothes for the bad weather. But here in Bari the weather was pleasant, and I decided to stay for a while to do laundry and make phone calls and plan for the journey ahead. I had run out of books to read. Bari seemed to me a useful city in every sense. It had bookstores and restaurants and inexpensive hotels. It had a concert hall and an ancient fort. It was small-scale, everything in the city was reachable on foot.

There was an air of unfussy helpfulness and goodwill in Bari that I put down to its being a Mediterranean port which dealt more with people than with cargo. With Ancona and Brindisi it was one of the great ferry ports of the Adriatic. The fact that it was a busy port meant that it had to be efficient. At the moment the ferries to Croatia were suspended, but there were numerous ferries to Greece and there were four a week to Durrazzo (Durrës) in Albania.

I ran into a man in Bari who said that if I stayed another week he would take me cross-country skiing.

"You mean there's enough snow in southern Italy for cross-country skiing in March?"

"Plenty," he said. His name was Ricardo Caruso, he was a fresh-air fiend after my own heart. He hiked, he rock-climbed, he skied.

I told him I had been to Aliano.

"That's a good place," he said. "Padula's also good. There's an old ruined abbey near Padula. Hidden – and so beautiful."

Having established some rapport, I asked Ricardo about the Albanians who had escaped from their country and come to Bari in their thousands in big rusty ships, so laden with refugees that the ships were on the verge of foundering. At first the Italian government had admitted many of them on political grounds. This charity provoked an outcry: What shall we do with these indigent Albanians?

It was only an over-nighter from Albania to Bari. What if thousands more came?

Thirty thousand more did arrive, very soon after. Some worked as waiters or manual laborers. Many joined the beggars on Bari's streets – panhandlers often advertised themselves on placards as "Albanian Refugee" or "Ex-Yugoslavia," meaning Croatian.

"It was terrible," Ricardo said, with such feeling that I dropped the subject.

I asked a woman at my hotel. What exactly was the story on the Albanians?

She made a grieving sound, and she was so ashamed, she said, she could not talk about it.

"A tragedy," she said, and turned away. "Please."

I finally found a man in Bari willing to talk, and more than that, he drove me to the Bari Stadium, where the Albanians had been held until they could be repatriated.

"Thirty thousand of them," Giacinto said. "Most of them young men, all of them screaming. But we have problems, we couldn't let them in."

There were Albanian graffiti still scrawled over the stadium door, the largest motto read in Italian: *We are with God, God is with us.*

"The worst was when some of them got loose," Giacinto said. "So they'd be running all over the place – in the city, all over the streets. Listen, this is a nice city. Then you'd look up and see some skinny strange Albanian guy, his eyes like a madman's. He'd run into a restaurant to hide, or into a hairdresser's. And the police would have to drag him out bodily, while he's struggling and screaming in Albanian."

Giacinto smiled at the weirdness of it.

"Misery turned them into fiends," I said, quoting *Frankenstein*.

"True. And this is a little country. Business is awful. What are we supposed to do?"

Three days of good meals in Bari set me up, too. Gnocchi was a local specialty, and so was risotto made with champagne; eggplant, olives, cauliflower, and fruit and fish. My laundry was done. I had books to read, among them one by Italo Svevo, who had lived in Trieste, where I was headed. I had some more maps. Everyone in Bari had been pleasant to me.

I went on my way up the Adriatic coast in a mood of optimism. For consolation and mothering, I thought, no country could match Italy.

The Ferry *Clodia* from Chioggia

With fascists in the Italian government for the first time since the war, I was interested to see whether the trains would be running on time. But even in Christian Democratic times they had nearly always been punctual. Italians told me that in the era of Mussolini, which boasted of railway promptness, the trains were often late. These days Italian State Railways were so eager to please that they printed *Buon Viaggio* in big blue letters on each square of toilet paper – under the circumstances creating a rather puzzling and ambiguous impression of farewell.

In the recent Italian election, the neo-fascists of the National Alliance Party had helped Silvio Berlusconi's Forza Italia party win a majority. The Minister of Transport was the neo-fascist who had called Mussolini "the greatest statesman of the century." Another party in Berlusconi's coalition was the Northern League, which was pledged to regain parts of Slovenia and Croatia and to create a Greater Italy once again. Rijeka in Croatia had once been the Italian city of Fiume. An Italian minister flew to Trieste and, directing his comments at Slovenia, screamed, "On your knees!"

It was so much like old times that I would not have been surprised to see a gesticulating politician call for another invasion of Ethiopia. I hated noticing politics, but this verged on surrealism and could not be ignored. It was the anti-communist element in Italian fascism, and the protection of the Vatican – in habitual collusion with fascists – that allowed Klaus Barbie and other Nazis to be spirited to Bolivia. There "Klaus Altman" formed "The Fiancés of Death," an underground organization which smuggled drugs and arms, and committed the occasional murder. After many years Barbie was caught and extradited to France, to the annoyance of the neo-fascists.

Having left Bari, I was in a noisy compartment, with a priest and several old women and some businessmen, on my way to Ancona via Foggia and San Benedetto del Tronto. It was such a crowded train that these passengers had no choice but to join the priest and his evil eye in this compartment.

"If Jesus came on earth to save souls, huh, why didn't he come sooner in world history?" a hectoring woman asked the elderly priest. "Eh? What about all the others before him, for all these thousands of years?"

"Good question," the priest said.

Some other people were chattering about politics, so I asked about the neo-fascists. What did they actually stand for?

"I'm not sure," one man said. He was middle-aged, tweedily dressed, possibly a lawyer, and was headed to Ancona. I addressed the question to him because he had the kindliest demeanor. "No one is sure. The neo-fascists say they have broken with the past."

And yet I had the feeling they idolized Mussolini. After all, the party was formed by old-line fascists. But I hesitated to say this.

"What's on their minds – race, imperialism, or immigration?"

"Probably all three. They also talk about the work ethic and crime and lazy people and wasted taxes."

The man sitting beside him was blunter. He said, "They want a police state."

Later on, a young man handed me a leaflet at a railway station. The message on it was that the neo-fascists were intent on suppressing personal freedom, democracy and the press, and on limiting rights generally.

At Foggia some people got off and two nuns got on. One with the meaty face and bulldog jowls of J. Edgar Hoover took a nip of brandy from beneath her robes and poured the whole thing into a glass of orange juice. She then glugged it down. Her black-robed companion, a dead ringer for the singer Meatloaf, quaffed a similar drink. It was 11:30 in the morning. They told the rest of the people in the compartment that it was the feast day of Santa Maria Antigua and with that they began saying the rosary in loud auctioneering voices for the next half-hour. After the last Hail Mary the nun who looked like Meatloaf burst into tears. The other nun comforted her until she said, "I am all right now," and changed her seat.

I was reading the Bari newspaper which had a story on Italy's birth-rate, one of the lowest in Europe. That was quite funny. The Pope had recently denounced condoms as sinful.

The very fat woman, who had joined in the nuns' loud rosary, took out a magazine and a sandwich. It was a health magazine called *Sta Bene*; the sandwich was mozzarella and ham. She read and munched all the way to Pescara.

Next to the railway line the calm and relatively shallow Adriatic gleamed, almost motionless even at the shoreline, all the way through the Abruzzi. And always the little ritual by the station-masters at the smaller stations: the man in his crimson peaked cap, brandishing his wand, blowing his whistle, finally saluting as the train clanked away, all the couplings ringing like hammered anvils. I saw fat sheep and grapevines and olive trees. There were back-yards, too, some of them with miserable-looking people in them. I remembered how for years in London, in the train home, I felt a sense of personal failure riding past the backyards of Clapham and Wandsworth. There was a point to be made about the way the trains in the Mediterranean traversed the rear of so many houses and their melancholy backyards. It was so revealing, if you could stand it.

Leaning against the window, in the corridor of the train, looking at the road that ran beside the tracks, I heard two young men beside me talking. They were noticing the more expensive cars. A large red motorcycle, a man and his woman passenger, swung out from behind a car and passed it, the shapely woman hugging and holding on.

"What a bike," the first boy said. *Che moto.*

"What an ass," the second boy said. *Che culo.*

I got off at San Benedetto del Tronto where, at the Center for Aquaculture and Mariculture at the University of Camerino, I looked for someone to talk to about the condition of the Mediter-ranean. San Benedetto advertised itself as a holiday destination – the coast was crammed with hotels and beaches – but I was interested in water quality and fish farms.

"Yes, we have fish farms," said Dr Gennari Laurent, who was

half French and half Italian. He said he was glad to see me. There was not a lot of public interest in fish farms. "We are growing sea bass and bream."

He was talking about small numbers – 300,000 fry compared with 200 million grown in the rest of Europe. But it took three years for a fish to grow to maturity in northern waters, two years in the south.

"We are mainly a research establishment. Still, we eat them."

"Do you put them into the Mediterranean?"

"It is very difficult to introduce fish into the sea," Dr Laurent said. "Take a fry that has been fed on dry pellets. You can't fatten him and put him into the sea, especially a sea bass. They have a particular way of feeding. A bream might possibly adapt. But that's not our purpose. We are studying a whole new area of fish farming."

"For commercial purposes?"

"Eventually," he said. "Greece has hundreds of fish farms – bass and bream. France raises trout. The British grow salmon. Italy is way ahead in eels – for eating, of course."

The decline in the eel population was a good indication of how bad pollution had become, he said. The European glass eel was once found all over the Adriatic, and was caught in great numbers around Venice; but now the eel did not travel farther north than Ancona, because of the vile water.

"The Yugoslavia side of the Adriatic is deeper, so there are more fish," he said. "One of the problems on the Italian coast is river pollution. The Po is very bad. I studied it myself. I found very bad water quality in the delta areas. Metals. Nitrates. Copper, for example. In fish it is immuno-depressive – it breaks down the fish's immune system, so they get diseases."

"I was under the impression that fish farms created pollution from all their accumulated excrement."

"Yes, that happens. The laws are lax here but strict in, say, Holland. But it is possible to reduce the level of ammonia through certain diets, or by using filtration."

"Do you think that some day there will be no fishermen in the Mediterranean, just fish farms?" I asked.

"There will always be some fishermen here," he said. "During two months in spring there is a ban on trawling, but after that everyone fishes twice as hard. It's hopeless!"

By the time I left the university and reclaimed my bag at the station it was dark, and so I spent the night in San Benedetto, a tourist town with no tourists yet. I caught an early train to the good-sized city of Ancona. This was also a large harbor and ferry port, with ships to Greece and Croatia. The district at the end of the railway line in Ancona was called Pinocchio. "As for Ancona," James Joyce wrote at the turn of the century, "I cannot think about it without repugnance. There is something Irish in its bleak gaunt beggarly ugliness." Some of that bleakness is apparent today, but it is softened by the friendly and apparently prosperous people of Ancona, whose luck it is to live on one of the great harbors of the Adriatic.

As soon as I found a hotel I went for a walk to the harbor. A fisherman at the port, Signor Impiccini, said that his catches were miserable. I told him I liked the fish they called triglia.

"They are best when they are small," he said. "Over eight or nine inches they don't taste nice."

"Are they found outside the Adriatic?"

"Oh, sure," he said. "The bottom of the Adriatic is sandy and muddy because of the rivers that empty into it. Triglia from the Adriatic are best in soup or baked. But the Tyrrhenian Sea has a rocky bottom. Triglia from that rocky bottom are best grilled."

As I walked along the harbor I saw a gathering of men, three men apologizing and explaining something to an older man, who was complaining. Then, having finished explaining, the men told him how much they liked him, and when the first one finished, he goosed the older man by driving a finger into his buttocks. The startled man jumped in anger. The second man did the same – a declaration of friendship and then a goose. The third man took a handful of the man's ass and twisted it, all the while talking in mock sincerity. Finally, they walked away, laughing in triumph, and muttering, "He can shove it" (*Va fan cul*) and "Unnerstan?" (*Eh, gabeet?*) and "To hell with it!" (*Mannaggia la miseria!*).

Few words are more vulgar than "ass" in Italy, and "shove it" sounds very coarse in Italian. Nevertheless, it was a fairly common refrain. I thought of the young men on the train ("What a bike"

... "What an ass") and how, ever since Sicily, whenever I bought a morning paper I was struck by the pornography on news-stands — not the fact of it, because of course it was everywhere, as common as postcards and devotional literature, but the kind of pornography; its themes and emphasis. There were videotapes and picture magazines. Most of it was prominently advertised as sodomy.

Top Anal and *Sex School* (*100% Anal*) were displayed along with the Donald Duck comics and the Sacred Heart prayer cards. *Capriccio Anale* was stacked next to Italian–English dictionaries, and *The Sights of Ancona* — or wherever. Some of it was euphemistic: *A View from Behind*; much of it was blunt: *The Seeker of a Deep Ass*. Often these combined women and animals, dogs mostly, in such videos or magazines as *Moscow Dog*, *Three Women and a Dog*, *Animal Instincts* (*Anal*), *Super Animal*, and so forth, displayed for anyone buying a newspaper to inspect. In Italy pornography was as publicly proclaimed, and as inescapable, as religion.

In Spain I had reached the conclusion that a country's pornography reveals an inner state and gives clues to a society's unconscious: its predilections and compulsions. What sells as pornography in one country would be laughed at in another. I happened to be in Ancona, but Italian pornography was pretty much the same all over the country. There were also unambiguous advertisements in Italy, such as the lovely woman appearing to fellate a penis-shaped fudgicle (motto: "Me and my Magnum!"). But what did this Italian obsession with sodomy and bestiality indicate? It was not a delicate subject but it was a delicate question.

I risked asking it in Ancona, in a bar the night that I arrived. I was among students — Ancona seemed to be full of schools and colleges. One was reading a thick book, *Il Fenomeno Burocratico*. On the little piece of paper she was using as a bookmark was scribbled the words, "*Chi si considera — vale poco; chi si confronta — vale molto.*" I fell into conversation with some of them, who were talking about the war in Bosnia, and after I said that I was an American they practiced their English with me. Eventually they got around to asking me what I thought of Italy.

"The food is wonderful, and I am grateful for the hospitality," I said. "People are also gentle with children, open-minded and appreciative. The newspapers are lively, the bookstores are excellent. Most of all, Italians are pleasant to be with because they are pleasant to each other."

I went on in this way, meaning what I said, and then, choosing my words carefully, I asked about the emphasis on sodomy in the porno I had been noticing.

"That's an old Italian method of birth control," one boy said, and they all laughed.

On my way to Rimini the next day I passed the seaside towns of Senigallia and Fano, the beginning of what Italians call *La Costa Tedesca*, "The German Coast," because of the annual visitation of Germans in the hundreds of thousands from May until September. There were German trailer parks at Marotta, and signs in German on most beaches. The train passed so near the sea I could clearly hear the sluggish Adriatic slosh against the jetties and the breakwaters that ran parallel to the shore. It was as heavily developed and as tacky as the Spanish coast, but unlike Spain, far lusher inland: hills of black pines, meadows bounded by junipers and poplars, modest vineyards and orchards, fields of hay being cut and baled.

The look of tragic absurdity in a resort out of season was epitomized by Rimini, so hopeful, so ready, so empty. No town in Italy, except Rome, is so Fellini-esque. Rimini was where the great director was born and grew up; it was deeply a part of his mind, it fueled his imagination, it was the scene of a number of his movies. Rimini, an ancient town that was also a cheap seaside resort, a blend of classical ruins and meretricious entertainments, was a perfect image for Italy, too. No wonder Fellini returned to it again and again to evoke his wildest imagery. (A vast fat woman dancing on Rimini's beach and chanting, "Shame! Shame!" to a little boy.) The town is justifiably proud of Fellini. After he died a pretty park near the sea front was named after him.

A faintly seedy place, Rimini is another resort that is noted for its throngs of German tourists. Yet some of the town is elegant, with boulevards of substantial villas, and the older part is ancient and lovely. There is a Roman amphitheater, a cathedral, several handsome churches. The local cuisine is also delicious. The area is well known for its whitebait and clam sauce and fizzy wines. I tried everything, but still felt somewhat uncomfortable. The problem is Rimini's small size. It was true of other towns on this coast. They were simply not built for this many people. The market overflowed the piazzas and streets and alleys, and on Saturdays there was no old town, simply stall after stall selling fruit and vegetables, cheese and meat, and stacks of clothes, as well as pots and pans, T-shirts, sweaters, and all sorts of Chinese knock-offs of US merchandise that are now sold the world over.

As the sun sank and the lights began to wink, Rimini became Fellini-esque – something about the lights twinkling in the emptiness under the moonless sky, the wind whipping at the seaside pennants and making the awnings flap. There were little chairs and empty pavilions, and the avenue along the shore was scoured by the wind hurrying off the sea, out of the Adriatic darkness, making Rimini seem like an abandoned carnival in the wilderness: small, weak, painted, futile, doomed. As Catholics said, and as Fellini insisted, the town was an occasion of sin.

I hiked up and down the sea front, liking the strangeness of all the hotels and cafés and lights, self-mocking in their abandonment. The beach was completely divided into horrible little fenced-off areas, the very sand taken over and planted with tables, chairs, beach toys, changing-rooms, playgrounds – everything evenly spaced, right out to the tide-mark, with signs and flags. But it was empty on this low-season night. I came to a better part of town, the Viale Principe Amedeo, with its villas side by side, the Villa del Angelo, Villa Mauro, Villa Jacinta, all looking wonderful and solid, family houses for the summer, the very image of bourgeois smugness, with palms and walled gardens.

And there this cold night, among the walls and the evergreens, on that street and the side streets, were numerous prostitutes, hailing the few passing cars, caught in the headlights' sudden gleam like deer dazzled in the road. Their long coats were flung apart by their urgent strutting – they wore cycling shorts and miniskirts and lingerie under these coats. They were big women – tall, not fat but imposing. Some were as big as men, and might well have been men – male transvestites. Seeing me they became animated, and called out, and sang, "Eh, baybee! I larf you!"

"Good evening," I said.

"You want something nice?" this laughing woman said.

"I just want to know how you are doing."

Another big one lunged at me and grabbed my crotch and said, "I want this!"

They all laughed at me, so bored and frustrated were they on a chilly night with no cars. There were more of them farther on, standing on the street, lurking in the driveways, in black slacks and blue suits. Some were Africans, a few might have been Germans or Slovenians, Bosnian refugees, recently liberated Albanians. Apart from me, they were the only pedestrians, and yet they were not walking, but rather actively standing, posturing, hallooing, waiting to be picked up by cars that went by. And after a while a few cars did go by, very slowly, the drivers appraising the women.

Fellini would have loved it: the bourgeois neighborhood, the expensive cars, the windy night, the whores scattered among the villas, the shrieks and cat-calls.

Seven or eight young boys went down the street and began teasing them, but the prostitutes stood their ground, jeering at the boys, questioning their virility.

"You've got nothing down there, boy!"

In the Via Gambalunga, also on a "nice" street (dentists' offices, villas, apartment houses), there was the "Club Riche Monde – Cabaret" and in small print, *No one under 21 admitted* and *Porno Show*. This also seemed Fellini-esque – degradation in a respectable neighborhood. As a younger man, ravenous for experience, I would have gone in. But it was after midnight, and I knew what was inside: expensive drinks and exhibitionism, and the kind of shakedown that makes you ashamed of how predictable the libido is. That, and the feeling of unease I got in the presence of public sex, like the irritation I felt when I saw comic books and porno mags all jumbled together on the news-stand. I went back to my hotel and read a book. Nowadays I did not want to put myself in the hands of pimps.

Another Fellini episode occurred the next day in Rimini. I was walking along one of the main streets when a bus lurched to a halt, and the passengers began banging on the windows. The driver had barricaded them in by locking the exit door, and a crowd gathered around the bus to watch the passengers arguing and struggling to get out. The police were summoned, and so were the ticket collectors from a nearby bus stop. There was fury inside the bus.

Ten African girls were gesticulating and howling in Italian. Then the doors opened and some old women got out. The African girls were still yelling at the driver. The police questioned them. "Where's your ticket?" "Don't touch me!" "We're all together!"

An Italian dwarf in a silk suit, smoking reflectively, stood near me to watch.

"What's up?"

"Tickets," he said.

The crowd grew around the bus, and now the African girls were screaming. They were Somalis or Sudanese or Eritreans, from the old Italian colonies and mission stations. It was hard to tell where they came from because they were so thoroughly urbanized, each one in an expensive wig and tight pants and heavy make-up – purple lips, glittering mascara. It was a showdown, and it went on for about twenty minutes; at the end the girls were triumphant, and they screamed abuse at the spectators and waved their bus tickets and swore at the driver. The police shrugged. The bus drove off.

Not all encounters between Africans and Italians are so jolly. The Violence Observatory, a Rome-based organization that monitors such incidents, reported that an average of at least one attack a day on foreigners was recorded in 1993, and the figures were higher in 1994. These were stabbings, shootings, beatings. All it took to provoke such an attack was a single episode – say, a carload of Moroccans running down an Italian girl (as happened the same month at the Tyrrhenian resort of Torvavianica) – and local people began assaulting any darkish foreigner they encountered. A few months after I saw this odd encounter in Rimini a fire destroyed a barracks housing hundreds of farm workers in Villa Literno near Naples. The victims were mostly Africans, who are now Italy's tomato-pickers.

A satirist like Fellini, merciless and impartial, would have had something to say. And I began to think once again that the great justification for traveling the shore of the Mediterranean, if such a justification was necessary, was that the foreground – these sudden strange encounters – was much more interesting than the Roman amphitheaters and the ruins.

From Rimini I took a branch-line train inland to Ferrara, via Cervia and Lido di Savio, detouring around the enormous low-lying delta of the Po. The train stopped everywhere, picking up old people and noisy schoolchildren from the farming communities in this tucked-away part of Italy crammed with fig trees and vineyards and fields tangled with artichokes.

I stopped in Ferrara and took a taxi to the nearby village – so it seemed from the map. It was called Dodici Morelli, and it was just a crossroads, some houses, a thicket of hedges, a small church.

"There is not much here," the taxi-driver said.

"My grandfather was born here," I said. "My mother's father."

"Bravo," the man said. "He did the right thing – went to America!"

"He used to write poetry," I said.

"Bravo." He said it with feeling.

It was a short trip by train from Ferrara to the little station at Rovigo. On the way a Portuguese couple in my compartment quarreled with the conductor. The woman had injured her arm, she said. The conductor doubted her. He asked her to fill out a declaration. The woman did not speak Italian. I gathered that she was drunk.

"Why you write I push de doors? I no push de doors! Geeve me, you dunno!"

"In Venice you go to police."

"Why? No! I no go! I escape from theese man!"

I stepped from that screaming into the green fields of Rovigo and caught another branch-line train, even smaller, the spur to Chioggia by way of the tiniest Italian villages I had seen so far, the farms and settlements that feed the appetites of Venice. It was a happy discovery: in the midst of all the celebrated cities, this obscure corner, reachable on a little rattling two-car train. The land was as flat as Holland; it had the look of a flood plain, and garlic and onions and lettuce sprouted from it.

At the end of this branch-line railway was the small, ancient seaside town of Chioggia, the last, most southerly island in the chain of narrow barrier islands that form the eastern edge of the lagoon of Venice. The lovely city hovers in the distance like a mirage on water, dreamlike spires and domes in the mist.

Chioggia is Venice with motor traffic. As a consequence it is scruffy and noisy, not livelier but more chaotic – few tourists, lots of locals, only dogs and children in the back streets, and only one hotel that I could see. I was not planning to stay. I had arrived early enough in the day to look around and then leave. With no splendid image to live up to, a rather ordinary town on the water, Chioggia was restful and pleasant. There were concerts and events advertised, but it was obvious that Chioggia had constantly to defend itself against the taunts of people who compared it unfavorably with Venice.

I left my bag with the ferry captain of the *Clodia* at the main quay and then limped from one end of town to the other, and across bridges and along the small canals. After lunch, I followed a nervous and exhausted bride and groom who were having their pictures taken; the family trailed behind with gently mocking friends, and onlookers, and all the while the bride's white gown and long train dragged through the mud of the quay.

I bought an antique postcard with a 1935 postmark in Chioggia, not for the picture – of Trieste – but the message: *Sei sempre nei miei pensieri. Baci infiniti* ("You are always in my thoughts. Infinite kisses.") Such tender sentiments lifted my spirits.

Workers from Chioggia commuted to the Lido on the *Clodia*. Anything but an easy trip, it was cheap but exhausting – over an hour and a half, involving ferries, buses, and in places legging it. The whole affair of transfer had the laborious efficiency of Italian travel. The ferry crossed to Pellestrina island, where at the quay a bus was waiting to transport the ferry passengers to the north end of Pellestrina. This island of somewhat recent, somewhat ugly houses and green meadows, and football fields, and schools, could have been almost anywhere in coastal Italy, except that the lagoon to the left and the sea-wall to the right were reminders that it was unusually slender and low-lying. The soil was sodden and water-logged, with that unnatural reclaimed look that Holland has. It seemed hardly land, it was so fragile and false; more like a raft or a carpet, not terra firma but something more easily drowned.

Arriving at the village of Santa Maria del Mare the bus rolled straight on to another ferry, the *Ammiana*, which had been waiting there at the north end of Pellestrina. This new ferry, with the bus on board, plowed into the lagoon and took us a half-mile to the south end of the Lido, another long and narrow island. The bus drove off the ferry ramp with us on it, and after a while we arrived at the Lido water-taxi station.

The Lido was residential; it is for people who want tree-lined streets, and cars, and the chance to swim. As a barrier island on the sea, it acts as Venice's shoreline; the word *lido* means "shore." Several hotels there are extravagantly grand, on their own Adriatic beaches; there are also many small hotels, and the usual boarding-houses. Today a rough sea was battering the beach of the elegant Hôtel des Bains, where Von Aschenbach leered at lovely little Tadzio and contemplated the meaning of life, in *Death in Venice*, the ultimate low-season narrative. Perhaps the masterpiece would have been more aptly titled *Death on the Lido*, since the Lido bears no resemblance at all to Venice.

I considered staying at the Hôtel des Bains or the Excelsior, but thought better of it. Apart from the fact that rooms were too expensive, I also felt that I would be isolated from the life of the Lido, in a gilded cage. Sometime in the future, when all I had to do was read a book and not write one, I would return and stay there. It seemed to me that the greatest Mediterranean comforts were available at those grand hotels on the Lido, but at a price: about $600 a night. On the lagoon side of the island I found the sort of ordinary hotel that in Italy was usually clean and pleasant, and the next morning I realized I had chosen well.

The first thing I saw the following day, as I walked down my side street to the lagoon, was a great flotilla of boats. Decked with pennants and banners, they were high-sterned wooden water-craft, larger and more elaborate than gondolas, with gold trim and bright paint, the lead boat with a tall crucifix instead of a mast and others carrying statues of saints, all of them manned by crews of oarsmen who were rowing them across the lagoon from Venice to the Lido. They bobbed busily in the early morning sunshine.

I had arrived at a good time, the Feast of the Ascension (the *Festa della 'Sensa* in Venetian slang), the day of the annual ceremony of marriage with the sea, *Ceremonia dello Spozalizio del Mare*. In former times, the Doge threw his ring into the lagoon and a young fisherman dived into the water and grabbed it. These days it was a regatta, followed by a mass at the Chiesa San Nicolo al Lido ("Here the emperor Barbarossa stayed before his meeting with Pope Alexander III in San Marco in 1177" – but perhaps we knew that already).

The ceremony was a ritualized blessing, the pretty boats with their bunting and flags and ribbons all fluttering in the wind drawn alongside the embankment; the muscular oarsmen still panting from the effort of the long row, their eyes lowered, standing in their splashed costumes, their caps doffed. A mass followed this, just like the sort of happy mass that followed a wedding ceremony. I associated this amount of piety and time with the sort of weddings I had preferred in my days as an altar-boy: there was usually a tip afterward from the harassed father of the bride. Tips and tokens were passing to the oarsmen, who were like acolytes at this ceremony. The so-called marriage of the sea "commemorated the Conquest of Dalmatia in A.D. 1000," my guidebook said: oars and pennants and blessings on this shore for almost a thousand years.

I took a water-bus from the Lido to Venice proper, and approaching this city in the sea, glittering in brilliant sunshine, I began to goggle, trembling a little, feeling a physical thrill and unease in the presence of such beauty, an exaltation amounting almost to fear.

Venice is magic, the loveliest city in the world, because it has entirely displaced its islands with palaces and villas and churches. It is man-made, but a work of genius, sparkling in its own lagoon, floating on its dreamy reflection, with the shapeliest bridges and the last perfect skyline on earth: just domes and spires and tiled roofs. It is one color, the mellowest stone. There is no sign of land, no earth at all, only water traffic and canals. Everyone knows this, and yet no one is prepared for it, and so the enchantment is overwhelming. The fear you feel is the fear of being bewitched and helpless. Its visitors gape at it, speechless with admiration, hardly believing such splendor can shine forth from such slimy stones.

Language cannot do justice to Venice and nothing can detract from its beauty. It floods regularly; its marble is damaged and decayed, its paintings rot, it has stinking corners. Its canals are green, some of it looks poisonous, it is littered, it teems with rats which not even the masses of Venetian cats can cope with. The graffiti on ancient walls and on church pillars – I noted *Berlusconi is Doing Harm* and *Berlusconi is the Assassin of Democracy* – are almost incidental. People still live in Venice, children play in its back streets, where families turn the cranks of pasta machines, men congregate to smoke, women scorch tomatoes. In the alleys beggar women cradle their children and hold signs: *Please Help My Family – Ex-Yugoslavia*. Even the fact that Venice is actually sinking and might one day be destroyed if not disappear altogether, gives it an air of fragility and drama, a passionate mortality.

The outdoor pleasures of Venice – walking, traveling on the water-buses, gloating over the architecture – are as intense as the indoor pleasures of browsing among the masterpieces of painting and sculpture. Both are hopeless too, because there is not enough time to see everything you want. To use my time, because I was just passing through, I made a project for myself. I looked for paintings in churches and galleries where the sea was specifically shown – the sea battles, the blessing of fleets, the sight of canals and gondolas in the background of religious pictures, the mythology of the sea. The best by far was in the Ducal Palace in St Mark's, Tiepolo's "Venice Receiving the Homage of Neptune" – the lovely woman personifying the city, *La Serenissima*, reclining while the ancient grizzled god empties a great horn-like shell of its treasure of gold coins and jewels.

At the western edge of Venice, towards the quays where the largest ships are moored, and next to the church of Santa Maria Maggiore, is a large medieval and mournful-looking prison. Being in prison in Venice seemed to me like the classical definition of hell – that you are near heaven but denied it absolutely.

That was also how I felt when I had to leave Venice, on a crowded train to Trieste.

All the way to Trieste I caught little glimpses of the sea, and after the train climbed to Aurisina in the hills that funneled the famous Bora wind into the city, I had a panoramic view of the enormous

notch in the Adriatic, called the Gulf of Venice on the map. It was
the last gasp of Italy – you could almost spit into Slovenia from a
window on the left-hand side of the train.

The late afternoon sun, misshapen by the risen dust, lost its
lightness and its gold, and thickening, growing orange as it descended, began to break slowly, the white sea dissolving the sun's
rich pulp.

With a little shudder the train, with far fewer passengers, stopped
at Trieste's South Station. I walked out and sensed that I was no
longer in Italy. It hardly looked like the Mediterranean any more.

Trieste was once the noble port of Austria, and it still looked to
me like Vienna-by-the-Sea. The city still had those gray Habsburg
buildings, every one of them looking like the headquarters of an
insurance company (and that included the Church of St Anthony
the Thaumaturgist), sloping up from the port in austere and
forbidding terraces. The structures of Trieste have big flat faces. It
is not a city of apartments and suites, nor private houses, nor any
small stucco dwellings on back streets. No chickens, hardly any
cats; all the dogs on leashes; like its sister cities in northern Europe,
composed of seriousness and gloom and the fragrance of sticky
pastries. It is the city closely documented in the novels of Italo
Svevo: *Confessions of Zeno*, the ultimate account of a man trying to
give up smoking, and *Senilità*, the story of an infatuation. Svevo's
friend James Joyce urged Svevo to call the latter book *As a Man
Grows Older*.

Joyce lived in Trieste off and on for about seven years, wrote
most of *Ulysses* there, gave English lessons, and fell in love with one
of his students. Sir Richard Burton, one of the world's greatest
travelers, was British Consul here in Trieste towards the end of his
career, and while his wife Isabel worried about the welfare of
Trieste's stray cats and overworked donkeys, Burton worked on his
books. They also spent time up the line at Villa Opicina. The
Burtons liked Trieste so well they eventually colonized seventeen
rooms in one of these large apartment blocks. Sir Richard filled
them with his spears and his dueling swords and collections of
pornography and incunabula; he wrote a dozen books, including
his translation of *The Arabian Nights*; and here in Trieste he died.

It was just a few hours by train from the incandescent lightness

of Venice to the lugubrious gray of Trieste, but of course being in
the Mediterranean was all about surprising transitions. Indeed,
ever since arriving on the Adriatic shore I had been anxious about
my next move, the onward journey to Croatia. I had seen the
ferries leaving for Split from Bari and Ancona. "No service to
Dubrovnik," I was told. None to Montenegro. I guessed the
reasons why. The thought of going there preoccupied me; I knew a
bit about it, just enough of the atrocities of its war and its recent
devastation for images of it to invade my dreams. Trieste was safe,
but Trieste was a more serious place than any I had seen, and it
seemed to be preparing me for something grimmer.

Just at dusk the city was almost empty of pedestrians. I walked
the length of the port and then back on the inside streets, and
found a place to stay.

"So what brings you to Trieste?" the clerk asked.

"I was curious about it," I said, and thinking of the writer who
had made the city real to me, I added, "and I have read Svevo. In
English, though."

"It is better to read Svevo in English. He's too confusing in
Italian."

Italians were full of compliments, even here at the edge of
Slovenia. The Spanish were too restrained to praise; the French
too envious and uncertain, the Corsicans too proud. For the more
generous and extrovert Italians, praise was normal, words cost
nothing, so the flow of daily life was eased. I had lost an important
ticket in Venice. At first the ticket collector mildly scolded me,
clucking, but when I said, "I am a cretin – I am really stupid," he
said, "No, no – it is usual to lose a ticket, don't be hard on
yourself."

More urgently than I intended, I said to the hotel clerk, "I want
to go to Croatia. Do you know anything about traveling there?"

"Nothing," he said. "But sometimes we get the refugees."

I saw some the next day – pan-handlers holding politely-worded
signs, and disoriented families with bags and boxes idling at the
port. After the Venetian capriccio, this sobriety. The Triestini
themselves were taller than the Italians I had been seeing, and
paler, and rather laconic. It was a city of suits, a businesslike place
with an air of solidity and prosperity.

James Joyce had been that most enigmatic of refugees, a literary exile in Trieste, sitting out the First World War in a Triestine apartment and writing his masterpiece about Dublin. But he had come there earlier. From 1904 to 1906, fleeing Ireland, practicing "silence, exile, cunning," he was an English teacher in Trieste's Berlitz School, while writing short stories. After a brief absence he returned to Trieste in 1907 and gave English lessons privately. One of his students, Hector Schmitz, was middle-aged (Joyce was a highly excitable 25-year-old), and a businessman, yet when Joyce showed him an early draft of his short story "The Dead," his student brought out two novels he had written under his pen name, Italo Svevo. He told Joyce that they were old hat – he had published *Una Vita* twelve years before and *Senilità* in 1898. The young Irishman declared him a neglected genius. *Senilità* especially pleased him.

It is easy to see why. The novel is about desire as self-deceiving, and it is firmly located in a city. The style is remorselessly plain, and every phase of the main character's infatuation is described. Emilio is a writer made susceptible by literary vanity, and obsessed by Angiolina, who both teases him and grants him the occasional sexual favor. Angiolina is a tricky and lovely young woman, who obviously has other lovers. The humiliations of passion in a labyrinthine city fascinated Joyce – both Schmitz and his hero were to become aspects of Joyce's henpecked hero, Leopold Bloom; and Schmitz's meticulous documentation of Trieste, must have impressed the Irish writer who was to fill *Ulysses* with the actual streets and pubs and theaters of Dublin.

Looking for Svevo's Trieste I realized how much a knowledge of the city mattered to an understanding of the novel. The city is Emilio's world. The love affair is enacted throughout the city. They meet in the center of town, on the Corso. Later, "They always met in the open air." Emilio woos Angiolina on the suburban roads, all of them named, and then they keep to the edge of the city, the Strada d'Opicina and the Campo Marzio.

I went to the Campo Marzio in the south-west corner of Trieste, where Emilio "saw the Arsenal stretching along the shore . . . 'The city of labor!' he said, surprised at himself for having chosen that place in which to make love to her." Some pages later Emilio is shadowing Angiolina on the opposite side of town. I went there too, to the public gardens, across to the Via Fabio Severo and down the Via Romagna. I climbed to the Castle and walked down the hill to the Piazza Barriera Vecchia and had a coffee and pastry on the Corso again, delighted to be able to guide myself through the city by using a novel that was almost a hundred years old.

There were no tourists in Trieste that I could see. That was a conspicuous absence, because Venice was so frenzied with them. But why would tourists come here? True, there was a Roman amphitheater in town – yet another – behind the Corso, and a broken Roman arch, the gate of the old city, but that was so ruinous and disregarded it simply stuck out of a seedy building in a back street, at the edge of a building site, and was somewhat in the way. There was no sign on the arch, only a recently scribbled exclamation, *Fuck the Fascists Forever!*

At just about the point when I had decided that Trieste was the quietest, most law-abiding place I had seen so far, I witnessed a vicious night-time street fight.

It was my second night in the city. I was walking through the lamplit Piazza Italia, having just eaten another good meal (and also thinking of the rationing in Croatia). I heard screams – a young woman howling; then men shouting, and loud bangs. It was outside a restaurant, the strange halting peristalsis of men nerving themselves to fight, like apes displaying anger. There were about eight or nine men, ill-assorted, first thumping on tables, then engaging in noisy sorties, drawing back and becoming more abusive with distance, then throwing the tables, a few chairs too. These were the economies of battle, just clatter and threats, a form of restraint; and all the while the young woman screeching. But at last there was no going back, and the men went at each other, kicking and punching, the wildest scene I had witnessed since leaving Gibraltar. It was the last thing I expected in Trieste.

That was an exception. It was a solemn and even dull place, but with the most attractive women I had seen so far, taller, more angular, brisker and better-dressed than elsewhere, not the duck-butted women of the Marches. Trieste's food was not highly flavored, but it was hearty: mussels and spaghetti, fruit and fish, and the fine wines of its region, Friuli. I began to understand why

Joyce had decided to live here and engage in the stimulating monotony of writing a novel.

Leaving Trieste meant leaving Italy, where knowing the language with reasonable fluency I had been happy — well treated and well fed. Now I was boarding the train into the unknown — the new nation of Slovenia and its neighbor, the crumbling republic of Croatia.

I I

The Ferry *Liburnija* to Zadar

My destination today was Pivka, "somewhere in Slovenia" (so I was told), reachable on the Budapest Express by my getting off very quickly at a thirty-second halt after about two hours' traveling from Trieste. It was a sunny morning, I was dozing in the midday heat. The border formalities brought me fully awake.

Until now I had hardly shown my passport anywhere, but leaving the European Community for the hastily improvised republics of former Yugoslavia meant that I was now under scrutiny. High in the Carso Mountains that formed the Italian frontier, Italian officials stamped my passport and looked through my bag. A few miles farther down the line, at Sezana on the Slovenian border, there was another search, but a stranger one. The Slovene customs man ordered me outside into the corridor, and then, kicking my bag aside, he set his sights on removing the seats from the compartment. He fossicked in the crevices where I might have hid lawyers, guns or money. He found nothing but dust. He jammed the seats back into the racks and said goodbye in English. In the matter of visas and border crossings, the smaller the country the bigger the fuss; like a tiny cop directing traffic.

It was such an empty train. Obviously no one wanted to leave Italian abundance for the relative deprivation of Ljubljana or Budapest, or any of the desperate little stations in between. For example, I was the only passenger to alight at Pivka, a railway junction.

After all that traveling and trouble I was nowhere. Yet I had to admit that it was a satisfaction being on this tiny platform, among unreadable signs, particularly after the celebrated places I had passed through. The pathetic name Pivka seemed curiously belittling and joyless, like a nickname for a dwarf. But because travel is often a sad and partly masochistic pleasure, the arrival in obscure and picturesquely awful places is one of the delights of the traveler.

It was like one of those remote junctions you see in depressing East European movies where people in old-fashioned clothes commit meaningless murders. It was now the middle of a hot afternoon.

I walked into the station bar, feeling like a conspicuous stranger, and ordered a cup of coffee. It was dark inside, and shabby, and the air was dense and stinging with the smoke of cheap cigarettes. I had no Slovenian currency, but Italian money was good enough – probably better. Citizens of these new little nations were forced by circumstances to be accommodating, and to speak English. I handed over a small Italian bill and received a wad of Slovenian money in return, with the newness and inkiness of inflated currency. I calculated that the large cup of coffee had cost me thirty-five cents, the cheapest I had drunk in fifteen years.

Pasty-faced men with greasy hair chain-smoked and muttered. I wanted to make a telephone call from the rusty phone on the wall but no one could sell me the token I needed to make the thing work.

"No tokens," the young woman said. Her name was Marta. She spoke English.

"I am a stranger here. I want to visit Pivka. Tell me, what is the best thing to see?"

"There is nothing," she said.

She was wearily wiping wet glasses with a dirty rag. She sucked her teeth. She pushed a loose hank of hair behind her ear.

"And the winter," she said.

"What is it like?"

"Bad."

"What about the summer?"

"Too hot."

"But there's no fighting here."

"No, that's –" She waved the rag to the east, slopping water on the bar's mirror. "There."

The men in the bar, drinking beer, smoking heavily, did not acknowledge me. Through the unwashed window I watched a dirty yellow engine shunting. I thought, as I frequently do in such places, *What if I had been born here?*

Leaving my bag with the station-master I walked into Pivka proper, which was a narrow road lined with empty shops. The town was sooty, just peeling paint and impoverishment, but it was not littered, simply fatigued-looking, like the people, like Marta at the bar. Now and then a car, always a small one going too fast, side-swiped me as I walked down the narrow pavement of Kold-voska Cesta. A rusty Wartburg, a Zastova, some gasping Yugos. It was like being attacked by weed-whackers. I could hear their whirring engines and frayed fanbelts, the sputter of their leaking radiators. But even these little cars proclaimed their nationalism. One had a sticker *Slovenia*, the rest were labeled *SLO*.

Walking along I heard a child crying inside a house, and a woman scolding; then a slap, and the child crying louder, and more scolding. Scold, slap, screech; scold, slap, screech.

I looked for a place to eat, I asked people – made eating gestures – "Station," they said. That horrible little bar? So I went back to the station and saw that there was a train in an hour or so for Rijeka. I talked to Marta again. She urged me to go to Rijeka, even though it was in the foreign country of Croatia. I sat in the sunshine, reading, catching up on my notes, and listening to the dusty sparrows of Pivka until the train came.

This two-car Polish-made train of Slovenian Railways was about twenty years old, filled with rambunctious schoolchildren on their way home. They shrieked at each other for a while, then shut up. There was a sort of hysteria here, probably something to do with political uncertainty and recrimination. Soon they all got off. There were now about eight of us remaining in the train: seven old people and me. And it was interesting that the countryside looked as seedy as the town, as bedraggled, not like nature at all, but like a stage-set designed to symbolize the plight of the country: thin, rather starved trees, ragged discolored grass, wilting wild-flowers. There was a 6,000-foot mountain to the east, Veliki Sneznik, but even that looked collapsible.

"Bistrica," the conductor said, clipping my ticket and motioning me out of the door.

At Ilirska Bistrica a youth in a baggy police uniform flipped the pages of my passport and handed it back. That was one of the irritations of nationalism – every few miles a passport check, just a ritual, at the frontier of another tinky-winky republic.

The train jogged on to a small station building with wisteria clinging to the walls. We sat there a while, the old folks muttering while I tried to engage one of them in conversation. There were no talkers.

"Just tell me where we are."

"We are leaving the Republic of Slovenia," an old man said. "We are entering the Republic of Croatia."

There was no sarcasm in his voice, yet the bald statement was sarcasm enough. We had gone – what? – about twenty miles from Pivka.

"You will require a visa," a policeman said.

This was Sapjane, the frontier of the Republika Hvratska (Croatia). It was a place much like Pivka or Bistrica. When a country is very small even these tiny, almost uninhabited villages are inflated with a meaningless importance. A breeze was ruffling the weedy tracks, and soughing in the pines; a cow mooed, its bell clinked. More sparrows. Customs! Immigration! You will require a visa! The officious but polite policeman laboriously filled in a form ("Father's name? Place of birth? Purpose of visit?") and stuck a pompous-looking Croatian visa into my passport, a scrupulous operation, taking fifteen minutes. I was the only foreigner. God help them when they had four or five foreigners on the train.

We were all ethnically approved: one American, seven Croatians. Before the break-up of Yugoslavia the train would have raced through this station at eighty miles an hour. But I did not complain about the delay. This was all experimental travel. If I had flown to Croatia from Italy I would not have been privileged to witness this sad farce.

Having done his duty, the policeman became pleasant. His name was Mario, he was from Rijeka – he commuted to this outpost – and he was a mere twenty-three. I remarked on the farcical bureaucracy – after an hour we were still at the station, waiting.

"Yes, there are delays, because we are all separate now,"

he said. "Slovenia. Croatia. Serbia. In Bosnia you have Mussulmans."

"They're different, are they?"

"Very much. You see, Slovenian people are much more like Germans or Austrians."

That became quite a common refrain: We are big bold Teutons, they are dark little savages. But in fact they all looked fairly similar and Slavic to my eye, untutored by Jugland's prejudices. I soon learned that a former Jug could spot an ethnic taint a mile away. Here comes a Bosnian! There goes a Slovene!

I said this in a polite form to Mario.

"That is because we married each other before," he said. "But we don't marry each other now."

"What a shame."

"Well, you see, it was Marshal Tito's idea to have one big country. But maybe it was too big." He was digging a big polished boot into the railway gravel. "Better to have our own countries, for political freedom. Maybe like America. One government in Washington and every state is separate."

"Mario, we don't need a passport and a visa to go from New York to New Jersey."

He laughed. He was intelligent; his English was good enough for him to understand that I had shown him the absurdity of what he proposed. And after all, the war was still on.

"Will I have a problem going to Montenegro?"

"I think, yes," he said. "And Serbia is a problem. Where do you come from?"

"Boston."

"Kukoc plays for the Bulls," he said. "Divac plays for the Lakers. But I am for the Bulls."

"They're not doing very well."

"They won last night," Mario said.

Here, in the farthest corner of Croatia, on the wrong side of the tracks at Sapjane, among mooing cows, the latest NBA scores.

"Michael Jordan," Mario said. "He is the greatest player in the world."

The Slovenian train had returned to Pivka, and at last a Croatian train arrived in Sapjane from Rijeka to take us on the return trip. I got into a conversation, speaking Italian with a Croatian. I remarked on the complexity of the republics that had sprung up.

"It's all shit," he said.

Rijeka had a reputation for being ugly, but it did not seem so bad, another Adriatic port city, rather steep and scattered, with an air of having been forgotten. Many people still spoke the Italian they had learned when the city was part of Mussolini's empire, and named Fiume (meaning "river", as did the word Rijeka). "Fiume is a clean asphalted town with a very modern go-ahead air," James Joyce wrote in a letter in 1906. "It is for its size far finer than Trieste." Within minutes of arriving I changed a little money and left the money-changer's a millionaire, in dinars.

Earlier on this trip I had read Nabokov's vivid memoir, *Speak, Memory*. He had remarked on his childhood visits from St Petersburg to a resort called Abbazia, much frequented by Russians at the turn of the century. I had inquired about the place while I was in Italy (*Abbazia* means monastery), but there was no such place on the coast. But I saw the name in parentheses on a Croatian map, and I realized that just a few miles away, down the coast, the penultimate station on the line to Rijeka, was Abbazia in its Croatian form, Opatija.

"There are dimples in the rocks, full of tepid sea water," Nabokov wrote of the place, "and my magic muttering accompanies certain spells I am weaving over the tiny sapphire pools."

It was 1904, Nabokov was five, and he was with his doting father and mother. His family rented a villa with a "crenelated, cream-colored tower." He remembered traveling to Fiume for a haircut. He described hearing the Adriatic from his bedroom: "The ocean seemed to rise and grope in the darkness and then heavily fall on its face."

This was my excuse to stay in Rijeka that night, eat another pizza, sleep in another bargain-priced hotel, and go to Opatija in the morning. The seaside resort was deserted. It retained its elegance, though, and looked like a haunted version of Menton. An old man swept the broad promenade with a push-broom. The boarding-houses looked abandoned. The restaurants were closed. The day was warm and sunny, the sea lapping at an empty beach.

"People come at the weekends," a Croatian woman at the news-stand told me in Italian.

Returning to Rijeka I made inquiries about the train to Zadar, which had recently been under heavy Serbian shelling.

"Ha! No trains these days!" the woman at the hotel said. But she took charge of me.

"You want to know the best thing to do? Leave this hotel right now. Go straight to the port. You can't miss it. In two hours the ferry leaves."

It was the coastal ferry to Zadar and Split.

"You think I'll get a ticket?"

"Ha! No problem!" she said. "No one comes here any more!"

I snatched up my bag and hurried to the port. Within fifteen minutes I was in possession of a five-dollar ticket to Zadar on the ferry *Liburnija*, with a hundred or so Croatians, and soon we were gliding past the islands of Krk, Chres, Rab, Losinj and Pag in the late afternoon sunshine, and I was happy again, on the move.

There were half-a-dozen German tourists on board who were taking advantage of the bargains created by the war – desperate hotel-keepers and empty restaurants, unlimited beach umbrellas, cheap beer. The rest were Croatians. I had the only ticket to Zadar; everyone else was going to Split.

The effects of the war were evident on the *Liburnija*, too: the chain-smoking adults, looking shell-shocked, the children in their mid-teens, a great deal more manic and aggressive than any I had seen so far – and I had seen a large number, since they often took trains home from school. These Croatian children acted crazed: they swung on poles, vaulted barriers, punched each other, screeched and wept – this was later, at eleven at night off the Dalmatian coast – and well into the early hours they kept trying to push one another over the rail into the Kvarneric channel.

I assumed it was an agitated state induced by the uncertainties and violence of the war that they had all experienced in some way, even if it was only hearing the thunder of artillery shells. They were returning to parts of Croatia that had been under fire. The Serbs had made their presence felt almost to the edge of the shore, and even many coastal towns had been shelled or invaded. The children were so hysterical at times that I expected one of them would succeed in tipping another over the rail and that we would then spend the rest of the night searching fruitlessly for the body.

The war mood was a species of battle fatigue, depression with brief periods of hyper-alertness. And it was as though, because the adults said nothing but only murmured and smoked, the children were expressing their parents' fears or belligerence.

I went into the cafeteria of the ship to escape them, but even there teenagers were running about and bumping into tables and overturning chairs. No one told them to shut up or stop.

"Those kids bother me," I said to a young man at my table.

He shrugged; he did not understand. He said, "Do you speak Italian?"

He was Croatian, he said, but lived in Switzerland, where he was a student and a part-time bartender in a club in Locarno, just over the Swiss border at the top end of Lake Maggiore. "I hate the French and the Germans. They don't talk to me anyway." Girls hung around the club – from Brazil, from Santo Domingo and the Philippines. "You could call them prostitutes. They will go with a man if the money is right. I am not interested in them."

He was on his way home to the island of Brac across the channel from Split for a long-delayed holiday.

"I didn't come last year because Serbs and Croats were fighting in the mountains, and there was trouble in Split. It is quiet now, but still no people come, because they are afraid of all this fighting they hear about."

"Are there good guys and bad guys in this war?"

"Look, we are Croats, but last year my father was robbed of almost five thousand US dollars in dinars, and the robber was a Croat!" He laughed. He was busily eating spaghetti. "Serbs are Protestants, Croats are Catholics, Bosnians are Mussulmen. Me, I can't understand Slovene or Montenegrin or Macedonian. It is like French to me. Bosnian and Serbian and Croat languages are almost the same. But we don't speak to each other any more!"

Having finished his meal he went to the cafeteria line and bought another meal, more spaghetti, salad, french fries and a slab of greasy meat.

"I'm hungry," he explained as he put this second tray down. "I'm a swimmer. I'm on the water-polo team at my school." He resumed eating and after a while said, "This food is seven dollars. Okay, maybe this isn't such a wonderful place, but it's cheap."

I went back on deck, where the youths were still running and shouting, and many people were bedded down in the open air, sleeping: stacks of bodies in the shadows. But even at nine o'clock there was some dusk left, a pearly light in the sky that made the water seem soapy and placid, and far-off to the west floating fragments of the sunken sun.

There were tiny lights on the coast, and fewer lights showing on the off-shore islands. Soon I saw the timed flashes of what could only have been lighthouses and we drew into a harbor that was empty and poorly lit; just a few men awaiting the ship's lines to be thrown to them.

This was Zadar, and it was midnight, and I alone left the *Liburnija* and went down the gangway. I saw a light burning at the shipping office, where there was a woman and man shuffling papers and smoking.

"I just got off the ship," I said. "I am looking for a hotel."

The man shook his head. The woman said, "There are just a few hotels and they are full with refugees."

"You mean there is nowhere to stay?"

"It is so late," the woman said. "Maybe the Kolovare Hotel. They have refugees, but they might have a place for you."

"Where is it?"

She pointed into the darkness at the end of the quay. "That way. Two kilometers – maybe three."

In fact it was more than a mile. The distance and even the late hour did not deter me from walking there; it was the thought of walking alone in a strange town that was twelve miles from the Bosnian Serb lines. Only someone looking for trouble would walk down these dark streets at that late hour.

"It is possible to call a taxi?"

"No taxis," the man said.

"Thanks."

But as I turned to leave, he said, "When the ship leaves, I will give you a lift."

So I waited on the dark quay at Zadar. It was like a quayside scene in a DiChirico painting, just as bare, just as bewildering.

There were no cars, no people, nothing stirring: it was the abnormal silence full of implication that is more typical in a war zone than noise, for war is nothing happening for weeks and then everything happening horribly in seconds.

The *Liburnija* did not leave until almost one-thirty. I thought: Is it any wonder I travel alone? I had no idea what I was doing. I seldom knew from hour to hour what my plans were. That trip to Opatija was a sudden decision, like the decision to plunge into Pivka and abruptly leave; ditto Rijeka. And now it seemed I had drawn a blank at Zadar. It was unfair to subject another person to this impulsiveness and uncertainty. I had started the day in Rijeka, had lunch in Opatija, had bought the ticket back to Rijeka, and had been sailing since late afternoon. Now, well past midnight, I had no place to stay, and my bag felt like a boulder. I would have been apologizing like mad to a traveling companion. Actually I was pleased. You're in Zadar, buddy, and that was something, still in the Mediterranean after all this time!

"See the holes in the buildings," the man from the agency said, greeting me and yawning after the ship departed. He spoke English mixed with German. His name was Ivo, one of many Ivos I was to meet in the next week or so.

Lumps of stucco had been blown off the walls, some of the walls had crater holes, and many windows were broken.

"From grenades," he explained. "The Serbs were in ships, right there, shelling us. This" — where his old car was parked — "was a crater. They filled it up. But the rest we still haven't fixed. The town is worse than this."

We got in and he drove, very slowly, like an elderly man uncertain of his route.

"All was dark. The whole of Zadar," he said. "And I was so afraid, and even now —"

He laughed in an urgent, mirthless way.

"I am very nervous now," he said. "My nervousness is serious. Look — holes, holes, holes."

We were passing blasted buildings and low ruined walls and pot-holes in the street.

"Do you think I should be nervous?"

"Maybe. I don't know," he said. "For me it was terrible. No water, no electricity. All dark. And it is still not over."

Not more than 125 miles across the Adriatic at Ancona, Italians, their bellies full of pasta and good wine, were sleeping blissfully; and all this Croat spoke of was bombing and war.

"Many people used to come here," Ivo said. "Now there is no one. They are afraid."

We were still traveling through the dark city, and I was grateful for this ride. It was hard to imagine my being able to find my way through these dark streets to the hotel.

"Now – only you," Ivo said.

"The last stranger in Zadar, that's me," I said.

"I hope they have a space for you," Ivo said, as he swung into the driveway of the Kolovare.

All I saw were sandbags. They were stacked in front of the entrance, two bags deep, eight feet high. They were stacked in front of the ground-floor windows. There was a wall of sandbags along the driveway. Some dim lights burned behind them. There were definitely refugees here; the unmistakable sign was laundry hanging from every balcony and most windows, so that the front of the hotel looked like a Sicilian tenement. All the doors were locked.

Ivo roused an old woman, and said something to her. He bade me farewell and disappeared behind the sandbags. The woman gave me a key and showed me to a back room. I tried to talk to her.

"Tomorrow, tomorrow," she said.

Zadar had been seriously shelled – there were signs of damage everywhere, and it was obvious that it had been hit from up close and vindictively: the ancient main gate of the old town, a Roman relic, had been shelled – for what reason, apart from malice? – and chunks blown out of it. The Serbs had set up machine-guns and howitzers in a nearby park, where they were dug in; and these marksmen shelled the high school that was sixty feet away. The high school was now in session, students chatting in the playground, but the front door was sandbagged, so were most of the lower windows, and many upper windows were broken. The entire front of the school was cicatriced by shells. There was major damage around the window frames, misses from their attempts to fire into the windows.

I talked to some of the students. Yes, it was fairly quiet now, right here, they said. But there were road blocks not far away. I asked about the shelling of the buildings. What was the objective?

"They wanted to kill civilians," a young boy said.

"Students?"

"Kill anybody," he said. "If they kill ordinary people in Zadar they think they would make us afraid."

But life went on. The old town of Zadar was not large, and it was contained within a high wall – shops, cafés, restaurants, a theater, some churches. The churches and most other buildings in the town were sandbagged, up to fifteen or twenty feet; but they were also damaged. There were many gun-toting Croatian soldiers in the streets. They were unkempt, they had long hair, many wore earrings; some of the soldiers looked middle-aged, and none of them seemed particularly healthy. They were pale and harassed, like the Zadar civilians.

In the Hotel Kolovare, refugee families killed time in the lobby – there was nowhere else to go, and this was now everyone's parlor. They looked at me without curiosity. Old men dozed in the lobby chairs, children chased up and down the corridors. They were over-excited, they were crazed, ashamed. The room doors were left open, so I could see women doing their laundry in the hotel bath-tubs, and dishes in the bathroom sinks, and ironing boards and household goods stacked in the bedrooms. There were whispers, and shouts. Life went on, but the moods were strange.

There was a cluster of small shops and cafés in the residential part of town about fifteen minutes from the hotel. "Residential" gives the wrong impression, though. The houses were dilapidated, many were scrawled with graffiti, or had broken windows. Some attempts had been made to grow vegetables in the yards. The apartment houses were in the worst shape of any. I walked there to look for a newspaper, but found nothing to read, though there were girlie magazines hung from clothespins along with comic books.

At a café I ordered a cup of coffee. A rock song was playing:

Take your bombs away
So we have today
Take your bombs away
Think about the way
You –

"Is that a local group?" I asked the young woman behind the counter.

"It's English – must be American," she said, and handed me my coffee.

It was none that I recognized, and they were wartime sentiments.

"You're American?" she said.

"Yes. And you're from Zadar?"

"No. My town is Zamunike," she said.

"Is that very far away?"

"Twelve kilometers," she said, and sounded rueful. "I can't go back there. I am a refugee here in Zadar."

Twelve kilometers was only about eight miles. Still, her house was behind Serbian lines, and that was another country, with a sealed and dangerous border.

"The Serbs are there."

"In your house?"

"Maybe."

"That's awful."

It amazed me – the nearness of everything: of war, of shelling, of nastiness, of dislocation, even of comfort, for the Italian Riviera was just across the water, and the stately solemnities of Trieste just up the coast. Zadar was a town which had been besieged and then abandoned. But the enemy was only a few miles away. Refugees had fled here, and no one really knew where they were or what was coming next.

We talked a while more, then an odd thing happened. When I gave her money for the coffee she refused it. She put her own money in the cash register.

"It's a little present," she said.

She did not let me insist. And I was moved. Since beginning this trip months before in Gibraltar it was the first time that anyone had given me anything that could be described as a present. Most of the time I was hardly noticed. I had passed through the Costa Brava and the Côte d'Azur, and Barcelona and Marseilles and Monaco. Nothing came my way. I had to travel here to find a token of generosity, from a skinny woman in a café, in a town full of shell holes, in the shadow of a war. Perhaps war was the reason. Not everyone was brutalized; war made some people better.

My map showed a railway line that went south to the coastal city of Split. It went farther than that, continuing through Montenegro to the Albanian border and beyond, deep into Albania. But a map was not much good here – maps are one of the casualties of war, the single purpose of which is to rewrite them. This was especially true here on the fuzzy border of Croatia and Bosnia-Herzegovina, which was in fact occupied by Serbian soldiers who were attempting to capture and so obliterate Bosnia-Herzegovina. They had tried and failed in Croatia: the shell holes in Zadar were proof of that.

There were many more shell holes in and around Sibenik, which I reached on a bus because none of the trains was running, for of course they all passed through Serbian lines. The bus left Zadar and stayed on the coast road, the choppy Adriatic on the right and pale gray boulders and cheese-white cliffs on the left. Soon we were in a landscape that resembled the Corsican *maquis*, low fragrant bushes and an intense litter of big stones, some in piles, some forming walls, the whole place weird with them.

There were not many passengers: the usual Croatian soldiers and nuns, some elderly people, a few youths. When the bus stopped, as it frequently did, the soldiers hopped off and smoked. At Biograd I attempted a conversation with a group of soldiers but was waved away. Rebuffed, I looked at the Kornat islands offshore, an archipelago of a hundred or so uninhabited and treeless lumps of stone in the sea. The whole landscape was stony, and the odd thing was that it had been demarcated into football-pitch-sized fields that served as goat pastures or great stony rectangles enclosing fruit trees.

I got off at dry, windy Sibenik for lunch – a cup of coffee and a slice of cold pizza – and to look at shell holes. It had been more lightly bombed than Zadar, but it was obvious from the random shelling that the Serbians had no scruples about bombing civilians. Like Zadar, like many of the towns on this coast, Sibenik wore a wounded expression and seemed to wince. I looked at these places but they did not look directly back at me. That was an effect of war, too.

The bus to Split took over an hour, though the place was only thirty miles away. I decided to stay here, to get my bearings. It was an industrial port, rather horrible-looking, enclosing the tiny ancient town of old Split in a maze of streets, with a Temple of Jupiter and a cathedral and a nearby market. All over the sea front of Split, and at the ferry landings and by the bus station (near another defunct railway station), there were old women plucking people's sleeves and offering rooms and nagging in German.

I saw those old women as my opportunity, and decided on a likely one and gave her the thrill of believing she had talked me into a ten-dollar room about a fifteen-minute walk from the ferry landing.

"Good room, cheap room," she said in German, and she made a "follow me" gesture by flapping her hand.

The room was on the third floor of a large, seedy apartment house, but I did not regret it until it was obvious that this old woman and I did not have any language in common. She could say "room" and a few other words in German and Italian, and was of course fluent in Croat. She lived alone. She was the envy of some other old women in the apartment house, because she had snared me.

I would not have minded being trapped there if we had been able to talk, but there was no conversation, I was not able to poke through the other rooms in my nosy way, the pictures of the crucified Christ and suffering saints on the walls depressed me, and I never found out her name. Some of the religious paraphernalia in the dark apartment – pictures of the Madonna and shiny rosaries – were, I later realized, souvenirs of Medjugorje, not far away, which the Madonna had been visiting fairly regularly to inspire the Croatians in their own religious nationalism.

"One week, two weeks?" the woman asked me in German.

"One night," I said.

It passed quickly. I fled in the morning to the greater comfort of the Bellevue Hotel, and tried to find a ferry south to Dubrovnik. None was running. "Forget Dubrovnik – go to Hvar," a ferryman said. Hvar was a nearby island. Instead, I wandered in the market, watching people selling some of their earthly goods in the Croatian version of a flea-market – but these people were refugees. In desperation I looked at the ruins of the Temple of Jupiter, and then I decided to make more travel plans. It seemed you could go almost anywhere from Split – to Ancona, to Rijeka, even to Albania. The one place that was unreachable was Montenegro. The border was only ten or fifteen miles south of Dubrovnik but it was closed. And there was no ferry traffic out of Dubrovnik. But I could bypass Montenegro by taking a ferry to Albania.

"We go to Durrës once a week," the young woman said at the shipping agency.

Since this Albanian ferry was leaving in a few days, I could go south to Dubrovnik, then come back here and catch it.

Split seemed aptly named: it made me want to split. The Bellevue was on a noisy street. After dark the streets of Split emptied. Most of the restaurants had no diners – no one had any money to eat out. I sat eating foul mussels and overcooked pasta. Even the wine was slimy.

But one of the pleasures I experienced in Split was entering a phone booth, inserting my plastic Croatian phone card, and then dialing an access code, my calling card number, and the phone number I wanted – thirty-one numbers altogether, and hearing a sleepy voice, *Hello, darling. I knew it was you. I'm so glad you called. I was worried . . .* Three in the morning in Honolulu.

Traveling from Split to Dubrovnik on a bus the next day I was thinking: What is Croatian culture that it gathered all these people into one nation? The food was a version of the worst Italian cooking. The language was the same as Serbian. What Croatian nationalism amounted to was fanatical Catholicism as a counter to the orthodoxy of Serbian Protestantism, and both sides had terrorist groups and secret societies. Croatians had abandoned the designs they had for annexing parts of Bosnia, because they had border problems of their own – most of the places on the Croatian map were in Serbian hands.

Yet with all the talk of Republika Hvratska, and all the national-
istic graffiti, and the flags and the soldiers and the empty nights in
their cities, it seemed to me that they had ceased to be individual.
Driven by war and religion, they had dissolved their personal
identities into the nation, and so they seemed spectral.

The ruined villages along the coast road looked like work-in-
stoppage, and even the landscape had the look of a building site:
whirling dust on windy bays, dry soil, broken boulders, crumbling
cliffs. Half the passengers on this bus were chain-smoking soldiers
who looked unfit for active duty.

We entered Bosnia. True, it was only the few miles of it that
reached to the coast – Bosnia's only shore – but thirty miles inland,
up the Neretva river, was Mostar, city of atrocities and continuous
shelling – it was being shelled today. After 428 years of being
admired by invaders and locals alike, intact through two world
wars, Mostar's single-span bridge over the Neretva, a masterpiece
of Ottoman architecture, had recently been blasted apart by
mindless Serbian artillerymen.

We soon came to a checkpoint, with Bosnian soldiers, and some
policemen who entered the bus and bullied civilians, denouncing
them for carrying doubtful-looking identity papers. There were
Croatian checkpoints, too, at Omis, Makarska and Podgora: the
same routine. Usually the victim of the policeman's wrath was a
squirming, cowering woman. In this sort of situation the cop had
absolute power: he could arrest the poor woman or boot her off the
bus, or send her back where she came from.

We reached Slano, farther down the road. You did not need to
be told that Slano had been the front line. The house walls were
riddled with bullets, many of the roofs were missing, some of the
houses were bombed flat. This was where the Serbians had dug in
for their attack on Dubrovnik. They had shot at everything. There
was not a structure on the road that did not have at least a divot of
plaster missing. Some had bright patches of tile where the roof had
been mended, and many windows were boarded up.

"Welcome to Dubrovnik" was repeated on a signboard in four
languages, and written across it in large letters, almost obliterating
the welcome, the Croatian word *HAOS!* – chaos.

*

Dubrovnik was famous for its beauty and its bomb craters; but it
was another empty city, with no traffic and no tourists, and even
Lapad harbor looked peculiarly bereft: no ferries running, no
fishing boats, no anglers. It was a gray day, the low sky threatening
rain.

I hopped off the bus in the newer part of town with the soldiers
and the nuns and the others. The soldiers laughed and stayed to
talk while everyone else scuttled away. That was another characteristic of the war: no one lingered anywhere − people arrived in a
place and then vanished. Apart from the groups of soldiers, there
were no street discussions or any public gatherings. As the only
non-Croatian on the street I was wooed by taxi-drivers, but it
would not be dark for a few hours and so I decided to walk around
the port, from hotel to hotel, to check the prices and get my
bearings.

Red Cross vehicles, UN Land-Rovers, and official cars of charitable agencies filled the parking lots of the first three hotels. The
desk clerks said, "We have no rooms."

This was not happy news. I kept walking. An aid worker,
probably Canadian judging from the maple leaf on his lapel pin,
sat in the lobby reading a paperback book. The woman at reception told me her hotel was full.

"Wish I could help you," the Canadian said.

The book he was reading was *Pride and Prejudice*.

Afterwards on the street, in a sharp attack of what the French
call "stairway wit," I realized I should have quipped to him, "Is
that a history of Yugoslavia?" He might have laughed and thought:
What a witty fellow!

Two more hotels were closed and looked damaged. The next
hotel that was open had been entirely given over to refugees. But I
eventually found one on a back street that had spare rooms. It also
had refugees. It was not a very good hotel. I was beginning to
comprehend another axiom of war: in a time of crisis the do-
gooders get the best rooms − five-star hotels for the UN and the
charities, one-star hotels for the refugees and me.

Again, as in Zadar, and on the *Liburnija*, and in Split, I was
among rambunctious children and dozy parents − locals and
refugees: more war nerves. The children played loud music and

chased each other and yelled. They raced up and down the hotel corridors, they congregated noisily in the lobby. Given the fact that they had been severely bombed, they remained indoors and seemed to have an obvious and perhaps understandable aversion – to not say phobic reaction – to being in the open air.

I had no such aversion. But before I could walk very far the rain began, first as a series of irregular showers and then as drizzle interrupted by thunder and lightning. I sheltered inside a grocer's shop that was so small I had to excuse myself and step outside when a customer entered.

Business was terrible, the grocer said. His glum wife agreed, shaking her head.

"Dubrovnik depended on tourists," the grocer said. "Now there are none."

That was the strange thing about a tourist resort without tourists. The town had been adapted for people who were not there. The hotels looked haunted, the restaurants and shops were empty, the beaches were neglected as a result and were littered and dirty. Few of the shops sold anything that a native or a townie would be likely to need or could afford. So the place was inhabited by real people, but everything else about it seemed unreal.

Apart from the shell holes and the closed hotels and the bullet nicks on buildings, the city was in good shape. The shattered roofs had been repaired. I had not yet seen the famously lovely old town of Dubrovnik, which had been heavily bombed, but I was told it had been restored.

"We have no income," said the grocer.

The stormy sky descended and darkened the town, and a while later the streets were black, the storm having obliterated the transition from day to night.

The hotel was so hard-pressed that for simplicity there was only one menu available, the refugee meal. I sat with these hundred or so people, mainly women and children, and had my refugee meal. It was one of the hours in the day when, stuffing their faces, the children were quiet. Elsewhere – but not far away, just across the mountains that hemmed in Dubrovnik, in Bosnia – food was being dropped from American planes or tossed out of the back of UN trucks; yet there was famine all the same. These refugees who had gotten to the shores of the Mediterranean were the lucky ones.

After dinner I began talking with a man in the lobby. First the subject of the weather – rain. Then business – no tourists. Then the war. He was aggrieved that America had not done more to help.

"Help who?" I asked.

"Help us in our struggle," he said.

I said, "Tell me why American soldiers should get killed in your civil war."

He did not like my tone.

"No one cares about us," he said.

"Everyone cares," I said. "No one knows what to do, and I don't blame them, because so far it has all looked so petty and unpredictable."

"Clinton is weak," the man said.

It irritated me very much that a tribalistic Croatian on this bombed and squabbling coast, with its recent history of political poltroonery, not to say political terror and fratricide, should criticize the American president in this way.

"Who told you that, Tudjman?"

Tudjman, the Croatian president, was noted for being a fanatical nationalist and moralizing bore, and an irritant generally.

"He's very strong, isn't he?" I said. I could not keep my eyes from dancing in anger. "You're so lucky to have him."

In sunshine, the old fortified town of Dubrovnik lived up to its reputation of being one of the loveliest in the Mediterranean: a medieval walled city, a citadel on the sea, with an ancient harbor. It was the Republic of Ragusa, so prosperous and proud that even when its buildings were destroyed in an earthquake in the mid-seventeenth century it was scrupulously restored, and has been so well preserved that the oldest paintings and etchings of it show it as it is today, unchanged. The town is listed as "a treasure" by UNESCO.

The worst damage since that natural disaster in 1667 had happened just recently, late in 1991 and well into 1992, when as many as 30,000 Serbian and Montenegrin shells hit the city –

there were cannons firing from behind the city, on the heights of the mountain range, and more cannons on warships just offshore, as at Zadar. There was no reason for this. The capture of the port meant almost nothing from the military point of view. The Serbian assault was rightly termed "cultural vandalism."

Most of the bomb damage had been repaired. Dubrovnik was a prettier place by far than Rijeka or Zadar or Split, or any of the other coastal towns, but there was something spooky about a preserved old town, one of the most venerable on the Mediterranean shore, that was totally empty. It was like Venice after the plague. Just after the Black Death, in 1345, when most of its citizens lay dead, Venice was begging outsiders to settle, and this queen of cities promised citizenship to anyone who became a Venetian: it must have looked something like Dubrovnik, with its empty streets and scarred walls and its air of bereavement.

But Dubrovnik was putting on a brave back-to-normal face and that made the whole place seem odder still, because it was empty – empty and handsome. Some stores were open, some cafés, even some restaurants. Art galleries sold pretty pictures of the town, sprightly oils of the glorious stone buildings and the harbor; watercolors of church spires, pastoral scenes of sweetness and light.

None of war, none of damage, or emptiness: no despair, no soldiers.

"Some artists came after the fighting and did sketches of what the bombs had done," a gallery owner told me. "They went away."

I asked a question about the siege.

"No," the woman said, and turned away. "I don't want to think about it. I want to forget it."

It was only twenty-odd miles from Dubrovnik to the border of Montenegro, the smallest of the improvised republics, then maybe another sixty or so to Shkodër in Albania, and that was – what? – a couple of hours.

No, no – not at all. Although these distances seemed in American newspapers to be enormous, the pronouncement, "We journeyed from the Republic of Croatia to the Republic of Montenegro and

then to the Republic of Albania" described a two-hour jog in a
car, a mere piddling jaunt, with plenty of time to stop and admire
the view. Geographically it was nothing, politically it was something else. It was, in fact, a political distance, like the eighty miles
that separated Cuba from Key West, or the few miles that divided
Mexico from California. You could not get there from here without
the danger of physical harm.

Montenegrins had allied themselves to Serbia and both had
designs on Croatia. So the border was closed. It was impossible to
tell whether the Albania–Montenegro border was open: probably
not. My hope lay in a ferry from Split to Albania, but even so I
looked for someone willing to take me to the checkpoint on the
border.

I found a taxi-driver, Ivo Lazo, a friendly man who had worked
for fifteen years in Germany and who spoke German and managed
some English.

He would say, "So the Serbian *chetniks* take the – *was ist
Messer?*"

"Knife."

"– take the knife and –" Mr Lazo passed a finger across his
throat to indicate how the *chetniks* slit them in their fanaticism.

"Can you take me to Montenegro?"

"Ha!" Mr Lazo exclaimed, meaning "ridiculous!"

"What about to the border?"

"Ha!"

"Maybe just to look at it?"

"Ha!"

"What do you suggest, then?"

"I will show you something interesting," Mr Lazo said.

Passing a sign reading *DUBROVNIK* on which was scrawled
To HELL, Mr Lazo drove me to the upper road, on the mountainside behind Dubrovnik, near where the Serbian artillery had
shelled the city. This was quite a different perspective from the one
I had had within the city itself. From this high position I had an
aerial view of the bombardment's effects – about a third of the roof
tiles were new, in great contrast to the old gray tiles; the repairs to
the walls were still visible – the new stucco-work left large pale
areas. Perhaps in time the colors would blend and the stone would

be uniformly mellow. At the moment it was a city wearing patches.

"Five hundred to seven hundred bombs hit it – you see?" Mr Lazo said.

"Where were you at the time?"

"Over there," he said, and pointed to the newer part of Dubrovnik, in the Lapad district, near the other harbor.

"Did you have any warning?"

"The first indication we had was from the Serbian families here," he said. "Four thousand of them – yes, many. The men started to go away, little by little. The old women stayed. They knew something."

"How did they know?"

"How did they know! How did they know!" Mr Lazo threw up his hands, and then began to explain the network of Serbian whispering, the foreknowledge of the attack.

He did not hate the Serbs, he said. He had lived with them almost his whole life. The *chetniks* of course were a different matter.

"They have long beards, they are dirty, they are – so to say – fundamentalists. They are like the Gestapo. They don't just kill. They torture. Women, children, all the same."

The *chetniks* were famous for their daggers and their muddy boots and their long hair, and there was something about their filthy faces that made them seem more ruthless and frightening, like the Huns and Visigoths – their distant ancestors – who had raped and pillaged their way through here at the end of the fifth century. *Chetniks* also were driven by the worst and most merciless engine for violence there is – religious crankishness.

In October 1991, the Lazo family in Lapad became very anxious, noticing that by degrees their Serbian neighbors had crept away. Soon the shelling began and lasted through November. They cowered in their house, twelve of them, Ivo and his parents and wife and children and some cousins. The shelling continued. It was now December. Many people had died, many houses had caught fire. The water was cut off. "We carried water from the sea to use in the toilet." They shared a well for drinking water. There was no electricity. It was cold, some days it snowed.

In a horrible and pitiless way it is interesting how gutless and patient soldiers can be, even when they have their enemy pinned down. The war all over the former Yugoslavia was – and still is – the epitome of this sort of cowardly onslaught. In almost every siege, in Sarajevo and Mostar and twenty other places, there has been no forward motion. The attacking army found a convenient position on a mountain or a road or at a safe distance at sea, and then for as long as it had artillery shells it bombarded the target, pinning people in their houses.

This was why the war seemed endless: instead of infantry attacks or guerrilla fighting or even aerial bombing, it was a war of sieges, like the oldest Mediterranean warfare. Every coastal town or port by this sea had been under siege at some point in its history: Gibraltar had fourteen of them; Malta had known even more – Turks attacking crusaders in Valletta harbor; British attacking the French during the Napoleonic wars; Phoenicians, Romans, Goths, Vandals, Turks, Nazis, the US Marines and my American uncles had all made war in these Mediterranean ports. But there was a significant difference between invaders and besiegers. Siege was hardly a military art; it was a simple method of wearing down and starving and demoralizing a civilian population. It was a massive and prolonged insult, carried on by a merciless army with a tactical advantage.

The Serbian army had massed their tanks on the north side of town, on the road near Slano, where I had seen the bomb damage. That was the forward line, the little villages of Trsteno and Drasac, where there were holiday homes and time-share bungalows built by Germans and British people in happier times.

There were also tanks on the road south of Dubrovnik, around Cilipi where the airport was – half an hour by road from Montenegro; and more tanks on the eastern heights that Lazo called Jarkovitze Mountain (it was not on my map). The ships were a mile or so off-shore. So Dubrovnik was completely surrounded, and shells were falling from the four points of the compass.

"My daughter Anita was very worried," Mr Lazo said. "I said to her, 'Go to the Old Town. You will be safe there.'"

There was an almost mystical belief in the sanctity and inviolability of the Old Town. Because of the enormous walls, ten feet thick and four stories high; because of the beauty of the town; because of its historical importance – its association with Venice, its great trading history, site of the oldest apothecary in the Mediterranean; because, most of all, of the town's religious connections – St Blaise had lived and died here, St Nicholas was its patron saint; for all these good reasons, the Old Town was a refuge.

Anita Lazo fled there with a number of others, and on 6 December, the Feast of St Nicholas – the timing was deliberate – the Old Town was shelled.

"I looked up and saw the tanks on the mountain," Mr Lazo said. "They were like matches lighting – the fire and then *whouf* – the bombs."

Hundreds were killed, as many as 250 civilians in that siege alone, and the destruction was enormous. Anita Lazo survived. Mr Lazo drove me to a point overlooking Lapad harbor and showed me the burned-down freezer plant, the ruined buildings, the rubble, the boats that had been shelled and had sunk, still lying dead in the water as hulks. This was the newer part of town, not a priority; about half the roofs had been repaired.

"They didn't come closer. They bombed. But to take the city – to capture it – that is very difficult," Mr Lazo said. "We had Kalashnikovs and other guns. We could defend it, man to man. But still the bombs fell."

The siege lasted three months – tension, noise, eerie silences, rumors; no water, no lights. Not long before they'd had as many as 70,000 tourists in a season. Now they had – how many?

"We have you," Mr Lazo said. "Ha!"

We went to Slano where there was hellish damage and more sunken boats.

"It will take ten years to go back to normal," Mr Lazo said. That seemed a popular number; many Croats mentioned ten years, and I was wondering whether they were quoting someone. "Even then there will be big differences. We are of the West. Croatia had 900 years of Austro-Hungarians, Serbia had 500 years of Ottoman Turks. They have the Eastern Orthodox, like the Russians. We have Rome – we are Catholics."

That meant, for example, that on 3 February, the Feast of St Blaise, they went to the church in the Old Town and a priest placed two lighted candles against their neck and said a prayer, because among other things St Blaise was the patron saint of neck ailments. I knew that from my childhood in Boston: the smell of beeswax, the flames warming my ears.

I avoided the theology of warfare and asked him why, after fifteen years in Germany, he had come here, to be bombed.

"I came home. Because home is home."

In a year of Mediterranean travel it was one of the most logical statements I heard.

"Tell people to come here," Mr Lazo said. "We are ready."

True, Dubrovnik was open for business, and like its women war had given it a gaunt beauty. But it was a city that had been traumatized and still looked patched up and fragile. My hotel was $18 a night, quite a bargain, even with the resident refugees and their manic war-nerves. The traffic in town was mainly the modern equivalent of camp followers – Mother Courage and her children: UN Land-Rovers, Red Cross vans, Caritas trucks, UNPROFOR and UNHCR vehicles. The beaches were foul. The casino was closed, many hotels were shut. It was not possible to count all the broken windows, nor had much of the broken glass been picked up from the ground.

The clearest sign that it was still a city of refugees was that laundry hung from every window and every porch and balcony, the sad scrubbed and faded clothes fluttering like battle flags.

I stayed a few more days in Dubrovnik, to catch up on my notes and for the pleasure of walking along the coast, the only tourist in town. One day I met an Italian taking a shipment of Red Cross medicine to Mostar. It was a day's drive from here. He had a Caritas truck.

"Mostar was very badly bombed, but there is no fighting in town now," he said. "A bit outside the town there is shelling."

"I'd like to go there, just to see."

"I can't take you, because of the insurance."

"I wanted to see the famous bridge."

"It's fallen," he said. *Caduto*.

On the way back to Split, the bus broke down at Slano. So while the driver made a mess of replacing the fan-belt – hammering the bracket with his monkey wrench, struggling with rusty nuts – I had another chance to examine the bomb damage. Then I sat beside the road, with the grumbling soldiers, and the bus-driver swore at the limp fan-belt.

I now understood why, the moment the bus had gasped to a stop, an attractive young woman had dashed out of the door, run into the road and begun hitchhiking. A few cars went by her, but within five minutes she had a ride. She was on her way and we were sitting at the edge of the broken road with a clapped-out bus. She exemplified another axiom of war: don't wait for your vehicle to be mended — just use your initiative; flash your tits and take off. It may be your only chance.

Back in Split I went to the Albanian ferry agency. The ferry for Durrës was scheduled to leave that night.

"Sorry. It was canceled," the young woman told me. "I cannot sell you a ticket."

"How do I get there?"

She shrugged. She did not know.

But I had a suspicion that if I took a ferry back to Ancona in Italy I could get one from there, or possibly from Bari, where I had been told there were regular departures. I bought a ferry ticket to Italy on the next day's sailing, feeling that I would reach Albania eventually, even if it meant criss-crossing the Adriatic. But it seemed a waste: in Dubrovnik I had been just two hours by road from Albania, but the trip was impossible. I was now faced with a four-day journey.

The point about atrocity stories, especially here, was that everyone told them. For a week I had been listening to stories about *chetnik* fanaticism; but, killing time in Split until the day the Ancona ferry left, I met an aid worker from Canada who told me about the Croatian fanaticism.

"Didn't you see them?" he said. "Weren't you here a few days ago?"

"I was in Dubrovnik."

"There were groups of Ustasha soldiers in the bars here in Split, all singing Nazi songs — the 'Horst Wessel' and all that."

The Ustasha were Croatian commandos, much like the Serbian *chetniks*. They modeled themselves on the Nazi SS and wore black shirts and a "U" insignia. Their ruthlessness and racism dated from the fascist Ustasha regime which had governed Croatia with Nazi help during the Second World War, and off its own bat, without Nazi control, had operated its own death camp. Serbian "ethnic cleansing" was now well enough known to be universally condemned, but this policy of Croatian "purification" was new to me.

"So what's going to happen here?"

"In ten years" – that magic figure again – "things will be quieter," he said. "And there will be a greater Serbia, a greater Croatia and a smaller Bosnia."

On the quay, having just bought tickets to Italy, was a family of refugees – a hollow-eyed man, his painfully thin wife and his child. The little boy looked robust, the parents half-starved, and so it was easy to conclude that the child had been given the parents' rations.

"We were airlifted by helicopter from Tuzla," he said, and since Tuzla was in Bosnia, the family obviously had been through the wringer.

They had escaped from Sarajevo, leaving their parents and their house and everything they possessed. All they had were two small suitcases, a pram for the child (who was too heavy for them to lift), and a bag of food. This family had been sponsored by a French organization, Solidarité, which had provided the helicopter getaway.

The family's story was not complicated, but in its simplicity it amply illustrated the despicable nature of this civil war, which was a border dispute fueled by ancient grievances (the assassination of the Croatian King Zvonimir in 1089, for example), wartime collaboration and score-settling, racism, and religious differences.

"I am a geologist," he said. His name was Dr Tomic; he was probably in his mid-thirties, but his haunted look made him seem much older. "I am from ex-Yugoslavia. My parents are Serbian, but I was born in Bosnia, so I am a Bosnian. Sarajevo is my home. My wife is a Muslim. That's the problem."

Mrs Tomic gave me a wan smile and shrugged her skinny shoulders.

"For eight years I had been at the university in Sarajevo, specializing in the geology of the area," Dr Tomic said. "Then my colleagues began to ask me questions as though to test me. Finally they said, 'We have lost confidence in you.'"

"Did they say why?"

"No – they couldn't. My geology is very local, just the thing that is studied there," he said. "My neighborhood was next. My neighbors began to make problems. They were blaming my wife for things. They know she is a Muslim. It got very bad."

"How bad? Give me an instance," I said.

"Dangerous – threats," he said, and seemed so shaken by the memory that I did not press him.

"We considered fleeing to Slovenia," he said. "They have camps here, but we don't qualify. They have Serbs in one camp, Croats in another, Muslims in a third. We don't fit in, because we are mixed."

"So what are you going to do?"

"Go to France," he said. "Take the ferry to Italy, then the train to Paris."

They were leaving everything behind, most of all they were abandoning hope for their country. It interested me that they had only two small bags and this folding pram; I imagined it to be the little boy's clothes, and a change of clothes for themselves. The average tourist in Italy on a short holiday – they would probably be sharing the train with many such people – had ten times this weight in baggage.

After that, whenever I read about troop maneuvers or politicians grandstanding or mortar attacks on cities or the pettiness and terror of the war, I thought about this skinny man and wife, each one holding a bag, pushing their little boy down the quay at Split, their starved faces turned to the Mediterranean, waiting for the ferry to take them away from here.

The next day I saw the refugee couple on the ferry *Ivan Krajc* standing in the rain by the rail watching the Croatian shore recede from view.

The rest of the passengers divided themselves into groups – Italian truck-drivers who joked and sang and ate, Italian pilgrims who had just come from Medjugorje and were still praying (dozens of them, standing on deck in the rain and chanting the rosary out loud), Croatians like the Tomic family, looking furtive and anxious; and aid workers down from Bosnia, with a few days to spend in Italy.

"We drove down from Zenica today," an aid worker told me. Zenica was about forty miles north-west of Sarajevo. "Last year it took us ten days to drive from Zenica to Split, because of road blocks and fighting. Today it took eight hours. Maybe things are improving!"

He was an Australian, traveling with his American wife, who was also an aid worker. She had a neighborly manner, and he was upright, mustached, and had a military bearing – he later told me he had been a soldier in South Africa. He was in his mid-forties, with the charity World Vision. His name was David Jennings. He and Theresa were making their first-ever visit to Italy, as a break from their aid project in Bosnia.

They asked me what I did for a living.

"I'm a writer."

"Journalists are a pain," David said.

"They all cover the same story – four guys in four separate cars go to the same place," Theresa said.

"They come for the big stories, when they can get their face on the camera, with shooting behind them," David said.

"I'm not a journalist," I said. "I don't work for anyone. I'm just looking around."

"I went back to Australia for about ten days last January," David said. "I looked at the paper, flipping the pages, and there was nothing about the war – nothing. I called the editor. I said, 'Hey, mate. I've just come back from Bosnia, and I've got some news for you – the war's still on!'"

"What sort of thing do you do?"

"I'm a logistician," he said. "But I do everything. I mean, we all do. We have heart specialists driving ambulances."

"Isn't logistics about making things happen?"

"Yes. I coordinate shipments of food and equipment. My military background is useful for that. It takes patience, though. I mean, like waiting for six hours at a checkpoint because some jumped-up little guy pretends there's something wrong with my papers."

The problem was that all the borders were so blurred. Serb, Croat and Bosnian lines were close and continually shifting.

"Because I'm working in Bosnia they see my work as helping the enemy," he said. "And they're fussy too. In my office I have a Bosnian Muslim, a Croat and a Serb. They get along fine. But my interpreter was dealing with a freight forwarder in Zagreb over the phone. After a few minutes my interpreter handed the phone to me. 'She doesn't want to talk to me.' The woman in Zagreb suspected – from the interpreter's Serbo-Croatian accent – that he might be a Muslim. I asked the Zagreb woman for a reason. She says, 'He is not speaking my language.'"

"I was thinking of going to Mostar," I said. "But I was warned that it was dangerous."

"You might have hit it on a bad day," he said. "Hey, I was standing talking with some UNPROFOR guys at Tuzla airport the other day. I felt a tug in my chest – a hard poke – and heard a bang and saw a slug spinning on the floor. Someone had fired at me."

"But it bounced off?"

"I was wearing a flak jacket."

"Who was the sniper?"

"Might have been anyone," he said. "Probably thought I was UNPROFOR. They all hate them. They suspect them of helping the enemy, whoever that might be."

Theresa said, "They try to demoralize people. That's how they think they'll win."

"Who is 'they'?"

"Each side," she said.

"Demoralizing" took the form of being beastly and unreasonable in uniquely horrible ways.

Later, in my cabin on the *Ivan Krajc* at midnight, twiddling my radio I found an FM station broadcasting from Split in English, for the benefit of aid workers and UN soldiers. It was a war report, and it sounded as bland as a stock market update.

"*– and three artillery shells fell just outside the city of Tuzla today. There were no casualties. Small-arms provocation was reported in Bihac lasting thirty-five minutes this afternoon. Twenty-five people are still listed as missing in Sarajevo. Two shells struck a house in Gorazde, demolishing* *it. No one was injured. Two mortar bombs exploded in Travnik. It was agreed that the left bank of the Neretva river in Mostar be officially reopened after six p.m. tomorrow. One member of UNPROFOR was critically injured by sniper fire in —"*

The soporific drone of the ferry's engines mercifully eased me to sleep. I slumbered all the way across the Adriatic, and in the morning I was back in Italy, looking for a way by ship to Albania.

12

The Ferry *Venezia* to Albania

It was not until I was on board the ferry *Venezia*, among dowdy women wearing long trousers under their thick skirts and grizzled cheese-paring men in cloth caps and frayed tracksuits — both men and women had the faces of fretful tortoises — that I realized that I was at last on my way to Albania. I had rehearsed it all mentally with such thoroughness that the whole business seemed inevitable. I had bought a ferry ticket from an agent in Ancona. The ferry was leaving from Bari, 200-odd miles down the coast. I went by train to Bari. Returning to a city, I always retraced my steps. In Bari this meant the same hotel, a certain laundry, a certain restaurant, a certain bookstore, a stroll down the Corso to the port. The women at the laundry remembered me, and one said, "We think you're an artist of some kind." That was nice. But they expressed amazement that I was going to Albania, which is regarded with horror by the Barese.

Another man in Bari was franker. "Albanians are the filthiest," he said. *Sporchissimi.* "And the poorest." *Poverissimi.* "Stay here!"

No argument could detain me. I was beyond being determined; I was programmed for Albania. I had my fifty-dollar ferry ticket. My clothes were washed. I had a stock of books and batteries for my radio. I even had a map of the place. I did not want to listen to any Italian's opinions about Albania — none of the ones I met had been there. But it was only on the deck of the *Venezia* as we headed east out of the harbor that I remembered that I had no visa for Albania, I hadn't the foggiest idea where I was going, or why. All I had done was offer myself as a passenger. I had merely shown up and said: *Please take me.*

But where? The importance of getting to Albania had preoccupied me to such an extent that I had forgotten why I was going.

On board, I wanted to ask people what their intentions were in Albania, thinking that it would offer some clue to why I was going. No one was very conversational. The passengers were seedy but calm. The Albanians muttered in Gheg or Tosk and ignored me. They crouched over little paper parcels of food, sinister-looking scraps of meat and crumbly crusts of bread and mousetrap cheese. There were not many children, though one family with two children had among its possessions, packed into cardboard boxes, a rocking-horse with green fur glued to it.

The decks of the ferry were crammed with stolen cars. I had been told by people in Bari that the cars on the ferry to Durrës had been snatched from streets all over Europe, given new documents, and exported to Albania where they would be sold on the black market and then vanish down dusty roads. There were the usual aid workers and the vans from various charities making their weekly food and clothing run. But Italian aid workers were the opposite of solemn – they were truck-drivers, smokers, shouters, practical jokers, goosing each other and laughing. They sprawled in the cafeteria, mocking the awfulness of the food (wet spaghetti, soggy salad, inky wine) and yakking, then one would say, "You recognize this song?" and would begin singing something sacrilegious in a falsetto voice.

I had the feeling that I was the only one on board who was just going for the ride. On deck I tuned my radio and listened to the news. "The trial of Ramiz Alia, former prime minister of Albania, started in Tirana today," I heard, and told myself that my trip was timely, yet knew that I was kidding myself. I knew nothing of Albania except that for fifty years the paranoid dictator Enver Hoxha had allowed few foreigners to enter and no Albanian to leave. Albania, cut off from everything, had a reputation for being one of the strangest countries in the world. With the great shake-up brought on by the Soviet collapse, Albania had changed – hadn't it? It must have, because here I was, *en route* to the coastal city of Durrës.

The moon was up, the ship passed parallel to the shore along a sea-level string of lights that were the street-lamps of the coast road south of Bari. Then the ship swung east, into the darkness.

Hurrying from Croatia to Italy to catch this ferry I had a sense of weariness, and wondered whether I had the stomach to push on. But the notion of going to Albania lifted my spirits, because I had never been there before and I knew nothing about it, and neither did anyone else. That in itself seemed a novelty, for here on the most heavily beaten path in the world, the shore of the Mediterranean, it was still possible to travel into the unknown.

At 6:30 in the morning I woke with a start in the tobacco-stink of my cabin and only then realized it had no porthole. I had to go on deck to see that we were in bright sunshine approaching the low green outline of what had been ancient Illyria. This dissolved as we drew closer, and now a brown cluttered headland loomed, the forehead of Durrës, ancient Epidamnus beneath it, with cranes and tenements. Nearer still, I could see the dome and minarets of a white mosque, my first glimpse of Islam on this trip. Another brown hill, and at its top a large white house, the palace of Ahmet Zogu who in 1928 had styled himself Zog the First, King of Albania. Ten years later, with an ultimatum from Italy (whose monarch Victor Emanuel called himself King of Italy and Emperor of Abyssinia and Albania), Zog was headed into permanent exile, Albania's whole treasury in his luggage.

"Passport control," a deck-hand said to me, and pointed to a card table that had been shoved under the broken TV set in the lounge. Two unshaven men in dirty sports shirts sat there with a stack of passports, looking tough as they took turns thumping the pages with their rubber stamp. It was as though the whole aggressive ritual was intended to erode your confidence: the shirts, the flimsy table, the grubby men, the jumble of passports. And their pad was so dry the men had to pound it to make even a feeble impression with the rubber stamp.

My passport was flung back to me and I went on deck to see the *Venezia* moving stern first towards the dock so that the stolen cars and aid trucks could be off-loaded. Beside us there was a hulk sunken to its gunwales, and a blond Albanian boy of about twelve or thirteen dived from it. He swam beside our ship, calling out for the passengers to throw money. He gagged and spat as the screws of our ship churned up swirling mud from the harbor bottom. The Italian truck-drivers flung balled up paper money and coins and soon there were four or five boys swimming for it and squabbling.

Knowing so little in advance I had mentally prepared myself for anything in Albania, but even so I was shocked by Durrës. My first sight as I walked off the ship was of a mob of ragged people, half of them beggars, the rest of them tearful relatives of the passengers, all of them howling.

It was hysteria, and dirt and dogs and heat, but what alarmed me most were the people snatching at me. No one elsewhere on my trip had noticed me. I was so anonymous I felt invisible wherever I went. No one had ever touched me. Here they pounced. They took hold of my hand, tugged at my shirt, fingered my pen. *"Signor!"* "Money!" *"Soldi!"* "Please! You geeve me!" "Meester!"

They fastened themselves to me, pleading. I could not brush them aside – they were truly ruined. They looked dazed, they were poor, ravaged, bumpy-faced with pox scars – mothers with children, blind men with boys, old hectoring crones, all of them plucking at me. "Geeve me theese!"

Third World, I thought, but it was the only Third World scene I had ever witnessed that was entirely populated by Europeans – the most dissolute and desperate and poverty-stricken and rapacious, lunging at me, following just behind me, demanding money.

I was a sitting duck for this attention. The Italian aid-worker passengers had vehicles. They drove through the mob. The Albanian passengers dragging cardboard boxes had nothing to give. But even travel-weary and plainly dressed I looked prosperous compared with the ragged mob at the port, and – worst of all – I was on foot. They were all around me, in my face, snagging my clothes, their hands in my pockets.

Hurrying on, I pretended I knew where I was going. I found a path cut through a junkyard, went across the railway tracks and followed them, hoping to get to the station, all the while passing curious people. Some beggars had stayed with me, still pleading, as I walked on into Durrës, which was a world of dust and ruination.

Nothing was right in Durrës. Even the trees were dirty and had rusted leaves; blighted and dying, most of them had the smashed, dilapidated look of the hideous tenements near them. Many limbs had been lopped and the ones that had been left were maimed. It was not that the trees looked dead, but rather that they had never been alive, just moth-eaten props on a cheap stage-set from a show that had closed long ago. High weeds grew in the railway yard, and the coaches that I could see were either tipped over or else derelict, with broken windows. Bright sun bore down on everything and the stink that I had first noticed as I walked off the ship still hung in the air – it was a shit smell in the heat, an odor of decay and dust, of rotting clothes, and even the earth – the dirt I was kicking as I hurried onward – had a rancid gasoline pong that was like the reek of poison.

In a filthy and deranged way it all fitted together – the toasted trees, the cracked buildings, the nasty earth, the trains that didn't run, and everywhere I could see people in rags. *Sporchissimi, poverissimi,* summed it up. When the people saw me it was as though they had seen The Man Who Fell to Earth, and they ran towards me and screamed for me to give them something – money, food, clothes, my pen, anything. The minute I made eye contact the person lunged at me and began pleading.

It was just as well I came here ignorant. If anyone had told me about this in advance – the way Durrës looked, the filth and desperation – I would not have believed them.

In the meantime I could not shake off these pleading people. I was still being followed and brayed at by two begging boys, a young woman holding a limp comatose child, and an old woman wearing leggings and a shawl. They were behind me as I walked down the tracks towards the station, and they stood with me at the station as I rattled the locked door. The station windows were cracked and broken, but I could see inside that it was empty, papers littering the floor, several chairs tipped over, the one-number pad calendar on the wall showing the wrong date.

A woman approached me, looking much like all the others: tortoise-faced, wearing a sweater in spite of the heat, trousers under her skirt, big broken shoes. But this one carried a bunch of keys – the badge of her authority.

"Train?" I asked.

"*Nuk ka tren,*" the woman said, and waved her hands with a flap of finality.

That was clear enough – anyway, I could have guessed there was no train, having seen the weeds growing over the tracks, and the vandalized coaches, and the wrecked station. Seeing me flummoxed, the beggars seized my hesitation as their opportunity and pleaded with me to give them something.

The woman with the keys was pointing to the front of the station. "*Autobusi*," she said.

That was plain too, but nothing else was as it should have been, not the thing itself, nor even a symbol of it: the station was not a station, the sidewalks were not sidewalks, the trees were not trees, the streets were not streets, even the buses I saw did not look like buses. The vehicles were ravaged and three of them together at the front of the station made the space look like a junkyard, not a bus depot.

The beggars stayed beside me, and there were other people squatting on the ground or standing in groups. Everyone was looking at me, waiting to see what I would do.

I'll go to Tirana, I thought. I knew from my map that it was only twenty-five miles away. *Come back here some other day*.

I went to one of the wrecked buses. Some more people followed me. I wanted to shake them all off.

"Tirana?" I asked.

"Tirana!" They pointed to another bus. And a ragged young man in his early twenties stepped over to me. I thought he was going to ask me for money, but instead he said, mixing English and Italian, "This bus is going soon to Tirana."

I climbed in and sat by the back door.

"It costs fifty leks," the young man said, and seeing that I was confused he took out a scrap of red rag that was a fifty-lek note and handed it to me. "You will need this."

Before the door clapped shut I managed to give the young man some Italian lire in return, perhaps its equivalent. For the second time on my trip I had received a gift from an unlikely person. He had given me, a stranger, what was in Albania a half-day's pay, knowing that I would never see him again. This sudden act of kindness, like the cup of coffee from the woman in the bar at Zadar, took the curse off the place, and though Durrës still looked horrific I was won over.

The bus was full. I was jammed on the long seat at the back being bumped by the passengers standing in front of me. There was a great stink of mildewed clothing and tobacco smoke, but I was near enough to the door to stick my head out when we came to a stop. It was a slow bus, the stops were frequent, but none of this mattered very much to me – I was on my way, fascinated by most of what I saw.

Men and women in the fields by the roadside worked with primitive implements – they wielded crooked-handled scythes and big sickles, they forked hay into heaps on horse-drawn wagons with ancient-looking tridents, and they plowed with yoked teams of horses. This was not even turn-of-the-century technology; these were the sort of farm tools that had been used in Europe hundreds of years ago. There wasn't an engine in sight, no tractors or cars – and no other vehicle on the road apart from this wheezing bus.

The fields were as rubbly and irregular as everything else. They were not flat, the furrows were not parallel, nothing was plumb. Since arriving in Albania I had not seen a straight line. That was true of the houses, too, the small collapsing hovels and sheds and tottering barns. And this absence of true geometry, this disorder, made Albania seem deranged and gave Albanians a suspicious and retarded look.

I had seen ruin before in other places, but it was odd to see farms that were so disorderly. Even in Third World countries where people lived in poor and misshapen huts their fields had order and there was always a symmetry in the plants, the wind-breaks, the ditches. But there was no harmony here.

That was simply strange, yet the landscape had another feature, and it floored me: the bunkers and bomb shelters. I had seen the first ones on the outskirts of Durrës and had wondered what they were. Most of them looked like igloos in cement, some big, some small; others were like pill-boxes, round or square. The smaller ones could not have accommodated more than one or two people. Twenty or more people could have fitted into some of the others, which were the size of bungalows. They were like stone lumps. They had no windows, though most of them had gunslits.

They were scattered all over the open, treeless landscape, rows of them on ridges, along the sides of the road, hidden in hollows, on the banks of stagnant creeks, and distantly, perhaps for miles – as far as I could see – they continued. They were everywhere.

These bunkers were unusual enough to have been remarked on by an Albanian writer, Ismaîl Kadaré. He is also the only Albanian novelist who has been translated into English. In his best-known novel, *The General of the Dead Army* (1970), Kadaré writes about a visiting Italian general who sees them: "The blockhouses were all silent and deserted . . . they looked like Egyptian sculptures with expressions that were sometimes cold and contemptuous, sometimes enigmatic, depending on the design of the gunslits. When the slits were vertical then the little forts had a cruel, menacing expression that conjured up some evil spirit; but when the slits were horizontal, then their strange petrified mimicry expressed only indifference and scorn."

"Egyptian"? "Cruel"? "Scorn"? No, most of this description is fanciful. They are mute and not very well made. The remarkable thing to me was how numerous they were – so many of them that they were the only landscape feature. A few had been converted into dwellings – their laundry unfurled in the sun was proof of that; but most of them looked abandoned and moldering, and there were clusters of them that had been vandalized.

That vandalism was the salient aspect of Albania that I noticed so far; that it was not merely poor – I had seen poor countries and deprived people elsewhere – it was brutalized, as though a nasty-minded army had swept through, kicking it to bits. It was not the poverty of neglect or penury. There was something melancholy about a neglected place – the sagging roof, the dusty glass, the worm-eaten door frame, the ragged curtains. This was not melancholy, it was shocking. But this was violent. Many of these roofs had been torn off, windows had been broken, curtains had been ripped. We passed a factory: it had been burned out. We passed a garage: buses were scorched and tipped over, as the train coaches had been. We passed twenty or more greenhouses: most of the windows were cracked or broken – there was broken glass everywhere, and only a few of the greenhouses were being used for growing plants, tomato vines strung up.

That unmistakable vandalism was upsetting because it was violent and illogical. I had just come from Croatia and seen shell holes and shattered roofs. Those were the marks of war; but this was worse, more thorough, more absurd, nightmarish. And adding to the impression of derangement were the people, standing near these broken windows and up-ended culverts and burned-out factories, wearing rags.

This continued all the way to Tirana: vandalism and cement bunkers and people fumbling with hoes and pitchforks in the lumpy fields. Masses of bunkers lay outside Tirana and in places they were so densely situated that these areas had the look of an extensive necropolis, so similar were the bunkers to mausoleums.

"There are 600,000 of them," a man told me in Tirana at the black market money-exchange. "One for each family – that is what we were taught. But what if we had used all that cement and iron and made houses with it? We would have no housing shortage now."

"Did anyone wonder why these bunkers were being built?"

"No. We were proud of them. We made them for a possible invasion – from our enemies."

"Who were your enemies?"

"Everyone," he said. "From every side. Revisionists from the east, imperialists from the west."

It was later that I met him. At the moment, as the bus pulled into town, I was still wondering what to do, for as soon as I got off more beggars lunged at me, and they followed me up the main street, whining and plucking at me.

My first problem was finding a place to stay. The only hotel I had found was full, and though at first I did not seriously mind being turned away because it was so dirty, it seemed there was nowhere else. The Hotel Tirana was closed – for repairs, one person told me; for demolition, someone else said. The only other possibility was the grubby Hotel Dajti.

"All full," the desk clerk told me. "Unless someone checks out."

"Is that likely?"

"Don't know. Please, I'm busy."

I walked some more, back to the main square, past the statue of the Albanian national hero Skanderbeg with his horned helmet, past the mosque, into some back streets, and spotted a hotel sign on another building. A man sitting on the stairs said he had space.

It was the worst hotel I had seen on my whole trip. I was not a hotel snob – I liked a bargain. But it was that Albanian look again, not of neglect but of vandalism; the place looked unhealthy, even dangerous.

The Dajti had at first looked grubby to me. Now that I realized that it was really the only place to stay it seemed desirable, even rather grand. The desk clerk told me to come back later in the day – he might have something for me. I couldn't call him. "The phones are not working." I left my name and considered offering him baksheesh; and then I perambulated again, thinking what a fix I would have been in traveling with someone else.

—*Where are we going to stay?*

—*Something might turn up.*

—*What if it doesn't? What will we do then?*

—*I don't know.*

—*Why didn't you think of this before?*

—*I don't know.*

—*You could have made a phone call.*

—*The phones don't work. You heard the guy.*

—*I'm scared, Paulie.*

—*Everything's going to be all right.*

I believed that. At the very worst, if there was nothing at the end of the day, there was the dump – the danger zone. There were also hotels in Durrës, awful place that it was; it was reachable by bus or taxi. There was also the last resort: to ask someone on the street if they knew of a little old lady who took in boarders. In such a desperate city that was probably the way most accommodation was handled.

At the enormous fountain at the Palace of Congresses children were companionably taking baths – they had soap and towels. Nearby stood a marble cone as high as a six-storey building. It was abandoned and partly wrecked (bricks missing, graffiti, kicked-over planters). A man saw me sitting and came over to talk. It had been a monument to Enver Hoxha, he said, and then: "Please give me money." On most street corners, in gutters, next to buildings, there were heaps of garbage, and people picking through it and scattering it. Whenever I paused and looked at something – a hedge, a bush, a state building, a wall, the gunky river that ran through town, someone got in my face. "Please – food! Give me something to eat!" I bought a bottle of nameless fluid to drink, but before I could raise it to my lips, a woman had her hand on it. "Please – water!"

These were serious beggars, ragged and deserving, cowering near the puny trees and in the shade of the brick walls. Some wore traditional dress – skirts, leggings, black shawls, slippers, a cummerbund, veils, wide sleeves, all in tatters.

Towards late afternoon I went back to the Dajti. Yes, they had a room. I swapped my passport for a key. The room was dirty, it had a rank smell, it overlooked a field where boys were yelling and kicking a football. I slept like a log.

In the bar the next day I met an American in Tirana on business who said, "This is the worst hotel in the world. I mean, officially. It's number one on a list of hotels that are, I guess, the best available in a given city." He smiled. "The pits!"

The general in Ismaîl Kadaré's novel stays in the Hotel Dajti. The Albanian novelist, who has been in exile in Paris for thirty years, makes it sound like the Ritz, a peaceful refuge, splendid among the pines of Tirana. *He collected his mail at the desk . . . asked for a call to be put through to his family.* In his otherwise macabre story, even the Dajti's phones work in the novel.

"But it costs forty dollars a night," I said. "It's not the worst forty-dollar hotel I've ever stayed in."

It was relative, too. Right outside it, because there were policemen and security men and usually groups of people, beggars had taken up residence under the trees. There was a homeless beggar under most of the trees. There were others in doorways, in the manner of homeless people in New York, who prefer to sleep in the doorways of Madison Avenue and the safer and better-lighted parts of New York City. At night, at the base of almost every street-lamp on the main boulevard of Tirana, Shqiperia ("Land of the Eagle"), there was a ragged child sleeping.

After this strange introduction to Albania – the beggars, the bunkers, the dereliction of Durrës, the horror of Tirana, the dirt – I went underground. I happened to be riding a bus from the Tirana railway station (wrecked, inhabited by lurking quarreling

Albanians) with no thought of where the bus was going – I was immersing myself in Tirana. I fell into conversation with a young man and his wife who were just returning from Durrës. His spoken English was excellent. His nose was bright pink.

"We have been to the beach," he explained.

Beach?

"Yes, it is a bit dirty. But we just sit. We do not know how to swim."

We talked a bit more; their names were Djouvi and Ledia. I rode with them to the end of the line, some miles from the center of the city, where they lived in a large and ravaged-looking apartment house. When they asked me what I thought of Tirana I told them frankly what I felt.

"The Tirana. that you see is much better than last year," he said. "We have touched bottom – a year ago we had nothing at all. Now there is some activity. There are goods in some shops. Before, there was no money, no goods, just desperation."

"How was it worse last year?"

"It was anarchy," he said. "There was no food, there was no government."

I tried to imagine Tirana looking worse than it did today.

"We had riots. Mobs of people roaming the city. Tirana was dangerous."

We had been walking down the road and were now in a slum of tottering eight-storey tenements, making our way – I guessed – to where Djouvi and Ledia lived. Djouvi told me he was twenty-four, Ledia was twenty. They had married a year ago, and yet both of them seemed older than their years. I remarked on that. Djouvi said, "I look older than twenty-four, yes, because so much happened to me. The hunger strike. The political troubles. We thought we might be shot. Also the fear of secret police."

Now we were at the last grim tenement in the cluster. Djouvi asked me to look at the satellite dishes on the wall. There were five mounted on the wall of the building.

"Albanians are individualistic," Djouvi said, "so each one gets his own satellite dish instead of one for the whole building, which would be cheaper. We get CNN, MTV. Italian channels are shown on Albanian TV, because it is cheap. I can speak Italian though I have never had a lesson. A quarter of the people in Tirana can speak Italian from watching TV."

"How long have you lived in this building?" I asked him in Italian.

Without hesitating, he said in Italian, "I have lived here my whole life. I was born in it. Look at those buildings – they are ugly and dirty. But if you go inside you will see the apartments are very clean, because they are privately owned. Inside they are beautiful, outside not so nice."

He invited me up the stairs to his fourth-floor apartment. It was spartan but clean – a bedroom, a kitchen, a sitting-room with a bookcase: books by Mark Twain, plays by Ibsen and Aeschylus.

"My father helped build this building. We paid rent for thirty years. So when the government privatized it was sold to us for $97. But we had paid for it many times over."

"You seem very optimistic," I said.

"I am optimistic – because I see changes for the better. Last year there was no one by the stadium selling soft drinks."

He called it a stadium. It was a ruined football field, trampled grass surrounded by faltering walls, with some tables in front where people sold bottles of orange soda.

"Now there are four people there. Next year they will have shops in town and someone else will be there – people are moving on, little by little. Individual enterprise. That is what we want."

But I said that I had not seen anything substantial for sale except pornographic newspapers – two-cent tabloids with large headlines over smudgy pictures of nude couples embracing or women on all fours. And Albanians did not seem to make anything except the rugs, copperware and knick-knacks that were for sale in one shop in town. Even postage stamps were in short supply. At the main post office where one woman sat at one window stamps were rationed, three to a customer. There were only two sorts of stamp; neither was good for an air-mail letter. The good-for-almost-nothing two-lek "Posta Shqiptare" stamp bore a portrait of Mother Teresa, herself an ethnic Albanian from the province of Kosovo.

"Those sexy newspapers on the street have become very common in the past six months," Djouvi said. "Before then we had many papers, political ones. But people now are sick of politics and sick of news. They want pornography."

Ledia made tea. Her English was not good enough for her to be able to follow the conversation, but Djouvi translated for her. After a while I felt self-conscious, pestering Djouvi with questions – after all, I had just met him on the bus, and here I was in his apartment, drinking tea and asking him to explain Albania. I said that I really had to go but that I wanted to meet him and his wife again, to take them to dinner, and that they were free to bring any of their friends. I was ignorant of Albania: I wanted to know more.

After thinking this over, Djouvi said that it was not such a good idea to sit in a restaurant talking about the past of Albania, even worse to speculate on the future. But a walk in the park, meeting at one of the outdoor cafés first, might be better. He had a few friends who might like to come along to practice their English.

We agreed to meet the next day, around five, after work. Djouvi was a clerk in an office. His friends were teachers and civil servants. I met them not far from the cone-shaped Hoxha memorial, which was no longer the Hoxha memorial but simply an embarrassment. It had not been hard to tear down the dictator's statue, but this enormous obelisk was another matter. They might have to learn to live with it, or else to rename it.

Late the next afternoon I sat on the bench that Djouvi had indicated on a neatly drafted map, and soon after five looked up and saw Djouvi and Ledia with three other Albanians about their own age. They were Nik, Ahmet and Alma. Djouvi explained that I had just arrived in Albania from Italy.

"There are many Albanians working in Italy," Nik said. "We work hard and earn little money. Even in Germany and Switzerland you will find Albanians."

"And Greece," Alma said.

"The Greeks don't like us," Nik said.

"Italians smuggle Albanians into Italy," Djouvi said. "They charge up to one thousand dollars. They pick them up on the beach south of Durrës. They use small fast boats and take the Albanians to the Italian coast and drop them."

"Let's get something to drink," I said. We walked across the boulevard where, under the trees, various entrepreneurs had set up cafés. There was a friendly-looking place near the road, but they said no and chose one of the cafés at the very back, surrounded by bushes. We were hardly visible here at our table, drinking coffee, eating cookies. It was clearly their intention to remain hidden with this nosy American.

"For years nothing changed in Albania," I said. "Then something happened, right?"

"After Ceaucescu was shot," Ahmet said, referring to the murder of Romania's dictator around Christmas, 1989. "The next day things began to change here. The people were talking, first small groups of them, and after a few days there were larger groups, and we knew something was going to happen."

"Was Hoxha in power then?"

"No, Hoxha died in 1985. His successor was Ramiz Alia. He is on trial now."

"Hoxha was a dictator in tandem with Mehmet Shehu," Ahmet said. "It is said that Hoxha shot Mehmet Shehu, though the official version is that Shehu committed suicide. I knew Shehu's son," Ahmet went on. "He told me his father was not suicidal. He went to the school in the morning – his father was fine. When he came home from school his father had a bullet in his heart."

"So you five are all friends, is that right?"

"We were students in 1990 and 1991. We helped form the Democratic Party as an underground movement. Alia was in power, but for some reason he was weak. Hoxha's widow was working behind the scenes, filling the posts with her relatives. We wanted to do something."

"I am so happy to be talking to the Albanian underground," I said. They laughed and instinctively looked around to see whether anyone had noticed them. "When I arrived I was really depressed, but it seems as though something promising is taking place."

"This was a hard place before," Nik said. "They would accuse us of being spies. People were afraid because of the police. The city was cleaner then. It was fear. It looked different. People are careless now because they know it is not their own property."

Yes, even from where we sat at this café we were within sight of the heaps of garbage and the broken tree limbs and the squatting, whining beggars.

"Tell me why it was a hard place. Was it just the police?"

"If Hoxha thought you were not on his side he imprisoned you," Ahmet said. "He labeled you as a spy. I remember when I was at university we spent one month a year doing work for the state. We were sent to a labor camp —"

"A concentration camp," Djouvi said.

"In the next room was the former Minister of Education, Todi Lubonja, and his family, doing forced labor. His crime was that when he was minister he allowed Western music to be played, decadent music, and Hoxha was furious. That was in 1974. Lubonja was finally released in 1989."

"What other famous prisoners were there?"

"The present President of Parliament, Pjeter Arbnori, a writer, was put in prison in the Stalinist time," Nik said. "He stayed there for almost thirty years. Longer than Mandela! He finally founded the Albanian Social Democratic Party. He was imprisoned in 1954, released in 1984."

"Were ordinary people imprisoned for political crimes?"

"There was a strange law here under the Hoxha regime," Djouvi said. "If a man was regarded as a spy or an enemy his whole immediate family went with him to the camp."

"Not just them," Ahmet said. "It did not stop there. Other more distant family members were barred from higher education or other things."

"They were pariahs," I said, and explained the word; yes, yes, that was the word – political pariahs.

"It was illegal to flee the country," Alma said. "But let's say you managed it. After the police discovered that you had gone they arrested your brother – they punished another family member for what you had done."

"Beards were banned," Ahmet said – he looked as though he had the beginning of a beard himself.

"Have you heard of Disneyland?" I said. Of course they all had. "Workers in Disneyland are forbidden to grow beards. And that's probably not the only obsession that Disney executives have in common with Albanian dictators."

Long hair was also banned, and Western music, and blue jeans, and pornography. Until 1990 no one in Albania was allowed to own a car. As soon as the government changed people started letting their hair grow, and playing rock music, and wearing blue jeans. Stolen cars were being imported from Italy or smuggled over the Greek border by the thousand. All over Tirana there were men sitting on stools near stacks of yellowing two-cent porno newspapers.

"So tell me," I said, "how did this horrible man Hoxha manage to stay in power?"

Djouvi said, "Hoxha made us believe that we were the best people in the world. There was crime and violence and poverty in every country except ours. We believed everything we were told. We did not question anything. We did not ask why we had water shortages in summer and power cuts in the winter. We had no taxes. We believed that we were the greatest country in the world, better than China, which we had rejected, better than the Soviet Union, much better than the West."

"At school we sang songs, praising Hoxha. What a wise and great man he was," Alma said. "We all did military service."

"We all had a weapon – everyone in the country had a gun," Ahmet said. "Each person had a personal weapon and a bunker. My weapon was a Kalashnikov, in the – what do you call it? – national arsenal? There were many weapons here."

It was hard to imagine anything so efficient as an arms industry in this country that did not even have tractors or plows or sewing-machines.

"Weapons is the one industry that has not stopped," Djouvi said. "The factory is in Elbasan. We made weapons, we had a Chinese factory and Chinese training."

Nik said, "All children love guns. We loved taking them apart and fixing them."

We talked some more, and I was resisting writing anything down, because I did not want to make them self-conscious, but at last I suggested that we meet again tomorrow, at the same place. It was cheap enough – coffee 20 cents, sandwich 50 cents, mineral water 80 cents, a beer $1. The waiter presented me with a bill for less than $5.

"We will see you tomorrow, at the same time," Djouvi said, shaking my hand.

"Come by the hotel," I said.

"It's better here," he said.

"Okay, but if I'm a bit late wait for me," I said. "I want to stop by the Embassy."

A querying expression came into his eyes.

"It's a good idea for Americans to register their names in the US Embassy in some countries," I said, and thought: *Especially in this country*. "But I'll try to be on time."

Off they went. The next day I found the Embassy, which was a lovely building in the style of a Mediterranean villa, creamy stucco with green and yellow trim, on a back street of Tirana. I spoke a while with the Deputy Chief of Mission, Douglas Smith, who had been in the country a year or so and was fluent in Albanian. He told me about the tradition of blood-feuds in the hinterland, wondering out loud whether they were somehow related to the concept of *besa*, which was a solemn Albanian oath. The feuds had been stopped by the old regime, but there was apparently a resurgence of them with the democratic reforms.

I was at the café table early to meet the Albanian underground. Five o'clock came and went. I drank a beer. I had the dinner special, rice with a glop of tomato sauce on it and meatballs made out of a dead animal and french fries. The meatballs were *quofta*: a Turkish word for ground meat or meatballs; many food words in the eastern Mediterranean were Turkish, though as *kofta* this one had gotten as far as India. I was reminded again of what truly disgusting food passed for Albanian cuisine.

There was no sign of the talkative youths of the previous afternoon. I should have known better than to say that I was planning to stop by the Embassy. Paranoia is a hard habit to break. I never saw them again.

After three days and three nights in the stifling darkness of the fish's belly, Jonah had an illumination. That is often the way with nightmares. After three days, Albania – which had started as a nightmare – took on the dimensions of a valuable experience. I had overcome my disgust and fear. Tirana was still as ratty, but I was calmer, fascinated rather than repelled, and so the city did not seem so bad. "It just looks dirty," as Jonah might have said.

The beggars were now recognizable. They slept at night in the places where they sat all day with their hands out. There was a legless woman, an old blind man, and a hectoring man who shouted at passers-by, demanding money; there were many children, scavenging in the day and curling up under the lights or in doorways at night. Two always slept together, one lying face down and his younger brother – perhaps – using the small of his back as a pillow.

Instead of leaving I stayed a few days more. One of the reasons for this was that it was not easy to leave. I had arrived by ship and I wanted to leave by ship. Studying the map I could see that in the deep south of the country a narrow channel separated Albania from the island of Corfu. It looked no greater than five miles: no distance at all.

"Yes, there are fishermen there, and they might take you across," a man told me in Tirana.

He was from that area and seemed to have Hellenistic sympathies.

"My family name was Stavro," he said. "We were orthodox. It means 'cross' in Greek. But the government made us change our name. So my grandfather took the name Çeliku – it means 'steel,' like Stalin."

"How could you be orthodox? Didn't Hoxha ban religion?" I asked.

"Yes. No churches. They were forbidden."

God was illegal. Albania enjoyed the distinction of being the only officially atheistic country in the entire world. But instead of flocking to churches after the fall of the government they went haywire on porno, which had also been banned.

I was not convinced that I would be able to find a fisherman in southern Albania to take me to Corfu, but there was another way of getting to Greece. Greeks had a tendency to close the border out of spite, because they disliked Albanians and had poor diplomatic relations with the government. If the border was open, there was a bus from Gjirocaster to the Greek town of Ioannina.

There was said to be a train to Vlore in the south, but it was not running. Çeliku said there was a bus that went. I had not seen a bus that looked capable of going such a distance. I walked towards the southern edge of town, where I had been told the depot was located. There were no vehicles in sight, but there was evidence of buses: great oil stains in the dust which spoke of big leaking gaskets.

I kept on walking, into a ruined park, past a stagnant reservoir where people were sunning themselves in their underwear. Their underwear had the same cast-off look as their clothes, just as ill-fitting and ragged and dated. Most of what Albanians wore these days had been supplied by Italian charitable agencies, and so it had come out of attics and closets in pious households up and down the Adriatic.

There were signs of vandalism even here – plaques torn off, signs defaced, dates obliterated, plinths cracked where they had held statues. About a mile beyond the reservoir there was a terrible smell, borne by a hot breeze. No sign indicated it, but it was clear that just ahead was the Tirana zoo.

I hate zoos generally, but never have I felt more like opening cage doors and setting the animals free. If they ate a few Albanians then it was poetic justice for the torments these animals had endured, though I had yet to see an Albanian fit to eat.

The cages were very small – about the size that they would be for a wicked criminal in the prison of a brutish country. This was how the animals were seen – as savage beasts; and because they were beasts they were treated like convicted murderers. An example of this was the magnificent tiger, his fur gone grotty in his foul cage; he was fatigued and desperate in this eight- by twelve-foot cage, which hardly contained him. An Albanian watering some plants tormented the tiger by squirting the hose into his face.

A wolf gnawed a bone in a small cell. Three eagles flopped in another cage, so small that it was impossible for them to spread their wings – one of them hobbled. A filthy crane, four sweating bear cubs, and worst of all a lioness, demented by captivity, pacing beside the bars, with still enough wit to flinch when an Albanian worker tossed twigs at her. Her mate, cowed by the twig-throwing, retreated to the back wall of the cage.

"Why are you doing that, you shit-head?" I said to the Albanian, and made gestures.

He grinned at me and muttered in his own language. Throwing

things at the animals was apparently one of the pastimes here. Among old bones and lion droppings and slime there was the other stuff that Albanians had flung through the bars – more twigs, balled-up paper, stones, a black cap.

But seeing this zoo was a way of understanding how the Albanians lived, in tiny apartments, eating bad food and not enough of it, putting up with water shortages and power cuts, tormenting each other, ignoring the filth in the streets. It was almost certainly the way their prisoners were treated, and these zoo animals were just another species of prisoner.

If I had abused that bullying man at the zoo in Italian he might have understood me. It was true that Italian was the second language here. I found an Italian-speaking taxi-driver, Ali, bargained a little, and went back to Durrës in his fairly new Lancia.

"Where did you buy this car?"

"Down the coast. The place has no name."

"So was this car stolen?"

"Probably. But not here. Italy maybe."

The bunkers by the roadside and on every hill did not look less strange, even days later. Ali said one of them was his – he had forgotten which one.

Past the ruined trees, the broken road, the cracked tenements, the locked railway station: I had fled from these on the old bus. The beach at Durrës was the nastiest I had seen in the Mediterranean. It was bouldery and black, littered with oily flotsam, broken glass and greasy plastic. This was the sort of beach that needed a great overwhelming tide to sweep it and scour its sand. Such a tide did not exist in this sea.

Its filth did not deter Albanians from swimming and sunning themselves there. Pale, in their underwear they had the look of people who had been forced to strip and undergo a cruel initiation.

Roman columns stood on the beach – in ancient times this was where the Via Egnatia picked up after it left Bari, one of the great spokes of the Roman road system. It was the remains of a temple, left to decay. Farther on, a war memorial to the Albanian dead – a twenty-foot-high bronze soldier charging off his plinth, and underneath it, spray-painted in red on the marble, *Nirvana* and *Guns 'n Roses* and *Fuck You.*

The construction of the memorial, the way the slabs were set up, the marble blocks a certain height and spaced just so, made it serve a dual function as war memorial and toilet. It had been fouled; it stank. This whole shore under the headland of the former palace of King Zog was a horror.

Ali said, "Want to see the amphitheater?"

We drove into a dead-end, and there among the houses of the slum was a Roman ruin. The slum was part of it, though the houses looked much frailer than the Roman arches.

An Albanian watchman, angling for a tip, began chattering in Italian.

"This is where the rich people came in on their horses," he said, showing me a cavernous entryway. "The poor people came in through that little door up there."

The slum-dwellers had simply encroached upon it in a distinctly Mediterranean manner, creeping up to it and snatching the marble slabs and the old Roman bricks and using these ancient building materials for their hovels.

"This was big enough for fifteen thousand people," the watchman said. "They had shows – animals, lions, tigers, and gladiators. Look, the original stone, these steps, this passageway went all the way around the perimeter, where you see these houses."

"The people used the stone for their houses," I said.

"But they didn't break it. An earthquake did that," he said. "There were two earthquakes. In the first one it was destroyed. People took the stone to put in their houses. Come, I will show you the chapels."

There were two Byzantine chapels in the lower passageway. There had been catacombs; there were mosaics of broken but still recognizable portraits of saints. The watchman knew them: St Sofia, St Irene, St Stephen, some angels. "This was used for baptisms and funerals."

"It's too bad so much of it is buried," I said.

"We only found it a little while ago."

"This Roman amphitheater? You didn't know it was here?"

"No. Like I said, it was buried in an earthquake. Then one day in 1966 a man's fig tree died. He dug it up to plant another, and in the hole he found this wall – these stairs." He showed me the marble staircase. "He dug further and when he found more stairs he reported it to the archeological department. And they saw that this whole slope was an amphitheater."

At that point it began to be excavated, and bits of it started to vanish, only to appear as elements in the nearby houses. The Roman amphitheater was a mess, like everything else, and the underground passages that had been dug out were flooded.

"Pump's broken!" the watchman said. Nevertheless, he had earned his five leks.

We went, Ali and I, to King Zog's palace. Ali said that it was now a government guest-house, like Hoxha's mansion in Tirana. "Sometimes visitors stay here." It was a squarish villa at the top of the hill, less impressive up close than it had seemed from the deck of the ferry *Venezia*.

Zog had a son, Ali said. He had been born in this palace, and the next day the infant had been spirited into exile with his father and mother.

"Do you want him to be your king?"

Ali laughed at the suggestion, and said, "He spent one day here. Then a few years ago he came back. Also for a day. So he's – what? – fifty-five or fifty-six, and in his whole life he's spent two days in Albania!"

I asked him whether it was true, as the youths in Tirana had told me, that all the borders of Albania had been closed, and that people were forbidden to leave.

Yes, Ali said, it was against the law – no one could leave.

"Why?"

"Why! Why!" he slapped his head to ridicule my pestering question. "You think it's strange that we couldn't leave this country. Look, when I was a little boy I couldn't leave the house! Everyone stayed in. My parents kept the door locked. I couldn't go out. You understand? No one went out of the house during Hoxha's time."

"They went to work, though?"

"Yes. Then straight home."

On our way back to Tirana we passed the decrepit factories. The biggest was a rubber factory.

"Is it working?"

"Destroyed," Ali said. "All the factories are destroyed. Rubber factory. Plastics factory. Machinery. All broken."

"Who did it?"

"Who! Who!" He smacked the side of his head again. "Who do you think did it?" He laughed, but it was a shameful laugh. "I did it! In 1990 and again last year! We were excited. We broke everything!"

However poor Tirana seemed, life was harder in the countryside. About thirty miles south of Tirana many people had taken up residence in the larger bunkers and bomb shelters. They had extended them at the entrance with a framework of poles covered with plastic or canvas sheets. It was bound to happen, with so many bunkers and such a serious housing shortage.

I had come here with Adrian Bebeti, a native of Tirana in his late twenties, who also owned a stolen car, a BMW with a tape deck and leather seats. I had met him near the Dajti and he agreed to take me on a slow trip to southern Albania for $100, stopping at Vlore and anywhere else I wished, and dropping me at Sarande, where ("perhaps," he said in Italian) I might find a boat to take me to Greek Corfu.

Himself, he hated Greeks, he said. They were scum who did little but persecute Albanians and lord over them the fact that they were members of the European Community. And look at them: the average Greek was just as pathetic as the average Albanian.

Adrian spoke Italian fluently. He had visited Italy twice. His brother worked there. He watched Italian television – he liked the game shows, the football, the music programs.

Driving south we passed a burned-out factory.

"Did you do that?" I asked him.

"Not that one," he said. "I burned another one!"

Traveling down the coast, about twenty miles south of Durrës Adrian pulled off the road near a huge parking lot. But it was not a parking lot.

"All stolen," Adrian said. *Tutto robato.*

It was the thieves' car-market, all the cars lined up in an orderly way beside the shoreline. The Mediterranean had some odd beaches, but this one was by far the oddest. There were about 500 cars and Albanians swarmed around them, kicking the tires, flashing money, making deals. Mr Lombardi, are you looking for your Fiat that was stolen in Rome a few months ago? It was here. Mr Schmidt, your Mercedes that was pinched in Munich, and Mr Wilson's Jeep Cherokee that was last seen in a hotel parking lot in Lausanne – these and many others were here under the scrubby pines by the Albanian shore. They were in good order, with new papers, and there were so many it was impossible for me to look at all of them. The prices were reasonable because, having been stolen, they had no book value, only what the market would bear. They were much cheaper, Adrian said, than what they would have cost in Italy or Germany. The number of them, and their excellent condition, and the remote spot on this grubby beach, nowhere near a town, all impressed me. It struck me that some of them might have come with me the week before on the ferry *Venezia* from Bari.

"Crooked lawyers in Italy fix them up with new papers, and off they go," Adrian said.

"Ask them how much this Mercedes is."

But he wouldn't. He said, "It is not a good idea to ask questions here if you are not intending to buy a car. They will wonder why you ask so many questions."

"I suppose that's my problem – asking questions," I said.

"In Albania we have learned not to talk too much," Adrian said. And he suggested we get back on the road.

It was a poor road, lined with rows of tree stumps. The trees, Adrian explained, had been cut and used for fuel. There were few other cars on the road – some carts, some horses and dogs and chickens, and people had the habit of walking in the road. The houses were much poorer than ones I had seen in Durrës and Tirana. But they had the same Doomsday look, as though at a certain point in the growth of these villages they had been stricken. The people were not ragged – no beggars here – but there was a definite look of deprivation: women carrying water in tin containers, families hoeing, groups of people selling small piles of vegetables or fruit by the side of the road. At the town of Fier we stopped and walked to the market, where Adrian bought a pound of cherries. They were in season. We sat and ate them, and then set off again.

Remembering what the American diplomat had said to me about the *besa* and the blood-feud, I asked Adrian.

"You're confusing two things," he said. "First of all, *besa* means a promise that has to be kept, no matter what."

"Give me an example," I said.

"All right. Suppose you give me your telephone number in New York and I go there, because you invited me and you gave me your *besa*. In that case, you meet me, you take me to your house, you feed me – because your *besa* was given with your invitation. You would never leave me on the street. You would look after me no matter what. You cannot abandon me!"

He was driving in a swerving, fast-slow sort of way. If private cars had been banned in Albania until 1990 that meant no Albanian had been driving for more than three years, and most of them much less, or not at all. The inexperience certainly showed.

"Revenge is another matter," Adrian was saying – gabbling in Italian and swerving to avoid pot-holes in the rutted road. "We call it *hakmari* or *jakmari*. *Hak* means blood, *mari* means take."

"Does it always involve killing?"

Adrian took both hands off the steering-wheel and cupped them, a gesture that meant, "The answer to that question is so obvious I do not believe it is worthy of a verbal reply."

I said, "Please give me an example of Albanian *hakmari*."

"All right. Someone does something to your brother. So you do something to him. Or, you just killed someone in my family, you miserable pig –"

Adrian became shrill and definite when he personalized these examples. I was uncomfortable again, as I had been when, illustrating *besa*, he had said, "You cannot abandon me!"

"In that case, I kill you," he said, his jaw set. "Never mind how much time passes. It could be twenty years later. By then you are happy. You have forgotten what you did. But I have not forgotten. It is there, the pain in my heart. One day you leave your house – happy! It is a nice day! I go to you and" – he whipped his fingers against his throat – "I kill you."

"Is it better if some time passes?" I said. "In English there is a proverb that goes, 'Revenge is a dish that is best served cold.'"

Adrian smiled. He liked that. But he said, "Any time is the right time for *hakmari*."

I saw from the map that we were approaching Vlore, where I had been intending to stop. I mentioned this to Adrian. He did not react. His mind was on other things.

"My grandfather was a victim of *hakmari*," he said. "He had an enemy. One day the man killed him. It was my mother's father, about 1952 or so."

"Was his death avenged?"

"What could be done? Nothing. Because there were no men in the family. My grandfather had three sisters and his wife, and only daughters. Women don't kill." He kept driving. He said, "That was in Scutari."

"Why weren't you told to kill the man?" I asked.

"I couldn't kill him. I wasn't born until 1966. By then it was too late. I was the wrong generation. The matter had been forgotten."

"I see. So vengeance has to be carried out by someone in the same generation as the victim."

"Exactly," Adrian said.

"Was *hakmari* practiced during the Hoxha times?"

"No, not in the Hoxha communist times. But in the past few years I have heard stories. Not a lot, but definitely there are families 'taking blood.'"

We stopped for the night at Vlore. We had gone more than half the distance to Sarande, and it was now late in the day. It was not a good idea to be on the road after dark in a country so inadequately provided for. Anyway, Adrian had a friend here, he said. Remembering my liking for the cherries he had bought at Fier, Adrian asked several people in Vlore where we could buy some. Thirty cents got us a kilo of ripe cherries.

The hotel at Vlore had no name, and many empty rooms. The only guests were two Albanian families. They had spent the day on the stony beach. Adrian said he would stay with his friend and pick me up at seven the next morning. He left me the cherries and a stern warning to be very careful. "Lock your door at night." I took his advice.

At Vlore there was a large villa on a headland which had belonged to Enver Hoxha. Before darkness fell I walked towards it, but I saw that it was guarded by soldiers and thought better of rousing their suspicions. Though people stared, no one in Vlore followed me; there was dire poverty here, but no beggars. The people on the beach, baring their bodies to the gray sky, risking death by poison in the water of Vlore bay, were bony and pale. It was so odd to see these skinny white people crouched on the sand, frail little families at play – and these were the well-off Albanians, at this seaside town.

Probably because Hoxha had come here often, there were slogans painted on the sides of buildings. They resembled the so-called "big character" Cultural Revolution slogans I had seen in China, and in some cases the words were identical. *Glory to Marxism and Leninism* had been painted carefully in red letters on a wall in Vlore, and other walls extolled Hoxha – *Glory to Enver Hoxha* (*Lavde Enver Hoxha*) and ditto with revolution, work, and Albania. No one had bothered to paint over the now out-of-date slogans, but in some cases whole walls had been smashed. On a mountainside outside Vlore, in stone letters forty feet high, were the words *PARTI ENVER.*

I drank a beer, I ate bread and stew, and in my room I listened to an update from the BBC about the trial in Tirana of Ramiz Alia, who was being tried on charges of "abuse of power" and "misappropriation of state funds."

There was no sound at night in Vlore. No wind, no passing cars, no music, not even a voice. The sea was silent: not even the mushburger waves that slopped on the shore of other Mediterranean places.

"So what did you call him?" I asked Adrian the next morning, as we drove out of Vlore past the slogans to Hoxha. "'Great leader'? 'Teacher'? 'Father'? Something like that?"

"*Shokut*," Adrian said. "*Shokut* Enver."

"Meaning?"

"Friend." *Amico*.

That was wonderful. The man who had put a wall around the

country and starved them and turned off the lights and terrified them and imprisoned them and wouldn't let them grow beards and lived in lovely villas while they stayed inside their huts eating sour bread or cleaning their personal weapon ("in the event of an attack by the imperialists"), this man was "Friend Enver."

"These days we don't use the word *shokut* at all," Adrian said. "It is not a good word, because of the way we used it before."

"Then if you don't use the word friend, how do you say 'Friend Adrian.'"

"We use the word *zoti. Zoti* Paul, I might say to you if I greet you," he said. "It means 'god.' No more friends, we are now gods."

Until Vlore we had been traveling on a shore road that was fairly flat, but the next day I saw that the southern part of the Albanian coast was mountainous. The steep cliffs dropped straight into the sea, and the road climbed behind them, becoming corrugated and unsafe, as it shook our car sideways to the edge. Rising to over two and a half thousand feet the road was also bleak and windy, in places precipitous, at the edge of rocky goat-haunted ravines, where the only settlements were clusters of stone huts, many of them ancient.

Above Vlore there were only tree stumps – the trees had been recently cut down. In the desperate and anarchic days of the previous year when there was no fuel, people had cleared the woods and cut even the cedars that had been planted beside the road.

"Perfume!" Adrian shouted as he bumped along the side of a ravine, and the heavy scent of rosemary from the mountainside entered the car.

Almost four hours of this narrow mountain road; Adrian had a tape machine in his car but only one tape, "The Greatest Hits of Queen," a rock group. Adrian liked the group. "Freddie Mercury," he said, "he died of AIDS." Towards noon, passing a remote spot, we saw a policeman hitchhiking. At first I thought he was at a road block, and my heart sank. But Adrian explained that the man was hitching a ride and that we were under no obligation to pick him up. Thinking that it might be useful to have a policeman on board, I said, "Let's take him."

The policeman had two containers of olive oil. They were so heavy he could scarcely lift them. Adrian helped him hoist them into the trunk.

"Ramiz Alia!" the policeman said. "He's on trial!"

Adrian said nothing. The policeman abandoned his attempt at conversation. Clearly, Adrian hated him. We drove about twenty miles. When the policeman got out at a crossroads Adrian discovered that some of the olive oil had leaked on to the carpet of his trunk, and he cursed and swore. It was obvious that the Albanians had few personal possessions, but they were maniacally fastidious about keeping them in good order.

The villages on the southern Albania coast looked Greek – blocky stucco huts on hillsides. We passed a ruined church.

"What religion are you?"

"None," Adrian said.

"What about God?" I asked, sensing that I sounded like a character in a Graham Greene novel.

"I really don't know – the whole thing confuses me," Adrian said.

We were soon back above the coast again – great bluey-green bays and steep sluices of whitish rock. There was no one in the coves. No boats, no people, no villages. There was no litter. These were the emptiest and most beautiful beaches I had seen so far. Most of them were only accessible by sea, the cliff walls too steep for any path. I was never to see such a coastline again in the Mediterranean. Nothing had happened here. Farther on there was a submarine base, with a large man-made cave cut into the mountainside at the shoreline for the sub to slide into. That was guarded, but that was the only man-made thing on this whole superb shore, that still had the look of Illyria.

The Greek island of Ithaca, home to Ulysses, was only a hundred miles due south of here. Sailing back to Penelope, Ulysses would have seen these same cliffs and bays of this unspoiled coast.

We reached Sarande in mid-afternoon. Adrian was edgy. He wanted to start back to Tirana immediately. I gave him the hundred dollars we had agreed on and he dropped me at the Hotel Butrinti at the edge of town, just above the harbor.

"Is there a boat to Corfu?" I asked the desk clerk.

"Oh, yes. It will be here tomorrow at noon," he said. "It is only one hour to Corfu town."

This was delightful news. The hotel was empty. I got a room and walked around the town, which was a strangely empty place, having been deserted by Albanians who had fled to Italy or Greece in search of work. There was a shirt factory and a carpet-weaving operation in Sarande. There was a hospital. There were schools. What Sarande lacked were people.

I met Fatmir, a friendly local man, whose parents had remained devoutly Muslim, he said, throughout the atheistic Hoxha years. He was fluent in English.

"I hope you will come back in ten years," Fatmir said. "You will find that the houses are better, the town is better, the port is better, the food is better, and I am better."

The strangest thing of all – stranger than the ruin of Albania, the bad roads, the skinny people, the rural poverty, the broken glass, the vandalism, the cruelty, the unexpected kindness – stranger than all of this was the sudden appearance the next day of a boat-load of tourists sailing into Sarande harbor on a day-trip from Greece. I had not seen any tourists for such a long time – none in Albania, none in Croatia, none in Slovenia, not even Trieste had tourists. I felt I had been through a mild ordeal and that I had made a personal discovery. At that point I bumped into a bus-load of package tourists on their day out.

I waited for them to return from their little tour of the ruins at Roman Butrinti, and then I sneaked on to the bus which was taking them back to their boat. I would simply pretend that I had been on their day-trip and, just like that, would find my way to Corfu with the tourists.

These were nicer than the sort that in Gibraltar I had had to distinguish from apes, but still the genuine sunburned beer-swigging article. They hated Albania. They were disgusted by Sarande – after my experience of the rest of Albania, Sarande seemed pleasant, if a bit spectral. The tourists were shocked by the Hotel Butrinti. They mocked the Roman ruins.

Most of them were hard-up Britons who had come to Corfu because it was, they said, cheaper than a holiday at home. Kathleen and Sally, two older Irish women who worked in the same clothing factory in Dublin, had paid a little over $400 (£267) for two weeks in Corfu. This included their round-trip air fare from Dublin, as well as bed and breakfast at the hotel in Corfu. ("We couldn't go for even a few days in Cork for that money.")

"I'm not impressed at all," one woman said, glancing at the town as we lined up on the quay.

"The food were filthy," a man said in a strong Lancashire accent.

"The tea, I couldn't drink it," his Lancastrian companion said. "They make it out of flour, you know."

"The Russians had something to do with this, I understand."

They were bored, scared, exhausted.

One man next to me looked very depressed.

"Are you all right?" I asked.

"Me wife died at Christmas," he said. Four months ago. "It was quite a blow."

"How long were you married?"

"Forty-two years," he said. He was asthmatic with grief, struggling for breath, poor old guy, looking so lost here on this Albanian shore.

"Oh, God."

"That lady over there is just a friend," he said. "I went out with her long ago, before I met my wife. I don't know what will happen now. I'll sell my motor-home soon." He looked sadly at me. "I don't expect you to understand. But you're kind to listen."

Fatmir had come to the quay to see the tourists leave.

"Come back to Albania, Mister Paul," he said. "When you come back it will be better."

The sad old man said, "That's a shocking big bag you've got there."

"I'm a stowaway," I said. I explained how I had come from Tirana and was sneaking aboard so that I could get to Greece.

"Good lad."

My passport was examined and stamped. I found a seat on the upper deck, feeling pleased with myself. Kathleen and Sally waved to me from another seat. But on board, among the tourists, I got gloomy. Spring had arrived and so had the trippers and the holidaymakers, the Germans, the cut-price package people, in their annual combat with the hectoring locals. "I geeve you good price!" "You eat here!" "The food were filthy." "Just ignore him, Jeremy." All that.

As we left Sarande on this boat to Corfu town, fifteen or twenty boys leapt from the pier and began swimming in the rolling water of the stern, yelling, "Money!" and "Give me your hat!" and "*Soldi!*" as a smaller number of them had done at Durrës.

Some of the tourists taunted them, just as the tourists had taunted the apes on the Rock of Gibraltar. Others threw bits of paper or peanuts. Some coins were flung from the rail – small-denomination leks which, although made of some sort of metal, were so worthless they could float in water. The Albanian boys began to complain. The tourists laughed. The boat gathered speed.

"Fuck you!" one of the boys yelled. He made a finger sign. Then they all took up the cry. "*Adio!*" "Fuck you!" "*Va fan cul!*" "Fuck you!" "Fuck you!" "Fuck you!"

"The universal language," Kathleen said in her lilting Dublin accent.

13

The MV *Seabourne Spirit* to Istanbul

On our third day at sea we were all given a printed directory, a little four-page brochure, as elegant as a gourmet menu, of the passengers' full names and where they lived. I kept it, read it carefully, used it as a bookmark, and as it became rubbed and foxed with use I scribbled notes – question marks, quotations, warnings to myself – beside some of the names.

From Richmond Virginia, then, came Mr William Cabell Garbee Jr and Mrs Kent Darling Garbee, and from Southold, New York, the Joe Cornacchias, whose horse, "Go for Gin," had just won the Kentucky Derby; from East Rockaway, the Manny Kleins, to whom on the quay at Giardini Naxos, near Taormina, I gave instructions in the use of an Italian public telephone. Mr Pierre Des Marais II and Ms Ghislaine LeFrançois had come from Île des Sœurs, Quebec; Ambassador Bienvenido A. Tan Jr and Mrs Emma Tan, from Manila, Republic of the Philippines – the ambassador, retired, now did "charitable work" in a public manner; and the Uffners, the Tribunos and the McAllisters from New York; all these had joined the *Seabourne Spirit* that day on the quay at Nice.

The Mousers were from Boca Raton, and smoked heavily and invented fabulous new destinations with their malapropisms, such as their cruise to "Rio J. DeNiro" and "Shiva, Fuji." And from Honolulu there were the Bernsteins: Mark, who had once been obliged to destroy on behalf of a client twenty-two million Philippine pesos (one million US dollars), a five-hour job on his office shredder; and his wife Leah, who represented the popular Hawaiian singer Israel Kamakawiw'o'ole, whose current weight was over 700 pounds. Mrs Sappho Drakos Petrowski from Simsbury, Connecticut (but formerly a dealer in fresh flowers in the Florida

Keys) was traveling as a companion to Mrs Mary P. Fuller, ninety-one years old, of Bloomfield, Connecticut, widow of brush tycoon Alfred Fuller, who sold brushes door-to-door and then founded the Fuller Brush Company.

There was Harry Jipping, a developer, from Reno, Nevada, who said, "Malta – is that an island, or a country? Isn't it part of Italy? You mean it's got its own money and all that?" and "That black stuff – what's it called? Right, caviar – that Cornacchia guy's always chomping on it." Harry was traveling with his wife Laverne, a Frisbie from Grand Junction. The Joneses from New York, the Smiths from Toronto, the Greens from Wootton Wawen, England, Mrs Doris Brown from Lauderdale, Florida, the Burton Sperbers from Malibu. And Jack Greenwald from Montreal, who wore a blazer with solid gold buttons, and the regimental tie of the Household Cavalry, and who addressed the waiters in French, usually to describe his personal recipes which he insisted on their delivering to the head chef, Jörg; he seldom spoke to another passenger on board except to say, "Can you tell me what a drongo is?" or "I'm down to two desserts." Mr Greenwald's wife was the former actress Miss Constance Brown.

The Zivots from Calgary, the Alfred Nijkerks from Antwerp, Belgium, the Sonny Prices from Sylvania, Ohio, and the Rev. Deacon Albert J. Schwind from Beach Haven, NJ, Señor and Señora Pablo Brockmann from Mexico City, Mr Ed and Mrs Merrilee Turley from Tiburon, California. Mrs Blanche Lasher from Los Angeles was on her twelfth cruise, and so were the Ambushes and the Hardnetts.

And Mrs Betty Levy of London and the Algarve was on her thirtieth cruise and had been up the Amazon. "I love your books, I've read every one of them," Mrs Levy said to me. "Are you writing one about this cruise?"

"No, unless anything interesting happens," I said, so confused by her directness that I realized that I was telling her the truth.

The Fritzes, the Norton Freedmans, the Louie Padulas – all these people, and more, boarded the *Seabourne Spirit* that day in Nice.

The summer had passed. It was low season again. I needed an antidote to Albania and the shock I had gotten in Greek Corfu, an island leaping with chattering tourists that reminded me of the rock apes on the slopes of Gibraltar. I had gone home and tended my garden, and then in late September I went to Nice. I joined this cruise. I had never been on a cruise before, or seen people like this.

Many were limping, one had an aluminum walker, Mrs Fuller was in a wheelchair, some of the wealthiest looked starved, a few were thunderously huge, morbidly obese. Like many moneyed Americans who travel they had a characteristic gait, a way of walking that was slow and assured. They sized up Greek ruins or colorful natives like heads of state reviewing a platoon of foreign soldiers, with a stately and skeptical squint, absolutely unhurried. That, and an entirely unembarrassed way of laughing in public that was like a goose honking ten tables away.

"You've got to be a mountain climber to get up these stairs!"

"Why don't they turn the air conditioner on?"

"Who's that supposed to be?" It was the color portrait on B Deck of the Norwegian king and queen – two of Scandinavia's bicycle-riding monarchs, King Harald V and Queen Sonja. The ship was Norwegian, registered in Oslo.

Some were rather infirm or very elderly or simply not spry, with a scattering of middle-aged people and only one child (Miss Olivia Cockburn, aged ten, of Washington DC, traveling with her grandparents). The majority were "seniors," as they called themselves, who had the money or time to embark on such a cruise. Hard of hearing, the passengers mostly shouted. Their eyesight was poor. Eavesdropping was a cinch for me, so was note-taking.

"This is our eighth cruise –"

"Did you do the Amazon?"

"Vietnam was very unique –"

Most of them, on this luxury cruise through the Mediterranean, were sailing from Nice to Istanbul. Some were going on to Haifa. Betty Levy was headed into the Indian Ocean with the ship. The cost for this, excluding air fare, was $1,000 a day, per person.

I was a guest of the shipping company. There was no disgrace in that. It often happens that a writer is offered free hospitality in a hotel or on a ship. Few newspapers or magazines actually pay a

penny for the trips their writers make, and so travel journalism is
the simple art of being slurpingly grateful. It posed no moral
problem for me, but because my writing made me seem as though
I was continually biting the hand that had fed me, my ironizing
was nailed as "grumpy" and I was seldom invited back a second
time. That was fine with me. In travel, as in many other experiences in life, once is usually enough.

In 1928, Evelyn Waugh was offered a free cruise of a similar sort,
through the Mediterranean on a Norwegian ship, the *Stella Polaris*.
Waugh's agent got free tickets for Waugh and his wife on the
understanding that Waugh "would write it up in a travel book."
The account of his cruise, *Labels, A Mediterranean Journal* (1930),
was one of the most celebrated travel books of the thirties, regarded
by many people – though not by me – as the heyday of the travel
narrative. (I think that travel books have had many heydays.)

Waugh "had no interest in foreign travel," Humphrey Carpenter
wrote in *The Brideshead Generation*. "He would have agreed with
John Betjeman's remark to Edward James: 'Isn't abroad *awful*?'"
Yet Waugh gave the Mediterranean mixed reviews, and admitted
to a frank infatuation with Corfu. *Labels* was full of snap judgments
and obnoxious opinions that helped make his reputation, and
because of its hearty snobberies the narrative became the model for
a certain kind of travel book that was much boosted recently by a
crowd of pedants who believed that there was a time in the past
when the going was good. It is actually a strange book.

But then a travel book is a very strange thing; there are few
good excuses for writing one – all of them personal – and these
days there are as many different travel books as there are travelers.
The fairest way of judging travel books is by their truth and their
wit. You can have quite a good time reading a harrowing book
like *The Worst Journey in the World*, by Apsley Cherry-Garrard,
without any further thought of traveling to Antarctica. It is less a
matter of geography than of your own taste. And some of the best
and most enjoyable travel books are studies in snap judgments. In
the end, all that matters is that the facts are generally true, so that
a historian, some Fernand Braudel of the future, will be able to use
your book as a source for, say, the condition of Albania in 1994

(". . . stolen cars . . . bad roads . . . poor diets . . . lived in bunkers
. . . Hoxha graffiti still legible on some walls . . ."). Historians are
on firm ground with primary sources, diaries and travelers' tales.

The most tedious travel book in my opinion is the one in which
the author is being vague about having a wonderful time. All that
jauntiness seems like boasting to me, and dishonest boasting too,
since the writers must be hiding so much misery. We all know that
a vast proportion of travel is accumulated nuisance; but if boredom
or awfulness is handled with skill and concrete detail, it is funnier
and truer than the sunniest prose.

Labels was written by a 26-year-old who had just published a
successful novel, *Decline and Fall* (and was about to publish *Vile
Bodies*); who had decided, like the character in Saki, that "the art
of public life lies in knowing when to stop, and then going a bit
further."

Here is Waugh on the French: "As a race, it is true, the French
tend to have strong heads, weak stomachs, and a rooted abhorrence
of hospitality." Germans are "ugly." Paris is "bogus." Monte
Carlo is "supremely artificial." Waugh even manages to be rude
about the pyramids ("less impressive when seen close") and the
Sphinx, "an ill-proportioned composition of inconsiderable aes-
thetic appeal." Majorca, Gibraltar and Algiers are no better,
though Waugh's way of dismissing them is highly amusing. Waugh
is no kinder to what he calls – and this has a certain resonance
today – "the mongrel kingdom of the Jugoslavs."

It is all eccentric opinion – Waugh is the last person who would
say that his book had the weight of scholarship as its justification,
or even the quest for adventure. "There is no track quite so
soundly beaten as the Mediterranean seaboard," he says, admitting
that this will be the opposite of adventure, as it is the opposite of
scholarship. At one point he begins to discuss Arab architecture
and then he apologizes and offers a whole paragraph of "silly old
me."

Labels is never predictable. When travel writers make cruises the
subject of books, the theme is often that of the Ship of Fools on yet
another pointless voyage. (Perhaps it has something to do with the
fact that writers tend to be solitary, if not downright anti-social.)
Waugh avoids that, and is impartial, as mocking towards the

English as he is towards the Maltese and the Algerians. In the narrative he develops a line in wine snobbery, too: "the wine of Crete is lowly esteemed," "I do not believe that Algerian wine is really very nice," Malaga is "very nasty," and as for Manzanilla, "the inferior brands taste like the smell of evening newspapers."

And so it goes, this parody of the Grand Tour, from Monte Carlo to Naples, from Haifa to Cairo, from Malta to Gibraltar, by way of Venice and Athens and Ragusa (Dubrovnik) and many other "labeled" cities that Waugh promptly re-labels. The book has no more authority than the eccentricity of its author who, on the verge of a divorce, was very unhappy at the time he wrote it. It is vindicated by its humor and its originality. Also, Waugh knew better than most people that there is a great deal of pleasure to be derived from a travel book in which the traveler is having a very bad time; even better if it is an ordeal.

I had not been lying to Mrs Betty Levy. My idea was to find a way of going back to Greece and Turkey, not to do a hatchet job on a ship-load of cruise passengers, supine on the sun deck, reading Danielle Clancy and Clive Grisham, novels with alarming titles: *A Clear and Present Client, Extreme Prejudice, Remorseful Storm Rising*. They yawned and turned the pages. The big books were propped on their bellies. I was reading *Gatsby*, as you know.

The *Seabourne Spirit* was a moderate-sized ship of 10,000 tons. Its 180 passengers were accommodated not in cabins – the word was not used – but in two-room suites: double beds, bath-tubs, a liquor cabinet, a television set, and not a porthole but a picture window through which you could see the Mediterranean. On various decks, there was a swimming-pool, several jacuzzis, an exercise room, a sauna room; a large marina unfolded from the stern, complete with two speedboats.

Tipping was forbidden on the *Seabourne Spirit*. You could eat whenever you liked, alone or with a group of people. You could host a dinner party at short notice and they would prepare a table for twelve. You could call room service and say, "Caviar for six and two bottles of champagne," and it was there in your suite in ten minutes.

I had always thought you worked and saved to put your kids

through college. I had now discovered that there were Americans who worked and saved to take vacation cruises on ships such as the *Seabourne Spirit*. A fourteen-day cruise in 1994 was about equal to what it cost the average student in the United States to attend a good private university for one academic year: that is, about $28,000.

As a train drudge and a ferry passenger, I had bumped and shuttled from Gibraltar to Albania, thinking of the coast of this sea as overdeveloped or sludgey or victimized by war or stupidity. As a cruise passenger I saw the Mediterranean as much bluer, the coast much tidier, and from the deck of the *Seabourne Spirit* Nice had great charm and even its shingly beach looked peaceful. Nice was not the overcrowded seaside resort of retirees and dog merds that I had passed through on a jingling train so many months before. It was no longer the site of my one-star hotel and my long, rained-upon walks. It was merely a backdrop, twinkling as I drank my complimentary glass of champagne. Night fell, the mist put the town out of focus and made it a Matisse, with yellow blobby lights reflected in the water. We glided out of the Old Port, south to Italy.

Down in my suite the phone was ringing.

"*Ja*, Mr Theroux, this is Jörg the chef, calling from the kitchen."

"Yes?"

"I hear you are a vegetarian," Jörg said. "I can tell you that we just had some nice salmon flown in from Norway. Was there anything special you wanted me to make for you?"

It seemed an auspicious start, and the next day, gliding along a perfectly flat sea that was blue and unwrinkled under a blue and cloudless sky, a slight breeze, Italy showing as a low smoky shoreline to the east, we passed between Elba and Corsica. The captain made an announcement to this effect, some people looked up and squinted past the rail, then returned to their reading.

There was a lecture in the lounge given by the *Seabourne Spirit*'s own on-board academic. I went to the lecture that first day and, along with the rest of the listeners – about thirty of us – made notes. The subject was "Mediterranean Civilizations."

– *Greece was resource-poor, and overpopulated. They needed to colonize all over the Mediterranean to get resources.*

– *But there was never a place called Greece. Just city-states.*

– *The Minoans were peaceful and progressive.*

– *The Myceneans were mercenaries.*

– *Spartans sent their children to military school at the age of seven. They never came home after a defeat. Better to die.*

– *The Romans did not practice moderation.*

– *Cleopatra was not Egyptian. She was the daughter of a Macedonian general.*

– *The Athenians were gentle and democratic. They woke up. They had no breakfast. They ate one meal – porridge. They wore a sort of diaper, and a sheet. They went to the forum and talked. It was not a life of luxury.*

At this mention of porridge, a huge man sitting behind me said to his wife, "Are you as hungry as I am?"

"The male passengers on this ship are so big," a woman said to me that first lunchtime, "I thought they must all be members of a team of some kind."

The white ship growled south bathed in full sunshine on the glittering sea, following the low shore of Italy that was never more than a long narrow stripe at the horizon, like the edge of a desert, a streak of glowing dust.

Our progress followed one of the oldest routes in the Mediterranean. "Coasting was the rule" in the Mediterranean, Fernand Braudel wrote in *The Structures of Everyday Life*. It was rare for any ship to risk the open sea, even as late as the seventeenth century, because the fear of the unknown was so great. "The courage required for such an unwonted feat has been forgotten." Mediterranean sailors usually went from one port to the next, along the coast, and it was a brave sailor of the high seas to venture out of the sight of land, from Majorca to Sicily, or Rhodes to Alexandria. "The procession of coasting vessels steered by the line of the shore, to which they were constantly drawn, as if by a magnet."

But our ship steered parallel to the coast for the pleasure of seeing it, and hovering, as a reminder of where we were.

The clear day of unobstructed sun became a blazing late afternoon, the western sky and sea alight, and at last in a reddening amphitheater of light, a buttery sunset.

An invitation had been clipped to my door: Did I wish to join the First Officer and his guests for dinner?

There were ten people, and the subject at my end of the table was, what did we do for a living?

Millie Hardnett said that her husband had made his fortune in specialty foods − canned fruit, jars of peaches in wine, exotic syrups, and after selling his business to a food conglomerate they now spent their time cruising.

Twisting his dinner roll apart, Max Hardnett asked me, "Someone told me you were a writer, Paul. Have you published anything under your own name?"

"My husband sold his company to Sara Lee," the woman to my left said.

This was Mary Fuller, whose husband had founded Fuller Brush. And another fact: Sara Lee was a real person, a middle-aged woman whose father had named the cheesecake, the company, and everything else after her. She had a last name, but no one could remember it.

Her companion Sappho said to me, "Alfred wrote a book, too. You say you're a writer? You should read it."

A Foot in the Door, by Alfred Fuller, described (according to his widow) how he had grown tired of being a poor farmer in Nova Scotia and took a hint from his brother, who worked for a brush company, and decided to sell brushes door-to-door. What's that? You mean I don't have the brush you require? Well, describe it to me and I will supply it to you. Alfred was open to customers' suggestions and created brushes to fill their needs. Bottle brushes, wide brooms, whisks and dust mops. This was pioneering salesmanship and soon Alfred had teams of men out there, ringing doorbells and hustling for commissions.

"It was a real Horatio Alger story," she said.

"What do you think about that?" Sappho asked me.

"I met Arthur Murray once in Honolulu," I said. Why was I telling her this? He was another famous name on a business. "I even know someone who danced with him. Arthur Murray taught her to dance in a hurry."

"Alfred thought up the idea of direct selling," Mary Fuller said. "It's not popular now because of crime."

She was ninety-one and kept to her wheelchair, but she was not at all frail, and she had a good appetite. At times, surveying the table, she looked like a sea-lion, monumental and slow in the way she turned her head. She kept her good health, she said, by visiting mineral baths in places like Budapest and Baden-Baden. She mumbled but she was lucid. She spent each summer in Yarmouth, Nova Scotia.

"How did you meet Alfred?" I asked.

"He courted me in New York," she said. "He was very determined. When he wanted something he got it. That's why he was so successful in business, too. My mother called him 'The Steam Roller.'"

She went on a cruise every year, she said. This simple assertion brought forth a torrent of cruise memories from the rest of the table.

"This is our sixth cruise in three years –"

"We were up the Amazon –"

"So were we. I wanted to go into the jungle in a canoe, but instead we shopped in Manaus –"

"I went to Antarctica. In the summer of course. Penguins –"

"We cruised China. That was special –"

"Down the Yangtze –"

"Vietnam on the *Princess* –"

In the morning we were anchored off Sorrento, high steep cliffs and pretty palms and dark junipers, the carved porches and stucco walls of hotels and villas. At the Hotel Vittoria Excelsior it was possible to see the suite where Caruso had stayed. Across the bay was Mount Vesuvius, Naples in its shadow, smothered in a cloud of dust.

This was a different Italy from the one I had seen in the winter. I had been traveling second class on trains, among working people and students; in my Italy of cheap hotels and pizzas I often lingered to watch people arguing, or goosing each other, or making

obscure gestures. I seldom saw a ruin or a museum. But this
Seabourne Italy was the Grand Tour of the Italy of colorful boatmen
and expensive taxis and day-trips. It was the coast of castles and
villas, but there was no need to go ashore: you could sit under the
awnings and simply admire Italy, its glorious seaside. Just look at
it, and then doze and let the ship sail you to a new coast. After all,
the Mediterranean shore was much prettier viewed at a distance.

Some *Seabourne* passengers bought ceramics in Sorrento, and
lace, and leather goods. Others, of whom I was one, went on the
Pompeii tour.

Pompeii was a Roman seaside resort which was buried, along
with Herculaneum, in A.D. 79, mummifying many of the inhabitants and wrapping them in the ashes of Vesuvius, so preserving for
posterity Roman frivolity and ingenuity, the passions as well as the
day-to-day life of these people, some resident and some on holiday.
Many of our images of Roman decadence, the salacious postcards
of big penises and scenes of buggery that are sold in Naples,
originate in Pompeii. An illustrated booklet in five languages,
Forbidden Pompeii, was stacked in every souvenir shop. The site itself
– just a glorified ground plan, all that remained of Pompeii – was
in an industrial area, full of garages and factories and auto repair
shops, in a suburb of Naples.

It had been plundered long ago. Even its so-called excavation –
which was recent: from the mid-eighteenth century – had been just
a form of looting and treasure-seeking. It had no studious or
archeological intention. No one cared to investigate the Roman
way of life or the organization of ancient households. Some bits of
pottery that were unearthed influenced Josiah Wedgwood's so-
called "Etruscan" pottery designs as well as creating fashions in
some English furniture designs. But that was all. Digging up
Pompeii was a quest for trinkets and corpses.

Sometimes the digging was ritualized. General Grant stopped in
Pompeii in 1877 on his triumphant trip around the world. To
honor his visit, the Italian authorities dug up a ruined house for
the general. This sort of excavation was "one of the special compliments paid to visitors of renown." General Grant was given a
chair and he sat and smoked a cigar while the workers began
shoveling. A loaf of bread (baked in A.D. 79) was unearthed. Then

some bronze ornaments. The Italians were disappointed and ashamed. They had hoped to find a human body. They eagerly offered to excavate another house in anticipation of perhaps finding a corpse or some old jewelry for General Grant. The general said he was hungry. A man in his party suggested going to a nearby restaurant, and he joked, "to excavate a beefsteak!"

Our guide was Ricardo. That was another aspect of this new cruise-ship Italy. Instead of the buttonholed strangers I had depended on before, I now had a guide showing me around. They were just as friendly but oddly irrelevant. Ricardo was a good-humored Neapolitan who had recently moved to Sorrento.

"Eight meters of volcanic ashes," Ricardo said. "Four square miles of city, where 25,000 people —"

Like the history lecture yesterday, the tour was anecdotal, filled with meaningless numbers and generalizations, but from this bouncy little Figaro they were like a salesman's obliging patter. "Big wine shop!" he said, as we walked down one of Pompeii's paved streets. "See wagon ruts in the road? These are stepping stones. See graffiti? Notice this is a bakery — just like the bakery oven we have today for pizza and bread."

We went through the Forum; we saw a toilet. "They called it a Vespasian, because he was the emperor who taxed the people for each peepee."

"I didn't realize there'd be all this walking," Mr Mouser said.

Ricardo said, "I will show you a brothel. A real one!"

We hurried after him, turning corners. Then Ricardo paused and said, "You see that big phallus on the wall?"

It looked like a peg on a coat-rack. To tease him I said, "You think that's a big one?"

"I think maybe normal," Ricardo said.

"In America we would call that a small dick." Out of delicacy I said this in Italian, using the word *cazzo*, enunciating it — not grunting *gatz*, the way I heard Italians doing in Boston when I was growing up.

"That word is a little vulgar," Ricardo said in Italian.

"What word would you use?"

"'Dick,'" he said. *Cazzo*. "But I don't raise my voice, eh?"

James Joyce believed that Italians were obsessed with their

private parts. "When I walk into the bank in the morning," he wrote, "I wait for someone to announce something about his *cazzo*, *culo*, or *coglioni*. This usually happens before quarter to nine."

The Pompeii brothel – a so-called *lupanare*, a house of the she-wolf – was filled with shuffling Japanese, young and old, men and women, giggling at the lurid frescoes depicting coitus, marveling at the pallets of stone – the shelves on which the act of love was performed; snapping pictures of the cubicles.

"Now I will show you the house of the bachelor brothers," Ricardo said. "They lived a bisexual life. We know this, from frescoes and statues."

One of the statues of Priapus, a small figure clasping a torpedo between his thighs, was in a side room. Thirty Japanese filed past it. I waited at the exit listening to the flashbulbs and the shrieks and giggles of the women, who emerged with their hands over their mouths, because an open mouth is considered rude in Japan. The Japanese men were silent, and they looked rueful as they shuffled out of the room. Not very long ago, women tourists were forbidden to enter that room.

In an unvisited corner of the same house there was a fresco showing the infant Hercules strangling snakes, and I thought again of the Pillars of Hercules, and how this god, the patron of human toil, was a suitable model for me in my journey.

"What do you think?" Ricardo asked me as we strolled along.

"Very interesting."

But I was being polite. I disliked it all for being a theme park devoted to Roman dissipation – just chat and speculation, a rather unsatisfying amusement, like Epcot's preposterous Italy-by-the-lagoon in Orlando, Florida. In the end, all that people will remember will be the statue and fresco of Priapus showing his torpedo. Pompeii was only that, a big dick.

We were soon on more fertile conversational ground when I saw a priest – an American, or at least non-Italian priest – was walking past us with another group.

"Ricardo, when you see that priest," I said, "do you think he's a *jettatore* who might give you the evil eye?"

"That is a superstition you find in Sicily and south of Naples," Ricardo said, laughing insincerely. "Not here very much."

"Don't some people do something when they see a priest?"

"You scratch your − somethings − and you make a cornuto if you see someone with the evil eye. A priest, maybe."

"What do you do?"

"I don't worry much, except −"

He was hesitating. I said, "Yes?"

"Nuns," he said with disgust. "I hate to look at them. Their faces can be frightening, especially the ones with a black cloth over their heads."

"What do you do when you see them?"

"I have a special thing that I do," he said. He winked at me, but he would not say what his precaution was against the evil eye of a black-shawled nun.

Whatever Ricardo devised in the way of counter-magic was something in the folklore of Italian superstition that had been proven effective against the evil eye. The belief was ancient and so were the remedies. Touching iron was recommended − keys, nails, a horse-shoe, the hinge of a door − because iron was associated with magnetism, to absorb the malevolent power. If no iron was immediately available, a man secretively grasped his goolies. Garlic worked − some people carried a few cloves in their pocket. Some people wore garlic on a string, or a piece of onion, or a saint's picture, or a necklace of pigs' teeth. They might carry a goat's horn, or a plastic imitation. Some colors repelled the evil eye: blue in the north of Italy, red in the south. Was there a *jettatore* standing on the road making a *mal'occhio* on your house? Sprinkling water sometimes helped. Even better, pissing on the spot where the evil-doer stood, because urine also acts as counter-magic.

Thin people, priests, nuns, gypsies were all potentially dangerous *jettatori*, suspected of possessing the evil eye. The *jettatore* was not to be confused with the Sicilian *strega*, a witch but a useful − probably indispensable − woman, who (observed by both Norman Lewis and the Sicilian reformer Danilo Dolci) "arranges marriages, concocts potions, dabbles a little in black magic, clears up skin conditions, and casts out devils."

The evil eye is probably rooted in envy; such fears predominated in places where people were more or less equal in their misery, where resources were scarce and there was heavy competition for them. It was also related to the struggle in such places of getting ahead without looking superior or stronger, the paradoxes of power and difference, and the fear of the unknown.

The shores of the Mediterranean, so divided in certain matters, are united in their fear of the evil eye. Compliment a Frenchman and he blows lightly, to ward off the curse. If someone says, "What a lovely baby!" to almost any Italian parent in the presence of their child, the parent will immediately (and covertly) prong their fingers at the speaker, as a way of fending off evil spirits. Or they might spit three times at the suspected *jettatore* as soon as the person's back is turned. In any case, the parent kisses the baby when he or she suspects it of an evil eye being projected on the child. Ricardo said that anyone who compliments a baby without adding "God bless you" (*Dio ti benedica*, or in dialect *Di' bendet*) is probably wishing evil upon the child.

Some chants worked in Italy, I was told. Fearing the eye, you muttered the words for the three blackest things in the world: "Ink! Black mask! And the buttocks of a female slave!" (*Inga! Mascaro! E natiche di schiava!*) or simply, "Away! Tuna eggs in France! Let bad luck go to sea!"

Maltese fishing-boats have the horned hands painted on the bow to deflect evil. Small replicas of finger horns were worn, or kept on key chains. Crusaders – the Knights of St John – had sculpted eyes in the watch-towers in Valletta as part of the harbor defenses. In Greece, not priests but people with blue eyes are dangerous as bringers of the evil eye, and it is perhaps significant that Greeks think of Turks as being blue-eyed people, a whole nation of evil eyeballs ablaze. The remedy is a glass blue eye that Greeks use as a pendant. In Turkey (where this remedy originates) the glass blue eye can attain the size of a dinner plate, and the glass eye, along with other necessities such as matches and cooking oil, is sold in every kiosk and shop. It is really a fish-eye, and plucking out a fish's eye and stepping on it is efficacious counter-magic in the eastern Mediterranean.

But I should not think of Italians as people who walked around worrying about the evil eye, Ricardo said. Did I know what a *gobbo* was? Yes, I said, a hunchback.

A *gobbo* got his hump by having been the victim of the evil eye in infancy. But it also meant that he was the repository of counter-magic.

"So it is good luck to touch the hump of a hunchbacked man," he said. "And if the hump is on a dwarf, that's even better. Some people go about with a hunchback all the time. Gamblers, for example."

The modern version of Pompeii is probably the nearby town of Positano, a small harbor shared unequally by the idle rich and the landladies and the fishermen. If Positano were to be buried in volcanic ash today, future generations would understand as much about our wealth and our pleasures and the prosaic businesses such as bread-making and ironmongery as Pompeii taught us. They might not find a brothel, but they would find luxury hotels, the San Pietro and the Sirenuse. The Roman author and admiral, Pliny the Elder, died in the Pompeii disaster; a Positano disaster could gobble up the film director Franco Zeffirelli, who lives in a villa there. It was perhaps this coast's reputation for wickedness that induced Tennessee Williams to make his decadent Sebastian Venable in *Suddenly Last Summer* begin to go to pieces in Amalfi, before he was finally eaten by cannibalistic boys in another Mediterranean resort, the mythical Cabeza del Lobo.

The *Seabourne* was not leaving until late, and so I paid a Sorrentino driver eighty dollars to take me to Positano. This was my expansive *Seabourne* mood: I would never have paid that money when I was jogging along on trains and ferries.

Along the Amalfi drive, winding along the cliffs and slopes of this steep coast – much too steep for there to be a beach anywhere near here – I told the driver my fantasy of Positano being buried in ash. The driver's name was Nello, and he was animated by the idea.

"It could happen," Nello said, and began to reminisce about the last eruption.

It was in 1944; he was twelve. "My madda say, 'Hashes!'"

Nello insisted on speaking English. He claimed he wanted practice. But that was another thing about travel in a luxurious way: the more money you had, the more regal your progress, the greater the effort local people made to ingratiate themselves and speak English. I had not known that money helped you off the linguistic hook.

"Vesuvio wassa making noise and zmoke. The hashes wassa flying. Not leetle hashes but ayvie, like theese," and he weighed his hands to show me how heavy they were. "We has hambrella. Bat. The weend blows hashes on de roof and − piff − it barns.

" 'Clean de roofs!' my madda say."

"It sounds terrible," I said.

"It wassa dark for two day. No san. Hashes!"

And it was certain to erupt any minute, Nello said. The volcano was long overdue.

We got to Positano. Isn't it lovely? Nello said. Yes, it was, a steep funnel-shaped town tumbled down a mountainside into a tiny port. What could be more picturesque? But it was a hard place to get to − the narrow winding road. It was expensive. It was the sort of place, like Pompeii, that you took a picture of and showed your friends and said, "We went to Positano." And they said, "Isn't it darling? Those gorgeous colors." It was the Mediter-ranean as a museum: you went up and down, gaping at certain scenes. But really I had learned more about Italy in the crumbling village of Aliano or the seedy back streets of Rimini.

On the way back to Sorrento and the ship Nello said he was too tired to speak English, and so, in Italian, we talked about the war.

"The Germans had food when they occupied Naples," he said. "We didn't have anything to eat. They threw bread away − they didn't give any to us. And we were hungry!"

"What happened after Liberation?"

"The Allies gave us food, of course. They handed out these little boxes with food in them. Delicious."

"So the war was all about food, right?"

"You're making a joke!"

But I was thinking that this precise situation was happening across the Adriatic: the Serbians had food, the Bosnians had none; the war was being fought as viciously as ever.

We sailed from Sorrento after dark, and some time in the night we passed through the Straits of Messina. This time I did not think of

Scylla and Charybdis. I was absorbed in my meal and probably being a buffoon, saying, "Yes, Marco, just a touch more of the Merlot with my carpaccio." The ship was silent and still in the morning. I pressed the button on my automatic window shade and it lifted to show me the coast of Sicily. Craning my neck I could see Etna, and on the heights of the cliffs on the nearby shore the bright villas and flowers of Taormina.

It was so beautiful from the deck of this ship anchored in the bay that it seemed a different town from the one I had trudged around some months ago. I had been a traveler then, looking for D. H. Lawrence's house. This time I was a tourist. I bought some ceramic pots, then I walked to the quay and showed Manny Klein how to use the public telephone.

"You're an old pro," he said.

Later, in the lounge, the *Seabourne Spirit* passengers said they were a bit disappointed in Sicily. But it wasn't really that. It was a growing love for the ship which eventually took the form of a general reluctance to leave it, to look at any ruins, to eat ashore, or even go for a walk on the pier when the *Seabourne Spirit* was in port. The ship had become home – or more than home, a luxury residence, a moveable feast.

"May I suggest the two salmon terrine with caviar and tomato, followed by essence of pigeon with pistachio dumplings?" the waiter, Karl, asked. "And perhaps the game hen with raisin sauce to follow?"

Karl, of Italian, German and Ethiopian ancestry, was the spit and image of the Russian poet Alexander Pushkin, one of whose grandmothers was a black Abyssinian.

"As I mentioned the other day, I try not to eat anything with a face," I said. "Which is why I had the asparagus and truffles last night, and the stir-fried vegetables."

"Yes, sir."

"Nor anything with legs."

"Yes, sir."

"Nor anything with a mother."

"No fish, then."

"Fish is a sort of vegetable," I said. "Not always, but this gravlax with mustard sauce, and the angler fish with lobster hollandaise, might fall into that category."

"Soup, sir?"

I looked at the menu again.

"I'll try the sun-dried blueberry and champagne soup."

For dessert I had a banana sundae with roasted banana ice cream, caramel and chocolate sauce. The man at the next table, gold buttons flashing, had just finished a plate of flamed bananas Madagascar and was about to work his way through a raspberry soufflé with raspberry sauce.

After dinner I went on deck and strolled in the mild air for a while. The night was so clear that from the rail I could see the lights of Sicily slipping by; the places I had labored through on the coastal trains were now merely a glow-worm of winding coast, Catania, Siracusa and farther down, at the last of Sicily, the twinkling Gulf of Noto.

It is only sixty or seventy miles from the coast of Italy to Malta, but that night it was a rough crossing, and for the first time the *Seabourne* rolled in the westerly swell. Sometime in the early hours there was peace again, my bed was level, and by dawn we were anchored on the quay at the edge of Valletta, in Grand Harbor, walls and turrets and watch-towers on every side. I could see the staring eyes that had been sculpted into some towers by the Crusaders as a defense against the evil eye.

Malta has been identified as Calypso's island in the *Odyssey* and was home to the Crusaders, the Knights of St John, and is still an impressive fortress. It is also low, almost treeless, dusty, hot, and priest-ridden. There is so much Christianity in Malta, and of such a kneeling and statue-carrying and image-kissing variety, that there is an old Arab proverb that goes, "He's calling to (Muslim) prayer in Malta!" (*Wu'ezin fi Malta!*) – in other words, asking for something utterly hopeless; trying to get blood from a stone, or as they say in Italy, "blood from a turnip."

Most of the *Seabourne* passengers had already gone ashore for the bus tour to Mdina. I decided to make my own walking tour of the town, though it would not have been difficult to include the whole island. It was about eight miles wide, and eighteen miles long. If you could take the heat and dust, much of it was walkable in a day. Apart from the forts and citadels there were small square houses and dusty streets, not very different from the place that Edward Lear described to his sister Ann when he passed through in 1848: "There is hardly a bit of green in the whole island – a hot sand stone, walls, & bright white houses are all you can see from the highest places, excepting little stupid trees here and there like rubbishy tufts of black worsted." The people were very kind, he added, "But I could not live at Malta."

But who could? Anthony Burgess and various British tax exiles had tried it in the 1970s but they were undone by the Maltese government, which harassed them. Burgess, an ardent and prolific book-reviewer, was accused of soliciting and receiving porno-graphic books – that is, review copies – and the books were frequently intercepted by Maltese customs. He eventually left and moved to Italy, though the government seized his house and confiscated his library. The Malta sections of Burgess's autobio-graphy are chapters of sorrowful accidents and misunderstandings and frustrations. It baffled me why writers chose the most irritating Mediterranean places in which to live and be creative – Maugham in Cap Ferrat, Greene in Antibes, Burgess in Malta. After writing his masterpiece *His Monkey Wife* (*or Married to a Chimp*) and a movie script for *The African Queen*, John Collier went to Cassis, near Marseilles, and wrote very little.

I walked down the gangway and up the cobbled street into Valletta, bought a map and some stamps and listened a while to a small sweating woman in a damp T-shirt shrieking into a bullhorn.

"Most important thing! Beauty with a purpose! You see? She is lovely but she is holding hands with two Down's Syndrome sufferers!"

"What's going on here?" I asked a Maltese man in a snap-brim hat.

"That's Miss Malta," he said.

The buxom young woman in the yellow ball-gown tugged the two shy, bewildered girls down the sidewalk, past an outdoor café of gaping Maltese.

"Beauty with a purpose!" the bullhorn woman yelled. "Beauty is in the eye of the beholder!"

She lowered the bullhorn to get her breath.

"Hello," I said. "Is that Miss Malta?"

"Miss Republic of Malta, yes," she gasped. "We are going to the Miss World Pageant in Johannesburg next month."

The Maltese seemed approachable, friendly, rather lost, a bit homely, dreamy, decent and well turned-out. The garrison atmosphere was much the same as I had found in Gibraltar. Even the Maltese who had never been in England had a sort of shy pride in their English connection and spoke the language well.

The English had found these people, used them to service their fleet and dance for their soldiers, educated them, made them into barbers and brass-polishers, turned over to them London lower-middle-class culture and the sailor values of folk-dances, fish-and-chips, BBC sitcoms and reverence for the Royal Family, and given them a medal. Every schoolboy – Maltese as well as British – knew that Malta had been awarded the George Cross for bravery in the last war.

But the British soldiers had left, the brothels and most of the bars were closed, business was awful here too, and at a time when most British war heroes were auctioning off their medals at Sotheby's – a Victoria Cross was worth about $200,000 – Malta's medal was hardly valuable enough to keep the economy going. The neighbor island of Gozo was the haunt of retirees living off small pensions. The only hope of making the islands viable was for Malta to join the European Union.

I never saw Lear's "stupid trees." Presumably they had all died in the severe drought that was still going on – there had been no rain for six months. The earth was so parched that the plowed fields had the same look as the nearby stone quarries, for the fields were littered with chunks and blocks of hardened clay. The fields were bounded by stone walls, cactuses, and spiky yucca-like plants. It was a fearfully rocky place, and still so dry that the islands five desalination plants were going at full bore.

After the Carmelite church and St Paul's Shipwreck church and the Crusader fortress, I went to St Paul's Anglican cathedral. In this island of 360,000 people, all were Catholics except for the 180 paid-up Protestants at St Paul's Anglican. Today the church was being prepared for the harvest festival: English ladies with the pallor and fretfulness of exiles were polishing brasses, arranging flowers and piling fruit.

"I'll put the bougainvillea on this wire frame and if it dies, there it is."

"Quite."

"And your maize cobs, Joan?"

"Trying to get them to spill out of this bally little basket."

Fussy, helpful, panting church helpers, brass polish in one hand, cut stems in the other, and surveying their labors the keen eye of a vicar, hoping to impress a bishop. With so many dead heroes and clerics and Crusaders and expired retirees in Malta, the church was thick with brass plaques all in need of a good polishing.

"This plaque is coming up a treat, Gina."

"I could do with a nice cup of tea."

We then learned the island was called Malta and the natives showed us unusual kindness, is written in Acts 28.1–2. In the King James translation Malta is given as "Melita," the Greek name (derived from *meli*, the Greek word for honey, for which the island was renowned). The rest of the Bible chapter is a good traveler's tale about shipwrecked Paul. Gathering some sticks for a fire, St Paul is bitten by a snake. Seeing this bad omen, the "barbarous" Maltese take the stranger to be a murderer. But Paul plops the snake into the fire and shrugs, and "they changed their minds and said he was a god." After some effective faith-healing, Paul is fêted by the Maltese and given all the provisions he needs to take him onward to Sicily and thence to Rome.

The cheeriest man I met in Malta was Mr Agius, "coffin-maker and undertaker," busy in his shop near the church. He had been taught the coffin trade by his father and grandfather and he told me that a good mahogany coffin with silver handles went for $1,000, while the cheapest one, of plain pine, cost $165.

"This is for poor people," he said, showing me the cheap one. "There are many poor people in Malta. They choose this one."

He disposed of three or four coffins a week. He nipped from one coffin to the next, pointing out their virtues, the flourishes, the angels, the crosses, the handles, the gilt, the panels.

All the while I talked to him his son sat with his face in a radio that was blaring old rock-and-roll songs – "Peggy Sue" and "Rock and Roll Music (Any old time you use it)".

Malta had the culture of South London in a landscape like Lebanon – newsagents selling the *Express* and the *Daily Telegraph*, video rental agencies, pin-ball parlors, pizza joints, and a large Marks and Spencer. All those, as well as fortresses and churches and many shops that sold brass door-knockers. But chip-shops and cannons predominated.

"I want to see the sights," I said to a man at a bus stop in Valletta in desperation.

"What about the salt-pans of Buggiba?" he said.

It was early afternoon. On the after-deck of the *Seabourne Spirit*, pecan pie was being served with vanilla bavarois, and coffee and armagnac.

I boarded the goddamned bus and rattled down the narrow road to Rabat and Mdina, across the island. The names were Arabic, like many others in Malta, and for all its Italian loan-words Maltese was a Semitic language. Even the people had an Arab cast to their features, though they sneered at such compar-isons, for the English had taught them to despise Gippos.

More fortifications and cannon emplacements at Mdina, a walled town on a hill looking over dusty fields and complaining donkeys; and seeing this landscape of powder and dead trees I began to understand Malta's serious water shortage. The brackish water from the faucets had forced nearly everyone to drink im-ported bottled water. Mdina and Rabat were parched and lifeless, like Valletta. It was as though only war, or talk of it – memories of plucky heroics – animated the Maltese. The war was advertised all over Malta in exhibits and museums and memorials; it was all that anyone talked about. But the war stories ranged from the earliest Crusades to the Second World War. The reason for this was obvious enough. The Maltese had only been useful during military campaigns, but in times of peace they had been ignored. This was a garrison.

Wandering down the street at Mdina, I saw some people from the ship.

"I don't think much of this place –"

"A little disappointing, like Pompeii –"

"I could use a drink –"

They were headed back to the ship, so I joined them on the bus, just got on after my ten-cent ride on an old British bus to Mdina.

The Maltese guide, haranguing on a microphone for the ship's passengers, was determined to make a case for Malta.

"This has become a very, very fashionable part of Malta," she said. We passed a low hill of square houses. And at a small row of shops: "This is a very trendy discothèque – all the young people in Valletta go here," and "Major shops. Your Bata Shoes, your Marks and Spencer, your Benetton."

After that she uttered the sort of sightseeing sound-bite I had started to collect.

"The Germans dropped a 228-kilo bomb on that church, while 500 people prayed. It did not go off. People said it was a miracle of the Virgin Mary."

At Valletta, the bus-load was offered a choice of visiting another church or going back to the ship.

"Ship" was unanimous. The feeling was that Malta – magnificent from the ship, with a drink in your hand – was rather disappointing up close. Afterwards, no one had a good word for Malta, even after having given it a good five hours of thorough scrutiny.

That night, as the *Seabourne Spirit* crossed the Ionian Sea at twelve knots, I dawdled over my note-taking and went to the dining-room late. On this ship, everyone had a right to eat alone, but the maître d' said that if I wished he would seat me with some other people – provided they did not object.

That was how I met the Greenwalds, who were from Montreal. Constance was demure, Jack more expansive – the previous night I had seen him polish off two desserts.

"What did you think of Malta?" I asked.

"If you wanted to buy a brass door-knocker," he said, "I guess you'd come to Malta. There are thousands of them for sale there, right? Apart from the door-knockers, it wasn't much."

"Did you buy one?"

He was a bit taken aback by my question, but finally admitted yes, he had bought a brass door-knocker. "I thought it was an eagle. But it's not. I don't know what it is."

"Isn't that a regimental tie you're wearing?" I asked.

"Yes, it is," he said, and fingered it. "The Royal Household Cavalry."

"They let Canadians join?"

"We are members of Her Majesty's Commonwealth," he said. "Though as you probably know, there's a secessionist movement in Quebec."

"What sort of work do you do?"

He semaphored with his eyebrows in disgust and said, "Scaffolding."

"Really?"

He smiled at me and said, "See, that's a conversation-stopper."

"Mohawks in New York City are capable of climbing to the top of the highest scaffolds," I said, to prove it was not a conversation-stopper.

"I'm not in scaffolding, I was just saying that," he said. "'What do you do?' is the first question Americans ask. But it's meaningless. 'I'm Smith. I'm in steel manufacturing.'"

He was a big bluff man, and his habit of wearing a blazer or a peaked cap gave him a nautical air, as though he might be the captain of the *Seabourne*, if not the owner of the shipping line. He seldom raised his voice, and he took his time when he spoke, and so it was sometimes hard to tell when he had finished speaking.

The waiter was at his elbow, hovering with a tureen of soup.

"Oh, good," Jack Greenwald said. "Now I'm going to show you the correct way of serving this."

After we began eating the conversation turned to the cruise. Most people on the cruise talked about other cruises they had taken, other itineraries and shipping lines and ports of call. They never mentioned the cost. They said they took ships because they hated packing and unpacking when they traveled, and a ship was the answer to this. It was undemanding, the simplest sort of travel imaginable, and this sunny itinerary was like a rest-cure. The ship plowed along in sunshine at twelve knots through a glassy sea by day, and the nights were filled with food and wine. Between the meals, the coffee, the tea, the drinks, in the serene silences of shipboard, young men appeared with pitchers of ice water or fruit punch, and cold towels. And there was always someone to ask whether everything was all right, and was there anything they could do for you.

"I was on a Saga ship, cruising to Bali," Jack Greenwald said. "Forty-one passengers and a hundred and eighty crew members. Can you imagine the number of times I was asked, 'Is everything all right?'"

Over dessert – again Jack was having two, and being very careful not to spill any on his regimental tie – and perhaps because I had not asked, he volunteered that he had been the producer of a number of plays and revues. The names he mentioned meant nothing to me. *Up Tempo* was one. It rang no bells. *The Long, the Short and the Tall* ? Nope. Titles of plays or musicals, because they were usually re-worded clichés, sounded familiar but inspired no memories.

"*Suddenly This Summer?*"

"Rings a bell."

"Parody of Tennessee Williams," Jack said. "Did very well."

"Before my time, I think."

"I sometimes have problems with writers," he said. "There was one that made problems. I had to pay him two dollars fifty a night for one joke he had written. Just one line."

"What was the line?"

"Someone in the cast says, 'Will the real Toulouse-Lautrec please stand up?'"

"That's not very funny," I said.

"No. And the writer complained that he was not being paid on time. His lawyer sent me a big long lawyer letter. I said to myself, 'Hell with it,' and took the line out. Writers."

"That's what I do for a living."

"Know the story about the writer?" he said. "Writer makes it big in Hollywood and wants to impress his mother. So he invites her out to visit him. She takes the train and he goes to the station with flowers, but he doesn't see her anywhere. Finally he goes to the police station to see whether they know anything, and he sees her there. 'Ma, why didn't you have me paged at the station?' She says, 'I forgot your name.'"

"That's not funny either," I said, but I was laughing.

"It's odd, isn't it, Brownie?" he said to his wife. "We've broken our rule. We've actually had dinner with another passenger."

"I hope that wasn't too painful for you," Constance said to me.

"Tomorrow I'll tell you how I made some lucky investments in the Arctic," Jack said. "Frobisher Bay. Making a deal with some Eskimos while they ate a raw seal on the floor. I'm not joking."

After a man has made a large amount of money he usually becomes a bad listener. Jack Greenwald was not a man in that mold; he was not in a hurry, and he was a tease, but with an air of mystery. "I happen to be something of an authority on Persian carpets," he would say. Or it might be Kashmiri sapphires, or gold alloys, or oil embargoes. If I challenged him I was usually proven wrong.

These deals in the Canadian Arctic, this talk of "my carver," "my goldsmith," and the billiard-room he was planning to build, with a blue felt on the billiard table, made him seem like the strange tycoon Harry Oakes, whom he somewhat resembled physically; but there was an impish side to him too, a love of wearing Mephisto sneakers with his dinner jacket, and a compulsion to buy hats, and wear them, and a tendency to interrupt a boring story with a joke.

"Hear the one about the eighty-year-old with the young wife?" Jack said, when the subject of Galaxidion, our next port, was raised in the smoking-room, where he had just set a Cuban cigar aflame. "His friend says, 'Isn't that bad for the heart?' The old man says, 'If she dies, she dies.'"

I had fled from Corfu after arriving there on the boat from Albania. I had tried and failed to get to Ulysses' home island of Ithaca. But there was only one ferry a week. The *Seabourne* passed south of it in the night and I felt I had returned to roughly where I had left off and was continuing my Mediterranean progress. I had felt a deep aversion to Corfu which even in the low season was a tourist island. The whole of Greece seemed to me a cut-price theme park of broken marble, a place where you were harangued in a high-minded way about ancient Greek culture while some swarthy little person picked your pocket. That, and unlimited Turkophobia.

We had sailed south of the large island of Cephalonia, and passed Missolonghi where Lord Byron had died, into the Gulf of Corinth, anchoring off the small Greek village of Galaxidion on a bay just below Delphi. Indeed, beneath the glittering slopes of Mount Parnassus.

Tenders took us ashore, where we were greeted by the guides.

"My name is Clea. The driver's name is Panayotis. His name means 'The Most Holy.' He has been named after the Blessed Virgin."

The driver smiled at us and puffed his cigarette and waved.

"Apollo came here," Clea said.

Near this bauxite mine? Great red piles of earth containing bauxite, used to make aluminum, had been quarried from the depths of Itea below Delphi to await transshipment to Russia, which has a monopoly on Greek bauxite. In return, Russia swaps natural gas with Greece. Such a simple arrangement: we give you red dirt, you give us stinky gas. Apollo came here?

"He strangled the python to prove his strength as a god," Clea went on, and without missing a beat, "the yacht *Christina* came here as well, after Aristotle Onassis married Jackie Kennedy, for their honeymoon cruise."

Through an olive grove that covered a great green plain with thousands of olive trees (not looking at all well after a three-month drought), we climbed the cliff to Delphi, the center of the world. The navel itself, a little stone toadstool *omphalos*, is there on the slope for all to see.

"I must say several things to you about how to act," Clea began.

There followed some nannyish instructions about showing decorum near the artifacts. This seemed very odd piety. It was also a recent fetish. After almost two thousand years of neglect, during which Greek temples and ruins had been pissed on and ransacked – the ones that had not been hauled away (indeed, rescued for posterity) by people like Lord Elgin had been used to make the walls of peasant huts – places like Delphi were discovered by intrepid Germans and Frenchmen and dug up.

Delphi had not been operational since the time of Christ. In the reign of Claudius (51 A.D.), "the site was impoverished and half-deserted," Michael Grant writes in his *Guide to the Ancient World*, "and Nero was said to have carried 500 statues away." Delphi was officially shut down and cleared by the Emperor Theodosius (379–95), who was an active campaigner for Christianity. It is no wonder that what remains of Delphi are some stumpy columns and the vague foundations of the temples – hardly anything, in fact, except a stony hillside and a guide's Hellenistic sales pitch. Anyone inspired to visit Delphi on the basis of Henry Miller's manic and stuttering flapdoodle in *The Colossus of Maroussi* would be in for a disappointment.

The Greeks had not taken very much interest in their past until Europeans became enthusiastic discoverers of and diggers in their ruins. And why should they have cared? The Greeks were not Greek, but rather the illiterate descendants of Slavs and Albanian fishermen, who spoke a debased Greek dialect and had little interest in the broken columns and temples except as places to graze their sheep. The true philhellenes were the English – of whom Byron was the epitome – and the French, who were passionate to link themselves with the Greek ideal. This rampant and irrational philhellenism, which amounted almost to a religion, was also a reaction to the confident dominance of the Ottoman Turks, who were widely regarded as savages and heathens. The Turks had brought their whole culture, their language, the Muslim religion, and their distinctive cuisine not only to Greece but to the whole of the Middle East, and into Europe, as far as Budapest. The contradiction persists, even today: Greek food is actually Turkish food, and many words we think of as distinctively Greek are in reality Turkish – kebab, doner, kofta, meze, taramasalata, dolma, yogurt, moussaka, and so forth: all Turkish.

Signs at the entrance to Delphi said, "Show proper respect" and "It is forbidden to sing or make loud noises" and "Do not pose in front of ancient stones."

I saw a pair of rambunctious Greek youths being reprimanded by an officious little man for flinging their arms out and posing for pictures. The man twitched a stick at them and sent them away.

Why was this? It was just what you would expect to happen if you put a pack of ignoramuses in charge of a jumble of marble artifacts they had no way of comprehending. They would in their impressionable stupidity begin to venerate the mute stones and make up a lot of silly rules. This "Show proper respect" business and "No posing" was an absurd and desperate transfer of the orthodoxies of the Greeks' tenacious Christianity as they applied the severe prohibitions of their Church to the ruins. Understanding little of the meaning of the stones, they could only see them in terms of their present religious belief; and so they imposed a sort of sanctity on the ruins. This ludicrous solemnity was universal in Greece. Women whose shorts were too tight and men wearing bathing suits were not allowed to enter the stadium above Delphi where the ancients had run races stark ballocky naked. In some Greek places, photography of ruins was banned as sacrilegious.

In spite of this irrationality, the place was magical, because of its natural setting, the valley below Delphi, the edge of a steep slope, the pines, the shimmering hills of brilliant rock, the glimpse of Mount Parnassus. Delphi was magnificent for the view it commanded, for the way it looked outward on the world. The site had also been chosen for the smoking crack in the earth that it straddled, which made the Oracle, a crone balancing on her tripod, choke and gasp and deliver riddles.

"'What kind of child will I give birth to?' someone would ask the Oracle," Clea said. "And the Oracle was clever. She would say, 'Boy not girl,' and that could mean boy or girl, because of the inflection."

"I don't get it," someone said. "If the Oracle could see the future, why did she bother to speak in riddles?"

"To make the people wonder."

"But if she really was an oracle, huh, why didn't she just tell the truth?"

"It was the way that oracles spoke in those days," Clea said feebly.

"Doesn't that mean she really didn't know the answer?"

"No."

"Doesn't that mean she was just making the whole thing up?"

This made Clea cross. But the scholar Michael Grant describes how the prophecies were conservative and adaptable to circumstances, and he writes of the Oracle, "Some have . . . preferred to ascribe the entire phenomenon to clever stage management, aided by an effective information system."

Clea took us to the museum, where one magnificent statue, a life-sized bronze of a charioteer, was worth the entire climb up the hill. As for the rest I had some good historical sound-bites for my growing collection.

– *The Oracle sat on this special kettle and said her prophecies.*

– *Pericles had very big ears, which is why he is always shown wearing a helmet.*

On the way back to the ship, while the guide was telling the story of Oedipus – how he got his name, and killed his father, and married his mother; while frowning and somewhat shocked *Seabourne* passengers listened – I began to talk to the Cornacchias, Joe and Eileen, who told me about their recent win at the Kentucky Derby. It was the second time a horse of theirs had triumphed – "Strike the Gold" had won in 1991, and "Go for Gin" this year.

"What's your secret?" I asked.

"I have a very good trainer who knows horses. He feels their muscles. I also have a geneticist, who checks them out. It's a science, you know."

The Cornacchias lived on the north shore of Long Island, some miles east of Gatsby country. Eileen was an admiring and pleasant person and Joe an unassuming man who did not boast. He was also very big. "I tell the horses, 'If you don't win, I'm going to ride you.'"

"What was the purse this year?"

"I won eight-point-one million bucks. Broke even."

"Where's the profit, then?"

"'Go for Gin' is starting to make money as a stud."

Back on the ship, we resumed our voyage, and as the sun set behind Corinth we slid through the narrow Corinth Canal, with just a few feet to spare on either side. Jack Greenwald stood on deck in his blazer, smoking a thick Monte Cristo, waving to the Corinthians on shore.

At the *Seabourne* dinners when black tie was requested, two or three times a week, it was impossible to tell the waiters from the passengers. The night before we arrived in the port of Piraeus, a variety of caviar was served that reminded Jack Greenwald of something he had once eaten in the Arctic. This became a long story about narwhal tusks, "an area in which I am one of the few living specialists."

"I have two very important things to do in Athens," Jack said to me on deck after dinner. "Make a phone call, and buy a captain's hat. I want one of those real hats – not one with braid. And the phone call is about my cat."

"Yes?"

"My cat is a diabetic," he said. "We must have a medical update. Isn't that right, Constance?"

On the quay the next day I said that we would save money and time if we took the train the twenty miles or so from Piraeus to Athens. Good idea, he said, and waved away the taxi-driver he had been speaking to. But on the way to the station Jack became bored, and he turned around to see the taxi-driver dogging our heels, still whining.

"Please don't say another word," Jack said. "I will give you a hundred dollars if you stick with us all day."

That was fine with the taxi-driver, whose name was Leonidas. He took us to a jewelry shop. Jack: "Is that your cousin?" Leonidas took us to a restaurant. Jack: "You have relatives everywhere." Leonidas had a blue eye on his key-chain, a talisman against the evil eye. Jack: "You actually believe that stuff?"

"I'm going to tell Leonidas I'm in love with him," Jack said. "Just see what he says."

In a wintry voice, Constance said, "Behave yourself."

"Tell me about your king," Jack said.

"King Constantine," Leonidas said. "Since one year he come to the Greek."

"Were you happy?"

"Some not happy. Some people say, 'Go!'"

"Did you say 'Go'?"

"No. That is not good, sir."

"You know Jackie Kennedy?"

"Mrs Kennedy, sir. She married Mr Onassis for the name, sir. For the name!"

Jack turned to me and said, "When Kennedy died I had to take two numbers out of my revue, *Up Tempo*. They mentioned him. They weren't funny any more."

We went to the Acropolis, but it was shut because of a strike by the municipal workers who staffed it. Still, it was possible to see the Parthenon, as white as though it had been carved from salt, glittering and elegant, and towering over the dismal city of congested traffic and badly-built tenements. Apart from what remained of its ancient ruins, and the treasures in its museums, Athens had to be one of the ugliest cities on earth, indeed ugly and deranged enough to be used as the setting for yet another variation on the Heart of Darkness theme, perhaps to be called *Acropolis Now*.

The *Seabourne* passengers we happened upon in the city were unanimous in sharing this view.

"Athens is a four-hour city," one man said, meaning that was all the time you needed to see it in its entirety. That hourly rate seemed to me a helpful index for judging cities.

"I think Athens is a toilet," a blunter man said.

"There's nothing to buy in Greece," a woman said.

While I bought lurid postcards of ancient pottery depicting bizarre sexual acts, Jack went to another jewelry store with Leonidas. I found them later, being pursued by the owner.

Hurrying into the taxi, Jack said, "When a jeweler tells you a stone costs $140,000 and then after some haggling says that he'll give it to you for $80,000 – a discount of sixty grand – does that inspire confidence?"

This brought forth a lesson in the form of a story from him in buying anything in the Middle East. This applied to Greece, Turkey, Iran, Israel, wherever one was possessed of a desire to spend.

"What I am about to tell you is very valuable," he said. But the story was complicated. It concerned his friend Ali who had sold him a carpet, then bought it back, and re-sold it, all at different prices.

"What's the point of the story?" he asked in a rhetorical way. It was this: Nothing in the Middle East has an absolute value. What a cousin is charged is different from what a stranger will be charged, and an old customer is told an altogether different price. There is no way of assigning a price to anything except by sizing up the buyer.

New passengers had arrived on board and were audible as they got acquainted with the old ones.

"– and then I'd be facing a $200,000 medical procedure."

"– so big it wouldn't fit in the safe in the house, so we had to take out a separate policy."

"– on a scale of one to ten my brother-in-law is a minus four."

"– our tenth cruise in two years."

"– up the Amazon."

"– Antarctica."

"– Galapagos."

The ship sailed south to the Peloponnesian port of Návplion, gateway to Mycenae. I had seen the Mycenaean gold masks and bracelets in the museum in Athens, and felt in need of a little exercise, so I stayed in Návplion and climbed the thousand steps on the hill behind the town to visit the fortress Palamidi. This brooding structure of eight bastions that dominates the skyline was pronounced impregnable by its Venetian architect, Agostino Sagredo. But he had tempted fate, because a year after it was finished, 1715, the Turks landed in the Peloponnese and immediately captured it. About a hundred years later, in 1822, the year of Lord Byron's death during the Greek struggle for independence, the Greeks wrested it from the Turks.

At the top, a sign: "Visitors are prayed to enter the site decently dressed." I knew this was another example of Greek Puritanism and misplaced veneration. I asked the young man at the entrance to explain to me what it meant. He was unshaven, in a grubby shirt. He was playing cards with his much grubbier friend.

"People come with bikinis and shorts. They don't look nice," he said.

Oh, sure, Demetrios, and you look like Fred Astaire.

Hiking farther on, outside town, I met a woman on the footpath and asked her if a village lay at the end of it. I apologized for not speaking Greek.

"Don't apologize," she said. "I am Italian."

So we spoke Italian. Her name was Estella.

"What part of Italy are you from?"

"I am from Uruguay," she said, and added, "Let me tell you, Uruguay is much cleaner and more orderly than Greece. Do you notice that Greeks throw paper and bottles all over the place?"

The litter in Greece was remarkable – the roadsides, the beaches, even the ruins were scattered with plastic bottles and candy wrappers and rags and tin cans. I wondered why.

"Because they are barbarians," Estella said. "They are different from every other European."

"You don't think Greece is modern?"

"I have lived in Návplion for three years. I can tell you it's not pleasant. Greece is decades behind in every way. Twenty or thirty years behind the rest of Europe."

"I am just visiting. I saw the fort."

"The fort is like everything else here. Interesting, but dirty."

From a nearby hill I had a good view of Návplion: the small old Venetian quarter, which was now just souvenir shops; the commercial part of the city, which had gone to seed; and the rest of it, ugly and recent and jerry-built and sprawling.

More than any other place I had seen so far on the Mediterranean, Greece was purely a tourist destination, a theme park of shattered marble and broken statues, and garbled history. But tourists did not really go to Greece for the history; they went for the sunshine, and these cautioning signs were in many cases meant to restrain north Europeans who in the Greek warmth became militant nudists – Germans, especially. The Greeks struck me as being more xenophobic than the French, and more ill-tempered and irrational, in a country more backward than Croatia. They sneered at the Albanians and deported them. They loudly cursed the Turks. They boasted of their glorious past, but were selective, for it was only yesterday – in the 1960s – that these passionate democrats had welcomed a military coup, and supported it in its creation of one of the most right-wing governments in the hemisphere, the seven-year dictatorship of the Greek Colónels.

Greece manufactured nothing except tourist souvenirs. It did not even clean its beaches of litter. It was famous for its pollution and its foul drinking water. Even its politics had become ridiculous, as its aging prime minister, famous for his moralistic rants, chucked his wife and ran off with an air hostess. But Greece had been redeemed. By being accepted as a member of the European Community, Greece had become respectable, even viable as a sort of welfare case. Membership meant free money, handouts, every commercial boondoggle imaginable; and the sort of pork that Italians had made into prosciutto the Greeks simply frittered away, all the while keeping their Mediterranean enemies out of the European Union.

As I walked over the hills above Návplion the sky lowered and it began to rain, and the complaints of the grazing sheep grew louder. In sunshine, at a little distance, Greece could look delightful, because the arid glaring rock was so bright and back-lit, the trash and garbage camouflaged, and even the most polluted parts of the Aegean had sparkle. The rain made it truly gloomy. In bad weather Greece was an awful place, of glum gray tenements and wrecked cars and rough treeless hills of solemn stone. Cloudy skies seemed also to throw the Greek dereliction into sharper relief – and so, to make matters worse, the sensational litter of Greece became visible in the rain.

Given these tetchy people and this insubstantial landscape and the theme-park culture, wasn't it odd that Greece was thought of as a country of romance and robust passion and diaphanous rain? In a land of preposterous myths, the myth of Greece as a paradise of joy and abundance was surely the most preposterous. How had that come about?

"The sea," wrote Kazantzakis, rhapsodizing in *Zorba the Greek*, "autumn mildness, islands bathed in light, fine rain spreading a diaphanous veil over the immortal nakedness of Greece. Happy is the man, I thought, who, before dying, has the good fortune to sail the Aegean Sea.

"Many are the joys of this world – women, fruit, ideas. But to cleave that sea in the gentle autumnal season, murmuring the name of each islet, is to my mind the joy most apt to transport the heart of man into paradise. Nowhere else can one pass so easily and serenely from reality into dream. The frontiers dwindle, and from the masts of the most ancient ships spring branches and fruits. It is as if here in Greece necessity is the mother of miracles."

Dreamy, sentimental, passionate Kazantzakis, of the purple prose and the purple nose! His Greece, especially his native Crete, is mostly gone now and the paradox is that (if I may borrow an empurpled leaf from one of the master's own books) it seems that Kazantzakis's Oedipal feeling for his motherland produced the inevitable Greek tragedy. Tourists came in droves to verify Kazantzakis's sensuous praise of the Greek sluttishness, and rumbustiousness, and good-heartedness, the cheap food and the sunshine.

The early visitors were not disappointed, but in the end Greece – so fragile, so infertile, so ill-prepared for another invasion – became blighted with, among nightmares of tourism, thousands of Zorba Discos, Zorba Tavernas, Zorba Cafés, and the *Zorba the Greek* bouzouki music from the movie soundtrack played much too loudly in so many souvenir shops; all the curios, the fake ikons, the glass beads, the T-shirts and carvings and plates ("Souvenir of Mycenae"); and regiments of marching Germans, resolutely looking for fun. Greece had needed a few metaphors. Kazantzakis provided the highbrow, or at least literary metaphors; movies and television provided the rest.

The *Seabourne* lay at anchor in the Cretan port of Agios Nikolaos ("Ag Nik" to its habitués). There were many Zorba businesses here, and the sign "As seen on the BBC" was displayed at various parts of town, for this place, specifically the nearby leper island of Spinalonga, was the setting for a popular and long-running series entitled *Who Pays the Ferryman*.

"You didn't see it?" a German said to me at a café in town. He was incredulous, and he mocked my ignorance. I was not offended. Since I spent many days mocking other people's ignorance, this was fine with me. "When this show was on television in Germany, the streets were empty. Everyone was at home watching it. Me, too. That's why I came here."

The port and the town and everything visible had been given over to tourists; there was not a shop, or any sign of human activity, or any structure, that was not in some way related to the business of tourism. All the signs were repeated in four languages, German taking precedence.

Writing about tourists – whether it is a harangue or an epitaph – is just pissing against the wind. There is a certain fun to be had from snapping the odd picture, or cherishing the random observation. But I had vowed at the beginning of my trip to avoid tourists and, whenever possible, not to notice them. Haven't we read all that elsewhere? I went ashore, bumped into the Greenwalds (Jack: "I've just been offered a genuine Greek icon for fifty dollars. Think I should buy it?"), walked around a little, and finding the crowds of milling tourists much too dense, I rented a motorcycle and left Agios Nikolaos at sixty kilometers an hour. I rode east, down the coast, then southward over the mountains to the opposite side of Crete, to the town of Ierapetra. This place looked very much like Agios Nikolaos, which I had fled: curio shops, tavernas, postcard shops, unreliable-looking restaurants, "Rooms for Rent!" "Bikes for Hire!".

There were plenty of Zorba enterprises here, too. And bullying restaurateurs and their touts brayed at passers-by at Ierapetra.

"Meester — you come! You eat here! *Sprechen Sie Deutsch?* Best food in Griss! Where you go? Not some other place — you eat here!"

Every five feet there was an insistent tout, hustling people off the pavement and seating them before any competitor could snag them. There was probably a more unpleasant figure one could be assaulted by than an unshaven Greek howling commands in ungrammatical German, but if so I could not think of one at the moment. They were seriously browbeating the perambulating tourists — just the mood to whet your appetite; and when the people kept walking they were insulted and abused by the touts they had passed.

All that and a foul beach; but the muddiest beach at Ierapetra was called Waikiki, a misnomer that was merely a harmless desecration compared with the violence of calling a boarding-house outside town "The Ritz." Elsewhere in Ierapetra the eighteenth-century mosque in a quaint part of town had been wrecked and partly rebuilt. The minaret was still standing. The Arabic calligraphy remained. But the interior was defiled, having been turned into a tiny auditorium. Chairs had been set up, facing music stands, and the bass drum was propped against the wall.

Was this worse than the Turks in Istanbul revamping the Byzantine magnificence of Santa Sophia and making it a mosque, along with any number of Christian churches? Probably not. But there were still Christians functioning in Turkey and there were no Muslims in Greece. Apart from the tourists and some retirees, there were no foreigners in Greece. There were Arabs in Spain, Albanians and Africans in Italy, Moroccans in Sardinia, Algerians in France; but there were no immigrants of any kind in Greece. The Albanians that came had been sent back. Whether it was Greece's feeble economy that kept everyone except Albanians (whose economy was abysmal) from wishing to settle there, or Greek intolerance, was something I did not know. Perhaps it was both – or neither, since the Greeks were themselves migrants, leaving in great numbers for America and Australia.

Was Crete the ancient homeland of the Jews? Tacitus thought so. His theory was inspired by the name of Crete's highest mountain, in the central part of the island: "At the time when Saturn was driven from his throne by the violence of Jupiter, they abandoned their habitation and gained a settlement at the extremity of Libya. In support of this tradition, the etymology of the name is adduced as a proof. Mount Ida, well known to fame, stands on the isle of Crete: the inhabitants are called Ideans; and the word by a barbarous corruption was changed afterwards to that of Judeans."

A Dutchman, Janwillem from Rotterdam, whom I met in Ierapetra, told me that he was here to look at buying a place for his retirement.

"I retire in a few years," he said. "I would like to over-winter here, or in Benidorm."

"What's the attraction here?"

Janwillem countered with a question of his own. "You've been to Holland?"

"Yes," I said.

"Very flat. Very expensive," he said. "But here" – and he gestured – "is cheap! You can eat at one of those places with wobbly tables, very old and nice, dinner for two, with wine – twenty guilders!"

"So you're moving here?"

"Maybe if I find a flat on the top of a house, with balcony, nice view of the sea."

Still, Janwillem seemed doubtful. Was he?

"I think it is very isolated in the winter," he said. "There is a Dutch group of people in Benidorm, in Spain. You have been there?"

"Yes," and I wanted to add *I hated it*, but why demoralize this Flying Dutchman in his hopes for a happy retirement?

"If you are bored in Benidorm, it is so easy to get the bus back to Holland," he said. "Here is harder. A ferry to Piraeus, then the train or the bus to Patras. Ferry to Italy. Another train to Rome. Train to Paris. What? Two or three days – maybe four!"

I had met Janwillem by chance, walking the back streets of Ierapetra, as he was looking for a likely dwelling in which to spend his retirement. By the end of this conversation he had convinced himself that retirement in Greece would be an enormous mistake.

Mounting my motorcycle I rode back to Agios Nikolaos, admiring the mountains and the blue bays, side-swiped by cars and trucks, as I made my way through the goat-chewed, sheep-nibbled landscape of sharp rocks and olive trees and cracked white houses, all of it screamingly signposted: For Rent! For Sale! Buy Me! Try Me! Rent Me! Eat Me! Drink Me!

Mike the Greek was still sitting at his motorbike rental agency, still reading the porno magazine he had been leafing through that morning.

"How do you say porno in Greek?"

"Porno!" he cried. "Same!"

Back on the *Seabourne*, I met Jack Greenwald who said that he had spent the afternoon in the jacuzzi on the upper deck with Ambassador Tan.

"We talked about what stressful lives we had led," he said. "I was lying but I think he was telling the truth. We were drinking and sitting there in the jacuzzi in the sunshine. It was very pleasant. He tells me he's on his way to Bangladesh, to help poor people."

"Was Reggie in the tub?" I asked, using the name we had assigned to one of the British passengers.

Jack wagged his finger at me and said, "No, no. Never trust an Englishman who doesn't shine his shoes."

*

After warm purple cauliflower with olives in white truffle vinai-
grette, chilled plum bisque, and marinated breast of guinea fowl
with juniper gravy – or did I salve my conscience with the
vegetable gratin? – I bumped into Mrs Betty Levy and asked why
she had been missing at dinner.

"I'm feeling a bit precious today," Mrs Levy said. "I had some
consommé in my suite. I don't want to get anything. They've all
got something."

Now, well into our second week of this Mediterranean cruise on
this glittering ship, we had learned a little about history (toilets
were called Vespasians in ancient Rome, Pericles had enormous
ears, Athenians ate porridge for breakfast), and found out a lot
about each other. In many ways it was like being an old-time
resident of an exclusive hotel. Passengers knew each other, and
their families, and their ailments, and were confident and hearty.

"How's that lovely wife of yours, Buddy?"

"Say, is your mother any better?"

"Lovely day. How's the leg?"

The only stress was occasioned by the visits ashore – not that it
was unpleasant being reverentially led through the ground plans of
ancient sites, and down the forking paths of incomprehensible
ruins, many of them no larger than a man's hand ("Try to
imagine that in its day this structure was actually larger than the
Parthenon"); it was rather that every daily disembarkation for a
tour was like a rehearsal for the final disembarkation, the day
when we would leave the comfort of the *Seabourne*, and that was
too awful to contemplate.

This ship was now more than home – it had become the
apotheosis of the Mediterranean, a magnificent vantage-point in
the sea which allowed us to view the great harbors and mountains
and cliffs and forts, in luxury. At sundown we were always back on
board, away from the uncertainty and the stinks of the port cities,
and the predatory souvenir-sellers. We were on our floating villa
which, in its way, contained the best of the Mediterranean. We
drank the wines of the Midi and the Mezzogiorno, our dishes were
better than anything we saw in the harborside restaurants, and
rather than risk the detritus of the beaches, we had our own
marina at the stern. Even with his billions, Aristotle Onassis had

felt there was no greater joy on earth than cruising these sunny islands, and his honeymoon trip with his new wife, Jacqueline, was the very journey we were embarked on, sailing – it must be said – in our vastly superior ship.

From Crete, we sailed through the islands called the Sporades, living up to their name as sporadic – isolated and scattered – and onward past the Greek island of Kos to the coast of Turkey, the port of Bodrum, with its Crusader castle and its crumbling city wall and its market, which contained both treasures and tourist junk.

It was immediately apparent, even in the swift one-day passage from Greece to Turkey, that we were in a different country. I compared them, because as old enemies they were constantly comparing each other. Turkey was both more ramshackle and more real. Travelers tended to avoid Turkey, which was not a member of the European Union (thanks in part to Greece's opposition), so Turkey had not depended on tourists for its income and had had to become self-sufficient, with the steel industry and the manufacturing that Greece lacked. Turks were calmer, more polite, less passionate, somewhat dour – even lugubrious; less in awe of tourists, and so they were more hospitable and helpful. Greeks were antagonistic towards each other, which made them hard for foreigners to rub along with; Turks, more formal, had rules of engagement, and also seemed to like each other better. Turkey had a bigger hinterland and shared a border with seven countries, yet Turks were less paranoid and certainly less xenophobic, less vocal, less blaming, perhaps more fatalistic.

We had crossed from Europe to Asia. Turkey is the superficially westernized edge of the Orient, Greece is the degraded fringe of Europe, basically a peasant society, fortunate in its ruins and (with most of the Mediterranean) its selective memory. But it was wrong to compare Greece with Turkey, since their geography and their size were so different. Greece's landscape was more similar to that of Albania, and if Greece was a successful version of Albania, Turkey was a happier version of Iran – and perhaps the only moderate Muslim country in the world.

After the assault by touts at Greek ports it was restful to walk down the quay in Bodrum and not have Turks flying at us. That restraint was an Asiatic virtue. Turks also had Asian contempt,

and were famously cruel, both knowing they were so and believing
that most people in the world were just the same. If you abused
Turkish hospitality (as I did frequently) and asked Turks whether
they tortured their prisoners, they spat and said, "Everyone tortures their prisoners!"

It was raining in Bodrum. Half the *Seabourne* passengers did not
bother to go ashore. But even in the rain the harbor looked alive,
an effect perhaps of being full of beautiful wooden sailboats in port
for a regatta. The Crusader castle was intact, except for the
occasional mark of an infidel's aggression. There were pious Latin
inscriptions over the battlements and gateways ("No victory is
possible without your help, O Lord"), a nice reminder that Christianity had kept its faith robust with its own *jihads* – holy wars that
had lasted for centuries.

Walking past a carpet shop – an unmistakable sign that we were
in Asia – I saw Jack Greenwald being harangued by the carpet
dealer.

"This is not a carpet! This is a piece of art!" he cried. "I am
selling art!"

Jack beckoned me in, introduced me to the dealer, Mr Arcyet,
as "my millionaire friend," and soon carpets were being unrolled
and were flopping one on another. It was another Greenwald tease
to abandon me to the hysteria of a Turkish carpet dealer who
believed he had an American tycoon captive in his shop, on a
rainy day in Bodrum.

His hysteria was short-lived, interrupted by a more dramatic
event. Outside the shop, a huge Turkish woman had collapsed on
the street, and she lay in the rain, her skirt hiked up, while a
Turkish man slapped her face in a violent attempt to revive her,
and other Turks sauntered by to stare. Soon there was a crowd of
murmuring Turks watching the supine woman, and when a taxi
came to take her away it required four of them to haul her into the
back seat.

That unscheduled event was the only drama in Bodrum that
day. It was too rainy to go anywhere. The phones would not work
without a Turkish phone card, and there were no cards for sale
anywhere in the town ("You come back next week"). I looked at
the old mausoleum and the new casino and the suburbs of bunga-

lows and condominiums of the sort that were being retailed elsewhere in the Mediterranean as holiday homes for Europeans from
less congenial climates. The prices of this Turkish real estate
ranged from $30,000 to $60,000 − cheaper, but just as hideous as
the ones in Spain, Malta and Greece.

Resolute about staying ashore, I had a Turkish lunch of eggplant, fava beans, stuffed peppers and a gooey dessert, and afterwards, back on the ship, realized that the people who had stayed
on board had had a better lunch, a drier time of it, and had still
enjoyed the thrill of seeing the castle and the sailboats and the
shapely Turkish mountains.

At dinner, the *Seabourne* was sailing north to Lesbos, and Jack
Greenwald was in unusually high spirits in anticipation of dessert −
one of his own recipes, *Fraises au poivre*, strawberries with black
pepper. Greenwald high spirits took the form of teasing, and as we
were at a larger-than-usual table, he was able to range over it,
poking fun. To the Panamanian, he said: "Noriega was a very
patriotic man, above all, don't you think?" To a woman wrinkling
her nose: "That is how Eskimos say no. They say yes by lifting
their eyebrows − here, do you think you can manage that, too?"
To a rationalist at the head of the table: "Of course, I believe in
ghosts, and our Prime Minister, Mackenzie King, believed in
ghosts, too."

This chatter was no more absurd than that of the other
passengers.

"− Harry and I were at the Barbara Sinatra benefit for abused
children," a woman was saying. "Tom Arnold was one of the
speakers. He talked about the man who had abused him −"

" figured, if you're in Turkey you've got to get a Turkish
carpet. I measured the spot in the house and I've got the measure-
ments with me. We're looking for something floral − my wife loves
flowers. We don't want anything geometric −"

"− a couple of icons. They swore they were genuine −"

"− stayed for a whole week in the Sea Shells − they're islands in
the Indian Ocean."

"− next time up the Amazon."

"− get to Rio J. DeNiro, during Carnival."

At last, the waiter rolled a trolley towards Jack Greenwald with several bowls, the strawberries, and in bottles and saucers various other ingredients for his dessert. Jack supervised and narrated the preparation.

. "Nine plump fresh strawberries – good," he said. "Now, take that pepper mill and grind twelve twists of pepper," and he counted as the black pepper fell upon the crimson strawberries. "Take a tablespoon of Pernod and macerate them, yes, like that. And a tablespoon of Cointreau. Macerate. Lift them, let it reach all the berries. Now a tablespoon of Armagnac. Macerate, macerate."

"Yes?" the waiter showed Jack the bowl of slick speckled berries.

"A few pinches of sugar and three-quarters of a tablespoon of fresh *crème*," Jack said. "Mix carefully, just coat them with the *crème*. You notice how I pronounce that word 'clem' – that's because I'm from Montreal."

There was a bit more business with the *Fraises au poivre*. The plates were wrong. No, not soup bowls – but flat plates were needed for the serving, and the sauce had to be dripped just so.

"What do you think?" he asked, after I had sampled some.

It was hard to describe the taste, which was both a slow sweet burn, and peppery and syrupy and alcoholic and fruity; and I did not want to tell him that no taste could compete with the pleasure of watching this dessert being concocted by him and the deferential waiter.

To add to my pleasure, Jack immediately ordered a helping of cherries jubilee, another Greenwald variation, flambéed, with ice cream, and tucking in, he said, "Doesn't this go down nicely after the strawberries?"

Afterwards, he said that he had joined the cruise – he was going on to Haifa after Istanbul – in order to lose forty pounds, "but I'm having my doubts."

Morning in Lesbos, dreary in a drizzling rain, but there were floods elsewhere. FLOODS! CATASTROPHE! the Lesbian headlines cried. DEATH IN CRETE! Torrential rains were general all over the Peloponnese: cars washed into the sea, stranded tourists, cliffs broken by erosion, roofs collapsed.

Because so little vegetation existed in Greece, whether on the mainland or the islands, the soil did not hold the rain. Lesbos was a study in erosion, the gravelly hills sluicing down their own gullies and washing into the street; dirt, mud, stones, silt, sand traveling fast in streams and pouring into the sea, reducing the island, making it starker and stonier.

Had Greece always looked like this? I began to think that there had to have been a time when it was forested, and that the loss of trees had given it this wasted and lined appearance. It had perhaps been quite a different landscape in ancient times, not the white wasteland of hot pockmarked stone and blazing sand, but a cooler place of shade trees and forests.

I traipsed through the town of Mitilini, bought a newspaper, made a telephone call, visited a church, and watched a fisherman plucking tiny fish from the thick folds of his net. It continued to rain. Few places are gloomier than a tourist town in a rainstorm. The weather seemed to make the Greeks crabbier, too; the frowning, chain-smoking men in the damp tavernas they had turned into men's clubs.

If I had arrived in Lesbos on my own, in a boat from Turkish Izmir, or on a Greek island-hopping ferry, with days to spend on the island, I would have tried to make it work for me. I would have buttonholed a Lesbian, needled a landlady, glad-handed a Greek, and tried to create some rapport. But this was a one-day visit. I jumped puddles all morning, had lunch on the *Seabourne* and made another foray in the afternoon, all the time watching the clock. The food on board was excellent; there was friendship and good cheer and comfort. It was so easy for me to turn my back on the island and wait for the ship's whistle to blow and for Lesbos to vanish astern.

Most of the passengers were getting off the ship in Istanbul. A few were going on to Haifa. Mrs Betty Levy was threatening to stay aboard for another month or more. Her dream, she told me, was to be at sea for weeks – no ports, no tours.

This impending sense of departure gave our progress up the Dardanelles the following morning a gloomy air of abandonment, and the funereal pall was not lightened by the knowledge that we were passing Gallipoli, and the graves of 200,000 fallen soldiers. The Dardanelles is like a canal, no more than a mile wide in some places, linking the eastern basin of the Mediterranean to the Sea of Marmara, where another canal – the Bosphorus – divides Istanbul, and so on to the Black Sea.

The Dardanelles is also the Hellespont of Leander, who swam back and forth to be with Hero; and of Lord Byron, in homage and in imitation. I had thought of swimming it myself – a mile was swimmable – but it looked uninviting in late October, with four- to five-foot breaking waves, and a heavy chop, with a cold wind blowing from Thrace on the north side.

"Freeze the vodka," Jack Greenwald was saying to the waiter in French, preparing him for the caviar course at tonight's dinner. "Wrap the bottle in a wet towel, put an apple in it for taste and keep it so cold it gets syrupy. Do you follow me?"

The bloody battlefield of Gallipoli was now the little Turkish village of Gelibolu, mainly fisherfolk, and where Xerxes and Alexander had marched their armies across on pontoon bridges, where Jason had sailed with his Argonauts in search of the Golden Fleece, there were rusty freighters, and more villages, and a town, Çanakkale – some mosques and minarets visible, along with the factories and the clusters of houses. But it was wrong to expect anything dramatic. It was an old sea, of myths and half-truths and sound-bites of history; its periods of prosperity and peace had been interrupted by even longer periods of disruption and pillaging. It was the center of many civilizations, but there had always been barbarians at the gates – and inside the gates.

Yet so little was left of the Mediterranean past that it was possible to travel the sea from port to port and never be reminded of the ancients. Even the recent brutality of Gallipoli was buried on the featureless shore – just another cemetery. There were so many graves on the shores of this sea.

Fog rolled in, dusk fell, blurred lights shone from the shore, some indicating the crests of hills. And then in this mist, a nocturne of misty light, there emerged and remained printed on the night a vision from the past, of a skyline that was purely minarets and towers, and mosque domes and bridges and obelisks, like a promise made in Byzantium that was being honored in the present. We had crossed the Golden Horn.

Closer to the European shore, which is the site of the old city, their features were more distinct, first the squarer lines of the Topkapi Palace, then Agya Irene, and the 1,500-year-old Agya Sophia, every brick intact; and behind its minarets, the six minarets of the Blue Mosque, and on the crest of the hill Nur Osmanye – the Light of God – the thick Byzantine fire tower, the Yeni mosque beneath it, at the end of the Galata Bridge, and, beyond, the vast, almost unearthly masterpiece of Sinan, the Suleiman mosque, pale and glittering even in this shifting fog.

Ferries were crossing the Bosphorus, passing the *Seabourne*, hooting, their lights illuminating the sea and giving the scraps of hanging fog the shimmering and golden texture of an antique veil, a little tattered and brittle, perhaps, but still usable for conveying mystery.

Just before I left the *Seabourne Spirit*, Jack Greenwald took me aside and gave me a gaily-wrapped present. Inside was a Turkish lapel pin and his Household Cavalry tie.

"Wear them both," he said. "The pin will be useful here in Turkey. The tie is helpful everywhere."

"I'll feel like an imposter wearing this tie."

"Don't be silly."

"And isn't it an insult to your regiment?"

"Not at all," he said. "My regiment wasn't half as impressive as that one."

"Jack, do you mean you weren't a member of the Household Cavalry?"

"Oh, no, I was in another regiment – you wouldn't be impressed by that one," he said. "I only wear ties from fancy regiments. I get good results, too. I'm always being saluted when I'm in London."

14

The MV *Akdeniz* through the Levant

Leaving the comfort of the *Seabourne Spirit* was so much like a secular version of the expulsion from Paradise that I thought I would brood less if I moved straight on to Syria. It seemed a prudent move, too. For all its physical beauty, Istanbul was passing through a turbulent phase. A recent bomb in the covered bazaar had killed many people, including three tourists. That caused an immediate 8,000 visitor cancellations to Turkey. The bazaar bomb might have been the work of Kurds of the Kurdish Workers' Party (PKK). But there were other bombers, fundamentalist ones, from the Great Raiders of the Islamic East and the Devrimçi Sol – the Revolutionary Left. Liquor stores were a frequent target; so were banks, because they charged interest on loans, and it is written in the Koran that "Allah hath blighted usury" (II:276).

There had been a rocket attack on the residence of the United States Consul-General. It missed, but if it had hit its target the building would have been demolished. Ten armed men guarded the house now, and the Consul-General and most foreign diplomats in Turkey did not stir outside without a bodyguard.

Istanbul, even under siege, was still magnificent. Never mind that W.B. Yeats had not actually seen the city – it was everything magical that he had written about it in his two greatest poems. It had known three incarnations: as Byzantium for a thousand years, then Christian Constantinople, and finally Istanbul of the Ottomans. It was a labyrinth, ringing with the voices of hawkers, of ferry horns, of muezzins and of the plonking music that was called "Arabesque." As Yeats implied, it was a place where there was no real distinction between life and art; it lay on both banks of the

Bosphorus, one continent nestling next to another – just a stretch of water, a ferry ride from Europe to Asia.

And though Turks moaned about the dangers in Istanbul, they were warier of the Turkish hinterland. My plan was to get a Syrian visa here, take the train to the south coast city of Adana and then trains and buses to Iskenderun, Hatay, Antakya (Antioch) and into Syria and down the Syrian coast.

"That is a bad area," I was told.

"Which area?"

"Every place you mentioned."

"But that's my route," I said.

"May it be behind you!" It was a Turkish expression: *Geçhmis olsun.*

Soon after arriving in Istanbul, I checked into a third-rate hotel and applied for a Syrian visa. Feeling sentimental, I walked down to the Galata Bridge and looked for the *Seabourne Spirit* on the quay at Karaköy. But it had sailed away. Another ship was in its place – Turkish, rusty, slightly larger, no one on board.

I seriously considered swimming the Hellespont.

Ömer Koç had swum the Hellespont, though he, of all people, could have found an easier way of crossing that stretch of water. His was the wealthiest family in Turkey. I looked him up, because I had an introduction and because my Syrian visa was taking a while to come through.

"I've also swum across the Bosphorus, to Europe, and back," Ömer said. The Hellespont swim was in homage to Byron. "It can be a long swim – three miles or more, because the current takes you."

"I was thinking of trying it."

"This isn't the month to do it," he said.

A handsome young man in his late twenties, Ömer spoke with an English accent acquired as a student in England. He helped run the family business, Koç Holdings. The walled compound of Koç Holdings was something of a landmark, in that its grounds had been scattered with Greek pillars and marble ornaments and statues. They had been gathered by his father, Rahmi, from sites all over Anatolia, to make it look like an ancient site.

"He had a wonderful sarcophagus, but in the end decided not to put it on the lawn," Ömer said. "He felt that it would be frightfully morbid."

Ömer lived on the Asian side of the Bosphorus in a palatial Turkish house known as a *yali*, a summer house. It was the narrowest point on the Bosphorus, where Darius had built a pontoon bridge and marched his army across in the fifth century B.C. On its carefully chosen embankment, the *yali* epitomized the great absorbing tendencies of Turkish culture – an appreciation of light and land and water, and a blend of East and West; the Ottoman house in its maturity.

Ömer's *yali*, built a hundred years ago, had been occupied by the princely son of a Khedive, one of the Turkish viceroys of Egypt. When Ömer's father Rahmi bought it in 1966, it had fallen into disrepair. Rahmi Koç totally revitalized it.

"I was very small when we moved in," Ömer said. "I spent my childhood here, and I still live in it most of the time."

I wondered whether Ömer had been intimidated by having been brought up in this pristine house with its delicate furnishings.

"My brothers and I realized that it was ornate, but my father didn't worry about us making a mess," Ömer said. "He's not bothered by that sort of thing."

He and his brothers, Mustafa and Ali, romped in the *basoda* – the formal living-room where guests were received, and climbed all over the banquettes, called *sedirs*. They especially loved being so close to the water, Ömer said. They dived off the landing-stage where their boat was moored, and this proximity to the Bosphorus turned them into great swimmers.

Like his father, Ömer too was a collector, a passionate bibliophile. His library was stocked exclusively with books on Turkish subjects. Evelyn Waugh used to joke that his relative, Sir Telford Waugh's book, *Turkey – Yesterday, Today and Tomorrow*, "sounded like Boxing Day." Ömer owned that book and a thousand more rare volumes, along with old maps, weapons, incunabula, and treasures such as Sultan Abdul Hamid's personal letter-opener, a simple dagger.

"This is interesting," Ömer said to me, and showed me a copy of Lew Wallace's *Ben Hur* inscribed to Sultan Abdul Hamid (1876–

1909). And he explained that Lew Wallace had been the American Cultural Attaché from 1881 to 1885.

Ömer's grandfather, Vehbi Koç, now in his eighties, was the patriarch of the family and a noted philanthropist. He had been called "the father of Turkish private enterprise." His name was as familiar to the average Turk as Henry Ford's was in America, and significantly Henry Ford II wrote a foreword to Vehbi Koç's autobiography. Ömer gave me a copy. The book was not a rags-to-riches story, because the Koç family was not indigent. It was a modest Ankara family whose house, like most others in Anatolia, had no lights or running water. A real bath was "a public bath. This was a monthly expedition."

In accordance with Turkish tradition, family members found Vehbi Koç one of his own cousins for him to marry. This arrangement was intended "to preserve the family fortunes, and with the hope that they would get along together." He saw his wife for the first time at the end of the marriage week when, on the seventh day, his bride Sadberk raised her veil.

As a youth, Vehbi went to Istanbul and served an apprenticeship. "I noticed that the minorities" – the Greeks, the Jews, the Armenians – "led a better life. Their standard of living was much higher than the Turks', so I decided to go into business." He progressed from being a contractor, to manufacturing, to the production of foodstuffs and steel, to the making of cars (Fords and Fiats), and railways. He became by his own report a frugal billionaire and his book contained, among other things, advice on how to stay healthy. For example, "Find the right weight, and stick to it for life."

"The best entertainments" from his youth, Vehbi Koç wrote, "were marriage and circumcision ceremonies."

"Oh, yes, circumcisions are great occasions in Turkey," Ömer told me. And it did not take place immediately after the boy's birth. His own *sunnet*, or circumcision party, occurred when he was two and a half; it was a joint one, shared by his brothers Mustafa (9) and Ali (7), and celebrated at the *yali* on the Bosphorus. It was an enormous party – 400 guests – and his parents indulged their sons.

"Normally the party is held the same day as the ceremony – to ease the pain, as it were," Ömer said. "But my parents wanted us to enjoy it, so it was held fifteen days later."

As we talked, and drank coffee, I felt I was experiencing an aspect of culture in the Turkish Mediterranean that had not changed in five hundred years. This was the ultimate country house. It was hard to imagine a more peaceful setting, a greater harmony of both natural and architectural elements, or − in this waterside culture of caiques and yachts and ferries − an easier place to reach, from almost anywhere. I had fulfilled the old Turkish idea of fleeing the city of shadows and hawkers' cries and music, and finding peace in its opposite, light and silence; sitting in comfort at the edge of Asia and contemplating Europe.

Frustrated that my Syrian visa was taking so long, I went back to the ship I had seen moored at Karaköy, the *Akdeniz*, a Turkish cruise liner. Was it headed somewhere interesting? I found the agent in a nearby office.

"Where is this ship sailing to?" I asked.

The man's English was inadequate to frame a reply, but he handed me the printed itinerary: Izmir, Alexandria, Haifa, Cyprus, and back to Istanbul. Perfect.

"What day is the ship leaving?"

"Today − now."

"Now?"

He tapped his watch. He showed me three o'clock.

It was now noon. I explained that my passport was at the Syrian Consulate, three miles away. If I could get it back from the Syrians and check out of my hotel (two miles away), was there room for me on board?

Plenty of empty cabins, he indicated. The price was 34 million Turkish liras − cash. This was $940, not bad for a twelve-day cruise. I wondered whether I could get aboard. I decided to try.

What followed was a bullying drama enacted by mustached men in brown suits, chain-smoking and muttering in broken English. There was also a manic pursuit through Istanbul traffic. The Syrians complained about my insistence on having my passport back prematurely. The hotel complained that I had not given them prior notice of checking out. The post office money-changers were on strike, and so I went to a usurer who laughed at my credit card and took nearly all my cash. Eventually I had my passport, my bag, and the money. I was panting from the effort, and I had less than an hour left to buy my ticket, buy an exit stamp from the police, get through customs and immigration, and board the ship. Then the police complained, the immigration officials complained, and so did the agent. The counting of the 34 million in torn and wrinkled bills of small denomination took quite a while.

Amazingly, just before the gangway was raised I was hurried aboard the *Akdeniz* and given my cabin key.

"My name Ali," the steward said.

That was his entire fund of English words; but it was enough. He was a short bulgy man, forty or so, in baggy pants and a stained white shirt. He seemed glad to see me, and I thought I knew why.

A large Turkish suitcase had been placed in my cabin. The suitcase alone filled the floor-space, and bulked in my fears. I imagined my cabin-mate. He would be called Mehmet, he would snore, he would smoke, he would natter in his sleep, he would get up in the middle of the night so often I would nickname him "Mustafa pee," and he would retch – or worse – in the tiny head. He would toss peanut shells on to the floor. He might be antagonistic; worse, he might be friendly. Indeed, he might not be Mehmet at all, but rather a big tattooed biker called Wolfie, with scars and a blue shaven skull; or a ferocious backpacker; or a demented priest, or a pilgrim, or a mullah with wild staring eyes. At these prices you got all kinds.

Ali was outside the cabin, waiting for me. He knew what I had seen. He knew what was in my mind. Ali may have had an infant's grasp of English but he had intuition bordering on genius.

"Ali, you find me another cabin," I said.

He understood this.

"One person – just me. This ship has plenty of empty cabins."

Just to make sure there was no misunderstanding I whispered the password, *baksheesh*.

He smiled and showed me his dusky paw: Welcome to the Eastern Mediterranean.

He narrowed his eyes and smiled and nodded to calm me, to

reassure me that he was going to deal with this matter immediately. Give me a little time, he was suggesting.

I looked at the rest of the ship. It reeked of rotting carpets and sour grease and damp Turks and strange stews and old paint and tobacco smoke. There were about a hundred passengers, all of them Turkish. Not a single backpacker, or German tourist, nor any priests nor pilgrims. The Turks on board, in thick shawls and brown suits, were drinking tea and smoking and fretting. And men and women alike, all bespectacled, had that Turkish look of uniform disguise that resembles someone wearing fake glasses attached to a false nose-and-mustache.

I was not alarmed by any of it until the Turks themselves began to complain about the ship.

"I was not expecting this," Mr Fehmi said. He had worked at a NATO base for sixteen years and spoke English fairly well. "This is a great disappointment."

We were among the few drinkers on the ship. We were soon joined by a ship's officer who explained that the *Akdeniz* was experiencing difficulty leaving the quayside. It was a forty-year-old ship with no bow thrusters, so a tug had to snag a stern line and spin the ship one hundred and eighty degrees to the edge of the Golden Horn, and only then could we get away.

But in this slow turning the whole skyline of Istanbul revolved, gray and golden in the late afternoon light, the sun setting behind the mosques and the domes and the minarets. I counted thirty minarets and a dozen domes, and with the ferries hooting, and the fishing-boats and the caiques and the freighters dodging us, everything at the confluence of these great waters – the Bosphorus, the Golden Horn, the Sea of Marmara – sparkled and rang with life. And then we were truly underway, passing the Topkapi Palace and the city wall that still showed breaches where it had been blasted open by the Ottomans in 1453.

In a stiff wind, we passed Haydarpasa railway station, where I had planned to take my train to Ankara and Syria. But that was yesterday's plan. I had changed my mind, and I was glad of it, for wasn't the whole point of a Mediterranean Grand Tour to voyage among the great cities – from here to Izmir to Alexandria and onward? And I liked being the only *yabançi* – foreigner – on board.

It was as though, among all these Turks, on this Turkish ship, crossing the Eastern Mediterranean, I had penetrated to the heart of Turkey.

I went back on deck to look at the last of Istanbul – "Look thy last on all things lovely, every hour" – and saw Ali creeping towards me. He signaled with his eyebrows, he pursed his lips, he dangled a key. That meant he had a cabin. He beckoned, and I followed him to a new cabin.

This is all yours, his hand gestures said. And when I passed him his *baksheesh*, he touched it to his forehead in a stagey show of thanks, and then slapped his heart, and I knew that as long as my money held out he was mine.

Then I was drinking fifty-cent beers in the smoky lounge and congratulating myself. It had been a frantic but worthy impulse, like leaping aboard a departing train for an unknown destination. Never mind the cigarette smoke and the filthy carpets and the Turkish muzak and the TV going at the same time. I found a corner to make notes in and read a few chapters of *Dr Wortle's School* by Anthony Trollope (scandal and hypocrisy in an English village), and then, just as night fell, I went on deck and watched the Sea of Marmara widen into an immense sea that might have been the Mediterranean.

Having my own cabin meant that I had a refuge. And because it was on B-deck I was entitled to eat in the Upper Class restaurant, the Kappadokya, where the captain and other officers dined. The captain was a pinkish Turk with confident jowls in a tight white shirt and white bum-bursting trousers, who looked like a village cricketer whose uniform had shrunk. He sat with six Turkish spivs and their preening wives. It was Upper Class, but like the Lower Class dining-room on the next deck down it was the same men in brown suits and old veiled women and frowning matrons in fifties frocks. Some of the older women looked like Jack Greenwald in a shawl, and their big benign faces made me miss him.

I was seated with an older Turkish couple. We had no language in common, but the man tapped his finger on Greenwald's Turkish pin that I had in my lapel, and he smiled.

"*Afyet olsen.*" That was from my small supply of Turkish phrases: "Good eating."

But the phrase was misplaced. The meal was not good, and a palpable air of disappointment hung in the room – silence, and then muttered remarks. It was generally a hard-up country, and these people were spending a large amount for this trip. We had that first meal: salad, pea soup, fatty meat and vegetables, and a third course of a great mass of boiled spinach; then fruit and cream for dessert. It was Turkish food but it also somewhat resembled an old-fashioned school meal.

The shawls, the brown suits, the felt hats, the clunky shoes and dowdy dresses and cigarettes were all part of the Turkish time-warp in which the Turkish middle class was still finding clothes of the 1950s stylish. Even the shipboard dishes of pickles and potato salad and lunch meat and bowls of deviled eggs were from that era, and appropriate to the old Packards and Caddies and Dodges that plied up and down Istanbul. (In a week in Turkey, the average middle-aged American sees every car his father or grandfather ever owned.) It was a sedate cruise so far, the non-drinking Turks all well-behaved, very placid, and so Turkish that it seemed like mimicry – a big smoky lounge of dour Turks in heavy clothes, heading for Egypt.

But I was grateful to them for making room for me, for allowing me aboard, for being hospitable. Turks made a point of greeting strangers in the common areas of the ship. I learned the greetings, I felt lucky.

And it gave the Mediterranean its true size. It was not the trip I had planned – five days through Turkey to the middle of Syria overland, with all the road blocks and hold-ups. Instead, it was a couple of days from Turkey to Egypt: overnight to Izmir, and then a day and a half to Alexandria; and a day from there to Haifa. The Eastern Basin contained many cultures, with sharp elbows, but in fact the area was rather small. It was just that the people on these shores were so combative that it made this end of the Mediterranean seem large.

From Bursa, then, came Mehmet Saffiyettin Erhan, an architect and historian of old wooden buildings, traveling with his shawled and aged mother, Atifet. And the Sags (Sevim and Bahattin), and General Mehmet Samih, three-star general and ace fighter pilot,

known to all as Samih Pasha, who boasted of the windows he had
broken with the boom of his jet engines over Nicosia, just before
the partition of Cyprus. And Mehmet Cinquillioglu and his wife
Fatma, the four Barrutcuoglu, including little Lamia, the three
Demirels, and the Edip Kendirs. And there were some Kurds, too,
ones I thought of as concupiscent Kurds, and . . .

Oh, give it up. But studying the names outside the Purser's
Office on the *Akdeniz* passed the time. We had traversed the
Dardanelles during the night, and now, in sunshine, I was standing
at the rail with Mehmet Erhan, the architect.

"If architecture is frozen music, that looks like a minaret in D."

"Pardon?"

We were sailing past a mosque, into the port of Izmir. The ship
was three hours late, Mehmet said, not that it mattered. Mehmet
was a fund of information. Çanakkale – the Dardanelles – meant
"cup" in Turkish. The Turks were rather proud of having slaughtered so many foreign troops at Gallipoli. Under the leadership of
Kemal Ataturk, the Turks had driven the Greeks out of Smyrna
(Izmir) in a decisive battle in 1923, and founded the Turkish
Republic. Ataturk's house was in Izmir, if I wanted to see it.

"What does *Akdeniz* mean?" I asked.

"White Sea," he said. "It is the old Turkish name for the
Mediterranean."

The Black Sea was *Kara Deniz*, the Red Sea *Kizil Deniz*, and
beyond that headland was the Greek island of Chios, where
Homer was born.

"If there was a Homer," I said. There seemed to be some doubt
whether Homer ever existed – that the poetry just accumulated
over the years, with recitation, and that the idea that Homer was
blind came from the description in the *Odyssey* of Demodokos, the
blind minstrel:

> ". . . that man of song
> whom the Muse cherished; by her gift he knew
> the good of life, and evil –
> for she who lent him sweetness made him blind."

Mehmet, who had read the *Odyssey* in Greek, said he had also
heard of that possibility.

The *Akdeniz* docked and we were told that it would not leave Izmir until late afternoon. I had time to take a taxi down the coast to Ephesus, the great Graeco-Roman harbor city, where St Paul had preached and was buried; and where the Virgin Mary spent her old age. Mary was not buried there; there was no body. At death she had been levitated from the planet earth in a cosmic transposition known as the Assumption, an article of faith among Catholics. It is an incident the New Testament neglects to mention — that Mary "was assumed body and soul into Heavenly glory," like Enoch and Elijah, was made official by Pope Pius XII in the 1950s — though you would have thought someone would have noticed it at the time. The idea of a little Jewish woman, known variously as the Mother of God and the Queen of Heaven, being propelled by divine force bodily into Outer Space ("angel wing'd, gorgeous as a jungle bird!") cannot be called unmemorable.

The Panayia Kapili, or House of the Virgin, five miles down the road from Ephesus, had been spruced up and was no more than a novelty, but it had a lovely view, which was all that mattered.

There were brothels in Ephesus, as there had been at Pompeii, and graffiti, too, but this was altogether a greater city, and more of it remained from antiquity. My problem was that the whole time I was in Ephesus I worried about the ship leaving Izmir without me, so I hurried back. At the gangway, a crew member said there had been a new change of plan — the ship would not be leaving until nine.

I needed money. The banks were closed, and so were the money-changers. But on a back street of Izmir I saw embedded in an old wall something that looked like a cash machine. I stuck in my ATM card issued by Fleet Bank in East Sandwich, Massachusetts, punched in some numbers, and out came ten million Turkish liras ($280), just like that.

Some screeching schoolchildren were leaving a large building on the sea front. A sign on the front door said that it was Ataturk's seaside house, the one that he had used in the 1920s, when he was leading the war against the occupying Greeks. I went inside and recognized my dinner companions from the previous night on the ship, and their children and grandchildren. One of the ten-year-olds spoke English. They were all from Ankara, he explained. They had taken the train to Istanbul to catch the ship. He said that his parents and grandparents were impressed that I had chosen to visit the house of their famous Ataturk.

The great man's old telephone stood on his desk. One of the children giggled into the receiver until he was reprimanded by a caretaker. Ataturk's bath-tub, his wash-stand, his sofa, his tables, his chairs. Some objects retain the aura – the personal magic – of the owner; others do not. Wood does, big fuzzy chairs don't; a bath-tub does, a bed does not; a desk does, and a telephone, but not curtains, or framed pictures.

A wooden, clinker-built rowboat was dry-docked in the reception-room, and it was so well made that it did not look out of place. Ataturk had rowed it in Izmir Bay, using those same oars that were counterbalanced with heavy upper shafts.

I left the house and walked down the promenade where, at the German Consulate, there was a long line of Turks, old and young, waiting for German visas. In spite of the dire news from Germany that Turks were being assaulted and their houses burned, that they were the target both of skinheads and opportunistic politicians, still there were plenty of potential migrants in Izmir.

As the sun exploded in its descent at the edge of the distant Aegean and became a slowly evolving incident, vast and fiery and incarnadine, I boarded the *Akdeniz* in time to eat, a dinner that was like the parody of a heavy meal: cold meat, beans, fish, more meat, more beans. Never mind. I had gorged on caviar on the *Seabourne*. This was a different experience.

Then I sat under the lights of the deck, in the mild evening, and read in the *Turkish Daily News* an item about the Turkish Foreign Minister, Mr Mümtaz Soysal. It was another act in the endless drama between Greece and Turkey, but it was timeless, too, and this episode could have occurred at any time over the past century, with the same phrasing.

"If Greece extends its territorial waters from six miles to twelve miles, we will go to war with them" – and Mr Soysal had actually used the word.

Mr Soysal had made himself popular in Turkey because of his

pugnacity. But the Greek Foreign Minister, Mr Kaolos Papoulias, met Mr Soysal in Jordan and they agreed in the future not to use the word "war."

After that the Greek Defense Minister, Mr Arsenis, accused the Turkish minister of "raving."

It was like old times, and old times here could mean anything from the Trojan War to the partition of Cyprus. The newspaper said that Greeks and Turks were holding talks on the future of Cyprus. To aid their cause the Greeks had sent to Cyprus a specially sanctified holy icon from a monastery on Mount Athos. The Greeks seemed confident that this icon would do the trick, but the Turks were not so sure.

As I read, the anchor was hauled up and we were tugged to sea and away from the twinkling lights of Izmir.

At dawn we passed the island of Patmos, where an angel appeared to John and the result was the Book of Revelation. Patmos was Greek. All the islands were Greek, in fact, even the ones that were only a mile or two from the Turkish mainland. Turkey, to its irritation, possesses only a handful of offshore islands, which is why any mention of Greece extending its territorial waters sounds provocative and maddens the Turks. We passed Kos, then quickly Nisiros, Tilos and Rhodes. Turkey was a persistent shadow behind – always a low layer of dirty air behind the islands.

"The islands are so empty," Mehmet said. He was again standing at the rail, with his mother. "Nothing on them. One town, or less."

He grinned at me.

"Because there are nine million Greeks," he said. "Maybe ten. Not many."

I asked Mehmet about the Kurds. On the BBC morning news on short-wave I had heard that thirty villages had so far been emptied of Kurds and fifteen more had been burned, with crops and animals, the goats suffocated in their pens.

"I know many Kurds," he said. "We have Kurds on this ship – some passengers. They look like us. Same face. They speak Turkish. We are friends."

After the Gulf War the Kurds, who had been fighting for forty

years or more, had become hopeful again of establishing a homeland. They fought with greater conviction, believing that the
United States would take up their case. It did not happen. It only
made the Turkish troops angry. They evicted Kurds from their
villages in the south-east and sent them into the mountains, and
when some Kurds straggled back the Turks burned their villages
to the ground. The radio program contained the voices of Kurds:
*We were given twenty minutes to leave by the soldiers. But some people were
too old to gather their belongings, and they lost everything – all they owned
was destroyed.*

I reported this to Mehmet.

"But some Kurds are not troublesome," he said. And then he
raised his eyes and said, "That is Karpathos, also in Homer."

We were alone on the deck. The Turkish passengers tended to
be heliophobic. They sat under the awnings, in the smoky lounges,
along the sheltered passageways. There were always six or eight of
them in a lounge watching videos, one of their favorites a cowboy
film, starring Charlton Heston. They gathered for the meaty
meals, which were usually mutton stews and thick bean soups and
mounds of rice, followed by fruit in iced syrup. Breakfast was just
olives and yogurt and cucumber slices. Even in this sunny weather
they remained heavily dressed, the men in ties, the women in drab
frocks and shawls.

"Put on your pantaloons," a waiter in an ugly black uniform
said to me, when I entered the dining-room one hot day in
shorts.

On the third night out there was a cocktail party, with non-
alcoholic punch, and the officers were introduced, just as on the
Seabourne, but these were solemn, rather robotic-looking men in
white uniforms, like ice-cream sellers being awarded prizes for
good sales. It was also a Turkish holiday – Republic Day – so we
got a special meal of shish kebab, stuffed eggplant and a special
dessert, and as usual the fat man at my table ate his wife's main
course and dessert. For most meals this woman sat toying with her
food, and when her husband finished his meal he swapped plates
and got hers.

No one read anything on the ship – not a book, not a newspaper,
nothing. Only Mr Fehmi and I touched alcohol. The rest bought

cups of coffee; they talked. They were then most sedate, as well as the politest people I had ever traveled with.

How polite would they be in an emergency? I pondered the question because we were so ill-prepared. A fire was always a possibility — everyone smoked. The ship was old, and poorly cared-for. But there was no lifeboat drill at all; no suggestion of where the mustering stations were located; no mention of where the life-jackets were stowed. I found mine in a tangle at the bottom of my closet. It probably did not matter. In the event of a sinking I felt sure that "My name Ali" would lead the stewards to their lifeboat and while he was stamping on the rest of the passengers' fingers and pushing them away he would signal to me and let me aboard. Watch Ali, I thought: he knows the drill. He was usually to be found hiding on the lower stern deck, scowling with hatred at the sea.

The night before we landed at Alexandria I was invited to another dinner table. Three men beckoned, then stood and welcomed me.

"I am Samih — people call me Samih Pasha," an older man said to me, and shook my hand. "I think I recognize that tie."

"Household Cavalry," I said.

"I am Fikret," the second man said. He looked haunted and shy. He was attempting to smile. He was a radiologist and his evasiveness suggested he was having a bad time on board.

"I am Onan," the third man said. He was young, soldierly, with an odd blaze in his eyes.

"There is another Onan in the Bible," I said.

He ignored this. "I am making a pilgrimage to Jerusalem."

The soldier, the medical man, the religious nut; and me. We became friends. After that, I ate almost every meal with them. At that first meal, Samih Pasha said, "I have been everywhere. Even Santa Barbara and Nevada and Singapore. Singapore is the clean-est city in the world, but it is not interesting. I am a military man. I should have liked that. But, ha! I wanted to leave Singapore after one day!"

"Tomorrow we will be in Egypt," Onan said.

Almost all my life, I had dreamed of Alexandria. Most of life's disappointments begin in dreams; even so, in the morning when the *Akdeniz* lay at anchor there, and I stepped ashore for the first time, I was horrified by the city – but wait.

Alexandria seemed filthy and flyblown until I saw Cairo, which was in many respects nightmarish; yet after a while the Cairene nightmare wore off, the frenzy in the foreground (*Meester!*) diminished, and my return to Alexandria was like being received into bliss. Thus some dreams can be reclaimed, and most culture shock is probably curable.

"But sometimes," a Turkish crewman said to me, "you have to do this," and he held his nose.

Drawing towards it on the *Akdeniz*, Alexandria seemed to me the ultimate sea-level city, at the very lip of the Nile Delta, the flattest city imaginable, in a flat landscape, flatter than Holland, with no high ground behind it for 2,000 miles to the Mountains of the Moon. Alexandria's flatness and its elongated shape had compressed it, forced it to become maze-like, a city of secrets, and its harbor and position had made it one of the most cosmopolitan cities of the Mediterranean.

Like the greatest cities in the world, Alexandria belonged to everyone who lived in it; shared by "Five races, five languages, a dozen creeds: five fleets turning through their greasy reflections behind the harbor bar. But there are more than five sexes." That is Durrell writing in *Justine*, the first novel in *The Alexandria Quartet*, a sequence about love, sensuality, intrigue, deception; and purple with Nubian slaves, child brothels, and cabals, and nearly always someone in the casbah wailing with meningitis. But this cosmopolitan aspect of the city is persistent. Everyone belongs. In the second novel, *Balthazar*, the narrator amplifies this theme, speaking of how "the communities still live and communicate – Turks with Jews, Arabs and Copts and Syrians with Armenians and Italians and Greeks . . . ceremonies, marriages and pacts join and divide them." And more: "its contemporary faiths and races; the hundred little spheres which religion or lore creates and which cohere softly together like cells to form the great sprawling jellyfish which is Alexandria today."

Or rather, yesterday; for today, Alexandria is a monoglot city of one race, Arabic-speaking Arabs; and one creed, Islam; and no sex. The foreigners had gone – the last had been expelled by

Colonel Nasser in 1960 – and the money was gone, too; there was certainly a connection. And another sign of the times was the large number of Egyptians who had migrated to New Jersey. This militant tribalism seemed to be the way of the world, and certainly the story in much of the Mediterranean. It was perhaps a depressing discovery, but it was news to me, and the desire for enlightenment seems one of the nobler justifications for travel. That was good. I was seldom prepared for anything I found on these shores.

The great multiracial stewpot of the Mediterranean had been replaced by cities that were physically larger, but smaller-minded. The ethnic differences had never been overwhelming – after all, these were simply people working out their destinies, often in the same place. But in this century they had begun to behave like scorpions – big scorpions, small scorpions, greenish, russet, black; and now the scorpions had sorted themselves out, and retreated to live among their own kind. I had yet to find a Mediterranean city that was polyglot and cosmopolitan.

Even under the Ottomans, Smyrna had been full of Armenians, Greeks, Jews, Circassians, Kurds, Arabs, gypsies, whatever, and now it was just Turks; Istanbul was the same, and so were the once-important cities of the Adriatic – Trieste was just gloomy Italians who advocated secession from the south; Dubrovnik was Croatians on their knees, praying for the death of the Serbs and the Bosnians. Greece seemed a stronghold of ethnic monomania, without immigrants. Durrës in Albania was a hellhole of pathetic Shquiperians, and if the Corsican clans had their way there would not be a French person from Bastia to Bonifacio. It was hard to imagine a black general named Othello living in Venice now, though there were any number of Senegalese peddlers hawking trinkets there.

Given his over-ripe imagery and his feverish imagination, it is wrong to expect to find Durrell's Alexandria. He says himself that his Alexandria, "half-imagined (yet wholly real), begins and ends in us, roots lodged in our memory." That is true. And events have changed the cityscape. The Rue Nebi Daniel, where Darley, the narrator, lives and so much of the action takes place, is easy enough to find on the 1911 Baedeker map (running north–south, from the Jewish synagogue to the station), but nowadays is Horreya (Freedom) Street. In Durrell's novels it is a dream-city, full of fantasies of food and sex, and even the descriptions are dreamlike, as in the evocation of the body of water that lies just behind Alexandria, "the moonstone mirror of Mareotis, the salt-lake, and its further forevers of ragged desert, now dusted softly by the spring winds into satin dunes, patternless and beautiful as cloud-scapes." But that fictional city was gone, if indeed it had ever existed; and so was Flaubert's Alexandria and E. M. Forster's.

The great Greek poet C. P. Cavafy, who lived most of his life in Alexandria (and worked for the Ministry of Irrigation), told a different story. In his poems he had celebrated the richness, the history, the squalor, the eroticism of the place as something human. His sense of reality caused him to be labeled decadent. In "The City" and "The God Abandons Antony" he had wisely emphasized that the city was something within us, sometimes as "black ruins" and sometimes representing human hope or failure. "The city is a cage ... and no ship exists/To take you from yourself." The English poet D. J. Enright wisely wrote, "It is not that Cavafy reminds us that we are merely human. He reminds us that we *are* human."

No one has ever described the place where I have just arrived: this is the emotion that makes me want to travel. It is one of the greatest reasons to go anywhere.

There were fleeting glimpses from certain books I had read, some aspects of dereliction, like a couple in tatters, and you think: That broken rag on her head was once a turban, and there were gaps on those shoes where there had once been jewels, and her shreds had once been silks. You could make out what it had been from what it was, like the town auditorium in Crete that had once been a mosque, and the claustrophobic church in Siracusa that had been a Greek temple.

The hookahs, the so-called hubble-bubbles, are still there in Alexandria, and so are the cafés where the men sit sucking on these water-pipes, while cripples and flunkies fill them and keep them alight; the tottering buildings, the Cecil Hotel, the Corniche and its cooling breeze, and the children fishing from the edge, swallows criss-crossing the heaps of garbage, the jetty of the Corniche ending in the fort that was built with the rubble of the Pharos, the lighthouse that was one of the Seven Wonders of the World, the "clang of the trams shuddering in their metal veins." The stalls of watermelon, and fish, and almonds, the men with pushcarts doling out the mucky fava-bean mixture they called *foul*. The air full of brick dust "sweet smelling brick dust and the odor of hot pavements slaked with water." The city was physically recognizable; the way life is lived outdoors on its streets and pavements makes the city visible and tantalizing, too, for what else remains indoors and hidden? At the very least, with the well-turned phrase, "a thousand dust-tormented streets," Durrell could be assured that in this respect his description of Alexandria would never be out of date.

Alexandria was a broken old hag that had once been (every other writer had said so) a great beauty; she was not dead, but fallen.

It was not quite true that no one had described the Alexandria that I saw. There was one man, Naguib Mahfouz. He wrote in Cairo, but his inspiration came from Alexandria, where he spent the summer months each year. "Only twice in his life has he been abroad," one of his translators wrote, "and after his second trip he vowed never to travel again." He had won the Nobel Prize in 1988, the Arab world's only Nobel laureate in literature. At the moment Mahfouz was in trouble.

Two weeks before I arrived in Alexandria, while I was still on the *Seabourne*, visiting Taormina, Mahfouz had been stabbed by a Muslim fanatic in front of his apartment house on Sharia Nil in Cairo. He had been in intensive care since then. Mahfouz had been denounced by the blind cleric, Sheik Omar Abdulrahman, and just as he had inspired the bombers who had tried to bring down the World Trade Center, he had filled another poisonous little apostle in Cairo with the resolve to murder Mahfouz.

It was a sudden stabbing on the street and had left a deep wound in Mahfouz's neck. Mahfouz was an old man, eighty-three, a diabetic, and he had been seriously injured. Blood pouring from his wound, he had been taken to the hospital, which was fortunately only a block away.

I decided to take the train to Cairo to see whether I could talk to him. It was either that or a visit to the pyramids with Samih Pasha, Fikret and Onan.

Meanwhile, Alexandria was having an odd effect on me, plunging me into dream-states, in which I was a sort of Prospero figure in a big rambling estate, among all sorts of Eskimos and Indians and old friends; and even odder unrepeatable sexual dreams. Was it the bright light of early dawn blazing through my porthole, the stillness of the ship at its berth in the Western Harbor, the mutters and bells and clangs? All that, and the city itself – everything I had read about Alexandria was feeding my imagination, provoking desires.

The news was bad. Tourists were being shot by fundamentalists in Luxor and Gizeh. Some had died of their wounds. The body count was fifteen this year, two last week. Some of the victims had been on tourist buses, others on trains.

"They shoot into first class – they know where the tourists are on the trains," Raymond Stock told me.

Raymond, an American poet, essayist and teacher, was Mahfouz's biographer. He was fluent in Arabic and had lived in Cairo for four years, keeping in daily contact with his subject, whose apartment was not far away. I called Raymond from a pay phone at the port of Alexandria soon after I arrived on the *Akdeniz*. He said that even though Mahfouz was in the hospital he had still been seeing the wounded man almost every day and that he was slightly improved.

"Is there any chance of my seeing him?"

"I'm just going to the hospital now," he said. "They might move him out of intensive care and if they do we could visit him this afternoon."

On this very slender possibility I made plans to take the two-hour train trip from Alexandria to Cairo. But there was nothing else I wished to do; the pyramids, the sphinx, the bazaar, the museums – they could wait. One of the aspects of the classical Grand Tour that I had always found attractive was the way the traveler sought the wisdom of great men. Naguib Mahfouz was certainly one of those.

"I have been driving a taxi for twelve years, and this is the first time I have ever taken a tourist to the main railway station," the taxi-driver told me.

"I'm not a tourist," I said.

"Why you take the train?"

"So I can look out the window."

And, I thought, so that I can verify something I had read: "Alexandria Main Station . . . the noise of wheels cracking the slime slithering pavements. Yellow pools of phosphorous light, and corridors of darkness like tears in the dull brick façade of a stage set. Policemen in the shadows . . . the long pull of the train into the silver light . . . the giant sniffing of the engine blots out all sound . . . a final lurch and the train pours away down a tunnel, as if turned to liquid."

That was *Justine*, and the nice image of "the giant sniffing of the engine" had to mean a steam locomotive. That was the only difference. If I had known what the station would be like I could have answered him: I want to go to the railway station because I want to enter a time warp.

But this was true of many railway stations. The two main stations in Istanbul had hardly changed at all. Haydarpasa was a hundred years old but the only difference was that diesels had now replaced steam. The same had been true in Trieste and Split, even in Tirana and Messina and Palermo, in Valencia and Alicante and Marseilles. Railway stations are not timeless, but – too well-built to modernize, too large and dirty to purify; often elderly, sometimes venerable – they retain a sense of the past.

The three classes of tickets, the confusion at the ticket windows, the pushing and shoving and the queue-jumping men cutting ahead, the texture of the cardboard tickets, the very smudges of the printing, made it seem an experience from a former time, from a paragraph in a book written long ago. The torn advertisements fraying from the wall, the "Women's Waiting Room," the filthy platforms, the beggars, the sweet-vendors and newsboys, and the shafts of dusty sunlight slanting on to the rails, the clopping of horses in the courtyard; these details, part of the present, might be found on the same old page.

Assuming that the Egyptian Muslim fundamentalist gunmen

traveled third, and their victims were in first, I decided to buy a second-class ticket to Cairo on a later train. This presented a difficulty which illustrated one of the dilemmas of Alexandrian life. Outside the station I was ambushed by men screaming at me, hectoring me to buy melons, or nuts, or crocodile-skin shoes. Inside, at the ticket window, I found myself begging a clerk to sell me a train ticket. It was perhaps an Egyptian paradox: the things you don't want are pushed in your face; the thing you want seems unobtainable. After some perseverance, and luck, I found the right ticket window. It was outside the station – not many people knew where the first- and second-class ticket windows were, which was perhaps a comment on how hard-up Alexandria had become. I bought a round-trip ticket.

Then, to kill time and see the city, I took a tram-car ten stops, west, into the old Arab Quarter. Here and there I spotted Turks from the *Akdeniz* haggling with Egyptians over figs, or fruit, or candy; or tourist junk – plaster sphinxes, beads, brass plates, leather purses, stuffed toy camels, crocodile-skin belts. Turk and Arab, with no language in common, screamed at each other in broken English.

"Fie dallah!" cried the Egyptian hawker.

"Free dallah!" the Turk yelled.

"Fuh dallah!"

"Duh wanna."

"Meester – best prass for you."

"Free dallah!"

On the way back to the railway station my returning tram became jammed in traffic so dense I had to walk or else risk missing my train.

The problem was a dead cart-horse on the tracks a quarter of a mile away at the center of Alexandria. I chanced upon it after passing through the stopped traffic of honking cars and taxis, the trams, buggies, trucks, buses and motorbikes. At the head of all this traffic was the dead horse, still in its traces, its wagon over-turned, on the tram-lines. It had been killed on the spot by being struck by the tram-car. One of the tram's front panels was dented and smeared with blood. The horse was a gray nag, very skinny, tortured-looking eyes and wrung withers, with a big red gash on its hip bone and another on its leg. The death of this one miserable creature had brought the city of Alexandria to a halt.

The train to Cairo passes through the heart of the delta, through suburbs and Sidi Gaber, past the shanty-town sprawl and the brick tenements hung with laundry, Arab boys kicking a football in a clearing between two vegetable patches; and then the railway line offers a panorama of the delta's agriculture – cotton fields, grape arbors, wheat fields, rice paddies, fields of leafy greens and bean stalks. Every foot of the delta was cultivated, all the flatness demarcated into gardens and fields. The canals were so choked with hyacinths and papyrus that water traffic was unthinkable. Even in the heat of the day there were people in the cotton fields, picking the cotton and hauling sacks. The animals sought shade, though. It was hot and dry, and goats were pressed against flat walls, their flanks against the brick, because that ribbon of shade offered the only relief against the sun overhead.

Only two branches of the Nile pass through the delta. The Cairo train crosses both of them, the Rashid branch at Kafr el Zaiyat, and nearer Cairo, at Benha, the Domyat branch. I had never seen the Nile before, but here there was not much of it. There are so many dams up-river that a relatively small flow of the Nile penetrates this far. And the most recent one, the Aswan High Dam of 1970, so reduced the flow of alluvial soil that the north-west edges of the delta towns that had always been gaining land (because of the easterly flow of the Mediterranean current here) were now being eroded by the sea. The Nile delta was shrinking.

Because they were so dusty and sun-baked and neglected, the towns of the delta, even the larger ones like Tantra and Banha, were impossible to date. They seemed to exist in that Third World dimension of poverty and neglect that held them outside of time.

The mob at Cairo station, people struggling to leave, people struggling to secure a taxi or board a bus, hustling, haggling, picking pockets, or simply standing and looking desperate, was the worst, most frenetic, I had seen anywhere in the Mediterranean. The taxi-drivers were the most rapacious by far. It is no surprise to learn that a great proportion of New York's taxi-drivers began their careers here in Cairo, and many of these same men would soon be joining them. It was not simply that they were rapacious –

rapacity becomes instinctual among the urban poor in the Third World, as a survival skill − but that the most straightforward transactions always turned into a tiresome bidding war, in which you were always cheated.

"Fifteen dollars," a cabbie told me when I said where I wanted to go. This was nine times the normal fare. Just being quoted a fare in dollars in this far-off country irritated me.

But my efforts were rewarded. I met Raymond Stock at the Semiramis Hotel and he greeted me by saying, "Mahfouz is expecting you."

He explained the stabbing, while we had coffee. Sheik Omar had issued the *fatwa* on Mahfouz in 1989 from his seedy little mosque in New Jersey. It resembled the *fatwa* against Salman Rushdie for *The Satanic Verses*, and coming so soon after that well-publicized one, it seemed as though Sheik Omar was trying to upstage the Ayatollah Khomeini. Mahfouz, too, was being accused of writing a blasphemous book. Sheik Omar called him "an infidel." The book was *Children of the Alley* (*Aulad Haratina*). In one reading it was just a neighborhood tale of life in Cairo, but it was poetic too, and much could be read into it. That was the problem − its allusiveness. It seemed to contain echoes of the Koran, and the Bible too. This was not as strange as it seemed. Time had done very little to change the Arabic language or the structure of Egyptian life. The character Qasim was a familiar figure in Cairo, but he had certain qualities in common with the Prophet Mohammed (and his chapter abounded with Koranic parallels). Rifa'a somewhat resembled Jesus, as the character Gebel resembled Moses. It was the story of a delightful family, said its most recent translator (my brother, Peter Theroux), but within this was a deeper story, of the spiritual history of mankind. The novel had 114 chapters; the Koran had the same number. "It is not a history of God," Mahfouz had said, "but rather a history of God the way Man has insisted on imagining Him."

The stabbing came about in this way. Mahfouz had an informal weekly meeting with his pals in Cairo. They were mainly old men and called themselves "the vagabonds" (*harafish*). But a few weeks before, there had been a quarrel − a trifling matter, but it kept Mahfouz at home the following week. When the dispute was patched up, Mahfouz was with his pals again – and that was the night the assassin came for him. He said he was an admirer. He was a member of Sheik Omar's Al-Gama'a Al-Islamiya, the fundamentalist Islamic Group.

"If you come here tomorrow at five, you will find him," Mrs Mahfouz told them.

No one, not even she, suspected that someone would try to kill Mahfouz. In any case, Mahfouz made no concessions. He was fearless. He walked every day in the open air. Everyone who knew him, knew his movements. He was a familiar figure in Cairo, he walked all over the city, and he lived without a bodyguard. There was a feckless doorman at his apartment house but that man was half-asleep at the time of the attack.

The attacker approached Mahfouz the following day, just before five o'clock, as Mahfouz was getting into a car. Seeing him, Mahfouz, in a reflex of courtesy, turned to greet him. The man drew out a knife with a seven-inch blade and thrust down, stabbing Mahfouz at the base of his neck on the right side, cutting the carotid artery and slicing the radial nerve.

In his haste, the attacker forgot to cry out "*Allah-u-akhbar!*" and this omission (so he told police afterwards) explained why he had failed in his mission to murder Mahfouz. For this lapse, Allah delayed the death. He remembered to say it afterwards. "That is why I got away." Other people said the man was simply unprofessional, since he had used a lowly kitchen knife for this important deed.

"I am being chased by a thief," the man said to the taxi-driver who, unsuspecting, bore him away.

Meanwhile, Mahfouz had fallen and blood was pumping out of his severed artery and on to Sharia Nil. The man who had come to give Mahfouz a ride compressed the wound, stanching the flow, and the wounded man was hurried to the Military Hospital, just a few minutes away.

Bleeding profusely but still standing, Mahfouz said to the doctor, "There's some blood here. I think you should look at it."

He was immediately given two pints of blood, and during surgery another eight pints.

In another part of Cairo, the attacker was caught and held by some people whose suspicions were aroused by his strange behavior. The man did not deny what he had tried to do.

He said, "If I am released I will try again to kill him."

In the newspaper *Al-Ahram*, Hasan Al-Turabi, the leader of the Sudanese Islamic Front, said, "The Egyptian fundamentalists' use of force is a legal and honorable action, as were the attacks in Tel Aviv [the recent bus bomb] by Hamas."

The most enlightened view – and it underlined the paradoxes of the issue – was that of Professor Edward Said, who wrote in *Al-Ahram*, "Mahfouz's stabbing highlights the total bankruptcy of a movement that prefers killing to dialogue, intolerance to debate, and paranoia in favor of real politics."

But the blame had to be shared: "It is hypocritical now to say to Mahfouz's assailants only that they are crude fanatics who have no respect for intellectuals or artistic expression, without at the same time noting that some of Mahfouz's work has already been officially banned in the Arab world. One cannot have it both ways. Either one is for real freedom of speech or against it. There is little basic distinction in the end between authorities who reserve the right for themselves to ban, imprison, or otherwise punish writers who speak their minds, and those fanatics who take to stabbing a famous author just because he seems to be an offense to their religion."

Children of the Alley had the distinction of being banned in every Arab country, and many of those same countries included other Mahfouz novels in this ban. Small wonder, as Professor Said had suggested, that the fundamentalists seemed justified in their murderous intentions.

"He's glad to see you," Raymond said. "I told him you helped get him into the American Academy."

"He got himself in," I said.

The smiling man, supine in his bed, his neck bandaged, his hand in a splint, who greeted me in the intensive care ward did not seem the dangerous man who had been vilified all over the Arab world. His expression was serene, his eyes clear. He was weary from what could have been a mortal wound, but he welcomed his visitors with animated conversation. He was modest, he teased, he even laughed and, soon after, this man who had been stabbed by a religious nut with a kitchen knife said, "It hurts when I laugh."

Raymond introduced me. He said, "This is the man I told you about. He was one of the people who supported your application to the American Academy of Arts and Letters."

Mahfouz began to laugh a little as Raymond repeated this in Arabic, as though a witticism had occurred to him that he was anxious to deliver.

"Raymond's exaggerating," I said.

Mahfouz said – his first words a joke – "I am the first person to be stabbed for being a member of the American Academy!"

He then uttered a dry chattering laugh that convulsed him and caused him pain. He was in a ward with about ten other men, all of them bandaged, with drip-feeds, and monitoring devices, and with plastic curtains around their beds. But Mahfouz's intelligence, and his sweetness, shone in his face.

"How are you feeling?"

"I can't write," he said, and swung his splinted right hand on its sling. "That is bad."

Doctor Yahyah el-Salameh said, "The hand problem was caused by nerve damage. The knife hit the radial nerve. So his hand is paralyzed."

"My eyesight is bad, and I can't hear," he said. "That wasn't the attack. That is because of my diabetes."

Some of this was in English, some in Arabic. His accent could have been the accent of one of the characters he had described: "like the smell of cooking that lingers in a badly washed pan." Raymond stood behind me, translating. Mahfouz understood most of what I asked him, though from time to time he needed Raymond's help.

"Tell the people at the American Academy that I am very grateful," he said, clutching my hand. "Please thank them."

"I know they're worried about your health."

"It was a shock, but –" He smiled, he laughed a little; he did not want to dwell on the attack.

"What do you think about those people?"

"I feel no hatred," he said, slowly, in English. "But –"

He was gasping, having a hard time getting the words out. Doctor Yahyah looked anxious, but Mahfouz waved him away.

"– it is very bad to try to kill someone for a book you haven't read."

He was sniggering again, and seeing me laugh, he kept on talking, gesturing with his wounded hand.

"If you read the book and don't like it," he managed to say, stopping and starting, "then, okay, maybe you have a reason to stab the author. Eh? Eh?"

It was as though he was turning the whole attack into a violent absurdity. Something of the same kind occurs in his strange story, "At the Bus Stop," where the passive onlookers to a series of disconnected intrusions and sudden incidents all die in a senseless hail of bullets. That story and some others in the collection *The Time and the Place* have the distortion of a nightmare, a blend of comedy and horror and the lack of logic that life confronts us with. He was saying: As a shy and peaceful man – elderly, deaf, half-blind, diabetic – wasn't it ludicrous that he had been knifed? He was old and physically shrunken, like the character of whom he wrote, "There's nothing left for death to devour – a wrinkled face, sunken eyes, and sharp bones."

"But I am sad," he said.

And he explained that the whole thing was pathetic. This was silly and futile. The fundamentalists were, most of all, ignorant.

"I thought they had learned something. I thought they were better than before. But they are as bad as always."

"I think he is getting tired," Doctor Yahyah said. "Maybe you –"

As though defying the doctor, Mahfouz said, "Fight thought with thought – not thought with violence."

It was what he had said when defending Salman Rushdie against the supporters of the Ayatollah Khomeini. The effort of his speaking, much of this in English, had wearied him. He saluted us. He said he would be better soon – "Come back to Egypt then – we'll talk" – and he gripped my hand in his left hand and tugged it with affection.

Afterwards, I realized that I had been the one who had raised the religious issue and harped on the attack. But in retrospect I had the feeling that Mahfouz would have been much happier talking about something else – his work, perhaps, or Islamic

aesthetics, or the weather, or Alexandria, or the French philosopher
Bergson (who had worked on a theory of humor), or music, for
which – before his deafness – Mahfouz had had a passion. He did
not regard himself as a victim. His fatalism was part of his humor,
and his modesty, and most of all it made him fearless.

My train back to Alexandria was *El-Isbani*, "The Spaniard,"
though no one could explain why it was called that. It was an
express, it rushed across the delta, stopping two or three times, and
Alexandria on my return seemed serene, as Mahfouz had described
it: "Here is where love is. Education. Cleanliness. And hope."

   I had a drink at the Cecil and walked down the Corniche in the
darkness, listening to the waves lap at the shore. "A great blue
mass, heaving, locked in as far as the Fort of Sultan Qaitbay by
the Corniche wall and the giant stone jetty arm thrusting into the
sea." This is Mahfouz, in his novel *Miramar*. "Frustrated. Caged.
These waves slopping dully landwards have a sullen blue black
look that continually promises fury. The sea. Its guts churn with
flotsam and secret death."

   Alexandria made sense to me now. It was not a derelict or
threatening place. It was an ancient city, founded by Alexander
the Great around 330 B.C., and rising and falling with the fortunes
of this end of the Mediterranean it had been many different cities
since then. Mahfouz had been born in 1911 and had witnessed the
violent 1919 revolution, the various occupations – Greek, Turkish,
British; the Second World War, the rise of Nasser, the fall of
Nasser, the assassination of Anwar Sadat, the humiliation of the
Israeli Six-Day War of 1967. He had seen E. M. Forster come and
go; he had been in Alexandria in the late 1940s when the action of
Durrell's novel had unfolded. He had watched these writers and
their characters depart. And it was right that after the romantics
and the fabulists had finished with the city, and the fantasies had
ceased to be credible, the city had been reclaimed by a realist like
Mahfouz, who possessed sympathy, and alarming humor.

   I slept in my cabin on the *Akdeniz*, and woke exhausted and
enervated by my dreams. Then I went into town again, bought
the newspaper, and went to a café to read it. An Alexandrian
joined me, Mr Mohammed Ali.

"Cairo people are not like Alexandria people," he said.

"Why is that?"

"We are Mediterranean people," he said. "We are used to so many other nations, so many other different people."

"But everyone in Alexandria is the same now. Isn't that so?"

"We are people of the shoreline and the water," he protested. "We have maybe three million people. Cairo has fifteen million!"

While I was in Alexandria, on the evening of my third day, the Arabic newspaper *Al-Ahali* (The People) published Naguib Mahfouz's offending novel, *Children of the Alley*, in a special edition that sold out within a few hours of its hitting the street. "After twenty-five years of its absence from the Egyptian people!" the headline said. The whole book, in thirty broadsheet pages, had been printed without permission, infringing Mahfouz's copyright. At first glance it seemed a challenge to the hard-liners, but Raymond Stock had lived in Egypt long enough to find a sinister motive possible. Remember when Mao started the Hundred Flowers campaign in order to get intellectuals and rebels out of the woodwork? he said. Well, this might be something similar, the publication of the blaspheming novel encouraged by the fundamentalist sheiks, to see who would applaud it; in this way identifying the infidels, and rousing potential stabbers of Mahfouz. Whatever, it was an event, and it seemed to electrify the city. All at once, in the space of a few hours, everyone in Alexandria was reading Mahfouz's novel.

"All gone," the newsboys told me.

Looking for someone to help me buy a copy, I met a man who had bought five. They were at his house, he said, or he would have given me one.

"I spent forty pounds [about $14] on one copy last year!"

This man, Mohammed Okiel, asked one of the newsboys who had turned me away earlier, claiming he did not have a copy. Browbeaten by Mohammed Okiel, he found a copy of the special edition under some movie magazines. He had the decency to say "Sorry" to me in English.

"He is ashamed," Mohammed said.

Mohammed was a lawyer. We found a quiet back-street café where young men were puffing on hookahs, and we drank cups

of coffee and talked about Mahfouz. I did not say that I had
seen him in the hospital in Cairo – it was too improbable, and
it was boasting. Besides, I wanted to know what other people
thought.

"Naguib Mahfouz is a great man," Mohammed said. "And he
is a very great writer."

"Have you read the novel?"

"Yes, *Aulad Haratina* is a great novel. I like it very much," he
said. "All the prophets are in it. Jesus, Moses, Mohammed. But it
is also about us – we people."

"Are you a religious person?"

"No. I have no religion," he said. "Religion is false. Christian,
Muslim, Jewish – all false."

"Why do you think that?"

"Because they cause trouble."

"Don't they bring peace and understanding, too?"

"People should be friends. I think it is easier to be friends
without religion," he said. "You can have peace without religion.
Peace is easier too, without religion."

The texture of Alexandria, all the metaphors and the romance
and the layers of history, were irrelevant to that simple reflection.
It seemed a salutary and humane thought, too, because in a
matter of hours the ship's lines were loosed from the quayside, and
we sailed out of this sea-level city, passed the lovely palace of Ras
el Tin, and the old yacht club, and the lighthouses, and the ships
at anchor. As the sun set directly behind our stern, we plowed east
along the crescent of the delta, towards Israel.

On deck, after dinner watching the Rosetta lighthouse winking
from the Egyptian shore, at the narrow mouth of the Rashid Nile,
Onan said – speaking as though I were not present – "Paul ran
away from Alexandria. Where did he go?"

"There is something about this man," Samih Pasha said, and
his mustache lifted as he smiled at me. He then tapped the side of
his nose in a gesture of suspicion. "Something – I don't know
what."

"I had business to attend to," I said.

"We saw the pyramids," Fikret said. "But for just a little while.

Fifteen minutes at the museum. Then the shopping. Women shopping."

"I was very angry," Onan said.

I said, "You can't leave Egypt unless you have a small stuffed camel toy and plaster model of the sphinx."

"You see? He is making a joke," Samih Pasha said. He tapped his nose again, once again drawing attention to its enormous size. "Something, eh?"

Fikret said, "I think Mr Paul is right. He does his business. He doesn't waste time."

"You are going to Jerusalem?" Onan asked me sternly.

"If I have time. Are you?"

Onan sucked his teeth in contempt, to demonstrate the absurdity of my question, and then he said, "The only reason I am on this ship is to go to Jerusalem. Not the pyramids, not the sphinx. I don't care about the Nile. But Jerusalem. It is a holy place!"

His tone was just a trifle shrill, combining something military with something obsessional, a touch of the *ghazi* – the warrior for God Almighty.

"Relax, Onan, of course I'm going to Jerusalem," I said. "I have the feeling you are making a pilgrimage."

"It is your feeling," he said. "I must find a concordance in Israel – for the Bible. I read Hebrew. I am interested in the Bible."

"Yet I feel that you are a devout Muslim."

"Once again, it is your feeling," Onan said. "I believe in the words of the holy Koran. I believe in heaven and hell."

This statement had an effect in the darkness of the Levantine night. We had passed beyond the sea-level lights of the shore and were traveling surrounded by dark water and dark sky, a cosmic journey on a rusty ship.

Fikret was muttering to Samih Pasha. He said, "General Samih knows a joke about hell."

"Thank you very much," Onan said tersely.

"A man dies and doesn't know whether to go to heaven or to Gehenna, as we call it," Samih Pasha said, smiling broadly. "So an angel comes and shows him two breeches."

He paused and smacked his lips, to make sure we had taken this in. I thought: Breeches? Then I thought: Yes, bridges.

"First breech is heaven. Very nice. Clean. Peaceful. Seenging," Samih Pasha said. "Second breech. Man looks. Is Gehenna. Music! Fun! People dancing! Boys! Gorl!"

"'Weech breech?' the angel asks him. Man says, 'Second breech! Thank you very much!' He find gorl right away. Nice! He begin to make love to her. Nice! But! Something is wrong. He cannot make love. He look — no holes!"

Onan frowned, Fikret squinted. I said, "No holes," and was interested that this Turkish man should use the plural.

"The man says, 'Now I see why this is Gehenna!'"

I laughed, but no one else did except the General, at his own joke. Onan continued to glare at him. Fikret said with his usual solemnity, "I understand."

That night, lying in my cabin, I thought of poor diminished Alexandria, and it seemed logical that it should look that way, after so much of it — streets and buildings and monuments — had been ransacked by writers.

Offshore, twiddling my radio, I got classical music — Beethoven's violin concerto from the Israeli shore — and remembered that the last time I had heard such music was in Mediterranean Europe. That was not so odd, for after all, Israel is an outpost of Europe, the moral high ground as a refuge and a garrison.

And because of the ethical commitment and the financial burden required by Israel of all Americans, it is impossible for Americans to go to Israel and not feel they have a personal stake in it — or more, that Israel owes them something: perhaps a hospitable attitude? Reflecting on the twelve-figure sum of approximately one hundred billion dollars that America has given Israel since 1967, that was my feeling. It was not a number I ever dangled in front of an Israeli, though on deck at the port of Haifa I said to Samih Pasha, "As an American taxpayer, I think I own that building." He laughed, and later in Turkish Cyprus, a place that is a drain on Turkey's budget, Samih Pasha said, "That building! I paid for it! It's mine!"

"Now Paul is going to disappear," Fikret said.

"Bye-bye," the General said.

Onan was busying himself with his maps and scriptures, in

preparation for his pilgrimage to Jerusalem. He looked more intense than ever, and even somewhat feverish, his eyes bright with belief.

The *Akdeniz* had hired a bus for those Turks who wanted to go to Jerusalem. A number of people had signed up for the trip, but many – as in Egypt – were interested in looking at Ottoman sights, whatever Turkish castles and fortresses they could locate. The passengers on the *Seabourne Spirit* were offered a four-hour tour of the whole of Israel, called "The Holy Land by Helicopter." It is a very small place, and so this was not as odd as it sounded, and the helicopter tour took in all the main cities, including Haifa, Tel Aviv, Jerusalem and Nazareth, and ended at the citadel of Massada – the scene of the famous massacre – with hampers of picnic food, and chilled champagne.

I had no particular plans in Israel, just a general desire to travel down the Mediterranean coast of Israel, to Tel Aviv and Gaza; to see Jerusalem; to pay a visit to a writer, who was Arab and Christian and an Israeli citizen. But this was all premature, because when I went into the *Akdeniz*'s lounge to collect my passport I found myself surrounded by armed men.

"Israeli security," one man said. "Is this you?"

It was my passport, the page with my goofy picture on it.

"Yes."

"Come with us."

I was taken to a corner of the lounge, while the Turkish passengers looked at me with pity. They were the problem, not me. Every one of the other passengers, the whole crew, the officers – from the captain to the lowliest swabbie – every person on board the *Akdeniz* was a Turk.

"You speak Turkish?" one of the Israeli security men asked.

"No."

"But everyone on this ship is Turkish."

"Some of them speak English," I said.

"Are you traveling with someone?"

"No."

A man flicking through my passport said, "You have been to Syria."

"No," I said. "That visa's been canceled. I had to pick up my passport early in order to catch this ship. Out of spite the Syrians wouldn't give me a visa."

"Why are you the only American on this ship?"

"I don't know," I said.

"What is your profession?"

I hesitated. I said, "I'm in publishing."

These men wore pistols; two of them had machine-guns. They did not wear uniforms, but they were soberly dressed and seemed very intent on discovering how an American could be traveling alone with so many Turks.

"And now I'm a tourist," I said.

It hurt me to have to admit that, but I thought generally that tourists got away with murder and that being a tourist was an excuse for any sort of stupidity or clumsiness. You can't do anything to me – I'm a tourist!

"What are you going to do in Israel?"

"Look around, then leave."

"What do you have in your pockets?"

"You want to search me?"

A woman approached. She muttered impatiently in Hebrew, and it had to have been, "What's going on here?" The men muttered back at her, and showed her my passport.

"Yes," she said. "This ship is Turkish. The people are all Turkish. But you – why are you on board?"

"Because they sold me a ticket."

"Where did you buy it?"

"Istanbul," I said.

And at this point, faced by Israeli security and having questions barked at me, I was on the verge of asking whether this was a traditional Israeli way of greeting strangers: sharp questions and even sharper gun-muzzles in my face.

"What are you doing here?" the woman was asking me, as she leafed through my passport, the sixty pages filled, as you know, with exotic stamps – China, India, Pakistan, Fiji, New Guinea, Rarotonga, Great Britain, Albania. She flipped to the first page.

"Are you the writer?"

"Yes."

She smiled. "I have read your books." She said something in

Hebrew to the security men. "Now I know why you are on this ship."

"Thank you. Does that mean I can go?"

"Okay. No problem," she said, and wished me well.

Meanwhile, elsewhere on the *Akdeniz*, the Cimonoglu family and others were being divested of their passports. "Because we are young – we have the whole family, even children, with us," the mother, Aysegul, told me later. "They think we want to stay in Israel and take jobs! But we have jobs in Turkey! I will write an angry letter to the Israeli Consulate in Istanbul."

What are you doing here? was a question I usually felt too ignorant to answer. My answer had to be: *Just looking.*

Curiosity was my primary impulse – sniffing around. But I also wanted to see things as they are, especially the aspects of any country that were likely to change. The look and the feel of a place, the people – what I could grasp of their lives. Politics seldom interested me, because there were too many sides, too many versions, too concerned with power and not enough with justice.

Most of the time I felt like a flea. I could not pretend that I was part of a place, that I had entered the life of it. I was a spectator, certainly, but an active one. I was also passing the time, and there was nothing unworthy about that. Most people like to think they are in search of wisdom. That was not my motive. Perhaps it was all very simple, even simpler than curiosity, and that, in every sense of the phrase, I was making connections.

I walked off the ship and around the harbor and looked for the *Seabourne Spirit*. It was due in Haifa the following week, I was told. That was a pity. I had thought I might see Jack Greenwald again. I continued walking into town to buy some envelopes so that I could send some accumulated books and maps back to myself.

Walking along I kept seeing the same series of books, the repeated title, *The Land of Jesus, Das Land Jesu, La Tierra de Jesus, La Terra de Jesus, La Terre de Jésus.*

The woman at the stationery store said, "Nine shekels."

It was a word I never got tired of. I found it a slushy and comical word, filled with meaning. Shekels was like a euphemism for money, but it had other similar-sounding words in it – shackles and sickles and Dr Jekyll, all money-lender's meanings. It was impossible for me to hear the word and not think of someone demanding money. At this point, I had no shekels.

"You can change dollars into shekels at the bank, or on the street – the black market," she said. "The rate is three shekels and twenty agorot."

But when I asked on the street, fierce men – Russians, Moroccans, Poles – said, "Two shekels, ninety agorot! Take it! That is the best price!"

"I want three shekels," I said, though I did not care. I liked saying the word "shekels."

A man selling hard-core porno videos from a pushcart on the street, shouted, "No one will give you three shekels! You change money with me!"

The way these Israelis spoke to me had more significance than what they were saying. It was as though they were always giving orders, never inquiring or being circumspect. Other Israelis I dealt with that first day in Haifa were the same, and I noted the tone of voice and the attitudes, because they did not change in the succeeding days.

They were gruff, on the defensive, rather bullying, graceless and aggrieved, with a kind of sour and gloating humor. They were sullen, somewhat covert, and laconic. They seemed assertive, watchful and yet incurious; alert to all my movements, and yet utterly uninterested in who I was. I did not take it personally, because from what I could see they treated each other no better.

This abrupt and truculent behavior surprised me, especially as I had become accustomed in my week on the *Akdeniz* to elaborate Turkish courtesy, the greetings, the gratitude, the rituals of politeness. Turks almost never raised their voices in polite company, and they had a number of expressions for taking the blame for a mistake rather than risk causing offense. Dealing with other people, Turks tended to seek permission. Casually bumping into someone they said, "*Kasura bakmayan*," "Please don't notice my mistake."

Some Israelis were as elaborate and Semitic in these courtesies as Turks and Egyptians had been, but there were few of these. They were silent or else muttering Sephardis, Moroccans, Algerians, Spaniards, with dark expressive eyes, and these people could be very polite. The rest were familiar in a Western way – European, Russian, Romanian, Hungarian; urbanized, exasperated. They sweated, they complained, they peered with goose-eyes and raised their voices. They looked uncomfortable and overdressed; they looked hot.

An address I had to find in Haifa was on Tzionut Street – Zionism Street. About ten years ago it had been called United Nations Street, because at the time Israel had been befriended by the UN and this was one of the ways they showed their thanks, crowning a city street with the name of the helpful organization. But in 1981 a resolution was passed by some countries in the General Assembly equating Zionism with racism. The Israelis were so annoyed that they changed the name of Haifa's United Nations Street to the hated word Zionism.

I was looking for the writer Emile Habiby, but he was not in his studio in Tzionut Street. He might be out of the country, a neighbor told me. Or perhaps I should try his home in Nazareth.

Haifa had the look of a colony, which is also the look of a garrison. Its new buildings looked out of place – imported, like foreign artifacts – on the heights of the hills, among them Mount Carmel, that bordered its harbor and its sea-level town of merchants. There were of course soldiers everywhere, and many people – not just the obvious soldiers – carried side-arms. The city did not have an obvious religious atmosphere either, and its secularism was jarring after all the expressive pieties of the Islamic world I had recently seen. The most conspicuous place of worship in Haifa was the enormous Baha'i temple – jeered at by Onan as "a ridiculous religion – not even a religion." (He had the same disdain for Sufism: "They take the Koran and just fly away with it!")

Just as I was surprised by the off-handedness and the truculence, I was pleased by many other aspects of Haifa that I had not expected. The food, for example. It was the cleanest, the freshest, the most delicious I had found since Italy – but it was less meaty than Italian food, and lighter. It was salads and fish and fresh bread, hummus and ripe fruit, just-squeezed juice and pure olive oil. It was not expensive. Everyone ate well.

The public transport was another pleasant surprise. There was a

train to Tel Aviv. There were buses. From the bus terminal in
Haifa you could go anywhere, every half-hour, and because this
was Israel there was not a town or village in Israel that was not
reachable in a few hours. Jerusalem was an hour and three-
quarters. The Dead Sea was two hours. Nazareth was an hour. Tel
Aviv about an hour. A bus to Cairo took half a day, which was
nothing. President Clinton had just visited the previous week to be
present at the signing of the Israel–Jordan Peace Accord. So there
were buses to Amman, too.

The intellectual life of Israel was visible in terms of public
lectures and bookstores – I had not seen such well-stocked bookstores since leaving Italy. Croatia's were pathetic, Greece's stocked
school textbooks and women's magazines, Turkey's were no use to
me, nor were Egypt's. Israelis sold every sort of book and magazine
in all the languages that Jews spoke, which was almost all the
languages of the world. There were museums with rich collections,
classical music on the radio, and symphony concerts. I liked going
to concerts, listening to live music; I went to two good ones in
Israel. I could have gone to many more if I had stayed longer.
Israelis complained of the high cost of living, and the high inflation,
but nothing in Israel struck me as being very expensive.

And there was a suburban atmosphere which also made it seem
peaceable, if not downright homely and dreary. This first impression was borne out by my travels to other towns and cities, for so
much of Israel had the texture and pace of a retirement community, and – alone among the Mediterranean countries I saw – the
whole land was noisy with the persistent whine of air-conditioners.

Strangest of all, I felt a sense of safety. Perhaps it arose from the
colonial look of the city, and the orderliness of the stores and
streets. I never felt at risk – or rather I felt that I was among
millions of people who were taking the same risk.

But of course you only feel very safe in Israel if you are ignorant.
I did not know it then – I learned it by degrees – but Israel was in
a terrible period, one of its worst cycles of murder and retribution.
What I took to be somnolence was suspense.

Another thing I learned about Israel: never question a date,
because everyone took liberties. A person might allude in one

THE MV *AKDENIZ* THROUGH THE LEVANT   385

sentence to something that happened last week, and in the next breath he would be in the Bronze Age, quoting the Torah and mentioning Egyptians at the time of Moses, making it all seem like it was yesterday. It was poetic license, but it was often the basis of Israeli political or military decisions. Egyptians claimed that on the walls of the Israeli parliament, the Knesset, was written "Greater Israel from the Euphrates to the Nile!" It was not merely a misquotation, but a misrepresentation of Genesis 15.18, in which God promises Abraham and his descendants all land from the Euphrates to the river of Egypt, which is not the Nile but the Sea of Reeds. On the other hand, "God gave it to us" is not usually the equivalent of a Purchase and Sale Agreement.

The same doubtful history and wobbly logic made it normal for Israeli immigrant citizens from Morocco and New York City and Kiev to think of themselves as Israelites, and Israeli life today as a rehash of the Torah, in which the chosen people were taunted and held captive and laid siege to by idol-worshipping pagans. They never used the word "Palestinians", always saying "Arab" instead, because it depicted an upstart horde and served to make Israelis seem the underdogs (there were so many more Arabs in the Middle East than there were Palestinians). Egyptians avoided the word "Arab" too. They were part of the same theater of self-dramatization. This was the land of the Pharaohs, they said; they were pharaonic. "We built the pyramids!"

So, the Israelis were not alone in taking liberties, but it made life rather confusing for a traveler when Mediterranean peoples were so busy misrepresenting themselves. Most inhabitants of its shores took the most fanciful liberties with their ancestry. In fact, though no one ever said so, the Mediterranean was almost devoid of aborigines.

Anyway, I took the train down the coast from Haifa to Tel Aviv. Israeli Railways was celebrating its centenary. A hundred years ago Israeli Railways did not exist, of course; but who had built this line? Probably the British.

Something that bothered me greatly were the numerous people traveling armed with rifles, usually large and very lethal-looking ones, and pistols. Most of those people were soldiers and one of the characteristics of Israeli soldiers on trains and buses was their fatigue. They always looked sleepy, overworked, and no sooner were they on a seat than they were asleep; I often found that their weapons bobbled in their arms were pointed directly at me.

This happened on my very first ride. A soldier in the seat opposite made himself comfortable to sleep, put his feet up and propped his Uzi automatic rifle so that it was horizontal in his lap, and it slipped as he dozed, and was soon pointing into my face.

I said, "Excuse me," because I was afraid to tap his arm and risk startling him and the weapon discharging.

He did not wake, but after a while I raised my voice, and asked him to take his rifle out of my face.

Grumbling, without apology, he shifted in his seat and moved his rifle so that it was pointing at the woman across the aisle, who was so engrossed in reading a medical textbook, *The Metabolic Basis of Inherited Disease*, that she did not notice the man's weapon.

"Now it's pointing at her," I said.

He slapped and pushed the rifle, and though it was still not upright as it should have been, he grunted and went back to sleep.

Walking up and down the crowded coach, I counted the weapons: two in the next row, a frenzied man in a white shirt with a nickel-plated revolver, a soldier two rows back with a pistol and a rifle, ditto the soldier next to him, a woman in uniform lying across two seats with her big khaki buttocks in the air – a pistol on her belt, seven more armed passengers farther down. My feeling is that all weapons are magnetic – they exert a distinct and polarizing power, and nearly all attract violence. The gun-carrier's creed is: Never display a weapon unless you plan to use it; never use it unless you shoot to kill.

For the first time on my trip I suspected I was traveling in a danger zone. I had never seen so many weapons. And yet, as I said, I did not feel that I was personally threatened. That was one of the many paradoxes of Israel: it was a war zone and yet it was one of the most monotonous places imaginable.

We passed Carmel Beach, some condos going up, and a sign, "The Riviera of Israel." It was rubble and rocks and, farther on, dunes. The coast had the look of a shoreline that had been leveled so that it could be defended. There were no obstructions, it was all visible, nowhere for a landing-party to hide. In military jargon such a landing was called "an insertion" – a rapid on-shore penetration by stealth under cover of darkness, men leaping out of small boats and hitting the beach. Many had been attempted, but few had succeeded. The very idea, though, that such military actions were contemplated here made this section of coast south of Haifa unlike its Riviera namesake.

At Binyamina and beyond was the reality of the country – that it was really very empty and under-populated, that the garrison mentality is strong (people living in places they can defend), and that it was agricultural, intensively cultivated in many places, banana groves set out with precision and order, grape and vegetable fields beneath the green and rocky hills of Har Horshan.

The orchards and citrus groves I had expected to see in Israel were there on the coast near Netanya, with rows of eucalyptus, the gum trees that were used everywhere as giant quick-growing fences and windbreaks. Plenty of fruit trees, and canals, and craters, and scrubby ditches; but where were the people? This coast was one of its most populous regions and yet it was thinly settled.

The settlement of Hertzliyya was celebrating fifty years of prosperity, and agriculture flourished there too. But with such subsidies, so it should have. It seemed to me much more extraordinary that Mediterranean countries that did not receive three billion dollars a year in foreign aid were growing fruit and running schools and defending themselves.

Approaching Tel Aviv, I saw for the first (and last) time on the shore of the Mediterranean a drive-in theater. It was beside the tracks, and also beside the sea. It was advertising a double feature in Hebrew on the marquee.

That was appropriate enough, for no city in the entire Mediterranean looks more like an American concoction than Tel Aviv. It was wrong to compare it (as many people did) with Miami and its tangle of suburbs. Tel Aviv was both more sterile and less interesting, and it was strangely introverted; its streets were lifeless, its different cultures, and its tensions, masked.

So what was it? Tel Aviv had no Mediterranean look, nor anything of the Levant in its design; it was Israeli in the sense that Israeli architecture and city planning are American derivatives. Somewhere on the east coast of Florida there must be a city that

Tel Aviv resembles, a medium-sized seaside settlement of ugly high-rise buildings and hotels, a shopping district, a promenade by the sea, not many trees; a white population watching gray flopping waves under a blue sky.

Did the appearance of it mean anything? I spoke to some people in Tel Aviv. I began to think that what was visible in Israel was less important than what was felt.

"You know about the bombing?" a man named Levescu said to me, utterly dismissing a question I had asked him about the look and the texture of Tel Aviv. He waved away what I had said with an irritable gesture. "Twenty-five people! On a bus! An Arab!"

"Yes, I read about it," I said. "Terrible."

"Terrible!"

This tragedy had put Tel Aviv in the news for having had one of the worst massacres in recent Israeli history; twenty-five dead, forty-eight people wounded. That had happened only a week before.

"It was revenge, wasn't it?"

"Revenge – for what? It was murder!"

Some months before, in Hebron, a man named Baruch Goldstein had entered the Shrine of the Patriarchs (a mosque, but also a synagogue, where Abraham, Rebecca, Leah, Isaac and Jacob are entombed) during prayers, perhaps with the connivance of Israeli soldiers – after all, Goldstein was heavily armed – and howled, "No Arab should live in the biblical land of Israel!" He machine-gunned twenty-nine men to death, severely wounded over a hundred men, and was himself beaten to death.

The members of the Palestinian group Hamas (an Arabic acronym but also meaning enthusiasm or ardor or zeal) had vowed revenge. The Tel Aviv suicide-bomb was their reply.

"There will be no dialogue with Hamas," Prime Minister Rabin had said on Israeli television. "We will fight to the death!"

I mentioned to Mr Levescu that it seemed there would be more violence.

"You didn't hear the news?" Then he told me.

Three Palestinians had been killed just that morning at a checkpoint in Hebron.

That night, watching television in Tel Aviv, I saw another

killing, and it had taken place either that day or some few days earlier. A video-tape taken by a freelance journalist showed an Israeli soldier giving the *coup de grâce* to an injured and unarmed Palestinian. The tape showed the soldier sighting down his rifle and firing a bullet at the struggling man's head and blasting the skull to pieces. It was explained that the man, Nidal Tamiari, had had a fist-fight with the soldier. The military denied that the soldier had shot the man in cold blood. The spokesman said, "He was verifying the kill."

It was too late to ask Mr Levescu what he thought, but in any case I had a feeling I knew what he would say. *This is war!* He had said it often enough in our conversation at the café by the sea in Tel Aviv. His sentiments were predictable, and his story was fairly typical.

"We left Romania in 1946," he said. "Father, mother, brother and me, and sister."

They crossed the border into Hungary, made their way by train to Budapest, where they hid. They were smuggled to Vienna, then into Germany. They stayed a while, they received some help, they headed south to France, moving slowly, and once on the coast traveled east, entered Italy and got a train to Bari. A ferry took them to Cyprus. They were among many Jews there, awaiting transfer to Israel. At last they arrived in Haifa. The trip from Romania had taken a year.

"My father joined the Hagganah ["Defence," the Jewish guerrilla army prior to independence] and we were given a house," he said. "The house is still there in Haifa. Arabs were our neighbors. We visited them. They came to our house. We liked their food better than they liked ours. We ate with Arabs!"

That reminiscence, like the Pilgrim Fathers befriending the Red Indians and being helped by them, was a frequent detail in stories of Israeli pioneers in Palestine.

"Weren't you fighting the Arabs?" I asked.

"Other Arabs," he said. "And British."

"Which other Jews were here when you arrived in 1947?"

"The first wave had been Russians. Then Poles. Then Bulgarians and Romanians," he said. "In the 1950s we got Moroccans and North African Jews – Algeria, Tunisia. And others."

"Americans?"

"Not many from America," he said. He laughed — not mirth: it was a nervous expression of the Israeli ambivalence towards America. "Americans come here. They look. They smile. They know they have something better."

"What do you think of America?"

"America is the grandfather of Israel," he said. Or it might have been "godfather."

The following day in Gaza, at the Palestinian settlement of Khan Yunis, a Palestinian journalist, Hani Abed, was blown up by a sophisticated bomb that had detonated under his car when he turned the ignition key. Such a bomb could only have been placed there by members of the Israeli secret service, Mossad. It seemed as though what Rabin had said just the other day about fighting to the death was being proven.

This was not denied; on the contrary, it was heavily hinted that this was so by the Hebrew newspaper, *Ha'aretz* ("The Land"): "Hani Abed . . . got the punishment coming to him, 'for they have sown the wind, and they shall reap the whirlwind,'" including Hamas in the denunciation.

Wiping someone out and then quoting a bit of blood-spattered scripture (this text from Hosea 8:7 was an old standby) seemed fairly routine. But of course that was not the end of it, for several days later a boy on a bike pedaled past an Israeli checkpoint into Gaza City and blew himself up, along with two soldiers, and he was instantly proclaimed a martyr for the Palestinian cause.

That was an about average week. I happened to be there, writing it down. It went some way towards explaining why the Israeli soldiers were anxious and fatigued, why strangers never chatted in trains or buses, and why the atmosphere was so sullen.

There had been no public expression of bereavement in Tel Aviv over the bus bombing. No flags at half-mast, no wreaths, no ribbons. There were angry letters to the *Jerusalem Post* in this regard: "What is wrong with us that we cannot express our own grief?"

That did not mean that no one grieved; there had to be great sorrow. But the silence meant there also had to be tremendous resentment, anger and frustration. Out of this bitterness came feelings of revenge, and support for any politician who vowed (as most did, *ad nauseam*) to avenge the deaths. This and the unforgiving attitude seemed an Israeli rather than a Jewish reaction.

There was not much public expression of joy either – not much laughter, no talking on buses and trains, no sense of animation; more a sort of sick-of-it-all, seen-it-all attitude that was laced with suspicion. After dark the Tel Aviv streets emptied, and the same was true of Haifa – almost no night-time pedestrians. That was a clear sign of high anxiety.

Even Tel Aviv, in spite of its long beach and leafy suburbs, had the look of a fortress, for its militarism gave it the same colonial garrison look that Haifa had. It looked out of place, built on sand, artificial and incongruous. It was both too big and not big enough, and only its traffic and loud music and air-conditioners gave it a Miami sound.

I went to the Tel Aviv Museum of Art, about a twenty-minute walk from my hotel. It contained a number of works which I had seen elsewhere – rusty shovels ("Untitled #34"), flashing lights ("Neon Fragment"), rags on hooks ("Work in Progress"), and the last resort of the artist barren of imagination, broken crockery glued to plywood ("Spatial Relationships") – perhaps the splinters and shards of the very plates the artist's spouse had flung in frustration, crying, "Why don't you get a job!"

This frivolity did not speak of Israel, but obviously someone – a wealthy person in Tel Aviv – had put up the money for this. One exhibit showed photographs of small naked girls, six- and eight-year-olds, smiling, with trusting faces, sitting with their legs apart. The expression "kiddie porn" did not describe such pathetic trust and violation.

We have all been in such art museums and said, "It makes me mad." And been told by the ludicrous supporters of such junk, "That's good. It's supposed to make you mad."

But the museum was not a total waste. There was also a one-person show by an Israeli artist named Pamela Levy – photographic paintings, all of them arresting, many of them upsetting. Some were scenes of battlefields, showing dead and dismembered soldiers, and the horror of war. Many were depictions of biblical characters, or Old Testament recreations of Israeli life, hairy men and chubby women in classic poses. Many of the naked men were shown hooded; "Lot and His Daughters" had a sinister carnality – naked girls and a supine old man, and the painting entitled "Rape" was disturbing most of all because it looked like a form of fooling that was about to turn violent.

The artist Pamela Levy had been born in Iowa in 1949 and had come to Israel in 1976. She was as much of an Israeli as anyone else but I felt that her painting said a great deal about the state of mind here: the repression, the aggression, the fantasies, the naked-ness, the sexual ambiguity, terror. Those paintings seemed to offer an insight into the turmoil in the country, and so her art was true.

Later, I had lunch with the Cohens from London. I bumped into them in a restaurant and we talked. They were an elderly middle-class couple, very polite to each other and pleased to be in Israel. It was their annual holiday.

"Every year we come, just about this time," Mrs Cohen said. "We've seen so many changes."

"Has Tel Aviv grown very much?"

"I can remember when none of this was here," Mr Cohen said. "Are you from London?"

"I used to live in south London," I said. "Clapham – Wands-worth way."

"Are there many Jews there?"

"I don't know," I said.

And as I was muttering to myself, How should I know how many Jews there are in Clapham? it occurred to me that perhaps I had been privy to a secret exchange. When Jews met in safe places they asked where each other was from and said, "Are there many there?"

"I think there's a synagogue in Putney," I said.

"Hammersmith," old Mr Cohen said.

Changing the subject, I mentioned that it was my first time in Israel and that I liked the food.

"Oh, yes," Mrs Cohen said. She mentioned several restaurants for me to try. "They're not very nice but at least they're kosher."

The streets were empty at nine o'clock, and Tel Aviv, which advertises itself as "The City that Never Takes a Break," is not much after dark. It was just a wall of unforgiving concrete; not pretty, not even very interesting, but like the rest of Israel in being clean and orderly and full of public buses. No graffiti, no apparent disorder, and so naive people who were unaware of what was going on were reassured by this appalling ordinariness.

The beach at Tel Aviv continued south to Jaffa where, within a few feet, it turned into an Arab town. But it was not a popular destination. Most people stayed right here at the center of town, and it made me think that this was perhaps more an Eastern European dream of the seaside than an American one, illustrating the Shakespearean solecism, the stage direction in *The Winter's Tale*: "the coast of Bohemia."

I woke early, and called Emile Habiby. He was still out of the country, so I checked out of my hotel, and got a ten-shekel bus ticket to Jerusalem. In this week of revenge killings I expected the bus to be filled with soldiers, and it was; but they were asleep, hugging their rifles, and when they woke up they looked cranky. The rest of the bus passengers were the assorted citizens of Israel – Moroccans in tracksuits, Hassids in black hats, followers of the Lubavitcher sect whose messiah, recently deceased, was Rabbi Menachim Schneerson. (An exact duplicate of the messiah's Brooklyn brown-stone, down to the iron rails and the aged brickwork, had been built in Jerusalem so that he would feel at home in the event that he should visit Israel.) There was a woman with a violin and another with a viola, students with textbooks, people with groceries, and pilgrims – but a pilgrim is just another sort of tourist.

Down the highway, into the semi-desert and Route One through the rocky hills. But it was all more familiar than it should have been. The guard-rails were American style, and so were the signs and barriers and arrows and signal lights, and all this hardware gave a distinct sense of being in the United States.

The four-lane road passed ravines and steep slopes, some wooded summits. Old-fashioned armored cars and rusty trucks had been left by the roadside as memorials to the men who had died in what the Israelis call the War of Liberation. The vehicles, so old, so clumsy, roused pity. It was rough country, and even with the stands of slender cypresses it looked pitiless, as the buildings did by the side of the road, plain, unornamented, with that same garrison look, the flat military façade which was Israeli architecture. Most buildings in Israel seemed as though they had been designed to withstand an attack.

Jerusalem is a city in the hills. The outskirts were steep and suburban, and the higher the bus climbed the denser the buildings. The bus station was like any old bus station, crowded, chaotic, with an added element of anxiety, for violence was an outdoor activity in Israel. Because Jerusalem's terrain is irregular the streets are twisty and steep. This makes it hard for someone on foot to get a good clear sight of the city – or rather the two cities. The Old City is the Jerusalem of postcards. But West Jerusalem is the city of politics and commerce; it is still being built and settled as the Israeli capital, as though a deliberate challenge to anyone who harbors the idea of internationalizing it.

Asking the way to the Old City, I met an Ethiopian Jew, Negu. The colloquial term for such people was Falasha ("stranger" in Amharic), but it was rejected by them as obviously contemptuous. He said he would show me the way. He had little else to do. He was not working.

"You could join the army, couldn't you?"

"I am too old for the army."

But he was hardly thirty, and as Israel was a country where, of necessity, soldiers were all ages and sizes, I could not understand why this was so.

"Would you be a soldier if they let you?"

Negu shrugged. He did not want to pursue this. He was thin and tall and quite black, with piercing eyes and an odd sloping walk with a twitch of alertness in it, always seeming to be aware of what was happening around him.

"When did you come here?" I asked.

"Six years ago."

"From Addis Ababa?"

"My village is 800 kilometers from Addis Ababa."

"This must be quite a change from that." Eight hundred kilometers had to be the remote bush, the very edge of the country, on one of the scrubby borders – of the Sudan, or Kenya, or Somalia.

We were walking through the busy precincts of West Jerusalem, where there were offices and agencies and shopping districts and hotels. Ahead I could see the domes of the Old City, an ancient skyline, but here it was all bustle – people, traffic, the same hectic anxiety that I had felt in the bus station, an air of apprehension; each person walked just a beat faster, and their voices were more insistent and a few octaves shriller.

"In some ways, Israel is better."

But he was doubtful.

"Better than your village in Ethiopia?"

"In some ways only. In other ways, no. Ethiopia is good."

"You're a Jew, though?"

"Yes. I am a Jew. We do not use these things on our head," he said. He pointed to a passer-by wearing a yarmulka.

"You have a family?"

"Yes. Wife. Children," he said. "We are Jews."

"Will you stay here?" I asked. "Do you like it?"

He shrugged, the same shrug, irked by my curiosity, wondering who I was and why I was asking.

"That is the gate you are searching for," he said, and left me.

It was the Jaffa Gate, which took me through the Armenian Quarter to the Church of the Holy Sepulchre. I went inside, jostled by hurrying visitors, and then walked to the real treasures of the city, Temple Mount, the Dome of the Rock and, a little farther on, the El Aqsa mosque. There I met Fikret, from the *Akdeniz*, who had lost the others.

"I was at the Crying Wall," he said. "I cried!"

"Where is Bible Man?" That was our nickname for Onan.

"He is looking for Hebrew books," Fikret said. "He has already bought one for sixty dollars."

We walked together through the Lion's Gate, to the edge of the Mount of Olives. Fikret reminded me that this was a city that was sacred to Muslims, which all believers tried to visit.

Jerusalem was a little jewel in the hills, a lovely city, certainly one of the most beautiful I had seen on my trip. But as a place of pilgrimage, inspiring a sort of breathless pilgrim eager to possess it, with that special intensity, Jerusalem merely glittered for me. I found myself resisting its power to cast enchantment. Praying there seemed like theater, requiring a suspension of disbelief or a self-conscious fakery. And the city was a symbol. In Israel symbols were always useful shorthand, and so they were chosen as targets – they were exaggerated, or destroyed; either way, they lost their reality.

Fikret stayed, saying he was going to look at the mosque again. I decided to return to Haifa. Back at the bus station I tried to buy a ticket to Gaza.

"No, no, no," the ticket-seller said, and waved me away.

I asked a policeman. He shook his head. He said that, because of the recent shootings and bombings, the territories were closed. I would not be able to get through a checkpoint at the border.

"That's too bad."

"That is not bad," he said. "You are lucky you can't go to Gaza. It is dangerous."

At the bus station when I was asking for directions, a man heard me speaking English and took me aside. He was thinking of emigrating to the United States. Did I know anything about Orlando? He wanted to become a driver there – not necessarily a taxi-driver, but something a little more colorful, perhaps a limo driver.

"I think I could be a success there, with my English accent," he said.

It was true, he had the ghost of an accent, but though his reasoning seemed preposterous, I said, "Sure, they're bound to think you're David Niven, but how is Israel going to manage without you?"

"There's no money here," he murmured, and slipped away.

To reassure myself that the *Akdeniz* would not leave Israel without me I talked to the purser. No, the day after tomorrow, he said; and so I was free to go to a concert, the Haifa Symphony Orchestra: Elgar's Introduction and Allegro for Strings, Tippett's "A Midsummer Marriage," Rachmaninoff's Rhapsody on a Theme by Paganini, and Stravinsky's Symphony in C.

Afterwards I saw six decorous prostitutes crouched at the corner of Sederot Ha'atzma'ut and little Lifshitz Street, and they were laughing and making kissing noises at me. I attempted to talk to them – they were bound to be fluent in English – but realizing that I was not interested in anything else they turned away. Besides, they saw some potential customers hurrying along: two young

Hassidic Jews with big black hats and black frock coats, velvet yarmulkas, side-curls and black pants tucked into black socks. They walked in a flapping flat-footed way, and quickened their pace when they saw the prostitutes, who just laughed.

I followed the Hassidic boys for a while, just to see where they were going – up to Mount Carmel or over to the crumbling buildings of Wadi Salib. Seeing them in the bus or the train, in the desert heat, these black-suited and bearded Hassidim always made me perspire. Dressed for chilly nineteenth-century Poland, they made no allowance for being in the desert of the Middle East. They also seemed out of place because Israel was so secular – Christian or Orthodox churches were more numerous in Haifa than synagogues. People were polite but pieties were rare, courtesy scarce. It was not rudeness; it was more a sort of truce. Everything was practical and measured. What was the fear? Was it that generosity, which is also goodwill, exposed you to strangers and thereby put you at risk?

Back at the *Akdeniz* all the Turks were on board. They were relaxing. After the tension and the seriousness of Israel, these Turks seemed the soul of jollity. The food was Turkish, the music was Arabesque syncopation and Turkish movie themes. The ship lay at a distant pier, a twenty-minute walk from Gate Five, Port of Haifa, the turnstile where we had to show our passports. For the passengers, the ship was Turkey.

I was still reading the Trollope novel, *Doctor Wortle's School*, about the fuss in an English village over an apparent impropriety. Tonight the embattled doctor was reflecting, "It is often a question to me whether the religion of the world is not more odious than its want of religion."

Emile Habiby had arrived back in Israel. When I telephoned him he said that he would get into his car and meet me in Haifa. I protested – no, he had jet lag. I would come to Nazareth. On my map, Nazareth was about halfway to the Sea of Galilee – about thirty-five miles, less than an hour.

"But how will I find you?"

"Everyone knows me! Just ask anyone for Habiby *sofer*."

Sofer is "writer" in Hebrew.

I found a taxi-driver, Yossi Marsiano ("like Rocky Marciano"). He was a Moroccan Jew, from the north Moroccan town of Ouezzane. He was edgy and impatient. He had a way of grinning that showed no pleasure at all, only pure hysteria. I told him Habiby's name.

"He's an Arab?"

"He's an Israeli."

This was true, and more than that he was a Christian and a Palestinian as well. Yossi was confused, and for a moment it looked as though he regretted having agreed to take me. Then he told me to get into the car, and to hurry.

"How much?"

We agreed on 160 shekels.

"Get in. We go," he said. "In, in."

Leaving Haifa and passing the populous bluff of Mount Carmel that dominates the city, it was impossible not to think of Habiby. He had written about those specific heights a number of times in his novel *Saraya the Ogre's Daughter* (translated by Peter Theroux, 1995). One of the glimpses is fanciful: Mount Carmel as "a bull with its snout turned up, ready to lunge at a matador come to him from the land of Andalusia. He disregards him in anticipation of matadorial carelessness; if he ignores him, the bull will not give him a moment's respite . . . [But] he is as patient as the Arabs."

In another part of the novel, Mount Carmel is remembered by the narrator as the wilderness of his childhood, "still a virgin forest, except for its lighthouse, which was, in our eyes, closer to the stars in the heavens than to the houses of Wadi al-Nisnas . . . The wild melancholy of al-Carmel took our breath away." Returning hopefully, he sees it as it is today, a promontory covered with apartment houses and condominiums, and fenced-in mansions. It is now denuded of trees; gone are the flowering plants, the terebinth, hawthorn, fennel and paradise apple that had protected it. The old spring has dried up, and the narrator reflects on "how mountains die – how Mount Carmel is dying!"

It is an oblique reference to the way that modern Israel has spread its new buildings over an ancient landscape, turning familiar contours into an unrecognizable (and unmemorable) urban sprawl.

The growth was still in progress. No sooner had Yossi and I reached the north end of Haifa than we were in a traffic jam.

"Road fixing," Yossi said.

While he reassured me that this was nothing, a matter of minutes, he continued to fret. That was an Israeli paradox, a person obviously troubled and anxious saying, "No problem!" Yossi was fretful. We inched along. He banged the steering-wheel in anger and became self-conscious and said in his unconvincing way, "It's okay. Don't worry."

I was not worried. Nazareth was not far. But to take Yossi's mind off the traffic jam I asked him how he had come to Israel. Every Israeli had a migration story. In the 1950s, Yossi's parents had not seen any future for themselves as a minority in the remote Moroccan town of Ouezzane, surrounded by Arabs, and so they had decided to take their small children and settle in Israel.

On the surface, it was a back-to-the-homeland story, but where was the work? Where was the money? It was all right for Yossi's father, who was a bank clerk, but Yossi and his brother did not discern any bright new Israeli dawn. The brother moved to Los Angeles and prospered. So much for the homeland as a refuge.

"I went to Los Angeles to visit him," Yossi said. "In California you can't walk on the street. Just Mexicans walk. Everyone else drives."

"Not exactly," I said.

"Yes! I was there! No one walks!"

"But your brother is happy there, right?"

"Right. And I want to live there. I want to work, get a Green Card. But how can I, if I can't walk on the street?"

Impatient in the stalled traffic, he had become shrill. I decided to agree with everything he said about the United States, no matter how offensive or inaccurate it was.

"Manhattan is better. You know that."

"It sure is," I said.

"Too many Jews in Manhattan," Yossi said, his grammar slipping. "That is good. I talk to the Jews, they talk to me. I think, maybe I go there and get some money. Here is no money."

"But this is the Jewish homeland, isn't it?"

"No money here," he said, smacking the steering-wheel. And he started to grumble. "America is dangerous. Guns. Trouble. Why I want to go there?"

"That's a good question."

"Because here is bureaucracy," Yossi snapped back. "Office. Papers. Application. Permission. 'Hello – no, sorry, is closing, come back in two hours.' 'Come back tomorrow.' 'Come back next week.' 'Sorry I cannot help you.' 'You pay 100 shekels.' 'Officer is not here now.' 'Where is your papers – you have no proper papers.' This is shit!"

It was quite a performance, and it certainly convinced me. I shut my mouth and let him fume until the traffic eased. But he was soon chattering again.

"This Habiby *sofer* – he is an Arab, you say?"

"He's an Israeli – Christian. Born in Haifa," I said, and resisted adding, *Unlike you, Yossi.*

"More road fixing!" Yossi said.

More traffic, a bottleneck; an hour went past, and then we were on our way, on a road that skirted a large village.

"That is an Arab city," Yossi said.

"What is its name?"

"I don't know."

I saw from my map that it was Shefar'am – small houses on a hillside, sprawling further, some animals grazing in the foreground; not much else.

"No streets, no numbers, no names – like this Habiby. 'Ask for me – ask for *sofer*.' No number, no street. In Haifa you can go anywhere – too easy. Jews have numbers!"

"I'll try to remember that, Yossi."

As the obstacles increased, Yossi became shriller and in his shrillness more anti-Arab.

"Look at the houses – not clean! The streets this way and that! No numbers!"

The road to Nazareth became narrower, the line of traffic slower, and Nazareth itself across the desert and occupying a high hill was like a distant vision, almost a mirage. It was physically different from any other of the places I had seen in Israel, not just the style of the houses, but the way they were piled up, some of them leaning, the look of accumulation over the years, added rooms and windows, wall upon wall, the layers of tiled roofs. The foundations were ancient, but higher up the third or fourth storey was more recent. It was the sort of growth that was characteristic of wonderful old trees – fragile shoots on young branches that crowned a thick immovable trunk. Nazareth had that same grip on its hill – it was something venerable, with deep roots, still growing.

People worked outside in Nazareth, too – some of them were following the sort of occupations that were usually pursued in the open air in the Middle East – carpentry, wood-carving, car repair; but there were men fixing televisions and painting signs, too. They were banging dents out of car fenders, and selling fruit, and stacking bricks. Unlike the indoor existence that people lived in Jewish Tel Aviv or Haifa, life in Muslim Nazareth spilled into its streets.

That was another difference between Jews and Palestinians. It annoyed Yossi.

"You see? Just people everywhere, and not clean, and what are they doing?"

They were working, they were sitting, they were dandling babies, they were exuding an air of possession and belonging.

"Look over there," Yossi said, and pointed to the east, another settlement, an extension of Nazareth, but newer, with whiter buildings and tidier roofs and emptier streets; the Jewish settlement of Natseret Illit.

"Jews! Jews! Jews! Jews!" Yossi cried.

We started up a hill ("Too many cars! All these Arabs have cars!"), entered an area of twisty streets ("So dirty!"), continued to climb ("Houses have no name, no number – like Morocco Arabs") and yelled at passers-by, "Habiby – *sofer!*"

The name did not ring any bells with the passers-by.

We kept going. Sunshine turned to twilight. Dusk gathered. The dust of Nazareth was reflected in car headlights, and people and animals wandered in the road ("Arabs!"). The lights did not help; their glare made it harder for us to see, and finally in the interior of the upper town instead of illuminating the road the lights blinded us.

"Haifa is not like this! Look at Arab streets!"

He was ranting, and it seemed we were truly lost when he asked a man and woman where Habiby lived and they said in a Scottish accent that they had only been in Nazareth for two days and had no idea.

"Forget it. Let's go back to Haifa. We'll never find the house."

"You must find your friend!" Yossi screamed, making a U-turn in the dark. "And I must smoke a cigarette!" He was very upset. He screamed again incoherently. He was saying, "Don't worry!"

The only lighted doorway on this street was a bakery. A man in flour-dusted overalls stood holding a squeeze bag of frosting and was using its nozzle to decorate some jam tarts. He had not heard of Habiby, but he said in Arabic, "Why don't we call him and ask him directions?" He did so. The street was not far, he explained. He sat down and smacked some flour out of a shallow cardboard box and turned it over. Very slowly, he sketched a map on the bottom of the box. Then he handed this box to Yossi, and off we went, higher, almost to the top of the hill of old Nazareth.

Emile Habiby's house was large and rambling, set along with others on a steep hillside, filled with people, mostly women and children, all of them Habibys. The author had three daughters and ten grandchildren; his first great-grandchild had just arrived.

He sat, the patriarch, surrounded by this energetic family. He was seventy-three, stocky, even bull-like, with a heavy sculptured head and a raspy voice and a booming laugh. He had the build of a Mediterranean fisherman – he had worked on a fishing-boat out of Haifa for many years; but he was also one of Israel's intellectuals. He had published a number of novels, among them *The Secret Life of Saeed* and *Saraya the Ogre's Daughter*, and he had won several literary prizes – the Order of Palestine in 1991 and the year before that the Jerusalem Medal. Two previous recipients of the Jerusalem Medal were so outraged by the fact that the prize had been awarded to an Arab that these thinkers (who had been singled out for their contribution to humanity) returned their medals in disgust. The absurdity was much enjoyed by Habiby, whose novels are excursions into the fantastic.

I had encouraged Yossi to come in with me and, welcomed, given a cigarette, he sat calming himself in this Palestinian household, a great nest of Habibys. Cups of coffee appeared and pastries and small children. In the kitchen other children were being fed, and the Habiby women were talking and laughing. I was moved as much by the size and complexity of the family as by its harmony.

And at last Yossi was smiling a real smile. In spite of all of his abuse and his shrieking, we had arrived, and he was happily smoking and we were receiving the best welcome imaginable, with food and compliments and solicitous questions.

There were pictures of Jesus on the wall, and portraits of the Madonna and Child. It was a reminder that this was a Christian family, and such pictures could not have been more appropriate since Nazareth was the home of Mary and Joseph. The Basilica of the Annunciation had been built over the house of St Anne, and even Joseph's workshop had been discovered and excavated in Nazareth − there it was for all the world to see, the workshop of the best-known carpenter in Christendom.

"It's good of you to come all this way," Habiby said. "Though you know I would have come to Haifa to see you."

"Yes. But I found the trip out here interesting," I said. Especially when Yossi had pointed to the Jewish settlement of Natseret Illit and howled, "Jews! Jews! Jews! Jews!"

We talked about the tension since the massacre in Hebron. Habiby had written an article in the *New York Times* about it in which he had said, "One cannot go on pretending that nothing has changed," and that the error many Israeli leaders and politicians had made was in refusing "to tell their people that they must reach out to the Palestinians; they have nobody else to rely on in the long run." He was encouraged by Foreign Minister Shimon Peres' condemnation of the assassin Goldstein.

What had happened afterwards had been inevitable, since both sides had vowed retribution. But his view was that both Palestinians and Israelis had a duty "to stand up to our own extremists."

"There is an old Arab saying," Habiby said, "that the Jews celebrate their feasts around gardens, the Christians around kitchens, and the Muslims around graveyards."

A peace conference was going on at that moment in Casablanca, to which Yitzak Rabin had been invited. I asked Habiby what he thought of the Israeli Prime Minister's contribution.

"He talked too much. He should have proceeded slowly," he said.

"You mean he was demanding too much?"

"No. He didn't realize where he was," Habiby said, throwing up his hands. "He was in Morocco, not Israel. He was among Arabs. But he talks to these Arabs as though he is talking to his own people." He was referring to Rabin's manners, his characteristic bluster.

"Being tough and businesslike, giving orders."

"That's it. But a little politeness would have been helpful."

"I suppose he is feeling confident now that he has made a peace agreement with Jordan."

"It should still be possible for him to show some politeness," Habiby said. "Now they are committed. But instead of all this public boasting and all the urgency, why not use a little tact?"

Tact was a scarce commodity in Israel. Suspicion was so ingrained, and fear so common, that every sphere of life was affected, and the absence of faith and goodwill made people brusque. Israelis had struggled to arrive at this point, but life was still a struggle, and they perhaps saw, as Habiby had said, that they had no one else to rely on; the only allies Israelis would ever really have would be the Palestinians.

"Charmless," I said. It was a word that summed up the atmosphere of Israel for me.

"Yes," Habiby said, and gestured with his cigarette. "As for the peace agreement, I am not hopeful. I have doubts. But there is no going back."

He had written, "We, Israelis and Palestinians, are already fated to be born again as Siamese twins . . . true solidarity with one is contingent on true solidarity with the other. There is no alternative."

"What brings you to Israel?" he asked.

"I'm just traveling around the Mediterranean. At the moment, I'm on a Turkish ship," I said. "It's in Haifa – leaving tomorrow."

"I have been traveling myself," he said. "I must stop traveling or I'll never write anything."

"I know the feeling. Monotony is the friend of the writer."

Yossi joined the conversation, first in English, then in Hebrew.

Several times I interrupted to say that we ought to be leaving – after all, I had visited at such short notice. More food was brought. We ate. Habiby roared, describing the pompous attitude of Israeli politicians. Yossi nodded – yes, he agreed, it was awful.

Later than I intended, Yossi and I left. The whole Habiby family turned out to see us off and make us promise that we would come back again.

"You see, Arabs? The door is always open," Yossi said in an admiring way. "We come there, the door is open. Cigarettes for me. Some food, thank you. Coffee, yes. Some more. Please, thank you. Take some extra."

"You like that?"

"Oh, yes. Is good," Yossi said. "The Arab door is always open."

We got lost again, but Yossi was calmer. He stopped and instead of shouting out of the window he got out of the car and asked for directions. A man said that he would show us the way, if we followed him. We were taken down a dark, narrow road through the Balfour Forest, and then on a different route to Haifa.

At Haifa, Yossi was reminded again of the hospitality at Nazareth.

"We lock our doors," he said. "Jews don't have open doors. No pastry. No food. No coffee."

"What do Jews have instead of open doors?"

"Just hello. A little talk. Then goodbye."

He kept driving, and he had second thoughts. He suspected that he had given me the wrong idea.

"But sometimes an open door is bad," he said. "You want to talk to your wife, eh? People doing – what is Ha! Ha! Ha!"

"Laughing."

"Yes. Laughing. It is bad. Open door can be bad. And look," he said, and nodded at the heights of Haifa just ahead of us, Mount Carmel, the populous cliffs. "Those streets have names. Those Jews have numbers."

He drove me to the port. He became sentimental again. "It was nice how they served us. Food. Coffee. That was nice," he said. "You know that man was talking politics to me?"

"What did you say to him?"

"I told him, don't ask me. I don't know about politics."

Instead of eating on the ship I found a restaurant and spent the last of my shekels on a meal. Every meal I ate in Israel was delicious, and I had found the Israeli countryside an unexpected pleasure. The restaurant was almost empty, like the streets; like everything else in after-dark Haifa. Everyone was home, watching TV, doing schoolwork, worrying.

All the Turks were on board the *Akdeniz*, so eager to leave, and in such a mood of celebration, that even from my cabin I could hear them singing, their voices and their plonking instruments vibrating in the ship's steel hull, making the thing throb with music of the Arabesque.

Some time in the night I heard the sounds of departure – clanking chains, the lines slipping and straining in the winches, barks in bad English from ship to shore and back again, and then the reassuring drone of the engines and the ship rocking slowly in the deep sea. Then uninterrupted sleep was possible.

Dawn was bright, the glare of a dusty shoreline and a fortress, a gothic church in the distance among rooftops: northern Cyprus. It was not a province of Turkey – silly me for thinking so – but a sovereign state, the Turkish Republic of North Cyprus, bankrolled and backed and guarded by Turkey, the only country in the world which recognizes it. It was about a third of Cyprus. The southern part was Greek, and the Green Line, guarded by United Nations soldiers, divided the two. Ever since this partition there had been peace on Cyprus.

Famagusta had been re-named by the Turks Gazimagosa – Gazi an honorific term for a warrior, since the town had come through the war with valor. It was a small town, and its port was located in the old part, surrounded by a Venetian wall. It was very ruinous, all of it, and my impression was that Turkish North Cyprus was having a very bad time. Walking slowly with Samih Pasha, Fikret and Onan, it took us thirty-five minutes to see the whole of Gazimagosa, including the church which was no longer a church: the gothic cathedral of St Nicholas had been turned into the Lala Pasha mosque by the grafting of a minaret on to one of the spires.

"This is it," Samih Pasha said, tweaking his mustache. "So we go to Girne."

"You come with us, *effendi*," Onan said. "We worried about you in Israel when we didn't see you."

Greek Kyrenia was now Turkish Girne. It was about sixty miles away. The four of us found a taxi, and I let the Turks haggle with the driver. They came away saying, "No, no. Ridiculous!"

The driver had said that he could not take us for less than 800,000 Turkish liras. This was $25 – an outrageous amount to the Turks. I did not say that it seemed reasonable, because I was curious to know what their solution would be. It was a seventy-five-cent ride in an old bus to Lefkosa (Nicosia), a city that had been bisected by the Green Line. From there we would have to catch another bus to Girne.

On a bus that swayed down an empty road, past unplowed fields in the November heat of Cyprus, the wobbly wheels raising dust, the passengers dozing, the landscape looking deserted and arid (water was scarce, the last harvest had been terrible, the little nation was ignored by everyone), I was thinking how odd it was to be here, traveling across this bogus republic. The bus was uncomfortable, the road was bad, the food was awful, the weather was corrosive. But I had never been here before, which was justification enough; and I felt a grim satisfaction in being with a little Turkish team of men who kept telling me they worried about me when I was out of sight.

It was only an hour and a half to Lefkosa. The onward bus was not leaving for another two hours. In spite of his age, Samih Pasha walked quickly into town. He said he was eager to see the Green Line.

"Have you been here before?"

"Yes, but not on the ground," he said, smiling. When he smiled his mustache lifted in a big semaphore of happiness. "I was flying."

In the ethnic fighting of 1964, and again at partition in 1974, it had been Samih Pasha's task to fly his F-100 fighter plane from one end of Cyprus to the other, from his airbase in Turkey. The object was not to engage Greek planes – the Turkish air force dominated the skies – but to break windows.

"I am flying at ten meters," Samih Pasha said, "and when I get over Lefkosa I let out the afterburner and make a big noise – an explosion, you can say – and all the windows break!"

"Greek or Turkish windows?" I asked.

"Both! Impossible just to break Greek windows!"

And he described with pleasure the way his fighter jet streaked low across Cypriot air space, scaring the bejesus out of the Greeks, and reassuring the Turks, who (so it was said on this side of the Green Line) had been systematically oppressed by them.

We walked down one rubbly street and up another, past some shops just closing for the lunch-time siesta, to the United Nations checkpoint: a sentry post, a shed, a barrier, and a bilingual English–Turkish sign, STOP/DUR.

"I'd like to pass through," I said to the soldier in the blue beret who stood holding an automatic rifle.

"No."

"I just want to see Greek Cyprus and come straight back."

"It is impossible."

"You see?" Onan said. The others had watched me. They were much too polite to ask the soldier.

A woman came out of her house nearby and said hello in English. Her house had a colonnade in the front, and a pretty porch. I asked her whether she had crossed the Green Line, which was fifty feet away. No, she said, not for twenty years.

"This house was given to me by my father," she said, when I complimented her on it. "That was in 1930. Over there" – she pointed across the street to some abandoned houses – "was an Armenian family, and some Greeks. But they left."

"Were they forced out of their houses?" I asked.

She got my point, and without replying directly to the question, she said, "My house in Limassol [in Greek Cyprus] is wrecked. They took my antiques. They took my Mercedes car."

I was sorry that I had gotten her on to the subject, because the others left me listening to her litany of complaints. I sympathized. This had been a prosperous capital and now it was a wreck of a place, and we stood on a blocked road, among deserted houses, and the old woman was saying, "They won't find a solution – not soon –"

A wall of atrocity photos was on display, under glass, on the Turkish side of the Green Line. They were blurred and smudged, some of them hard to make out. But the captions told the whole story, sometimes with sarcasm:

– *A Greek Cypriot priest who forgot his religious duties and joined in the hunting and killing of Turks*

– *A mother and her three children murdered by Greek Cypriots in the bath of their house in Nicosia*

– *Mass grave*

– *Refugees*

– *Burned village*

– *Frenzied Greek Cypriot armed bandit*

– *Dead bullet-riddled baby – life was hell for us in 1963–74. We cannot return to those days.*

"That is true," Fikret said. "It was really bad. They tortured people. The Greeks burned Turkish villages. They made us suffer."

"Aren't you glad you had General Samih, three-star window-breaker, to help you?"

"This man," Samih Pasha said, tapping his head, and squinting at me, "he is always writing things down. I ask why?"

He had seen me scribbling atrocity captions. I said, "Because I have a bad memory."

We walked to a restaurant, Sinan Café, farther down the Green Line. It was half a café, for it had been split in two by a wall that blocked the street; this main north–south road was now a dead end. On the wall a sign said, "1st Restricted Military Area – No Photographs!", with a skull and cross-bones.

Fikret and I drank a coffee. The owner said, "Want to look over the wall? There's a good view from upstairs."

We went to the second floor of his house and peered over the Green Line into Greek Cyprus. I could see ruined rooftops, broken tiles, no people; but in the distance was a tall pole flying the Greek flag, in defiance. As though in reply, from the Turkish side there was a Muslim call to prayers, the long groaning praise of Allah.

"Fikret, what do you think of Greeks?"

"Greeks in Turkey were prosperous because they were good businessmen," he said. "We do not hate each other."

"But Greece is in the EU."

"They don't belong there, but neither does Turkey," he said. "We are still a backward country. Does the EU want another headache?"

The four of us bought fifty-cent bus tickets at the Lefkosa bus shed and went another twenty miles over a mountain range towards Girne, on the north coast. The shoreline was rocky, and the land rose to black and rugged cliffs. Samih Pasha described how Turkish troops had landed just west of here in 1974. He pointed out the caves in the cliffs where they had hidden themselves and ambushed the Greeks, driving them south. We stopped at Bellapais.

"The quietness, the sense of green beatitude which fills this village," Lawrence Durrell wrote of Bellapais, high above Girne, not far from the Crusader castle of St Hilarion, where Richard the Lionheart spent his honeymoon. In his house there, described in *Bitter Lemons*, Durrell began writing his Alexandria Quartet. Nowadays Bellapais is perhaps more remote and dustier than it has ever been, but it is still very pretty. Villages endure destitution better than towns, and rural poverty can perversely seem almost picturesque.

But the town of Girne had the same look of desolation as the larger settlements I had seen in this embattled corner of the island. Empty streets, scruffy shops, empty hotels. I went to the largest hotel, on the sea front, just to see whether I could make a telephone call. The woman at the switchboard said it was impossible.

"You can't call outside of here," she said. "No one recognizes us!"

Samih Pasha and Onan and Fikret commiserated with the woman, saying it wasn't fair. Yet it interested me that this portion of an island in the Mediterranean was regarded as such a pariah that it had no contact with any country beyond its borders; and its greatest enemy was on the other side of the Green Line.

Suddenly Onan said, "We have to go. We will see you later."

Watching him hurry away with Samih Pasha, Fikret said, "They will go to the Officers' Club to eat."

"Onan's a soldier?"

"I think, yes. Bible-man was in the army before."

"What about us? Bean soup at some awful place, eh?"

Fikret shrugged. He did not complain. We went to a restaurant and had bean soup and salad and rice. The waiter was perspiring in the heat, his hair plastered to his head. A man carved slices from the upright log of grilled meat chunks called a *doner kebab* and mocked us for not trying some of the greasy scraps. A beggar woman crawled inside the door and sang pathetically, *I am in trouble – Allah sent the trouble to me*, until the man standing at the meat log threatened her with his meat fork.

"I want to ask you about marriage," Fikret said.

Now I knew why he had seemed so preoccupied. I said, "What's on your mind?"

"I have been thinking about marriage."

"How old are you?"

"Forty-six. But I have never been married," he said. "How old should the woman be?"

"Have you had a woman friend?"

"A young one. She was twenty-eight, a nurse," Fikret said. "She was too young for me. I told her to go back to her young man. But she was nice. And she was my height."

The height issue was important to Fikret. He was rather short. I said, "Why do you want to get married?"

"I don't like to be alone. I live with my brother," he said. "He is not married. He is discreet. But –" He leaned closer. "Please tell me what to do."

"Find a friend, not a wife," I said. "Don't think about her age. If you like her and she likes you, everything will be fine. Maybe you will marry her."

This did not console him. He was still fretting.

"My life is not getting any better," he said.

"Fikret, don't look so desperate."

"I think my life is getting worse."

We went to a café down on the sea front for dessert and were served by a pretty waitress. Fikret smiled. I urged him to talk to her. She was a Turkish immigrant, having fled from "Bulgaristan" – Bulgaria was full of Turks, Fikret said. He named six former

Soviet republics as Turkish, and the Chinese province of Xinjiang
– "That's Turkish, too." He talked a while with the waitress. But
she was married. She had gotten married just a month ago. Fikret
shrugged. Just his luck.

"This seems a sad place," I said, as we walked along the shore
afterward. "Why is that?"

"It is isolated," he said with such suddenness I realized that the
word was in his mind. He felt isolated too, and sad.

On the way back to Gazimagosa, across the plains, Fikret said
that one of the most famous Turkish fortune-tellers lived in that
town. Her name was Elmas – the Turkish word for diamond – and
she was noted for being so prescient that people came from all over
to have her read their palms. Not just Turks, but people from
many countries.

"They send her plane tickets and money, so that she can visit,"
he said. "She knows everything."

"Let's find her," I said. "We can ask her about your future."

But, looking for her in Gazimagosa, we were told that we were
too late.

"After five o'clock Elmas does not say anything," a Turk in
town told us. "You can find her, but she will not speak."

We walked in the failing light through the town towards the
port. When night fell, Turkish Cyprus was in darkness because
electricity was so scarce. Children chased each other in the dark,
screeching miserably, the way children in the water howl and
thrash, pretending to be drowning.

How strange that a place that had been so important, even
illustrious in history, could be so decrepit. The north coast was
associated with Richard the Lionheart, who had led his Crusaders
in a victory that gave them command of three castles at the edge
of the Kyrenia Mountains, which they held. The Venetians had
built the town's fortifications. The original of Othello had done
some of his soldiering here. More recently, this eastern coast was
noted for its beaches. Lawrence Durrell had written his book *Bitter
Lemons* not far from the spot in Girne where Fikret said, "It is
isolated." Now it was a backwater, with UN soldiers guarding the
Green Line and 27,000 Turkish troops hunkered down in the
hinterland.

This was one of the few places the *Akdeniz* stopped where the local food was worse than that on the ship. At dinner we saw Samih Pasha and Onan, who had just arrived back from Girne and the Turkish Officers' Club.

Onan said, "I have been feeling bad because we left you."

"You had to do your duty," I said. "I had not realized that you were a *gazi*."

"I am not a *gazi*," Onan said. Samih Pasha had begun to laugh.

I said, "I know it must be important to you to discuss your battles with the other *gazis* in the Officers' Club. And of course the Pasha had to do the same, reliving his famous window-breaking attack on Lefkosa."

I kept it up, jeering at them for abandoning Fikret and me in Girne. Onan remained stern and apologetic. Fikret laughed – it was good to hear: he laughed so seldom.

Samih Pasha peered at me and said, "There is something about you."

The weather turned windy after we left Cyprus, but there were fierce storms elsewhere in the Levant, the captain told me. Storms could be terrible here. "The waves breaking across the ship, so it is like a submarine." Alexandria was a difficult harbor to enter in a storm. "One time I spent five days going back and forth, one hundred miles east, one hundred miles west, before we could go in."

The *Akdeniz* became for me like a seedy hotel in which I was an old-time resident. A Turkish hotel: the food, the music, the greetings, the courtesies, the wives in their old-fashioned frocks and shawls, the old soldiers, the young boy who spoke English well and was funny, the old woman – possibly crazy – who ranted at me in Turkish, "My Name Ali" doing my laundry and overcharging me, then pretending to be surprised when I tipped him, the waiter who looked like Tom Selleck, the barman who said, "The usual?" The round of odd meals, cucumbers for breakfast, big meaty lunches, obscure stews at night.

The General, Samih Pasha, was always at the head of the table. I encouraged him to tell us war stories, and he obliged. His stories usually emphasized the courage of Turkish fighter pilots in NATO exercises. Where accuracy was concerned, the crucial factor in fighter bombing was nerve.

"You have to be brave," Samih Pasha said. "Going maybe 500 miles per hour. If you are not brave, you release the bombs too soon. The brave ones release bombs at the last minute for a hit, then count one-thousand one, one-thousand two, one-thousand three, and pull the stick." He grinned, the tips of his mustache rising. "The G-force take you. Maybe you black out. But you are climbing."

The Italian pilots were appalling, the Greeks even worse. The Turks on the other hand were so deadly that in a bombing raid of four planes the first two planes obliterated the target, leaving nothing for the last planes to bomb.

Samih Pasha's high military status as a three-star general had gotten him a special passport. He did not need a visa to enter Germany. He had a multiple-entry visa for the USA. He showed me his military passport.

"Good passport," he said.

"That's not just a special passaport," I said. "That's a Pashaport."

He thought this was screamingly funny, though neither of the other Turks laughed.

At another meal I began baiting them about the Greeks. We had just been to Cyprus and seen the misery of the Turks on this divided island. And what about the Armenians?

"Ignorant people in Turkey might say things," Fikret said. "But if you live with Greeks and Armenians you see they are good people. You understand them. Prejudice is ignorance."

"I agree," Onan said.

"And people who live far away from them have images of them that are untrue. But we like them."

"But what about their Turkophobia?" I said.

"That is understandable," Fikret said. "Why should we blame them? Armenians too – we should understand, though I am sorry to say they believe that part of Anatolia belongs to them."

In spite of my needling, the only criticism they offered was that it was said that Greeks and Armenians did not trust each other. "But we don't know if this is true."

It was relaxing to travel among people with so few prejudices, who were so ready to laugh, who could let themselves be mercilessly interrogated by me. They had a rare quality for people so individualistic – politeness. I also believed Samih Pasha when he claimed that Turkish soldiers were brave. Many had been sent to Korea, to fight on the US side in the Korean war. Some had been captured and, refusing to talk, had died under torture.

I thought I might tap a vein of cruelty if I spoke about capital punishment. Mentioning the candidates in the US elections who had campaigned advocating hanging-and-flogging policies, I asked how they would vote.

"I am a military man – a general," Samih Pasha said. "All my life my job was to kill people. But I am against all hanging."

"Because it is cruel?" I asked.

"It is cruel, yes, but it is also unjust," he said. "That is most important. How can you be so sure? And for people to be sentenced and then wait ten or fifteen years on appeal is horrible."

"In Iran they do it all the time," Fikret said.

I said, "We do too."

"But not so much," Onan said.

"Clinton believes in it," I said, and told him the Florida and Texas figures; that thirty-seven states had the death penalty; and that New York was probably going to get it, as their new governor had promised it.

The Turks were silent. Samih Pasha said, "Terrible."

That night the storm grew worse, and Istanbul was still two days off. Fikret got seasick. "I don't like this weather," he said. "I think I should get off the ship in Izmir." It was not only a rough sea with a stiff wind, the air temperature had dropped. Just a few days ago we had been in the heat of Haifa, and now everyone was wearing heavy clothes and complaining.

The Turkish songs in the lounge after dinner were tremulous and plangent and repetitive, and all of them in their lovelorn way reminded me (in Samih Pasha's translations) of how long I had been away. The musicians played: a drum, a zither, a violin, a clarinet; and the sad woman sang,

> The months are passing –
> I am waiting.

> Why don't you come?
> Don't leave me alone . . .

The Turks sat mournfully listening, eating ice cream, drinking coffee.

> Every night
> I want to stroke your hair
> Every night
> To touch it
> Your hair
> Every night.

At Izmir I hurried into town and called Honolulu and was reassured. I strolled to the bazaar and sat under a grape arbor and had lunch, a fish kebab and salad. I read an item in the *Turkish Daily News* which said that the government was thinking of doing away with "virginity tests on female students and the expulsion of 'unchaste' ones from school." Virginity tests?

In the afternoon the *Akdeniz* sailed into another storm, and Fikret hugged himself in misery on deck, regretting that he had not gotten off at Izmir and taken a train back to Ankara. With fewer people on board (half had disembarked at Izmir, including Samih Pasha and Onan), the ship had a somber air; and the cold weather made the mood bleak. The next day in the iron-colored Sea of Marmara under a gray sky it was even worse.

I stood with Fikret at the rail. The sea air, however cold, was fresher than the foul air down below on this ship of chain-smokers. We passed Üsküdar, where Florence Nightingale had tended the sick during the Crimean War; it was now a prison. That gave me an excuse to ask Fikret the ultimate Turkish question.

"Do you think they torture people in Üsküdar?"

He shrugged. The movement of his shoulders meant "probably."

"How do you know?"

"All countries torture," he said.

I let this pass. I asked, "What do they do in Turkey?"

"Beating on the feet — bastinado," he said. The word was

precisely right, and I was amazed that he knew it. "Also electricity and hanging by arms."

"This would be, what? Crucifixion?" I said, as blandly as I could manage.

"Whatever," he said. "To get information."

I said, "But people lie under torture, so what good is it?"

He got agitated, and his seasickness made him groggy. He repeated that everyone did it. He said, "The Germans executed the whole Baader-Meinhof gang in prison and then called it a mass suicide!"

"I think it was suicide."

"The British government tortures Irish people!" he said.

"They used to," I said. "But it was sleep deprivation — keeping prisoners awake at night to question them. And I think they used noise, too."

"That is worse than the bastinado!" Fikret cried. "That can make you lose your mind!"

He looked at me reproachfully. He was seasick and upset, and I had offended him by taking advantage of our friendship to ask him nosy questions. But that was the nature of my traveling: a quest for detail, conversation as a form of ambush, the traveler as an agent of provocation.

The mood passed as Istanbul came into view, a whole hill of exotic features — the palace, the minarets, the domes, the steeples, the tower; and below it the bridge, and the water traffic in the Golden Horn.

"I am going home," Fikret said.

"I hope you find that woman you're looking for."

"Yes," he said, and gulped as he tried to swallow his anxiety. "And where are you going?"

"Two weeks ago I was headed for Syria, when I saw this ship leaving and decided to join it," I said. "Now I really am going to Syria."

15

The 7:20 Express to Latakia

There was undoubtedly a more hallucinogenic experience available in poppy-growing Turkey than a long bus ride through Central Anatolia, though it was hard for me to imagine what this might be after a twenty-three-hour trip in the sulfurous interior of a bus of chain-smoking Turks, as day became twilight, turned to night, the moon passing from one side of the bus to the other, gleaming briefly in the snow of the Galatia highlands, fog settling and dispersing like phantasms, glimpses of dervishes, day dawning again, another stop, more yogurt, children crying in the back seats, full daylight in Iskenderun, rain in Antioch, all windows shut, the stale smoke condensing in brown bitter slime on the closed windows as fresh blue fumes rose from forty-nine burning cigarettes in this sleepless acid trip on the slipstream of second-hand smoke.

Being Turks, the smokers were courteous. I was repeatedly offered a cigarette. *Yes, plenty for you – please take two!*

On a train I would have been scribbling. That is impossible on a bus, which is only good for reading. I was jammed in a seat, a pain in my lower back that crept to my shoulder blades as we bumped from Ankara to Adana. I retreated into books. I re-read the whole of *Hindoo Holiday*. I read Maugham's short novel, *Up at the Villa*. I read *Myles Away from Dublin*, by Flann O'Brien. I read *The Man Who Mistook His Wife for a Hat*.

In the blue haze of cigarette smoke I reflected on the warning I had had not to take this long route through Turkey.

"What's the worst thing that can happen?" I asked.

"That the bus will be stopped by Kurds and you'll be dragged out and held hostage," said my knowledgeable friend.

That happened frequently in south-eastern Turkey, near enough to my route for me to be alarmed. Also, I was headed for Syria, a country very friendly towards the embattled Kurdish people.

"*Gechmis olsen.* May it be behind you."

But it had seemed a matter of urgency that I leave. Istanbul was also having its problems. In the previous few days in the Istanbul suburb of Gaziosmanpasha there had been a riot between Muslim fundamentalists and the somewhat schismatic and more liberal-minded Alevi sect. The matter had started with a drive-by shooting – fundamentalists plinking at Alevis at a café. Two Alevis dead. Then rival mobs gathered. Twenty-one people had been killed and many more wounded, mostly by the police and commandos who had intervened. Encircling the rioting mobs the police began firing at each other, like Keystone kops using live ammo.

The funerals that followed were massive parades of screeching mourners, and hundreds of police and soldiers. At the same time more riots broke out on the Asian side of the Bosphorus, at Umraniye. That resulted in eight dead, twenty-five wounded and "400 listed as missing" – so the local newspaper said. There was more rioting in Ankara: more funerals, much more disorder. Buses and ferries, bearing furious or sullen passengers, heading from the Asian side were halted and turned back. In other parts of Istanbul there was fighting between fundamentalists and Alevis.

"A foreign power is behind this," said Mrs Çiller, the Turkish Prime Minister. She meant Iran, but Greece was also blamed for "withholding information."

"What next?" I asked my Turkish friends.

"After Friday prayers tomorrow there's supposed to be trouble, when people come out of the mosques."

I said, "Then I think I will leave on Friday, before prayers."

The ticket from Istanbul to the Syrian border was twenty-five dollars. It seemed a bargain until the bus filled with smoke. And because the weather was cold, the windows stayed shut.

"Ten years ago this was all open fields," a Turk named Rashid said to me on the bus.

It was all high-rise housing now, and no trees, and in the bare stony fields tent camps had been put up by gypsies – the tents made of blue plastic sheeting – and these urban poor, with their ponies and dogs, fought for space with the Turks in the tenements.

These were the Alevi neighborhoods. Rashid was a believer. Among his beliefs was metempsychosis, the transmigration of souls. Rashid as a good Alawite might be reborn as a star in the Milky Way. A bad Alawite might end up back on earth as a Christian or a Jew. He worshipped sun and fire – a legacy of Zoroastrianism. Orthodox Islam was based on five pillars – prayers, the Hajj, the Ramadan fast, charity and the confession of faith. Rashid rejected these. It was only later, in Syria, that I was told that one of the more peculiar Alawite beliefs is that women do not possess souls. It seemed just as peculiar to me that Alawites believed that men, and especially Alawite men, had souls.

Altogether it was not surprising, perhaps, that the fundamentalists, who had contrived to follow an equally bizarre but different set of beliefs and symbols, had declared war on them.

Speaking of symbols, the bus passed a market where a man was selling cucumbers. The cucumber is a potent symbol in Turkey. *Hiyar* – cucumber – is a synonym for penis. One of my Turkish friends had said to me, "No one uses the word cucumber in Turkish, because of the vulgar associations." It was a bit like an English speaker being very careful to give a context when using the loaded word "balls." But in Turkish a whole set of euphemisms was substituted for cucumber. Most people called them "salad things" (*salatalik*) so as not to offend polite taste.

Every so often there is a bomb scare in Turkey, sometimes involving the American Embassy. A telephone threat is made, a location is described. A man describing himself as a bomber hangs up. Then the counter-terrorists go into action. Sophisticated thermal imaging equipment is brought to bear on an ominous-looking parcel left in a doorway. As many as a hundred men might surround the parcel, to provide cover for those disarming it. In many instances the bomb-disposal experts find a large ripe cucumber in the parcel, with a note saying, *This is what you are!*

A television set at the front of the bus began showing a violent video of a sub-Rambo sort, all explosions, gunfire and mutilation. I read *Hindoo Holiday*. I gagged on the cigarette smoke. The smoke gave me a headache. If the bus were stopped by Kurds they would look for a foreigner (so I was told) and find only me. I would be held captive and used with the utmost brutality. I wondered whether the Kurds smoked? If not, being their prisoner did not seem so bad.

After dark, at a cold windy pit-stop, I bought a glass of yogurt.

"What did you pay for that?" Rashid asked me.

"Twenty thousand," I said. Fifty cents.

"Life is so expensive here," he said. "In Antakya you could get that for eight thousand." Twenty cents.

He was making a return trip. He had arrived in Istanbul the day before to receive an order for his metalworking shop in Antakya. To save money he slept at the bus station and came straight back. He hated Istanbul anyway.

"And these," he said, waving a pack of cigarettes. "Fifty thousand! Go ahead, take one –"

I read *Up at the Villa*, in which a pretty widow gets a proposal of marriage from a distinguished man about to take an important post in India. She needs time to think about it. The man departs. That night the woman goes to a party, where a young rascal proposes marriage to her. She laughs at him, saying she does not believe in love, but would like to use her beauty and make an unfortunate man happy for just one night. That same night she picks up an impoverished man who had been a waiter at the party. She takes him to her villa, prepares a meal for him, makes love to him, and then tells him why. The young man is so insulted he shoots himself. She panics and calls the rascal, who helps her get rid of the body. The distinguished man is scandalized when he hears what has happened, and the pretty widow ends up with the rascal, who spirits her away before the body is found.

I liked the idea of a great scheme (marriage to an ambitious and successful man) being undone by a single unthought-out act, but this frantic night was unbelievable. And I objected to the book because it did not sufficiently remove me from the irritating reality of noxious smoke and bad air and coughing passengers and the lurching bus.

Into Ankara, out again, through mountain passes, under snowy cliffs, past cold fields where low fog had gathered in ghostly wisps, and onward between black crags, and above it all a huge ivory cue-ball moon.

"I worked in Saudi Arabia," a man named Fatih told me at another pit-stop in the darkness. "I went to Mecca and Medina."

"So you made the Hajj?"

"No, no, no. If you do that, you can't drink alcohol and what-not afterwards."

He would purify himself with a Hajj some other time, when he was older, and past any carnal desire.

We eventually came to the middle of Turkey, Tuz Gölü, a great lake, with the moon gleaming upon it; and another stop at two in the morning in cold clammy Aksaray, an area well known for its desolation and monotony and mud houses. I stood and stamped my feet and took deep breaths, and then re-boarded and read *The Man Who Mistook His Wife for a Hat*, a collection of neurological case-histories. It was a salutary book – Oliver Sacks is full of sympathy for afflicted strangers and he usually determines that these people have developed strengths and gifts as compensation for the supposed defects. Also: "There is often a struggle, and sometimes more interestingly a collusion between the power of pathology and creation." That was certainly true. If you were happy and normal, why would you ever want to write a book? Indeed, why would you be on this bus at all? There was an aspect of dementia to the act of writing as there was to a desire to travel, but as Sacks pointed out, dementia was nothing to be ashamed of, and indeed was often a useful spur to imaginative or creative acts.

As I read this book, dayspring in the shape of a rising tide of pinkness gathered in the sky over the low hills of Anatolia, and the moon still showed in the clear sky. Then, towards Adana, bright daylight heated the bus, and field workers and vegetable-pickers traipsed down the road all bundled up, carrying hoes. Farther on, people bent double were already working in the fields. This green and fertile part of Turkey was chilly and sunny and flat, in the delta of the Ceyhan river, the tucked-in corner of the Mediter-ranean, next to the Bay of Iskenderun.

Iskenderun itself, its puddled streets lined with thick palm trees, lay at the foot of a range of the dark Amarus Mountains, and beyond its small houses and its onion fields was the sea again, small waves slapping, the surface hardly disturbed, like the shore of a lake. It was the old sloppy Mediterranean Sea, not a body of water with many moods, but looking shallow and tame and almost exhausted. There was no fishing here, not even any swimming. And this place which Alexander the Great had founded after a great battle – until fairly recently it had been known as Alexandretta – was just a little tile-roofed town. Its beach was littered with wind-blown trash and dumped junk; when "the Lord spake unto the fish, and it vomited Jonah upon the dry land," that land was reputedly this very beach. But here, as elsewhere, the sea is now no more than a backdrop to olive groves and fruit trees.

This province, Hatay, is disputed. The Syrians claim it as rightfully theirs, but the Turks control it. The people themselves speak a heavily guttural Arabized Turkish, and the markets both in Iskenderun and in Antakya – where I gave up and got off the bus and, followed by hawkers and small boys, staggered through the market to a hotel – seemed as Middle Eastern as it was possible to be, without many veils.

Recovering from the bus ride to this town on the border of Syria, I stayed here in Antioch for a night and the next day hiked from monument to monument – the Roman bridge, the mosque and aqueduct, the church of St Peter. There were ruined fortresses outside the town, and one of them, the castle of Cursat, had been built by Crusaders.

More impressive to me than anything else was the market at Antakya, which was almost medieval in its bustle and its mud, small boys quarreling and fooling among the fruit and meat stalls, and the full, floppy costumes of the country people, the women in pantaloons and shawls, the men with beards and gowns. The commerce was brisk – the selling of fruit and fish, the retailing of tonics and potions – and it was also a meeting-place of people from the mountains and the seashore, from Turkey and Syria and Lebanon. It was not a covered bazaar but rather a large area of rough ground, where people were yakking and striking deals and watching staticky television and talking over bundles and sacks of lemons and heaped-up blankets; boys rushed around selling glasses of tea on trays, or dried fruits and nuts from barrows. Cripples, beggars, beards, deformed people with boils and knobs on their faces, all the sects of Islam, and mud puddles and flaming braziers and the sizzle of meat, and a great sense of filth and life.

In this remote place people came up to me, often either a shaven-headed boy or else a hobbling old man, and they greeted me in Turkish, asking "*Saat kach?*" ("What time is it?") because I was wearing a wrist-watch. I was perversely gratified because they had asked in Turkish, which proved that my long bus trip had had the effect of making me as rumpled and muddy as the rest of them. So I went about feeling anonymous and happy. The disciples of Jesus spent a year in Antioch preaching and it was in Antioch (Acts 11.26) that, perhaps in answer to a puzzled question, "What sort of Jews are you?", they first began to call themselves "Christians."

Looking for another bus to the Syrian coast I was told that the western border was closed and that I would have to enter Syria by the Bab el Howa – the Gate of the Wind – and proceed to Aleppo, before heading for Latakia, on the coast. It was hundreds of miles out of my way, but it was all right with me. I had been told that Aleppo was a pleasant place with a famous bazaar. And there was a railway train from there through the mountains to the Mediterranean.

There were only four of us on the Aleppo bus. Turks are not welcome in Syria, and not many Syrians ever get across the border. I sat with Yusof, a talkative and untruthful-seeming Tunisian who gave me several conflicting reasons for going to Syria.

"See this? Tunisian passport," he said, shuffling the thing. "And this is an Iraqi passport. Why? Ha! You have so many questions."

But even when I stopped asking questions he volunteered some strange information.

"I have a US visa. I have lived in Verona. You speak Italian? *Buon giorno!* I sell gold – no, not always."

The young couple making up the four were Turks from Bulgaria. They sat holding hands, looking nervous.

We passed through a pretty countryside, the road just wide enough for one vehicle, poplars and stone cottages, and plowed fields, and soon the Syrian border – the no-man's land, fenced with barbed wire, the meadows filled with crimson poppies and leggy asphodels.

"That is a Kurdish village," Yusof said, indicating a cluster of huts. How did he know that? Farther along the narrow road he said, "Mister, have you been to Israel?"

I hedged, and denied it, and Yusof smoked and told me a few more lies, and the bus broke down.

The problem was the fuel line. The driver yanked up the floorboards and played with some rubber tubes, blowing on them. An hour passed. I got out and marveled at the wild-flowers, and then sat and scribbled some notes. Another hour passed. The sky was gray. Surely the border would be closed if we waited too long? I was pacing up and down the side of the road, though the others, fatalistic Muslims, simply sat and waited.

"Yusof, why don't we flag down the next car that comes through and take it to the border."

"Best thing, mister, is be very careful," he said. And he pointed cautiously and became conspiratorial. "Over there is Syria. That is another country. You hear what I am saying? Another country. So we wait."

The driver tried the engine. It farted and died. He kept trying, stamping on the accelerator, twisting the key. I reckoned that very soon the battery would be dead. But after some minutes he fired it up and we got aboard and jogged along to Turkish customs. That was simple enough, a rubber stamp, a farewell. But the Syrian border was an obstacle course.

Yusof said, "Be careful."

Now I noticed how weirdly he was dressed, in a shiny shirt and flared pants and clopping high-heeled shoes and gold chains around his neck and dense sunglasses. In spite of this, he was doing his best to be inconspicuous.

A small number of people jostled for attention at a desk, where a bored and rather indifferent soldier ignored them. I thrust my passport over their heads and, as though amused by my insolence, he snatched it and said, "American!" and laughed. I did not see my passport again for about an hour.

In the meantime, I found Yusof lurking. He said he wanted to buy me a drink. We had coffee, while he held a chattering conversation with some Syrians. I noticed that there were large portraits of President Assad all over the frontier. He was a man with an odd profile – beaky nose, big chin, surmounted by the squarest head I had ever seen. His portrait at its most accurate was like a cartoon parody: misshapen and villainous. His comb-over hairdo varied from portrait to portrait. His suit was too tight, his neck too thin, his tie ridiculous, his smile insipid. As for his politics (to quote 1 Kings 11), "He was an adversary to Israel . . . and he abhorred Israel, and reigned over Syria."

But there was another portrait − a younger man, with a slim, stubbly face and sunglasses and army fatigues.

"Who's that, Yusof?"

"No," he said, meaning, *Don't ask*. He paddled with one hand in a cautioning gesture.

The delay at the border today was caused by a group of Syrians smuggling shirts and pants in large suitcases. The absurdity of it was that while these smugglers opened their cases, revealing stacks of shirts in plastic bags, huge trucks rumbled past. They were German, and they were loaded with crates of German machinery, from a firm called Mannesmann. The crates were stamped *For the Ministry of Technology, Baghdad, Iraq*. Six of these vast flat-bed trucks. They were headed towards Iraq, through Syria − and they were waved through by Syrian soldiers. It seemed to make little difference to anyone that Iraq was subject to UN sanctions and such a shipment of German machine parts was illegal. In the meantime the shirt-smugglers were bullied and denounced.

Yusof took me aside. He put his hand over his mouth and muttered, "That is Assad's son. He died. Don't talk."

We were summoned to the office and handed our passports. And then we were on our way. Those men wearing dark glasses and sipping tea, Yusof said, they were not travelers. They were members of the *mukhabarat* − Syria's secret police. All this in a whisper, Yusof's hand over his mouth.

"Here I like," Yusof said. We were in a rocky landscape, with wide stripes of green. "Aleppo is good. I drink. I eat. I disco. I fuck. But" − he leaned over − "I don't talk."

Across the low hills some miles farther on were minarets and a citadel on a bluff, and squat buildings: Aleppo. After all the small towns and villages of Turkish Hatay, this was like my myopic mirage, the distant vision which blurs and produces a sort of Middle East capriccio, blending beautiful rotting buildings with ugly new ones, the whole of it sifted and sprinkled with dust. Many places in the eastern Mediterranean looked that way to me, a hotchpotch of building styles surmounted by earthen-colored domes and the slender pencils of minarets.

"Come with me," Yusof said. "I know this place."

"I'm busy," I said.

We were standing by the roadside, among honking taxis and buses, and within sight of twelve billboard-sized portraits of President Hafez Assad, Father of the Nation. But that was not as odd as the smaller but far more numerous portraits of his son. They were pasted to walls and to poles, they were airbrushed and stenciled on to masonry, they were stuck in every shop window; and every car in Aleppo displayed the young man's picture, many of them gilt-framed, on a rear-window shrine.

"You're busy?" Yusof looked very puzzled, which was my intention.

It's that man again, I thought, and asked Yusof his name.

He gave me a pained smile, and I realized that I did not need a ruse to drive him away. All I had to do was ask him my usual questions.

Yusof covered his mouth, and on the pretext of drawing on a cigarette, he muttered, "His son." Yusof, although not Syrian, had the superstitious Syrian horror of speaking Assad's name. He glanced around and added, "His name is Basil."

"Basil?"

A wild look distorted Yusof's features. I had said it too loud. He compressed his face in a furtive frown for a moment and then hurried away.

The cult of Basil had taken possession of Syria. Though it was a touchy matter, and politically suspect, I looked into it a bit. It was not easy. Syrians were voluble about everything except matters pertaining to their president. They hung pictures of Assad everywhere, they looked at Assad's face constantly – that square head, that mustache, that insincere smile of fake benevolence, that hairpiece. A Syrian was never away from the gaze of this man. Assad had been staring at them for twenty-five years. He was as large as life and twice as ugly. But they rarely spoke about him, they almost never uttered his name.

"Big Brother is watching you," a witty young Arab woman said to me later in Damascus. His titles are Father-Leader (*El Ab el Khaad*), and also Comrade, Struggler, General Secretary, President, Commander of the Nation.

"Or you just put 'First' in front of a word and that is a title," a rebellious Syrian said to me in a low voice. "For example, First Teacher, First General, First Commander."

Like many torturers, dictators, monomaniacs and tyrants, the most sinister and popular of Assad's titles was "Friend." Recently he had given himself a new honorific: *Abu Basil* — "Father of Basil."

I asked Syrians to translate the inscriptions under Basil's portrait. *Basil the Martyr!* was very common. But they also said, *Staff Sergeant! Martyr! Cadet! Parachutist! Comrade! Beloved! Son! Knight!*

"Martyr" — *shaheed* — was an interesting word to use for the dead Basil. The term was full of Koranic implications, usually describing a warrior who is sacrificed to the faith, going smiling to his glorious reward in Allah's heaven. Palestinian suicide bombers are martyrs. Any victim of the Israeli secret police, the Mossad, is a martyr. The young man who knifed Naguib Mahfouz was described by his fanatic friends as a martyr after he was hanged in Cairo.

Basil's martyrdom took place in January 1994 on the road to Damascus airport as the young man, habitually driving fast, sped to catch a plane for Frankfurt where he was embarking on a skiing holiday in the Alps. He reached the speed of 150 miles per hour (the figure 240 km/hr was part of the mythology of Basil's death) and he lost control of his car, and was killed instantly when it crashed. He was thirty-two and was known as someone who liked fast cars. After forty days of mourning, an enormous statue was erected to him in his father's home village of Qardaha. The statue depicted the young man being propelled upward on a beam of light, his father (Father-Leader) standing at the bottom of the beam, and the son (Martyr, Cadet, Parachutist) taking flight.

A younger son, Bashar, twenty-nine, took Basil's place as his father's successor. He had been studying quietly in London. He was summoned home, and is now next in line to the throne of his dynastic-minded father. Meanwhile, Assad's rambunctious brother Rifaat (who, asserting the secularism of Syria, killed 20,000 of the Muslim Brotherhood in 1982 in Hamah) also has ambitions but keeps to himself in a villa on a hill outside Damascus. Rifaat's portrait is not to be seen anywhere.

I had arrived by road from rural Turkey and had been plunged into Syria, in the chaotic and friendly city of Aleppo. I liked it as soon as I arrived. But I was too tired to take in anything except the cult of Basil. I found a hotel and had a nap. I woke in the dark, then went back to sleep until the next day.

Aleppo was gritty, ramshackle, and not very big. It had busy, dusty streets, dust everywhere in this sprawling, itching place that is everyone's idea of a city in the Middle East, rotting and unthreatening, mysterious, filled with the smells of food and scorched oil and damp wool and decaying bricks. It was not like a city at all, but rather a large provincial town, with a mixed population of Arabs, Armenians, Kurds and even a community of Jews. It had landmarks – the park, the citadel, the bazaar, the mosque, the railway station. I took a bus to St Simeon's basilica. Simeon Stylites, as he is sometimes known, sat on a tall pillar for thirty years to mortify his flesh, haranguing the faithful from the top of his column.

I am not a pilgrim – I dislike the word in fact – and as with other religious sites I detected no odor of sanctity at St Simeon's, only a slight whiff of piety: humility, not holiness and the definite sense of theater that I had felt in Jerusalem. I had sensed this often in places reputed to be holy – not sanctity at all, but a turbulent suggestion of passion and conflict.

Back in the crooked streets of Aleppo I realized that what I liked best about the place was a liberating sense that everything in the city was reachable on foot. Also Syria had the worst telephone system I had so far seen in the Mediterranean, and so I was never tempted to use the phone or send a fax. This also freed me from worrying that I had anything urgent to attend to; communication with the outside world was impossible. It invigorated me to feel out of touch, and it concentrated my mind on where I was.

I had been anxious about my trip to the coast until I walked to the railway station – a funny little Frenchified station with the

usual Assad hagiography in any number of ludicrous murals – and
saw that there were three trains a day to Latakia. At the station I
engaged three young men – medical students – in a conversation
about the murals. They immediately clammed up and made eye
signals and hand gestures and all sorts of non-verbal suggestions to
change the subject. This was what Albania had been like under
"Friend" Hoxha.

It was not fidgeting caution but real fear – of, I supposed, the
mukhabarat. Until late in 1994 there were 6,000 political prisoners.
Assad released some old, sick prisoners, to impress the United
States and to make himself seem magnanimous. But it was clearly
not a country in which there was any dissent.

The pride of Aleppo is its bazaar, a vast covered souk criss-
crossed with narrow lanes and the usual demarcations – silver
here, gold there, carpets somewhere else; small, cramped neigh--
borhoods selling shoes, or scarves, or fruit, or spices. Tinsmiths,
weavers, glass-blowers. It served much more than its city. Everyone in northern Syria used the bazaar at Aleppo.

"Meester – I have sold nothing today. You must buy
something!"

Winter was colder in Syria than I had expected. The days
started almost frostily; at noon it was warm, then the temperature
dropped through the afternoon, and at night it was cold again,
everyone in sweaters and jackets. I decided to buy a scarf in the
bazaar, not a two-dollar polka-dot Palestinian keffieh to wrap
around my head, but perhaps the sort of five-dollar wool keffieh
that served the nomads.

One of the characteristics of a Middle Eastern bazaar is that
thirty stalls sell exactly the same merchandise, but the hawkers
differ in their sales pitch, which are thirty kinds of attitude ranging
from a silent glowering from a man squatting on his haunches at
the rear of the shop, sulking because you are walking past, to the
active nagging of the stall-holder chasing you and plucking your
sleeve – "Meester!"

I was looking for a warm scarf, but I was also looking for
English-speakers. I soon found five of them sitting among bolts of
silk.

"Come here, Meester! Hello! Good evening, and how are you?"

This man introduced himself as Alla-Aldin – "Aladdin" – Akkad, and his friends and colleagues, Moustafa, Mohammed, Ahmed and Lateef. They were all young and insolent-looking, yapping at each other.

"You are a French?"

"American," I said.

"You are a Yank," Akkad said. "That is what people call you. Please sit down. Drink some tea."

I intended to buy a scarf and therefore accepted the invitation. I would have been more careful in a carpet shop. I sat with them and we talked about the cold weather, how damp it was in the bazaar, my travels in Turkey, my impressions of Syria, and so forth.

Moustafa said, "Do you mind if we call you a Yank?"

"Not at all. But what do people call you?"

"They call us donkeys," Akkad said, "because of the donkeys wandering around the bazaar. We don't care. Donkeys are good animals. And we wander too."

"What do you call Turkish people?"

"'Mustache,'" Mohammed said. And to his friends, "Yes?" Akkad explained, "Because they all have mustaches."

"What about Egyptians?"

"We call them 'Take-Your-Watch,' because they are thieves."

"Jordanians?"

"'They-Only-See-Themselves,'" Moustafa said. "They are self-ish, they think about themselves all the time."

"What about Israelis?" I asked.

"Worse than Jordanians," Akkad said.

"'The sun shines out of their arseholes,' we say. It is an Arabic expression for snobbish," Moustafa said. "They think it, you see. So we call them 'arseholes' for short."

"I don't like to say this word," Akkad muttered. "But it's true they are very snobbish. They think they are better than everyone."

"Are you married?" Moustafa asked me.

"It's a long story," I said.

"I am married and so is he," Akkad said, indicating Moustafa. He pointed to Lateef, who apparently did not speak English – he smiled but said nothing. "He is a horse's hoof."

"Not a donkey?" I said.

"And I am a ginger beer," Akkad said. "Although I am married."

"I don't get it."

"It is slang," Akkad said, and took out a book. He wagged it at me and said, "This Yank does not understand!"

The book was titled *Australian Slang*, and it was inscribed to Akkad from Ray, an Australian, in big affectionate blue loopy handwriting.

"My old boy friend," Akkad said. He batted his eyelashes at me. "He was a traveler like you."

I leafed through the book of slang. *Horse's hoof – poof. Ginger beer – queer.* Over a year paddling in the Happy Isles and I get a lesson in Aussie slang from a Syrian in Aleppo?

"I get it," I said. "But didn't you say you were married?"

"Yes. I just found out I am a homosexual one month ago, after five years of married life."

"Isn't that a little inconvenient?" I asked.

"Only for my wife," Akkad said.

"But I like women," Moustafa said.

"I like men," Akkad said. "So does he. And he. And you see this man there" – another young man had paused in the lane of the bazaar to mutter to Lateef – "he was my boyfriend once. You see how he is ignoring me?"

"I agree with Moustafa," I said. "I prefer women."

"Women smell like omelets," Akkad said.

"Do you like omelets?"

"No," he said. "I like men. They smell like watermelons."

"'A woman for duty. A boy for pleasure. A melon for ecstasy.' Isn't that an Arab proverb?" I said.

"I have never heard it," Akkad said. "I don't understand."

Moustafa cupped his hands at his chest to suggest breasts and said, "I like these melons on a woman!"

"I don't like them," Akkad said. "How old are you?"

I told him.

"No," he said. "But if you are that old you must be happy. Very happy."

"Yes, he is happy," Moustafa said.

"I am happy," I said. And thought: Yes, drinking tea in this bazaar on a chilly evening in Aleppo, in the farthest corner of the Mediterranean, listening to their silly talk, sensing a welcome in it, the hospitality of casual conversation, feeling I could ask them almost anything and get an answer; I am happy.

"Why did you come here?" Akkad said.

"To buy a scarf," I said.

"I will not sell you a scarf now. Moustafa and Ahmed will not sell you a scarf. You know why? Because we want you to come back here tomorrow to talk with us."

"That's fine with me."

Later I went to a restaurant and had hot bread and hummus, baba ghanouj and eggplant, salad and spicy fish chunks. I was joined by a student, Ahmed Haj'Abdo, who was studying medicine at the Aleppo medical college. He said he wanted to get high marks, so that he could study abroad and specialize. I introduced the topic of Assad, hoping to get more colorful information about the cult of Basil. Mr Haj'Abdo got flustered and searched the restaurant desperately with his agitated eyes.

"Sorry," I said.

He just smiled and then we talked about the weather.

The next day, my last in Aleppo, I went back to Akkad and bought a head scarf and asked him the best way to Latakia. There were so many ways – buses, "pullman," minivans, taxis, shared cars, the train.

Akkad said, "The best way. You mean quickest? Safest? Most comfortable? Cheapest? What?"

"What does 'safest' mean?"

"The road is dangerous. It winds around the mountains. Sometimes the cars and buses go off the road and into the valleys. People die."

"Train is safest and best," Moustafa said.

"That's what I always say."

My first-class ticket to Latakia on the early train the next morning was two dollars.

There were a hundred or more Syrians in the waiting-room of the railway station the following morning. In cold countries that are poor there is often a sartorial strangeness, people dressed differently and weirdly, abandoning fashion for warmth. Syria this winter morning was that way. There were women in black drapes, their faces covered, looking like dark Shmoos, and others like nuns, and still more in old-fashioned dresses and old fur-trimmed coats. Men wore gowns and women wore quilted coats and many people wore leather jackets and odd hats. There were gypsies in brightly colored dresses, with thick skirts, and there were soldiers. The well-dressed and watchful secret police looked very secure and went about in pairs.

There was no such thing as a Syrian face. There were many faces, of a sort that was common in Europe and America – pale skin, red hair, blue eyes, as well as nose-heavy profiles and dark eyes and swarthy skin. Some could have been Spanish or French or even English. There was a Syrian Huck Finn face with freckles, and tousled hair. There was a Semitic face – nagging auntie with a mustache. There were people who looked like me. I was sure of this, because every so often I was approached and asked questions in Arabic, and the questioner was puzzled and abashed when I replied in English.

It was a cold sunny day in Aleppo, six in the morning, hardly anyone on the street, and so the rats were bold, foraging in the gutters as I kicked along noisily to keep them away. I wore a sweater and a jacket and a scarf. The rats ran ahead of me, nibbling garbage. One scampered on, glancing back at me at intervals, and panting, like an over-excited pet.

The 7:20 express to Latakia was a beat-up train, with terrible coaches in second class and passable ones in first. But all the windows were so dirty it was hard to see out, and many were cracked, the sort of dense spider web of cracks that prevented anything from being clearly visible.

With my notebook on my lap, I wrote about the fellows in the bazaar and then, because I was short of books, re-read *The Man Who Mistook His Wife for a Hat*, the chapter on "street neurology," thinking how resourceful Oliver Sacks was in walking the streets of New York City, diagnosing the ills of the people raving or chattering. In another place he quoted Nietzsche: "I have traversed many kinds of health, and keep traversing them . . . And as for sickness: are we not almost tempted to ask whether we could get along without it? Only great pain is the ultimate liberator of the spirit."

The ticket-collector wore a dark suit and well-shined shoes and he smoked a cigarette. In his entourage were two soldiers and two flunkies. He snapped his fingers at each passenger, and under the gaze of the soldiers – who were fat older men, straight out of Sergeant Bilko's motor pool – he directed one of his flunkies to retrieve the ticket. Without touching it he examined it, and the second flunky tore it and returned it to the passenger. Five men, each with a particular role: a miniature bureaucracy in the aisle of the railway train.

Many offices I had seen in Syria were like that: several people doing one job, consulting, discussing, sharing the problem; or just being social, drinking tea, smoking, taking no responsibility.

Showing through the cracked windows of the train the suburbs of Aleppo had a fragmented and cubist quality, a wall of tenements as assorted puzzle pieces. We were soon in the countryside, and the Syrian countryside in the mountains that rise parallel to the west coast, the Jebel al Nusayriyah, is among the loveliest in the Mediterranean. Eastern and southern Syria is desert, but this was a landscape of green cozy valleys and stone cottages – gardens, shepherds, wheat fields, olive groves and fruit trees. I had not expected such a fertile and friendly-looking land. Later, when I saw the desert, I realized that my stereotype was that – what the Syrians called the *sahara*, a limitless waste.

But here it was peaceful, meadows of sheep nibbling flowers. I had expected gun emplacements and artillerymen glowering through binoculars, not these stolid rustics clopping along on donkeys, and the lovely white villages of small domed houses; each settlement, surrounded by plowed fields, had a well and a market and a mosque.

A man strode through my railway car, climbed on to a seat, removed a light bulb from a ceiling fixture, and plugged in a tape deck. For the rest of the trip he fed tapes of screechy music into this machine.

The meadows in the distance were like crushed velvet, and seen closer they were scattered with wild-flowers and banked by stands of sturdy blue-green pines. Even that loud music could not distract me from admiring a landscape I had never seen or heard about, and the thrill was that it was ancient, biblical-looking, the land of conquering, slaughtering David and the Valley of Salt. At Jisrash Shugur on the Orontes river there were flowers everywhere and the town itself lay on the crest of a distant hill, as white as the white stone ridge it was built upon. We were hardly any distance from the Turkish border, and passing alongside it, but these villages were not at all like Turkish ones either in the design of their houses or in the way the people were dressed.

We penetrated the big green mountain range on our way to the shore, and circled the slopes of these peculiarly Middle Eastern-looking heights – so old were they, having been mountains for so long, so tame and rounded, they seemed domesticated by the people who had been trampling them and letting their goats and sheep canter over them, nibbling them since the beginning of the world. They were gentle slopes, with soft cliffs and unthreatening gullies and no peaks, green all over, with pine woods and villages in their valleys. They were not at all like the fierce mountains in the wilderness, with their sharp peaks and sheer cliffs and their raw and serrated ridges and their cliff faces gleaming like the metal of a knife blade.

That was something that I had learned about the Mediter-ranean. There was not a single point anywhere on the whole irregular shore that had not known human footprints. Every inch of it had been charted and named – most places had two or three names, some had half a dozen, an overlay of nomenclature, especi-ally here in the tendentious and rivalrous republics of the Levant, that could be very confusing.

Three and a half hours after leaving Aleppo we were speeding across a flat sunny plain of date palms and orange and olive trees, towards Latakia. It had been a long inland detour, but I was back on the shore of the Mediterranean.

I walked from the station to the center of Latakia and found a hotel. After lunch, I walked to the port. I was followed and pestered by curb-crawling taxis in which young men sat and honked their horns. The only way to discourage them was to hire one – and anyway, I wanted to go north of Latakia, to see the ruins of Ugarit.

That was how I met Riaz, an unreliable man with an unreliable car. He spoke a little English. Yes, he knew Ugarit. Yes, we would go there. But first he had a few errands to run. This allowed me to see the whole of Latakia in a short time. It was not an attractive place. The only beach was some miles outside the city at the laughably named Côte d'Azur, where on an empty road a deserted hotel, the Meridien, sat on a muddy shore. That area had the melancholy of all bad architectural ideas exposed to the full glare of the sun.

"Who is that?" I asked Riaz as we passed statues of Assad. There were many statues of Father-Leader here.

Riaz laughed, but it was a nervous laugh. It was not a joking matter to stare at the statues, however silly they seemed. One statue in Latakia showed Assad hailing a taxi – his hand raised. In another he was beckoning   "I have a bone to pick with you, sonny!" – and in yet another he looked, with both arms out, like a deranged man about to take a dive into a pool, fully clothed. "I will crush you like this!" could have been inscribed on the plinth of a statue which depicted Assad clasping his hands rather violently, and a statue at the abandoned sports complex at Latakia showed the Commander of the Nation with his arm up, palm forward, in a traffic cop's gesture of "Stop!".

Any country which displays more than one statue of a living politician is a country which is headed for trouble. Leaving aside the fact that nature had not endowed this spindle-shanked and wispy haired man in his tight suit to be cast in bronze, the unflattering statues still seemed provocative and irritating. In a hard-up place how could anyone be indifferent or willingly justify such expenditure? Syria was another country, like those of Mao and Stalin and Hoxha, of silly semaphoring statues of the same foolish old man, and in time to come they too would end up being bulldozed on to a scrap heap.

"What is his name?" I asked Riaz.

Riaz said, "Ha! Ha! Ha!" and looked wildly around in the traffic.

Two or three miles north of the city was Ras Shamrah. It had been an unimportant village until, in 1928, a farmer plowing on a nearby hill bumped his plow blade against the top edge of a symmetrical wall, buried in the ground. Further digging revealed it to be the wall of a large building, a palace in fact, and in time the foundations of an entire city were uncovered, thirty-six hectares of a royal town which was dug up in stages throughout the 1930s. That sort of discovery – even the detail of the plow-blade – had happened many times before in the Middle East (and it was also a poor farmer in China who – with a hoe – found the terracotta warriors at Xian); peasant plowmen were probably the world's first archeologists. But Ugarit yielded a real treasure in the form of small bead-like clay tablets on which was inscribed the precursor of the alphabet I am using now. (Guidebook: "The writing on the tablets is widely accepted as being the earliest known alphabet. It was adapted by the Greeks, then the Romans, and it is from this script that all alphabets are derived.") There were trinkets, too, bracelets and beads and spear points and knives; but the implications of the tablets the shape and size of a child's finger bone were the earliest examples of human jotting.

Ali the caretaker apologized before charging me four dollars in Syrian piastres – it was almost his week's pay – to look at the ruins. And he followed me, pointing to the crumbled walls and weedy plots, saying, "Palace . . . library . . . well . . . aqueduct . . . flight of stairs . . . house . . . archway . . . stables . . . mausoleum . . ."

It was no more than a mute ground-plan, spread over several hills, where with their narrow hooves balanced on the flinty walls goats cropped grass and pretty poppies grew wild. Having been excavated, it had been so neglected it was becoming overgrown, with rubble obscuring many of the walls; no pathways, no signs, no indication at all of what had been what. Ugarit ("once the greatest city in the entire Mediterranean") was turning back into a buried city. It had been looted of all its trinkets and artifacts – they were on display in the Damascus museum.

I liked being here alone, and felt it was all a throwback to an earlier time on the Mediterranean shore, when a traveler might stumble upon an ancient site and be shown around by a simple soul who lived nearby. The temples and villas of rural Italy, and Carthage and Pompeii, and the ancient marble structures of Greece, had once been treated like this – just crumbling curiosities, where goats and sheep sheltered. Every so often a peasant would raid them for building blocks or marble slabs. That was definitely a feature of the Mediterranean – the temples turned into churches, the churches into ruins, the ruins buried until they became quarries for anyone who wanted to build a hut. In the eighteenth and nineteenth centuries – we have the evidence of splendid engravings – Greece and Italy looked just like Ugarit did today; the ruins were novelties, broken cellars and fallen walls and stairs leading nowhere and tombs robbed of their artifacts and bones.

Sitting on a wall to admire it – the sun on the flowers and the grass that grew higher than the ruins – I was approached by Ali again.

"Alphabet there!" he said.

He pointed to a small enclosure, where in a shady, muddy corner, in a clump of weeds, the tablets had been found. It was as though it was sacred ground. In a sense it had been hallowed, by printed words, some of the first in this hemisphere. Five thousand years had passed since then. And here, in Syria, the very place that had given the world this elegant script, half the people were still illiterate.

On the way back to town, I asked Riaz, "Are there any ships that go from here to Cyprus?"

"No."

"Are you sure?"

"No."

"So can I get a ship to Cyprus from Latakia?"

"I think."

"You think yes?"

"I think no."

He was right – no ferries ran any more, though there were plenty of container ships in the port. The town was small and tidy and sunny, and with vaguely European architecture, unlike cold, dusty and oriental Aleppo. It seemed to me amazing that in the space of a single morning I had passed from one climate to another; and not only the weather here, but aspects of the atmosphere, were identical to a hundred other places I had seen on the Mediterranean shore. Latakia was another example of a town that had much more in common with a port in Greece or Albania or Sardinia than any of its own inland towns, the sunny Mediterranean culture of the languor, the bougainvillea and palms and stucco houses, the seaside promenade.

"You want to see Lateen?"

He meant a Christian church, a Latin. (Christians in Syria are called *Masihi* for their belief in the Messiah.) There was one in Latakia, a Frenchified two-steeple cathedral dating perhaps from the 1930s. (The French had controlled Syria from 1926 until independence in 1946.) There was a sense of life in Latakia that was self-contained; the town was seldom visited by any foreigners – foreigners hardly came to Syria and when they did they kept to Damascus and avoided the rather stagnant and vandalized coast. Better than any bricks and mortar were the tangerines and oranges of Latakia. I paid off Riaz, and bought some fruit, and walked the streets, and went to bed early.

Sixty miles down the coast, two hours on the slow bus, was Tartus, a new town enclosing an ancient walled city. I walked around it and thought: How has it changed? The people still lived among goat turds and foul garbage piles and they scrubbed their laundry in wash-tubs and hung it from their windows, where the sun struck through the archways. The children played in the narrow lanes where open drains bore foul water to the sewers. Rats darted between bricks and in the ruined nave of a church there was more laundry. There were old and new parts of the walled city, but it was hard to tell them apart. People had extended the old houses, added rooms and stairways and vaulted ceilings and cubicles. Old men still sat under the arches of the city gate. I imagined that people here on the Syrian coast had more or less always lived like this, apparently higgledy-piggledy, but actually with great coherence, using all the available space, protected by the city walls and the privacy of their solid stone houses, this honeycomb of an old town.

There was an island just offshore called Arwad. I wanted to look at it, but I could not find any boatman willing to take me there. So I walked along the beach. Tartus had the filthiest beach I had seen anywhere in the entire Mediterranean: it was mud and litter and sewage and oil slick. Perhaps that too was just as it had always been, the disorder and filth and carelessness. Swimming as a recreation and the craze for a suntan were recent novelties. In terms of its being regarded as an enormous sewer by the people who lived on its shore, the Mediterranean was perhaps no different from any other sea in the world.

"The sea in Western culture represents space, vacancy, primordial chaos," Jonathan Raban wrote to me, when I asked him why every sea on earth is treated like a toilet. Jonathan, one of my oldest friends, was the editor of *The Oxford Book of the Sea*. The biblical "waters" implying emptiness and chaos is specifically the Mediterranean. Jonathan indicated a passage in *The Enchaféd Flood* in which Auden warmed to this theme of the disorderly sea: "The sea, in fact, is that state of barbaric vagueness and disorder out of which civilization has emerged and into which, unless saved by the efforts of gods and men, it is always liable to relapse. It is so little of a friendly symbol that the first thing which the author of the Book of Revelation notices in his vision of the new heaven and earth at the end of time is that '*there was no more sea.*'"

"Put rubbish into it, and it magically disappears," Jonathan said. "Water being the purifying element, you can't pollute it – by definition." Before the middle of the eighteenth century, "the sea was a socially invisible place; a space so bereft of respectable life that it was like a black hole. What you did in or on the sea simply didn't count, which is partly why the seaside became known as a place of extraordinary license." And he went on, "The sea wasn't – isn't – a place; it was undifferentiated space. It lay outside of society, outside of the world of good manners and social responsibilities. It was also famously the resort of filthy people – low-caste types, like fishermen ... It was a social lavatory, where the dregs landed up."

Nothing held me in Tartus. Wishing to see the great Crusader castle known variously as the Krac des Chevaliers and Qal'at al-Husn, I made a deal with a taxi-driver named Abdullah who said he would take me there and then on to Homs, where I could get a bus or a train to Damascus.

"Lebanon!" he cried out after twenty minutes or so, gesturing towards the dark hills to the south.

And then he turned north off the road and headed for the heights of the mountain range that protected the interior of Syria and commanded a view of the whole coast. At a strategic point, above the only valley that allowed access, was the most beautiful castle imaginable. After a childhood spent reading fairy-tales, and believing in valiant deeds, and associating with them every act of love, chivalry, piety and valor – however specious they seemed in retrospect – it is impossible to belittle the Crusader castles of the Mediterranean, the scenes where such deeds were first defined for such a child as I was.

The knight in armor, a sword in one hand, his crested flag in the other, is such a potent symbol of virtue that I never questioned it. I was inspired by the fantasy and the idea, not the historical truth of the Crusader knights. To a great extent, Westerners derive their notions of self-sacrifice and morality and romantic love from stories of the Crusaders – and incidentally our prejudices against Muslims and Jews – and a sense of style, too, of jousting and armor and pennants and castles. The Krac was the epitome of that sort of dream castle, with ramparts and dungeons and symmetrical fortifications, and a chapel and stately watch-towers.

"Neither a ruin nor a showplace," T. E. Lawrence wrote of the Krac in his obscure book on Crusader castles. In 1909 Lawrence walked 1,000 miles in the three hottest months to do his survey of these magnificent structures. And he was not exaggerating when he called it the "best-preserved and most wholly admirable castle in the world."

Leaving the castle, I said to Abdullah, "How far is it to Damascus?"

He gave me the distance in kilometers, and it seemed to be little more than 100 miles. There were still a few hours of daylight. We made another deal. He would take me there for forty dollars.

It was a rash move. I should have looked more closely at his car. The road passed behind the mountains that border Lebanon, Al Jabal ash Sharqi. More importantly, the road passed along the edge of the Syrian desert.

"*Sahara!*" Abdullah yelled at the wasteland out the window.

Sheep cropped grass on the western side of the road. On the eastern side they would have starved. Camps of nomads, dark tents and flocks of animals, were visible in the distance.

Just before darkness fell the engine faltered and Abdullah cursed, and the car replied, coughing one-syllable complaints, and then we were stuck.

"Okay, okay," Abdullah said. To prove he was confident he took my picture and he screamed into the wind.

His high spirits were unconvincing. It was an electrical fault, he said. He waved to a passing car and said he would be right back. Then he was sped into the failing light, and dusk fell. I sat in the car, tuning my short-wave radio — news of the Israelis shelling southern Lebanon and blockading the fishing-ports. Every so often a large truck went by, and the thud of its slipstream hit Abdullah's car and shook it, and me.

Cold and unsettled at the edge of this desert, feeling thwarted, this enforced isolation filled my mind with memories of injustice — put-downs, misunderstandings, unresolved disputes, abusive remarks, rudeness, arguments I had lost, humiliations. Some of these instances went back many years. For a reason I could not explain, I thought of everything that had ever gone wrong in my life. I kept telling myself, "So what?" and "Never mind," but it was no good. I could not stop the flow of unpleasant instances, and I was tormented.

From time to time, I laughed to think I was so removed mentally from Syria, but then I concluded that being in the middle of this desert had something to do with it. It was pitch dark and silent except for when the occasional truck thundered by. I supposed that I was fearful and disgusted; I disliked the desert, I had been abandoned by Abdullah in this howling wilderness, where there was darkness and no water.

A pair of oncoming headlights wobbled off the road. Abdullah got out and approached the car laughing, carrying a gas can. Saying it was an electrical fault had been a face-saver.

It was late. Returning his gas can to the town of Deir Atiyeh he stopped the car and I told him I was bailing out. There ensued a great whinging argument, as he pleaded, berated, complained and demanded more money than we had agreed on. "I bought you oranges!" he howled. I thought: I hate this nagging man. Then I said: "Do I care?" I gave him what he wanted and swore at him, and afterwards realized that the whole incident irritated me because I had been planning to tip him the very amount he had demanded.

In Deir Atiyeh, where I stayed the night, I had time to reflect on Assad's personality cult. There was a large statue of the Father-Leader skating — perhaps on thin ice — in the center of Deir Atiyeh. There were also signs which a helpful citizen translated for me: "Smile! You are in Deir Atiyeh!" "Be happy — we are building the country!" and "We in Deir Atiyeh are all soldiers of Hafez Assad."

I have to call my informant Aziz, which was not his name, or else he will be persecuted and thrown into prison — the Syrian cure for dissenters — when the Commander of the Nation reads what I have written. "Aziz" was defiant. He said Assad's vanity was ridiculous. He was saluted at school each morning, he said, when the kiddies entered the classroom. They chanted, "Hafez Assad, our leader for ever!" and another one that started, "With blood, with soul, we sacrifice ourselves to you!" And it was he who told me that his palace in Damascus, built at a cost of 120 million dollars — and of course no one but the Commander was allowed to enter it — was called Kasr el Sharb, the People's Palace.

This glass and steel monstrosity, like a massive airline terminal, on a high bluff overlooking Damascus was almost the first thing I saw the next day when I reached the city. It can be seen from every part of the city; that is obviously one of its important features. The structure was as truculent and unreadable and unsmiling, as forbidding, as remote as the man himself. Vast and featureless, it could be a prison or a fortress, and in a sense it is. Assad has almost no contact with the people, and is seldom seen in public. He is all secrets, a solitary king-emperor. There are rumors that he is sick, that his son's death was a shock, that he is in seclusion. Some days he is shown on the front page of the *Syria Times* sitting rather uncomfortably in a large chair, apparently nodding at a visiting dignitary.

Beneath Assad's palace, Damascus lay, biscuit-colored, the chill of morning still upon it, the new suburbs, the ancient city, the souk, the mosques and churches, the snarled traffic, the perambulating Damascenes. For reasons of religion and commerce, for its shrines, its mosques, its churches, Damascus is heavily visited. It is an ancient city, so old it is mentioned in the Book of Genesis

(14.15–16) – Jerusalem is not mentioned until the Book of Joshua (10.1–2). Unlike Jerusalem, which as an old walled city and bazaar it somewhat resembles, Damascus is the destination of few Western tourists; but it is dense with its neighbors from the desert and the shore. It is the souk and the shrine for the entire region. "Damascus is our souk," a man in distant Latakia told me. It is everyone's souk. And the great Omayyad mosque, built 1,300 years ago to a grandiose design, is the destination of many pilgrims. Beirut is only a short drive – two hours at most – and so there were Lebanese here too; and Iraqis, stifled by sanctions, shopping their hearts out; Nawar people, gypsies from the desert, and the distinctly visible women with tattooed chins and velveteen gowns from the Jordanian border; gnomes in shawls, scowling Bedouins, and students, and mullahs with long beards, and young girls in blue jeans, and hectoring touts in baseball hats.

In one corner of the walled city was the house of Ananias, who in Acts 9.1–20 had a vision which commanded him to go to the house of Judas to receive Paul.

"Original house," said a caretaker.

Perhaps it was. Perhaps this was Straight Street. But I was dubious. It was true that this was the oldest continuously inhabited city in the world, but it had also been besieged and wrecked and pillaged and burned at various times. The shops in the souk, which was larger than Aleppo's, and better lit and airier, sold brassware and tiles, inlaid boxes and furniture, rugs, beads, huge swords, bad carvings, knick-knacks, and Roman glassware.

"Original glass," the hawkers said.

They were small mud-encrusted perfume bottles which had recently – so these stories went – been excavated. There were small terracotta figures, too, and pint-sized amphorae. For just a few dollars I could be the owner of a priceless collection of Roman artifacts.

The head of John the Baptist is said to have been interred at the Omayyad mosque. Anyway, there is a shrine to it in the interior of the mosque, which lies at one end of the covered bazaar. I walked there and saw a group of Iranian pilgrims squatting on the carpeted floor, all of them sobbing, as they were harangued by a blubbing mullah doing a good imitation of an American TV evangelist in a *mea culpa* mode, yelling, preaching, weeping, blowing his nose, wiping his eyes, while his flock honked like geese in their grief.

Looking on were incredulous Syrians, secretly mocking, smiling at the exhibitionism and looking generally unsympathetic.

"Are you religious?" I asked an Arab in the mosque.

"Not at all," he said. He had come to look at the renovation of the mosaics and pillars in the courtyard of the mosque. It was a horrible job the workmen were doing, he said – an act of vandalism, they were defacing it.

"What is that man saying?" I asked, indicating the howling, sobbing mullah. He was standing stuttering and speechifying, and at his feet the sixty or more people sat with tear-stained faces, their shoulders shaking.

"He is telling the story of Hussein."

Hussein, Ali's son, was the grandson of Mohammed, and was beheaded in the year 680 by an army of the Omayyad caliphate at the Battle of Karbala in Iraq. It was a violent and dramatic story which involved Hussein witnessing the slaughter of his wife and children, surrounded by a hostile army, besieged, urging his horse onward, and at last apologizing to his horse as – helpless – Hussein is beheaded.

"And those sweet lips, that the Prophet himself kissed – peace and blessings be upon him! – was then brutally kicked by the soldiers –"

A great shout went up from the passionate pilgrims, and a tiny Smurf-like woman shrouded in black handed a wodge of tissues to the mullah. He blew his nose and continued.

"They kicked Hossein's head like a football –!"

"*Waaaa!*"

What startled me was the immediacy and power of the grief. It was more than pious people having a good cathartic cry. It was like a rehearsal for something more – great anger and bitterness and resentment, as though they had been harmed and were nerving themselves to exact revenge. The howls of the grieving Muslims had the snarl of a war-cry.

Assad was a dismal individual but, impartially intolerant, at least he could claim credit for keeping religious fanaticism in check. He had persecuted the religious extremists with the same grim brutality he used in suppressing political dissent. It was perhaps his only real achievement, but he was characteristically ruthless, which was why the massacre at Hamah claimed so many lives. That was the trouble with dictators: they never knew when to stop.

This subject came up at lunch the next day with some Syrians I had been introduced to. It was one of those midday meals of ten dishes – stuffed vegetables, salad, kebabs, hummus, filled bread, olives, nuts and dumplings – that lasted from one until four and broke the Syrian day in half. But one of the pleasures of Syria was its cuisine, and the simplest was among the best. Each morning in Damascus I left my hotel, walked three blocks and bought a large glass of freshly-made carrot juice – twenty carrots, fifty cents.

"Oh, yes, this is definitely a totalitarian state," one man said. "But also people here are civilized. We are able to live our lives."

How was this so?

"I cannot explain why," another said. "There is no logic in it that you as a Westerner can see. But in the Arab world such contradictions are able to exist."

"We allow for them," the first man said. "It is very strange. Perhaps you would not be happy here."

"Are you ever afraid?" I asked.

"There are many police, many secret police. People are very afraid of them."

"Do people discuss Assad?"

"No one talks about him. They do not say his name."

I said, "So what we're doing now – this conversation – it's not good, is it?"

They all smiled and agreed. No, it was not a good idea. And, really, in a totalitarian state there is nothing to talk about except the obvious political impasse.

"Do you think I should go to Beirut?" I asked.

"You know the Israelis are shelling the south?"

"How would that affect me?"

"Many of the fundamentalists have retreated to Beirut. They associate Israel with America – after all, America allows this to happen. They might accuse you of being a spy. It is not a good time."

"What would they do to me?"

"Kidnap or –" The man hesitated.

"Shoot me?"

Out of delicacy, they were not explicit, but I had the distinct feeling they were saying, "Don't go." They lived in Syria. They visited Beirut all the time – it was such a short distance to travel, no more than sixty miles, and of course the border formalities.

"The last time I was in Beirut – just a few days ago," one of them said, "Israeli jet planes were flying over the city, buzzing the rooftops, intimidating people, breaking the sound barrier – and windows."

I was losing my resolve. That made me linger in Damascus. One of the happiest experiences I had in Damascus was at the house of a man named Omer, the friend of a friend. Omer was a Sudanese cement expert who worked for the Arab Development Corporation. He lived with his attractive Sudanese wife and three children in an apartment block about a mile from the center of Damascus.

We were drinking tea and eating sticky buns when he summoned his eight-year-old son, Ibrahim, to meet me. The boy did not speak English. He was tall for his age, wearing rumpled blue buttoned-up pajamas. He looked solemn, he said nothing, he stood and bowed slightly to show respect.

Then, without a word, he went to a piano in the corner, and sat down and played a theme and variations by Mozart. It was plangent and complex, and sitting upright on the stool the boy played on without a duff note. In that small cluttered apartment I experienced a distinct epiphany, feeling – with Nietzsche – that "without music life would be an error."

The fighting in southern Lebanon and the strafing of Beirut made me reconsider my jaunt along the Lebanese coast. I called the American Embassy in Damascus and asked for information. By way of response I received an invitation to a recital at the ambassador's residence. On this particular Arabian night, the performance was given by a visiting American band, Mingo Saldivar and His

Three Tremendous Swords. Saldivar, "the Dancing Cowboy," played an accordion, Cajun and Zydeco music, jolly syncopated country-and-western polkas. At first the invited guests — about a hundred Syrians — were startled. Then they were amused. Finally they were clapping.

Afterwards, I found the ambassador talking animatedly in Arabic to a tall patrician-looking Syrian. I introduced myself and asked my question.

"Don't go to Beirut," the ambassador replied. "Not now. Not with your face. Not with your passport."

The American Ambassador to Syria, Christopher Ross, a fluent Arabic speaker, is a highly-regarded career diplomat, and an amiable and witty man. He is also a subtle negotiator in the delicate peace talks involving Israel and Syria. The sticking point was the Golan Heights. This large section of eastern Syria was captured by Israel in 1967 and has been occupied by them ever since, and partly settled — something that quite rightly maddens the Syrians. In this connection, Ambassador Ross saw a great deal of President Assad, had been to Assad's bunker and would have been a fund of information for me, except that he skillfully deflected all my intrusive questions.

"I think the ambassador is right — stay away from Lebanon at the moment," the tall man said. He was Sadik Al-Azm, from an ancient Damascene family. His professorial appearance — tweed jacket, horn-rimmed glasses — was justified, for he was a professor at Damascus University. He was noted as the author of an outspoken defense of Salman Rushdie.

"That seems rather a risky thing to have done in a Muslim country," I said.

"What do I care?" he said, and laughed out loud. "This is a republic, anyway. Even our president defended Rushdie!"

"It doesn't worry you that Syria is crawling with Iranian fundamentalists."

"What do they know?"

"They know there's a *fatwa*, they idolize Khomeini," I said. "It seems to me they'd like to stick a knife in your guts."

"The Iranians you see here haven't read anything," Professor Al-Azm said. "They haven't read what I wrote about Rushdie,

and they certainly haven't read *The Satanic Verses*. I'm not worried.
In fact, I am updating my book at the moment for a new edition."

"Fearless, you see?" Ambassador Ross said.

"What do I care?" the professor said.

"I think this phrase 'Islamic fundamentalism' is misleading,"
the ambassador said. "I call it 'political Islam.'"

He went on to say that he felt it was related to many other
movements that in my opinion were now actively obnoxious in the
world – the Christian Coalition, the Moral Majority, the Pro-Life
assassins, and so forth. The militant moralizers in the United
States who represented a new Puritanism were ideologically similar
to the Muslim Brotherhood and the Party of God. Ambassador
Ross did not say so, but it was logical to conclude from this that
the Reverend Pat Robertson and the Ayatollah had a great deal in
common.

In Syria and elsewhere, unexpectedly, political Islam was growing. More people – many of them young – wore veils, fasted at
Ramadan.

This severely orthodox reaction had something to do with the
waywardness of governments and the crookedness of politicians.
Instead of working within the system, people were adopting a
religious scourge, which was a simpler remedy involving denunciation and murder. It was perhaps understandable, but I found it
depressing.

I wandered away while the ambassador was challenging Professor Al-Azm on another recondite matter, and I fell into conversation with a Syrian, Mr Hamidullah. After a while I asked him
about the cult of Basil.

"Father-President groomed him for leadership," Mr Hamidullah
said.

"Isn't an election usually a more reliable way to pick a leader?"
I asked.

"In your country, maybe. But Syria is much different. Here it is
necessary to have a golden formula to govern."

"I see," I said. *Golden formula?* I said, "And President Assad has
the golden formula."

"I call it the Secret Key," Mr Hamidullah said. "Without it,
Syria cannot be governed. Father-President was passing this on to

his son. He knew that when he died the next leader would need to have the Secret Key."

"And this Secret Key is necessary because –"

"Because this country is so difficult!" he said. "We have Druses, Alawites, Christians, Jews, Shiites, Assyrians. We have Kurds, we have Maronites. More! We have Yezidis – they are devil-worshipers, their God of Bad is a peacock. We have – what? – Chaldeans! How to govern all of them? Secret Key!"

He grinned at me, having demonstrated to his satisfaction that Hafez Assad's dictatorship was necessary and that, in the absence of Basil, his second son Bashar would be the possessor of the golden formula, the Secret Police – sorry, Mr Hamidullah! I meant to say, the Secret Key.

On my way to Ma'aloula, a village in the mountains north of Damascus, I saw picked out on a hillside in white boulders a motto in Arabic.

"What does that say?"

"'*Hail to Our Glorious Leader*.' Meaning Assad," said Munif, and shrugged and puffed his pipe.

Munif is the author of a dozen novels. His *Cities of Salt* trilogy – *Cities of Salt*, *The Trench*, and *Variations on Night and Day* – had been translated into English, to great praise, by my younger brother Peter Theroux, who suggested I meet Munif when I passed through Damascus. Munif showed me a limited edition of the first book. It was a de luxe large format with loose pages, boxed, with signed and numbered wood-block prints by a famous artist, Dia al-Azzawi. I marveled at the prints. Munif smiled. Yes, he said – he had recently finished writing a volume of art criticism – they were very good.

He was born in Amman of mixed Saudi–Iraqi parents, and was raised in Saudi Arabia. Vocally out of sympathy with the Saudi leadership, who have banned his books and revoked his citizenship, Munif has lived in many places in the Middle East – as well as Paris – in his sixty-odd years and has held eight different passports-of-convenience, including Yemeni and Omani. Munif is an exile of a sort that hardly exists any more in the Western world but is fairly common (at least as far as intellectuals are concerned) in the

Middle East. He is essentially stateless, but remains unbending. In his last communication with the Saudi government he was told that he could have his citizenship back but he had to promise to stop writing and publishing.

"No conditions. I will not accept a passport with conditions," Munif said, and that was the end of the discussion.

I liked him from the first. He was laconic, kindly, generous, hospitable. If there was anything I wished to see or do, he was at my disposal. Was there anything I wanted to buy? I had no desire to buy anything, I said. Did I wish him to drive me to Beirut? I said I had been told it might be dangerous. But what suggestions did he have?

"Ma'aloula," he said. "Saydnaya. There are lovely and very historic places you should see before you leave Syria."

One of the curious features of Ma'aloula was that Aramaic was still spoken there by three-quarters of the population, who are Christians. Jesus spoke Aramaic. When he said, "Blessed are the meek, for they shall inherit the earth," it was in Aramaic. When he said, "God is love," it was in Aramaic. In the Bible, Jesus's cry on the cross, "*Eloi Eloi, lama sabacthani*," is Aramaic.

It was hard to find a person in Ma'aloula who spoke English, but Father Faez Freijate spoke it well. He was a plump cheery soul with tiny eyes and a white tufty beard and side-whiskers, like a comical old Chaucerian friar. He wore a brown robe and carried a staff. His face was pink-cheeked and English-looking, but he roared with laughter when I mentioned that to him. "I am Arab and my family is Arab for three thousand years!" He was from Hauran, in south Syria, and was the pastor of the Ma'aloula church of St Sergius and St Bacchus, soldiers in the Roman army who had been martyred in A.D. 300. The church was built in 320.

"Do you speak Aramaic?" I asked.

"Yes, listen. *Abounah* –" He clasped his hands and began muttering very fast. At the end he blessed himself with the sign of the cross and said, "That was the Lord's Prayer."

"How do you say, 'God is love,' in Aramaic?"

"I do not know."

I wanted very much to hear Christ's words as they were originally spoken. I said, "How about, 'Let he who is without sin cast the first stone.'"

"I do not know."

"'I am the light of the world.'"

"I just know a few prayers. Ask someone in town," Father Freijate said with an air of exasperation. Then he said, "Have you seen the altar?"

Small and horseshoe-shaped, it looked like a shallow sink from which the drain has been omitted. It was the proudest ornament of the church, though it looked to me unprepossessing, until the priest explained it.

It was made of marble that had been quarried in Antioch. Its design had been adapted from the pagan altars of the animistic desert faiths – worshipers of bulls and cats and snakes. Such altars had been used for animal sacrifices, which was why their sides were necessary; and the pagan altars had a hole in the center for draining away the animal's blood. This altar was made before the year 325, Father Feijate said, because that was the year that the Council of Nicaea said that all altars had to be flat. It was unique. There was not another one to be seen anywhere else in Christendom.

"Why are there so many caves in Ma'aloula, Father?" All over the mountainside and in the passages and corners of the cliffs there were carved holes and shelves and caverns.

"The peoples were troglodeeties!"

"They lived in them?"

"Yes! And they had necropoleese and antik toombis!" He laughed at my ignorance and hurried away to help another visitor.

We went to Saydnaya. Saydnaya had two sides. One was a political prison, the other a church and convent. The prison, another bunker, was built on a hill but was mostly underground and surrounded by three perimeter fences of barbed wire. It had watch-towers, but it hardly needed them for the prison was absolutely escape-proof, but more than that, its dampness and its windowless cells shortened the prisoners' lives by causing pneumonia and arthritis. There were said to be thousands of political prisoners at Saydnaya. A Syrian political prisoner was simply an enemy of Assad – sorry, Friend Assad.

The cathedral of Saydnaya was some distance from the prison, at the top of the hillside village. It was a happier place. It contained a convent and an orphanage – smiling nuns doing laundry, yelling children scampering in the back precincts. The nuns dressed like Muslim women in black draped gowns and black head-dresses.

The history of the church was given in a set of old paintings, which could be read like a strip cartoon. A *malik* – king – out hunting, saw a gazelle. He drew his bow, but before he could shoot it, the creature turned into the Virgin. The king prayed. Afterwards, the king won a great battle. He returned to the spot where he had seen the Virgin and built this church.

I was about to enter a chapel when a friendly but firm little man insisted I take my shoes off. Surely that was done in mosques and temples but not in Christian churches? No, he said, I should read Exodus 3.5, the injunction, "Put off thy shoes."

This was Mr Nicholas Fakouri from Beirut, who had come with his wife, Rose, to bring a sacrifice.

"What sort of sacrifice?"

"A sheep."

Munif's daughter Azza translated my specific questions. The Fakouris had come by road from Beirut and had stopped in the bazaar in Damascus and bought a hundred-pound sheep for the equivalent of about ninety dollars. They had taken it here and presented it to the nuns at the church.

"They will kill it and eat it at Easter."

"That is a present, not a sacrifice."

"It is a sacrifice," he insisted, using the Arabic word.

Rose Fakouri said, "I was very sick. I prayed to the Virgin. When I got better, I came here with my husband to give thanks."

Driving out of Saydnaya we passed the prison again, and I imagined all the men in those dungeons who had been locked up for their beliefs. Munif said that they allowed some of them out, but only after they had been physically wrecked by their imprisonment. He said, "They are sick, they are finished, they are ready to die."

"Writing is difficult in a police state."

He laughed and shouted, "Living is difficult!"

We returned to Damascus. He asked me to wait while he removed something from the trunk of his car. It was a large flat parcel, one of the limited-edition prints that I had admired in his apartment the first day we met.

Standing at the juice stall, drinking my last glass of Damascus carrot juice, I realized that I liked this dusty, lively, rotting, uncertain, lovely-ugly place, and that I was sorry to leave, especially sorry that I was not heading the sixty miles to Beirut, but instead through the desert, the back way, through Jordan to Israel again. That was my fall-back position – a ship that was leaving Haifa in a few days. Like a surrealistic farewell, a bus went by while I sipped the carrot juice, and on its side was lettered HAPPY JERNY!

16

The Ferry *Sea Harmony* to Greece

Down Moussallam Baroudy Road, past the blue *To Beirut* arrow and the lovely semi-derelict Hejaz railway station to Choukri Kouwatli Avenue, and following the arrow *To Jordan*. Instead of the short trip to Lebanon I had to take a much longer one, around its back, south into Jordan and hang a right into Israel, and keep on going to the coast and the waiting *Sea Harmony* that was sailing in a few days. It sounds like an epic, but in fact if I had made an early start, I could have had breakfast in Damascus (Syria), lunch in Amman (Jordan), tea in Jerusalem (Palestine; disputed) and dinner in Haifa (Israel).

These countries were so small! One of the more marvelous atrocities of our time was the way in which the self-created problems of these countries, and their arrogant way of dealing with them, made them seem larger, like an angry child standing on its tiptoes. They were expensive to operate, too, they had vast armies; they indulged in loud and ridiculously long-winded denunciations of their neighbors. All this contributed to the illusion that they were massive. But, no, they were tiny, irritating, shameless and vindictive; and they occupied the world's attention way out of proportion to their size or their importance. They had been magnified by lobbyists and busybody groups. Inflation was the theme here, and it was just another tactic for these quarrelsome people to avoid making peace.

Lovely roads, though. That was how I managed to cover so much ground. I was thinking: Why isn't Route 6 as good as this – why can't I get to Provincetown this fast? And then I reflected: We paid for those roads and bridges from Jordan to Jerusalem and on to Tel Aviv, and they are a hell of a lot better than ours!

After the last shrine to Basil, a triumphal arch at Der'a (where

T. E. Lawrence was captured, fondled by a Turkish commander and then abused and whipped – one of the great chapters of *Seven Pillars of Wisdom*, ending "in Deraa that night the citadel of my integrity had been irrevocably lost"), and Syrian customs, I was held up by a car-load of Arab smugglers. Cartons of Marlboros, about fifty of them, had been crammed into the car's chassis, and they were being removed and stacked at Jordanian customs, under the eyes of the suspects. Then the green hills of Jordan, the queer Taco Bell architecture of the repulsively spick-and-span city of Amman and – since Jordan does not have a Mediterranean coast – a ten-dollar taxi ride from there to the Jordan–Israel frontier at the Allenby Bridge (thirty feet from end to end, another bit of Middle Eastern magnification) and into the West Bank, real desert under brooding mountains and Israeli fortresses and gun emplacements; a bus to the Israeli checkpoint, and another ten-dollar taxi to the Damascus Gate in Jerusalem.

All the way through Jordan and well into Israel, the truth of this expensive farce was evident in the sight of the tent camps of Palestinians – shepherds with their animals, displaced, hardly tolerated, snotty-nosed children and their ragged elders, despised by Jordanians and Israelis alike, who roar past them in Jeeps and buses, sending up clouds of dust, making a vivid frontispiece for the diabolical next edition of the Bad News Bible.

I stayed in Arab East Jerusalem and made a circuit of the old city again. It was another average day in Zion. Israeli police were in the process of arresting three Arabs near the entrance to the Damascus Gate, and a Jewish protester was being dragged away for holding a "pray-in" at the Temple Mount. At the sacred sites people assumed all the odd postures of piety, on their knees, in their stocking feet, bowing, sobbing, and – at the Western Wall – hundreds, carefully segregated by sex, men here, women there, separated by a steel crowd-barrier, gabbled over their paraphernalia of scrolls and books, men wearing shawls on their heads like the Haurani crones of south Syria, while others had paper yarmulkas, like squashed Chinese take-away cartons, on their heads.

On a blocked back lane a hysterical Lubavitcher in a black hat and black frock coat and billowing black pants hoisted his orange mountain bike in order to squeeze past a van and, struggling through the narrow gap, knocked over an Arab's stack of cabbages. The men began a futile argument in different languages.

On the Via Dolorosa, near the Flagellation chapel, I heard a man say to a woman, "So now we do everything you say and you make all the decisions!"

And around the Fifth Station, where the Via Dolorosa ascends steeply to Golgotha, a woman was saying to a man, "Are you sure it's this way? You're not sure, are you? You're just too embarrassed to ask someone directions."

And farther down the Via Dolorosa, a child screaming, "But you said I could have one!"

Near the Lion Gate there were some Intifada graffiti, which a young Mujahadeen helpfully translated: *Long Live Al-Fatah* (Arafat's Palestinian organization), *This Land of Flowing Blood*, and *In Memory of the Hero and Martyr Amjad Shaheen!* (shot by Israeli soldiers).

Politicians tended to simplify the sides into Jews and Arabs, but such designations were totally misleading. A Jew might be a Moroccan, fluent in Arabic and Hebrew and French, raised in Marrakech and educated in Tel Aviv; or a Russian from Odessa now living in a settler village in Gaza, or a monoglot girl in pigtails from south Florida. An Arab might be as complex and interesting as the man I met over coffee in east Jerusalem – a Christian named Michel, born in Jaffa in 1933, his father Palestinian, his mother Italian. "Many Italians used to come and stay here, because it was a holy land for them, too." He said that since 1948 there had been nothing but trouble. The influx of militant Jews had made it impossible for him to go on living in Jaffa, so he had had to come here to Jerusalem, where there was safety in numbers. He had been married in the church of St Anne in the Old City and believed (as I did) that Jerusalem should be an open city, internationalized, and not an Israeli stronghold. The Israelis had knocked down walls and put up offices and rearranged and rebuilt Jerusalem to suit their political ends.

His twenty-year-old son was in Iraq, studying engineering.

"Because I have no money," he said. "And Saddam Hussein gives scholarships to Palestinians."

There were some Palestinians at the Hebrew University in

Jerusalem, and there was a Palestinian university at Beir Zeit in Nablus. But in general Israel took no responsibility for educating the underclass of Palestinians any more than they saw the Palestinians as having a right to their own portion of the country. Not much was being asked – at most about twenty per cent of what was rightfully theirs. Without partition there will be no peace, but in the present atmosphere peace was a long way off.

It was an atmosphere of conflict, a joyless unrestful place in which from the simplest transactions, like being ripped off for a taxi fare, to the highest levels of government, there was no finesse. It was all sour looks, suspicion, the sharp elbows, the silences, the soldiers, and fundamentalists of all descriptions. Both sides were fearful, racialist, intolerant and paranoid. Israelis ignored the fact that they snatched and settled land that was not theirs. Their usual reply to any complaints was: You hate Jews.

The worst turn of events was the recent rash of suicide bombers. Ironically, it was an Israeli, Baruch Goldstein, who initiated this new form of warfare, when he killed twenty-nine Muslims at prayer at a mosque in Hebron. He knew when he opened fire that he would never leave the mosque alive; he was beaten to death. Soon after him there were three Palestinian suicide bombers, in separate incidents, who managed to bring Israelis down with them, and this has become the principal tactic, and the most violent so far, in the war between the extreme Palestinian groups (Hamas and Hezbollah) and the Israelis. There are few defenses against the person who is willing to sacrifice his life to kill others.

There was always a violent reply. The Israelis, obsessively retributive, had an absolutely unforgiving rule of retaliation, and always with greater force. It assured a continuing hopelessness and an impasse.

A new development was that their dislike and fear of Palestinians had reached such a pitch that their answer now to Palestinian demands was the hiring of immigrant laborers and field hands from Thailand, the Philippines and Poland – desperate so-called "guest workers" – to bring in the harvest. In the absence of Jews willing to perform the menial tasks that had been assigned to Palestinians, there were now 70,000 such immigrants, a new element in the society, and a new underclass of non-Jews.

In a crowded almost silent bus, jammed with passengers, I rode to Haifa. Only one person spoke, an old Ethiopian Jew – a patriarch, traveling with his large family. He carried a fly whisk and called out in Amharic when he saw anything unusual. It was very easy to translate his exclamations. We passed the airport. *Look at the planes!* he cried. We passed the railway line. *Look at the train!* We were stuck in traffic. *Look at all the cars!* And nearer Haifa, traveling along the coast, the old man was delighted. *The sea! The sea!*

The blue water lapped at the low shore of tumbled dunes.

Intending to be early, in order to catch the *Sea Harmony*, I went directly from the station to the pier. In the event, I very nearly missed it.

"Come with me," an Israeli security officer said to me as he leafed through my passport.

I was then subjected to the most intense and prolonged interrogation and suitcase search it has been my experience to receive in thirty-four years of traveling. This time I was not rescued by a helpful bookworm who knew my name. Instead, I was made to wait. And then I was questioned. Why had I gone to Turkey? Who did I know there? Who did I visit there? Where had I stayed? These specifics were noted. The same questions were asked of my time in Syria and Jordan. Then I was taken to a side room. My suitcase was gone through a third time, by a new official. He pointed to a plastic chair.

"Sit down."

"If you say please."

"Sit down!"

"I find this very unpleasant," I said after two hours in the chair, when the man returned with my passport.

Another man began trawling through my little bag. I stood up to stretch.

"Sit down!"

I was then summoned to receive my passport. I said, "What do you think?"

"I don't sink nossing."

"Know what I think?" I said. "I don't like being treated like this."

"No one likes," he said sourly. He hated me for my impertinence.

He hated his job. He hated the Palestinians. He hated his life in a country where everyone is a possible terrorist and where life in this state of siege is a turbulent and terrifying nuisance.

The disgust and pessimism is so palpable that after a dose of it, the *Sea Harmony* ship-load of shouting, boasting Greeks, swaggering on deck and plucking at their private parts and smoking and guzzling ouzo and snarling at each other, was peaceful by comparison.

The Mediterranean War Report: Fighting in Turkey – Turks against Kurds; fighting in Bosnia – Serbs against Bosnian Muslims; fighting in Algeria – most recent death toll, 40,000 in the past three years, ten thousand of them since I had started my trip. The Israelis were shelling south Lebanon and continuing a blockade of south Lebanese ports and fishing-grounds; the terrorists of Hamas were continuing their suicide missions against Israelis in Hebron and Gaza – and Israelis were answering each attack with one of their own. And a stand-off between Greeks and Turks in Cyprus.

The *Sea Harmony* was headed to Greek Cyprus, steaming out of Haifa and its hill of lights. I was sitting at the stern, with my feet jammed against the rail. A man approached and stood a bit too close to me.

"Excuse me," the man inquired. "Are you Guy Lupowsky?"

He had a plump pink face and a pot belly, and he stood awkwardly, his short arms hanging. He wore a gray suit, but it was rumpled; and a shirt and tie, but they were soup-stained. He said "Lupowsky" in a slurping and delicious lisp, all spittle and slush.

I said no, I was not Guy Lupowsky.

"I am sorry. I see you and I fink you is him. Classical guitarist from Belgium. I am a musician. I play Jewish." He said the words "musician" and "Jewish" as though he were masticating the wet pulpy segment of a juicy orange.

After every few words he swallowed. His English reflected the way he was dressed. It was well intentioned and almost formal in many respects, like his suit and tie, but also like his suit and tie it was mangled and at times comic.

He introduced himself as Sam – that is, Shmuel – Spillman. He said he divided his time equally between Belgium and Israel, going back and forth, nearly always on the *Sea Harmony* on this leg, and the rest by Italian ferries and trains. He did not have a home in either country, nor even an apartment. "I get a room, just a small one. A big one confuses me. I rent a room by the week in Tel Aviv, and another one in Brussels. I cannot own a place. That would confuse me."

In a sense he was the ultimate voyager, shuttling across the Mediterranean from Brussels to Tel Aviv and back. He had no permanent home – he did not want one. He had few possessions, he said; they rattled him. What to do with them? He had his music and his mother. That was enough, said Spillman.

"I cannot stay with my mother, or there will be trouble. She is very rich but we quarrel. She makes problems. Is better that I get a room and visit her. I have some presents for her." He thought a moment. And he slurped and lisped the spattering word, "Chocolates."

"How do you decide when to stay and when to go?" I asked.

"It is the sunshine," he said.

"You like sunny weather?"

"I need sunshine," he said, and the word on his tongue was like a gum drop, "for my depression."

"I see."

"I need to come here."

But "here" was far astern to the east, for we had plunged seaward, and the lights of Haifa were just a little row of lighted dots that made a yellow horizontal line across the night. Israel was that perforation in the darkness.

"For my depression I need the sunshine, and I need the Jews," Spillman said. "I am very Jewish." He swallowed and went on, "I am very, very Jewish."

"So you visit Israel when you get depressed in Brussels?" I said. "But when do you visit Brussels?"

"When I get depression in Israel," he said. "When it feels dark to me. I take medication but the real medication is to leave. Every six months or less I feel it, and it gets bad, and I see my doctor. He prescribes medication and I come."

"Isn't it sunny most of the time in Israel?"

"Sometimes it is dark," he said. "I am not speaking of the sunshine. I wanted to settle in Israel but I did not want to give up my Belgian residency. It was such a big decision and it was giving me depression. My psychiatrist said to me, 'Don't decide, go back and forth, as you wish. It is better.' So I do that."

"That's a wise doctor," I said.

"He is my friend."

He hesitated.

"He knows I am a gay people," Spillman said. He looked at me sadly. "But I have no more desires. I had a friend but now I have no friend. Are you going to eat?"

"Is it time?"

"From six-thirty to seven-thirty they serve dinner. Then it is closed. You can buy coffee or biscuits or sweets, but not foods. In the morning at seven –"

After so many voyages, Spillman knew the whole routine of the ship. He knew some of the crew, and they knew him. He knew every feature of the ship, that they did not do laundry, that the coffee was good, that the food was expensive, that the deck chairs were always dirty, that the crew smoked too much. He knew the arrival and departure times. More than that, he knew the high points of each port of call – the fruit market in Limassol, specific hotels where you could get an inexpensive shower (Spillman had a seat, not a cabin, on the ship and had nowhere on board to have a bath), the best eating places *en route*, a particular café in Rhodes that sold roast chicken. Spillman said the word "chicken" with a gasping and slushy hunger.

All this I learned over dinner, spaghetti and cabbage salad, glopped on to plates by the five Burmese who served in the cafeteria. It was prison food.

The stewards, the waiters, the menials, nearly all the underlings on this Greek ship were either Burmese or Indian. They spoke no Greek. Orders were always given in English and carried out by these efficient, muttering flunkies. They swept, they painted, they mopped, they cooked and served. A Burmese made the moussaka, another Burmese shoveled it on to plates, an Indian handed it over, a Burmese rang the cash register. It was not their fault that the ship served prison food. And none of them had been on the ship long – a year at most. The Burmese were from Rangoon, the Indians from Bombay. They were desperate for employment. They were also loners on the ship – men without women.

Greece, like Israel and Italy, had high unemployment, around ten per cent. It interested me that Burmese were making moussaka on this Greek ship, and Filipinos were picking oranges outside Tel Aviv, and West Africans were harvesting tomatoes near Salerno, in Italy. It was the Third World in the Mediterranean, proving that there were even poorer and needier countries than Tunisia and Egypt and Morocco. These people and others had come from half-way around the world to help these developed countries, members of the European Union, to scrub its floors and harvest its crops. The Burmese and Indians lent the ship a melancholy air and made the Greek crewmen seem like overlords, as they loudly issued orders in badly pronounced English. They made the class system explicit by giving it a color. The Mediterranean had always had an underclass of remote or provincial people, but they had never come from so far away.

"Maybe you'll meet someone," I said to Spillman over lunch the next day. Speaking of his marriage he had begun to slip into another depression.

"Yes?"

He stopped eating. The thought of meeting someone seemed not to have occurred to him. He became reflective, a problem clouding his face, taking some of the pinkness from it.

"Perhaps."

"What's the problem with your mother?"

"My marriage, also. I made such a great scandal with my marriage. It was a big catastrophe, *mamma mia*. You know Jewish women? No sex before marriage! Don't touch me!" He dabbed a balled-up hanky at the spaghetti sauce on his lips. "On our wedding night it was such a disaster." He was silent for quite a long time. Months, perhaps years, were passing in his mind. Events, too. He was nodding, reviewing these events as, great and small, they passed before him. At last he winced and said, "We got a divorce."

He followed me on deck afterwards. Having just left Israel for

his health he was in a particular mood, one of rejection, as he
headed to his other home.

"Israel is no more a Jewish country," Spillman said disgustedly.
"It was special before, but now it is like all other countries. Just
wanting money. Everyone talks about money."

He was speaking into the darkness. Israel was somewhere in that
darkness.

"I think there will be civil war," he said. "Jews against Jews, the
orthodox ones against the other, the settlers against the others. The
Arabs will just watch us fighting."

Spillman was in the cheap seats in the big smoky lounge at the
center of C-deck, surrounded by his heap of bags — shopping-bags
mostly, in which he carried all his possessions. One of them was an
instrument he called a "melodeon" — a fat flute with a keyboard
which made a kazoo-like sound. Good-hearted man that he was,
he spent part of the day serenading the others in the cheap seats:
Jewish songs, gypsy songs, and old favorites such as "Blue Moon"
and "O Sole Mio."

There was a bald toothless Israeli with a dog on his lap in the
cheap seats, and a German family with a small baby, and some
backpackers, and some Greek Cypriots, and part of a group of
pilgrims to the Holy Land, and a Dutch couple who had just been
on a kibbutz. There were some Arabs, too. The Israeli with the
dog said that he had been a soldier his whole life. "I have fought
in three wars!" The German family had set up a field kitchen in
some spare seats and were forever dishing up food for their baby
and themselves. The Slovakian pilgrims traveled with a small
bearded friar who said mass in one of the lounges every day. The
prettiest pilgrim was a girl in her twenties who carried a wooden
cross as tall as she was. Tacked to it was a holy card, the size of a
baseball card, with a saint's picture on it. She heaved the cross in a
slightly defiant way, the winsome Slovak, smiling, carrying this
enormous cross among the querulous passengers.

There were other passengers, too, in the cabins. Some of them
had strange stories to tell, but I met them later. The *Sea Harmony*
was an unusual ship in the way people were spilled together. The
bad weather did not help either — it was cold and windy, the sea

unsettled. It was not a cruise, but rather a way for these people to get from one side of the Mediterranean to the other, or to stop on the journey.

I had paid a little extra to have my own cabin. That was my only luxury. The food was awful. The weather was grim. The Greek crew were truculent and unhelpful, and the Greek passengers even worse – two of them sat in the lounge shouting into cellular phones, making interminable calls. They smoked. They demanded that the Burmese play tapes of Greek music very loudly. Because the decks were cold and windswept, there was no refuge anywhere. But I had my cabin.

The wind was blowing the rain sideways on our approach to Limassol, and the weather continued cold and rainy – such a novelty, after the parched landscapes of Syria and Israel, all these muddy sidewalks and puddled streets and weeping trees. I had been eager to see the Republic of Cyprus, after having traversed Turkish Cyprus. It had been impossible for me to go directly from one to the other, and so this thousand-mile detour had been necessary. But had it been worth it? Yes, I thought so, because I had seen how lifeless and deprived Turkish Cyprus was; and now I saw that it hardly mattered, for Limassol, with its tourists and its Royal Air Force base at nearby Akrotiri and its embittered Greeks, was unattractive and seedy. Turkish Cyprus was like a Third World island of soldiers and self-help; Greek Cyprus was a rather ugly and bungaloid coastline, the most distant outpost of the European Community, another welfare case.

The French historian Fernand Braudel said that the larger islands in the Mediterranean are miniature continents. He cited Corsica, Sardinia, Sicily and Cyprus as good examples of this. I could see how this might be so. A single island might have many micro-climates, and regions and dialects, if not separate languages; and a mountain range that was like a continental divide, and a wild or sparsely settled interior. They were so complex they seemed vast, and each section of coast was different. But the partition of Cyprus had made it smaller. It had broken into two mean frag-ments, a pair of true islands, each with its own culture and language. The large, complex island of Cyprus had become two simpler and much less interesting places in the twenty years since the Turks had asserted themselves in the north and the Greeks in the south.

I walked from the port to the town, buying my breakfast on the way, fruit here, juice there, and at last I bought a copy of the day-before-yesterday's *Daily Telegraph* and read it over a cup of coffee in a café across from Limassol's front, while the wind whipped the waves on to the promenade.

Limassol was as unlike a town in Turkish Cyprus as it was possible to be, and yet if anything it seemed more hollow and dreary. It was, I suppose, the cheesy funfair atmosphere that tourism had brought with it, and the weird jauntiness, the forced high spirits and fake geniality that can make a visitor lonely to the point of depression. Spillman had told me he was going fruit shopping at his favorite market and then straight back to the ship. There was nothing else to buy, only horrendous souvenirs, un-painted plaster statues, mostly nude women, but also animals, busts of anonymous Greeks; paperweights made of varnished stones, copper salt-cellars, toy windmills, dishcloths depicting Cypriot costumes and maps, dolls in traditional dress, doilies, tablecloths, egg-timers, letter-openers, ashtrays labeled *Limassol*, and every souvenir plate imaginable. There were many images, in plaster, on dishes, or modeled in plastic, of the goddess Aphrodite. Legend had it that Aphrodite had risen from the waves off the west coast of Cyprus. "The sanctuary of Aphrodite at Old Paphos was one of the most celebrated shrines in the ancient world" (*The Golden Bough*). The images on sale depicted a sulky, misshapen Barbie doll rather than the goddess of love.

The day-before-yesterday's *Mirror*, the *Sun*, the *Daily Mail* and other British papers were available. Bus tours were advertised to various parts of the island. Signs said "Traditional English Pub," and "Full English Breakfast," "Fish and Chips," and "Afternoon Tea." There were bleak hotels on the promenade and some derelict mosques on the back streets. There was something old-fashioned and fifties-ish about Limassol, as though like the newspapers the town too had an air of the day-before-yesterday.

The Greek Cypriots I spoke to were friendly and forthcoming, and as angry with the Turks as the Turks I had met on the north side of the island had been with them. Each side expressed their anger in the same words.

"I have a lot of property in the north, but I have no idea what happened to it," a Greek woman told me. I had heard something similar from a Turkish woman, her exact counterpart, in the north, on a street in Lefkosa, who had fled from Limassol.

And there was Mrs Evzonas. Twenty years ago, in Famagusta (now Gazimagosa), she said to her husband, "Let's get out of here." There were Turkish planes flying overhead, and Turkish ships in the harbor. They took a two-hour drive to Limassol and hunkered down. "We'll go back when it's safer."

She told me, "We thought it would end soon. How did we know that it would last this long?"

In two decades the Evzonases have not been back, nor have any of their friends. But this is a legitimate republic, recognized by other countries. I made phone calls to the United States from the public phone booths. And because of the brisk tourist trade it was possible to earn a living here in a way that in Turkish northern Cyprus was out of the question.

"I would like to go back, but how can I?" Mrs Evzonas said. "With my passport it is impossible." She shrugged. "We are stuck here."

"This was once a small town," a man named Giorgio said to me in Limassol. "In 1974 it was nothing. But so many refugees made businesses, so it began to get bigger."

I told him I had been to the town he knew as Famagusta.

"They say it is a ghost town," he said.

He wanted me to agree, and he was right of course, but how could I tell him that in its ghostly way the town was more weirdly attractive than this?

The *Sea Harmony* was not leaving until late that night. The driving rain had discouraged me from leaving town, and so I hung around, and when the rain slowed to a thin drizzle I walked east along the coast, working up an appetite, and then returned and had a traditional English beer in a traditional English pub and met Mr Reg MacNicol from North London, who was on a two-week holiday ("We come for the weather"). When I asked too many questions he exploded and his florid face grew redder and he said, "You Yanks give me the pip! Life's a compromise! Utopia doesn't exist!"

I took a bus back to the ship, where the Slovakians were kneeling in the midst of another solemn mass in the lounge bar.

"I bought these for you," Spillman said, handing me some Cyprus tangerines.

A woman nearby said, "I know you. I saw them interrogating you in Haifa. They took you away."

"You're very observant," I said.

"I was afraid for you," she said. "Hi. I'm Melva. From Australia. I've lived a really cloistered life. All this is new to me."

She was another loner on this ship of loners, a solitary traveler, and she was as pleasant and as odd as the others. Tall, calm, observant, she shared a cabin with two other women, strangers to her. She had been cheated in Turkey and ill with suspected pneumonia in Egypt and had spent two days in an Israeli hospital. "They threw me out. I had a temperature of a hundred and two and they said, 'You must go now.' I went to one of those grotty hotels and nearly died." But she was game. I asked how she was now. "I'm coming good!

"Want to play cards?" she asked.

She taught me an Australian card game called "Crappy Joe," which was a version of two-handed whist that had interminable variations. Each successive game became more complicated in terms of the combinations needed to win. Her parents had played it almost every night for years in the western Sydney suburb of Emu Plains.

"Aw, I was married for twenty-six years myself, but my husband and I just went in different directions. I had to get away."

She was dealing the cards for another hand of Crappy Joe.

"You make it sound urgent," I said.

"He was stalking me," she said. "At night I'd look out the window and there he'd be, staring in, his face so frightening. I'd be driving somewhere and look in the rear-view mirror and he'd be behind me. I went out with a chap – a very nice man. My ex-husband went to his office and threatened him. 'Don't you dare go out with my wife.'"

"He sounds dangerous," I said.

"That's what I told the police. That he was obsessed. He's got three rifles. But they said, 'He hasn't done anything, has he?' 'He keeps stalking me and staring at me through the window,' I said. But that wasn't enough. I couldn't prove anything. He hadn't done anything physical, see."

In the rain and wind the ship pulled out of Limassol harbor, and I was glad I was here and not there.

"I got so worried I decided to leave," she said. "I went to India, to Egypt, to Greece. Maybe he'll leave me alone when I get back."

She won the hand, gathered the cards, let me cut them, shuffled them and leaned over.

"Maybe I'll never go back," she said.

The ship was rolling as it sailed around the coast of western Cyprus, past Aphrodite's birthplace and Cape Drepanon and the last horned cape on this island of horn-like capes, Arnaoutis, and then into the darkness towards Rhodes.

Rhodes — Colossus of Rhodes, one of the Seven Wonders of the World, a giant bronze figure: was this my compelling interest on this island? No, it was not. How could it be? It was just an old story. The thing had been erected 2,300 years ago, it had been knocked down sixty-five years later and sold off as scrap. So much for the Colossus of Rhodes.

But not far from where this monstrous statue once stood, Spillman the Belgian was saying to me, "I will buy a chicken. I will drink some water. I will play music for the people in the town square. After one cup of tea I will return to the ship. At six o'clock I will take food. Some fruit. Some cheese."

"You are very well organized, Mr Spillman."

"I do make planations of my daily life," he said, his English faltering, "so I do not make a depression."

As he walked along, distracted — perhaps hungry — his English became a sort of homage to Hercule Poirot.

"You can tell by my visage that I am a Jewish? Attention, I buy some parfum for my muzzah!"

This and more was my experience of Rhodes. The old walled city of Rhodes was one of the most beautiful I had seen in the Mediterranean; the Palace and Hospital of the Crusader knights were graceful as well as powerful. The water was brilliantly blue, and mainland Turkey was visible just across the channel. But all this was a backdrop for my walk with pigeon-toed Spillman. I admired him for having ingeniously compensated for his spells of depression. He liked his life, and provided he did not deviate from this route through the Mediterranean in which fruit markets and cheese stalls loomed larger than ruins, his life was happy. I began to reflect on how in the way I was traveling there was an unusual and apparently disjointed process at work. There was something immensely more interesting to me in hearing about Melva and Ted's divorce, and the spooky behavior of her crazed ex-husband, than in hearing a story of – well, as we had just left Limassol, let us say the tale of Richard the Lionheart's marriage to Berengaria of Navarre in 1191, at Limassol Castle, a building that had been practically demolished.

I could not deny that the setting mattered. The Rock of Gibral tar to me was a French tourist on a ledge at the top pinching an ape. I remembered Van Gogh's Arles because I was almost run down by a high-speed train at Arles station, while entranced by almond blossoms. In Olbia, Sardinia, a Senegalese scrounger told me in Italian how in Africa (which he visited regularly) he had two wives and six children: "Not many." In Durrell's Kyrenia, Fikret the Turk suffered over his bean soup and said, "I have been thinking about marriage . . . Please tell me what to do." I could not now think of Jerusalem without seeing a Lubavitcher Jew in a black hat and coat hoisting his orange mountain bike into an angry Arab's cabbages. My lasting impression of Dubrovnik was not its glorious city, but rather its bomb craters and broken roofs and the Croat Ivo saying, "I came home. Because home is home."

Places had voices that were not their own; they were backdrops to a greater drama, or else to something astonishingly ordinary, like the ragged laundry hung from the nave of a plundered Crusader church in Tartus, on the Syrian coast. Most of the time, traveling, I had no idea where I was going. I was not even quite sure why. I was no historian. I was not a geographer. I hated politics. What I liked most was having space and time; getting up in the morning and setting off for a destination which at any moment – if something better compelled my attention – I could abandon. I had no theme. I did not want one. I had set out to be on the Mediterranean, without a fixed program. I was not writing a book – I was living my life, and had found an agreeable way to do it.

In this way I was exactly like the others on the *Sea Harmony*. We only looked like lost souls, but we had our achievements: Spillman, who had solved the problem of his depression; Melva, who was free of her husband's threats; the Bratislava pilgrims, for whom prayer was a way of life; the German, Heinz, who traveled with his little family. And more.

Delayed in Rhodes, I ran into Yegor, the bald and toothless Israeli who was always boasting how he had fought in three wars. He wore old tattered clothes and his only luggage was a small canvas bag. He slept in the cheap seats, where Spillman played, and sometimes he spoke French to Spillman. On board the first day he had said to me, "You have a cabin? I want to sleep with you!" And he laughed a loud toothless laugh, his lips flapping at me. He was obviously excitable. So I had not encouraged conversation.

But he ambushed me. I left Spillman looking for his chicken restaurant and his fruit stand; I had headed out of the walled city to the windy bay on the fringes of which tourist-resort Rhodes lay as new and ugly as every other new Greek seaside town. The Greek genius for tacky construction surpassed anything I had seen – surprising in people who claimed the Parthenon as part of their heritage.

Even Yegor remarked on the flimsy construction. It was the strong wind, battering the hotel signs and tearing at the power lines. None of the hotels was open and, absent of people, they looked abandoned and vulnerable.

"I think the wind will make them crash down!" Yegor said. His whinnying laugh was bad, but the sight of his toothless mouth was worse. I also thought: Why do apparently weak-minded people take such delight in disasters?

His dog, young and strong, tugged him along on its rope leash.

"What's your dog's name?"

"Johnny Halliday."

Hearing its name, the dog hesitated and glanced back at his master. Then he trotted on.

"But I call him Johnny."

Again the dog turned its soulful eyes on Yegor.

"I take it you're a soldier, Yegor," I said.

"Three wars," he said. "In '67, the Egyptians had swords and tried to cut us" – he flailed his arms – "like this, our heads off! But we beat them! I was given a free apartment. I pay only forty shekels for one month."

"You're lucky."

"But I have a big problem," Yegor said. "I drink."

"You get drunk?"

"I get drunk. I go to jail."

"What are Israeli jails like?"

"Jews in one room, Arabs in another room. In each room, twenty men," Yegor said. "One toilet only."

"That's not very nice."

"Horrible. And they fight, the prisoners."

"What do they fight about?"

"On your first day, they take your food, to make you frightened. So you have to fight. What else can you do?"

We were walking down Papanikolaou in the new part of Rhodes city, a block or so from where waves were being blown on to the bright deserted shore. We had passed the edge of Mandraki harbor, where on one corner – so it was thought – the Colossus had stood. But speculating on this Wonder of the World meant a great deal less than the reality of Yegor's saying, *On your first day, they take your food, to make you frightened.*

"The police arrested you because you were drunk?"

"Because I broke a table," Yegor said.

"An expensive table?"

"Not expensive, and not big. Made out of glass."

"How did you break it?"

"I used a man to break it," Yegor said.

"You used a man?"

"I took him and crashed him down, so I broke the man, too. Ha! Ha! Ha!" That laugh again, those gums, those lips. "I was drunk, so they arrested me."

"Were you in prison long?"

"Some months," Yegor said. "But I have been seventeen times in prison. I can't help it – I drink too much!"

He jerked his dog's leash, the dog made a strangled noise, and they walked on, the dog yapping in a sharp imitation of his master's laugh.

Later that day, back inside the old castellated city, I was admiring the medieval walls and the carved escutcheons when Yegor accosted me.

"I told you lies," he said. "Ha!"

"About going to prison?"

"If you go to prison in Israel they take your passport, and I have a passport, so how could I go to prison? Ha! You believed me!"

The problem with a liar is not his frank admission of lying but rather when he robustly asserts that he is telling the truth.

Another of the loners was leaving the ship in Rhodes. This was a young fellow named Pinky, who congregated with the Germans and Spillman and Melva and others in the cheap seats. The name Pinky was short for Pinsker. He made a living in Canada working as a teacher in settlements of the Ojibway and Ojib-Cree people. The villages were in remote parts of Canada. The job was well paid but stressful. Burned-out, was the way he put it.

"For example, the kids are real delinquents sometimes."

"How does an Ojibway teenager express his delinquency?"

"You wake up in the morning and you see that they've covered your house in graffiti – names and swear-words and everything. And they go nuts with snowmobiles. You're a writer, aren't you?"

I smiled at him in what I hoped was an enigmatic way.

"I can tell by the way you're always asking questions. And you're the only one who listens to Spillman."

Pinsker told me he was rather lonely. It was about time he found someone to share his life. He had not found much romance in the Ojibway settlements of northern Canada, and so he had set out on an extended trip, hoping to meet someone. His month working on a kibbutz had not improved his situation, and it had surprised him in other ways. As a Jew he had been shocked by some of what he had seen.

"The kids knew nothing about Judaism. Can you imagine that, in Israel?" he said. "A lot of them had never been to a synagogue. They were pre-Bar Mitzvah age, but they didn't study. I've never seen Jews like that — I was surprised by their ignorance."

"But better behaved than the Ojibway kids?"

"Not really. Some of them were really obnoxious — always fooling," he said. "What do you think of Israel?"

"The land of contradictions," I said. I mentioned some of what I had seen. Small land, big contradictions.

"When I was on the kibbutz someone told me a really interesting theory," Pinsker said. "It's like this. In the Diaspora, Jews realize that non-Jews are always looking at them and so they strive to be religious. They work, they study difficult subjects, they try to get ahead in the community — they want to excel, and they usually succeed. They know they are seen as Jews and that it's important that they succeed. Don't you think that part of it is true?"

"If you say so."

Pinsker said, "But when they get to Israel they consider that they've arrived. They don't have to prove anything to anyone. They sit around and complain — there's no need to do anything. Who's looking? Who cares? They abandon their ambitions and get lazy. That's why Israel is the way it is, and why it doesn't seem Jewish."

Pinsker was staying in Rhodes, hoping to catch a ferry to the Turkish town of Marmaris in the morning. He said goodbye and wandered away to look for a hotel, while I went back to the ship, thinking how little I had learned of the island. But it had been importantly a backdrop for the lives of these travelers, and as a gorgeous location it gave their stories an exoticism that made them memorable. There was, as always, a poignant interplay between the melancholy banalities of the travelers' tales and the locale of this lovely island.

We were at sea, making for Piraeus all the next day, through the Cyclades — never out of sight of an island, and usually within sight of a half a dozen. On the bridge the captain dreamed of invading Turkey and reclaiming land that he felt belonged rightly to Greece. There was bouzouki music inside and cold, raw weather outside. There was nowhere to sit on deck. The twenty-eight Slovakians from Bratislava were on their knees in one lounge, praying; the Greeks in another, smoking. The squalor in the cheap seats became remarkable, a piling-up of bags and garbage and supine bodies.

Three nights in a row I had the same dream. I was an actor in a Shakespearean play that might have been *Hamlet*. I was the main actor, probably Hamlet. This was unclear in the dream because although it was a large and elaborate production I did not know any of my lines – not one. I did not even know the names of the other characters. It was all a muddle and mystery, especially as I had never been in a play in my life. Perhaps it was an anxiety dream about being unprepared and having to improvise. My method of travel was all about improvisation.

Each time I had the dream I was arriving at the theater – a sort of open-air affair, with many people in the audience, and lots of actors and stage-hands, most of them greeting me with high hopes. None of them had the slightest idea that I did not know my lines. I would covertly pick up a copy of the play and leaf through its several hundred pages and realize that there was no way that I could learn my part between now and ten minutes from now when the curtain was going up on the first act. I experienced a sense of absurd humiliation and panic, as people greeted me and congratulated me, telling me how much they were looking forward to my performance.

Most dreams are merciful. Each night, just before the curtain rose, I awoke.

I continued to play games of "Crappy Joe" with Melva. She was feeling optimistic and fitter than she had in Egypt and Israel, though still on antibiotics. "I'm coming good!" she said. She wanted to be independent. "I'm not a bludger," she said. "Don't look back!"

When we arrived at Piraeus we announced where we were going and realized that we were each going to a different place – Melva was staying in Athens, hoping to meet some Australians; the Germans were going to Crete, Spillman to Brindisi, Yegor was vague, Pinsker was gone. The Israelis whose names I never learned were speeding away in their car, heading for Croatia, they would not say why. Spillman said he was depressed – it was cloudy, and cloudy days were awful for him. And then Yegor handed his dog's rope leash to him. The Greeks laughed. Spillman grew furious as the dog, agitated and confused, nipped other passengers. Then "Johnny Halliday" bit Spillman on the groin. Spillman's fly was usually open – it was open this morning. He clasped himself and sat down and began to cry, and at that moment someone turned up the bouzouki music.

I hurried to a train, and a bus and a ferry; to Bari, and more trains. All the while I heard Spillman's shout of hurt and complaint, as Yegor's dog yapped. But I had not hesitated on the quay. I had been there before.

17

The Ferry *El-Loud III* to Kerkennah

Tunisia is another Mediterranean island, surrounded on one side by water and on the other by pariah states: fanatic Libya on the south-east, blood-drenched Algeria on the west, and the blue Mediterranean on its long irregular coast, scalloped by gulfs and bays. Foreigners do not enter Tunisia by road. There are planes, of course, and there are ferries from France and Italy. I sailed into Tunis on a ferry from slap-happy Trapani in Sicily, entering the harbor at La Goulette in the late afternoon and passing Carthage, the little that remained of it, just a rubble-pile of marble where the glorious city had once stood.

I had now been on enough Mediterranean islands to sense that Tunisia was deeply insular. People said that Turkey and Syria were isolated, but that was not strictly true – there were buses from Turkey to Egypt, and from Syria to Jordan and Lebanon. Even poor miserable Albania had road and ferry access to Greece and Macedonia. My road and rail trip from Istanbul to Haifa had been slow and fairly awful at times – six border crossings and lots of irritation – but I had been safe; no one had attempted to cut my throat.

Islamic militants in Algeria had carried out their vow to kill foreigners. Their aim was to destabilize the country by frightening foreigners, who were Algeria's mainstay in running their oil-based economy. Seven Italian sailors – the entire crew of the ship *Lucina* – had recently had their throats slit as they slept in their bunks in the Algerian port of Jijel, not far from the Tunisian frontier; and a few months before that, twelve Croats had been found dead on their ship, their throats cut. Visitors to Libya sometimes simply disappeared. Such stories were a strong inducement to treat Tunisia as an island, and even Tunisians treated it that way. They never suggested crossing one of these borders; they seldom did so themselves – when they left Tunisia it was to go to France or Italy, to work at menial jobs.

Walking through the small, pleasant city of Tunis to shake off the effects of my sedentary trip, I was reminded by the street names of events here. There was Rue 18 Janvier 1952, Boulevard du 9 Avril 1938, Rue du 2 Mars 1934, Place 3 Août 1903, and many others. I noticed that the sky was full of birds. They were like dark, madly twittering sparrows or swifts, and they swooped and roosted in enormous noisy flocks, blackening the sky and wheeling back and forth. As they rose in the air, they shat in tremendous squirts that splashed on virtually everyone strolling on the Avenue Habib Bourguiba. These pestiferous birds are called *asfour zitoun* by the Tunisians – "olive birds," for their habit of snatching the olives from the great coastal crop.

I felt pleased with myself: I had arrived slowly by sea; I had discovered there was a railway network throughout the country; I was now resident in a 35-dollar hotel. I liked the food, Tunis was the right size – not much more than a big town – and the people were approachable. Already I had met the Taoufiks – Mr was Tunisian, Mrs was from Birmingham – and their 16-year-old son. After seventeen years in the country none of them had been to either Algeria or Libya. "And nothing has changed here in seventeen years!"

Another man, Ahmed, had lived and worked in New York City for three years, at 42nd between 7th and 8th. "I was working in a shop selling smoking things, like water pipes and souvenirs." He had a Green Card. So why was he back in Tunisia? He hated New York City: "Too many people and too dangerous, because," he said pointedly, "of black people and white people." I met Mr Salah who had gone to college in Baltimore. "I was there, like, four and a half years, studying business management. It was a neat place." Most of all, he missed basketball – the heroes, Jordan, Ewing, Rodman, O'Neal.

Tunisians seemed to me hospitable and pleasant, especially Ali, whom I bumped into at the railway station. He asked in Italian, "You're Italian?"

This was another country, like Malta and Albania and Croatia, within range of Italian TV broadcasts, so that many of the people who owned televisions also spoke Italian. But Ali had also worked in Rome for a while. Then he came back, got married and now had three lovely girls — he showed me their pictures.

We were walking along, chatting in Italian. He spoke it well. This was not some tout who wanted an English lesson, or a loan, or to offer me a deal on some local merchandise. He spoke about his children. He had an enlightened view of women and was eager, he said, for his girls to have the same chance as a boy in Tunisia.

He looked up and pointed ahead, beyond the people crowding the sidewalk. "The Medina is at the end of this street," he said. "Incredible place — you've seen it?"

"I just arrived yesterday."

"You're in luck. There's a big event this morning — the Berber carpet-sellers' market. You've heard of the Berbers? I'm a Berber myself, from a village near Gafsa."

He unfolded my map of Tunisia and showed me the exact location of his village. I really ought to visit him there sometime, he said. He would introduce me to the elders and take me around. Berber culture was real Tunisian culture, and carpets were their masterpieces.

"But we haven't got much time at the moment. This Berber market closes at noon and look — it's eleven-fifteen. Berber carpets are lovely — but then I am biased, being a Berber myself. Right through here."

It was a classic entrance to a bazaar, narrow, with fabrics hung up and fluttering like flags, and all sort of brassware and carvings stacked near it, and a beckoning fragrance of perfume and spices. Entering it reminded me of the souk at Aleppo — once I stepped out of the city heat and dust I was in the humid shadows of this labyrinth, in the passageways, where men in gowns sipped coffee at the entrance to their tiny shops.

Ali moved so fast through the crowd that I had to hurry to keep up with him, dodging some people and squeezing past others. Fortunately he was a tall fellow, and so much bigger than the other Tunisians that I could see him above the crowd of shoppers.

"I don't want you to be late," he called out, glancing back and moving a bit faster. "The Berbers will all be going home with their carpets pretty soon."

We passed a shop selling books and papers.

"I need to buy a notebook."

"Later," he said, stepping up his pace. "When you have time to look calmly you will be able to buy many good things."

He used a nice Italian phrase, *tante belle cose*, and I was reassured once again. He seemed the most sensible and helpful person I had met on my whole trip – not just in Tunisia but in the Mediterranean; he had the right priorities, he was the perfect host.

Fifteen minutes later in the middle of the souk, and I was utterly lost. Following Ali I had not paid any attention to landmarks, and so I stayed as close to him as I could. We passed carpenters and barber shops and shops selling bolts of silk and finished clothes, bakeries, jewelers, tourist curio shops selling dead scorpions ("for good luck"), amber beads, crimson coral made into beads and necklaces, old muskets, brassware, inlaid boxes, carved boars' tusks and more.

Seeing these robes, the Benedictine-monk garb of the Berber, covering body and head like a monk's cowl, I contemplated going into Algeria as Sir Richard Burton would have done – as he did do in Mecca, totally in disguise, in the forbidden place that was dangerous to any unbeliever. But Burton spoke fluent Arabic, and he would have learned Maghrebi Arabic for such a venture, and his *cojones* were of a legendary size.

"We're almost there," Ali said, turning a corner.

Just around the corner was a colorful shop, larger than any other, and stacked with carpets. Ali greeted the smiling man in the doorway.

"You're just in time," the man said in Italian – he spoke it even better than Ali. "Everything closes in twenty minutes."

We hurried upstairs and I was offered a soft drink. I said no thanks, since I knew that accepting any sort of gift in a carpet shop would obligate me – a cup of coffee, a drink, food; anything.

"Where are the Berbers?" I asked. Somehow I had been expecting a compound where scores of men in robes were muttering encouragement for me to examine their carpets.

"There – there."

He motioned me past a bed. Very large, with inset mirrors and ivory carvings, it stood against one wall, like a museum piece.

"The king's bed. Why is it so large?" the manager said. "He slept there with his four wives. But when Tunisia became modern and got rid of kings they also got rid of polygamy, and we bought the bed. As you can see, it is very beautiful and very expensive. Fine work."

"Please sit down," Ali said. "Time is short."

But it was only noon and we were in a carpet shop. I said, "I don't understand why time is short."

"The promotion – the carpet sale," the manager said.

"What promotion? I thought the Berbers were going home with their carpets. Where are the Berbers?"

"Please look," the manager said, growing irritable.

Small nimble men began unrolling carpets – lots of them, and the carpets were tumbling at my feet, being flapped apart and stacked. They were all colors, all patterns and sizes, rugs, prayer mats, kilims, runners. The manager was narrating this business, saying that this carpet was red because it was a marriage carpet, and this one was blue because blue was a favorite Berber color, and this was a kilim that was the same on both sides – see? And this carpet had a design to ward off the evil eye.

"Is there an evil eye in Tunisia?" I asked.

"There is evil eye in the whole world," the manager said. "Which one do you like?"

"The red one, the blue one, this one – they're all nice."

"This is 500 dollars. This is 900 dollars. This is –"

"Never mind."

"You want to buy this one?"

"No."

"Four hundred – what do you say. Go on, make me an offer."

"I'll think about it."

"You can't think. You have to buy it by noon. When the promotion ends."

Now, much too late, I realized that I had been hustled; so I resisted.

"I'll come back."

"You can't come back. What do you offer me?"

"Nothing right now. Maybe tomorrow."

"No! No!" he said. "There is no time. Just say a number!"

Just say a number? Hearing that, I laughed. The manager got angry and muttered harshly to Ali, who whispered back at him, and they began bickering in whispers, and every so often the manager howled, "Not much time!"

I thought: I am a fool. I am sitting here with one man howling and the other whispering and a third and fourth still unrolling carpets. I got up to leave. I said I would come back.

"You can't come back – you can never come back!" the manager screamed at me, still in Italian – *Mai, mai!* Never, never!

Back in the twisting passageways of the bazaar, Ali – who was somewhat subdued – said, "Let's say hello to my father," and stopped in front of a perfume shop. There was no one in the shop. Ali snatched a vial of perfume.

"Jasmine! Special to the Berbers!"

"Not today." I wondered whether he would persist.

"This is a present. No money! Take it!"

"I am afraid it will spill in my pocket," I said, and defied him to answer this.

He shrugged and turned as the perfume-seller, who was not old enough to be Ali's father, entered the shop and exchanged greetings with him.

I walked away, but Ali was next to me. He said, "So, how much will you give me for taking you around?"

"I don't want to be taken around."

"I just took you around. What about *baksheesh* for everything that I showed you?"

"For everything that you showed me?" I said, thinking: Here is another pair of mammoth *cojones*. "Nothing."

He left, grumbling, yet I did not dislike him really. I hated myself for falling for the line, *We don't have much time!* But it was a brilliant gimmick.

In the souk, in the street, at the station, the faces of Tunis were the faces of the Mediterranean in a much more remarkable way than anywhere else I had been on the shores of this sea. The Arab face predominated, but Arab faces ranged from pasty freckled and pale-eyed to utterly dusty almost Dravidian masks. The faces of Tunis could have been Italian, Spanish, Greek, Sardinian, Turkish, Albanian – and probably were. In Tunisia, Europe and all its colors met North Africa and all its colors, and one blended into the other. With its great ports and its easy proximity to Italy, the country had always been a crossroads. When the Vandals conquered Spain and North Africa they sacked Carthage and re-entered Europe by hopping over from here to Italy. It was an easy distance, for which Sicily was the stepping-stone.

Racially it was not monochromatic, and the clothes too were still reminiscent of orientalist paintings, the shrouded women, the veils, the shawls – as well as pale pouty girls in blue jeans and big bossy women in sunglasses and frilly dresses.

I went by train to Al Marsa via Goulette, Salambo, Carthage (Hannibal), Carthage (Amilcar), Sidi Bou-Said and the Corniche. At Sidi Bou-Said, a small town on a hill overlooking the sea, all whitewashed houses, I hiked around. The houses had blue shutters, blue doors, blue porches: the blue was supposed to keep the mosquitoes away. Down by the sea, the shore was littered – as bad here as it had been a thousand miles away on the Syrian beaches. In the thin woods beside the shore there were Tunisian lovers – couples smooching in the oleanders, and a profusion of stray cats.

There seemed to be nothing else at Sidi Bou-Said. The vestiges of Carthage's memory were remote conquests of the Phoenicians, Hannibal's battles, the Punic Wars, St Augustine (he had been a student there), and the Barbary pirates. The traditional date of the founding of Carthage was 814 B.C. But there were more recent memories. Robert Fox writes how, after the mysterious death of three Israelis in Cyprus in 1985, Israeli planes appeared in the skies on this part of the coast and bombed the PLO compound, intending to kill Yassir Arafat. Seventy-two people died in this Israeli bombing. Arafat was not one of them. Fox goes on, "Two years later Israeli raiding parties landed from the sea at the village of Sidi Bou-Said, the St Tropez of Tunis, to murder a senior PLO figure, Khalil al-Wazir, whose *nom de guerre* was Abu Jihad, in his bungalow; the Israeli government believed, erroneously, that he had organized the Intifada in the Occupied Territories."

Black, yellow-streaked clouds loomed over Carthage (Baedeker in 1911: ". . . the beauty of the scenery and the wealth of historical memories amply compensate for the deplorable state of the ruins"), and soon the rain began. It was as strong as monsoon rain, and as sudden and overwhelming, casting a twilight shadow over the coast and hammering straight down with a powerful sound, the water beating on the earth, smacking the street. At once the gutters were awash. Then the streets were flooded. The train halted, the traffic was snarled. *Look, it's like a dam!* a woman cried out in French, at the sight of a field. There was a kind of hysteria as the rain came down. People were gabbling, they were confused. The city began to drown, and then it simply failed.

It was a turning-point in my trip, though I did not realize it until quite a while afterwards. From this moment onward the weather deteriorated. It went bad. It thwarted me. It frustrated my plans. Short periods of sunshine were separated by long spells of low cloud and wind, until the wind became a spectacular Levanter. The low pressure and all the damp rooms and shut windows and stale air also seemed to make me ill. Within a few days I had a severe cold – a sore throat, stomach trouble, aching muscles.

Deciding to leave Tunis, I solicited advice from Tunisians. *See the desert!* they said. *See the cave-dwellers at Matmata! Go to Tozeur and Djerba. There are Jews in Djerba! See the nomads and the camel-sellers and the weavers! See the mystics who fondle scorpions! Go to Sousse – tourists love Sousse! Whatever you do, don't go to Sfax. There is nothing in Sfax.*

So I bought a ticket to Sfax. The ticket was ten dollars for first class, and another dollar for the Comfort Section of first class. Sfax was about 200 miles away, down the coast, where I hoped the weather was better. My idea was to go there and convalesce until I felt well enough to continue my traveling.

I would have preferred to take the train west to the Algerian border, to Bizerte, then Jendouba and on to Annaba (Bône) on the Algerian coast. In a more peaceful time it would have been a wonderful trip, from Tunis to Tangiers, along the coast. Before I started traveling in the Mediterranean it had been my intention to take this route. But then I had discovered that Tunisia was an island. Some other time I would return, and go to Beirut and Algeria and perhaps to Libya. It was impossible to be exhaustive on any trip – even living in another country had not allowed me enough time to go everywhere, to see everything. After eighteen years in Britain, much of it was unknown to me. For example, I never went to Shropshire, and I had always wanted to go there. After a year's travel in China I had failed to get to Hainan island. In the Pacific I never achieved my goal of sailing to Pitcairn island. I was not dismayed. I turned them into ambitions. It was something to dream about, for unvisited places inspired greater dreams than places I had seen. The existence of the unknown was the wellspring of my dreams. And I also thought, *I'll be back*.

The train was almost empty. The only people in the Comfort Section were a Vietnamese woman and a chain-smoking Tunisian man who was trying to woo a young Tunisian woman traveling on her own.

We were out of Tunis, beyond the slums, the suburbs, the refuse heaps and scavengers in shacks, in a matter of minutes, and then it was all olive groves for sixty miles. Like so many other parts of the Mediterranean shore, olive trees predominated. There were more here, and they were more orderly and fruitful, than in Greece. They were organized on terraces, with cactuses and spiky century plants arranged around them as perimeter fences, and with so much space between the trees the olives could be picked mechanically.

I saw an old woman riding a donkey through a herd of goats, I saw shepherds strolling behind flocks of sheep, and stumbling lambs, and in the geometric settlements there were low square houses on grids of streets. I had known nothing about Tunisia before I had gotten off the Sicilian ferry, and so I was pleased to see how orderly and apparently self-sufficient it was. And it was another secular place – at least there was no state religion, either theological or political.

Greener and tidier as we continued south, the countryside was flat and agricultural. It seemed a very peaceful land, in spite of the stormy weather. Passing through Sousse – the railway line went right down Sousse's main street, along the promenade, around the port – I was reminded that it had been recommended as a nice place to visit. It was clearly a tourist town.

Thirty or forty miles south of Sousse we came to El Djem. The town was insignificant, but the Roman amphitheater in El Djem was more impressive and better preserved than the coliseum in Rome, which it much resembles. It is also said to be bigger.

"It's in better shape and there's more of it than the one in Rome," an American man said to me, at El Djem. He was Mike from Louisiana.

Mike's friend Steve said, "This thing is real old."

They could appreciate the handiwork in El Djem because they were in construction themselves. They had been living in Sfax for almost two months, living alone – going slightly crazy, they said – supervising the building of an oil-drilling platform offshore.

Steve went on. "It was built in something like 1720."

"Isn't it Roman?" I said.

"The guy didn't say, but I'll tell you one thing. This sucker is well built."

"That's for sure," Steve said, and leaned way back to admire the complex arrangement of arches.

"Is this A.D. or B.C.?" Mike said.

"What's the difference?" Steve replied.

Exactly, I thought. Surely the point was that it was about a thousand years older than any other building in the town and yet was stronger, more handsome and symmetrical and would probably outlast all the rest of them.

I got a later train onward to Sfax, and was at first alarmed by the ugly suburbs and tenements, but at last I was reassured. It was a more somber and quieter place than Tunis, with just a few main streets, a boulevard and a harbor. Mike and Steve told me that the medina – the bazaar – was worth seeing. There were some islands fifteen or twenty miles offshore but they had not been there. It's kind of a quiet place, they said. And they added, *We're going nuts here.*

It was right for me. There was no traffic. There was a sea breeze. The hotels cost almost nothing. There were no tourists here, because the town supposedly lacked color. Yet people lived here, and they worked and prospered. They traded in salt and fish and phosphate and sulfur, as well as in the products of the poorer inland places – spices and handmade goods from Kairouan and Gafsa. On this cool damp night there was a crowd of milling men along the main boulevard of Sfax that resembled the *passegiata* of Sicily and Calabria. I felt that I was outside the mainstream, on the sea. I liked the briny odor of the breeze, and the great clammy blankness at the shore that was like a black wall at night.

I did not feel well. I went through the medina the next day and had to ask permission of a carpet-seller to sit in his shop for a while – I was dizzy and weak. While I sat and perspired, feeling ghastly, he unwrapped a Berber kilim. It was striped, vividly colored, hand-woven of wool.

"I'll wrap it for you, so you can carry it."

"I am too ill to carry anything."

But three days later I went back and bought it, for sixty dollars. It was ten feet by six feet. In a year and a half of travel on the shores of the Mediterranean, it was the only thing I bought; indeed, it was the only thing I saw that I wished to buy.

In those three days I vowed to get better. I knew I had a bad cold and some sort of low-grade infection in my lungs. I took aspirin. I tried to clear my lungs by eating spicy food, the soup they called *h'lalem*, couscous with hot pepper sauce, and glasses of Tunisian mint tea.

Reading about the anniversary of Nietzsche's birth, I had a context for examining my own bad state of health at the moment. I had become interested in him since reading about him in the Oliver Sacks book. "Fritz," as his sister called him, had been born 150 years ago, in Rocken, Germany. He wrote *Beyond Good and Evil* and *Thus Spake Zarathustra*. He loved music. Somewhat unfairly, he had been taken up by the Nazis who admired his saying, "What fails to kill me makes me stronger." He went insane in 1889 and returned home to live with his mother and sister. He spent his last seven years as a vegetable, and died in 1900 at the age of fifty-six. But some years before the end, there were signs of eccentricity.

"He was fond of playing the piano, splashing in the bath-tub and occasionally carefully removing his shoes and urinating in them."

This strange case-history had the effect of making me feel that I was perhaps not so ill after all.

*

All my life I have hated being asked to explain what I am doing. I hate the question because I very seldom know the answer.

It was Sunday in Sfax, and everything was closed. After three days supine in the seedy grandeur of the Hôtel des Oliviers I was feeling slightly better, though I was far from well. I woke thinking: What about Djerba? It was a whole day's traveling south by train. Gabès was halfway. What about Gabès? But I hesitated when I realized there was a ferry this morning to Kerkennah. The two islands of Kerkennah were about fifteen miles offshore from Sfax. It took an hour and a half. It cost fifty cents. The ferry was leaving shortly and it was called *El-Loud III*. All these details, especially the name, helped me make up my mind to go to Kerkennah.

I grabbed my bag and hurried to the ferry port. How would I have explained this apparently indecisive behavior to a traveling companion, who would ask the reasonable question, *Where are we going?* I would have to answer, *I'm not sure.*

Traveling in a general direction, without a specific destination, it was necessary for me to be alone. It wasn't fair to expect anyone to put up with that much indecision or suspense. I was not sure why I had come to Sfax, until I got there. This may be another difference between a traveler and a tourist: the traveler is vague, the tourist is certain. But I was vindicated in my ignorant decision. My two-day trip to Kerkennah was pleasant.

There were about 300 passengers on the ferry, all Tunisian; many of them were returning to their island home for the day, some of them were picnickers, a few had gone along for the ride. Being Tunisians they were all sorts, but this was also a feature of the Mediterranean coast. There was no place that I had seen on my entire trip that was one thing – a single people, the same face, the same religion, all dressed the same. One of the pleasures of the Mediterranean was the way in which the complex cultures had intermingled, though what was true of the shoreline was not the case in the inland villages.

The passengers were old, young, light, dark, orthodox, liberated, some in shawls, some in fezzes, others in baseball hats. One of the youths had a saxophone, and with a drummer he improvised Arabic melodies on the open deck. It was a good-humored and friendly crowd. They treated each other with courtesy, didn't push, and were easygoing, high-spirited and respectful. One man had a sprig of jasmine stuck over his ear, like a Tahitian wearing a blossom.

There were cormorants diving into a flat sea and there were distant fishing-boats, but there was nothing else for almost an hour. It was not the distance of the islands that made them hard to see; it was that they were low-lying, the highest one just a few feet above sea-level. They came into view as smudges on the sea, and then began to look like atolls, Gharbi first and then the edges of its sister island, Chergui.

Some old buses and taxis were parked in the dust at the ferry landing, waiting for passengers. The drivers sat on stacks of palm fronds that had been trimmed of their stalks. These palms were the only vegetation on the islands.

"Where do you want to go?" a driver asked me in French.

"To the town."

"No town. Only villages."

"Is there a hotel?"

"Get in."

Where are we going, Paulie?

There were five of us in the taxi. Kerkennah was too small to show as anything but a dot on my map and so I really had no idea where we might be going, or what places existed on the islands. The only landscape I could see was perfectly flat and arid, stony yellow ground and dying palms with ratty fronds.

"Where are you going?" I asked the other passengers.

"Remla."

"Is that a nice place?"

"Very nice," they said.

"I want to go to Remla," I said to the driver.

"No," he said.

"Oh, all right," I said.

We passed two or three settlements of small square houses, some with flat roofs and some with domes, and scattered shops, and chickens in the road. It was the simplest place I had seen so far on the Mediterranean coastline. The land was flat, the trees were few, the houses were small. It was not run-down, just silent, empty, lonely, one-dimensional. There were no power lines, apparently no lights.

What I took to be a village was a cemetery with hut-like tombs, each one with the face of the deceased painted on the side, the size of a political poster, the same empty gaze.

We came to a crossroads, took a left, a right, a left. There were no signs. We were on gravel roads now. Then there were no villages at all, just those battered, withered palm trees. There were no people. We drove on for half an hour and then came to a sign, "Grand Hotel," with an arrow. A high wall, a gate, a plaster building, a man.

"Welcome." It was a Tunisian in his pajamas, speaking English.

There was no one else around. After the taxi left there was silence, like dust sifting down, a bird's chirp that was so slight I realized that only this tremendous silence made it possible for me to hear it.

"Very quiet today."

"No people."

"Are they coming?"

"Later."

"Today?"

He frowned. "No. Two months, three months from now."

"But I am here."

"You are welcome, sir."

This was not the first time on my trip that I had achieved the distinction of being the only guest in a hotel, but it was the first time I had managed it in a hotel this large.

"This way, sir."

I was taken through the hotel to the dining-room and shown to table 23. I counted the other tables: there were seventy-two.

"I am Wahid Number One," the waiter said, bowing.

"From Kerkennah?"

"From Kerkennah, sir. Is nice."

In this utterly empty place I felt optimistic. I thought: I'll stay here until I get well.

Wahid Number One served me *brik*, which was thin fried pastry, with canned tuna fish and a fried egg. That night's dinner was turkey. It was a pressed slab of old turkey parts, with gravy. The next day it was *brik* again, and spaghetti, and French fries made with bad fat. They were disgusting, ochreous meals, with cold wobbly desserts.

"Is there another hotel nearby?" I asked Wahid Number One.

"Farhat Hotel."

"Nice place?"

He shrugged. "Farhat Hotel they come French."

"And Grand Hotel?"

"They come English."

"In a few months," I said.

"Two or three months," he said.

Instead of retreating I decided to find out as much as I could about Kerkennah – give it a few days and then move on. In the meantime, two days here in this empty place was an experience unlike any I'd had on my trip. The ocean was gray in this threatening weather; the narrow sandy foreshore of the island was stacked with weed. I walked for several miles. Much of the shore was used as a dump – rusty cans, old cars, plastic bottles, trash. There were some houses, there was an old ruin. There were some date palms on the flat desert-like land. They had short orange fronds with clusters of dates. The dates had fallen and rotted, and so there were masses of buzzing flies.

Oleanders, and date palms, and a green stagnant swimming-pool. Except for the flies and the chirp of birds, not a single sound. Except for the manager and Wahid Number One, not another person. The houses a mile up the beach were empty. Amazingly, I was on the Mediterranean – the emptiest part I had so far seen, emptier than the emptiest part of Albania. There had been people here; they had come and gone. It was like a colony that had gone bust, an experiment that had failed.

All that I worked out on my first day. On my second day I went bird-watching. For all the reasons it had seemed dead and abandoned it was attractive to birds, and amounted to a bird sanctuary the like of which I had not seen anywhere on the Mediterranean shores – many different birds in great profusion. A number of them must have been migrants, since this had to be one of the stopping-off places for birds in their seasonal transit between Africa and northern Europe; others I took to be resident shore birds. The largest was a gray heron, about four feet tall and looking patient and important in its slow-motion strutting at the shoreline. I saw a little egret, and a quail that called out, "Wet my lips!" Farther on I spotted a wader that turned out to be a curlew, some plovers, a crested lark, a linnet, a red-rumped swallow. A whitish bird with a black mask and a gray cap and black wing-marks was definitely a great gray shrike. I had no bird book. I sketched them and wrote descriptions of their peculiar marks and later identified them. In this way, by spotting birds, I have given the flattest days of travel some meaning and a sense of discovery.

Later that second day I went to Remla, in the old bus that passed by the Grand. Remla was like a town at the end of the world. Apart from the subsistence fishing there was nothing else. The soil was too poor to support vegetable gardens. There were no lights. The town itself was a huddle of square huts set in a maze of damp passageways.

"What about water?"

"We have fountains."

The brackish undrinkable water came from wells. On the road there was a bar, Al Jezira, where the local people congregated. When a motorbike crepitated past the bar, the boys and old men looked up. These were the men who owned the fishing-boats. The boats had lateen sails, but the fishing was no good, the men told me. The desolation here surpassed anything I had so far seen. Experiencing it I regarded as a personal achievement. And on the third day, wishing greatly to leave Kerkennah, I told myself I felt much better. I said goodbye to Wahid Number One and left the empty hotel on the deserted beach and took the bus to the ferry landing. There I met Mourad, who was heading for Sfax, to visit his wife who was ill in the hospital there.

My first impression of Kerkennah was of a great emptiness – hot gravelly earth and dying trees and poor huts. But that appearance of nothingness was misleading. Everything here had a name. Remla was an important town, and without realizing – without knowing it – I had also been to El Attaïla and Oulad Kacem and Melita. This ferry landing was not just a ferry landing. The three decrepit houses here and the rutted road comprised the settlement of Sidi Youssef.

"What do you think of these islands?"

"This is my home," Mourad said.

Like most other Tunisians he had an air of uncorrupted courtesy.

And so we sailed back to Sfax on *El-Loud III*, and the morning light floated a russet color across the surface of the sea, while lambs bleated on the trucks below decks.

In Sfax I tried to solve the problem of traveling from Tunisia to Morocco without stopping in Algeria. I was given the name of a company in Tunis which acted as the agent for a Libyan ship, the *Garyounis*. This ship took both passengers and cargo and sailed from Tripoli to Tunis to Casablanca. I did not really want to leave Tunisia. I liked it here, and now I was ready to follow all the advice I had been given, about seeing the desert and the cave-dwellers at Matmata, and Tozeur, and the Jews in Djerba, and the nomads, and the camel-sellers, and the weavers, and the mystics who fondled scorpions. I called the agent. He said the *Garyounis* would be leaving in a few days for Casablanca.

I picked up my sixty-dollar kilim from Ahmed Khlif in the medina of Sfax, in his narrow shop at the Souk des Étoffes. I took the train back to Tunis.

Tunis was busy with two important events – the Carthage Film Festival and a decisive soccer match, Tunisia against Togo, to determine which country would qualify to play in the Africa Cup. I watched the match on television at the café in a back street, with about 200 people, men and boys. They were attentive, there were no outbursts, only murmurs. Tunisia was ahead, one to nil for most of the match, and towards the end, when Togo kicked the equalizer, not a word was spoken. The only interruption came when the strangled cry of a muezzin gave his call to prayers. A number of people got down, faced east, and prayed – five minutes of this – then back to the match, which ended in a draw.

The Carthage Film Festival was promoted under the slogan "A Hundred Years of Tunisian Cinema!". This seemed to me as unlikely a claim as the centenary of Israeli railways that was being celebrated when I was in Haifa. Never mind. I pretended to be a movie critic and went to two of the movies. In spite of the name of the festival, the movies were shown in Tunis. Most had been made in the Mediterranean; France, Algeria, Lebanon, Libya, Morocco, Egypt and Palestine were represented. There were ten films from Turkey. The rest were from places as distant as Brazil and China.

My interest was the Mediterranean. I chose two films about places I had been. But I had not been able to penetrate the countries to this extent. *Couvre Feu* (Curfew), directed by a Palestinian, Raschid Masharaoui, was an insider's account of simple bravery and defiance against great odds, the stone-throwers of the Intifada facing the machine-guns of the Israeli soldiers.

Throughout the Mediterranean, the most-quoted atrocity of Bosnia was not a list of the number of dead but rather the deliberate shelling by the Serbs of the ancient bridge over the river at Mostar. The destruction of the bridge symbolized everything that was wicked about the war – the stupidity and meanness in the conflict, and all the atavistic cruelty that was still present in the Mediterranean. In *Bosna* (Bosnia), directed by Bernard Henry, I saw the bridge destroyed – and much else. This documentary showed the carnage of the war, the pitiful, merciless slaughter, the inert corpses by the roadside, the blood and broken glass and decapitations; the mass graves, weeping children, terrified adults and brutalized soldiers – snow, rain and ruin. But no atrocity in the film stirred the audience more than the shells – about a dozen of them altogether – falling on the bridge, and the bridge itself, which had stood for 500 years, finally falling to pieces into the river. The people in the theater gasped, there were pitiful groans, and when the lights came up there were tears in their eyes.

I went back to my hotel after the film about Bosnia and listened to the news on my short-wave radio. "Serbian forces are advancing on Bihać to reclaim territory they lost to the Bosnians in the past two weeks," I heard. The casualty figures for the dead, wounded and missing were given, and the news that Sarajevo (which I had seen shelled in the year-old documentary *Bosna* just an hour ago) was being shelled again.

The weather was rainy and cold. I was eager to move on. I returned to Mr Habib, the agent for the shipping lines.

"We are waiting for notification," the agent said. He was

friendly. He spoke English well. He said that it would be an interesting voyage.

I said, "As it's a Libyan ship, I think I should tell you that I am an American."

"No problem. I'll talk to the captain, just in case anyone thinks of doing something stupid to you."

I kept trying. But three days later Mr Habib was still waiting for notification, and there was no word about the *Garyounis*.

18

To Morocco on the Ferry *Boughaz*

This lake-like sea with such a tame coast had so habituated me to
sunshine and mediocre weather that it did not occur to me to stick
my face into the wind today and fathom its force. Surely the whole
point about picturesque landscapes was that they were not dangerous? But if I had simply wetted my finger and held it up I would
have known a great deal. As the rain and wind increased, I waited
for the *Garyounis* to take me to Morocco. I saw only that the wind
was lifting the flags higher and straighter than normal. A seasoned
Mediterranean sailor would have seen more muscle in that wind
than I had seen, sensed something darker and chillier, a turbulence
from the Levant, a dolphin-torn and gong-tormented sea. It was
the weather we had been having for a week. Mediterranean
weather usually came and went. But this did not go.

One day, Mr Habib said, "The *Garyounis* was put into dry-dock.
The Libyans are sending a different ship. It does not take passengers. Therefore, you will have to go some other time."

I muttered an insincere curse. This was not good weather for the
three-day voyage to the far side of Morocco. It was not good for
the short voyage to Sicily. There were no other ships to Morocco,
and I had vowed not to take any planes. The Marseilles ferry was
leaving next week. I decided to make my way by train through
Italy to France, where I might find a ferry to Morocco. It was a
very long detour, but what was the hurry?

My travels soon became what an exasperated English person
would call a bugger's muddle. Refusing to leave the ground, I
traveled from Sicily to Naples again, to Rome; and north by train
to Livorno and Pisa. Crossing from Nice to Corsica I had missed
this section of coast, which was dramatic, and dignified by rocky
cliffs and blasted by the wind. This was one of the loveliest

coastlines in the entire Mediterranean. It was another place that I would be happy to return to. I consoled myself by thinking that on the *Garyounis* I would have missed it – the houses clustered on the great plunging rock-cliffs of seaside Cinqueterre, the villas and precipices south of Antignano, the enormous blocks of marble piled at the station of Massa, near Carrara, which had supplied raw material to almost every Italian sculptor.

On the coast, all the way from Chiavari – where I was proud to have relatives – to Portofino and Rapallo and Genoa, the cliffs were too rugged to be vulgarly modernized, too sharply angled to serve as the foundations for condominiums. They had that in common with the cliffs of the Costa Brava in Spain, and the seaside heights of Croatia, and sections of the Turkish coast, and north Cyprus. But wherever the Mediterranean coast was flat it was over-built; the low-lying shores had been deemed suitable for hotels and mass tourism, and had been destroyed.

The rarest sight in the Mediterranean was surf, but at Imperia Porto Maurizio, approaching Ventimiglia, I saw six-foot rollers dumping foam on to the beach. Something unusual was happening in the Mediterranean this week; and still the wind was blowing from the east.

There were six older American couples in the train, bewildered by the weather, burdened by seventeen heavy suitcases. They were from Jackson, Mississippi, and they soon became embroiled with some Spanish students in a fuss about seats. The blustering turned to abuse. It was a blessing that these gentle people were not aware of what was being said to them in Spanish. They were the sort of patient Americans whom I had seen being taken advantage of and overcharged all over the Mediterranean. It did not matter that they said Antibes as though it rhymed with "rib-eyes," and pressed their faces to the window and chanted "Monny Carla." After all, no one else here could have pronounced the grand Mississippi name Yoknapatawpha.

"You're a yella-dog Democrat," Billy Mounger said to me, concluding – correctly – that I would vote for a yellow dog before I'd vote for a Republican.

I said, "I think I'd vote for a yellow dog before I'd vote for a Democrat, too."

He laughed at that. He said, "We're yella-dog Republicans. We're probably the most right-wing people you probably ever met."

"Go on, then, shock me, Billy," I said.

"I'm chairman of the Phil Gramm for President Committee."

"That is pretty shocking." Mr Gramm claimed to be the most conservative candidate of all the Republicans.

"That ain't the story," Mounger said. "One of our guys back there is against Phil Gramm. Says to me, 'I don't want no oriental damn woman as the First Lady in the White House.'"

Mrs Gramm, born and raised in Hawaii, was of Korean descent.

"You said it, Billy, he's one of your guys."

They all got off at Cannes, rhyming it with "pans," and I stayed aboard, rattled down the track to Marseilles, where I was told there were no ferries to Morocco. I got into my berth and slept until Port Bou, the frontier, changed trains at dawn, and at Barcelona got another train to Valencia. Twenty-six hours ago I had left Rome.

Gently rocking around the edge of the Mediterranean once again, in the opposite direction, this Spanish train stopped at the town of Tortosa. It was exactly opposite – that is to say, at the far end of the Mediterranean – from the Syrian town of Tartus, where I had been over a month ago. Tartus had once been given the name of Tortosa by the Crusader knights. We passed Xilxes which, printed boldly on its station signboard, had the appearance of an obscure Roman numeral. I stayed only long enough at the lovely station at Valencia to buy some oranges and a ticket through the fields of fruit trees, past a small chapel-like building lettered *Urinario*, to Alicante. I would have continued, but I was too late for the Malaga train, so I slept there and went to Malaga the next day.

At Malaga I bought a ticket on the ferry to Melilla, the Spanish enclave in Morocco; then I went out and had dinner of local pickled eels.

"Where are you from in America?" the bartender asked me.

"Boston."

"The Boston Strangler." *El Estrangulador del Boston*.

"That's me."

*

The ferry *Ciudad de Badajoz* left Malaga at one in the afternoon for Melilla. It was a gray windy day, and only about twenty of us were making the trip. Most of them were Moroccans, the men looking like Smurfs in djellabas, the women like nuns in habits and hoods, traveling with gunny-sacks for luggage. A handful of Spaniards had cars or trucks down below. It was a large ferry, five storeys from its plimsoll line to its top deck. I regretted that I had not been able to take one like it from Tunisia, but anyway I would be in Melilla in seven hours.

Leaving Malaga's outer harbor the ferry pitched and began sailing aslant the wind, the shoulder of the easterly hard against its port beam. Seasickness bags were distributed by the crew. The Moroccans used theirs, and some of them could be seen tottering along, bearing these little sacks to the deck where they were jettisoned over the rail. This was a lesson to me. After a year and a half of glaring at the Mediterranean and writing "tame," "lake-like," "a vast pond," "sloshing waves," "almost featureless," "wearing a dumb green look of stagnation," and so forth – heaping abuse on the Mediterranean the way you might insult someone lazily snoring on a sofa – the sea had come alive and was howling in my face, the way someone lazily snoring on a sofa would react if unfairly abused.

It was not a long swell and a distant fetch between waves, but rough irregular waves and a strong wind – a sea that was more confused and noisy than many oceans I had seen. The storm was not an illusion. This large ferry was tossing in it like a chamberpot.

"Windy," I said to a man at the rail.

The seasick passengers inside had made me feel queasy and had driven me outdoors.

"It is the Levanter," he said. I had not heard that word spoken before, though I had read it in books about the Mediterranean. It was the weather-changing wind from the east that could blow at gale force. But I had only known sunny or gray or rainy weather; no storms, nothing to interrupt my plans.

"Going to Melilla?"

"I hope so."

"Why 'hope'?"

"Because this weather is very bad."

He looked worried. It had not occurred to me that the wind was anything but a nuisance. How could it be a danger? This was the Mediterranean, after all. Yes, I had read of severe storms in the *Odyssey*, but that epic was famous for its hyperbole.

"This is a large ship," I said.

"Some ships are not large enough for the Levanter," he said.

To change the subject I said, "Isn't Melilla a bit like Gibraltar? It is a little piece of Spain in Morocco, the way Gibraltar is a little piece of Britain in Spain."

"That is true. It is the same. But we still want Gibraltar."

"Maybe the Moroccans want Melilla."

"Yes, but so do we. And Gibraltar too."

He laughed, seeing the contradiction, but refusing to concede.

It was cold on deck, and though there was wind but no rain the deck was wet with spray and spoondrift. The wind had raised the sea and lowered the sky. The visibility was poor. The smack of the waves against the ship was as loud and violent as though the hull was being struck with metal, the sound like the clapper in a cracked bell.

The man's name was Antonio. He was from Mijas. I told him that I had been to a bullfight in Mijas over a year ago. I had found the whole thing generally disgusting and brutal, but in the hope of eliciting an opinion about bull fever I refrained from telling him my true feelings. Besides, this storm did not create an atmosphere that was conducive to the free flow of ideas.

"Mijas is becoming very famous," he said. "The young matadors start there, like the ones you saw, and they soon make a reputation."

"But the most famous matador in Spain is from Colombia, isn't that so?"

"No. The best one now – the real hero – is Jesulin de Ubrique. Every man and woman loves him – every girl wants to meet him."

"Ubrique is near here, isn't it?"

"Down the coast," Antonio said. He gasped and clutched the rail as a wave crashed against the deck below. He raised his voice. "And another one is the son of the famous El Cordobes, though El Cordobes refuses to say that he is his son."

"What's the son's name?" I shouted over the wind.

"Manuel Diaz el Cordobes, and he is crazy like his father. More crazy! His father used to play with the bull, but this Manuel Diaz puts his face against the bull's face. He is double crazy!"

"I have a theory that Spanish people prefer football to the *corrida*."

"Not true. We love the *corrida* more."

"But it's not a sport."

"No. It is a spectacle," Antonio said.

In the course of our little conversation the weather had grown much worse. Spray flew into the windows and salt grains frosted the glass. Sea water ran across the upper decks, and the lower decks were awash. Now and then you hear about a storm sinking a ferry, because they are not built for storms. But you don't remember those news items until you are on a ferry, in a serious storm.

"I have lived around here my whole life. I cross to Morocco a lot. I have never seen it this bad," Antonio said.

"We ought to be there soon."

"No. It's many hours away."

"It's only a seven-hour trip, and we've been sailing for five."

"Going slowly," he said.

"Maybe the weather is better in Melilla."

"With the wind in this direction it will be worse. The Levanter blows against it."

The fury of the sea, the height of the waves, the screaming wind – they all defied me, author of the words "junk waves," "mush-burgers," "slop and plop of the Mediterranean." It was a maddened sea and this huge ferry was having trouble negotiating it. From the hold came the sound of clanking chains, the creak of cars and trucks, the rolling clatter of steel barrels and the rattle of loose bolts on the steel gangways.

Antonio said, "I am afraid about my car. I think it will crash into another one."

I stayed on deck. True, it was cold and windy on deck. But it was stifling in the cargo hold. It was nauseating in the lounges. Now and then someone would stagger out to the deck to practice projectile vomiting. I held on, pressed into a corner, trying to read an old fluttering copy of the *Guardian* I had found in Malaga.

I thought: When we get to Melilla this will just seem like a bad dream.

Soon after, as it was growing dark, the captain made an announcement: "Because of the wind and the poor conditions we are not proceeding to Melilla. We are returning to Malaga."

The vast squarish bulk of the ferry turned clumsily into the wind, twisting as it went, the sea-spray flying, and then the vessel was in full retreat from the storm.

The phlegmatic Spaniards, used to bad news, took this well. The Muslim Moroccans, contrary to all the teachings of Islam, took the announcement badly and shouted and threw things and argued and slammed the hatchways. Their children cried. The menfolk ranted. The women sulked. They did not want to go back to Spain.

Hours later, in darkness, we were back in Malaga. I was frustrated by the return, but I was also relieved. The captain knew these seas; he would not willingly abandon the voyage if he had confidence in his ship. So he had feared for the ship. The port was closed. All further ferries were canceled.

Antonio gave me a lift to the bus station. He said, "These Levanters usually last three days."

Perhaps there would be more of it. My response was to go into full retreat myself, back to where I had begun my trip. It was only an hour and a half from Algeciras to Ceuta, the southern Pillar of Hercules. I was disappointed that I had not been able to sail from Tunisia, but it was interesting, was it not, that I had been forced to go all the way back to the Straits of Gibraltar to make my crossing? It had not really spoiled my plans, because – always improvising – I had never had much of a plan.

The coast was stormy all the way to Algeciras. This time Torremolinos was wild and wind-blown, and so was Torreblanca, the sea gray and the heavy surf smashing thick suds on to the deserted beach. I was heading back to where I had begun, and the signs went from Spanish, to bilingual, to English as we traveled south. Then it was "Liquor Shop," "Property Brokers," "Video Rental," "Hairdresser," "Music Café," "Insurance Broker," "Real English Breakfast," the *Sun* on the newspaper racks, "Ironmonger's Shop," "Legal Advice."

This was the sort of coast that had inspired the witty last line in Harry Ritchie's book about the Costa del Sol, *Here We Go*. Looking up from the deranged coast of yobboes and package tourists, and seeing the sunset on the mountains, the author reflects, "Spain. It looked a beautiful country. Someday, I thought, I really must go there."

To Fuengirola again – "Everything for Your Pets," "Real British Pub" – and then on to Marbella via trailer parks and the hills of white condos, beside the white raging Mediterranean, reminding every frail dwelling on shore that this old sea, the actual water that had been described on the first page of the Bible, was not to be underestimated, and nature was greater than anything manmade. Goodbye to your beach umbrellas and your ridiculous signs and your awnings and your gimcrack fences; goodbye to your condos and your haciendas; goodbye to the very shoreline of fragile soil. Nature was also the Sunderer of Delights and the Destroyer of Dreams.

The storm gave the sea a symmetry I had never seen in it before, the order of sets advancing on the shore from the horizon. These waves pounded the beaches and the promenades, and scoured the dark sand, and dragged trash away.

Seventeen months after leaving Algeciras in sunshine, on the road to Morocco the long way, I arrived back, in a high wind. There is something about a seaside town on a stormy night. This was not any old wind, this was the Levanter, and the official weather station in the port of Algeciras clocked its gusts at 93 miles per hour (150 kilometers per hour). On the Beaufort Scale 72 mph is the strongest wind for which there is a designation. It is a hurricane, force 12. Most of the time the Levanter was blowing in the 50s and 60s – gale force, occasionally rising to storm force 11. This was the third day of the storm. The hurricane gusts had knocked down electrical wires and put Algeciras in darkness.

The wind was news. Like Malaga and Melilla, the port of Algeciras had shut down. So had Tangier. So had Ceuta. This entire end of the Mediterranean was closed. In Algeciras, traffic had accumulated at the ferry landing. People were sleeping in the lobbies of the terminal; they picnicked beside their cars. There were few vacant rooms to be had at the hotels, and this normally quiet town was full of people waiting for the ferries to leave.

Just down the coast at Tarifa the loose sand and gravel had blown off the beach, leaving a hard, smooth, packed-down surface. One of the proverbs relating to the violent Levanter wind was that of the Portuguese sailors, "When the Levanter blows, the stones move" (*Quando con Levante chiove, las pedras muove*). Along the coast road plastic bags were plastered against the sheep fences; billboards had blown down, so had some trees and power lines. In the narrow back streets of Algeciras obscure objects rose up and smacked me in the face. The palms on the promenade were noisy, their fronds smashing. Large metal signs were knocked from buildings and clattered into the street.

The other thing about constant wind, which is one of the worst forms of bad weather, is that it can drive you mental. It is more deranging than rain, a greater nuisance than snow; it is invisible, it pushes, it pulls, it snatches your clothes, it twists your head, and finally your mind. That night and the next day passed. The wind did not cease. It seemed odd to go to sleep hearing the wind blowing hard, and to wake up with it still blowing. On my second day in Algeciras it seemed to be blowing harder.

"I've been to Morocco twenty-three times," a bird-watcher named Gullick told me. "That's forty-six crossings. Only one of them was canceled – New Year's Eve, out of Tangiers."

Gullick was conducting a birding expedition to Morocco. His Range-Rover was hung up on the quay, his passengers were becoming agitated.

"We're all birders," the only woman in the group told me.

Her name was Debbie Shearwater.

"That's an amazing coincidence, for a bird-watcher to have a bird's name."

"I changed it from Millichap, for personal reasons," she said. "But also I hated having to spell Millichap all the time."

"Everyone spells Shearwater right, then?"

She laughed. "No! They call me Clearwater, Stillwater, Sharewater –"

"That flag's not flapping as strong as it was yesterday," one of the other bird-watchers said, looking up at the flag on the *Boughaz* ("The Straits").

But it was, it was whipping hard.

"Where I come from," Debbie Shearwater said, "a wind like this would be news. It would be on the front page."

Later that day, Gullick proudly passed around an item from *El País* about the Levanter. The facts were that the port had been closed for two and a half days. The gusts had been clocked at 150 kph. There were fifteen-foot waves in the Straits. Some fishing-boats had been lost. The other news concerned the large number of people waiting in Algeciras – travelers, truckers, Moroccans, Spaniards. These travelers milled in the town like displaced people, unable to move on.

One hotel in Algeciras was fairly empty – it was the best one, located at the edge of town, the Hotel Reina Cristina. I was staying near the ferry landing so that I could watch the progress of the ships as well as the storm, but one day I walked out to the Reina Cristina to kill time. This hotel had a pool, and gardens, and was surrounded by trees, and was more like a villa in the country than a hotel in this port town. On the lobby wall were the bronzed signatures of some of the hotel's more illustrious guests: Franklin Delano Roosevelt, 20 July 1937; Cole Porter, 1956; Lord Halifax, Estes Kefauver, 1957; Alfonso XIII, Orson Welles.

W. B. Yeats spent the winter of 1927-8 in Algeciras. He had gone to Spain to recover from a bad cold. In the somber and posh Hotel Reina Cristina, nursing his cold, Yeats wrote a poem, "At Algeciras – a Meditation upon Death," which begins with a pretty portrait of the Straits:

> The heron-billed pale cattle-birds
> That feed on some foul parasite
> Of the Moroccan flocks and herds
> Cross the narrow Straits to light
> In the rich midnight of the garden trees
> Till the dawn break upon those mingled seas.

Back in town the optimistic bird-watcher was saying again, "I don't think that flag is flapping as hard as it was this morning."

Gypsies, Germans, Moroccans, Africans, sailors, families, small children, motorcyclists, dogs, truck-drivers, bus passengers – everyone was waiting. Some were drunk. Many slept in their vehicles. Backpackers lay on the floor of the terminal in their sleeping-bags. And people were still arriving by car in Algeciras to take the ferry to Tangier or Ceuta.

It was just over an hour to Ceuta, about two hours to Tangier. But now three days had passed without any ferries. And still the wind blew. I took the bus to Tarifa, to kill time. It was a pleasant little town buffeted by wind. Spray blew from one side of the harbor to the other, drenching the bronze statue erected to "Men of the Sea."

The wind gave me a headache that would not go away. It made me irritable. It woke me in the middle of the night and made me listen to it damaging the town and scraping at the window. During the day it made me feel grubby. It hurt my eyes. It exhausted me.

Algeciras was such a small town and I was there such a long time that I kept seeing the same people. I got to know some of them. The ceramic-seller with the terracotta piggy banks, the many Moroccans selling leather jackets. The dwarf selling lottery tickets. The scores of agencies selling ferry tickets; the fruit-sellers and market butchers and fishmongers. Some born-again Christians who had once been hippies ran a café that offered Bible study with its sandwiches; I got to know them. The Indian watch salesmen who had lived in Spain for ten years, "and no Spanish person ever said to me, 'You fucking Indian,' like they did to me in London – or four or five men come up to me in the tube train and say things. Spanish are good people" – I met him, too.

And there was Juana. She stood on the sidewalk near Bar El Vino. She was twenty, or perhaps younger. But a serious drug habit made her look much older – haggard, red-eyed, wild-haired. The wind tore at her hair and snatched at her skirt as she clutched her jacket and searched passers-by with her pockmarked and pleading face. She was cold and impatient, and sometimes plainly desperate.

"*Señor – hola!*"

Most of them hurried past. She was harmless, but there was something dangerous and witch-like about her appearing from the shadows beside Bar El Vino in this wind.

Juana became a familiar face, and so I usually said hello to her. This friendliness encouraged her. "Fucky-fucky?"

"No thank you."

"Three thousand." That was twenty-five dollars.

"No thank you."

"Anything you want to do, I will do."

"No thank you."

"The money includes the room at the hotel!"

"No thank you."

"It is cheap!"

And following me down the street, bucking the wind, she would be summoned back by a big growly-voiced woman, calling out, "Juana!"

It was too windy for me to read. I couldn't think in this wind. Listening to music was out of the question, and so was conversation. After dinner I watched TV in the neighborhood bar, and it seemed as though I had begun to live the life of a lower-middle-class resident of Algeciras. *Crocodile Dundee* was on one night, dubbed in Spanish. We watched that. We watched wrestling and football. One night there was a bullfight. A matador mounted on a horse wounded a bull, then rode back and forth poking the bleeding animal with a pikestaff. The bull turned and gored the horse, then flipped the horse and rider and trampled them. The matador lay motionless, next to the crumpled horse, until the bull was distracted and run through with a sword. It was possible that this ten-minute *corrida* produced the death of the bull, the horse and the matador.

We watched cartoons. That was what I had been reduced to by five days of Levanter wind: a middle-aged mental case sitting on a wobbly chair in the filthy Foreign Legion Bar, watching Tom and Jerry cartoons.

The Levanter was as strong on the sixth day as it had been on the first. But there was nothing new about this. In 1854, in a book called *The Mediterranean*, Rear-Admiral William Henry Smyth wrote, "The hardest gale of the neighborhood is the Solano or Levanter of the Gibraltar pilots . . . That the winds in the Straits of Gibraltar blow either from the east points or west points of the

horizon (technically termed *down* or *up*) in general has been imme-
morially remarked; and the conformation of its coasts on both sides
renders the reason palpable. Of these winds, the east is the most
violent, being often the cause of much inconvenience in the bay,
from its gusty flows and eddies, besides its always being found raw
and disagreeable on shore: hence Señor Ayala, Historian of Gibraltar, terms the east wind 'The Tyrant of the Straits' and the west
their 'Liberator.' "

The morning of my sixth day, sickly yellow-gray clouds with
shafts of dawn appeared over Gibraltar. Though from La Linea
the Rock had the appearance of the Matterhorn, and from the
heights of Algeciras Gibraltar seemed like a fortress, glimpsed from
the port here the complicated rock looked like a mutt snuffling on
a hearthrug.

"I think that flag's starting to droop a bit," the bird-watcher
said.

He was wrong again, but that afternoon the wind did abate,
and by evening it had slackened enough for the port authority to
give the order to start loading the ferries. After that, everything
happened quickly. The whole port came awake, people began
running to their cars, gathering their children and dogs. The
truckers started their engines. And Algeciras, which had been
scoured by wind for six days, just slumped and lost its look of
defiance. The storm was over. The town was as limp as its flag and
it reassumed its guidebook description: "An ugly town of very
slight interest."

After all this, the ferry trip was an anticlimax; from Algeciras to
Ceuta, the southern Pillar of Hercules, took just one hour. The
pillar stood at right angles to Gibraltar. Hardly more than a hill, it
was said to be Gibraltar's "rival in antiquity if not in splendor."
Neither photogenic nor remarkable, it was upstaged by its gera-
niums, another two-star relic that made me reflect again that what
matters is the journey, not the arrival.

That glimpse of the other Pillar of Hercules should have meant the
end of my grand tour. But I had waited so long to get to Morocco
I decided to stay in Tangier. Besides, David Herbert had just died,
at the age of eighty-six. "End of an era," the obituaries said,

writing of his frivolity: "He became the toast of Tangerine society. In that 'oriental Cheltenham' (as Beaton called it) he was often to be found arranging flowers for one of Barbara Hutton's rooftop parties in the casbah." I had been urged to look him up. "He's awful – you'll love him." He was colorful, he wore a wig, his sister was lady-in-waiting to the Queen Mum, he had known everyone who lived in or had ever visited the place, and every pasha and pederast in Sodom-sur-Mer.

David Herbert's father was Lord Herbert, elder son of the 15th Earl of Pembroke and 12th Earl of Montgomery – he was also bankrupt. The old man had inherited Wilton, "perhaps the most beautiful house in England." As second son, David Herbert had no title, though to irritate his brother he called himself Lord Herbert. He was known as the "Uncrowned Queen of Tangiers."

I rode from Ceuta to Tangier with a pair of terrified tourists, a husband and wife, in a bus-load of Moroccans. "I'm a surgeon and my wife is an attorney," the man said, with uncalled-for pomposity. They were from Minneapolis.

"Both those professions will come in handy here," I said.

It was raining very hard when we entered the city, and at the Avenue d'Espagne, where it met the Rue de la Plage, the pelting drops turned the puddles that mirrored the bright piled-up medina into dazzling reflections.

Almost at once I was set upon by four men.

"Big welcome, my friend –"

"Listen, I not a guide. I want to practice my English –"

"I am student. I show you what you want –"

"I take you to hotel –"

They followed, haranguing me, and it was hard to shake them off; but by walking resolutely in the rain as though I knew where I was going they dropped by the wayside. Farther on I was accosted by beggars, but the street grew steeper – Tangier is spread across several hills – and soon there was no one except the Moroccan men and women, Smurfs and nuns, their pointed hoods up against the rain and cold. I passed the medina. Medina in Arabic means "the city," and is usually the walled city in any Arab settlement; kasbah means "citadel." The most convenient definition is this: a medina is a walled city with many gates, both exits and entrances; a kasbah, being a fortress, has only two, an entrance and an exit.

I was headed for the Hotel El-Muniria, the hotel in which William Burroughs wrote *The Naked Lunch*, and where Jack Kerouac and others had stayed. On the way, as I stepped out of the rain into a lighted doorway to read my map, a man appeared and asked me what I was looking for. When I told him, he said, "This is a hotel." He showed me a room. It was pleasant enough and cost fifteen dollars (140 dihram), and besides, my feet were wet and I really did not want to go any farther.

From the beginning of my trip I had hoped to drop in on Paul Bowles, who was as important to the cultural life of Tangier as Naguib Mahfouz was in Cairo. David Herbert had been no more than a colorful character, but Bowles had written novels that I had admired – *The Sheltering Sky*, and *Let It Come Down* and *The Spider's House*. Many of his short stories I regarded as brilliant. Some of the strangest and best writers of the twentieth century had come to Tangier; Bowles had known them all, he represented the city. He had known Gertrude Stein and William Burroughs and Gore Vidal and Kerouac and all the rest; he was a writer and a composer. He had translated books from Spanish and Mahgrebi Arabic. Most of the world had visited. Everyone had left. Bowles remained, apparently still writing. In a world of jet travel and simple transitions, he refused to budge. He seemed to me the last exile.

"Mr Bowles is very ill," a Moroccan told me.

It was not surprising. Bowles was in his mid-eighties. The weather was terrible – first the six-day Levanter, and now this rain. It was cold enough for me to be wearing a jacket and a sweater. I needed the radiator in my hotel room. But I dreaded Bowles's illness too, his being sick. I did not want to pester a sick man, and it also seemed to me that any illness in this damp, cold city could have serious consequences. Besides, I had no introduction to him. I did not know where he lived.

This Moroccan, Mohammed, who claimed to know Bowles, said, "He has no telephone."

Would he deliver a letter for me? He said yes. I wrote a note, telling him that I was in Tangier, and asking him whether he was well enough to have a visitor. I handed it over to Mohammed for delivery.

"We meet tomorrow at three o'clock," Mohammed said. "I will tell you the answer."

The rain continued to crackle all night on the cobblestones, blackening the narrow streets of the kasbah, emptying the medina of pedestrians or else forcing them to shelter in doorways, and giving the city an air of mystery: in the rain Tangier was gleaming and unreadable. In such bad weather all Moroccans pulled their hoods up over their heads and it looked like a city of monks.

I could understand why certain foreigners might gravitate to Tangier. It was full of appealing paradoxes. The greatest was that it seemed so lawless and yet was so safe. It was also superficially exotic, but not at all distant (I could see solid, hard-working Spain from the top floor of my hotel). Tangier had an air of the sinister and the illicit, yet it was actually rather sedate. Except for the touts, the local people were tolerant towards strangers, not to say utterly indifferent. Almost everything was inexpensive, and significantly, everything was available – not just the smuggled comforts of Europe but the more rarefied pleasures of this in-between place that was neither Africa nor Europe.

If you decided to stay in Tangier there were other people just like you, writing books, composing music, chasing local boys or foreign girls. The city was visually interesting but undemanding. I realized that as I waited for a response from Paul Bowles. It was an easy city to kill time in. Its religion was relaxed and its history was anecdotal. The rough, real Morocco was behind it, beyond the Rif mountains. A foreigner might have to be careful there. But everyone belonged in Tangier. "Cosmopolitan, frowsy, familiar Tangier," Edith Wharton had written in her travel book *In Morocco* (1925), "that every tourist has visited for the last forty years."

From 1923 until 1956 Tangier had been officially an International Zone, run by the local representatives of nine countries, including the USA. But even its absorption into Morocco at independence in 1956 did not change Tangerine attitudes or its louche culture. In addition to the kasbah and the drugs and the catamites that hung around the cafés, Tangier had the lovely

Anglican cathedral of St Andrew and the Grand Mosque. It seemed to me not Moroccan but Mediterranean – a place that had closer links to the other cities on the Mediterranean than it did to its own country. The great Mediterranean cities had much in common – Alexandria and Venice, Marseilles and Tunis, and even smaller places like Cagliari and Palma and Split. Their spirit was mongrel and Mediterranean.

I met Mohammad at the Hotel El-Minzah, one of the landmarks of Tangier, an elegant place but untypical in being rather expensive.

"Mr Paul Bowles is ill," he said.

"You told me that yesterday. Is he sicker now?"

"Perhaps," Mohammed said.

"Did you deliver my letter?"

"Yes."

"No answer?"

"You can ask Mr Paul Bowles."

"And how will I do that?"

"You can meet him."

The problem was finding him. And it was odd that everyone knew him and yet no one could say exactly where he lived. Even odder was the fact that he had been living in the same apartment block for almost forty years. He did not get out much. He had sought exile in Tangier; he had also sought exile in his apartment. Mohammed knew the name of the building in which Bowles lived, and the street, but no one seemed to recognize these names. My taxi-driver had to ask directions. The street had been re-named – it was no longer Imam Kastellani. The building had no number. It was about a mile from the center of Tangier, in what counted as a suburb. And it was not much of a building – four nondescript storeys; you entered by the back, and the ground floor was occupied by two shops.

A small girl playing in the foyer told me in French, "The American Bowles is upstairs in number twenty – the fourth floor."

I went up and rang the bell and waited. I rang it four times, standing in the semi-darkness of the hallway. Except for the jangling of the bell, there was no other sound inside. The afternoon was cold and damp, the building smelled gloomily of stewed meat.

I thought: If I am spared, if I attain the age of eighty-five, I do not want to live in a place like this. Give me sunshine.

"One time I visited Bowles and when I entered his apartment he was being thrown into the air by an Arab," my friend Ted Morgan had told me.

Historian and biographer (Maugham, Churchill and FDR, as well as William Burroughs), Morgan had lived in Tangier in his previous incarnation as Sanche de Gramont. His descriptions of Tangier in his Burroughs biography, *Literary Outlaw*, had rekindled my desire to visit the city, which he regarded as lurid but fun. But what was this about Bowles being thrown into the air?

"The Arab was muscular and had a very serious expression, and he was bouncing Bowles the way you might throw a baby in the air to make it laugh. That was what struck me. Bowles was giggling madly as he went up and down."

But there was no answer from Bowles's apartment. I turned to buzz the elevator when the door of number twenty opened and a dark and rather tough-looking Moroccan in a black leather jacket stood facing me.

"Yes?"

I said, "I would like to see Mr Bowles."

The Arab stared at me. Why had it taken so long for him to answer the door?

I said, "I want to ask him if he received my letter."

It seemed a lame excuse, but the man nodded. "Wait here. I will ask him."

He had left the door ajar, so I could see into the shadowy apartment, to a room with cushions and low chairs, a sort of Moroccan parlor, with shelves but not many books. There was a small kitchen to the right, a stove with a blackened kettle on it; but it was cold – nothing cooking. I nudged the door with my foot, and as I did so the Arab returned.

"You can go in," he said. He was abrupt, neither polite nor rude. And he was strong. I could just imagine this Arab as the man in Ted Morgan's story, tossing the distinguished writer in the air and making him giggle. The Arab vanished, leaving me to find my own way.

The parlor was dark – I could not read the titles of the few books on the shelves. Another small room beyond it was darker still, but its shadows were an effect of the brightness in the last room, where Paul Bowles lay in a brown bathrobe, on a low pallet against one wall, propped up, like a monk in a cell.

My first impression of the room was that it was very warm and very cluttered. The heat came from a hissing blow-torch attached to a gas bottle, a primitive heater shooting a bluey-orange flame at Bowles from a few feet away. The litter of small objects included notebooks and pens, as well as medicine bottles and pills, and tissues. There was an odor of camphor and eucalyptus in the air that gave it the atmosphere of a sickroom.

"Come in, come in," Bowles said. "Yes, I know your books. Take that chair."

He had a genteel American voice, rather soft, with one of those patrician East Coast accents that is both New York and New England – but in fact placeless, more a prep-school than a regional accent.

"I'm not well at the moment. I had a blocked artery in my leg. The doctor operated immediately, and I think it worked. But here I am. I can't walk. I don't know whether I'll be able to."

Yet, apart from lying there on his pallet, he did not look ill and he certainly did not seem elderly. His face was almost boyish, his hair was white but there was a lot of it – he had the look of a parson or a schoolmaster. What he had just said was precise. He spoke carefully, sometimes ironically, and was responsive. His hearing was excellent, his mind was sharp. Only his posture – supine, and his thinness, indicated that he might be ill. Otherwise he looked like someone whom I had disturbed in his nap, which was possibly the case.

Everything he might need was within reach. He was surrounded by books and papers and medicine, by a teapot and spoons and matches; and the wall facing him was divided into shelves and cubbyholes, in which there were stacks of sweaters and scarves and manuscripts. Some of the manuscripts were typed, and others were musical scores.

On the low table near where Bowles lay there was a large metronome, and bottles of capsules and tubes of ointment, and cassette tapes and a tin of Nesquik and cough drops and a partly eaten candy bar and a crumpled letter from the William Morris Agency and another note folded and jammed into an envelope on which was scribbled, *Paul Bowles, Tanger, Maroc,* a vague address but it had obviously found him, as I had, with little more information than that.

That metronome reminded me of something Bowles said in a letter to Henry Miller. The letter is in his collection *In Touch,* and it relates to his choosing to live in Tangier. "I agree with you about doing things slowly," he wrote. "Now that I think of it, it's one of the reasons why I'm still here. One can set one's life metronome at the speed that seems convenient for living. In the States the constant reminder that time is passing, that one must be quick, removes all the savor of being in the midst of living."

Black-out curtains covered the window. That impressed me. You would not know in this small back room whether it was night or day, or what country you were in.

"I am very sorry to disturb you," I said. "It was kind of you to see me. I won't stay long."

He had blue piercing eyes. His thin hands were folded over his brown robe, and some papers lay on his lap. The blow-torch hissed and fizzed.

"I'm glad you came," he said.

"But I can see you're working. I know I'm interrupting."

"I wish I could get up," Bowles said. "I'm doing a translation – Roderigo Rey Rosa, a Guatemalan. And I have some work to do on a piece of music. What brings you to Tangier?"

"I've been traveling in the Mediterranean, trying to make some sense of it. Going to places I've never been before," I said. "But you've been here since – when?"

"I first came here in 1931," Bowles said, tugging his robe closer to his throat. "I was planning to go to Villefranche. Gertrude Stein said, 'Go to Tangier.' I didn't know Tangier from Algiers. She had been here. She was very interested in a local painter."

Gertrude Stein – hadn't she also sent Sir Francis Rose, and Dorothy Carrington to Corsica? And Robert Graves to Majorca? And Hemingway to Spain? My impression of her now was of a big bossy lesbian, queening it in her salon in Paris, directing literary traffic, sending writers to unlikely destinations in the Mediterranean.

"I came with Aaron Copland," Bowles said. "He hated it. There is often drumming at night here – you must have heard it. Aaron couldn't sleep. He used to hear these drums and say, 'The natives are on the warpath.' He was very worried. He went away, but I stayed."

"But you must have traveled a great deal. I love your Mexican stories, especially 'Pastor Dow at Tacate.' Pastor Dow and his wind-up phonograph, playing jazz so that the Indians will stay and listen to his sermon."

"I was in Mexico from '36 until – when was Pearl Harbor?" – I reminded him – "Yes, until 1941," he said. And he smiled. "My favorite part of 'Pastor Dow' is the little girl with the small alligator dressed up as a doll."

"Have you done any traveling lately?"

"I went to Madrid last June to hear a performance of my music."

"What about the United States – do you have a home town?"

"New York is my home town, if New York can be called a home town," Bowles said. "But I haven't been back to America for twenty-seven years. I'm not afraid of flying. It's just that it's a lot of trouble – all the delays and waiting. And you can only bring one suitcase. I liked traveling in the great days, by ship, when I could bring half a dozen trunks – two of them might be filled with books. Now that is impossible."

"How long has this been home for you?"

"I moved to this apartment in 1957, if that's what you mean."

"I meant Tangier."

"Years," Bowles said. "I had a house in Sri Lanka for a while. But I like it here. I like Islamic countries. It's very corrupt here, but not as corrupt as some of these Central American countries."

"Has it changed you, living here so long?"

"Living here, among Muslims, I suppose I've become more patient and fatalistic," Bowles said. "You have no control over things, so what can you do? Muslims live their faith, they are seldom hypocrites. But hypocrisy is part of Christianity."

"What is it about Tangier that attracts so many foreigners?"

He shrugged. The question did not provoke him. He had perhaps heard it ten thousand times. He said, "They don't stay. The Beats came here twice, first in '57, and then in '61. Orlovsky, Gregory Corso, Allen Ginsburg."

"And William Burroughs?" I said, prompting him.

"Burroughs was here," Bowles said. "For a long time he didn't know where he was. Then he was writing *Naked Lunch*. He'd finish a sheet of foolscap and drop it on the floor. Allen gathered them and put them in order."

It was well known that Bowles kept his distance from the Beats. These people were simply passing through. But Bowles was a respectable exile — superficially, at least. He was married, for one thing. Jane Bowles was another famous figure of Tangier. Her novel *Two Serious Ladies* was one of the strangest books I had ever read; accomplished, but odd. They kept an alligator as a pet. They had no children. Jane was frankly lesbian and towards the end of her life had been confined to a wheelchair. Daniel Farson wrote in his biography of Francis Bacon, "She drank; he preferred drugs like *majoun*. She called herself, with self-lacerating cruelty, 'Crippie the Kike dyke.'" Bacon said that Jane "Died in a madhouse in Malaga, it must have been the worst thing in the world. Looked after by nuns, can you imagine anything more horrible?"

"Sex, for Bowles, appears to have been an embarrassment rather than a relief or a consummation of more delicate feelings," the poet Iain Finlayson was quoted as saying in Farson's book. "His fondness for young men can perhaps be better viewed as somewhat pedagogic and paternal."

But that was obviously the past — and probably the distant past. He seemed to me a man who masked all his feelings; he had a glittering eye, but a cold gaze. He seemed at once preoccupied, knowledgeable, worldly, remote, detached, vain, skeptical, eccentric, self-sufficient, indestructible, egomaniacal, and hospitable to praise. He was like almost every other writer I had known in my life.

Talking about the Beats, Bowles had mentioned Allen Ginsburg. "Ginsburg is a rabbi manqué," he said. "He looks like a professor of chemistry. I read *Howl*. I didn't love it. I read *Kaddish*, his next, and liked it more."

"What about *Naked Lunch*?"

"Burroughs had a sense of humor," Bowles said. "No jokes in the others."

"What do you read for pleasure?"

"Recently I re-read *Victory*. It is very sinister when those three men show up. And *Passage to India*. I re-read that. I didn't like it as much as the first time."

"You said a moment ago that you had a place in Sri Lanka," I said.

"It was an island," Bowles said. "I loved it. I happened to be visiting the Earl of Pembroke at Wilton —"

"David Herbert's father," I said.

"Yes, and I met Sybil Colefax. I told them I wanted to go somewhere warm. They suggested Ceylon. It was an awful trip on a Polish ship. I went to Colombo and then down to Galle and then on this island. It was small, not more than an acre, but covered with wonderful plants that a Frenchman had brought from all over the world. When the island was put up for sale I wired my bank and bought it."

And now in this small hot room, with the shades drawn, he was on another island. No living space could have been smaller than this back room where he obviously lived and worked; he ate here, he wrote here, he slept here. His books, his music, his medicine. His world had shrunk to these walls. But that was merely the way it seemed. It was another illusion. His world was within his mind, and his imagination was vast.

I said I ought to be going. He said, "You're welcome to stay," and opened a flat tobacco can and took out a hand-rolled cigarette and offered me one.

"Go on. It's a *kif* cigarette," he said. *Kif* was marijuana, *majoun* was hashish jam. He added, "I always have my tea at four. And look, it's almost five-thirty."

We puffed away, Bowles and I, and now I recognized one of the odors in the room that earlier I had not been able to put a name to. We smoked in silence for a while, and then my scalp tightened and a glow came on in my brain and behind my eyes.

"I take it for health effect," Bowles said. "They should legalize it of course."

"Of course," I said. "I was going to bring you a bottle of wine."

"I don't drink. Next time bring me chocolates."

We kept puffing, companionably, saying nothing. Then I saw what Bowles's real strength was: he was stubborn. People came and went. Bowles stayed. People started and abandoned their symphonies and novels. Bowles finished his own. People got sick and neglected their work. Bowles took to his bed and kept working. His life was a masterpiece of non-attachment, of a stubborn refusal to become involved in anyone else's passions. I could just imagine his blue eyes narrowing and his thin lips saying, *I'm not moving*.

Bowles said, "People come every day. There are film and TV people. The *équipe* takes over. Some Germans stayed for eleven days and dropped food and sandwiches everywhere. Some people want me to sign their books. The ones with the most *chutzpah* say to me, 'Since we were in Tangier we didn't want to leave until we saw what you looked like.'"

"I suppose because you keep to yourself, people seek you out."

But another reason that people sought him out was that he had no telephone.

"I work all the time," Bowles said. "Malraux said to me, 'Never let yourself become a public monument. If you do, people will piss on you.'"

"That's good."

Bowles leaned over, snatched at the black-out curtains, missed, and then gathered his bathrobe again.

"Is it dark?"

"It must be – it's after seven," I said. "I ought to be going."

"I don't know whether I'll go anywhere with this leg," he said, staring at his thin shanks under the blanket. He looked up at me. "We'll meet again, inshallah. Are you staying in Tangier?"

"I might leave tomorrow."

He took a puff on his *kif* cigarette and kept the smoke in his lungs.

"Everyone is always leaving tomorrow."

Darkness had fallen. I had to grope my way out of Bowles's apartment, and I stumbled down the stairs – the elevator was not working. But I was elated. I had met Bowles, he had been friendly and he seemed to typify a place that had been something of a riddle to me.

Pleased with myself for this pleasant encounter, I kept walking, down Bowles's road that had once been called Imam Kastellani, up to the main road and past the Spanish Consulate, and into town, about a twenty-minute walk. I needed to find a quiet place to write everything down, the whole conversation. I entered a bar, the Negresco, and ordered a glass of beer and began writing.

"You're a writer," the bartender said. His name was Hassan. He asked to see the page, and smiled at my handwriting. "Do you know Mohammed Choukri? He is a writer. He is over there."

I was introduced to a small smiling man with a big mustache. He was slightly drunk, but he was alert and voluble. His books, he said, had been translated by Bowles, and he had known Bowles for over twenty years. His best-known novel was *For Bread Alone*, but he had published other books, in Arabic and French. One was a diaristic account of his meetings with Jean Genet.

"Genet preferred me to Bowles," Choukri said, a twinkle in his eye, as though defying me to guess the reason. He was small, fine-featured, smoking heavily, in his late fifties or early sixties. He wore a tweed jacket and a tie and seemed almost professorial.

"Why?"

"Because I am marginal," Choukri said. "Bowles is from a great family. He has money. He has position. But I am a Berber, from a little village, Nador. Until I was twenty I was illiterate." He licked his thumb and pretended to stamp a document with it. "I had thirteen brothers and sisters. Nine of them died of poverty — tuberculosis and other diseases."

"How long have you known Bowles?"

"Twenty-one years," Choukri said. "He is a miser. In twenty-one years he has not bought me even one cup of coffee."

You're not difficult; you're simply mean, a friend of Bowles once said to him. Bowles reflected: *I've thought about it for some years, and have decided he was probably right. The meanness however is not personal; it's just New England parsimony, and I've never questioned its correctness.*

"Do you think he's happy here?"

"You can't ask that question now," Choukri said. "You should have asked him that thirty years ago."

We stood at the bar, drinking beer. The beer slopped on my little notebook. I had been interrupted writing about Bowles. Now there was more – this sudden encounter with one of Bowles's oldest friends in Morocco. It was dream-like, too. All those names: Gertrude Stein, Aaron Copland, the Earl of Pembroke, William Burroughs, Jean Genet – familiar and intrusive and unreal in this smoky Tangerine bar, another unlikely interlude in the hello–goodbye of travel.

"He is a nihilist," Choukri said.

That seemed to sum him up, the man who had once owned an island and visited Wilton House; who now stubbornly lived in a room, warmed by a blow-torch.

"Did Tangier do that to him?"

"Tangier is a mysterious city," Choukri said. "When you solve the mystery it is time to leave."

I could not have imagined a better exit line to serve my departure – from Tangier, from Morocco, from the Mediterranean. But the line vanished from my mind the next morning as I boarded the ferry *Boughaz* for the trip across the Straits.

I was thinking of an aspect of Mediterranean travel that was like museum-going, the shuffling, the squinting, the echoes, the dust, the dubious treasures. You were supposed to be reverential. But even in the greatest museums I had been distracted and found myself gazing out of the windows at traffic or trees, or at other museum-goers; places like this were always the haunt of lovers on rainy Sundays. Instead of pictures, I often looked at the guards, the men or women in chairs at the entrances to rooms, the way they stifled yawns, their watchful eyes, their badges. No museum guard ever resembles a museum-goer, and my Mediterranean was like that.

Herculean was a word I kept wanting to use but never did; the only Herculean part of my trip was every night having to describe how I had spent the day, without leaving anything out; turning all my actions into words. It was like a labor in a myth or an old story. I could not sleep until the work was done. Mediterranean travel for me – for many people – was sometimes ancestor-worship and sometimes its opposite. This was unlike any other trip I had taken, because although the journey was over, the experience wasn't. Travel was so often a cure; I was cured of China and Peru, by going; I was cured of Fiji and Sri Lanka. Cured of Kenya and Pakistan. Cured of England, after many years. But my trip had not cured me of the Mediterranean, and I knew I would go back, the way you went back to a museum, to look – at pictures or out the window – and think; back to some Mediterranean places I saw, and more that I missed.

The mooring lines of the *Boughaz* were hauled aboard just as dawn broke. I thought of what Bowles had said. Don't become a monument or people will piss on you. There was no danger of my becoming a monument, but Gibraltar was another story. Perhaps that explained why I had been so flippant when I had seen it the first time, and maybe so many monuments explained the mood of my Mediterranean travel, or some of it.

The darkness in the sky dissolved, as though rinsed in light. Into that eastern sky leaked yellow-orange, pinking to paleness, a whole illuminated day ahead, looming behind the Rock to the north-east, grander at this distance, and then the pair of pillars big and small on the facing shores. The sea was calm, and glittered under limitless sky – it was going to be a wonderful morning, the sort of restful brilliance you get, the sky exhausted of clouds, after days of storms. The light grew brighter, revealing the day, and it just got better, as this rosy dawn became a sunset in reverse.

READ MORE IN PENGUIN

In every corner of the world, on every subject under the sun, Penguin represents quality and variety – the very best in publishing today.

For complete information about books available from Penguin – including Puffins, Penguin Classics and Arkana – and how to order them, write to us at the appropriate address below. Please note that for copyright reasons the selection of books varies from country to country.

In the United Kingdom: Please write to *Dept. EP, Penguin Books Ltd, Bath Road, Harmondsworth, West Drayton, Middlesex UB7 ODA*

In the United States: Please write to *Consumer Sales, Penguin USA, P.O. Box 999, Dept. 17109, Bergenfield, New Jersey 07621-0120.* VISA and MasterCard holders call 1-800-253-6476 to order Penguin titles

In Canada: Please write to *Penguin Books Canada Ltd, 10 Alcorn Avenue, Suite 300, Toronto, Ontario M4V 3B2*

In Australia: Please write to *Penguin Books Australia Ltd, P.O. Box 257, Ringwood, Victoria 3134*

In New Zealand: Please write to *Penguin Books (NZ) Ltd, Private Bag 102902, North Shore Mail Centre, Auckland 10*

In India: Please write to *Penguin Books India Pvt Ltd, 706 Eros Apartments, 56 Nehru Place, New Delhi 110 019*

In the Netherlands: Please write to *Penguin Books Netherlands bv, Postbus 3507, NL-1001 AH Amsterdam*

In Germany: Please write to *Penguin Books Deutschland GmbH, Metzlerstrasse 26, 60594 Frankfurt am Main*

In Spain: Please write to *Penguin Books S. A., Bravo Murillo 19, 1º B, 28015 Madrid*

In Italy: Please write to *Penguin Italia s.r.l., Via Felice Casati 20, I 20124 Milano*

In France: Please write to *Penguin France S. A., 17 rue Lejeune, F–31000 Toulouse*

In Japan: Please write to *Penguin Books Japan, Ishikiribashi Building, 2–5–4, Suido, Bunkyo-ku, Tokyo 112*

In Greece: Please write to *Penguin Hellas Ltd, Dimocritou 3, GR–106 71 Athens*

In South Africa: Please write to *Longman Penguin Southern Africa (Pty) Ltd, Private Bag X08, Bertsham 2013*

BY THE SAME AUTHOR

Saint Jack

Variously a sailor, ship's chandler, hustler, pornocrat and benevolent pimp, Jack is able to offer visitors 'anything you want, anything at all', and it is his proud claim that he never fails to satisfy his customers. At first Jack was the youngest drinker at the Bandung Club, but now at fifty-three he is almost a fixture at the bar, an institution. Expatriates like him begin to fear dying, alone and vulnerable, in an alien tropic. And Jack still dreams of success.

'A very funny book about a deeply serious subject ... marvellous, warm, intelligent writing' – *Sunday Telegraph*

The Family Arsenal

Paul Theroux's novel of violence in the tradition of Brighton Rock is set in the grimy decay of south-east London.

'An uncomplicated pleasure ... with this writer the thrills are never cheap and obvious' – *Guardian*

'Brilliant and haunting ... the ingenuities of the plot, the London setting ... the trapped and interwoven people, and the balefully witty observation, have an undistracted force' – *Observer*

Picture Palace

For over fifty years Maude Coffin Pratt has levelled the peepstones of her Third Eye at the beautiful, obscure and obscene, and at the private places and public parts of the famous, from Gertrude Stein to Graham Greene. At her retrospective exhibition her life, measured by camera spools, is rolled out for inspection. Except for the frame that really mattered: the exposure that should have been there, but wasn't.

'Maude's voice, harsh, coarse, and yet surprisingly innocent, remains in the ear long after the book has been put down' – *The Times*

BY THE SAME AUTHOR

The Mosquito Coast

Allie Fox was going to re-create the world. Abominating the cops, crooks, scavengers and funny-bunnies of the twentieth century, he abandons civilization and takes the family to live in the Honduran jungle. There his tortured, quixotic genius keeps them alive, his hoarse tirades harrying them through a diseased and dirty Eden towards unimaginable darkness and terror.

'An epic of paranoid obsession that swirls the reader headlong to deposit him on a black mudbank of horror' – *Guardian*

'An adventure story of the most exemplary kind ... A work of genuine inspiration, intensely realized' – *New York Magazine*

The London Embassy

An American diplomat has been promoted and posted to London. In these episodes from his career – dinner with Mrs Thatcher, a meeting with a Russian defector, gossip, love affairs – he infiltrates the public lives and private events of the capital's rich and famous and, in doing so, draws us a memorable map of the metropolis.

'Paul Theroux is a Somerset Maugham at heart; telling a story, conveying an atmosphere, getting an emotion dead right' – *Sunday Express*

The Black House

A reign of terror begins for Alfred and Emma Munday when they take their failing marriage to the solace of an old country house. There, in the peace and quiet of the Dorset countryside, a strange and beautiful apparition enters their life, disrupts it ... creates a fatal triangle of fear, fantasy and eroticism.

'Theroux skilfully brings out the strangeness, even menace, lurking beneath the homely and familiar ... beautifully written' – *Sunday Telegraph*

BY THE SAME AUTHOR

Millroy the Magician

When Jilly Farina walks into the tent at the Barnstable County Fair to see Millroy the Magician her life is transformed. Fixing her with his steely, hypnotic gaze, Millroy performs miracles in front of her spellbound eyes. And when he 'magics' her into his trailer and tells her he will train her to be his assistant, for the first time in her lonely life Jilly feels safe.

'Magical ... the real success is Millroy himself, who acts unpredictably whenever the reader feels that he has his measure' – *Daily Telegraph*

Chicago Loop

'This is the cleverest and most exhaustive picture of a psychopath since Patricia Highsmith's *Ripley*' – *Spectator*

'A very powerful and absorbing novel ... he holds the reader every step of the way' – *Financial Times*

Waldo

Monogamy, marriage and honest toil are all out as life-options for Waldo. What he *thinks* he wants is a nice simple girl, white and soothing as an aspirin. What he gets is a sleazy hotel roomful of insatiable Older Woman. Then he dreams of a typewriter helpless under his hands and, sure enough, is suddenly discovered as journalism's sunniest new talent ...

On the Edge of the Great Rift
Fong and the Indians • Girls at Play • Jungle Lovers

Three comic and sinister novels set against Africa's vibrant landscape.

Also published (not available in the USA)

World's End
O-Zone
My Secret History

BY THE SAME AUTHOR

The Kingdom by the Sea

Paul Theroux's round-Britain travelogue is funny, perceptive and, said the *Sunday Times*, 'best avoided by patriots with high blood pressure ...'

After eleven years living as an American in London, Paul Theroux set out to travel clockwise round the coast and find out what Britain and the British are really like. It was 1982, the summer of the Falklands War and the royal baby, and the ideal time, he found, to surprise the British into talking about themselves. The result is vivid and absolutely riveting reading.

Travelling the World

Paul Theroux has spent a lifetime travelling through Asia, Africa, North and South America, the British Isles, Europe and the Middle East, and his fascinating journeys have become bestselling travel books. Now he has authorized a book of his favourite travel writing, complemented and illuminated by photographs taken by those who have followed in his footsteps.

Riding the Iron Rooster
By Train Through China

'[*Riding the Iron Rooster*] finds Theroux chuntering round China for a year, initially with an organized party, later with only a series of semi-official watchdogs for company. His obsessive curiosity brings him into contact with numerous oddities, from the melancholic Mr Fang to the mountaineer Chris Bonington, but we learn most of all about Theroux himself – the armchair traveller's ideal companion' – *Sunday Times*
(Not available in the USA)

Also published (not available in the USA)

The Old Patagonian Express
Sunrise with Seamonsters

BY THE SAME AUTHOR

The Happy Isles of Oceania

'He voyaged from the Solomons to Fiji, Tonga, Samoa, Tahiti, the Marquesas and Easter Island, stepping stones in an odyssey of courage and toughness ... Not since Jack London has a writer described the Pacific islands so eloquently and informatively. This is Paul Theroux's finest, most personal and heartfelt travel book' – *Observer*

'Panoramically accomplished ... Theroux is never happier than when paddling his little craft to unpopulated spots as far from human company as he can get ... the writing is cool, the reportage industrious and the research rock-solid. Theroux's control of his material is a wonder to behold' – *Financial Times*

The Great Railway Bazaar

Fired by a fascination with trains that stemmed from childhood, Paul Theroux set out one day with the intention of boarding every train that chugged into view from Victoria Station in London to Tokyo Central, and to come back again via the Trans-Siberian Express.

'In the fine old tradition of purposeless travel for fun and adventure ... compulsive reading' – Graham Greene

From Penguin Audiobooks

The Old Patagonian Express
Riding the Iron Rooster
The Pillars of Hercules
all read by William Hootkins

Forthcoming from Penguin Audiobooks

The Kingdom by the Sea
The Happy Isles of Oceania